2nd Edition

COUNSELING AND PSYCHOTHERAPY

integrating skills, theory, and practice

ALLEN E. IVEY
University of Massachusetts, Amherst

MARY BRADFORD IVEY
Amherst, Massachusetts, School System
Amherst College

LYNN SIMEK-DOWNING
University of Massachusetts Medical School

ALLYN and BACON
BOSTON LONDON TORONTO SYDNEY TOKYO SINGAPORE

Library of Congress Cataloging-in-Publication Data

Ivey, Allen E.
  Counseling and psychotherapy.

  Includes bibliographies and index.
  1. Counseling. 2. Psychotherapy. I. Ivey, Mary
Bradford. II. Simek-Downing, Lynn. III. Title.
BF637.C6I93 1987   158'.3   86-20464
ISBN 0-13-183138-0

Cover design: 20/20 Services, Inc.
Manufacturing buyer: John Hall

Cover photo: Copyrighted
  M.C. Escher heirs
  % Cordon Art–Baarn–
  Holland.
Manufacturing buyer: John Hall

Grateful acknowledgment is made to the following sources for permission to reprint:
Charles C Thomas, Publisher and Microtraining Associates for permission to reprint materials
and pictures throughout the text. In addition, Norma Gluckstern and Jerry Authier, who
participated actively in previous writings are acknowledged for their personal support and
many substantive contributions to this text. (Continued on p. 466.)

Printed in the United States of America

10 9 8 7 6 5   95 94 93 92 91

ISBN 0-13-183138-0 01

CONTENTS

SECTION I: BASIC STRUCTURES FOR INTENTIONAL COUNSELING AND PSYCHOTHERAPY

2 DECISIONAL COUNSELING 25

3 THE SKILLS OF INTENTIONAL INTERVIEWING 49

4 INDIVIDUAL AND CULTURAL EMPATHY 91

11 THE COGNITIVE-BEHAVIORAL MOVEMENT 301

12 SYSTEMS THEORIES AND METHODS 333

SECTION III: THEORY INTO PRACTICE: "WHICH THEORY FOR WHICH INDIVIDUAL UNDER WHAT CONDITIONS?"

13 RESEARCH ON THEORY AND PRACTICE 379

14   INTEGRATING SKILLS AND THEORY   413

APPENDIXES

INDEXES   468

ACKNOWLEDGMENTS

People are the stuff of counseling and psychotherapy, and a variety of individuals have been most helpful in the construction of this book. We'd like to recognize some of the important contributions.

Fred Borgen and Harold Engen have been especially welcome as friendly critics. Their insightful comments throughout have led to increasing clarity and the reconstruction of several chapters.

An effort has been made throughout this book to have relevant authorities review the content and method of this work and make suggestions for revision. Important among these have been:

Chapter 2: William Matthews, codeveloper of the five stages of the interview, and Leon Mann of Flinders University, South Australia, for useful insights into the decision-making process.

Chapter 3: Joann Griswold for her superb demonstration of quality therapy.

Chapter 4: Paul Pedersen and Derald Sue for critical reading of the newly expanded cultural definition of empathic understanding.

Chapter 5: Barbara Partee for a deeper understanding of the linguistic issues underlying the therapy process.

Chapter 7: Viktor Frankl, Alfried Längle, Elisabeth Lukas, and Joseph Fabry for their critical and incisive comments on the role of logotherapy.

Chapter 9: Beth Sulzer-Azaroff, John Krumboltz, and Sharon Bower for suggestions on modifying the chapter on behavioral thought; Robert Marx for providing a critical reading of the chapter and supplying new material on relapse prevention specifically designed for this book.

Chapter 10: Viktor Frankl, Alfried Längle, Elisabeth Lukas, and Joseph Fabry for critical commentaries on the presentation on logotherapy.

Chapter 11: Albert Ellis for suggestions and comments on the material on rational-emotive therapy; John Krumboltz for his conceptions of career counseling, which have many broad implications for the cognitive-behavioral movement; and the Institute for Reality Therapy for comments on relevant portions of the manuscript. Robert Marx also read the chapter and made extensive suggestions for clarification.

Chapter 12: Natalie Garber for suggestions on updating and expanding material on transactional analysis; William Matthews for a helpful reading of the material on family therapy; and Derald Sue, Bailey Jackson, and Mary Ballou for their material and comments on the new consciousness-raising therapies.

Chapter 13: Nicholas Cummings for his suggestions on summarizing his work at Kaiser-Permanente; Stanley Baker for comments on psychoeducational meta-analysis; and Fred Borgen for critical commentary on the entire chapter.

Chapter 14: Nancy Baron for her clear commentary on ethical procedures in structuring the clinical interview; and Machiko Fukuhara for providing an excellent case example with which to summarize this book and for providing a model of intentionality in action.

Dwight Allen, Jerry Authier, Norma Gluckstern, Frank Reilly, Joe Litterer, and Bruce Oldershaw are especially recognized for personal and professional support over the past several years.

GENERAL THEORY OR METATHEORY

General theory is theory created for the purpose of understanding underlying constructs of differing theories—specifically, the searching for harmony and connections between and among alternative theories and methods. As applied to counseling and psychotherapy, general theory is the development of an integrated and systematic formulation of *skills, theory,* and *practice* in the helping process.

Skills

The Japanese Samuri were naturally skilled individuals who were taught the intricate complexities of swordsmanship. The skills were taught one-at-a-time and practiced until thoroughly mastered.

When the Samuri completed their course of training, they retreated to the mountaintop to contemplate and to forget about the skills just learned.

Upon returning, they had naturally integrated the skills into their being.

Lanette Shizuru

Theory

There is nothing so practical as a good theory.

Kurt Lewin

If you don't know where you are going, you may end up somewhere else.

Kenneth Blanchard

Practice

What treatment, by *whom,* is most effective with *this* individual with *what* specific goal, under *which* set of circumstances, and how does it come about?

Gordon Paul

Well, if you don't like that idea, I've got another . . .

Marshall McLuhan

INTRODUCTION: STEPS TOWARD GENERAL THEORY IN COUNSELING AND PSYCHOTHERAPY

Well over 250 theories of counseling and therapy compete for attention in the marketplace of ideas and practice. The task of wending one's way through a maze of sometimes antagonistic views of the world can leave one confused and discouraged. Alternatively, you can view the wealth of ideas for helping others develop and grow as a magnificent contribution to human progress.

Most likely both a positive and a negative view of the current state of counseling and therapy are accurate—the complexity of our theory and practice is overwhelming, but it simultaneously speaks to vigor, enthusiasm, and promise.

This book seeks to bring some order to the occasional chaos of therapeutic theory and method. This search for a comprehensible understanding can be termed "general theory," the search for connections and harmony among many alternative ways of presenting theory and practice. The basic organizing principle for this book is stated in the following general premise, which you will find repeated at the beginning of each chapter in this book:

GENERAL PREMISE

An integrated knowledge of skills, theory, and practice is essential for culturally intentional counseling and therapy.

Skills form the foundation of effective theory and practice: The culturally intentional therapist knows how to construct a creative decision-making interview and can use microskills to attend to and influence clients in a predicted direction. Important in this process are individual and cultural empathy, client observation skills, assessment of person and environment, and the application of positive techniques of growth and change.

Theory provides organizing principles for counseling and therapy: The culturally intentional counselor has knowledge of alternative theoretical approaches and treatment modalities.

Practice is the integration of skills and theory: The culturally intentional counselor or therapist is competent in skills and theory and is able to apply them to research and practice for client benefit.

Undergirding integrated competence in skills, theory, and practice is an intentional awareness of one's own personal worldview and how that worldview may be similar to and/or different from the worldview and personal constructions of the client and other professionals.

ORGANIZATION OF TEXT

The General Premise is designed to provide you with a summary of where you are going and where you have been, and the chapters themselves reflect its content. Chapter 1, for example, focuses on the conceptions of *intentionality* and *general theory* and is designed as an introduction to an integrated view of counseling and therapy.

Chapters 2 through 7 examine the foundation *skills* of counseling and therapy. If you master the practical skills of Part I, you will have a solid foundation for understanding theory and then demonstrating it in practice. (Chapter 2 presents decisional counseling, a basic theoretical model that will facilitate your work in many other orientations to change.)

Chapters 8 through 12 present twelve additional theoretical formulations to the change process organized into five chapters—focusing on psychodynamic, behavioral, existential-humanistic, cognitive-behavioral, and the newly evolving systems therapies. Each theory is presented in sufficient detail so that worldview, basic constructs, and techniques may be understood and mastered. You will find a variety of exercises in this section, the most important of which are detailed suggestions on how to structure a practice interview in many differing theoretical orientations.

Chapters 13 and 14 review the extensive research in counseling and therapy; Chapter 14 then takes the skills and theories of the preceding chapters and shows how an initial interview may be planned and how a long-term treatment plan may be organized. Special attention is given to a detailed analysis of a series of counseling interviews and how this interview may be examined from several theoretical perspectives.

Important in Chapters 13 and 14, but also throughout the text, are exercises and ideas oriented to helping you think through your own general theoretical orientation and your own personal decision as to how to become a counselor or therapist.

Critical to the entire text is the question, *Which* treatment is best for *which* individual under *what* conditions? And "best" can at times be misleading. Turn to the cover of this book and examine the Escher print. Then turn the text to one side, then upside down. View the text from above or from an angle. Each alternative perspective, like the alternative theories you will be examining, contains a piece of the "truth." But, saying which is the "best" way to view and interpret either the Escher print or the complex world of counseling and psychotherapy is not an easy task, for there are many differing ways that may be useful and may broaden understanding.

Our desire, then, is to tell you neither what to do nor precisely the best way to help clients grow and develop. Rather, we are concerned with developing an intentional counselor or therapist, a person who can view the learnings from the field, study one's self, and initiate an independent but responsible general theory of the counseling and therapy process. General theory in counseling and therapy is only in the beginning stages. . . . What are your contributions to its growth?

1

CULTURAL INTENTIONALITY IN SKILLS, THEORY, AND PRACTICE

GENERAL PREMISE

An integrated knowledge of skills, theory, and practice is essential for culturally intentional counseling and therapy.

Skills form the foundation of effective theory and practice: The culturally intentional therapist knows how to construct a creative decision-making interview and can use microskills to attend to and influence clients in a predicted direction. Important in this process are individual and cultural empathy, client observation skills, assessment of person and environment, and the application of positive techniques of growth and change.

Theory provides organizing principles for counseling and therapy: The culturally intentional counselor has knowledge of alternative theoretical approaches and treatment modalities.

Practice is the integration of skills and theory: The culturally intentional counselor or therapist is competent in skills and theory, and is able to apply them to research and practice for client benefit.

Undergirding integrated competence in skills, theory, and practice is an intentional awareness of one's own personal worldview and how that worldview may be similar to and/or different from the worldview and personal constructions of the client and other professionals.

GOALS TOWARD INTENTIONALITY

Developing an integrated worldview and orientation to counseling and psychotherapy is a central goal of this book. This chapter presents an overview of central concepts leading toward this objective and seeks to:

1. Present the concept of worldview. (There are many different ways that you may work with the client toward positive change.)
2. Point out how skills, theory, and practice may be integrated in a general theoretical approach to counseling and therapy.
3. Define the concept of cultural intentionality as a general, integrated goal for both therapists and counselors and clients.
4. Define the concepts of interviewing, counseling, and psychotherapy.
5. Raise the important issue of ethical practice in the helping professions.

YOUR UNIQUE PERSONAL STYLE OF THERAPY AND COUNSELING

The cover illustration, "Relativity," by M. C. Escher, the Dutch artist focuses on two individuals located on the stairs at the top and center:

> . . . two people are moving side by side and in the same direction, and yet one of them is going downstairs and the other upstairs. Contact between them is out of the question, because they live in different worlds and therefore have no knowledge of each other's existence. (1960, p. 15)

You, as a counselor or psychotherapist, may be considered a bit of an artist. Your task is to observe the troubled client walking down life's path, perhaps in a wrong or ineffective direction. If you can join that client's world for a time and walk with him or her on that journey, you may find a new understanding and respect for a way of being different from your own. Furthermore, you may find that the client has a desire to change and wants you to help find new ways of being and acting.

Let us imagine that a client has come to you for help. After some preliminaries, the client tells the following story:

> I feel so inferior . . . you know I work in the cafeteria. I go out and wipe tables in these little loose white jackets . . . with a rag in my hand, going around and wiping tables. I feel so self-conscious and that people are staring at me. Maybe they aren't, but I feel that they are. I hate the job. It's a little better behind the serving line, but still it feels low and unimportant to me.

It is important that you take a moment now and think through what you consider to be the central issues in this situation. Imagine you are the counselor or therapist. *Write down what you would say to the client.*

(At this point, you may have glanced ahead in the chapter to find the "correct" answer. We don't have the correct answer, nor do we believe that there is one most appropriate sentence to say to a person who may be coping with conflict. However, it is highly likely that some responses are going to be more helpful than others.)

The chances are that you do have a response to the client, one which offers something of yourself, is potentially helpful, and leads to personal growth. If you can "walk" with clients and understand their different view of the world, you may be able to help them find more useful ways to think and manage their lives.

Before you go any farther, have several other people respond to your client's statement and record what they say. Are their responses the same as yours? Would they lead the client in a different direction than you? Is one response necessarily "the best"?

Could it be that what you say to another person in a counseling or therapy session says as much about you, or more, than it does about the client?

COUNSELING AND THERAPY AS A PROCESS OF INTERPERSONAL INFLUENCE

How you as a counselor or therapist respond to the client greatly determines what will happen next. Your answer to the client from the cafeteria determines what will be said next, whether the problem will be treated at a surface or deep level; in fact your response determines whether the discussion will continue at all. The manner in which we respond and conceptualize the world of others can have a great influence on how clients (and friends and family) think and act in the future. Even the simple act of encouraging a person to continue talking, as opposed to ignoring what has been said, may influence a person's life greatly over time.

Counseling and therapy are processes of interpersonal influence. But, *what is to be the direction and method of our influence?* Let us examine some alternative responses to the client from the cafeteria and, later, we can consider some critical cultural implications of our responses.

1. "You sound like you feel terribly nervous and self-conscious in your job." (This focuses on key emotions of helpee and may lead to further discussion of feelings toward the self.)
2. "Could you describe another situation where you have felt this way?" (This helps determine whether or not the feelings are a common thread throughout the helpee's life, and it provides additional data to clarify the picture.)
3. "Inferiority feelings? Think about those feelings of insecurity and self-consciousness. Then let your mind flash back to the earliest childhood experience you can think of and tell me about it." (This technique seeks to find the roots of present day experience in childhood and is oriented to therapeutic change.)
4. "You say you felt insecure. What did you do just before you had this feeling? Give me the whole sequence of events leading up to and following a situation *today*

where you were wiping the table." (Searching for specificity of behavioral sequences may lead to action training to work against the problem.)

5. "That's an irrational idea. We've talked about that before. It's solely in your head. Now let's get on to working some more on how you think." (This helps in examining how a person thinks about her or himself. In this case, the counselor and client have obviously worked together on parallel issues before.)

6. "I think I can understand how you feel. I've worked on tables too, and felt terribly self-conscious and embarrassed when I was serving. Is that at all what you feel like?" (Self-disclosure of one's own parallel experiences can facilitate client talk.)

7. "I'd say what you need to do is relax and forget it. Doesn't sound that bad." (Advice and suggestion is one possible lead and is a common reaction given by people to others who need assistance.)

Which of the above responses was most like yours? Which of the above responses is the correct one? It is difficult to say because each leads the client in a very different, potentially valuable direction. There are obviously hundreds of other possible responses that could be developed from an array of personal experiences and counseling theories. Given the right person and the right timing, there are many potentially useful responses.

This book assists you in becoming a constructive helper, counselor, or psychotherapist. While we argue that there is no one "right" way to help and that you must determine your own personal style and manner of counseling, we also urge you to become aware of what you *are* doing and how it may influence the direction of another person's life. Helping is a process of interpersonal influence, and the therapist can have great power in the life of the client. The more responses you have in your personal repertoire, the more possibilities you have for being a helping person, and the greater the chances are for the client to grow and develop.

Worldview and Theory in Counseling and Therapy Expanding one's response repertoire for helping is not enough; it is also necessary to examine one's conceptual framework or *worldview.* Put in simplest terms, how do you think the world works?

If you have not thought about this before, a beginning clue may be in your response to the first question of this chapter where you identified the central issues about your client who works in the cafeteria. The manner in which you identify these central issues provides a small picture of how you view the world. It is out of this worldview or *theory* that you make a decision on how to act. Your worldview and theories determine how you relate to others and probably led to what you said to your client.

To give a more precise idea of how important the concept of worldview is in the helping process, examine some of the central issues identified by others who were given the same excerpt about the cafeteria.

1. "The problem in this case undoubtedly relates to feelings of inferiority and inadequacy. Adler talks about these terms and how childhood experiences often provide the clue as to why these feelings are present now."

2. "This person is a victim of the economic system where some people have enough money to go to college and play around, drive big cars, etc., while others have to struggle. The issue is not feelings, but an unjust society."

3. "A smock is pretty ugly and it makes people stand out. I think I'd feel that way too. Maybe what we need is a less conspicuous uniform."

4. "Lucky to have a job at all. I couldn't find one. This student has no problem and ought to shut up and be happy about what is happening."

5. "The actions of cleaning and serving aren't important. What is important is how one feels about oneself and what one is doing. This student needs to become aware of the self as person and not as an object."

Each of the above definitions of the key issues reflects a different world-view and leads to very different actions on the part of the therapist. The first response comes from a psychodynamic approach and could lead to long-term psychotherapy. (The psychodynamic approach examines childhood experiences and feelings to see how they present themselves in adult life.) The second world-view or theory is that of a radically oriented approach and could lead to economic consciousness-raising techniques as the mode of influence. The third worldview comes from a practical business administration approach and seeks to make environmental changes. The fourth theory denies the feelings and risks leading to an angry exchange. The final view presented is a humanistic worldview that emphasizes emotion and could lead the client to enter an encounter group or seek person-centered counseling.

Careful examination of interview typescripts, films, audiotapes, and videotapes reveals that counselors have their own *typical patterns* of responding to clients. As a counselor, you can start to identify your pattern of working with people. Out of examining your definitions of key issues and your typical responses, you can eventually evolve a fairly accurate picture of your typical way of looking at other people and their concerns.

Psychological theories, such as psychoanalysis, behaviorism, and existentialism, discussed in this book represent theories or worldviews and are means of conceptualizing and thinking about people and the world. Out of Freud and the theory of psychoanalysis comes not only an explanatory set of concepts to view human behavior but also a relatively clear set of intervention techniques through which people may be helped. Similarly, the many other approaches to counseling have a worldview, explanatory concepts, and intervention techniques to achieve specific ends. The task is to use what you think and feel are the most accurate ideas from each theory and to build your own theory about the world.

THE DEVELOPMENT OF YOUR OWN THEORETICAL ORIENTATION

Some in the helping professions are overly zealous in their commitment to their own theoretical frame of reference or worldview in therapy. Commitment and belief are essential if one is to be competent and make a difference in the lives of others, but a single-minded rigidity may make it impossible to help those who may not respond to your first effort at providing assistance. The task is to be flexible in your use of skills and theory and to remain open to new ideas. There are several routes that you may use to develop your own integrated theory of practice in counseling and therapy.

Eclecticism. One organizing worldview that has shown increasing popularity for practice in recent years is eclecticism, and approximately half of currently practicing therapists and counselors describe themselves as adopting some form of this approach. The eclectic recognizes that many theories and methods are of merit and deliberately sets up to select aspects of different theories that may be useful to a varied clientele. The strength of eclecticism lies in flexibility and breadth. At the same time, there are those who criticize this position as overly flexible, lacking systematic thinking, or even being "lazy" in that the counselor or therapist has not taken the time or effort to know one orientation well.

A Single Theoretical Commitment. The contrasting orientation to eclecticism is represented by the many therapists who may have adopted a strong and studied commitment to a single theory, such as behavior modification, psychoanalysis, or structural family therapy. The strengths of this approach are in-depth knowledge of technique and method and an ability to modify the theory to meet individual client needs. Some criticize those committed to a single theory, however, as being rigid and unwilling to change their methods when clients don't respond to the approach.

General Theory. George Kelly, the personality theorist, has pointed out that as eclectics become more systematic in their thinking, they are developing their own theory or *general theory* of helping in which they have integrated several different orientations into one unified approach. General theory or metatheory may be described as a larger conceptual view than either eclecticism or adherence to a single theoretical orientation. General theory seeks to connect and organize pieces of theory in a coherent and systematic framework. General theory could be described as a systematic "eclecticism."

However, it is possible to be primarily committed to a single theoretical orientation and still be a general theorist. A general theorist from a behavioral orientation, for example, might work primarily from this point of view but, at the same time, could *respect* different theories and adapt portions of them in practice. For example, you will find that the cognitive-behavioral theorist Albert Ellis (Chapter 11) has a clear central theoretical commitment, but he is nonetheless able to draw on concepts of humanistic psychology and psychodynamic theory at times to enrich his basic orientation.

As a therapist and counselor, you face a choice. You may become a "lazy" eclectic, drawing in a somewhat random form from different theories. Or you may decide that one orientation to helping is *the best* and refuse to consider alternatives. Or you may take a general theoretical orientation through the route of systematic eclecticism or flexible commitment to a single theory. Both systematic eclecticism and flexible adherence to a single theory are forms of general theory. What they have in common is (1) an awareness that clients respond differently and may need the techniques of an alternative orientation to one's own regular method at times; (2) a respect for worldviews and theories different from one's own; and (3) the ability to see how different theories may be systematically related one to the other for client benefit.

You, as a beginning counselor or therapist, will find that the helping field offers a bewildering array of competing techniques and theories. Many at this stage find it wise to focus on one favorite orientation. Later, as you gain more expertise, you can broaden and learn in more depth about alternative methods. Most beginning therapists and counselors find behavioral theory, Rogerian person-centered theory, or cognitive-behavioral theory the most comfortable single theories for initial study. Psychodynamic theory, the most complex, may be brought in later, particularly through some of its theoretical views of child development and object relations theory.

However, at this point, there is no single correct way to begin a theoretical commitment, although some will strongly suggest what you *should* do. Your task, we suggest, is to examine the field and make your own decision as to how you systematically will organize your counseling and therapy work.

Figure 1.1 *RESEARCH BRIEF: DO COUNSELING AND PSYCHOTHERAPY HELP?*

The answer to the above question is complex and the subject of much argument in the field. Recognizing that researchers and writers have a vested interest in the results (for example, if counseling and psychotherapy don't work, why conduct therapy, study it, or even write this book?), the following seems to be most central in the findings.

1. Counseling and psychotherapy do seem to make a difference and a wide array of different types of methods can help your clients grow and develop.
2. Current research evidence suggests that cognitive-behavioral methods of helping are most effective. However, research on these techniques tends to focus on more limited objectives than humanistic and psychodynamic theories. Many feel that no real difference between and among different therapeutic theories has truly been demonstrated.
3. Not only can psychotherapy help, it can also harm. Ineffective helping techniques in which you fail to indicate an understanding of the client's worldview, make technical errors, or move too quickly may harm the client.
4. A major controversy in the field exists as to the importance of long-term professional training. Several studies exist suggesting that nonprofessionals can produce as much positive change in clients as experts.
5. Currently, many experts are coming to believe that different theories are differentially effective with different clients. Thus, you may wish to gain knowledge and expertise in more than one counseling and therapy theory.

These particular research results are discussed in more detail in Chapter 13, and you may wish to refer to pages 381 through 384 for elaboration.

INTEGRATING SKILLS, THEORY, AND PRACTICE

Skills form the reality of counseling and therapy. *Theory* provides the ideas that organize key principles of helping. *Practice* occurs when you take your skills and theories and apply them directly to clients. If you have a solid foundation of skills and an intellectual understanding of theory, you are well prepared for the practice of therapy and counseling.

Chapters 2 through 7 of this book focus on basic skills of counseling and therapy. Each chapter focuses on skills and concepts that are important in many theoretical orientations. For example, regardless of your theoretical orientation, you will find that listening skills are necessary if you are to walk with—that is, to understand your clients. All theoretical orientations stress listening to clients, and thus you will find that skills such as questioning are useful regardless of where you commit yourself theoretically. If you are behaviorally oriented, you need listening skills to obtain the behaviors and behavioral sequences of your client. If your orientation is psychodynamic, these same listening skills are necessary for drawing out a dream or the client's early childhood experience.

If you achieve a basic mastery of skills and concepts in the first seven chapters, you will come to the later chapters on theories well prepared to develop a beginning understanding of seemingly very different orientations to counseling and therapy. We say "seemingly" because, as you orient yourself to basic helping processes, you will find that you start developing connections between and among different theories. This is the beginning of general theory.

The theories described in this book represent varying worldviews and perspectives, each of which provides a useful frame of reference for looking at a situation differently. If you take the Escher print on the cover of the text, turn it on its side, view it upside down, or attempt to see the three-dimensional aspects of the print, you will note that each change of viewpoint offers a richer way of looking at and understanding the print. Similarly, the theories in Part II of this book offer unique ways to frame and understand the reality of therapy. At some point, you will want to commit yourself to an orientation, either to a single primary theory or to an eclectic or general point of view; without some stable basis for work, you and your client will end in chaos.

At times, you will find that we discuss concepts from chapters that you may not have yet read or have just finished reading. This is particularly so in Chapter 7, which provides a vital integrating bridge between skills and theory. These forward and backward references are designed to point out to you how skills and theories are related, how different theories and their techniques are related one to another, and how you use general theory to integrate different points of view.

One example of the integrated general theory approach would be the "positive asset search" of Chapter 7. Here you will find that many theories of therapy focus on helping clients reconstruct their worldview from a more positive orientation. The words may be different, but the underlying skills and process in each are closely related. Thus, you will find Rogerian person-centered theory talking about "positive regard," logotherapy about "modulation of attitudes," Tyler's minimum change therapy about "exploration of resources." Each of these formulations offers something unique to the helping process and an integrating awareness of general theory will enable you to move across theories and use them in practice more easily. For example, you may be intervening with behavioral assertiveness training and discover that Tyler's work in exploration of resources helps your client grow more positively. But, if Tyler's system does not work, you can work toward the same objective via person-centered or logotherapy methods.

General theory is about moving systematically and knowledgeably from theory to theory using trans-theoretical skills and concepts. The final chapters of this book focus on research and practice, the application of skills and theories for the practical benefit of clients. *Skills and theories that are not manifested in direct practice are likely to be lost and forgotten.* Underlying the final chapter of this book is Gordon Paul's important axiom, "*What* treatment, by *whom,* is most effective for this individual with *what* specific goal, under *which* set of circumstances?" (Paul, 1969).

In Gordon Paul's classic statement we would emphasize the important word "whom," which refers to *you* in the helping process. What is to be *your* selected set of treatments, what are to be *your* conceptions of the goal of helping, and what circumstances will *you* find *yourself* in as *you* enter the helping field? Furthermore, what is *your* awareness of client individual and cultural uniqueness? All these dimensions and more constitute the critical construct of intentionality, the deep awareness of *yourself* and others with a specific commitment to action.

The major goal of this book is increasing your flexibility in viewing the world and maximizing your ability to respond to others. But what would we want for the client? What is the goal of our helping? Why should we help?

AN OVERALL GOAL FOR COUNSELING—CULTURALLY-INTENTIONAL INDIVIDUALS

When asked about the purpose and long-term goals of psychoanalysis, Freud replied, "to love and to work." In a broad sense, most helping theories seem to accept the idea that effective daily living and positive relationships with others are the goals of helping. Specific theories over the years emphasize such key terms as self-actualization (Maslow, 1971; Rogers, 1961), self-efficacy (Bandura, 1982), development (Mosher and Sprinthall, 1971), okayness (Berne, 1964; Harris, 1967), clarified values (Simon, Howe, and Kirschenbaum, 1972), effectiveness (Carkhuff, 1969, 1982; Gordon, 1970), an increased behavioral repertoire (Alberti and Emmons, 1973; Wolpe 1973), and an I and Thou relationship (Buber, 1970). These are only a sampling of the many alternative descriptions of what helping is about.

A common theme underlying most approaches to interviewing, counseling, and psychotherapy is expansion of alternatives for living—the development of *intentionality* or purpose. The intentional individual, or the fully functioning person, can be described in the following way:

> The person who acts with intentionality has a sense of capability. He or she can generate alternative behaviors in a given situation and "approach" a problem from different vantage points. The intentional, fully functioning individual is not bound to one course of action but can respond in the moment to changing life situations and look forward to longer term goals.

The broad construct of intentionality underlies the several descriptions of theoretical goals for counseling discussed. Even more important, the goal of full-functioning intentionality for clients is directly analogous to the book's goal for counselors. Specifically, this is concerned with producing counselors who are capable, can generate alternative helping behaviors in any given situation, have several alternative helping modes available to respond to the needs of the client at the moment, and the ability to utilize these responses to assist others to reach long-term goals. *Both counselor and client seek intentionality.*

Intentional living occurs in a cultural context (Ivey, 1977). Cultural expertise and intentionality imply three major abilities on the part of individuals:

1. *The ability to generate a maximum number of thoughts, words, and behaviors to communicate with self and others within a given culture.*

Common to people who come for assistance on personal issues is immobility or the inability to act intentionally and resolve problems, or the experience of feeling fixed in one place.* This immobility is described differently among the several helping theories. For example, you will find that Gestalt therapy talks about splits and impasses; Rogerian therapy talks about discrepancies between ideal and real self; psychodynamic theorists discuss polarities and unconscious conflicts; and those committed to transactional analysis talk about crossed transactions or routinized "games people play." The inability to respond creatively and intentionally is a common issue with which all helping approaches must cope. The task of the helper is to free the client to respond and initiate intentionally. An array of techniques and modes of relationships exist for this purpose and will be discussed in some detail in later chapters.

Let us return to our client from the cafeteria. Immobility in this case is manifested in the sentence, "I feel so inferior," which repeats itself in a variety of ways throughout the conversation. Our task as counselors and therapists is to assist this person to generate new verbal and nonverbal ways to communicate with

---

*The basic concept of immobility, the inability to act effectively and intentionally, will appear in many forms in this book among many types of clients. Words and phrases such as "stuckness," "inability to respond," "polarized emotions," "frozen behavioral pattern," "indecision," "rigidity," "fixated" and many others all represent the loss of intentionality and resulting immobility.

self and others. The feelings of inferiority show themselves verbally through routinized sentences of self-depreciation and nonverbally through defensive behaviors, such as lack of eye contact, hunched shoulders, and deliberate physical distance in space from others.

There are many alternative ways for helping this client generate new verbal and nonverbal behaviors. Assertion training could be used to expand ability to deal with difficult situations and to enable the person to express thoughts and feelings freely. A person-centered helper, such as those who follow Rogerian theory, might focus on discrepancies between real and ideal self through listening to feelings and attitudes about self and work. A psychodynamically oriented individual might look into childhood for the roots of the present impasse. A humanistic helper would tend to look at the person's self-concept, and a radical therapist would examine the person's historical, cultural, and social context. These are only a few of a myriad of possibilities. Any one of them used effectively is capable of freeing our client to generate new behaviors and to be more fully functioning.

Thus, an underlying purpose or overall goal of all counseling and therapy would be to increase response capacity and the ability to generate or create new behaviors and thoughts.

The discussion thus far has omitted the key word *culture*. The assumption of most helping theories is that they are appropriate regardless of the cultural background of the individual. Too often, helping theory omits these critical considerations. At this point, let us turn to the second dimension of the overall goal of cultural intentionality:

2. *The ability to generate a maximum number of thoughts, words, and behaviors to communicate with a variety of diverse groups and individuals within and without the culture.*

It has been demonstrated in several research studies that 50 percent of Third World or minority individuals do not return for a second counseling interview (c.f., Sue, 1977). In addition, a large number of majority individuals also fail to complete the helping process. When these data are combined with the many individuals who need help and never seek it, a failure of considerable dimensions is apparent. One reason for this problem is lack of awareness and training given to counselors in issues of cultural awareness. The effective therapist must become aware of the fact that different client populations may use different verbal and nonverbal sentences and cues.

If the person described earlier in this chapter were of Hispanic background and working in a cafeteria in a predominantly white institution, the counselor must be able to deal with and be aware of issues of possible cultural racism and discrimination. Helping theories have tended to develop from white middle-class orientations. Evidence is rapidly accumulating that culture, religious background, socioeconomic status, age, and gender can be as important as the unique personality of the client and the problem itself.

Treatment of individuals without awareness of age, race, and sexual differences is naive. People from different backgrounds respond and are responded to differently. Well-dressed people obtain more attention and better service in a welfare office or a department store. Physically attractive and tall people are likewise better treated than their shorter or less attractive counterparts. Given standard middle-class United States culture, it is most preferable to be young, male, white, of high socioeconomic status, tall, and physically attractive. Similarly, it is less advantageous to be old, female, nonwhite, of lower socioeconomic status, short, and unattractive.

Traditional helping theories do not typically give enough attention to culture. Generating new behaviors in relating within one's own culture and other cultures is not enough in itself. The third aspect of intentionality requires commitment to action.

3. *The ability to formulate plans, act on many possibilities existing in a culture, and to reflect on these actions.*

Unfreezing an individual so that he or she is able to generate new behaviors is vital, but the simple generation of new ways of responding and acting creatively is not enough. At some point, the person must become committed to action and decide on an alternative. Not all counseling theories have a commitment to action as a goal.

Behavioral approaches to counseling are particularly strong on action. Clear, observable goals are developed with followup and evaluation. The rational-emotive therapists often assign specific "homework" assignments so the ideas generated in the interview are taken home and practiced. Most approaches to psychotherapy do not get this specific, but all therapeutic approaches encourage clients to look at their plans and the results of their actions.

Most counseling theories operating in the United States are based on a white, middle-class culture. What is appropriate behavior for a white individual may be unsuitable for a Black or Hispanic person. Individual behavior is partly determined by cultural norms. The expression of emotions as necessary in client-centered and psychodynamic therapy may be totally inappropriate and alien for some Asians and Native Americans. Not only the goal but the very process, style, and techniques of helping may be inappropriate.

Fortunately, most theories and approaches stress the importance of reflection on the appropriateness of their methods. This requires the counselor to reflect, analyze, and choose appropriate responses and techniques. The therapist who is skilled and knowledgeable in many theories and who has a concise approach to general theory and its application has a strong beginning for cultural intentionality.

Intentionality is a broad framework that provides an all-encompassing goal for the psychotherapy process while simultaneously providing specific frameworks which may assist both therapist and client in deciding how they want to be and act in their culture. Given such a large range of possibilities, it seems that intentionality is oriented toward total individual freedom *and* cultural respect.

TOWARD A DIFFERENT VOICE IN PSYCHOTHERAPY AND COUNSELING

Theory in counseling and psychotherapy is currently in a time of rapid change and development. In this book you will find several new ideas and chapters; important among them are the newly evolving systems therapies including cultural identity development and feminist therapy. You will find that the major traditional theories of counseling and therapy (psychodynamic, behavioral, existential-humanistic) have been primarily developed by white males from the Western world. The degree to which basic theories will be changed and adapted with the new challenges they face remains to be seen.

Given the new movements and ideas in therapy and counseling, the importance of your determining your own direction and integrated theory may be even more critical. It has become clear that culture influences our view of counseling and therapy at its very core, and you will find included in Chapter 4 a reconstituted definition of empathy—one that takes culture and cultural differences into account.

One important and highly influential scholar effecting change in this movement is the developmental psychologist, Carol Gilligan (1982). Although therapy and counseling are not her specialty, she has pointed out clearly that male and female constructions of and beliefs about the nature of reality are very dif-

Carol Gilligan, Associate Professor of Education, Harvard Graduate School of Education.

ferent. Before her writing, much important research and thinking about moral and cognitive development tended to be writing about *male* moral development.

Gilligan has pointed out the obvious—*men and women are different*. They tend to have varying patterns of psychosocial development that result in varying patterns of thinking. At the risk of oversimplifying a highly complex issue, men may be said to be "linear" or "if-then" thinkers. The male model of thinking tends to focus on results and achieving a specific goal. Gilligan describes women as "relational" thinkers, individuals who think about possibilities and relationships between possibilities before they take action.

The point is illustrated in the case of Jake and Amy, two 11-year olds who Gilligan uses to compare linear or hierarchial thinking to the more complex relational mode of being. A typical problem you will face in therapy or counseling is the issue of attribution of responsibility when your clients feel interpersonal conflict. Gilligan asked each of the youngsters the following question and obtained these responses:

> *"When responsibility to oneself and responsibility to others conflict, how should one choose?"*

JAKE: You go about one-fourth to others and three-fourths to yourself.
AMY: Well, it really depends on the situation. If you have a responsibility with somebody else, then you should keep it to a certain extent, but to the extent that it is really going to hurt you or stop you from doing something that you really want, then I think maybe you should put yourself first. But if it is your responsibility to somebody really close to you, you've just got to decide in that situation which is more important, yourself or that person, and like I said, it really depends on what kind of person you are and how you feel about the other persons involved. (Gilligan, 1983, pp. 35–36)

While Jake's and Amy's answers may too cleanly stereotype male-linear and female-relational responses, the general points should be observed: (1) Women do tend to have different ways of thinking about the world than men. (2) In many cases the direct, straightforward approach of the male model may be insensitive to others. (3) When viewed from an alternative perspective, the relational female model may be the more conceptually advanced.

In this book you will be exposed to a variety of theories. The major theories have tended to be written by males but, since this text is coauthored by both men and women, we hope we will be able to suggest alternative constructions of the helping process. In addition, you will find examples of both males and females who have influenced the growth of the helping process.

One critical cultural dimension of intentionality is your awareness of and respect for sex differences. Beyond that, cultural differences must become increasingly important in your thinking. If men and women construct the world of reality differently, it is even more so among varying cultural groups. Most of the influential theorists in therapy come from mainstream white culture. There is a

Lynn Simek-Downing

need for increased participation in revising the therapy process not only from a female perspective, but also from a Black, Asian, Hispanic, and multicultural perspective.

Those reading the second edition of this text will note a strongly increased emphasis on cultural and male-female differences. In the future, we can anticipate more emphasis on these core areas of the helping process. Counseling and psychotherapy are cultural processes. Our research and theory over time will inform us in more depth as to how we can intentionally modify, adapt, and use new data to grow over time.

ETHICS AND RESPONSIBILITY

The core of ethical responsibility is to *do nothing to harm the client or society.* The bulk of ethical responsibility lies on the counselor. A person who comes for help is vulnerable and open to destructive action by the counselor. Carefully developed ethical guidelines for professional therapists exist that examine and make specific recommendations for the issues of ethical responsibility. Ethical statements of the American Psychological Association and the American Association for Counseling and Development are included in Appendixes I and II. Here are some simple guidelines for counseling:

1. *Maintain confidentiality.* Respect your client's rights and personal privacy. Do not discuss what is said during an interview with others. If you are unable to maintain confidence, the client must be told *before* you begin talking; the client can then decide whether or not the data should be shared. If information that indicates a definite danger to the client or society is shared, ethical guidelines suggest that confidence may be broken to protect the

Figure 1.2   The Intentional Counselor Compared to the Ineffective Counselor

ATTRIBUTES	INTENTIONAL COUNSELOR	INEFFECTIVE COUNSELOR
1. Goals of helping	Seeks to help client achieve client goals and follows client agenda. Willing to suggest alternative perceptions and provide direction in some cases.	Seeks to impose own goals on the client and follows own agenda. May be unwilling to provide clearly needed direction and support.
2. Generation of responses	Can generate and create many responses to a wide variety of situations and issues.	May have no response or cling rigidly to one typical response mode.
3. Worldview	Understands, works, and acts on many worldviews.	May have no clear worldview or able to work within only one framework.
4. Cultural intentionality	Able to generate a maximum number of thoughts, words, and behaviors to communicate with one's own culture and a number of other cultures as well.	Able to function within only one cultural frame.
5. Confidentiality	Maintains client's privacy.	Discusses client's life with others without permission.
6. Limitations	Recognizes limitations and works with supervision. Shares theories, concepts, and personal work in the interview with other counselors.	Acts without recognizing own limitations and works without supervision. Unwilling to share professional work with others.
7. Interpersonal influence	Realizes how own response influences the client and how the client's responses influence counselors.	Lacks awareness of interpersonal influence. May even deny that the client is influenced in the counseling process.
8. Human dignity	Treats clients with respect, dignity, and honesty.	Treats clients dishonestly, disrespectfully, without feeling, and in a manner that may be harmful.
9. General theory	Actively involved with examining own self and worldview, constantly mastering new theories, and systematically developing a unique personal theory of counseling. After study, may decide to become fully committed to one theoretical approach.	Slavishly adopts a single theoretical position with no thought to alternatives, or may be unable to consciously define any systematic approach at all.
10. Attitude toward theory	Views theory as a construction of reality with awareness that one's personal beliefs are often based on one's culture and sexual background of thinking.	Ignores sexual and cultural issues underpinning the therapy process.

safety of the client or others. One must always be aware, however, that the prime responsibility of the therapist is to the individual client.

2. *Recognize your limitations.* There is a certain intoxication that comes when one first learns some techniques of counseling. Beginning counselors are tempted to delve deeply into their friends' or clients' inner selves. This is potentially dangerous. A beginning counselor should work under a professional's supervision and seek advice and suggestions for improvement of work and style. The first step toward professionalism is knowing one's own limitations.

3. *Avoid asking irrelevant details.* Beginning counselors are often fascinated with the details and "war stories" of client's lives. They will sometimes ask extremely personal questions about the client's sex life, intimate couple relations, personal travel experiences, etc. A sure sign of a beginning or poor counselor is giving prime attention to the details of the client's life while simultaneously missing how the client feels and thinks. Counseling is for the client's gain; not for your expansion of information.

4. *Treat the client as you would like to be treated.* Put yourself in the place of the client. Every person desires to be treated with respect, dignity, kindness, and honesty. A deep relationship and the building of good rapport begins by making the client feel accepted by respecting the client's thoughts and feelings and by treating the client as a person. A trusting relationship develops from the abilities of both client and counselor to be honest.

5. *Be aware of individual and cultural differences.* Ethical practice demands awareness of individual, ethnic, and cultural differences. It may be suggested that the practice of therapy or counseling without understanding of the cultural group with which you work is itself unethical practice. Are you equipped with sufficient understanding to work with people different from yourself?

Here are some situations where professional ethics arise:

- You are working as an intern in a halfway house for troubled adolescents. You see one of the teenagers smoking a joint in the backyard.
- During a practice counseling session in a small group in this course, one of your classmates tells you about an abortion and her feelings about the situation.
- While talking with a friend during the past few weeks, he has shared with you the fact that he is gay and thinking of "coming out."
- You are counseling a Black student as part of your work in the student volunteer program for academic counseling. He mentions racism as a problem on this campus. You are white.
- You are working in a college counseling center on career issues and discover that one of the staff members is having sexual relations with a student client.
- You are teaching sex education with high school youths and a 15-year-old girl tells you that she is pregnant and that her parents would throw her out if they knew.

Issues such as these are real and not imagined. They test the ability and good sense of every counselor. Discussion of these and other issues is needed to ground any therapist with an intuitive-conceptual grasp of what to do when a difficult situation arises. Use the above examples as a beginning to a lifetime examination of ethics in the psychotherapy process.

THE DEFINITION OF HELPING AND ITS CONTEXT

Helping can be defined as one person giving aid to another or offering a hand. The offering of assistance comes in many forms, as diversified as someone listening to a friend or a professional working in a mental health clinic. For the purposes of this book, however, more precise definitions may be useful. Helping will be defined as a general framework in which one person offers another person or group assistance, usually in the form of interviewing, counseling, or psychotherapy. *Helping,* then, is a broad term that may encompass any of the more precise concepts.

Throughout this book, the terms *helping, interviewing, counseling,* and *psychotherapy* will be used at varying points, sometimes interchangeably, sometimes with specific meanings. *Interviewing* is defined as a method of information gathering and will typically be characteristic of information gathering in a welfare office, employment agency, or placement service, or in career counseling. *Counseling* is a more intensive process concerned with assisting normal people to achieve their goals or function more effectively. *Psychotherapy* is a longer-term process concerned with reconstruction of the person and larger changes in personality structure. Psychotherapy often is restricted in conception to those with pathological problems. The distinctions between these words often becomes blurred in practice. As an interviewer discovers serious problems, he or she may move with the client into "Touches" of psychotherapy. Counseling specialists often have longer series of sessions and go into more depth than psychotherapists. Psychotherapists do interviewing and counseling. Although the definitions suggested here will work for general purposes, completely satisfactory definitions of distinctions are usually considered impossible. *Therapy* currently is a word that

Courtesy VISTA

Figure 1.3 Counseling Occurs in Many Settings: a One-to-One Session in an Office.

Figure 1.4 *Helping and the Distinctions Among Interviewing, Counseling, and Psychotherapy*

Helping may be considered the broader generic process. Most interviewers, counselors, and psychotherapists seek to help the client.

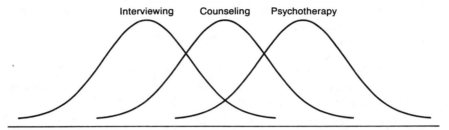

In the above figure, the following important points should be noted:

1. Interviewing is most commonly associated with data gathering, decision making, and brief sessions. Interviewing is almost exclusively the province of "normal" individuals.
2. Psychotherapy, by contrast, is associated with behavior and thought change, personality reconstruction, and long-term contacts between client and therapist. Psychotherapy ordinarily is concerned with "clinical" or "abnormal" populations.
3. Counseling occupies the broad territory between interviewing and psychotherapy. Therefore, the distinctions between counseling and the other two fields are most difficult. Counselors may conduct therapy, they often interview as well. While concerned with normality, they often work with clinical issues.
4. Regardless of how this chart is viewed, the overlap is considerable. At times, *psychotherapists conduct interviews and, similarly, many interviewers will do something therapeutic.*

is becoming more popular and may become the generic, common description of both counseling and psychotherapy. Some professionals use the terms interchangeably (see Figure 1.4).

Helpers and their clients enter into the interviewing, counseling, or psychotherapy relationship usually by mutual agreement. In some cases (public schools, prisons, state hospitals), people may be placed in a counseling relationship without their consent with counselors who have been assigned to them. Establishing a mutually beneficial relationship in such situations is, of course, difficult.

The many forms of helping span the world in both diversity and scope and range from C.A.R.E. programs to feed children internationally to camp counselors to self-help groups such as Alcoholics Anonymous. The functions, skills, training, and backgrounds of the many helpers vary extensively. Training in counseling skills has been provided for medical professionals, salespersons, tutors, volunteers, Salvation Army workers, volunteers for handicapped children, consciousness-raising groups, and religious communes.

You, as a prospective counselor, may be considering a career in clinical psychology, school guidance, social work, with the federal government, or with a private business enterprise. You may be interested in working in a community mental health center, a hospital, an alternative street clinic, a personnel office, or a volunteer agency. You may be interested in private practice, or you may wish to donate part of your time to a community action agency. You may take only one course in counseling skills, or you may involve yourself in a 4-year or longer graduate program leading to the Ph.D. and follow it with a postdoctoral internship and further study.

Some forms of counseling are concerned with molding the individual to fit into socially prescribed guidelines. This is especially true of institutions where counseling and therapy are provided without mutual consent. Other forms are concerned with radical change in society. The verbalized goal of most forms of psychotherapy is "to help the person find her or his own direction and then to achieve the goals associated with that direction." However, counselors vary in their ability to make this general goal happen.

Often, the barriers of language and culture can interfere with an individual's receiving help. Traditionally, counseling has been a profession that relies heavily on both the counselor's and the client's verbal skills. While some therapy is based on nonverbal communication and others on bodywork and mind and body integration, most require that people talk. The barriers of language, culture, and finances can be constraining factors. People who speak English only as a second language are less likely to seek help from English-speaking counselors.

Courtesy Contemporary Studio, Fort Lee

Figure 1.5   Counseling Occurs in Many Settings: a More Informal Session on the Streets.

If they do seek help, they are more likely to discontinue counseling early in the relationship. There is an increasingly obvious need for training to equip counselors and therapists to fill the needs for bilingual and trilingual helping.

The person seeking help is in a less powerful position than the counselor. Intentional counselors will always keep this in mind as they offer their services to others and will be sure to evelute their position as one of power as well as one of helping. Humility and wisdom on the part of the therapist are required. We do not yet know precisely how to assist all people to meet all their needs; the issues are simply too complex for the present state of the art. Further, the actual time spent between a therapist and a client is miniscule compared with the amount of time the client spends in the rest of the world. Even a series of thirty interviews over 30 weeks is but 30 hours out of a lifetime. It is remarkable that counseling and psychotherapy do make a difference in the lives of clients, considering the time constraint.

Despite these cautions, it is still possible for you to become an effective, intentional counselor, interviewer, or therapist. Helping can be a way of life, but it requires the ability to change, grow, and develop with your clients. Faith in humanity and humility on your part are two basic ingredients for this process. The remainder of this book is concerned with sharing some basic constructs important in intentional counseling and may serve as a beginning to your increased ability to enrich the lives of others.

OBJECTIVES OF THIS CHAPTER

For mastery of the content of this first chapter, you should be able to:

1. *Recognize that your response to the client is unique and represents you and your view of the world.* You may wish to start the unfolding process of discovering yourself as you interact with another in a counseling relationship.

2. *Define counseling as a process of interpersonal influence.* We have stressed that whatever you say or do in reaction to clients may determine what they will say or do next. As counselors, we are influenced by what our clients say to us simultaneously as they are influenced by what we say to them.

3. *Understand and discuss the concept of worldview and conceptual framework and theory in the counseling process.* We take the position that counseling theories, such as Rogerian, psychodynamic, and Gestalt, represent views of humankind that determine the likely interventions that a counselor will use with a client. Examination of interviews can help you to understand professional therapists' actions as well as your own. Later, as you examine yourself in the counseling process, your worldview may begin to unfold and lead you to develop your own general theory.

4. *Define and discuss the concepts and issues relating to eclecticism, orientation to a single theory, and the general theory/metatheoretical orientation.* It was suggested that any of the three orientations to therapy and counseling are appropriate, but that it is desirable to have an understanding and respect for other theoretical orientations beyond one's own conceptual frame and worldview.

5. *Define and work with the concepts of intentionality.* The generation of alternatives for creative responding is based in the belief that the effective counselor will have more than one way of responding to a client. A prime goal of the counseling process is to help clients develop the ability to generate new ways to describe and cope with their life situations. A tendency of many approaches to counseling, however, is to underplay important cultural differences among clients. Different cultures may be expected to generate different sentences and constructs. Further, women may differ from men, religious groups may vary, and ethnic and racial groups may participate differently in the therapeutic process.

6. *Discuss differences in male and female constructions of the world and their implications for cross-cultural counseling.* Theory is still in a constant state of development. Data indicate that men and women view the world differently, as do those of different cultures. What is to be your own consideration of these critical issues?

7. *Utilize basic ethical principles.* Some basic guidelines for responsible ethical behavior are presented with the suggestion that these principles be supplemented by study of professional association statements. Case examples for application of these principles were supplied with the suggestion that you add issues of your own for further discussion.

8. *Discuss the framework and context of counseling. Helping, interviewing, counseling,* and *psychotherapy* were defined. The many alternative settings and agencies in which helping occurs were discussed. Stress was placed on the importance of mutual consent between counselor and client before initiated counseling. *Helping* was defined as a verbal process that may present problems with bilingual individuals or those of a background different from that of the counselor. The first interview was outlined as particularly important in the development and maintenance of an effective, intentional counseling relationship.

9. *Define and use key terms in this chapter.* Particularly important concepts in this chapter are response repertoire, interpersonal influence, worldview, general theory, typical patterns, intentionality, culture, eclectic, ethics, responsibility, helping, interviewing, counseling, and psychotherapy.

We would like to state that this book will not discuss all the alternatives to helping. Some key theories and methods will be introduced, and other important approaches to counseling and psychotherapy will not be discussed. We can introduce only a sampling of theory and practice in the material we do present. Referral to methods and concepts beyond the scope of this introduction will enrich your potential as a counselor and enable you to decide upon the frameworks and methods most appropriate to you.

REFERENCES

ALBERTI, R., and M. EMMONS, *Your Perfect Right.* San Luis Obispo, CA: Impact, 1982.
BANDURA, A., "Self-Efficacy: Mechanism in Human Agency," *American Psychologist,* 1982, *37,* 122–147.
BERNE, E., *Games People Play.* New York: Grove, 1964.
BUBER, M., *I and Thou.* New York: Scribner's, 1970.
CARKHUFF, R., *Helping and Human Relations.* Vols. I and II. New York: Holt, Rinehart & Winston, 1969.
GILLIGAN, C., *In a Different Voice.* Cambridge, MA: Harvard, 1982.
GORDON, T., *Parent Effectiveness Training.* New York: Wyden, 1970.
HARRIS, T., *I'm OK—You're OK.* New York: Avon, 1967.
IVEY, A., "Cultural Expertise: Toward Systematic Outcome Criteria in Counseling and Psychological Education," *Personnel and Guidance Journal,* 1977, *55,* 296–302.
MASLOW, A., *The Farther Reaches of Human Nature.* New York: Viking, 1971.

MOSHER, R., and N. SPRINTHALL, eds., "Deliberate Psychological Education," *Counseling Psychologist,* 1971, *2* (4), 3–82.

PAUL, G., "Strategy of Outcome Research in Psychotherapy" *Journal of Consulting Psychology,* 1967, *31,* 109–118.

ROGERS, C., *On Becoming a Person.* Boston: Houghton-Mifflin, 1961.

SCHUTZ, W., *Joy.* New York: Grove, 1967.

SIMON, S., L. HOWE, and H. KIRSCHENBAUM, *Values Clarification.* New York: Holt, Rinehart & Winston, 1972.

SUE, D., "Counseling the Culturally Different," *Personnel and Guidance Journal,* 1977, *55,* 422–425.

WOLPE, J., *Behavior Therapy.* Elmsford, NY: Pergamon Press, 1973.

SUGGESTED SUPPLEMENTARY READING

Integral to this book is the concept that alternative points of view regarding the counseling and therapy process are valid. The following suggested readings represent enjoyable and important background reading and illustrate the philosophies of methods of the main psychological approaches. All present strong statements about alternative views of the world.

GILLIGAN, C. *In a Different Voice.* Cambridge, MA: Harvard, 1982. Male-oriented theory and practice may not be fully sensitive to complex sexual and cultural differences. Gilligan's highly influential work suggests a frame of reference for constructing theory from an alternative perspective.

HUXLEY, A., *Island.* New York: Harper & Row, 1962. Huxley is better known for his negative view of the future expressed in *Brave New World. Island,* however, is his statement about an ideal world of the future where poverty and injustice have been eliminated.

MALCOLM X, *The Autobiography of Malcolm X.* New York: Grove, 1964. The movement of a young man oppressed by racism in the northern United States, through crime, to his eventual discovery of the Black Muslim movement, and to his rejection of white society and the finding of his own identity. As Malcolm X moves toward ever-increasing enlightenment, he shows increased tolerance to the ideas of others.

NEILL, A., *Summerhill.* New York: Hart, 1960. The educational system of a unique alternative school in Great Britain is described. Neill's program may be described as psychodynamic in background and represents a full flowering of humanistic belief. His free school beliefs will seem unique to virtually all and outrageous to many. One of the most entertaining and thought-provoking books in the educational field.

SARTRE, J., *No Exit.* New York: Vintage, 1946. The great French existentialist play about the need for existential commitment and the resulting hell that occurs without relationship. Perhaps one of the best ways to grasp the essence of the existential approaches is a play reading in a small group, followed by a discussion of the meaning of the experience for counseling and psychotherapy.

2

DECISIONAL COUNSELING

GENERAL PREMISE

An integrated knowledge of skills, theory, and practice is essential for culturally intentional counseling and therapy.

Skills form the foundation of effective theory and practice: *The culturally intentional therapist knows how to construct a creative decision-making interview and can use microskills to attend to and influence clients in a predicted direction. Important in this process are individual and cultural empathy, client observation skills, assessment of person and environment, and the application of positive techniques of growth and change.*

Theory provides organizing principles for counseling and therapy: The culturally intentional counselor has knowledge of alternative theoretical approaches and treatment modalities.

Practice is the integration of skills and theory: The culturally intentional counselor or therapist is competent in skills and theory, and is able to apply them to research and practice for client benefit.

Undergirding integrated competence in skills, theory, and practice is an intentional awareness of one's own personal worldview and how that worldview may be similar to and/or different from the worldview and personal constructions of the client and other professionals.

GOALS TOWARD CREATIVE DECISION MAKING

This chapter presents decisional counseling as a modern reformulation of trait and factor theory. In decisional counseling, you seek to facilitate client decisions through considering the many aspects (traits and factors) of important decisions.
The goals of this chapter are to:

1. Present creativity as an underlying process of effective decision making, therapy, and counseling.
2. Demonstrate how trait and factor theory can be modernized into current decision theories and practices through a systematic five-stage model of the interview.
3. Discuss important decisional theory and practices of Janis and Mann who supplement and broaden the decisional model of this chapter.
4. Provide you with an exercise in decisional counseling which will enable you to conduct a basic counseling interview using the constructs of this chapter.

Thus, you are asked to orient yourself toward a view of counseling and therapy that is centrally directed at the making of decisions. It is suggested that all clients need to make decisions in therapy and that this model may be useful in organizing other models of helping as well. In later portions of this book, examples will demonstrate how to use basic decisional counseling with many differing theoretical orientations to helping.

DECISIONS, DECISIONS, DECISIONS

A man traveling across a field encountered a tiger. He fled, the tiger after him. Coming to a precipice, he caught hold of the root of a wild vine and swung down over the edge. The tiger sniffed at him from above. Trembling, the man looked down to where, far below, another tiger was waiting to eat him. Only the vine sustained him.

Two mice, one white and one black, little by little started to gnaw away the vine. The man saw a luscious strawberry near him. Grasping the vine with one hand, he plucked the strawberry with the other. How sweet it tasted! (Reps, 1957, pp. 22–23)

In life we constantly face decisions. On one hand, we face tigers endlessly challenging us. Yet, on the other hand, we have the sweet taste of strawberries before us if we will intentionally grasp what is near and make a creative decision for being.

Decisions are the stuff of life. Decisions are both our problems and our opportunities. To make decisions we need to be aware of the many *traits and factors* that we can examine and balance before deciding. Intentional decisions involve generating creative possibilities for choice.

A client will come to you stuck and immobilized between tigers and strawberries, although sometimes it is difficult to decide what aspects of the problem are tigers and which are potential strawberries. Should the client obtain an abortion or marry? Should the young couple that once was so in love get a divorce or seek to work it out? Should the student major in engineering—as the parents wish—or perhaps drop out of school for a year and work? How can the depressed individual enjoy a lovely summer day? These are but a few of the many problems to which creativity and effective decision making may be applied.

Intentional decision making involves several dimensions. First, we need to define the problem and have a method through which a solution may be achieved. Second, it is critical to clarify the many aspects of the problem, the traits and factors that must be considered. From this basis we can then create new ways of thinking and behaving. If the problem involves a marriage, the specific aspects of that marital problem need to be defined clearly. Then through the structure of the counseling interview, the therapist and client can creatively construct new ways of considering the marriage and new ways of behaving.

Creativity underlies the decisional process of the interview and requires a disciplined freedom, an openness to change, inventiveness, and imagination. When faced by life's tigers, you can take the given situation and generate a "strawberry," a solution . . . or you can remain fixed and let problems defeat you. To accomplish these objectives requires making creative, intentional decisions, and this involves skills and knowledge of theory, imagination, and practice—and some magic.

This chapter presents a creative interview structure that will make it possible for you to organize a systematic helping plan to facilitate your own and the client's creative potential. The model presented here, derived from recent decision-making theory and practice, is also related to one of the oldest theories of counseling—trait and factor theory. But decisions almost inevitably require some of the magic of creativity, too.

CREATIVITY AND MAGIC

It is difficult to will creativity, intuition, or new ideas. They seem to appear out of nowhere. A person may be faced with an unsolvable problem, then leave it for a time. On returning, the "bell rings" or the "light dawns" and a new answer has been generated. Creativity depends on spontaneity and a willingness to "let go." The classic alternating goblet/face of Gestalt psychology (Figure 2.1) is one representation of this fact. Some individuals have considerable difficulty seeing both possibilities within the figure. They, in effect, are immobilized and frozen with one view of the world. Given time and prompting, they can become freed and see the alternatives existing in the situation. That moment of "letting loose" and the accompanying insight ("aha!") is the essence of creativity—the ability to generate something new out of old pieces.

The Necker cube in Figure 2.2 illustrates the same point. Most people

Figure 2.1

immediately see a cube, then another cube, and with further examination the two cubes "moving" from one to the other. However, with further study it is possible to generate many more physical images (flat plane figures, triangles, etc.).

The "magic" in creativity is the spontaneous generation of something new out of already existing pieces. By analogy, consider the client who enters the counseling relationship. He or she may have the pieces, the traits and factors of the problem, fairly clear in mind but be unable to loosen and generate new ideas. In rigidity, immobility, and fixation comes the loss of magic or creativity. The task of the therapist is to help the client create new alternatives for being.

In the counseling process, creative thought is essential to both helper and client. Based on the information that the client presents, the counselor can then help generate alternative definitions of the problem and alternative solutions, de-

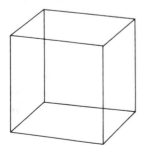

Figure 2.2

cide on a course of action, and generate interpretations of the possible consequences of the proposed action. Critical to developing new insights with the client is knowledge of the many skills, qualities, dimensions, and theories of helping. These may be developed first through conscious effort. As they are absorbed and practiced, this knowledge may be stored and called for when needed during the therapy hour.

Viewed from this perspective, then, the magic of the effective and intentional therapist is not necessarily magical at all. What has been accomplished is the result of long-term and systematic study in the counseling profession, coupled with careful observation and listening to the client in the office or street setting. Out of this experience and study the intentional counselor or therapist is able to trust intuitions and reach creatively into both the conscious and unconscious to assist the client.

A central objective of helping is to produce a more creative and generative client. The client comes with literally *pieces* of her or his life that don't make sense. The client may be able to present the ideas and facts consciously but is often unable to reorganize them into a more workable whole. The task of the therapist is to help the client examine the pieces consciously and unconsciously and to assist the client in generating more creative responses to life.

DECISIONAL COUNSELING: A REFORMULATION OF TRAIT AND FACTOR THEORY

Trait and factor theory could be best summarized as *decisional counseling,* in which the task of the counselor or therapist is to assist the client in making better choices for living more effectively. Historically, the roots of trait and factor counseling can be traced to Frank Parsons, who founded the Boston Vocational Bureau in 1908. Parson's model for vocational choice is simple but undergirds the reality of most vocational counseling and much of personal counseling as well.

> In the wise choice of a vocation there are three broad factors: (1) a clear understanding of yourself, your aptitudes, abilities, interests, ambitions, resources, limitations, and their causes; (2) a knowledge of the requirements and conditions of success, advantages and disadvantages, compensation, opportunities, and prospects in different lines of work; (3) true reasoning on the relations of these two groups of facts. (Parsons, 1909, 1967, p. 5)

This model may be paraphrased and expanded to take into account a wide range of personal issues as well. For example:

> In any decision there are three main issues: (1) a clear understanding of the client and the client's ability and perceptions; (2) a clear understanding of the environment important to the client's decision; and (3) true reasoning on the relationship of the client to the environment for effective decision making.

Despite numerous and incredible errors of analysis of both the person and environment, trait and factor counseling has survived, perhaps because Parson's logic is virtually impossible to fault. The emphasis on person-environment interaction stands in contrast to the person-centered theories predominant in most counseling fields. In Parson's framework, the environment is as important to analyze as the individual.

The logic of trait and factor theory is heavily rooted in an American pragmatic philosophy of "what works." Parson's statement and its paraphrase do describe the situation of the client before you, perhaps in a more realistic sense than any other theory. You will find that the emphasis on *both* the individual and the individual's environment tends to be stronger in trait and factor theory than in many other approaches.

When you meet with your high school or college counselor, talk with your adviser about a decision about courses, meet with your banker or lawyer about a financial or legal problem, they inevitably are using some form of trait-and-factor, decisional counseling. In making a wise decision, you and your adviser (counseling, financial, or legal) clearly need to know the specific traits you have as a person and the factors needed to predict success in the school, financial market, or legal issue. Furthermore, you want an adviser who *knows* the environment. Just because you are a good person doesn't mean you will succeed as a psychology major, in paying off your car loan, or in making an appropriate will. Environmental factors may override all personal factors. The difficult task of the decisional counselor is to consider the full complexity of issues underlying a problem and help the client to make an "effective decision."

Decisional counseling can be the most complex of all counseling methods despite the fact that it has the most simple structure—that of basic decision making. Complexity increases the possibilities of a general theoretical approach, and you will find that psychodynamic, cognitive-behavioral, person-centered, and other theoretical approaches can be used compatibly with decisional theory.

Effective decisional counseling is one of the most difficult, yet most needed modes of counseling, in that we all constantly make decisions but fail to make them systematically. It is *difficult* because sometimes so many factors impinge on decisions that effective decision making is extremely complex. Trait and factor theorists (Williamson, 1939; Paterson and Darley, 1936) have been criticized for failing to cope with the full complexity of the human condition but, when viewing their works carefully, their insights into people and their settings are impressive. They have failed, however, to communicate trait and factor counseling as a decisional process.

In recent years a variety of decision-making models have appeared on the counseling and therapy scene. (Brammer, 1985; Carkhuff, 1973; Ivey and Simek-Downing, 1980; Janis and Mann, 1977) While each of these independently developed models talk about decisions (which are central to trait and factor theory), these models have not been systematically related to the important historical work of Parsons and the trait and factor theorists.

This chapter suggests that trait and factor theory may indeed benefit from an infusion of recent thinking and research in the decisional process and that perhaps it is time to reformulate trait and factor theory as *decisional counseling*. Whether the words "trait and factor" are needed in today's counseling and therapy world may be arguable. Perhaps it is time to consider the more dynamic decisional process as central to the helping process, for it is decisions in the moment that must balance the many traits and factors in both the person and the environment.

DECISION MAKING IN THE INTERVIEW: A FIVE-STAGE STRUCTURE FOR ORGANIZING DATA AND THEORY

It has been proposed recently that most counseling and therapeutic methods can be studied and conceptualized within a five-stage, decision-making model (Ivey, 1983; Ivey and Matthews, 1984). This five-stage model (see Figure 2.3) will reappear at several points in this text illustrating how to conduct a successful interview using many differing theories. The decisional model has been found to be workable not only in decisional theory, but is also useful in understanding therapeutic methods as varying as psychodynamic dream analysis, reframing techniques, and behavioral assertiveness training (Ivey, 1983).

The great American inventor Benjamin Franklin, was one of the first scholars to study decision making systematically. He was concerned with a clear definition of the matter that must be decided, a listing of the alternative resolutions to the problem, and the *weighing* of the positives and negatives of each alternative in a simple decision balance sheet. Systematic decision-making models all deal with the same issue as concerned Benjamin Franklin. The interview itself,

William Matthews

Figure 2.3 The Five-Stage Structure of the Interview

DEFINITION OF STAGE	FUNCTION AND PURPOSE OF STAGE	CULTURAL AND INDIVIDUAL ISSUES
1. *Rapport/Structuring.* "Hello."	To build a working alliance with the client and to enable the client to feel comfortable with the interviewer. Structuring may be needed to explain the purpose of the interview. Structuring functions to help keep the session on task and to inform the client what the counselor can and cannot do.	With some clients and some cultural groups, rapport development may take a long time so that trust can grow. Methods of rapport development and decision making will vary with individuals and cultures.
2. *Data Gathering. Defining the problem and identifying assets.* "What's the problem?"	To find out why the client has come to the interview and how he or she views the problem. Skillful problem definition will help avoid aimless topic jumping and give the interview purpose and direction. Also to identify clearly positive strengths of the client.	Not all clients appreciate the careful problem delineation typical of middle-class helping. However, once goals are clearly established, it may be helpful to return to this stage.
3. *Determining Outcomes. Where does the client want to go?* "What do you want to have happen?"	To find out the ideal world of the client. How would the client like to be? How would things be if the problem were solved? This stage is important in that it enables the interviewer to know what the client wants. The desired direction of the client and counselor should be reasonably harmonious. With some clients, skip phase 2 and define goals first.	If work is clear and concrete here, specific resolutions may be immediately apparent. Some cultural groups and individuals prefer to start here.
4. *Generating Alternative Solutions.* "What are we going to do about it?"	To work toward resolution of the client's issue. This may involve the creative problem-solving model of generating alternatives (to remove stuckness) and deciding among those alternatives. It also may involve lengthy exploration of personal dynamics. This phase of the interview may be the longest.	It is critical that individual and cultural differences in decisional style be acknowledged. What is the "correct" decision from your point of view may be highly inappropriate to another. With some groups, a highly directive style on the counselor's part may be appropriate.
5. *Generalization. Transfer of learning.* "Will you do it?"	To enable changes in thoughts, feelings, and behaviors in the client's daily life. Many clients go through an interview and then do nothing to change their behavior, remaining in the same world they came from.	The degree of generalization will also relate highly to how effectively you took cultural and individual differences into account in the early stages of the session(s).

it is suggested in this chapter, follows a highly similar structure and uses many of the age-old concepts of Franklin, but it is organized in accord with newer models of creative decision making.

Rapport and structuring

A client cannot be creative unless the counselor or therapist provides an atmosphere of sufficient warmth and support. At the beginning of the interview, attention must be given to developing a rapport with the client. In some cases it may take several interviews before an adequate relationship is established.

In addition, clients often benefit from knowing what to expect in an interview. Briefly stating the purpose of the interview can be helpful in establishing a joint focus. The structure may be provided by the client (for example, "I'm here to look at how to handle my children and need to talk things through.") and/or by the therapist ("In my work with problems of this type, we usually do the following. First, I'd like to listen and understand how you view the problem, later we can look at solutions. Is that OK?").

Rapport development and structuring of the interview will always be unique to the individual and the cultural/historical background. Johnson (1978), for example, has pointed out that each individual has a unique decision-making style. Some have a holistic response to events and problems and prefer to make their decisions quickly and not think about them too much. Others, more systematic in nature, will break the problem down and explore it carefully step-by-step. Which of these styles is yours? If you have a spontaneous style, will systematic clients respond as well to you as if you tried to enter their more deliberate frame of reference or worldview? Obviously, you will want to recognize individual differences in decision-making style as you work through this model of the interview.

In the following interview, which we will follow throughout this section, you will note that rapport and structuring can sometimes be very brief. Let us consider rapport development and structuring as they might operate in a decisional counseling context.

HELPER: Hi, Jane. I hear you want to talk a little about how things are going in the new job. (The helper smiles, invites Jane to sit down. Jane appears eager and willing to talk.)

JANE: They're not going. (Jane scowls and forces the words.)

HELPER: They're not, huh? Let me listen for awhile and see what's up and perhaps we can come up with a better understanding.

As you can sense, Jane is anxious to start talking about her difficulty and the interview can proceed at once. The structure of the session is provided in a few short words. Needless to say, rapport doesn't always develop that easily. With adolescents that have been in trouble with the law, solid rapport useful for changing behavior may not appear for months. Further, if the cultural group you are working with is different from you, rapport may not come easily due to lack of trust between the two groups. Jane, for example, might not fully trust a male helper. If Jane were from a Native American background, considerable more attention to rapport development might have been necessary. Some cultural groups consider the "easy rapport" of many Americans superficial and offensive.

Data gathering

The client comes with a verbalized "problem." Is the problem presented the main issue that should be discussed? Your task in this phase of the interview is to listen to the presenting problem and to help the client create a clear and accurate definition of the problem and/or issues. Needless to say, the problem your client presents may not be the actual problem that needs creative resolution. What you are searching for here are the many traits and factors underlying the problem.

Lets continue with Jane:

HELPER: What's going on?
JANE: My boss has been on me ever since I walked in the door. He doesn't think I know one end of a screwdriver from another. The guys have been almost as bad. They laugh at me a lot. In fact, last week, I just took after one guy and wanted to punch him out. They just laughed all the louder. Bastards! I'll get them though.

What are the major issues in this case? What problem would you work on if you were the counselor? What are some of your hypotheses on what may be causing the problem? Does the problem stem from Jane, the possibly sexist culture of the workplace, or some combination of the two?

The temptation is to accept the problem as given by the client and then head for an immediate solution. The client's definition may be only a limited picture of what is happening. If the key issue for Jane is defined as "Things are not going well on the job," then the effort of the helper will be directed toward making things better on the job. This is, of course, a necessary part of the solution, but perhaps the problem is more complex. Before moving to immediate solutions, the counselor continues seeking to create possible alternative definitions and expansions of the problem:

HELPER: So, Jane, the job is really lousy . . . so bad, you feel at times like fighting. Could you tell me a little bit more about what's going on in your life lately?
JANE: Yeh, Joe can't stand my working. He just got laid off, you know. He thinks I ought to sit home like him, but I like to get out. Yet, I hate this bunch I'm working with. I am *so* fed up!

Given these additional facts, some of the definitions of the client's problem that we have considered may be less useful than we thought. Obviously any client has multiple issues and problems . . . if we try to solve them all, confusion will result and very little will occur as a result of our efforts. One definition of a working problem is sufficient at this phase. Other issues can be "flagged" and worked on later.

HELPER: So, Joe and you have a real problem to face. Could you tell me a little more about what he's been doing and how you see the situation?

JANE: Yeh, let me tell you about last night . . . (continues)

If the counselor had accepted the first definition of the problem (a poor job situation), important additional data would have been missed.

Gathering data involves more than problems, however. Clients grow from strengths, and positive assets of the client need to be identified. Consider Jane. She is obviously a competent, worthy person. But, she is only talking about her difficulties. Clients place themselves in a vulnerable position when they become *clients*. It is often very helpful to conduct a *positive asset search* so that you and the client are aware of strengths. At a minimum, the client will feel more comfortable and you may find useful attributes that can be used to promote growth and to solve the problem at hand. The positive asset search is detailed extensively in Chapter 7. An example follows:

HELPER: I've been listening to you for quite awhile talking about problems on the job and with Joe. I think you are doing fairly well, all considered. But, let's take a moment—I'd like to know some of the things that are going well, that you feel good about.

JANE: Well, I've done a good job in the shop. I'm proud of the work I do. For example, . . . (Jane continues)

HELPER: That's great . . . and I sense from what you are saying you and Joe have had some good times in the past.

JANE: Oh yeh, I remember . . . (Jane continues)

HELPER: So, not only do you have some real problems right now, but you do have several important strengths. Important among them is your ability to do good work and your past good history in many ways with Joe. Do I hear you correctly?

In such a fashion, the client is permitted to contrast problems with past and present successes. People grow from strength; the discussion of these positive strengths throughout the interview can be immensely helpful to clients.

Testing.   Therapy and counseling can be enriched through psychological testing. A wide assortment of personality inventories, intelligence and interest tests, value inventories, and other instruments are available to assist you in the data-gathering process. Assessment and psychological testing are important facets of the work of the therapist and counselor.

Testing can provide ideas about a client's strengths and possibilities that can help to focus on opportunities the client had not thought of before. Jane, for example, might find, via an interest test, that she had potential as a manager and perhaps could benefit from supplementary evening study, thus promoting career advancement. Intelligence and aptitude testing might demonstrate that she indeed has the abilities required for such studies. Personality testing might reveal patterns of thinking and feeling that were not immediately apparent through the dialogue of the interview. Furthermore, personality inventories may reveal unnoticed potential difficulties and assist the therapist in planning a more comprehensive and long-term treatment plan.

However, testing is not an answer within itself. Tests are sometimes accused of cultural, racial, and ethnic bias. Women have sometimes been falsely categorized by testers who fail to note the social context of testing. While often important in counseling and therapy, testing must be used with some caution.

Careful and culturally sensitive use of tests can benefit the counseling and therapy process. Tests help identify specific traits and factors of the client that can broaden both your understanding and the client's. Tests are a very real part of counseling. You will want to develop expertise in this field if you are eventually to make your personal decision on the proper use of testing in the data-gathering phase of the interview.

Determining outcomes

Once you have a clear definition of the problem, it is tempting to start problem resolution. However, your ideas about what an ideal solution is may be quite different from your client's. An example may help clarify this point:

HELPER: Jane, we've heard your feelings and thoughts about the job and about the problem with Joe. Could we stop for just a moment and think about *what would be your ideal solution to these issues*?

JANE: Well, I'd like to get along on the job. . . . I don't need to be buddy-buddy with the guys, just some simple respect is all I need. In a way, respect from Joe would be helpful too.

HELPER: What does respect mean to you?

JANE: No bugging from the guys, perhaps some help now and then without being so condescending. I don't really think I can demand too much from Joe . . . he feels so bad. But it would be nice, and help me to stand it, if he would help around the house a little.

Goal definition can proceed in very precise ways or it can remain somewhat general. What is important is that the goal is relatively clear. Jane might have said, "Well, I would really like to quit my job, get pregnant, and stay at home for awhile." Needless to say, such a radical shift in goals would suggest the need for problem redefinition and the return to stage 2, more data and information gathering. Asking clients their ideal outcome often changes the direction of the counseling and therapy process.

Defining the problem first works well with most middle-class clients, but some individuals and some cultural groups prefer getting a clear definition of goals before problem exploration. In some cases, you will find that the clear statement of goals makes problem definition almost unneeded. A good example of the above point would be for the counselor to have asked Jane early in the session what her ideal life would be like; her response (if it involved pregnancy and a change of workplace) would make the extensive problem-definition phase less necessary.

It is critical that you take time to ask the client's goals for satisfactory problem resolution. If you and the client don't know where you are going . . . you may end up somewhere else.

Generating alternative solutions

Many inexperienced counselors and therapists like to start by suggesting solutions: "So, you've got a problem with sex with your husband . . . here is what I suggest you do." But clearly effective rapport and listening must precede any attempt at problem resolution. It does very little good for you to solve a problem that the client feels no need to solve.

However, once you have defined the client's problem and the desired outcome, you are now ready to facilitate problem resolution through exploration of alternatives. It is this phase of the interview that draws most heavily on the creative process stressed in the early phases of this chapter. Remember that the client comes to you stuck and immobilized; your task is to free that person for creative responding. Encouraging creative responding in the client does *not* mean providing the client with your ready-made solution.

How can you facilitate creativity in the client? One route is simply summarizing the client's problem and assets as you have heard them, repeating the desired outcome, and contrasting the real, present situation and the ideal future. In *abbreviated* form, the following illustrates how this might be done with Jane:

HELPER: Jane, let me summarize to this point. I've heard you talk about the problem on the job and the difficulty with the guys and the boss. . . . I've also heard you have some really solid assets in your work. For example . . . you've said you would like to gain more respect from the people with whom you work. What comes to your mind as alternatives which may help you realize your goal?

Your summarization, in your own natural manner, of the contrast of the real situation and the ideal solution clarifies and structures the problem for the client's creative responding. You will find that many clients need only your careful listening and structuring. Once you clearly have outlined the present and the ideal situation, clients generate their own new answers.

But, many clients can develop only limited creative ideas for resolution. It is here that your knowledge of the environment, skills, and theory become ever more important. You may, for example, generate some of your own creative ideas for the client and share them. Good advice, well timed and used sparingly, is sometimes helpful. But—employed inappropriately—even the best advice may be rejected. Usually, people who come for counseling and therapy have already had *too much advice.*

The counselor in our sample dialogue shifted to a different helping style. Rather than create new ideas by announcing them, the counselor moved to a Rogerian person-centered style of reflective listening:

HELPER: So Jane, we seem to have a fairly good grasp of some key issues on the job. The plan we developed looks promising. However, I heard back there a bit that you and Joe have some problems. (Note that the counselor did not change topic to family concerns when these issues were raised, but "flagged" them for later discussion. Another alternative might have been to leave the job issue and work on the family concern and return to the job later. Either is probably appropriate, but working on both issues simultaneously may be unwise and confusing.)

JANE: Yes, he seems so discouraged and angry. Sometimes I almost feel frightened of him. I thought he was going to hit me.

HELPER: You're very concerned with his feelings, yet as I listen to you, you sound and look frightened for yourself.

JANE: I'm scared. He did hit me. . . . He can't stand the fact that I've got a job and he doesn't. I try and try to please him—I still do all the work at home. I don't know what to do.

HELPER: You desperately want to please him, yet your efforts are almost futile. I sense some anger as well. (Hearing the vocal tone.)

After working through the emotional issues, the counselor could return to basic creative decision making and assist Jane in generating ideas for action in her marriage.

HELPER: In summary, we seem to have things fairly clear. You seem very clear about your anger at Joe. You don't intend to allow yourself to take his verbal and physical beatings any more. At the same time, you also feel sad—in fact deeply hurt—because you still love him despite it all. Have I heard you correctly?

JANE: Yeh . . . until we put it together over the last half hour, it was all so confusing. Things seem clearer somehow.

HELPER:	So . . . given that you have real deep feelings of both love and anger, what are your alternatives for action? You've said you don't want to go on as you have in the past. What are some ideas which you might use to change your situation?
JANE:	Well, I've thought of leaving him, but then I want to stay, too.
HELPER:	Two alternatives, then, are staying and leaving. Let's assume you leave. What are some of the alternatives and possibilities.
JANE AND HELPER:	(Over the next several helpee responses and helper leads, an array of possibilities for living effectively with a separation are generated. Some reflective techniques may be used to help Jane sort through her feelings and attitudes toward the ideas that are developed.)
HELPER:	To sum up to this point, you seem to believe you could leave Joe and "make it" on your own. It would be tough and hurtful, but you feel confident you have the ability to do it. Now . . . earlier you were saying that you also had some feelings you wanted to stay with him. Let's sort through the possibilities and alternatives here. Let's brainstorm again and think through possibilities for staying as well. Later we can compare the possibilities in each.

It may be seen that the task of the counselor in this case is to work with the client, Jane, to help her think through as many possibilities for action as can be developed. A person with only one or two choices really does not have full opportunity for exercising control over her or his life. However, a client who becomes aware of three or more choices and their implications is in a position to become intentional and create and direct her or his own life rather than being directed by external forces.

To summarize, the fourth phase of the interview is critical to client growth and development. The object of this phase is to enable the client to generate creative ways of responding to the old immobilized forms of coping with the problem. These ideas may come from the client or from your own creative self as therapist. Furthermore, your knowledge of theories (for example, cognitive, psychodynamic) may be helpful at this point to facilitate client generation of alternatives.

Generalization

You may do a wonderful job of gathering data, defining goals, and generating and sorting alternatives but, unless a specific commitment to action is obtained, your efforts may be to no avail. Stories of wonderful insights and understandings in the interview abound, but the acid test is *does your interview make a difference in the life of the client? Does the client do something different as a result of counseling?*

Having worked through problems and clarified them, most counselors, therapists, and clients are tempted to close the interview and move on. Data clearly show that clients often, perhaps even usually, lose the benefits of counseling and therapy rather quickly; specific steps must be taken to ensure that your and the client's constructive efforts do not get lost (Marx, 1982; Marlatt and Gordon, 1980, 1985).

You as therapist must also give special attention to generalization and work with your clients to ensure that difficult gains in the interview are not lost in the ensuing days and months. For the beginning stage of interviewing, one simple method may be helpful: Simply ask the client, "What one thing today stands out for you? What one specific thing/action could you take tomorrow or next week to act on what we discussed?" Simplistic though this may seem, the discussion of an explicit or implicit contract for action will be helpful in maintaining client learning. These client followup actions are helpful ways to begin the next interview and provide additional data about client development.

Change and generalization that is not planned and does not carry a definite commitment for action is very likely neither change nor development, but the avoidance of true intentionality. However, the definition of change and development varies from culture to culture and from individual to individual. As a professional helper, you cannot assume your definition of change matches that of the client.

HELPER: Jane, we've come to the conclusion that you do have several things which could help your situation. There are many possibilities. Let's contract for just one change, one thing to do differently next week. Then when we meet we can see if it helped. What would you like to *do?*

JANE: Well, I think I would most like to speak up directly at work when the guys bug me. That assertiveness training you told me about sounds good. If my speaking up doesn't work, I'd like to try that. I'd like to do something different with Joe, but perhaps the situation is just too confusing at this moment for action.

The more specificity you as counselor can produce around commitment for change, the more likelihood your intervention and helping have in making a difference in the client's life. You will often find that one planned change results in many unplanned changes among your clients.

In this section, a general model for decision making and structuring the interview has been presented. The decisional structure offers a successful interview format that can be reordered and restructured in many ways. Different theories and therapies give differential attention to various aspects of the model. You are encouraged to mix and match the several stages to meet the uniqueness of your client. Later portions of this text will illustrate how this five-stage metamodel can be applied to theories as diverse as psychodynamic, behavioral, Rogerian, and others.

INDIVIDUAL OR ENVIRONMENTAL INTERVENTION? THE NEED FOR A COMPREHENSIVE VIEW OF THE HELPING PROCESS

The importance of *how* a client's problem is defined or redefined cannot be over-emphasized. We have seen that the problem as stated in the entry phases of the interview may not be the most important issue. The counselor must be alert to an infinite array of ways of defining the problem presented by counselees.

> Though women do not complain of the power of husbands, each complains of her own husband, or of the husbands of her friends. It is the same in all other cases of servitude—at least in the commencement of the emancipatory movement. The serfs did not at first complain of the power of their lords, but only of their tyranny. (John Stuart Mill, *On the Subjugation of Women*)

Returning to the case of Jane, it can be seen that many of her difficulties stem from being a woman in a man's world. She faces sexism and discrimination on the job while her husband is reacting to societal stereotypes, rejects her success in a nontraditional job, and beats her severely. Jane's relationships on the job and in her marriage are heavily affected by environmental sexism. Changing a massive system of institutionalized attitudes and behaviors is arduous work. Small wonder that most counselors prefer to work with individuals and ignore the surrounding environmental influences!

There are, however, some very immediate and practical techniques that a counselor can use that would represent beginning attempts to consider environmental influences. At the data-gathering phase, the counselor can help Jane realize that her problem is not solely *her* problem, but is also a problem of environmentally based sexism. The counselor can show the client that there are other ways to define her problem. For example:

HELPER: Jane, we've been talking now for three interviews. I hear you talking about how you want to manage better on the job and cope with the men who are bugging you. I also hear the same dimensions in your relationship with your husband. And . . . underlying that struggle, I keep hearing you say, "It's Jane's fault. If only Jane tried harder, somehow it would work out." Yet, the more I listen to you, the more it seems that what is really happening is that "Jane's problem" is also a "woman's problem." Women have been victimized by sexism and it sounds like you're getting victimized at home and on the job. How do you react to that?

The counselor here makes an interpretation of Jane's statement and provides an opportunity for her to react. Other alternatives for the counselor would include simply summarizing the facts and seeing if Jane could make the interpretation herself, giving her clear and direct advice about how to cope with the issue as a problem in sexism, adding bibliotherapy to the process, or suggesting that Jane participate in a feminist consciousness-raising group.

Truly intentional counseling always considers the potential environmental factors that may underlie immediate client problems. Racism is another major problem in current society. Any Asian, Black, Hispanic, or Native American client will have suffered the ravages and oppression of racism. Individual therapy theories tend to ignore this crucial underlying issue. However, new consciousness-raising therapies such as feminist therapy (see Chapter 10) now offer highly specific theories and methods to deal with these issues.

DECISIONAL STYLE AND THEORY: SOME ADDITIONAL IMPLICATIONS

Vigilant decision making has been defined as the most effective decision-making style. As Janis and Mann have observed, in vigilant decision making "the person is sufficiently aroused and motivated to engage in all the essential cognitive tasks of decision making, but is never so highly aroused that his cognitive capacity becomes impaired" (1977, p. 76). A vigilant decisional style is closely allied to the concept of intentionality and may be contrasted with other decisional styles such as "hypervigilance" (too extensive emotional arousal and limited search for alternatives), "defensive avoidance" (procrastination), "unconflicted adherence" (staying with the decision regardless of consequences), or "unconflicted change." At issue is finding a balanced intentional or vigilant style in which alternatives are considered and a decision is made within a reasonable emotional climate.

Out of their theoretical model of decisions and decisional style, Janis and

Leon Mann. One route toward effective counseling and therapy and planned change is psychoeducation. Psychoeducation or "training as treatment" is now recognized as a viable alternative and supplement to traditional one-to-one or family therapy (see Chapter 12).

Mann have generated some highly useful and specific techniques for personal growth and change that provide helpful variations and techniques for the five-stage model of decisional counseling.

Mann and his colleagues at Flinders University in Australia (Mann, Beswick, Alloucache, and Ivey, 1982) have developed workshops to help people develop more effective decisions. The sessions start with presentations of alternative methods of decision making, and clients are encouraged to recognize their typical way of deciding. Vigilant decision making is emphasized as a desired goal.

The third session of the Mann workshop focuses on the decisional balance sheet (Figure 2.4), a sophisticated version of Benjamin Franklin's early model. Here clients take the creative alternatives they have brainstormed and examine the positives and negatives of *each* decision. It may be noted that the balance sheet includes not only the client's gains and losses, but also how decisions

---

Figure 2.4   *The Balance Sheet Grid*

ALTERNATIVE # _____

GAINS	LOSSES
MATERIAL GAINS FOR ME	MATERIAL LOSSES FOR ME
MATERIAL GAINS FOR OTHERS	MATERIAL LOSSES FOR OTHERS
GAINS IN SELF-APPROVAL	LOSSES IN SELF-APPROVAL
APPROVAL BY OTHERS	DISAPPROVAL BY OTHERS

The client completes one of these grid sheets for *each* alternative for action under consideration. The first two items focus on the facts of the decision, the last two on how the client and others would feel about that decision. Source: Mann, 1982; based on Janis and Mann, 1977, reprinted by permission.

will affect others. This feature is important as it helps clients develop greater sensitivity and empathy in their decisional process.

The final sessions of the workshop deal with a future diary. Clients write out a typical day that they might anticipate a year from now, given the selection of particular alternatives. The future diaries often bring out emotional issues that were not brought into awareness by the decisional balance sheet. Mann has found that unless the decision maker considers both emotional and cognitive components, the decision is flawed and might not be implemented.

Once decisions have been made, specific action plans and followup for implementation are included in the training program. While the decision workshop represents a psychoeducational approach, in that it takes groups through the decisional process, it must be recognized that the systematic process could serve as a decisional model for counseling itself. You, as counselor or therapist, could follow the basic Mann model and adapt it with various clients.

Janis (1983) has recently extended the ideas of decision making to his own counseling model, which may be found summarized in Figure 2.5. Primary attention in his *decision counseling* is given to maintenance of behavior after the interview is completed. With careful attention to key factors, Janis has found that the counselor can produce lasting change in *one interview* with clients who wish to stop smoking or lose weight.

The decision-counseling model follows a three-phase framework, not unlike the five stages presented in this chapter. However, Janis is oriented toward achieving specific impact on decisions around a specific topic. Phase 1 of the model, "Building up motivating power," roughly corresponds to the first three stages of the model in this chapter. Janis and his colleagues have found that positive feedback (closely related to the positive asset search) is helpful in establishing relationship and in helping clients later to maintain change. This discovery, backed by several research studies, is particularly important as it demonstrates that the transfer of learnings in the interview can be facilitated early in the session by the nature of personal relationships.

Phase 2 of the Janis model focuses on specific actions to change behavior. For example, Janis stresses the importance of eliciting client commitment to change. Many clients state a wish to change, but if you listen carefully, you will discover that the final commitment to change is clouded by a series of "yes, but's . . .". When you notice a client closing off from you with "yes, but . . . ," you know that change is very unlikely to follow.

At Phase 7—"Giving selective positive feedback *versus* giving noncontingent acceptance or predominantly neutral or negative feedback"—Janis does something that most counseling and therapy theories tend to pass over and/or recommend against. Rogerian counseling theory (see Chapter 10) tends to emphasize unconditional positive regard as basic to successful helping. Janis provides a critical and important challenge to this hallowed belief of the helping profession. This does not mean that Janis would threaten or be negative. Rather,

---

Figure 2.5   *Critical phases and key variables that determine the motivating power of counselors as change agents*

Phase 1: Building up motivating power	1. Encouraging clients to make self-disclosures *versus* not doing so 2. Giving positive feedback (acceptance and understanding) *versus* giving neutral or negative feedback in response to self-disclosure 3. Using self-disclosures to give insight and cognitive restructuring *versus* giving little insight or cognitive restructuring
Phase 2: Using motivating power	4. Making directive statements or endorsing specific recommendations regarding actions the client should carry out *versus* abstaining from any directive statements or endorsements 5. Eliciting commitment to the recommended course of action *versus* not eliciting commitment 6. Attributing the norms being endorsed to a respected secondary group *versus* not doing so 7. Giving selective positive feedback *versus* giving noncontingent acceptance or predominantly neutral or negative feedback 8. Giving communications and training procedures that build up a sense of personal responsibility *versus* giving no such communications or training
Phase 3: Retaining motivating power after contact ends and promoting internalization	9. Giving reassurances that the counselor will continue to maintain an attitude of positive regard *versus* giving no such reassurances 10. Making arrangements for phone calls, exchange of letters, or other forms of communication that foster hope for future contact, real or symbolic, at the time of terminating face-to-face meetings *versus* making no such arrangements 11. Giving reminders that continue to foster a sense of personal responsibility *versus* giving no such reminders 12. Building up the client's self-confidence about succeeding without the aid of the counselor *versus* not doing so

From I. Janis, *Short Term Counseling.* New Haven: Yale University Press. Copyright 1983. Reprinted by permission.

---

clients seem to profit when they are made aware of what is likely to work and what isn't when the counselor selectively reinforces certain types of verbalizations and behavior.

Finally, it should be noted that Janis gives extensive attention to the final phase of the interview, that of maintaining change (Stage 5 of the decisional model). Specific techniques of support—such as arranging for peer contact, phone calls, and the potential of followup—appear to be useful in promoting and maintaining change.

The Janis model of decision counseling may be termed a "coaching style." Janis himself describes the model as follows:

> When the client regards the health-care practioner as an Olympic coach, she conveys the idea that in some sense, she thinks of the coach as treating her like an Olympic star. (p. 41)

Figure 2.6   *An Exercise in Decisional Counseling*

     Find a friend or family member who has a decision to make. Ask your "client" if you may take him or her through a systematic decisional program. Good topics for your first attempt include a major purchase, a forthcoming job search, or how to resolve a current problem with a friend or colleague. The following exercise includes the five-stage structure of the interview.

1. *Rapport/Structuring.* Spend some time developing rapport and telling your "client" about the structure of the session that will follow.
2. *Data Gathering.* Define the problem clearly and include a positive asset search. You will want to ask about the client's past history with this problem and how he or she has gone about making decisions. Search for the important traits and factors underlying the problem and assets.
3. *Determine Outcomes.* Ask the client what an ideal and specific solution to this problem might be. Your goal for client decisional style is that of intentional, vigilant decisions.
4. *Generate Alternative Solutions.* Use creative decisional models presented in this chapter. Given the clear definition of the problem and the ideal outcome, what alternatives can you and the client generate? Brainstorm as many ideas as possible.

     Then, systematically list the alternatives generated and fill in balance sheets as presented in Figure 2.4. Follow this by prioritizing the goals and selecting one alternative for action.

     Ask your client to think ahead a year from now and to creatively anticipate how life would be, given the implementation of the favored alternatives. This future diary may be written if you wish. Talk with the client about the future diary and give special attention to the emotions the client has toward this alternative. Will the client be satisfied and comfortable? You may find that serious examination of the future may bring up new issues and new concerns. For the purpose of this exercise, stay with the original problem as defined and note other problems for a possible followup chat.

     If the alternative selected does not *feel right* emotionally, consider other alternatives in the client list of priorities.

     Finally, ask the client to select one possibility for implementation.

5. *Generalization.* Make a contract with your client to implement the decision or a part of the decision. This may itself take some creativity. Followup on your client in the next few days to see how the decision is going and, if necessary, encourage the client to "fine tune" the decision so that minor problems and setbacks do not undermine the total effort. Depending on the issue, develop a systematic long-term plan for generalization.

     Decisions do not occur in a vacuum in the counseling office. You and your relationship with the client will impact the client's life. The five-stage model presented here—when coupled with specific decisional research and other models of systematic decision making—can make an important difference in the client's life. The client who becomes a vigilant decision maker is a result of your own vigilance and intentionality in your decisions in the helping process.

SUMMARY OF THIS CHAPTER

Competencies required for mastery of concepts in this chapter include the abilities to:

1. *Act creatively. Creativity* may be defined as "letting go" and spontaneously generating something new from already existing pieces. The somewhat more systematic, but analogous, task of the therapist is to help the client organize "bits and pieces," or traits and factors, of the decisional problem into new and creative alternatives for action.

2. *Understand and describe the major themes of decisional counseling.* Decisional counseling has been presented as a modern version of trait and factor theory and, also, as a model underlying other counseling and therapy systems. All clients make decisions drawing on factors in their individual personhood and from information in the environment.

3. *Define and demonstrate the five basic interviewing stages.* The basic structure of the interview includes the following five stages: rapport and structuring; data gathering; determining outcomes; generating alternative solutions; and generalization (transfer of learning from the interview to the "real world").

4. *Modify the interview structure to meet the needs of individually and culturally distinct clients.* Decision making underlies the helping process, but different individuals and different cultural groups may have different decisional styles. In addition, you have your own unique style that you must respect as you work with others.

5. *Describe the major aspects of Janis' and Mann's decisional models for counseling.* Mann presents decisional counseling as a psychoeducational/prevention technique and uses groups to teach decisional skills. Janis' decision-counseling model is divided into three phases with major emphasis on clients changing their behavior (for example, weight loss, stopping smoking) in their daily life beyond the immediate confines of the interview.

6. *Define and use key terms and concepts of this chapter.* Among the important ideas in this chapter are creativity, decisional counseling, Frank Parsons' Vocational Bureau, the relationship of person and environment in decision making, trait and factor theory, the five stages of the interview, culturally sensitive use of tests, vigilant decisional style, balance sheet grid, and the importance of followup in the interview as demonstrated by Janis' decision counseling.

REFERENCES

BRAMMER, L.,   *The Helping Relationship.* Englewood Cliffs, NJ: Prentice-Hall, 1985.

CARKHUFF, R.,   *The Art of Problem Solving.* Amherst, MA: Human Resource Development, 1973.

IVEY, A.,   *Intentional Interviewing and Counseling.* Monterey, CA: Brooks/Cole, 1983.

IVEY, A., and W. MATTHEWS,   "A Meta-Model for Structuring the Clinical Interview." *Journal of Counseling and Development,* 1984, *63,* 237–243.

IVEY, A., with L. SIMEK-DOWNING,   *Counseling and Psychotherapy.* Englewood Cliffs, NJ: Prentice-Hall, 1980.

JANIS, I.,   *Short-term Counseling.* New Haven, CT: Yale, 1983.

JANIS, I. and L. MANN,   *Decision Making: A Psychological Analysis of Conflict, Choice, and Commitment.* New York: Free Press, 1977.

JOHNSON, R., "Individual Styles of Decision Making: A Theoretical Model for Counseling." *Personnel and Guidance Journal,* 1978, *56,* 530–536.

MANN, L., G. BESWICK, P. ALLOUACHE, and M. IVEY, Decision Workshop for the Improvement of Decision Making Skills. Adelaide, South Australia, Flinders University, 1982.

MARLATT, A., and J. GORDON, "Determinants of Relapse: Implications for the Maintenance of Behavior Change." In P. Davidson and S. Davidson (eds.), *Behavioral Medicine: Changing Life Styles.* New York: Brunner/Mazel, 1980, pp. 410–452.

MARLATT, A., and J. GORDON (EDS.), *Relapse Prevention: Maintenance Strategies in the Treatment of Addictive Behaviors.* New York: Guilford, 1985.

MARX, R., "Relapse Prevention for Managerial Training: A Model for Maintenance of Behavior Change," *Academy of Management Review,* 1982, 7, 433–441.

PARSONS, F., *Choosing a Vocation.* New York: Agathon, 1909; 1967.

PATERSON, D., and J. DARLEY, *Men, Women, and Jobs.* Minneapolis: University of Minnesota, 1936.

REPS, P., *Zen Flesh, Zen Bones.* New York: Doubleday, 1957.

WILLIAMSON, E., *How to Counsel Students.* New York: McGraw-Hill, 1939.

SUGGESTED SUPPLEMENTARY READING

IVEY, A., and W. MATTHEWS, "A Meta-Model for Structuring the Clinical Interview." *Journal of Counseling and Development,* 1984, *63,* 237–243.
A practical and theoretical presentation of the five stages of the interview.

JANIS, I., *Short-term Counseling.* New Haven: Yale, 1983.
A scholarly, yet readable, summary of research and practice covering several years of Janis' work. The book is brief, yet provides an excellent overview of how to integrate decision making in the interview *and* produce results.

JANIS, I., and L. MANN, *Decision Making: A Psychological Analysis of Conflict, Choice and Commitment.* New York: Free Press, 1977.
This book is a highly sophisticated and carefully documented study of the decision process. Theory and research are blended into an interesting and important view.

SHALLCROSS, D., *Teaching Creative Behavior.* Englewood Cliffs, NJ: Prentice-Hall, 1981.
This slim book is one of the better sources for creativity exercises and for attuning the individual to the central methods and constructs of creativity.

3

THE SKILLS
OF INTENTIONAL
INTERVIEWING

GENERAL PREMISE

An integrated knowledge of skills, theory, and practice is essential for culturally intentional counseling and therapy.

Skills form the foundation of effective theory and practice: The culturally intentional therapist knows how to construct a creative decision-making interview and *can use microskills to attend to and influence clients in a predicted direction.* Important in this process are individual and cultural empathy, client observation skills, assessment of person and environment, and the application of positive techniques of growth and change.

Theory provides organizing principles for counseling and therapy: The culturally intentional counselor has knowledge of alternative theoretical approaches and treatment modalities.

Practice is the integration of skills and theory: The culturally intentional counselor or therapist is competent in skills and theory, and is able to apply them to research and practice for client benefit.

Undergirding integrated competence in skills, theory, and practice is an intentional awareness of one's own personal worldview and how that worldview may be similar to and/or different from the worldview and personal constructions of the client and other professionals.

GOALS OF ATTENDING AND INFLUENCING MICROSKILLS

This chapter* presents a full interview conducted by Joann Griswold, a graduate student who made a typescript of an interview as a course requirement. This session, held with a 72-year-old man, produced significant change in one interview. Through the use of effective decisional counseling and the microskills of attending and influencing, it is possible to make a significant difference in the life of your client.

Joann Griswold

Some goals of this chapter are to:

1. Present both the basic interview microskills of attending, listening, and influencing and their potential impact on the client for change.
2. Illustrate how microskills and the five-stage decisional model of Chapter 2 can be integrated into a complete interview and produce change in a client that is maintained over time.
3. Present an important chart in which the differential use of microskills in different theories of counseling and therapy may be compared.

As a foundation to skills in counseling and therapy, you will want to examine the core construct of attending behavior and how it is played out among different cultures. When you have grasped basic attending and influencing skills and behaviors, you have a solid foundation for building more advanced skills and techniques that can facilitate your client's growth and development.

---

*Concepts in this chapter are derived from A. Ivey, *Intentional Interviewing and Counseling* (Monterey, CA: Brooks/Cole, 1983) and are used by permission of the publisher.

IDENTIFYING NONVERBAL SKILLS

Before reading this chapter, turn to Figure 3.1, which illustrates a counselor listening to a client in two different ways. Which of the counselor styles do you prefer?

List on a separate sheet the specific behaviors of the two counselors. Be as precise as possible and identify observable aspects of their behavior.

Through body language and words, the skilled counselor communicates that he or she is attending to the client. In Figure 3.1, we see in counselor b poor eye contact, a slouched body position, and closed arms and legs. In counselor a the forward trunk lean, direct eye contact, and relaxed body style communicate interest and assurance.

It is possible through such analysis to identify highly specific verbal and nonverbal behaviors of the intentional and the ineffective counselor. This process of identification and selection of specific skills of counseling is termed the *microskills approach.* Using the microskills approach, we will break down the complex interaction of the counseling interview into manageable and learnable dimensions.

By the time you have completed this chapter, you should be able to: (1) identify and describe the several microskills used by successful counselors; and (2) use these microskills to score interview behavior of both clients and counselors. With further experience and practice, you can become proficient in these skills yourself and apply them in an interview. The skills approach is invaluable to all counselors regardless of theoretical framework, style, or technique.

Figure 3.1
Photos by John Ivey

a b

THE BASIC MICROSKILLS OF ATTENDING AND INFLUENCING

Through examination of the intentional and ineffective examples of counselor eye contact and body language, you have just participated in a basic exercise in microskills training that leads to the central concept of *attending behavior.* If you are going to interview or counsel another person it seems obvious that you should look at them and maintain natural eye contact. Further, your body should communicate interest. Once it was believed that counseling was solely a verbal occupation but, with the arrival of videotape and increased use of films in interview training, it has become obvious that nonverbal communication is basic in any interviewing, counseling, or therapy session. Thus eye contact and body language are the physical fundamentals of attending behavior.

A third aspect of attending behavior is vocal tone. Does your voice communicate warmth and interest, or boredom and the lack of caring? Even though you may be physically attending, your voice often indicates the quality of your willingness and interest in listening.

Moreover, if you are to attend to someone else, you must also "listen" to them. Listening, however, is not an observable behavior. Intentional therapists not only maintain attentive body postures, they also stay on the topic of the client and seldom change topics abruptly or interrupt. A major mistake of beginning counselors is to change the topic of discussion and ignore or fail to hear what the client has to say. For example:

CLIENT:	I've been downtown this afternoon and I really got anxious. I wanted to run when I saw a friend even. I simply don't want to be with anyone.
NONATTENDING COUNSELOR:	Let's see now, you're a sophomore this year?
ATTENDING COUNSELOR:	You say you wanted to run when you saw your friend. Could you describe the situation and what was happening in more detail?

It is seldom necessary or desirable to change the client's topic. Attend carefully and the client will tell you all you need to know. However, attending behavior varies from culture to culture and from individual to individual. Do not assume that your pattern of attending (or influencing) is appropriate for each individual whom you may meet. See Figure 3.2, which illustrates this point.

Attending behavior, then, is a simple but central aspect of all interviewing, counseling, and therapy. It involves four key dimensions: eye contact, appropriate body language, vocal tone, and verbal following.

Selective attention is a concept closely related to attending behavior. Observation of counselors reveals that they selectively attend and selectively ignore certain portions of client statements. Here, for example, is a longer client statement in which it is obviously impossible to attend to and respond to the total mes-

Figure 3.2 Nonverbal Attending Patterns in U.S. Middle-Class Culture Compared with Patterns of Other Cultures

NONVERBAL DIMENSION	U.S. MIDDLE-CLASS PATTERN	CONTRASTING EXAMPLE FROM ANOTHER CULTURE
Eye contact	When listening to a person, direct eye contact is appropriate. When talking, eye contact is often less frequent.	Some Blacks in the U.S. may have patterns directly opposite and demonstrate more eye contact when talking and less when listening.
Body language	Slight forward trunk lean facing the person. Handshake a general sign of welcome.	Certain Eskimo and Inuit groups in the Arctic sit side by side when working on personal issues. A male giving a female a firm handshake may be seen as giving a sexual invitation.
Vocal tone and speech rate	A varied vocal tone is favored, with some emotionality shown. Speech rate is moderate.	Many Hispanic groups have a more extensive and expressive vocal tone and may consider U.S. middle-class styles unemotional and "flat." Speech rate is faster among many Hispanic groups.
Physical space	Conversation distance is ordinarily "arm's length" or more for comfort.	Common in Arab and Middle-Eastern cultures is a six- to twelve-inch conversational distance, a point at which the middle-class U.S. individual becomes uncomfortable.
Time	Highly structured, linear view of time. Generally "on time" for appointments.	Several South American countries operate on a more casual view of time and do not plan that specified, previously agreed-upon times for meetings will necessarily hold.

Note: This figure is intended to provide an overview of some key cultural nonverbal patterns in middle-class U.S.A. and to provide an example from another culture to illustrate some major differences. Further study of other cultural patterns is highly recommended. It is also critical to remember that individuals within a single cultural group vary extensively.

sage. Read the client statement and select the item or items you think most important:

CLIENT: Things have been going pretty well. The business has been having some problems, though—I think one of the floorpeople is ripping us off. But I can't figure out who is doing it or how. It's been better with my wife, too—we even had sex this last week. She's getting into this women's lib stuff. I don't know what to make of it. Got a letter from Mom last week and Dad is sick and that night I had the weirdest dream about Dad smoking a broken cigar . . . (pause) I dunno . . . (pause) My daughter's coming home from college this weekend. I will really be glad to see her. Perhaps she'll calm things down around here.

Write down the idea(s) from the preceding passage that you would respond to.

Many client statements provide the counselor with a wide array of potential items for attention. In the example above, the client has suggested several potentially important areas for further examination (business, stealing, sexuality, women's liberation, parents, dreams, family relations). Depending on your theory of what is important, you selected one of the above or some other alternative. Similarly, different theories stress different information as most important and, through selective attention, determine what the clients are most likely to talk about. Therapists tend to selectively attend to information provided by the client, and the pattern of selective attention may say more about the counselor than it does about the client. Psychodynamic therapists often respond to sexual material, behavioral counselors to concrete issues that need resolution, and humanistic-existential counselors to relationship issues. As you begin to examine your own interviewing style, you will find that you have certain areas of a client's life that interest you more than others. This is not inappropriate, but it is critical that you are aware of your patterns of selective attention. Some counselors have clients who talk only about sex (or dreams, or male-female relationships, or feminist concerns, etc.) while other counselors may have clients who never talk about sex. The reason tends to lie more in the counselor than in the client.

Influencing behavior is the involvement of the therapist in effecting client growth or change. Attending behavior is critical for client growth, but if used as the sole vehicle for change, client growth can be slow and arduous. When the therapist takes direct action and involves herself or himself in the process of the interview, change can occur more rapidly. All theories of counseling in some way incorporate the idea of the counselor as an agent of change and growth. By their very presence, counselors influence clients.

The specific observable behaviors of influencing are closely correlated with those of attending. If one is to influence others, one must look at them and maintain eye contact: the body posture of the influencing counselor often has a slightly more forward trunk lean, while gestures tend to be those of direction and suggestion rather than of attention. Verbal following is again important, but the topic may be that of the counselor giving advice, suggestion, or direction. In effect, the subject of conversation is determined by the therapist.

Figure 3.4 illustrates examples of the role of the hands in influencing behavior. One might first notice the direct eye contact and the increased forward trunk lean. In picture 1 we see the hands relatively closed while in picture 2 they are more open. Picture 3 presents open palms as if presenting a gift, and picture

---

Figure 3.3 *Exercises in Attending and Influencing*

1. *Observation of intentional and ineffective listeners.* Search your environment for people who are clearly capable and effective listeners. They are the ones people like to talk to and seek out when they have a problem or concern. Note their patterns of eye contact, body language, and verbal following.

   Then seek out those whom you consider less effective and compare them on the same dimensions.

   Finally, look back in your own past and think about those who have been helpful to you and those less helpful. Examine their specific behaviors.

2. *A practical experiment with attending.* When talking to friend or family member, deliberately engage in negative attending behavior (look away, jump topic, slouch) and then at another time deliberately engage in positive attending. Note the effects attending and nonattending have on the other person.

3. *Classroom example.* Give special attention to the instructor via eye contact and a forward trunk lean. Very shortly you will find the teacher talking to you. It is possible he or she may even ignore the rest of the class. People talk to those who listen to them.

   Similarly, you will note that people who attend to others intentionally are noted and receive better service and warmer response than those who fail to engage in attending skills.

4. *Selective attention.* When talking to a friend or to a counseling client, note carefully the several things that are being said to you in any message you receive. Select an item of interest to you and attend to that. Later move back to another item in the same statement and respond. You will find that you can direct the flow of a conversation by your patterning of selective attention. This is a basic skill of any successful counselor, regardless of theoretical orientation.

5. *Influencing observation.* Select a person whose interpersonal influence you respect. It may be a friend or an acquaintance or it may be a film or television personality. Examine their verbal and nonverbal behaviors when they are trying to influence someone or presenting a point of view.

6. *Influencing and an exercise in assertion.* Go to a store and use ineffective influencing skills (look at floor, turn away from the clerk, mumble) and notice the service you receive (if any). Try positive influencing behavior and note your reception. This basic exercise can be used in any situation where you feel uncomfortable and not as intentional as you might wish to be.

---

4 represents even more openness (the bend of the fingers in the left hand may represent "Come back at me. What's your opinion of what I have just said?"). Such a series illustrates that many fine discriminations are possible in nonverbal observations. The first picture represents a stronger direction and "boxing in" while the last is more open. Which posture is "correct?" This, of course, depends on the context of the client-counselor communication. In some cases none would be appropriate; in others one way of presentation would be more effective; and in still others the pattern of nonverbal communication might make no difference at all. It remains important to realize that nonverbal communication through postures of influence or attention are influential on the content and process of counseling.

Figure 3.4 Alternative Uses of the Hands
Photos by John Ivey

56

Attending and influencing behavior—listening and talking—are further divided in the microskills approach into a series of communication skills such as questions, paraphrasing, interpretation, and self-disclosure. These specific verbal skills form the bulk of this chapter. However, before going further into their definition, it seems appropriate to present a complete counseling interview as a context for examining the attending and influencing skills.

AN INTERVIEW WITH MR. S.

The intentional counselor or therapist will know what he or she is doing and its impact on the client. One route toward more intentional and effective counseling is the careful analysis of your own interviewing style. The following interview was conducted by Joann Griswold and illustrates what can happen to benefit a client in one short interview. The interview also illustrates how knowledge of your microskill usage and decisional process can enable you to understand and describe, rather clearly, your own interview behavior.

This interview is representative of what you can do to analyze your own interviewing behavior. It also illustrates the impact of the several microskills and theories of this text on client growth and change. Important in this interview is that it is *real* and produced a change in one person's life. Furthermore, the client's age is 72, illustrating that client growth does not stop with old age; all individuals can respond to effective helping.

Background Information

At the time of the interview, the *counselor,* Joann Griswold, was a married 45-year-old graduate student working toward her M.S. degree in mental health nursing at the University of Massachusetts. She received her R.N. status and B.S. degrees at age 22 and actively practiced nursing for 4 years before "settling down and having a family." Over the next several years, Joann Griswold raised a family of four children. During that time she was active in community affairs and enjoyed a variety of hobbies ranging from sewing and reading to the writing of short humorous essays. As her family grew older, she became interested in volunteer work with mental health agencies and also worked as a social health educator with a migrant project. This led to her returning to school. The interview transcript with Mr. S. was completed as part of an assignment in her first course in counseling theories and techniques.

At varying times in this text you will be referred back to portions of this interview, so you will want to become familiar with it and the skill classification system outlined in this chapter. The skills listed will be outlined later in this chapter. *For the present, simply read the ongoing text of the interview, note Joann's commentaries, and observe how the five stages of the interview from Chapter 2 are illustrated. Later, you can return to the skill analysis for more detailed study.*

The *client*, Mr. S., is 72 and widowed. He is a retired postman and sought counseling in an alternative care agency for senior citizens, complaining about depression and an "inability to get started." This is the second interview. Key identifying data in the case have been changed.

Stage 1: Rapport/Structuring

In the first seven exchanges below, Joann quickly reestablishes rapport with the client. Each of us develop rapport with others uniquely. Basic to Joann's rapport development were solid attending behaviors of culturally appropriate eye contact, vocal tone, body posture, and verbal following. The microskills used by Joann are marked following her comments. The client's verbalizations are classified as well so that the specific impact of Joann's counseling can be noted. (Joann appears as "J" and Mr. S as "S.")

1. J:	OK if we tape this session?	1. Closed question
2. S:	Sure, that would be fine.	

It is critical that you inform clients and obtain permission before you tape a session, even if it is a practice session.

3. J:	Well, look at your smile.	3. Feedback
4. S:	*Today*, I feel pretty good.	
5. J:	You feel pretty good today, and that helps me feel good. What has happened since we last talked?	5. Reflection of feeling/self-disclosure/open question
6. S:	Things are a lot better now because I'm getting a lot more done—a lot of my problems that I didn't have finished, I've taken care of now. I'm more relaxed.	

Joann's analysis: It might have been helpful to have asked Mr. S. to identify concretely and specifically what is going well. Such an emphasis would give him a more solid base for the interview to follow.

7. J:	You're more relaxed; you're feeling better about yourself. I sense a feeling of relief and I hear you've taken care of some unfinished business. Am I hearing you?	7. Reflection of feeling/paraphrase followed by a checkout
8. S:	Um-hummmm.	

Joann's analysis: Mr. S. appeared uncomfortable at this point and this surprised me. So I went into a summary of the previous interview to provide a structure for the session and to help us discover alternatives for exploration and action. At 7, I was not fully with Mr. S.

9. J:	As we talked last time, we discussed the pressures you've been under—from many places.	9. Summary

Your sister, many projects, old friends, new friends, and the fact that this pressure finds you in the lifelong habit of doing for others before you do for yourself. You'd like to think of yourself as a fun-loving person who would like to get out of the rut of feeling overly committed to others.

I admire your strength and your commitment to your family—raising children, taking care of your wife when she was so terribly ill, and now helping your invalid sister-in-law. I feel very fortunate to know you—you show a great deal of love and caring. I'm happy things are going better for you.

Feedback/self-disclosure about relationship

Joann's analysis: The summary and positive feedback seemed to brighten Mr. S. up. He sat up straighter and smiled as I talked.

When I saw this, I felt we had adequate rapport and thus I could begin the data-gathering and problem-exploration phase of the interview. The two questions below represent the beginning of the next stage of the session.

Can you tell me more about what is happening with you? Can you tell me how things can continue to get better?

Open question

Stage 2:   Data Gathering

Joann's last two questions in 9 above represent the beginning of the data-gathering phase. It can be seen that transitions between stages are subtle with counselor and client moving among and between the stages, recycling information as needed. In the following segment, you will note Joann giving considerable attention both to problems and to strengths of the client through variations of the positive asset search. She will use listening skills as the primary mode of problem definition.

10. S: Well, for instance, ummm, I started to get involved in the past three or four months . . . when my wife first died, *I didn't do anything.* Now, I find myself getting out a bit more and that I feel better—especially if I do things on my own. A lot of these people I'm involved with are still getting me to do more than I want to do. *I don't know how to turn them down.* They expect a lot from me and I think I end up doing what they suggest just to keep busy so I don't think of my wife. Yet, *I'm alone* so much.

Comment: The client here summarizes in brief form the essence of his problem. His wife has died and he is sad and alone. Others come in to help, but he has mixed feelings about that

. . . he both wants to do things on his own and to be with others and keep busy. Ultimately, he is not making his own decisions. Joann could go in many different directions from this statement. Note that she focuses on the feelings.

11. J:	Now that you're alone, ah, I sense what you're saying is that you are lonely or alone quite a bit of the time . . .	11. Reflection of feeling
12. S:	Yes! (Emphatically)	
13. J:	. . . and that you thought that maybe some of these activities would serve the purpose of filling up your time and you wouldn't feel so lonely. How does this sound? Does it make sense?	13. Paraphrase/note checkout as closed question
14. S:	Yes, that's right, hummmm . . . and perhaps I have gone into the wrong things. These new friends think they are helping me and doing me a favor because *I am* so lonely. It helps, but at the same time I don't get to choose what I do. Other people are choosing for me.	
15. J:	Mmmmm . . . friends think they are helping you. I see you like to be with people and they like to be with you. Now, doggone it, if some of them would just realize you have the right to choose what to do.	15. Paraphrase/confrontation

Comment: Joann is using basic listening skills of paraphrasing and reflection of feeling to further clarify and specify Mr. S.'s difficulties. Confrontation is scored as a discrepancy between S.'s and others' desire.

16. S:	And *when* I want to do it, I would like to get the courage to just say *no* . . . but I just go along thinking, well there will be a solution somewhere, sometime. (laughs)	
17. J:	You're laughing, but I sense from the tone of your voice and the look on your face that underneath it isn't a laughing matter.	17. Reflection of feeling/confrontation

Comment: Joann has used basic listening skills of paraphrasing and reflection of feeling to clarify Mr. S.'s difficulties. Response 17 is a particularly important counseling lead in that she here confronts the discrepancy between what Mr. S. says and how he says it. At this point, Mr. S. lacks genuineness. Failure to observe and confront client discrepancies fully can result in a superficial interview. But, one must have solid rapport before one can confront such discrepancies. Mr. S.'s body and words mirror the discrepancy identified at 15.

18. S:	No, it really . . . isn't a laughing matter.	
19. J:	I sense you get angry.	19. Reflection of feeling
20. S:	Yes, it bothers me . . . (pause)	
21. J:	. . . bothers you . . . (pause)	21. Encourager
22. S:	. . . Ummmmmmm . . . and, ah, when my wife was alive, I didn't have these problems because I	

was so busy with her. Now in these last two or three months, the loneliness is facing me. I'm in trouble.

Joann's analysis: In the last few statements, Mr. S. has come more to the heart of his concerns. His last comment refers to the months when Mr. S. took care of his wife during her failing health. Emotionally, at that time he felt that his wife was "with him" everywhere he went. I note that in my next comment I failed to attend and the topic jumped. Does this tie in with my own tendency always to make things a little more pleasant than they really are and avoiding the difficult conflicts? In some ways, I am like Mr. S. myself. I think the confrontation at 17 opened things up for me a little faster than I was comfortable with. As often happens, the encourager/restatement opens up a key issue.

23. J: I hear you saying that, uh, that these new friends are infringing on your time. And I hear that you feel pulled in directions you don't want to go in. Is that right?

23. Paraphrase/checkout

24. S: Yes, that's it! You're right!

Comment: *Clients often exclaim "that's right" when the counselor offers an accurate paraphrase.*

25. J: And you feel you are being controlled by others; you're resenting this control. You'd like to break loose and do as *you,* yourself please. I don't like it when others try to control me. I get frustrated and angry and then resentful when others try to plan for me.

25. Interpretation/self-disclosure/confrontation

26. S: Ummmmmmm, I would like to break out of it and I would like to be able to choose my pastimes and go do things at times that I feel I want to do them. I don't want to be pressured . . . do this, do that.

27. J: Ummmmmmm . . . pressure . . . when you talk about pressure, I sense you can feel it now. How do you react to pressure? Can you tell me how pressure affects you?

27. Reflection of feeling/open question

28. S: I get *depressed.* I don't sleep well, it's on my mind. I haven't slept well since my wife died.

29. J: So you . . . you go to bed at night and you think about your problems and you get depressed and its a vicious cycle. (Mr. S.: Right.) And instead of looking forward to a project or something, you're going to enjoy, it feels more like a "should."
(Mr. S: Ummmmmmm . . .) Shoulds are obligations to other people and things seem to be like a leash leading us around. We all get in these traps. But when we get obligated to someone else, we need to think, "What about me?"

29. Summary/interpretation/self-disclosure/confrontation

Comment: With this summary, Joann closes the phase of data gathering. She puts the problem in perspective and clarifies the general issue. Underneath problem definition is a strong emphasis on Mr. S.'s positive assets and strengths. Joann moves to the third stage of the interview with her continuation of 29.

What is the best thing that could happen if for one whole day you chucked all your other people obligations and . . . ?	Open question

Stage 3: Determining Outcomes

With the above question, Joanne moves toward problem solving. The importance of having some idea of a goal for your unique client cannot be overstressed. With Mr. S., for example, he talks of self-direction and being alone at times. But, with another client, the "problems" of too many people might be an ideal solution to loneliness. Some want company all the time, others are more comfortable by themselves. Do not assume your ideal outcome will be the client's happy life. We all vary in our goals.

30. S:	I sometimes like to go off by myself and just fish and fish. Other times, I like to be comfortable with just a few old friends I've known a long time and just play cards. I like to dance, but only now and then.	
31. J:	Being by yourself and with a few special friends is enjoyable. Those who know you enjoy your company. I enjoy being with you too. These are some real strengths. Some people can't stand to be alone.	31. Paraphrase/self-disclosure about relationship
32. S:	I guess I am lucky. I still have some real friends, but these other people . . . I don't like to hurt their feelings . . .	

Comment: Over the next several interchanges, which are deleted, Joann and Mr. S. talk about how he might develop a more comfortable balance of being alone and being with others. The purpose of the discussion here was to clarify more precisely what Mr. S.'s ideal outcomes are. At this point, Joann has a grasp of the real situation facing Mr. S. and his ideal solution. It is possible to turn to the next stage of the interview.

Stage 4: Generating Alternative Solutions

The fourth stage of the interview is oriented to problem solving. Note that Joann might have solved the wrong problem if she had not waited to gather data on problems, assets, and desired outcomes. The goal of this stage is to generate several possible alternative solutions.

As counselor, you have the possibility of using your own theory and concepts to help the client generate ideas; or you can place the responsibility for new ideas on the client. If you are going to place responsibility for problem solving with the client, a clear summary of the situation, assets, and major discrepancies between the real and ideal situation would be helpful. In this case, such a summary might be:

J: Mr. S., I've been listening for awhile. It sounds as if your central concern is taking more charge of your own life. You've said you'd be most happy if you could be alone and fish when you'd like and spend most of your time with close friends. On the other hand, what is happening is that people who are less important to you are taking a lot of your time and you simply can't do what you want to do. A lot of this has to do with your effort to please others. You've got many strengths . . . people like you, you are able to find things you enjoy, I admire your courage. Given all this, what comes to your mind which might be useful in finding solutions?

This summary of the real and ideal situation is strengthened by the addition of the positive assets that implicitly say to the client, "You have the ability and strength to do it." Many clients find such a summary at the beginning of Phase 4 of the interview critical in enabling them to find satisfactory resolution.

      In the segment that follows, however, Joann chose a more active influencing style. You will note that her usage of influencing skills markedly increases. In the first portion of the interview, relatively few influencing skills may be found. Joann also draws from assertiveness training theory (Chapter 9) and psychodynamic theory (Chapter 8). It is the latter theory that proves to be most helpful with Mr. S. and allows him his first good night's sleep since his wife died. (As mentioned, some of the preceding interchanges have been deleted.)

42. J:	So you want to be yourself and stand up for what you want. Let's imagine that your friends Joe and Mary have called and want to take you to an auction, something that you do enjoy. Then, imagine that I am one of your busy acquaintances and I call and say, "Say there's a meeting and dinner at the lodge for our members' children who are graduating from college next semester. I'll pick you up at 1:30." I know you don't like large meetings. What are you going to say?	42. Paraphrase/directive
43. S:	I should tell you, "Well, I'm sorry, but I want to go with Joe and Mary." But, if I had made my new friend think I was interested (even though I wasn't), I would feel I *should* go with him. I just seem to go with the pressure. I don't want to hurt anyone's feelings.	

Joann's analysis: A full-blown assertiveness exercise might have been useful. Here we are just talking, but the information is still useful.

44. J:	Do you feel that Joe and Mary's feelings would be hurt?	44. Closed question
45. S:	No, ah well . . . they would understand . . . they are real friends. They understand I get into these things. I guess I just feel comfortable with them and they will not think badly about me if I cancel.	

Comment: In the next few exchanges, Joann and Mr. S. explore possible ways in which the problem could be resolved. Mr. S. continues to repeat the pattern of stating a wish to do something but then being unable to change his behavior. He is clearly immobilized or stuck, he lacks intentionality. Furthermore, he now understands his problem more clearly, but a beginning insight into one's difficulties doesn't change one's actions.

In the next series, Joann uses some directives and free association techniques derived from psychodynamic theory.

50. J:	. . . And so, how does it feel when you give in like that again and again in different situations?	50. Open question
51. S:	Miserable, it makes me depressed . . . with the exception of the people I'm helping . . . that isn't so miserable. I do like to help others.	
52. J:	I'd like you to try something. Just relax and close your eyes. Relax and think back—think about that miserable feeling just after the door was closed. You had the realization, you are going to do once again what you don't want to do . . . (pause) . . . Get with that feeling of misery . . . (pause) . . . Now think back to a time in your life when you felt miserable . . . (pause) . . . You look like you've got something to share with me.	52. Directive
53. S:	I'm thinking of something from away back. I borrowed something from my brother without telling him. And when he found out, he just cursed me and wished me dead and lost his temper and screamed at me. I think I was about six . . . . I just went into my room and cried. I was *miserable.* (Mr. S.'s eyes are moist and his voice is very sad.)	
54. J:	I would have been miserable too. Right now, I can sense how miserable you were.	54. Self-disclosure/reflection of feeling
55. S:	It seems ridiculous, but I was so miserable. He really hurt my feelings and made me feel guilty. He hurt my feelings, but I didn't hurt his.	
56. J:	What did you say to him?	56. Open question
57. S:	Like always, I said I was sorry and I didn't mean it. But it didn't help, he just swore some more . . . he had a terrible temper. I just cried it out. And so it seems, Joann, that I just never dared hurt people since that day . . .	

58. J: What I'm hearing (Mr. S: Ummmmmmn.) is that   58. Interpretation
          you are afraid you'll hurt people in the same
          manner you were hurt.
59. S: (softly) That's right, that's part of the answer.

Joann's analysis: I was surprised at myself when I used the focused free association exercise (see page 220). *It was the first time I had used it and I was surprised at its power. I don't usually think in psychodynamic terms, but it is clear that Mr. S. was repeating a long-time life pattern. Our earlier discussion seemed stuck. However, I wonder if I had used the assertiveness-training exercise* (see page 239), *if I might have done just as well or better?*

60. J: Has . . . have you thought about how you hurt   60. Open question
          yourself in this process?
61. S: Um . . . ah . . . (tearfully) subconsciously, I don't
          dwell on myself too much. I haven't thought
          about the incident with my brother in years. I
          don't dwell on myself much.
62. J: You don't dwell on yourself too much . . . you   62. Encourager/interpreta-
          care for others. Even in the situation with your   tion/feedback
          brother, you tried to understand him. You come
          across as a pretty courageous person both then
          and now.

Comment: This is a clear example of a positive reframe or interpretation. In virtually all situations, one can find positives. Locating the positive in negative events often enables clients to deal more effectively with difficulties.

63. S: Thank you . . . (sadly) No, it seems my life has
          always been to live for others, but I should have
          a change, but its difficult to change . . . I'd like
          to do fun things (very softly), but there is always
          someone demanding . . . demanding.
64. J: You . . . you just feel the pull. I can relate to that   64. Paraphrase/self-disclo-
          . . . I feel the pull from my family and other com-   sure/open   question/con-
          mitments and sometimes I never seem to have   frontation
          time for myself and what I enjoy. Sometimes that
          pull doesn't leave much room for you. Who or
          what in particular helps you relieve the tension?
65. S: My children are a real comfort . . . they call me
          often . . .

Comment: In the next few exchanges, Joann and Mr. S. confront the tug and pull of life and his assets to cope with the problems. Together they list his family, love of fishing, ability to be alone, and his commitment to others as critical positive ingredients of a problem solution. The discussion then turns to his wife's death. It should be noted that this is a cycling back to the problem definition phase of the interview even though it occurs late in the session.

71. S: I feel guilty; I don't know why I feel guilty. I'm
          beginning to realize as we go back to this hurting
          people that I don't do enough of what is good for

	me. I'm realizing that I would sleep better and not be so depressed if I would go out and do what is good for me, but . . . I'm not.	
72. J:	For most of your life, you've been taking care of other people ahead of yourself. Since your wife's death, you have tried to keep from being lonely by being very involved, but this isn't working. You've got many strengths, friends and family. I also see you getting tired of not standing up for your rights in certain situations. Does that make sense to you?	72. Summary followed by checkout/confrontation
73. S:	(With surprise) . . . Why yes, that's about it. I don't think you missed anything.	
74. J:	Then you are growing impatient with yourself? I'd like to see you get out and have all the fun you want, or stay at home in peace, or go out and go fishing. Is this the way you feel? Tell me . . .	74. Selective paraphrase/self-disclosure about relationship/checkout
75. S:	I should like that, but after all these years . . .	
76. J:	I sense that maybe it isn't as hard as you imagine. I like your laugh and your sometimes high spirits. Now let's get going . . . let's make a list of all the happy things you can do for yourself.	76. Feedback/directive

Joann's analysis: I see myself becoming quite aggressive here. Am I allowing Mr. S. to be self-directed or am I laying "my trip" on him? My personal style is to get on with it and do it. Is it right to impose that on him?

77. S:	It would be strange for me (laughs). I enjoy doing things like trips with the seniors to the ice show. Things like that make me feel good.	
78. J:	Could you tell me how you feel when you feel good?	78. Open question
79. S:	I'm relaxed and not depressed (very clearly and firmly). (Joann: Mmmmmmm.) . . . and especially if I'm looking forward to a trip . . . say to New York or the ice show. Then I'm not depressed, I'm doing what I want to do. But, if someone needs me, I'll stop doing what I want to do and go with them because they seem to feel unhappy when they can't go. I should do what I can do to make them happy.	

Joann's analysis: After all these years, he is still trying to please his brother. This I hadn't realized before. He repeats the pattern with his brother with people around him. He needs to have permission to have a good time.

Stage 5: Generalization

In this final phase of the interview, Joann becomes quite directive and uses some Gestalt repetition techniques (Chapter 10). Her effort here is directed to moving the understandings generated in stage 4 to the real world. It does little good if nothing comes of the interchange. Note the increased use of directives common at this stage.

80. J:	Do you ever say to yourself, I should do what I can to make myself happy?	80. Closed question
81. S:	I don't . . .	
82. J:	Repeat this after me. "I, John S., should do what I can to make myself happy."	82. Directive
83. S:	I, John S., should do all I can to make myself happy. (A little weakly)	
84. J:	Try it again.	84. Directive
85. S:	I, John S., should do all I can to make myself happy. (More firmly)	
86. J:	Let's try it again, only this time, "I, John S., *am* going to do what I can to make myself happy.	86. Directive
87. S:	I, John S., am going to do what I can to be happy. (A little more softly again.)	
88. J:	You look a little worried or sad over that.	88. Reflection of feeling
89. S:	Can I do it? Like I said, will it be easy or will it be a fight? How will I get the power in me to do it after all these years?	
90. J:	You have the power, you have a lot of power. You have a lot of strength. Can you tell me about your power and your strength? Tell me about the power and strength that you have.	90. Feedback/open question/ directive
91. S:	I have always had a lot of power and strength to do things for others, so if I can get the power and strength to do things for others, maybe I can get the power and strength for myself . . . maybe this is the solution? Would it be so?	
92. J:	Hallelujah! I do believe you're on the track. You are rearranging your priorities and saying, "I, John S., am a very important person. I, John S., have to take care of myself first."	92. Reflection of meaning
93. S:	And, then the rest will follow . . . (without direction and firmly, Mr. S. comments) I, John S., have the power and strength to take care of myself first after all these years.	

Joann's analysis: His response at this point surprised me. I didn't expect it quite so soon and firmly. I am impressed by his desire to "get on with it," which is so similar to my personal constructs. I also surprised myself. I believe in the humanistic school of self-direction and careful listening (Chapter 10), but I seem to have moved almost as fast as Fritz Perls. Maybe we humanistic types need not be afraid to act?

94. J:	Mr. S., I like the way you say that. I feel better about the way you said it that time. You seem very serious. Now, what one thing will you do differently next week to follow up on this?	94. Feedback/open question
95. S:	I've got a history of never quitting. I shouldn't quit on myself either. For 72 years I've been doing what others want, but this week I think I'll	

cancel that auction trip and go fishing. . . . I just hope it doesn't rain.

96. J:	You will take care of yourself first. The time is now. Is that what I hear you saying?	96. Reflection of meaning/checkout
97. S:	I hope so—no, I *will*. Thanks . . .	
98. J:	We'll talk about fish next week.	98. Social conclusion

Discussion of Interview with Mr. S.

That evening Mr. S. had the first full night's sleep since his wife's death, and this continued throughout the week. He returned the following week from a successful fishing trip.

A 6-month followup revealed continued normal sleeping patterns, much less depression, and found that Mr. S. was taking care of himself and making his own decisions. However, he still found himself in occasional double binds due to overcommitment and agreeing to do things he really didn't want to do. He discusses this now as "my nature, it helps me stay in contact with people. I just can't let them run over me anymore."

The microskills used by Joann follow a pattern common to many counselors and therapists in their interviews. Note that she has a predominance of attending skills in the first three stages and moves toward increased use of influencing skills in the later portions of the interview.

The general pattern of Joann's interviewing style closely resembles that of the humanistic counselor, particularly in terms of the early emphasis on attending and listening skills and the self-disclosures in which Joann discussed her own experience and impressions of the client. However, her interview contained more directives drawn from behavioral and psychodynamic theory than would be expected in a humanistic or Rogerian orientation.

This is a remarkable interview by a remarkable counselor; substantial and useful change can be brought about in a client in a single, well-designed session. Joann used most of the microskills in this chapter in an intentional fashion. She was also able to use the basic decisional model of the five-stage interview to organize the session in a useful structure. *It is important to note that Joann completed this interview before the model of the five-stage decisional interview was developed.* Examination of many skilled interviewers will reveal that this five-stage structure exists, even when it is not specifically planned.

It was once believed that only clients 40 years and younger could truly change their behavior as a result of counseling. The client, Mr. S., clearly demonstrates the strength that clients of all ages have at their disposal. Joann, through consistent use of the positive asset search and its variations, emphasized strengths in the client that permitted growth and development.

You, yourself, will want to conduct an interview and analyze your own ability to follow the five-stage model and produce predictable change in client behavior. It will be most helpful if you make a typescript and organize and analyze the in-

Figure 3.5

INTERVIEW STAGE	ONE	TWO	THREE	FOUR	FIVE	TOTAL
Attending Skills						
Closed questions	1	—	—	1	1	3
Closed questions as checkouts	1	2	2	3	1	9
Open questions	2	2	2	5	2	13
Encourager	—	1	2	2	—	5
Reflection of feelings	2	4	2	2	1	11
Reflection of meaning	—	—	—	—	2	2
Summary	1	1	1	—	—	3
Influencing Skills						
Feedback	2	—	—	2	2	6
Advice/information/ suggestion	—	—	—	—	—	—
Self-disclosure						
Relation to client	2	—	1	2	—	5
Relation to counsel	—	2	—	2	—	4
Interpretation	—	2	—	2	—	4
Logical consequences	—	—	—	—	—	—
Directives	—	—	—	5	4	9
Confrontation	—	4	—	4	—	8
Percent attending	64%	70%	89%	48%	50%	
Percent influencing	36%	30%	11%	52%	50%	

terview in a fashion similar to that of Joann Griswold. The typescript exercise is time-consuming, but is critical in terms of your own self-understanding and growth.

THE MICROSKILLS HIERARCHY

Culturally and individually appropriate attending behavior has been presented as the foundation skill of counseling and therapy. Rapport and meaningful client relationships rest on a basis of verbal and nonverbal listening. This section builds on the concepts of single, identifiable skills of counseling and therapy. Specific skills of interviewing that have specific goals and often predictable results in client verbalizations and behavior will be presented.

The skills are presented in the framework of the microskills hierarchy. This hierarchy assembles aspects of the interview into foundation skills (attending behavior and client observation), skills of attending or listening, focus, influ-

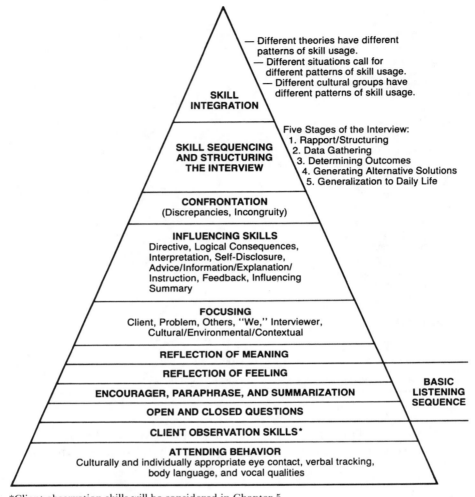

*Client observation skills will be considered in Chapter 5.

Figure 3.6 The microskills hierarchy. Copyright 1985. Allen E. Ivey.

encing, and confrontation, skill sequencing, and, finally, integration of skills into the natural interview. The microskills hierarchy may be viewed in Figure 3.6.

You will note that the microskills and skill sequences of the hierarchy will be later utilized to present several theoretical models of counseling and therapy. Once you have mastered the structure of the interview and the microskills, you can assemble the skills into the several types of counseling and therapy methods outlined later in this text.

Attending or Listening Skills

Attending behavior may be amplified with specific types of verbal leads that focus on the client and the problem, and enable you to bring out the major facts, feelings, and constructs a client brings to the interview. These specific leads or counselor statements are termed "attending skills" or "listening skills." After rapport development, your goal with most clients is to find out the nature of the problem.

Open questions are considered by some to be the most valuable of the attending skills. Open questions usually begin with "what," "how," "why," "could," or "would." Questions that begin with these words *usually* require the client to provide a longer, more open response and are not easily answered with a "yes" or "no." An open question is an invitation to talk.

Each open question will predictably result in a rather specific client response, thus providing you with important data about the problem (or strength). For example, note the following series:

> "Could you tell me what you'd like to talk about today? ("Could" questions tend to be the most open and help clients generate their own unique answers.)
>
> "What happened then?" ("What" questions tend to bring out the specific *facts of a problem.*)
>
> "How did you feel about the situation?" ("How" questions often lead toward process discussion; when the word "feel" is added, you may predict the client will talk about personal feelings regarding the problem.)
>
> "Why do you think it happened?" ("Why" questions tend to lead clients to talk about their past or present reasoning around an event or situation.)

Following the predicted results of each of these questions, the counselor can obtain rather rapidly: (1) a general picture of the situation; (2) the central facts; (3) how the client feels about those facts emotionally; and (4) the client's reasoning process. *A central goal of data gathering is to accomplish just that—specifically, What are the client's general impressions of a problem, the specific facts, the feelings, and the thinking process?* Systematically using the basic question "stems" will provide the basis for information gathering.

But, many counselors do not like questions. Some clients from some cultures are "turned off" by the rapid-fire questioning style of American culture. This is especially so in a situation where natural trust does not occur. A juvenile delinquent with a probation officer will, of necessity, be suspicious of questions and how they may be used against him or her. Similarly, some Black and female clients working with a white male counselor may be suspicious of what is behind the question-asking process. In such cases, moving directly to Stage 3 of the interview (Determining Outcomes) may be more useful. Interestingly, the same questions may be used more safely if you ask the client what their goals are, how they feel about the goals, and so forth.

Closed questions usually begin with the words "is," "are," "do," or "did." A closed question can be answered with a "yes" or "no" or just a few words. A closed question can be used to gather information, give clarity, gain focus, and narrow the area of discussion. It may stop a client's talking if he or she is straying from the topic.

However, closed questions used too extensively can work as a deterrent to conversation. Who enjoys the barrage of questions that puts the power in the hands of the other person? If used too extensively, closed questions can destroy a relationship.

"Why" questions are particularly troublesome and can produce client defensiveness. But some theories (for example, psychodynamic, rational-emotive) may use them extensively. Rogerian and client-centered therapists often object to the use of any questions at all. If you will turn to the data-gathering phase of the interview conducted by Joann, you will note that she is able to obtain critical data from her client, Mr. S., and still only use two questions in the process. She obtains a good picture of the client's reasoning process without asking "why?"

How can you obtain data from the client without asking questions? The skills of encouraging, paraphrasing, and reflection of feeling can accomplish the same goals as questions and are generally seen as less intrusive.

Encouragers or restatements are direct repetitions of what the client has said or are short comments such as "uh-huh," "so," or "tell me more . . ." that punctuate the interview and provide smooth flow. The skill, a simple one, is too often ignored as unimportant. However, encouragers and restatements offer the least intrusion into the client's world and have been demonstrated by research to be characteristic of successful counselors and therapists. Encouragers and restatements are active ways of letting clients know that they are heard and can go on.

An encourager is a powerful mode of response that represents the counselor's attention to key utterances of the client. Consider the following dialogue from the interview with Mr. S.: Which two or three words would you pick from it to repeat as encouragers?

MR. S: I really enjoy being alone. It bugs me when people try to direct my life. It bothers me that no one lets me decide.

Encouragers here could be "being alone," "bug you," "people decide your life," plus others. Each encourager leads the client into differing directions . . . and each of those directions would be in more depth. Depth is a characteristic and predictable response to the effective use of encouragers and restatements.

Joann, the interviewer, uses the encourager ". . . bothers you . . . ," and this particular response was central to defining the problem and understanding the world of Mr. S. In response to this encourager Mr. S., at 22, elaborates in detail, relating how being with his wife was important and how lonely he feels. *Each minimal encourager can be considered a reinforcer to the client that will have influ-*

ence on what the client will talk about next in more detail. Encouragers and restatements are by no means minimal in their impact on clients.

A *paraphrase* is an encapsulated repetition back to the client of the client's main words and thoughts. Selective attention is given to objective content that is restated in the counselor's own words, but the "touchy" and most important main words of the client are still used. The paraphrase helps the counselor to clarify, to bring together recent comments or threads of discussion and to concisely present ideas. Paraphrasing gives the client the opportunity to explore old issues again, to establish new connections, and to talk further in more depth. In addition, paraphrasing is often helpful to clients who have a decision to make, for the repetition of key ideas and phrases clarifies the essence of the problem. Many clients are able to make more effective decisions once they have been listened to.

An example of a paraphrase that clarifies Mr. S.'s decisional issues is found at response 23.

JOANN: I hear you saying that, uh, that these new friends are infringing on your time. And I hear you don't want to be pulled in directions you don't want to go in. Is that right?

The client exclaims excitedly, "Yes, that's it! You're right!" With this paraphrase, the client's diverse and sometimes confusing thinking has been distilled to its essence and now both Mr. S. and Joann understand the problem more fully.

Paraphrases also have the function of supporting clarification of facts gained through factually oriented "could" and "what" questions. They provide you with an opportunity to make sure you understand key facts surrounding a problem.

But clear understanding of facts is not enough. What about the emotional underpinnings of problems? *Reflections of feelings* provide you with an opportunity to "check out" where the person is emotionally on an issue. A reflection of feeling is closely akin to a paraphrase and, in practice, the distinction between the two is often impossible as they frequently appear together. Paraphrases are concerned with facts, and reflections of feelings with emotions, usually emotions associated with those same facts.

In learning the skill of reflecting feelings, it is first helpful to learn to label emotions. Words of feeling include *angry, fearful, glad, cynical, joyful, sad,* and innumerable others. Some beginning therapists have difficulty in recognizing emotions, and training in simple labeling must precede learning the skill.

A reflection of feeling often consists of three or four basic parts: (1) the pronoun *you* or the client's name (which personalizes the reflection); (2) the emotional label(s) or word(s); (3) a sentence stem ("You seemed to feel . . .", "I sense you are feeling . . ."); and (4) a context is often added to provide the setting for the emotional experience ("You feel angry *when your son rebels.*). The adding of context or situation, of course, is what brings paraphrasing and reflection of feeling so closely together, because the fourth dimension of reflection is essentially a paraphrase. ("Pure" reflections of feeling will tend to include only the first three dimensions above.)

Intentional reflections of feeling can set the tone and mood of an entire interview. In Joann's work with Mr. S., several reflections provide the groundwork for exploration and eventual resolution of his difficulties in sleeping and with his relationships with his friends.

17. J: You're laughing, but I sense from the tone of your voice and the look on your face that underneath it isn't a laughing matter.
19. J: I sense you get angry.
27. J: Ummmmm . . . pressure . . . when you talk about pressure, I sense you feel it now. How do you react to pressure. Can you tell me how pressure affects you?

Response 27 is a particularly interesting lead as it illustrates the relationship between reflection of feeling and the "how" question. "How" questions are often, but not always, associated with emotions.

Studies in short- and long-term memory reveal that nothing is stored in the brain unless it is emotionally meaningful. In effect, we perceive the world as it affects us emotionally in *immediate experience*. Thus emotional words are critical cues in telling us how the client is reacting to the problem, both in the past and in the present. When Joann says, "I sense you can feel it now," Mr. S. is actually recreating in the immediate moment the experience of the past.

This recreation of the past in the present is important in many types of therapy, particularly Rogerian and psychodynamic. While not made explicit in those theories, the central route toward recreation of experience lies in first attending to the facts of the problem, and then to the feelings.

Reflection of meaning is another important microskill. Once you have recreated a past or present experience in the interview, it is helpful to explore what the situation means to the client. As you read the case of Mr. S. in this chapter, you saw that he gave a negative meaning to the facts: he saw the problem as "his fault," and one of his critical meanings in life was to please and satisfy others. Through the skillful use of a psychodynamic directive, termed focused free association, Joann helped Mr. S. see the parallels between an incident with his brother at age 6 and his present behavior at age 72.

Mr. S. had previously felt that it was his responsibility to do what others wanted, to please them (a common problem for many of us). But as he developed new meanings, he saw the need for taking more responsibility on his own part, and Joann reflects that *new* meaning at response 92 (. . . "I, John S., have to take care of myself first") and at response 96 ("You will have to take care of yourself first. The time is now. Is that what I hear you saying?"). This meaning is a new cognition, a new worldview change for the client.

Distinguishing between a reflection of meaning and a paraphrase/reflection of feeling is not easy. In a reflection of meaning, the deeper, underlying meaning of the client is identified. The client reframes or reinterprets experience on his or her own. Reflections of meaning are very closely allied with interpretations from the influencing skill portion of microskills. An interpretation provides the client with an alternative frame of reference from which to view the problem. But the therapist has provided the interpretation. In reflection of meaning, the client has been enabled to find a new interpretation or meaning in old data or old situations.

Summarization is the gathering together of a client's verbalizations, facts, feelings, and meanings and the presenting of them to the client in outline form. Summarization involves attending to the client, experiencing the feelings and thoughts of the client, and integrating and ordering the complex content of the interview. The summary reviews the content and main feelings expressed in the session, brings together common elements, and clarifies. Summarization also gives the counselor a chance to hear if his or her thinking is accurate and gives a "breather," or a break, to the interview.

Examples of summarization may be found at several points in the interview with Mr. S. For example, at response 9 Joann summarizes the key facts and feelings from the previous interview and adds some positive assets as well. The summary at response 29 brings together data from the second stage of the interview and sets the stage for determining outcomes. Periodic paraphrases and summarizations through Phase 4 of the interview provide coherence and organization as alternatives for resolution are examined (for example, see response 72).

The Basic Listening Sequence. Attending skills can be organized into a coherent and systematic frame, termed the *basic listening sequence*. Figure 3.7 summarizes the specific skills and illustrates how the client's problem can be organized into key facts and emotions (and reasons, if you desire) and then can be summarized clearly for further examination.

Many counseling and therapy theories use the basic listening sequence to draw out data. While the skills are not sequenced so clearly as they are in Figure 3.7, you will find most therapists and counselors using variations of this basic model as they get to know their client and the client's life and concerns. Whether you are helping a client with a vocational decision, deciding about a divorce, or conducting a psychodynamic dream analysis, you will find you need to know the facts, how the client feels about those facts, and then organize them for further analysis. You will find the basic listening sequence and its accompanying microskills most useful as you enter different therapeutic approaches later in this text. Whether you become a behavioral counselor, a reality therapist, or a family counselor, you will find the basic listening sequence critical in all that you do.

Reflection of meaning is not included here as part of the basic listening sequence. As a more interpretative, reflective skill, it usually follows from effective use of the basic listening sequence, rather than being a part of it.

The basic listening sequence is most useful in the second and third stages

Figure 3.7   The Basic Listening Sequence

SKILL	DESCRIPTION	FUNCTION IN INTERVIEW
Open questions	"What": draws out facts "How": process or feelings "Why": reasons "Could": general picture	Questions can be used to bring out major data and facilitate conversation.
Closed questions	Usually begin with "do," "is," "are," and can be answered in a few words.	Closed questions can quickly obtain specific data; close off lengthy answers.
Encourager	Repeating back to client a few of the client's main words.	Encourages detailed elaboration of the specific words and their meanings.
Paraphrase	Repeating back the essence of a client's words and thoughts using the client's own main words.	Acts as promoter for discussion; shows understanding; checks on clarity of counselor understanding.
Reflection of Feeling	Selective attention to emotional content of interview.	Results in clarification of emotion underlying key facts; promotes discussion of feelings.
Summarization	Repeating back of client's facts and feelings (and reasons) to client in an organized form.	Useful in beginning interview; periodically in session to clarify where the interview has come to date; and to close the session.

of the interview, where you are interested in gathering data about the problem and the client's assets and in determining goals with the client. The interview with Mr. S. illustrates the importance of the basic listening sequence as Joann Griswold "draws out" the facts, feelings, and some reasons for Mr. S.'s situation. Griswold's responses also illustrate the obvious fact that you need not follow the basic listening sequence in a precise order to obtain the desired results. Most important in the use of the basic listening sequence is your ability to obtain *results* in terms of clear, organized data.

Focus and Selective Attention

Beginning helpers often focus on problems instead of the people in front of them. It is wiser to first focus on the client and later on the problem. For example Mr. S. says the following at response 10:

S: Well, for instance, ummm, I started to be involved (with other people) in the past three or four months . . . when my wife first died, *I didn't do anything.* Now, I find myself getting out a bit more and that I feel better—especially if I do things on my own. A lot of these people I'm involved with are still getting me to do more than I want to do. *I don't know how to turn them down.* They expect a lot from me and I think I end up doing what they suggest just to keep busy so I don't think of my wife. Yet, I'm alone so much.

J: Now that you're alone, ah, I sense what you're saying is that you are lonely or alone quite a bit of the time.

S: Yes! (Emphatically)

Note that Joann's response contained three personal pronouns—"you"—or variations. The client's name and the pronoun "you" focus the session on the person in front of you as counselor/therapist. Beginning helpers are often tempted to focus the interview anywhere but on the person before them. It would have been possible to focus the interview on others—for example, on a spouse ("Tell me about your wife") or on yourself ("I get lonely too sometimes. Let me tell you . . ."). At some point in the interview, both of these foci may be useful; but for the most part counseling and therapy are about the client. Focus on the person immediately in front of you. *Counseling is for the client,* not for the counselor, nor for absent parties, and sometimes not even for problem resolution.

Focus analysis is an elementary microskill, yet awareness of the issues related to focus are important in interview analysis and to successful counseling and therapy. Examination of the interview conducted by Joann with Mr. S. will reveal that the vast majority of her counseling leads focused on Mr. S., the client.

Focus analysis, however, is also useful to help us ensure that we have indeed considered all possible aspects of a client's problem. For example, it would be possible to respond to Mr. S. with a variety of foci:

1. *Client focus:* "Mr. S., you feel confused and lonely. You're unsure of what you want to do." In this example, there are four personal references to Mr. S.
2. *Other-person focus:* "Tell me more about your wife." Here we can predict that Mr. S. will start telling us about his wife and her death. That may be valuable information, but it does not tell us about Mr. S. and his *reaction* to the present or past situation.
3. *Problem/main-theme focus:* The presenting problem or main theme of the session was balancing time demands made by friends, so the counselor could have asked, "What do the people say when they ask you to do something? How often does this happen?" Again, this is important information, but it does not tell us much about how Mr. S. responds. As counselors we can do very little about the problem; that is Mr. S.'s task. Our concern as therapists is to encourage others to solve their own difficulties. As we listen to Mr. S., the problem emphasis on time demands changes to loneliness for a lost wife.
4. *Interviewer focus:* "That reminds me of my experience when I was lonely. I know how it hurts." Focusing on oneself may be useful as a self-disclosure or feedback technique, and it may help develop mutuality with the client. As rapport develops, such responses may be increasingly helpful. However, they must not be overdone.
5. *"We" focus:* "Right now *we* seem to be getting somewhere. *I* like the way *you* are sharing *yourself. The two of us* ought to be able to get somewhere with that." This type of mutual sharing frequently appears in humanistically oriented interviews. Joann uses the mutual focus of herself and Mr. S., for example, at response 9, where she talks about her positive feelings.
6. *Cultural/environmental/contextual focus:* "This sounds like a concern facing many older people. Society does not always make it easy." Undergirding our client's

problems are long histories of interaction with sociopolitical systems. With some clients, this can become an important focus for discussion. Helpers with a Black or feminist orientation often use this focus with real effectiveness to produce change. Yet counseling often tends to forget the cultural/environmental context and the historical background of the individual. Few therapies and counseling theories consider this dimension adequately.

These six dimensions of microskill focus analysis are critical for understanding what is happening in any therapy session. Focus analysis is concerned with the *subject or main theme of the client and counselor sentence structure.* For practical purposes, the actual grammatical subject of the sentence will indicate the focus of the counseling intervention to the client's statement. Counseling is centrally concerned with getting clients to make "I statements" in which they discuss themselves and their concerns. Counselors produce "I statements" in their clients by using the personal pronouns "you, your," etc. and by using their clients' names. Yet, it must again be underlined that the other types of focus in the interview remain valid at times and, in fact, must be included for counseling to be relevant to life experience.

The interview typescript has not been classified into focus dimensions. By far the bulk of Joann's responses focus on Mr. S., the client. However, she also focuses on herself, the interview, others, and on mutual focus. She did not focus on the cultural/environmental dimensions, although this would have been possible. It would be helpful for you now to review the session and locate the several types of focus used by the counselor. *And,* try to maintain constant awareness of how *you* would focus the session.

Influencing Skills

Clients can profit and grow from you using *only* attending skills. A basic competency you will want to achieve is the ability to conduct a full five-stage humanistically-oriented interview (see Figure 10.1), using just the basic listening sequence. You will find that verbal clients can often work through problems and concerns very effectively if you do not give advice, directions, or suggestions. The early theories of nondirective counseling (see Chapter 10) advocated using only listening skills and even went so far as to severely criticize the use of questions.

However, sole use of attending and listening skills can make growth slow and arduous. When you become an active participant in the interview, you can influence and speed the change process. Through your knowledge of theory and skills, personal life experience, and specific understanding of the unique client and his or her culture, you can share more of yourself and your knowledge to the benefit of your client.

The influencing skills discussed here include *feedback, advice/information/ other, self-disclosure, interpretation, logical consequences, directives,* and the *influencing summary.* These skills will be presented in terms of their use in the interview with Mr. S. The skills and their functions are summarized in Figure 3.8. Influencing

Figure 3.8   Influencing Skills

SKILL	DESCRIPTION	FUNCTION IN INTERVIEW
Interpretation	Provides an alternative frame of reference from which the client may view a situation. May be drawn from a theory or from one's own personal observations. *Interpretation may be viewed as the core influencing skill.*	Attempts to provide the client with a new way to view the situation. The interpretation provides the client with a clear-cut alternative perception of "reality." This perception may enable a change of view which in turn may result in changes in thoughts, constructs, or behaviors.
Directive	Tells the client what action to take. May be a simple suggestion stated in command form or may be a sophisticated technique from a specific theory.	Clearly indicates to clients what action counselors or therapists wish them to take. The prediction with a directive is that the client will do what is suggested. Figure 3.9 lists several specific directives drawn from different theories that will have differing anticipated results with clients.
Advice/information/ other	Provides suggestions, instructional ideas, homework, advice on how to act, think, or behave.	Used sparingly, advice and related skills may provide client with new and useful information. Specific vocational information is an example of necessary use of this skill.
Self-disclosure	The interviewer shares personal experience from the past or may share present reactions to the client.	Closely allied to feedback, this skill emphasizes counselor "I statements." Self-disclosure may build trust and openness leading to a more mutual relationship with the client.
Feedback	Provides clients with specific data on how they are seen by the counselor or by others.	Provides concrete data that may help clients realize how others perceive behavior and thinking patterns, thus enabling an alternative self-perception.
Logical Consequences	Explains to the client the logical outcome of thinking and behavior. "If, then."	Provides an alternative frame of reference for the client. This skill helps clients anticipate the consequences or results of their actions.
Influencing Summary	Often used at or near the end of a session to summarize counselor comments; most often used in combination with the attending summarization.	Clarifies what has happened in the interview and summarizes what the therapist has said. Designed to help generalization from the interview to daily life.

skills are complex and often are more effective if used sparingly and in careful concert with listening skills.

Interpretation may be considered the central influencing skill. It provides a new and alternative way through which clients may view their problems and themselves, and it leads to a cognitive change in worldview. The frame of reference for a paraphrase, reflection of feeling, or reflection of meaning is the client. The frame of reference for an interpretation (and the remainder of the influencing skills) is the therapist. Interpretation, the most complex of the influencing skills, is used sparingly by most effective therapists and counselors. Two or three skillful interpretations are likely to be maximum for any session. Clients can take only so much challenging to their existing frame of reference, and overuse of interpretation will result in a client denying your wisdom or, perhaps, leaving the interview completely

An example of Joann using interpretation followed a focused free association directive: Mr. S. had brought out new, clinically useful material and talked about a situation at the age of 6 in which he was troubled by his relationship with his brother. Joann offered the interpretation, "What I'm hearing . . . is that you are afraid you'll hurt people in the same manner you were hurt." (response 58). In this style of interpretation, Joann has *linked* past behavior in childhood with present behavior at age 72. This linkage is clearly from the psychodynamic model (Chapter 8), which holds that we repeat behavioral patterns learned in our childhood in present, daily experience.

Joann's interpretation of the linkage between the two events provides Mr. S. and Joann with a new perception of the reasons and emotions (Mr. S. was tearful as he described the past event) underlying current behavior. This alternative interpretation of life experience provides the groundwork for the later change in behavior and illustrates how cognitions can lead to behavior change.

The *directive* is, of course, the most "influencing" of the influencing skills. Despite extensive belief to the contrary, counselors often tell their clients what to do. Most directly stated, directives are those therapist statements that direct a client to do something, say something, or act in a certain way. The counselor may provide a directive by guiding a client through a fantasy (humanistic counseling), suggesting specific behavioral changes (assertiveness training), or making focused free association suggestions (psychodynamic theory). Even telling a client to complete an action homework assignment is a directive. Seventeen different types of directives are listed in Figure 3.9. There are many alternatives available to you once you master the basic listening skills and theoretical models.

Joann used several directives that had real impact on Mr. S. The focused free association directive at response 52 asked him to relax and free associate to an earlier life experience. This brought out data for the interpretation discussed above and was critical for the eventual breakthrough that happened in this session. However, the psychodynamic exercise does not provide behavioral change. Assertiveness training could have accomplished this task, but Joann chose Gestalt directives to make the need for behavioral change and action apparent. Note her

Figure 3.9 *Example directives used by counselors of differing theoretical orientations*

1. Specific suggestions/ instructions for action
"I suggest you try . . ."

2. Paradoxical instructions
"Continue what you are doing . . ." "Do the problem behavior/thinking/action at least three times."

3. Imagery
"Imagine you are back in the situation. Close your eyes and describe it precisely. What do you see, hear, feel?"
"Describe your ideal day, job, life partner."
"Imagine you are going on a trip into your body . . ."

4. Role-play enactment
"Now, return to that situation and let's play it out." "Let's role it out again, only change the one piece of behavior we agreed to."

5. Gestalt hot seat
"Talk to your parent as if he or she were sitting in that chair. Now go to that chair and answer as your parent would."

6. Gestalt nonverbal
"I note that one of your hands is in a fist, your other is open. Have the two hands talk to each other."

7. Focused free association
"Take that feeling and free associate back to an early childhood experience . . ."
". . . to what is occurring *now* in your daily life."
"Stay with that feeling, magnify it. Now what flashed into your mind first?"

8. Reframing/Gendlin focusing
"Identify a negative experience, thought, feeling. Now identify something positive in that experience and focus on that dimension. Synthesize it with the problem."

9. Relaxation
"Close your eyes and drift."
"Tighten your forearm, very tight. Now let it go."

10. Systematic desensitization
a. Deep muscle relaxation.
b. Construction of anxiety hierarchy.
c. Matching objects of anxiety with relaxation.

11. Language change
"Change 'should' to 'want to.' "
"Change 'can't' to 'won't.' "
Any new word/construct addition.

12. Staying with feeling/ emotional flooding
"Go back to that feeling, get with it, make it totally you."

13. Meditation
"Be still. Focus on one point. Relax. Concentrate on breathing. Let all thoughts slip from your mind."

14. Hypnotic trance
"Fixate on that point. Relax. Note your breathing. Focus your awareness . . ."

15. Group work
"Now I want you to do this . . ."

16. Teaching/homework
"Practice this exercise next week and report on it in the next interview."
"Turn to page . . ."
"Take out a sheet of paper . . ."
"Take this vocational test . . ."

17. Family therapy communications
"Don't talk to me . . . talk to him *now.*"
"Change chairs with your wife and sit closer to your daughter . . ."

use of Gestalt repetition at responses 80 through 86. Here Joann has Mr. S. repeat himself several times. Out of such repetitions, clients often get in touch with basic emotions. Joann reflected that feeling and then provided another directive, simply asking Mr. S. to tell her about positive strengths in his life (the positive asset search). When Mr. S. responded in the emotionally charged situation, he was able to make a breakthrough that led not only to insight, but also to behavioral change.

This series of directives is a particularly dramatic example of the value of counselor or therapist action. But, remember that this action came after Joann had carefully established rapport and used attending skills to hear out the client. Furthermore, she used the positive asset search throughout the interview so that the client had the base to encounter the very real difficulties of the past. Too many therapists expect clients to grow from a negative base of only problem discussion.

A useful, but potentially dangerous, set of influencing skills centers around *advice, information,* and *others.* This is a grouping of skills in which the counselor provides suggestions, may provide instructional information, and may even say, "If I were you, I would . . .". At times, you must give advice because you have important information that the client needs. Vocational counselors must give advice or provide vocational information. Transactional analysis therapists often teach the basis of their theories to their clients. Reality therapists often teach young people skills and knowledge they need to survive.

But, as you know, advice and instruction can be overused. Advice must be used carefully, and mainly at the request of the client; otherwise the client will say, "yes, but . . .". Anytime, the client responds with "yes, but . . .," it is generally time to change your style and move to an attending skill such as questioning or paraphrasing. (For example, "You feel that suggestion isn't helpful. What might be more useful to you?")

Self-disclosure occurs when you share your experience with the client. Two types of self-disclosure are noted in the interview Joann has with Mr. S. The first type is in relation to the client and is closely allied to, and sometimes indistinguishable from, feedback. A clear example of this form of self-disclosure and its relation to feedback occurs in the following:

J: . . . I admire your strength and your commitment to your family—raising children, taking care of your wife when she was so terribly ill, and now helping your invalid sister-in-law. (Feedback) I feel very fortunate to know you— you show a great deal of love and caring. I'm happy things are going better for you. (Self-disclosure)

In both the examples above, Mr. S. is receiving information about how the counselor views him. The self-disclosure emphasizes how Joann, the counselor, feels toward the client. The feedback statement centers more on objective data, although "I admire . . ." is close to a self-disclosure.

Both feedback and self-disclosure are helpful to clients in knowing how they are "coming across" to others. Distinctions between the two are obviously somewhat arbitrary, but both can help clients feel more comfortable and more willing to self-disclose. Too much personal feedback and self-disclosure may close off client talk. Some therapists become so enamoured of these two skills that they may use little else. For some clients, this open counselor is helpful and reassuring; but for others it is even more intrusive than a barrage of questions.

A second type of self-disclosure is easier to separate from feedback. Here the therapist talks about personal experience that may relate in some way to the client's topic. At response 64, Joann provides a classic self-disclosure from her own experience:

J: You . . . you just feel the pull. I can relate to that . . . I feel the pull from my family and other commitments and sometimes I never seem to have time for myself and what I enjoy. Sometimes that pull doesn't leave much room for you. Who or what in particular helps you relieve the tension?

Joann has done some important things in this self-disclosure. First, she has self-disclosed *very briefly*. Some therapists give long and extensive self-disclosures that take the focus away from the client. Note that Joann *immediately* changed the focus from herself to the client through the pronoun "you." Finally, she provided an open question so that she could see whether or not the self-disclosure was relevant.

You will find self-disclosure of your feelings to the client helpful if you are working in a modern Rogerian theoretical framework. In other theories its use may be less effective. The sharing of related personal feelings and experience *may* be helpful if used sparingly.

Feedback has already been discussed and an example provided. The purpose of feedback is to help clients see themselves as others do. When you share how you feel or view a client in an interview, the focus of your feedback statement is on yourself and, in this moment, it is almost impossible to separate feedback from self-disclosure. However, when you provide data about how others perceive the client (focusing on "others," as in focus analysis), classifying the skill as feedback is more apparent.

Feedback is the stuff of encounter groups and much other group experience. Here the client learns how others perceive him or her. Feedback may be an important skill of the family therapy treatment program. In family therapy, the client may need to learn how other family members view behavior.

In *logical consequences,* a complex skill, clients are led to understand the possible consequences of their actions. This skill was not used in the interview with Mr. S. But, if Joann had used the skill, it might have appeared as follows:

J: Mr. S., you've talked about your desire to please others consistently for the last 15 minutes. I've also heard you talk about how it tears you up inside and leaves you lonely despite the company you have. The consequences of your continuing not to stand up for yourself are clear: You'll have trouble sleeping and you may find yourself starting to feel a bit angry and bitter. How does that sound to you?

It may be seen that the structure of a logical consequence statement is basically one of paraphrase and reflection of feeling, with the addition of the logical consequences of continuing the behavior. The statement above also contains a check-out that provides room for the client to react and lessens the imposition associated with this skill.

Looking ahead to the consequences of one's actions can help one change behavior in the present. Rational-emotive and cognitive-behavior therapies (Chapter 11), and Adlerian counseling (Dinkmeyer and Dinkmeyer, 1979) all may be expected to use this skill. It is also important in reality therapy (Chapter 11), particularly with acting-out, delinquent-prone youth. Needless to say, this skill may meet with extensive client resistance and anger unless a solid rapport has been established.

The *influencing summary* often is used by therapists at the end of the interview. Here what the therapist has said and introduced during the session is reviewed. Influencing summaries usually appear in combination with the attending summarization. The critical distinction between the two lies in *whose* data are being summarized—the clients (attending summarization) or the counselor's (influencing summary).

Confrontation

The dictionary defines *confront* as "1. to stand or come in front of; stand or meet facing 2. to face in hostility or defiance, oppose." (Barnhart, 1950) These are two very differing meanings and are sometimes confused in the teaching of intentional counseling. At its least effective operation, a confrontation can represent an open or subtle display of hostility from the counselor.

As Ivey and Gluckstern have observed, a confrontation can be more subtle: "A confrontation is defined as . . . *the pointing out of discrepancies between or among attitudes, thoughts, or behaviors.* In a confrontation individuals are faced directly with the fact that they may be saying other than that which they mean, or doing other than that which they say." (1976, p. 46) A confrontation is *not* telling a client that he or she is in error or a bad person. In counseling, the first dictionary meaning of confrontation, cited above, is central; the second meaning is potentially destructive.

Critical to understanding confrontation are the words *incongruity* and *discrepancy*. Clients often give "double messages" in the interview. They may say, "I really love my husband, but . . . ," or "I want that job, but I don't want to work that hard," or "You're a fine therapist, but you're off your rocker on that last comment." In each of the above statements the client offers two comments in one sentence or paragraph indicating mixed thoughts and feelings about some matter of importance. An intentional, empathic counselor will point out to the client the existence of the mixed or double message, thus enabling the client to "come in front of" and face issues. Double messages, incongruities, and discrepancies may also show in body language when the client says, for example, "I have a terrific boss" while simultaneously crossing legs and arms tightly.

Some examples of confrontation from the interview typescript of Mr. S. and Joann include:

17. J: You're laughing, but I sense from the tone of your voice and the look on your face that underneath it isn't a laughing matter. (*Here Joann confronts the discrepancy between the two nonverbals. This moves him to a more indepth discussion of his problem.*)

25. J: And you feel you are being controlled by others; you're resenting this control. You'd like to break loose and do as *you*, yourself please. (*The confrontation here focuses on discrepancies between Mr. S. and his relationships with others. It leads him to talk about his feelings in this bind, leading him toward stating, at response 30, his own goals that would resolve the discrepancy he feels.*)

72. J: For most of your life, you've been taking care of people ahead of yourself. (*confronts discrepancy between self and others*) Since your wife's death, you have tried to keep from being lonely by being very involved, but this isn't working. (*discrepancy between actions and results and between feelings that can't be hidden*) You've got many strengths, friends, and family. (*confronts discrepancy between positive assets and problems*) I also see you getting tired of not standing up for your rights in certain situations. (*confronts real situation with ideal situation*) Does that make sense to you?

In the above series of confrontations may be seen the general structure of the interview Joann had with Mr. S. In a few short sentences she catches the essence of the case. It can be argued that the purpose of counseling and therapy is to identify and confront major discrepancies in the client. Following each of the confrontations, Mr. S. was able to generate further thoughts that led to his eventually resolving the issues of the interview.

One model sentence not used by Joann is often helpful to the beginning counselor or therapist: "On one hand, you think (feel, behave) . . . , but on the other, you think (feel, behave) . . .". This model sentence provides the essence of confrontation statements. It is nonjudgmental and provides an often clarifying picture of the confusing situation faced by the client.

Confrontation is a skill that balances and utilizes both attending and influencing skills. Yet, it seems to be most effective when it appears as a complex paraphrase or reflection of feeling. The examples above from Joann are predominantly attending or listening skills. It is possible to confront using influencing skills but, when the confrontations are framed in the form of paraphrases, summarizations, and the like, they provide maximum room for client growth.

Finally, it should be noted that confrontations are combination skills that are scored both as paraphrases, interpretations, or other microskills *and* as confrontation. When a confrontation occurs, use double-skill scoring.

It seems that most schools of psychotherapy pay special attention to incongruities and discrepancies. However, each theory has its own means of coping with these issues and uses vastly different routes toward meeting the common objective of resolving and coping with the inevitable incongruities and double messages we meet throughout life.

There is evidence that the overly confronting, charismatic therapist can be damaging to client growth. Similarly, there is evidence that the overly cautious therapist may accomplish very little growth. Intentional counseling demands a careful balance of confrontation with supporting qualities of warmth, positive regard, and respect. It is suggested that the empathic therapist is one who can maintain a balance of "push-pull" and support, utilizing a wide variety of counseling skills and theories. However, this balance must be authentic to the counselor's true self.

As noted to the right of each counselor "lead" in Griswold's interview, one may classify each helping lead into one or more microskill classifications. A confrontation does not exist as a separate classification and may be contained in a reflection of feeling ("On one hand you feel angry toward your parents and on the other you really love them"), a paraphrase ("You think you want to major in biology, but on the other hand you like psychology"), interpretation ("The behavior of arguing with authority seems to be important right now with your boss, but on the other hand you have a similar pattern with your own father"), or any other skill(s). In classification, score first with the microskill, then determine if a confrontation *also* occurs.

DIFFERENT SKILL PATTERNS FOR DIFFERENT THEORIES

Over 250 theories of psychotherapy and counseling have developed over the years, many of them claiming the "final answer." Nonetheless, each was developed for a reason and appears to meet the interests and needs of a special clientele. While the theories included in this book have clearly stood the test of time or are currently thriving, it should be stated clearly that many useful alternatives beyond those described here are available.

Microskills theory holds that all systems of counseling and therapy borrow some skills and structure from the five-stage interview. If you master the specific skills *and* the five-stage structure of Chapter 2, you can "mix and match" these foundational patterns so that mastery of many alternative theories of therapy is possible. Figure 3.10 summarizes several theories in terms of their differential usage of microskills. Note, for example, that "nondirective" theory (an early form of Rogerian theory) almost exclusively uses attending skills and very few questions. By way of contrast, note that rational-emotive and feminist therapy make extensive use of influencing skills.

		Nondirective	Modern Rogerian encounter	Behavioral (Assertiveness training)	Psychodynamic	Gestalt	Decisonal counseling	Rational-emotive therapy	Feminist therapy	Business problem solving	Medical diagnostic interview	Traditional teaching	Student-centered teaching	Eclectic/metatheoretical
	MICROSKILL LEAD													
ATTENDING SKILLS	Open question	○	○	◐	◐	●	●	◐	◐	◐	◐	◐	●	◐
	Closed question	○	○	●	○	◐	◐	◐	◐	◐	◐	●	◐	◐
	Encourager	◐	◐	◐	◐	◐	◐	◐	◐	◐	◐	○	◐	◐
	Paraphrase	●	●	◐	◐	○	●	◐	◐	◐	◐	○	●	◐
	Reflection of feeling	●	●	◐	◐	○	●	◐	◐	◐	◐	○	●	◐
	Reflection of meaning	◐	●	○	◐	○	◐	◐	●	○	○	○	◐	◐
	Summarization	◐	◐	◐	○	○	◐	◐	◐	◐	◐	○	●	◐
INFLUENCING SKILLS	Feedback	○	●	◐	○	◐	○	●	◐	◐	○	◐	◐	◐
	Advice/information/ and others	○	○	◐	○	○	◐	●	●	●	◐	●	●	◐
	Self-disclosure	○	●	○	○	○	○	○	◐	◐	○	○	◐	◐
	Interpretation	○	○	○	●	●	○	●	◐	◐	◐	○	◐	◐
	Logical consequences	○	○	◐	○	○	◐	◐	◐	●	◐	●	◐	◐
	Directive	○	○	●	○	●	◐	●	◐	●	●	●	◐	◐
	Influ. summary	○	○	◐	○	○	◐	◐	●	●	◐	◐	◐	◐
	CONFRONTATION (Combined Skill)	◐	◐	◐	◐	●	◐	●	●	◐	◐	◐	◐	◐
FOCUS	Client	●	●	●	●	●	●	●	◐	◐	◐	◐	●	◐
	Counselor, interviewer	○	◐	○	○	○	○	◐	◐	○	○	○	◐	◐
	Mutual/group/"We"	○	◐	○	○	○	○	○	◐	○	○	○	◐	◐
	Other people	○	○	◐	◐	◐	◐	○	◐	○	○	○	◐	◐
	Topic or problem	○	○	◐	◐	○	●	◐	◐	●	●	●	●	◐
	Cultural/ enviromental context	○	○	◐	○	○	◐	○	●	◐	○	○	◐	◐
	ISSUE OF MEANING (Topics, key words likely to be attended to and reinforced)	Feelings	Relationship	Behavior problem solving	Unconscious motivation	Here and now behavior	Problem solving	Irrational ideas/logic	Problem as a "women's issue"	Problem solving	Diagnosis of illness	Information/ facts	Student ideas/ info./facts	Varies
	AMOUNT OF INTERVIEWER TALK-TIME	Low	Medium	High	Low	High	Medium	High	Medium	High	High	High	Medium	Varies

Legend

● Frequent use of skill
◐ Common use of skill
○ May use skill occasionally

Figure 3.10 Examples of microskill leads used by interviewers of differing theoretical orientations

87

Each therapeutic system appears to have varying patterns that must be mastered if you are to work within that orientation. However, all systems use the basic listening skills to some extent and, once you have mastered those skills, you will find it easier to move across theoretical orientations into a new way of functioning. When you learn new methods of therapy, you then may build on these skills and frame them into a wide variety of techniques and strategies, appropriate to the system you are studying.

You may also note that microskills are not used solely by counselors and therapists. Workers in medicine, management, and teaching may also benefit from competence in the communication skills. One increasingly important role of the therapist or counselor is that of teaching others the effective interview skills.

Focus of therapy may also vary from theory to theory. A feminist therapist will focus extensively on the cultural/environmental context while this may receive only limited attention in Gestalt therapy, for example. Virtually all methods of counseling and therapy stress the importance of focusing on the individual in the interview. While it may be helpful to obtain information on family and friends, the task is to work with the *person* sitting in front of you.

If you gain a mastery of the attending or listening skills, you have a solid foundation on which to build specific theory at a later point. You will find that influencing skills vary more from theory to theory than do listening skills.

Quality in helping comes from taking the generalized framework of decisional counseling in Chapter 2 and adding competence in the microskills presented here. However, a few skills and some decision theory do not make a fully competent counselor, although they provide a useful beginning. Quality in helping comes from applying the theories and skills in an individually and culturally sensitive manner. This issue is explored in some depth in the following chapter.

SUMMARY OF THIS CHAPTER

Because this book will focus constantly on skills as they are applied in the counseling and therapy interview, it is important to master the concepts in this chapter before moving further into the text. It is critical that you be able to:

1. *Define and discuss the concepts of attending behavior and influencing behavior.* Dimensions of eye contact, body language, vocal tone, and verbal-following behavior were stressed. It was stated that clients of different racial and cultural backgrounds may vary on these important dimensions underlying the counseling process.

2. *Outline the several attending skills.* Flowing from the general construct of attending behavior are several listening skills: open and closed questions, the encourager, reflection of feeling, paraphrasing, reflection of meaning, and summary. These skills represent specific ways you can indicate to the client that you have heard him or her and facilitate drawing out the client's story. Many therapists would argue that these skills are the most important dimensions of the counseling process.

3. *Outline the several influencing skills.* The act of counseling also includes influencing the direction of the interview or activities the client follows after the session is terminated. The skills of directives, interpretation, feedback, self-disclosure, advice/information, and influencing summary were presented.

4. *Define and identify the six focus dimensions:* client, interviewer, others, problem or main theme, "we" or "mutual," and cultural/environmental/contextual.

5. *Score and classify an interview based on your knowledge of the preceding skills.* For the moment, this is the most important objective of this book thus far. If you can score and classify counselor interviewing leads according to the microskills taxonomy, you are well on your way to a detailed understanding of the counseling process.

6. *Understand that different theories use the several skills presented in this chapter with different frequency.* Some counselors and therapists will use the attending dimensions almost solely while others will use influencing skills as their primary mode of operation. Most counselors use some balance of the two dimensions. As you move through this book it will be important that you begin to sense your own favored usage of skills and theory.

7. *Define key terms and ideas presented in this chapter.* As the following key terms and ideas will appear repeatedly throughout this book, it is particularly important that you be able to use them and understand them thoroughly: attending behavior; microskills approach; microskills hierarchy; cultural implications of microskills; the several attending skills; focus dimensions; the influencing skills listed in summary points 2, 3, and 4 above; the basic listening sequence; and the way in which different skill sequences and patterns may manifest themselves in different styles of counseling.

Effective intentional interviewing requires more than the ability to use a wide array of skills appropriately with different clients. Intentional counseling and therapy also require the ability to provide high-quality interviews. The following chapter examines several aspects of quality in the interview with emphasis on the concept of empathy.

REFERENCES

BARNHART, C., *American College Dictionary.* New York: Harper and Row, 1950.

DINKMEYER, D., and D. DINKMEYER, JR., *Adlerian Counseling and Therapy.* Belmont, CA: Wadsworth, 1979.

IVEY, A. *Intentional Interviewing and Counseling.* Monterey, CA: Brooks/Cole, 1983.

IVEY, A., and J. AUTHIER, *Microcounseling: Innovations in Interviewing, Counseling, Psychotherapy and Psychoeducation,* 2nd ed. Springfield, IL: Thomas, 1978.

TURNER, S., D. BIEDEL, and J. HERSEN, "Effects of Race on Ratings of Social Skill." *Journal of Consulting and Clinical Psychology,* 1984, *52,* 474–475.

SUGGESTED SUPPLEMENTARY READING

BRAMMER, L., *The Helping Relationship,* 3rd ed. Englewood Cliffs, NJ: Prentice-Hall, 1985.

An excellent, brief summary of the helping relationship. Special attention is given to microskills in the interview as well as a presentation of an interesting alternative problem-solving model.

EVANS, D., M. HEARN, M. UHLEMANN and A. IVEY, *Essential Interviewing: A Programmed Approach to Effective Communication.* Monterey, CA: Brooks/Cole, 1984.

A programmed text based on microskills concepts. (Microskills emphasized in this chapter are taught in a linear programming model.) This book is an especially appropriate method to facilitate positive learning of the several skills in this chapter.

IVEY, A., and J. AUTHIER, *Microcounseling: Innovations in Interviewing, Counseling, Psychotherapy, and Psychoeducation,* 2nd ed. Springfield, IL: Thomas, 1978.

The basic research and theoretical statement underlying the concepts of this chapter are found in this book. Extensive discussion is given to analysis of the counseling and therapeutic interviews, cultural issues, and the psychoeducational approach to counseling. Includes a major review of over 175 data-based studies made of the microskills model.

IVEY, A., and N. GLUCKSTERN, *Basic Attending Skills.* N. Amherst, MA: Microtraining, 1982.

A series of videotapes and training manuals working through the basic listening sequence. Detailed instructional material for mastering the attending skills. Videotapes illustrate each skill and concept.

IVEY, A., and N. GLUCKSTERN, *Basic Influencing Skills* N. Amherst, MA: Microtraining, 1983.

Videotapes and training manuals on the several influencing skills. Logotherapy, reframing, vocational counseling, and assertiveness training are demonstrated as systematic skill sequences using microtraining approaches.

4

INDIVIDUAL AND CULTURAL EMPATHY

GENERAL PREMISE

An integrated knowledge of skills, theory, and practice is essential for culturally intentional counseling and therapy.

Skills form the foundation of effective theory and practice: The culturally intentional therapist knows how to construct a creative decision-making interview and can use microskills to attend to and influence clients in a predicted direction. ***Important in this process are individual and cultural empathy,*** client observation skills, assessment of person and environment, and the application of positive techniques of growth and change.

Theory provides organizing principles for counseling and therapy: The culturally intentional counselor has knowledge of alternative theoretical approaches and treatment modalities.

Practice is the integration of skills and theory: The culturally intentional counselor or therapist is competent in skills and theory, and is able to apply them to research and practice for client benefit.

Undergirding integrated competence in skills, theory, and practice is an intentional awareness of one's own personal worldview and how that worldview may be similar to and/or different from the worldview and personal constructions of the client and other professionals.

GOALS FOR INDIVIDUAL AND CULTURAL EMPATHY

Empathy requires you to enter the worldview of clients, to see things from their eyes, and "to walk in their shoes." This chapter seeks to facilitate the development of empathy through asking you to consider the following issues. The goals are to:

1. Present a definition of empathy as it has been defined historically by the field.
2. Examine how empathy may be broadened to include you and your client's cultural and ethnic background. You will be asked to examine your own cultural and ethnic background and to consider how empathy may be manifested differently among varying groups of individuals.
3. Present concepts such as concreteness, immediacy, and genuineness as useful ways to specify the nature of individual and cultural empathy.

THE BROAD CONSTRUCT OF EMPATHY

Empathy has a long and honorable history in the helping professions. In an important 1957 paper entitled "The Necessary and Sufficient Conditions of Therapeutic Personality Change," Carl Rogers made a strong case that empathy and related constructs are all that is needed to produce change in a client. To help another person grow, Rogers said, requires: (1) an integrated congruent relationship with the client; (2) unconditional positive regard for the client; and (3) the communication of empathy from the counselor to the client.* "No other conditions are necessary" (1957, p. 27).

Rogers has referred to the following as a good contemporary definition of empathy:

> This is not laying trips on people. . . . You only listen and say back the other person's thing, step by step, just as that person seems to have it at that moment. You never mix into it any of your own things or ideas, never lay on the other person anything that person didn't express. . . . To show that you understand exactly, make a sentence or two which gets exactly at the personal meaning this person wanted to put across. This might be in your own words, usually, but use that person's own words for the touchy main things. (Gendlin and Hendricks, *Rap Manual,* undated, cited in Gendlin, 1978)

This definition closely parallels attending behavior and the attending skills of paraphrasing, reflection of feeling, and summarization cited in the pre-

---

*The three specifics listed are a condensation of Rogers six conditions for personal growth. A useful summary of theory and research backing up Rogers's statement on empathy may be found in *The Counseling Psychologist,* volume 5, number 2, 1975, which contains a series of major articles on empathy including a brief and compelling statement by Rogers himself.

vious chapter. Furthermore, factor analytic studies of empathy (Zimmer and Park, 1967; Zimmer and Anderson, 1968) have shown that counselors who demonstrate high levels of empathy tend to use the attending skills frequently. Moreover, nonverbal components of attending behavior, such as eye contact, body posture, and physical distance, have been shown to relate to empathy (Haase and Tepper, 1972). *Thus, an elementary understanding of empathy may be achieved through effective use of attending behavior and the attending skills.*

Egan (1975) has defined two types of empathic understanding. The first, *primary empathy,* is directly related to ideas about empathy as presented by Carl Rogers and involves primarily attending skills. The second, *advanced accurate empathy,* requires that the counselor give more of himself or herself and often requires a direct attempt to influence the client. Through the use of influencing skills such as self-disclosure, directives, and interpretation, the counselor can reach higher levels of empathy. It may be useful to describe the two types of empathy as manifested in the interview with Mr. S. in the preceding chapter:

53. S: I'm thinking of something from away back. I borrowed something from my brother without telling him. And when he found out, he just cursed me and wished me dead and lost his temper and screamed at me. I think I was about 6. . . . I just went into my room and cried. I was *miserable.* (Mr. S.'s eyes are moist and his voice is very sad.)
Example of primary empathy—53. J: . . . Right now, I can sense how miserable you were.
Example of advanced accurate empathy—53/59. J: I would have been miserable too. . . . What I'm hearing . . . is that you are afraid you'll hurt people in the same manner you were hurt.

The example of primary empathy involves a reflection of feeling: Joann recognizes that the client is experiencing a similar feeling at this moment to one he felt some 66 years ago. The comments of Joann at this point are "interchangable" with those of Mr. S. and come from his frame of reference. In the example (later in 53 and in more depth at 59) of advanced accurate empathy, Joann adds a self-disclosure and an interpretation that influences Mr. S.'s thinking toward a new level. Used judiciously, this type of helping lead can truly facilitate client growth as it did in this interview. However, with poor timing and lack of understanding, the same lead could be potentially destructive. Advanced accurate empathy and the influencing skills add a dimension of risk to the helping process. Careful attending to the client will result in a relationship where appropriate counselor judgment about counseling interventions is increased.

Carkhuff (1969a, 1969b) considers the same issue under a different set of terms. He talks about five levels of empathy ranging from destructive (level 1) to "interchangeable responses" (level 3) to "additive empathy" (levels 4 and 5) that closely correspond to Egan's advanced accurate empathy and careful use of influencing skills in the interview. Figure 4.6 presents an adaptation of the Carkhuff/Egan approaches to empathy in the form of a scale that you may wish to use to rate general empathy and its more specific subcomponents.

The popularity of the empathy construct has led to extensive research. Early work strongly supported Rogers's statements. However, later reviews of the research have questioned whether empathy and the "core conditions" of effective helping are quite as central as once believed. You will want to review the summary of empathy research in Chapter 13 to examine this controversy. Parloff, Waskow, and Wolfe, for example, have criticized empathy and state that "the field is moving, albeit slowly, . . . toward studying a broader range of therapist activities as they interact with differentiated patient groups under a variety of specified treatment conditions . . ." (1978, p. 252).

Nonetheless, it is hard to imagine counseling or therapy being conducted without some minimal level of empathy. What does seem apparent from recent theory and research is that the core conditions of helping and empathy are more complex than originally believed. One important aspect of this complexity is increased awareness of cultural factors that may influence one's understanding of another person.

THERAPEUTIC EMPATHY: TWO PEOPLE BUT FOUR "PARTICIPANTS"*

Counseling and therapy are usually thought of as a two-person relationship—specifically a counselor and the client. Historically, it has been believed that only therapist empathy is needed with the client. There is now reason to believe that empathy requires a broader understanding. There may be *four participants in the interview: the counselor/therapist and her or his cultural/historical background and the client and his or her cultural/historical background.*

The theories of Jacques Lacan (c.f., Clement, 1983; Lacan, 1966, 1977) suggest that the interview is not just a relationship between the two people physically present in the session. The individual client before you brings with him or her a specific cultural and historical background that may affect rather powerfully the session. Needless to say, you as therapist have your own unique background. It could be argued that there are at least four major presences involved in counseling and therapy and that what sometimes appears to be the therapist talking with the client may actually be two cultural/historical backgrounds talking with each other. The figure at the top of the following page illustrates the possible complexities of the Lacanian point of view.

Important in this piece of writing for the book is that counseling is far more complex than just counseling an individual. The culture is there as well and must be considered.

*Material presented here taken from A. Ivey. "The Multicultural Practice of Therapy: Ethics, and Dialectics" © A. Ivey. To appear in a special issue of the *Journal of Social and Clinical Psychology* in 1987. Used here by permission.

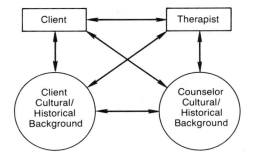

In the above figure, the client and therapist are what we see and hear communicating in the interview. But neither can escape the cultural heritage from which they came. Some theories of counseling and therapy tend to be ahistorical and give little attention to the power of history and culture on the client. They tend to focus solely on the client/therapist interaction and omit the importance of broader factors. Schneiderman (1983) has stated that "Those who attempt to erase cultural differences, who wish to create a society in which Otherness is nonexistent, come to be alienated. . . . The moral condemnation of Otherness is racist; of this there is little doubt" (p. 174).

Empathy requires that you be aware of both individual uniqueness and "Otherness" (cultural/historical factors) in your clients. Historically, empathy has focused on uniqueness to the point that social and related cultural/historical factors have been forgotten. For example, in much of counseling and therapy in the United States and Canada today, the assumption is still that all clients, regardless of culture, may be expected to respond to the same treatment. If one agrees with the Lacanian analysis presented here, such therapy or counseling may be viewed as follows:

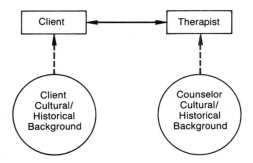

Thus, cultural and historical forces do impinge on the interview, but the counselor and client tend to be unaware of these issues and close off these critical data.

Unfortunately, in cross-cultural counseling the following sometimes occurs:

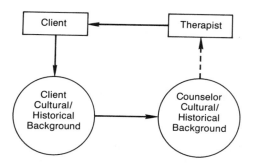

In this example, the client is aware of the special nature of his or her cultural/historical background and includes it in plans for the future. The counselor, however, operates from a theory focusing on individual empathy and does not take these important factors into account. In addition, the client sees the therapist as only a cultural stereotype. This example is not unusual, as many nonwhite clients who try counseling with ineffective white therapists will readily agree.

The desired model, then is for counselor and client to both be aware of and use culture and history in an empathic manner. Empathy can no longer be considered "necessary and sufficient" without specific attention to cultural issues.

The Lacanian model provides further additional stimulation for the constructs of empathy. At times, counselors and their clients think they are talking with each other. However, as the following diagram suggests, what is happening is that the counselor and the client are relatively passive watchers as the two sets of cultures and histories interact. You personally may recall unusual reactions you have had with some people, only later to discover that you were having a difficult time communicating due to different cultural styles and meanings.

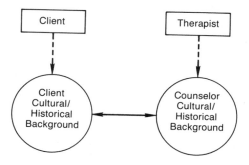

Another example of the above might occur when the client is a recently arrived Vietnamese and the counselor is a middle-class individual. The two may be talking to each other, but the degree of understanding may, at times, be so slight that in truth two cultures are talking "by" each other and the individuals are lost in the process.

Lacan offers a specific model for psychoanalytic theory in which the communication goal of the therapist is to reach the cultural/historical background of the client and to seek eventual personality reconstruction. The task of therapy is to generate an increased awareness of how cultural/historical factors are played out in the concrete life of the individual. This model below may be of French psychoanalytic origin, but it also describes the role of the feminist therapist or Black counselor in consciousness raising, or of any counseling and therapy procedure that attempts to show clients how cultural and historical factors affect their situation. The question raised in this model of therapy: "Is the client acting . . . or is the cultural/historical background causing the action?"

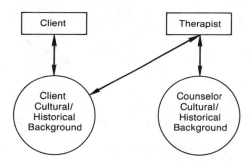

You as counselor or therapist, as you seek to be empathic, must take more than the individual into account. No longer can empathy be considered effective alone. It is suggested that empathy should only be considered part of counseling and therapy if it also includes the constructs of cultural and historical history. This may be recognized by some as a radical statement, given the ancient and illustrious history of empathy in the helping profession. However, research suggests that empathy has not been as successful as Carl Rogers once believed it would be; it seems logical that the basis of empathy is still correct, but may need modification to take into account new data on culture and counseling.

Let us now turn to an examination of examples of cultural empathy that remains an important and useful part of the helping process. This chapter will later consider in more depth the constructs of individual empathy.

EXAMPLES OF CULTURE AND EMPATHY

The intentional counselor or therapist has the ability to generate a maximum number of thoughts, words, and behaviors to communicate with a variety of diverse groups within and without a culture. You, as an intentional counselor, are a product of your cultural

FIGURE 4.1
a. Empathy requires understanding many individuals who are vastly different from you.
Photos by Irene Springer

Figure 4.2   *Characteristics of the Culturally Skilled Counselor or Therapist*

BELIEFS/ATTITUDES	KNOWLEDGE	SKILLS
1. . . . has moved from being culturally unaware to being aware and sensitive to his/her own cultural heritage and to valuing and respecting differences.	1. . . . has a good understanding of the sociopolitical system's operation in the United States with respect to its treatment of minorities.	1. . . . able to generate a wide variety of verbal and nonverbal responses.
2. . . . aware of his/her own values and biases and how they may affect minority clients.	2. . . . possesses specific knowledge and information about the particular group he/she is working with.	2. . . . able to send and receive both verbal and non-verbal messages accurately and "appropriately."
3. . . . comfortable with differences that exist between the counselor and client in terms of race and beliefs.	3. . . . has a clear and explicit knowledge and understanding of the generic characteristics of counseling and therapy.	3. . . . able to exercise institutional intervention skills on behalf of his/her client when appropriate.
4. . . . sensitive to circumstances (personal biases, stage of ethnic identity, sociopolitical influences, etc.) which may dictate referral of the minority client to a member of his/her own race/culture.	4. . . . is aware of institutional barriers which prevent minorities from using mental health services.	

Edited from Sue, D., et al., "Cross-cultural Counseling Competencies," *The Counseling Psychologist,* 1982, 10:2, p. 49. This is a report, developed by the Division of Counseling Psychology Committee, on key competencies of those who would counsel or provide therapy to various cultures.

and historical background; your client most likely comes from a related, but still different cultural background. No two individuals have the same cultural/historical background. Part of effective empathy is moving through differences toward understanding that others view the world very differently from you. Figure 4.2 summarizes issues of culture and counseling.

How well are you equipped to have empathy with people of different races (white, Black, Native American, Asian), different religious faiths (Jewish, Catholic, born-again Christians, Moslem), sexual preferences (gay, lesbian, heterosexual), ages (children, teenagers, elder citizens), ethnic groups (Italian, British-American, Lithuanian), and those who may be handicapped or have experienced special problems such as divorce or drugs? Furthermore, it is clear that men and women have varying developmental needs and counseling and therapy problems. As a counselor or therapist, you are expected to work effectively with people different from yourself.

There are several ways to prepare for a deeper understanding of the diverse clientele that we all face. The first involves a commitment to understanding differences and may be followed by study of empathy and listening skills. If you listen effectively, your client will eventually indicate to you how he or she feels comfortable. But, as research suggests, a warm, empathic skillful counselor is often not enough. As such you will want to begin a program of lifelong study considering some key aspects of individual and cultural differences and examine which theories of therapy are likely to be helpful to those whose background may be different from yours.

Ethnic and Other Group Differences

Those who read this book come from a wide variety of ethnic or racial backgrounds—this may be Irish, Italian, British, Jewish, Black, or Russian. Very often, you may be "bicultural" and have expertise, knowledge, and experience in more than one culture. The United States and Canada are sometimes referred to as "melting pot" cultures, but in truth they are a varied "stew" in which we are all mixed together. We have much in common, but differences in taste remain over the years. In addition, you may be gay or straight, young or old, or any of a variety of groupings that give a person some joint identity with others but a distinctness from "mainstream culture."

An ethnic group may be defined as "those who conceive of themselves as alike by virtue of their common ancestry, real or fictitious, and who are so regarded by others" (Shibutani and Kwan, 1965, p. 23). As such, ethnicity is a broader concept than race or religion. We group ourselves according to "we and they"—a way individuals and groups develop strength. But ethnicity may also result in persecution and lack of understanding of people different from ourselves. The definition of ethnicity above may be changed slightly to represent any of a variety of groups such as women, lesbians, the handicapped, the aged, or any other special group that has some identity within itself.

The goals of the clients you face will vary with their unique ethnic/cultural background. Most counseling theory and practice is oriented toward helping individuals self-actualize. But "self-actualization" and the individualism it represents may be inappropriate with clients who come from a "relational" ethnic group, one that believes problems are best solved *together*. A traditional Asian family, for example, will often seek to resolve individual concerns in the family in terms of family *harmony* rather than one individual meeting his or her "selfish" individual wishes. The goal of effective therapy varies with the culture and background of the client.

The relational, family, or group orientation will often manifest itself strongly in clients who may be rooted closely to Black, Native American, Asian, or Italian backgrounds. The family is the repository of the culture. If you were raised in an Italian family, the chances are far greater that you live in the same city (perhaps even on the same block) as your parents or grandparents (Rotunno and McGoldrick, 1982). If you are British-American and live in the eastern United States, you may be expected to live away from your parents but within a day's drive. Western British-Americans, on the other hand, may not be considered successful unless they live at least 500 miles from their home (McGill and Pearce, 1982). Black families who live in a hostile, racist environment tend to support one another from within and reject with suspicion help offered by outsiders (Pinderhughes, 1982). To be empathic requires an understanding of the unique individual and his or her cultural/ethnic background.

Given this complexity, it is important to remember that techniques that work well with one cultural group may be offensive and rude in another. Attending patterns differ; the use of questions may be considered intrusive; rapport may be more or less important; one theory from this text may be useful, another inappropriate. The desired goals for therapy with a handicapped client, a born-again Christian client, a recently arrived Cambodian, and an Irish-American may be very different.

Personal history is also very important in the development of an individual. If your client has experienced childhood sexual abuse, parents who have divorced, poverty, severe discrimination in the form of racism and sexism, the traumas of service in Vietnam, that client will respond differently from others. Developing understanding and empathy toward those who have experiences vastly different from your own is a lifelong task.

A useful first step toward cultural empathy is awareness of your own personal background. For some people in the United States, a person with an Irish heritage would be considered virtually identical with an individual who comes from a British-American history. However, closer examination reveals that even these two cultural backgrounds result in very different types of individual belief systems. Figure 4.3 presents the work of one counseling student who examined his own family background. One parent came from an Irish heritage and the other from a British one. Due to cultural differences, the parents gave the student differing messages and values. Note particularly the perceived "fatalism" of his Irish heritage as compared to the belief in personal action represented by the British heritage. It is this type of cultural difference that illustrates that intentionality is played out very differently among different cultures. As you read the statements, attempt to recall *empathically* that this is the way this individual views the world. You do not have to agree with those views; your goal is to understand and not to judge.

If you were counseling this student about a possible divorce, it is likely that his attitude would be shaped by his cultural background of mixed messages. If he identified more strongly with his British roots, the decision to divorce might not be so difficult; but if he believed more strongly in his Irish background, he might not even be there for counseling as divorce would not be a viable option. As many people in the United States and Canada come from bicultural backgrounds, it is most likely that some conflict between the two value systems will appear in counseling. Often this conflict is an internal struggle without awareness on the part of the client or the counselor. Your task may be to facilitate awareness of the relationship between culture and individual consciousness.

And, we must not forget that the student is also American, influenced by

Figure 4.3 *A Student Looks at His Mixed Family Heritage*

The following discussion was generated by Mark Darling, a student in crosscultural counseling. Mark comes from a family which most would consider "typically American." One parent is Irish, the other British-American. Mark, himself, is a third-generation American. Until the course in crosscultural counseling, Mark saw himself solely as "American." With reading and study, he came to realize that many of his beliefs and values were not just American, but were the result of long-term Irish and British values. He also found that some internal conflicts within himself were not solely his own individual "problems," but were also the result of variant cultural messages he received from his parents.

The analysis below presents a summary of his personal observations plus reading in cross-cultural counseling and family therapy (c.f., McGoldrick, Pearce, and Giordano, 1982). It should be obvious that cultural intentionality on the part of the therapist requires empathy to the cultural background of the client, an empathy that can only be built through long study and effort on your part into the spifics of varying cultures. Then, armed with that knowledge, you still face a unique individual before you with unique personal syntheses of cultural background. Given this information, would you say that Mark is predominantly Irish, British, or American?

IRISH-AMERICAN MESSAGES	BRITISH-AMERICAN MESSAGES
LIFE EXPECTATIONS.	
People are basically evil; life is determined by fate. You are the victim or beneficiary of luck; you have no say in the matter.	Good and bad are an individual choice. You are responsible for your fate. Live by the rules and work hard. Therein lies success.

These two basic attitudes underlie the belief system of an English-Irish individual. One of these will probably be dominant, yet both will be present. The combined message could likely be, "Win or lose, it's not your choice, but you are responsible for your failures." In this case, the individual would consider success to be luck, and failure to be a personal lack of initiative or ability. Thus the individual comes to feel like a failure with *certainty* of failing again, and *no expectation* of success.

FAMILY RELATIONS	
The family is your source and your strength. Family is identity and your obligation. To leave is to be alone and powerless.	You are an individual, strong and self-reliant. Leave home to make your fortune; establish your own family. Your life is up to you.

The conflict created by these two attitudes is very important. One possible synthesis of these is, "You are old enough to leave now, but you do not have the necessary strength to make it on your own." Thus the individual will feel a strong desire to set out on his own, but a corresponding inability to leave.

GENDER ROLES	
Women are morally superior to men. Men are morally weak, given to uncontrollable weakness. The mother is the strength of the household.	Women are fragile and must be protected. The father is the strength of the household.

The conflict here becomes one of role in the household. This may be synthesized as, "You are expected to be strong and virtuous, but you are incapable by nature of being so." In this way, individuals will feel the need to be something they cannot see themselves as being, and may experience a tremendous sense of inadequacy.

MARRIAGE

Marriage is a necessity, and you are bound by it for life. If you have problems in your marriage, they are your due, and you must accept them.

Marriage is a social contract. Both parties are responsible to maintain the agreement. If one is in violation, divorce is acceptable.

These two messages are very hard to reconcile. "You made a bad contract, and you have the right to a divorce, but divorce is wrong." The practical result may be that the individual will get a divorce, yet feel that action to be illegitimate and wrong.

LANGUAGE

Words are poetry, an expression of emotion. They have beauty but no reality, and may always be traded for better ones. Words are dreams through which you create an internal reality.

Language is law, the structure of reality. Words are specific and binding. Language is the means by which life is directed, and our plans are the key to growth and our gain. Through words you create your external reality.

In this conflict is the expression of a major source of misunderstanding between English and Irish culture. The English function by contracts, and contractual agreements demand that words be specific and binding. The Irish, on the other hand, see words as defined by the context in which they are used. These messages may be synthesized by the individual as, "Your daydreaming is a waste of time. You never do what you say you are going to do. Plan for the future, but it's all idle dreaming." The result can be an individual who is unable to follow through on agreements and is not generally relied upon.

A common tendency today is to stereotype and condemn "white males," particularly those of "Anglo-Celtic" background. But, as may be clearly observed here, British and Irish backgrounds are very different. It is not possible to stereotype any one individual because of color or ethnicity. Mark Darling is a unique person, in some ways bicultural, who works his way through the maze of cultural messages uniquely. As a young white male, he does not suffer the problems of sexism, racism, or ageism. Yet, it should also be clear that every client comes from a cultural background with special implications. Understanding variations in ethnicity and religion, race and sex, and many other factors will enrich your understanding in the counseling interview.

materialism, television, and the enthusiastic free choice emphasized in this culture. In a sense, this student is tricultural. Many, perhaps most of your clients will represent some form of bicultural pattern. When issues of age, sex, religion, handicap, and so forth are added as additional cultural groupings, the complexity you face as a helper with special populations should be readily apparent.

Clearly, North America is not a monolithic culture. Differences abound, varying peoples with differing family structures and expectations. Think about your own family. How does it respond to issues such as where children are expected to live after marriage? How much emotional and financial support does your family offer? What is the family attitude toward intellectual achievement? What are the expected roles of men and women? Beliefs about drinking? What are attitudes toward pain? *Then,* look at yourself and your life. How are your constructs similar and different from your own family? Figure 4.4 presents a framework within which you can examine your own cultural/ethnic heritage.

Chances are that you as a unique individual have some beliefs in common with your family and some significant differences. This is one simple illustration of the danger of taking general group characteristics, such as those identified above, and assuming everyone in that group is the same. A Jewish individual would not appreciate your expecting him or her to have the same values toward education similar to all other Jewish people (education is, however, a general value in Jewish culture) (Herz and Rosen, 1982). The particular person in the

---

Figure 4.4   *An Exercise in Cultural Awareness*

It is difficult to be understanding of others without an awareness of yourself as a cultural being. The following questions are designed to begin some thinking on your part about how your cultural/historical heritage may affect your work in the counseling and therapy interview.

1. *Ethnic heritage.* With what ethnic background do you first identify? You will first identify your nationality—U.S. citizen, Canadian, Mexican, etc. Beyond this first answer you may find the words *white, red, Black, Polish, Mormon, Jewish,* and others coming to your mind. Record those words.

   Then, where do your grandparents come from? Great-grandparents? Can you trace a family history, perhaps with different ethnic, religious, and racial backgrounds?

   Identify in list form or in a family tree your heritage. Do not forget your heritage from the country within which you live.

2. *Are you monocultural, bicultural, or more?* Review the list you developed and pick out the central cultural, ethnic, religious, or other types of groups that have been involved in your development.

3. *What messages do you receive from each cultural group you have listed?* Take time to list values, behaviors, and expectations that people in your group have come to emphasize over time. Figure 4.3 illustrates the process of how to list some key life messages given by your family or other cultural groups. How have you personally internalized these messages? If you are aware of the message, the chances are you have made some deviation from the family, ethnic, or religious value. If you are unaware, the values from outside may be so incorporated within yourself that you are a "culture-bearer" without knowing it. Becoming aware of these obvious but unconscious culture-bearer messages may become the most difficult task of all.

4. *How might your cultural messages affect your counseling and therapeutic work?* This final question is the most important of all. If you believe in individuality as supreme, given your family history, you may tend to miss the relational, family orientation of many Asians, Blacks, and Italians. If you come from a relational orientation, you may have difficulty in likewise understanding individualistic WASPs (White Anglo-Saxon Protestants) and label them as "cold" and "calculating." As we all come from cultural histories, it is easy to think that our way of being in the world is the way things "are and should be."

   The development of empathy requires a deeper understanding of ourselves and our cultural heritage so that we do not unconsciously impose our beliefs on others.

counseling interview remains unique and you cannot expect group differences to predict each person you meet.

However, a basic understanding of group differences may help you understand that a gay or lesbian client is likely to suffer from job discrimination and may sometimes have a family that rejects him or her. This is *not* true of all gay and lesbian clients, but an understanding that this may be an issue can be helpful. Many older people face problems of loneliness, but not all. You may see as inappropriate a young Italian family living with parents if that is different from your cultural background. Similarly, it is possible for an Italian family therapist to view a Jewish, Irish, or British-American client as strange and different in that they may not be as close as an Italian family. Let us now turn to aspects of individual empathy.

THE CORE CONDITIONS OF THE EMPATHIC ATTITUDE

Empathy requires one to see the world from a perspective different from your own. Skills in listening such as paraphrasing and reflection of feeling are critical in this process. However, key core conditions of helping have been identified as central if you are to *communicate* to others that you understand them. Understanding and an empathic attitude are not enough, you must communicate to your client the sense of empathy that you feel.

Important constructs from the helping professions that can help communicate your feelings of understanding and empathy for the client include: *positive regard, respect and warmth, concreteness, immediacy,* and *congruence, genuineness,* and *authenticity.* In addition *confrontation*—reviewed with the microskills in the preceding chapter—is often considered as one of the core conditions of empathy (see Figure 4.5).

Positive Regard

This term closely approximates the positive asset search of decisional counseling in Chapter 2 (reviewed even more extensively in Chapter 7). Succinctly stated, it is an empathic attitude that meets all clients positively and emphasizes their strengths. In cultural terms, it means that you as therapist are able to recognize values and strengths in clients different from yourself, even when the client holds attitudes far different from yours.

If you want to help a client change, you must believe that he or she can change and that he or she has positive aspects. In its most simple form positive regard may be defined as *selective attention to positive aspects of client verbalization and behavior.* All intentional therapists operate on the assumption that the client can be helped. If you do not believe that people can be helped, your clients will sense this message and will not be assisted by therapy or counseling.

Figure 4.5   *Qualitative Conditions of Intentional Counseling*

Empathy	Seeing the client's world from the client's perspective.
Primary empathy	Using attending skills of reflective listening to hear the client accurately. Your comments may be described as interchangeable with those of the client.
Advanced accurate empathy	Using influencing skills as well as attending skills and sharing yourself and your expertise with the client, but always within what the client can absorb and within her or his frame of reference.
Positive regard	Giving selective attention to positive aspects of client verbalization and behavior. Drawing on the positive assets of the client.
Respect	Offering enhancing positive statements to the client and encouraging him or her to move forward. Where differences occur, open and honest appreciation and toleration of those differences.
Warmth	Using primarily nonverbal means, such as vocal tone, posture, facial expression, to express caring for the client. Smiling has been shown to be especially important in the communication of warmth.
Concreteness	Being specific, obtaining details, getting clarification of facts and feelings.
Immediacy	Using the three dimensions presented—speaking in the present, past, or future tense. Clients who are moving intentionally will often spontaneously start using all three tenses as they look at themselves.
Confrontation	Meeting a client directly and pointing out differences, mixed messages, incongruities, and discrepancies in verbal and nonverbal behavior. Confrontation is *not* expressing your differing opinion no matter how helpful. The discussion of these same differences, however, may be a confrontation. Presented previously in Chapter 3.
Genuineness	Being truly oneself in relationship with others.
In relationship to self	Being oneself authentically and spontaneously. It is possible to be genuine and not relate to others.
In relationship to others	Being sensitive to the needs of the client and her or his ability to be-in-relationship *and* still being truly oneself.
Cultural empathy	Sensing and noting that your cultural background is not that of the client. Learning to become aware of differences and similarities in groups, without sacrificing personal uniqueness.

Carl Rogers does not just talk about his beliefs; he demonstrates them in his counseling:

> From a first glance, one would think the helpee has no assets, no hope. But, out of a dark morass of discouragement, Carl Rogers always seems to find something positive in an individual and highlights that positive dimension via a reflection of feeling and (more recently) direct personal feedback. (Ivey and Gluckstern, 1976, p. i)

Other theories operate within the same framework. You will find transactional analysis counselors talk about "strokes" and the giving of "warm fuzzies"; family therapists believe that people can change and grow in what appears to be a dismal, hopeless interaction; and behaviorists believe firmly that virtually all clients can learn to cope with their situation, by offering reinforcement to facilitate personal development. The words and methods may vary, but all effective therapies and counseling frameworks believe that they can make a positive difference in the life of clients.

The exchange below illustrates the importance of positive regard:

DONNA: Yeh . . . so tired, everything is coming down at once. If it were just one problem . . . but I can't stand my parents either. Mom cries every time she sees me and my father won't talk to me anymore—he just glares at me. It's like they disowned me or that I don't even exist.

HELPER: So, lots of things are going on. *You seem to paint a pretty accurate picture of the issues.* You're pregnant, you don't know which way to go about an abortion, you've got ambivalent feelings of love and anger toward Ronnie, your parents aren't providing any support. *Yet through all this I see you struggling to maintain yourself,* yet you feel weak and need support.

In this example the positive regard statements have been italicized. Donna has portrayed a generally discouraging picture. The beginning counselor, often overwhelmed, tends either to cover up the problem and thus avoid dealing with real issues or to see the problem as very discouraging and emphasize only negative aspects. An overly optimistic response which is *not* positive regard might have been "Donna, you've got lots of assets, things will turn out OK." Such a response by itself may be satisfactory, but if continued over an entire interview it actually results in a demeaning of the client's problem. The other pole would be represented by "Donna, the situation is pretty discouraging . . . you just move lower and lower." While this may be accurate in one sense, if continued over the entire interview, the client would wallow in discouragement and confusion. Both overly positive and overly negative approaches to the counseling interview are potentially destructive.

In short, positive regard demands that you constantly search for assets and strengths in your clients but at the same time deal frankly and clearly with their very real life issues. Counseling does not exist to smooth things over, but to help people cope with the world as it is. To help people cope with this world, the concepts of respect and warmth are essential ingredients of intentional counseling and psychotherapy.

Respect and Warmth

Cold, distant counselors and therapists may appear professional and competent, but underlying that facade of professionalism may be unconscious hostility and dislike for the client. The intentional counselor likes and respects other people and communicates these feelings to them. In this short section, respect and warmth are considered needed parts for true empathic understanding.

Counselors who lack respect for their clients may call them names behind their backs, devise manipulative games to "help," brag about their effectiveness to clients and colleagues, offer racist or sexist slurs, or show any of a host of behaviors indicating lack of regard and respect for other human beings. It would be pleasant to be able to say that these behaviors are rare in the counseling profession, but unfortunately they are all too common. The clearest indication of lack of respect occurs in the "put-down," where counselors offer negative statements about the client either directly or in subtle form. In addition, there are counselors who put themselves down and thus lessen their ability to counsel others.

There are some positive ways through which respect may be communicated:

> Two basic types of comments communicating respect are *enhancing* and *appreciation-of-differences* statements. Enhancing statements include "You express your opinion well" and "Good insight." Appreciation-of-differences statements include "I don't see it that way, but I can imagine how you could arrive at that opinion" and "I may disagree with what you say, but I will support your right to say it." It may be seen that respect and positive regard are closely related. (Ivey and Authier, 1978, p. 136)

Let us assume that Donna asks the counselor for an opinion. How should the counselor respond?

DONNA: You've listened to me for quite awhile. What do you think I ought to do? I'm so confused.

HELPER: I see you now leaning toward keeping the baby. I like that, I value life. If I were in your shoes, I suspect I'd be feeling much the same as you. Frankly, I hope you have the baby—yet I think it is your decision. What are your reactions to my thoughts? I think you can handle it.

Did the counselor respond appropriately in the above self-disclosure? Depending on one's value stand and theoretical persuasion, the answer can range from a resounding "yes" to an absolute "no." In such situations, counselors do not find easy answers available and perhaps choose not to share their opinions. Whether one should share one's opinion in the interview is open to argument; however, almost all would agree that answering such a question early in the interview would be inappropriate. Later in the session, answering the question may be more appropriate.

Respect is clearly vital to the interviewing and therapy process. It is a different construct from warmth. It is possible to respect another person's point of view but still lack the critical dimension of personal warmth. Together, however, respect and warmth present a powerful combination.

Warmth of counselor response has been demonstrated to be an important factor underlying an empathic relationship. But what is warmth? Warmth may be defined as an emotional attitude toward the client, expressed through nonverbal means. Vocal tone, posture, gestures, facial expression, and the ability to touch when appropriate are how the warmth and support of a counselor is communicated to a client. Smiling has been found to be the best single predictor of warmth ratings in an interview (Bayes, 1973). Warmth, then, appears to be one form of your self-expression in the world. Are you a warm person? How do you communicate your warmth?

Separating warmth, respect, and the earlier concept of positive regard is perhaps not really possible. Yet, one can imagine a person expressing positive feedback, respect, and positive regard to a client in a cold, distant fashion. The lack of warmth can negate the positive message. The communication of warmth through smiling, vocal tone, and other nonverbal means adds power and conviction to counselor comments.

Concreteness

HELPER: Could you give me a specific example of what happened when you and your parents argued about Ronnie?

Clients often begin therapy with vague, ambiguous complaints. A task of the intentional therapist is to clarify and understand vague ideas and problems expressed by the client. Effective interviews tend to move from vague descriptions of global general issues to highly concrete discussions of what happened or what is happening in the daily life of the client.

DONNA: Well, my parents don't help me. (Vague)

HELPER: Could you share one specific place where they didn't help you? Could you give me a specific example from last week? (Concrete)

DONNA: Well, when they found out I was pregnant, they just yelled and yelled and want me to get rid of it. (More concrete)

HELPER: What, specifically did they say? What did you say? (Concrete)

Through leads of this type the helper can move from a general opinion to a clear understanding of what actually did happen. Becoming empathic and understanding the other person is easier, obviously, when you understand specific facts. The tone and depth of an interview is often set by the degree of specificity and concreteness employed. Generally speaking, most clients will welcome concreteness as "objective facts" are less susceptible to personal or cultural distortion. Furthermore, specificity and concreteness will provide a more solid base for client and therapist problem solving.

But, sometimes the emotional experience may have been too intense for immediate discussion of concrete specifics. In cases of rape and abuse, the search for concreteness may sometimes wisely be delayed. North Americans in general tend to prefer discussion of concrete specifics of a problem, but the concreteness and directness of this approach can put off many Europeans, Asians, or Africans whose culture may be oriented more toward a subtle approach.

The search for concreteness underlies many, perhaps even most helping interviews. The client lacks full understanding and often has labeled a situation incorrectly. By asking the open question, *Can you give me a specific example?*, you can slow down and clarify a confusing interview.

Immediacy

The English language divides time into past, present, and future tenses. Generally speaking, the most powerful counseling leads are in the present tense and are considered the most *immediate*. Yet, different theories discussed in this book give different emphasis to different time dimensions. For example:

Psychoanalytic theory (at least in the early years of a long-term analysis) operates primarily in the *past* tense and focuses on past experience. Gestalt therapy and existential helping focus on the *now* and give special attention to what is happening to the client in the immediate "here and now" world. Behavioral helpers and vocational counselors may delve into the past, but are often primarily interested in facilitating client self-expression in the *future*.

The tense of discussion in the helping interview determines heavily the nature of the client-counselor interaction. Consider the following:

CLIENT:	I'm scared.
ANALYTIC HELPER:	Free associate to your earliest childhood experience which relates to that feeling.
EXISTENTIAL HELPER:	You're scared. What does that mean to you right now?
BEHAVIORAL HELPER:	What do you want to do about it? (Ivey and Authier, 1978, pp. 141–142)

Which of the above counseling leads is most effective? It will depend on your worldview and your idea of the objective(s) of the therapy interview. Each lead moves the client to more concrete expression but looks at the world in a very different time sense.

Immediacy is discussed by Carkhuff (1969a, 1969b) and by Egan (1975) as immediate discussion of issues between the counselor and the client and their relationship. The microskills of feedback and self-disclosure are important in this definition of immediacy. As you move toward a more present-tense orientation in helping, you will find yourself using more self-disclosure and feedback statements. This type of helping is characteristic of Rogerian, existential, and encounter types of helping. Common to this form of helping is, "What's going on with you, right now?"

Whether you define immediacy as the relationship between counselor or client or the more direct use of present-tense language, you will find this concept heavily used by Joann in her interview with Mr. S. For example:

3. J: Well, look at your smile. (4. S: *Today,* I feel pretty good.)
5. J: You feel pretty good today . . .
17. J: You're laughing, but I sense from the tone of your voice and the look on your face that underneath it isn't a laughing matter.
27. J: I sense you can feel the pressure *now* . . .
96. J: You will take care of yourself. The time is now. Is that what I hear you saying?

In each of the above, Joann uses present-tense language that enlivens and enriches the session.

But, although our clients live in the present tense, they also have experience from the past and plan for the future. We saw in Mr. S.'s case that he was in part reliving the past in the present and had to break that connection if he was to live differently in the future. Joann Griswold's use of immediacy made the session more impactful.

Yet, sometimes it is appropriate and desirable to be less immediate and less concrete. If a situation is too threatening and demanding, the counselor can move to the past tense and become vague to remove tension and threat.

DONNA: (visibly trembling and about to break into tears) I'm feeling so crumby. Nothing seems to make sense . . . it all seems so hopeless.
HELPER: Last week you seemed to be feeling better . . . different than now.
DONNA: Yeh, I had it together—I thought—but it seems to be falling apart again.
HELPER: Let's go back and look at one thing that you did last week that seemed to work with your parents.

The helper's second statement is nonimmediate and primarily in the past tense. The client responds with a similar pattern, showing less immediacy and concreteness. The counselor then focuses the client on the past tense with a positive experience. At this point, it is again feasible to become concrete and specific. It should be pointed out that retreating from strong client expressions is not always wise. A consistent pattern of avoidance of client emotional expression may be identified in some counselors and therapists. The intentional therapist learns when to become immediate and concrete and when to use these same concepts to take pressure off the client. Furthermore, different theories have differing ways to handle this issue. It is necessary that you examine your own life experience, commitment to counseling, and the several alternative theories to psychotherapy, and generate your own position on this critical issue. Regardless of where you stand on this issue, an awareness of the power of these constructs is mandatory.

Congruence, Genuineness, and Authenticity

Central concepts of the helping field, congruence, genuineness and authenticity were introduced by Carl Rogers who stated that the therapist in a counseling relationship should be a

> congruent, integrated person. It means that within the relationship he is freely and deeply himself, with his actual experience represented by his awareness of himself. It is the opposite of presenting a facade either knowingly or unknowingly. (Rogers, 1957, p. 97)

It would seem difficult to fault such a statement, and it is clear that openness and honesty on your part are central to your effectiveness. There are times, however, when complete openness and spontaneity of expression may damage the client. This point was brought home forcefully in 1972 when Lieberman, Yalom, and Miles studied encounter group casualties. They found that "open," "authentic" group leaders produced more casualties than more conservative types of counselors who developed relationships *with* their groups.

Two types of authenticity may be considered. The first type is authenticity to yourself. This may be fine, and you may be truthful and open as a model, but your client may not be ready for such behavior. The more important type of authenticity is when you have a genuine, congruent relationship *with* your client. This means noting where your clients "are at," listening to them, and opening a dialogue of empathy.

Critical work by Strong (1968)—followed by extensive research summarized by Corrigan, Dell, Lewis, and Schmidt (1980)—has helped redefine the parameters of what genuineness in a counseling relationship is. In addition to authenticity, we now must also think of how the client perceives our *expertness*, *trustworthiness*, and *attractiveness*. Strong's work shows us that if we are to influence a client, we must be seen as worthy of providing influence. Thus, with many clients it has been found that, for example, the professional degrees hung on the wall, a neat professional office, a professional demeanor, physical attractiveness, and demonstrated ability to win trust are equally important, if not more important, in the success of counseling than the traditional views of authenticity expressed by Rogers.

Given these warnings, it is still relevant to consider how genuineness in communication can best appear in the interview. Two concepts of genuineness and authenticity have been suggested: (1) genuineness in relation to self and (2) genuineness in relation to your client.

The following exchange with Donna about the abortion problem illustrates some issues in regard to genuineness:

DONNA: Yes, I can't decide what to do about the bab . . . I mean abortion until I know where I stand with Ronnie. He used to treat me nice, especially when we were first dating. He came over and fixed my car and my stereo, he liked to run errands for me. Now if I ask him anything, he makes a big hassle out of it.

HELPER: At this moment, I can sense some confusion. Let me check this out with you. . . . When someone is nice to me, I get to trust them and feel comfortable. But—then—if they let me down, I get low and lost and really confused. Is my experience at all like yours?

DONNA: I guess I have felt like that. I know I blame him for getting me pregnant and he wouldn't do anything to prevent it. It makes me damn mad!

HELPER: Right now, you *really* are angry with him.

The counselor illustrates genuineness in relationship to self through the skill of self-disclosure. The counselor shares her or his feelings and thoughts in a very real and personal manner. It may be noted that the self-disclosure is relatively vague and nonconcrete. Let us suppose the counselor is thinking of a past event in relation to his or her parents. If that concrete event had been presented, the counselor would still be genuine in relation to self; but the introduction of the parents' letting their child down is rather distant from this client's immediate personal experience. This is an example where genuineness in relationship to self actually could disturb the counseling relationship. In this interview, the counselor is genuine not only to self, but also in the relationship. The congruent self-disclosure is helpful to the interviewing process.

Genuine self-disclosure on the part of the counselor produces further genuineness on the part of the client. Intentional counselors tend to produce intentional clients. Let us now turn to an examination of client behavior as it relates to ideas of empathy.

USING EMPATHY IN THE INTERVIEW: DIALECTICS

Your empathic response to one client may represent insensitivity to another. Just as the microskill of attending must be used differentially with different individuals and those of varying cultural backgrounds, so you must be flexible in providing empathy throughout the interview.

Figure 4.6 *Empathy Rating Scale*

Instructions: Before rating a counselor's statement for its degree of empathy, it is critical that the context of what the client has been saying be considered as well. Therefore, examine what the client has just said before determining how well the counselor is "tuned in." Rate each counselor statement on the following seven-point scale for degree of empathy. It is also possible to examine several counselor statements or an entire interview segment and rate that for empathy.

Level 1: The counselor or therapist is overtly destructive to the interviewing process. He or she fails to attend (sharp body shifts, major topic jumps) in a way that sharply disrupts client flow or attacks the client or discounts information.

Level 2: The counselor or therapist may be implicitly and subtly destructive, even though overtly trying to be helpful. The distinction between levels 1 and 2 is a matter of degree and sharpness. The disagreement or lack of attention doesn't seem as unusual here and is seen in the daily life of most people in some form. (Also see level 5.)

Level 3: At first glance, the session appears to be moving normally. However, on deeper analysis, one sees that the counselor or therapist is *detracting* slightly from what the client has been saying. The paraphrase is close, but still misses the client's meaning. Much of our daily conversation fits this pattern. As a result of the interaction, the client is not damaged and has been listened to minimally, but counselor responses take away from what the client says or minimizes statements.

Level 4: Considered by many, the *minimal* level for counseling, level 4 responses are *interchangeable* with what the client is saying. An interchangeable response is best exemplified by an accurate reflection of feeling, paraphrase, or summary that catches the essence of what the client has said. An open question or a self-disclosure that aids client responding is another example of a level 4 response.

Level 5: At this point, counseling becomes truly additive in that the counselor or therapist is adding something beyond an interchangeable response. In addition to an accurate paraphrase or reflection of feeling, the therapist adds a mild interpretation or a probing question or interpretation that not only catches the major meanings of the client, but *adds* something new to facilitate growth and exploration. Generally speaking, level 5 requires the use of influencing skills or questioning techniques. Ineffective use of these skills at this point, however, may return the counselor or therapist to level 2. As one employs the influencing skills, the possibility for error increases.

Level 6: The counselor is truly becoming an intentional person. Attending and influencing skills are used in combination with the many qualities of empathy (concreteness, immediacy, etc.) to provide a more effective and facilitating level of counseling. Patterns of movement synchrony and movement complimentarity often are manifested.

Level 7: The highest level of counseling is one that relatively few counselors and therapists attain. In addition to solid, effective intentional manifestation of the many microskills and qualities of empathy, the counselor is totally "with" the client, yet apart and distinct. For some, this can be termed a "peak experience" in relationship. Direct-mutual communication is shown at this stage in its full dimensions.

(Circle appropriate number for each below.)

Empathy (global impression)	1	2	3	4	5	6	7
Positive regard	1	2	3	4	5	6	7
Respect	1	2	3	4	5	6	7
Warmth	1	2	3	4	5	6	7
Concreteness	1	2	3	4	5	6	7
Immediacy	1	2	3	4	5	6	7
Confrontation	1	2	3	4	5	6	7
Genuineness							
In relation to self	1	2	3	4	5	6	7
In relation to others	1	2	3	4	5	6	7
Cultural empathy	1	2	3	4	5	6	7

How can you cope with the variety of clients and their many diverse cultures when no formula or theory will provide a totally useful answer, that is, the "correct" response and action? The following three-step dialectical model of empathy provides you with a framework for balancing the uniqueness of the individual before you with your own general knowledge and with that of counseling and therapy theory:

1. Listen to and observe your client and her or his response.
2. Draw your response from the client's main words and constructs. When in doubt, generally use the attending and listening skills. But when culturally and individually appropriate, add your own experience, knowledge, or intuitions.
3. *Check out* your statement or intervention by asking, "How does that sound?" "Is that close?" or some other statement that allows the client to respond to you.

At this point, recycle to the first stage and change your style and comments as necessary until you and the client are both comfortable. Empathy is best considered a process in which counselor and client explore the nature of the client's worldview and beliefs about the problem together. There is no final standard of "superior" empathy; rather empathy requires you constantly to attune yourself to the wide variety of individual clients with whom you will work.

The interview in Chapter 3 that Joann had with Mr. S. provides useful examples of this basic dialogical/dialectical process. Joann listened carefully to the client, Mr. S. She used extensive attending skills, particularly in the first three stages of the interview. Having listened carefully to Mr. S., Joann made judgments about the possible use of influencing skills and of moving toward advanced accurate empathy. Almost invariably, Joann provides an opportunity for Mr. S. to respond to her through the checkout ("Does that make sense?" "Am I hearing you correctly?") or by asking "How do you respond to that?" This checking-out is especially helpful as it allows the therapist to change course in response to further client statements. The checkout may be done explicitly as above or implicitly through a questioning tone of voice as you make a self-disclosure or interpretation.

Note the following examples of Joann with Mr. S. that illustrate this process.

11. J: Now that you're alone, ah, I sense what you're saying is that you are lonely or alone quite a bit of the time . . .

12. S: Yes! (Emphatically)

13. J: . . . and that you thought that maybe some of these activities would serve the purpose of filling up your time and you wouldn't be so lonely. How does that sound? Does it make sense?

23. J: I hear you saying that, uh, that these new friends are infringing on your time. And I hear that you feel pulled in directions you don't want to go in. Is that right?

60. J: Has . . . have you thought about how you hurt yourself in this process?

90. J: You have the power, you have a lot of power. You have a lot of strength. Can you tell me about your power and your strength?

These statements are random selections from the typescript. If you examine the interview, you will find that virtually every lead in the interview opens up a dialogue or dialectic of understanding in which we move more closely to the "truth" of Mr. S.'s life. At the same time, no final truth is determined and the 1-2-3 process of "listen," "react," and "checkout reactions" provides a constant flow to the interview. In this way, empathy may be seen as an interactional flow.

We would argue that empathy has been misdefined by the helping profession by focusing too narrowly on what the interviewer does to promote understanding. While this is important, the dialectic of open discussion is the result of the basic process, and this dialogue itself becomes part of the process for later growth and future understanding.

SUMMARY OF THIS CHAPTER

To master the ideas of this chapter, it is important to:

1. *Define empathy as a foundation of counseling.* The concepts of primary and advanced accurate empathy were presented. Primary empathy is most often associated with the attending skills, and advanced accurate empathy, with the influencing skills. Recent summaries of research have suggested that issues surrounding empathy and the "core conditions" are more complex than once was believed.

2. *Delineate empathy as it relates to cultural intentionality.* The characteristics of the culturally skilled, intentional therapist were presented, and extensive discussion of

the importance of cultural awareness was discussed. It was pointed out that all clients come from unique personal and cultural backgrounds. An exercise in cultural awareness was presented.

3. *Understand and discuss the concepts of positive regard, respect and warmth, concreteness, immediacy, and genuineness, and identify where they are manifested in an interview.* The several subcomponents of empathy were presented. A related aspect, confrontation, was discussed in the preceding chapter as a microskill combination of listening to the client and pointing out critical discrepancies in client thoughts and behaviors. The specific conditions of empathy listed here will support your confrontation of client issues and help you develop and define a warm, empathic relationship with your client.

4. *Utilize the three-step empathic process to test the effectiveness of your interventions.* Empathy was presented as a three-step process between counselor and client of listening and observing the client, responding from your experience of the client and theory, and "checking out" with the client how effectively you communicated and/or heard the client. Through this process, you can shift your style and work with many differing types of individuals and groups.

5. *Define key terms and ideas presented in this chapter.* Key terms and concepts in Chapter 4 include empathy, primary empathy, advanced accurate empathy, culture and empathy, characteristics of the culturally skilled psychologist, biculturalism in clients, positive regard, respect and warmth, immediacy, concreteness, congruence, genuineness, and authenticity, and the three-step process of dialectic empathic awareness.

REFERENCES

Bayes, M., "Behavioral Cues of Interpersonal Warmth." *Journal of Counseling Psychology*, 1972, *39*, 333–339.

Carkhuff, R., *Helping and Human Relations*. Vol. I and II. New York: Holt, Rinehart, and Winston, 1969 a,b.

Clement, C., *The Lives and Legends of Jacques Lacan*. New York: Columbia, 1983.

Corrigan, J., D. Dell, K. Lewis, and L. Schmidt, "Counseling as a Social Influence Process: A Review," *Journal of Counseling Psychology*, 1980, *27*, 395–441.

Egan, G., *The Skilled Helper*. Monterey, CA: Brooks/Cole, 1975.

Gendlin, E., and M. Hendricks, *Changes*. Rap manual: mimeographed, undated. Cited in E. Gendlin, *Focusing*. New York: Everest House, 1978.

Haase, R., and D. Tepper, "Nonverbal Components of Empathic Communication," *Journal of Counseling Psychology*, 1972, *19*, 417–424.

Herz, F.,and E. Rosen, "Jewish Families." In M. McGoldrick, J. Pearce, and J. Giordano (eds.), *Ethnicity and Family Therapy*. New York: Guilford, 1982, pp. 364–392.

Ivey, A., and J. Authier, *Microcounseling: Innovations in Interviewing, Counseling, Psychotherapy, and Psychoeducation*. Springfield, IL: Thomas, 1978.

Ivey, A., and N. Gluckstern, *Basic Influencing Skills*. North Amherst, MA: Microtraining, 1976, 1983.

Lacan, J., *Écrits*. New York: Norton, 1966, 1977.

McGill, D., and J. Pearce, "British Families." In M. McGoldrick, J. Pearce, and J. Giordano (eds.), *Ethnicity and Family Therapy*. New York: Guilford, 1982, pp. 457–482.

McGoldrick, M., J. Pearce, and J. Giordano, (eds.), *Ethnicity and Family Therapy*. New York: Guilford, 1982.

Parloff, M., I. Waskow, and B. Wolfe, "Research on Client Variables in Psychotherapy and Behavioral Intervention." In S. Garfield and A. Bergin (eds.), *Handbook of Psychotherapy and Behavior Change*. New York: Wiley, 1978, pp. 233–282.

PINDERHUGHES, E., "Afro-American Families and the Victim Syndrome." In M. Mc-Goldrick, J. Pearce, and J. Giordano (eds.), *Ethnicity and Family Therapy*. New York: Guilford, 1982, pp. 108–122.

ROGERS, C., "Empathic: An Unappreciated Way of Being," *The Counseling Psychologist*, 1975, *5* (2), 2–10.

ROGERS, C., *On Becoming a Person*. Boston: Houghton-Mifflin, 1961.

ROGERS, C., "The Necessary and Sufficient Conditions of Therapeutic Personality Change," *Journal of Consulting Psychology*, 1957, *21*, 95–103.

ROTUNNO, M., and M. McGOLDRICK, "Italian Families." In M. McGoldrick, J. Pearce, and J. Giordano (eds.), *Ethnicity and Family Therapy*. New York: Guilford, 1982, pp. 340–363.

SCHNEIDERMAN, S., *Jacques Lacan: The Death of an Intellectual Hero*. Cambridge, MA: Harvard, 1983.

SHIBUTANI, T. and K. KWAN, *Ethnic Stratification*. New York: Macmillan, 1965.

STRONG, S., "Counseling: An Interpersonal Influence Process," *Journal of Counseling Psychology*, 1968, *15*, 215–224.

ZIMMER, J., and S. ANDERSON, "Dimensions of Positive Regard and Empathy," *Journal of Counseling Psychology*, 1968, *15*, 417–426.

ZIMMER, J., and P. PARK, "Factor Analysis of Counselor Communications," *Journal of Counseling Psychology*, 1967, *14*, 198–203.

SUGGESTED SUPPLEMENTARY READING

CARKHUFF, R., *Helping and Human Relations*. Vol. I and II. New York: Holt, Rinehart & Winston, 1969 a,b.

Two influential books on the helping process that detail Carkhuff's framework. Included in volume II are the well-known five-point subjective rating scales for empathy.

KATZ, J., *White Awareness: Handbook for Anti-Racism Training*. Norman, OK: University of Oklahoma Press, 1978.

Racism and oppression have long been a part of many cultures. This book provides a series of useful exercises for coming to terms with issues of racism and oppression.

MARSELLA, T., and P. PEDERSEN, *Cross-Cultural Counseling and Psychotherapy*. New York: Pergamon, 1981.

A summary of current theory and research in crosscultural counseling and psychotherapy. Outcome variables, specific treatment techniques for varying problems, and conceptual frameworks for this expanding field are presented.

McGOLDRICK, M., J. PEARCE and J. GIORDANO (eds.), *Ethnicity and Family Therapy*. New York: Guilford, 1982.

This book perhaps is destined to become the classic of crosscultural counseling literature. Presenting nineteen chapters on different ethnic/cultural groups and family patterns, it also provides solid connections with theory and suggestions for treatment. While oriented to family therapy, it will be a most useful text for those oriented to individual helping.

ROGERS, C., "Empathic: An Unappreciated Way of Being," *The Counseling Psychologist*, 1975, *5* (2), 2–10.

This represents one of Rogers' more recent comments on empathy and is a succinct and lucid discussion of issues. This article is followed by a series of helpful commentaries on empathy by several authors.

SUE, D., *Counseling the Culturally Different*. New York: Wiley, 1981.

This book provides a theory of crosscultural counseling and then presents specific chapters with history, suggested counseling procedures, and perspectives on counseling Asian-Americans, Blacks, Hispanics, and Native Americans.

5

CLIENT OBSERVATION SKILLS

GENERAL PREMISE

An integrated knowledge of skills, theory, and practice is essential for culturally intentional counseling and therapy.

Skills form the foundation of effective theory and practice: The culturally intentional therapist knows how to construct a creative decision-making interview and can use microskills to attend to and influence clients in a predicted direction. Important in this process are individual and cultural empathy, *client observation skills,* assessment of person and environment, and the application of positive techniques of growth and change.

Theory provides organizing principles for counseling and therapy: The culturally intentional counselor has knowledge of alternative theoretical approaches and treatment modalities.

Practice is the integration of skills and theory: The culturally intentional counselor or therapist is competent in skills and theory, and is able to apply them to research and practice for client benefit.

Undergirding integrated competence in skills, theory, and practice is an intentional awareness of one's own personal worldview and how that worldview may be similar to and/or different from the worldview and personal constructions of the client and other professionals.

GOALS OF CLIENT OBSERVATION SKILLS

"Relativity," on the cover of this book, presents two focal individuals who are walking the same direction on the same stairs, but one of them is going up and other is going down. The difficult and complex task of the counselor or therapist is to *observe* the direction of thought and behavior of the client and to "walk with" the client and understand that client's unique worldview. Once having "walked with" the client with individual and cultural empathy, you may need to assist the client to move in a new direction.

This chapter has the following key goals for practice in counseling and therapy.

1. To summarize key nonverbal factors that you will wish to observe in the client.
2. To present a system for examining client language and examining meaning underneath the "surface structure" of sentences.
3. To discuss the concept of client discrepancies, incongruities, and mixed messages as one of the central issues of therapy and counseling. How can these issues be identified and resolved?
4. To summarize and demonstrate the concepts of "pacing" ("walking with" the client) and "leading" (helping the client find a new direction).

The goal of this chapter, then, is the ability to "walk in more than one direction"—to learn more about understanding clients and how you might facilitate their development of intentionality.

INCREASING YOUR CLIENT OBSERVATION SKILLS

A man, aged twenty-five, is brought into the staff room of a community psychiatric clinic. His face is gaunt, his eyes are dull, his shoulders hunch, his hands scratch the back of his neck almost constantly, his shirt is partially unbuttoned, and his shoes are untied. Immediately on entering, he slumps into a chair and continues to scratch the back of his neck. The staff psychiatrist, psychologist, and social worker sit before him. One asks him why he is at the clinic. He continues to look at the floor and answers in a dull monotone: "sad . . . so sad . . . so sad . . . ." Further questioning brings no further data, only the words "sad . . . so sad . . . so sad . . . ," sometimes given slowly and deliberately; other times in an agitated, rushed fashion.

The young man above shows signs of deep depression. He lacks intentionality, which was presented in Chapter 1 as a central goal of the therapy process. The first aspect of intentionality was defined as the ability to generate a maximum number of words, thoughts, and behaviors to communicate with self and others in a given culture. The task of the therapist is to help free this man for intentional, creative responding. While the methods and theories of counseling vary extensively, this overall goal of therapy is basic.

A woman of seventeen visits a street clinic in a large city. She is neat and well kept and strides briskly into the corner cubicle where a volunteer peer counselor waits. After an initial friendly exchange of greetings, her voice becomes tight and tense as she talks about her lover's impotence and lack of interest in her. Her body becomes increasingly rigid as she states, "I love him so much. Why won't he respond to me? I've done everything for him. I bring home the money; I clean the apartment. What more can I do?" She breaks down into tears.

This woman presents a fairly "normal" problem of interpersonal relationships, yet the structure of her difficulties is close to those of the depressed patient in the psychiatric clinic. She, too, is frozen into repetitive patterns and is unable to create new verbal and nonverbal behaviors to respond to and direct her present situation. Again, the task of the counselor is to assist her in creating new answers, alternative behaviors, and taking intentional control of her own life.

THE SILENT LANGUAGE OF THE INTERVIEW

If our goal is to facilitate the personal and social development of the depressed man or the woman facing difficulty with her lover's impotence, we seek to enter their world and understand how they function in it. One of the first and most important dimensions is understanding and noting their nonverbal behavior.

Counseling consists of verbal and nonverbal interactions. Nonverbal communication and body language are foundations on which the language of counseling and therapy are based. Nonverbal language functions at three significant levels:

1. Definition and condition of the interaction: for example, timing of session, place, arrangement of office, clothes, and so forth define what is important, much of what will be said in that context, and the power relationship between two individuals.
2. Information flow: for example, often specific information passes in the form of nonverbal communication, but more often nonverbal communication *modifies* the meaning and places emphasis on verbal content.
3. Interpretation: each culture and each individual has significantly different patterns of meaning in nonverbal language. What means one thing to you may mean something totally different to someone else.

These three points comprise the major findings of extensive research in nonverbal communication summarized by Harper, Wiens, and Matarazzo (1978).

Extensive work in listening skills revealed that standard middle-class patterns of direct eye contact, forward trunk lean, and a medium vocal tone may be most inappropriate with some clients. When you are working with an extremely distressed individual, such as the young man in the example or someone talking about a delicate issue, direct eye contact may temporarily be harmful to the interaction. Avoiding the eyes of the person talking about a difficult topic may be wise at times.

What nonverbals should you focus on as you begin to study client behavior? While there are many ways to organize nonverbal behavior, it often proves helpful to begin with concepts that are already familiar to you. *Attending behavior* has been presented as a suggested way of your interacting with a client. The same four central dimensions of attending behavior provide a useful map for noting client nonverbals.

Eye Contact.   Given cultural differences, it is still important to note *when and in what context* the individual breaks eye contact. It is the shift of the pattern of eye movements that gives a clue to what is going on in the client's mind. Difficult issues tend to cause eye contact breaks. The young woman at the introduction of this chapter for example, may break eye contact when talking about impotence but not when she talks about her caring for her lover. This *may* be a sign of a real desire to maintain the relationship. However, precise meanings of changes in nonverbal behavior or eye contact require more than single observations, or you may make critical interpretative errors. Some clients fear certain topics (for example, sex, hostility, child abuse) and will avert their eyes when these topics appear on the horizon. Each client and client culture is different.

Body Language.   The vast array of body gestures, motions, and expressions cannot be detailed here. Clearly, they vary from culture to culture—witness the Western style of saying "no" by shaking the head sideways and the Russian style of saying the same thing by shaking the head up and down. Different groups ascribe different meanings to the same gesture, and you will also find each client has unique patterns.

The body language of the depressed young man discussed earlier illustrates many characteristics of the clinical manifestations of depression: poor eye contact, hunched shoulders, hands in constant movement, monotone voice, and a physical appearance of "not caring." These aspects of nonverbal communication are easy to observe. But the young woman's more subtle rigidity may require more careful observation in order to note a specific individual nonverbal style.

The most useful type of body language, however, is the *shift* or change in body posture. The client may be sitting naturally and then, for no apparent reason, close the arms, sit back in the chair, or cross the legs. Often these seemingly irrelevant shifts are indicative of conflict in the person. What is being said and what is being felt may not be the same thing.

Vocal Tone and Speech Rate.   A person's vocal tone and speech rate can say as much about people's states of being, particularly their emotional state, as the words they speak. Loudness and softness on certain topics may be important clues to the strength of feelings. A fast speech rate is often associated with nervousness and hyperactivity, while a slow speech rate may be associated with lethargy and depression. As in eye contact and body language, sudden voice changes around certain topics of discussion should be noted. Vocal tone is an indication of the degree of warmth. The voice is an instrument that conveys many subjective feelings and emotions.

Topic Jumps. Changes and shifts in topic are clues that your client has something else on his or her mind. You may enter a serious discussion of the woman's feelings toward her impotent lover and suddenly find she is talking about something totally different, perhaps problems on her job or maybe even the weather. Your ability to note a client's topic jumps and cope with them is critical to your success as a helper. Complicating this is the fact that sometimes it is wise to support clients in their changes of topic, as a temporary shift to a less difficult topic may help develop trust and allow you to return to the central issue in more depth at a later time.

The depressed client at the beginning of this chapter has, as is typical of many depressives, only one topic . . . himself and his depression. Your task with this type of patient may well be to change the topic and introduce new concepts for discussion. You will find many of your clients quite adept and skillful at controlling what is talked about in the interview.

Ultimately, your skill as a therapist and counselor will rest on your ability to "control" the topic and discussion flow. While you want to "walk with" the client and understand their view of the world, it is important to remember that most clients come to therapy in the hope that their worldview will be changed toward a more positive direction. The word "control" is used deliberately here as it brings out a difficult and complex issue. Control can be manipulative and unethical. However, if the client controls all conversation in the session, your ability to produce change may be impaired. It may be useful to think of control in the interview as a joint issue of both counselor and client. In the long run, clients must regain control of their own lives and, as such, overcontrol on your part is not desired.

Mirroring Nonverbal Behavior. One route toward balanced control of verbal and nonverbal behavior is the deliberate mirroring of your client's behavior. You will sometimes find yourself aware of nonverbal behavior that simply doesn't make sense to you, and you may feel awkward and distant from the client. One route toward understanding the other person is to consciously imitate or mirror nonverbal behavior for a brief time. If you attend carefully to your own body once you assume a mirroring position, you will find that changes in the client's movement actually produce stimulation or desire to move in your own body. These "electrical potentials" may be noted through mirroring and produce an even higher level of empathy.

Examination of films and videotapes reveals fascinating patterns of nonverbal communication. In a successful, smoothly flowing interview, *movement complementarity* or *movement symmetry* often occurs between counselor and client. Movement complementarity is represented by a "passing" of movement back and forth between client and counselor. The client may pause in the middle of a sentence, the counselor nods and the client finishes the sentence. Movements between counselor and client pass back and forth in rhythm.

Movement symmetry is exciting to view. Counselor and client unconsciously have assumed the same physical posture: their eye contact is usually direct; their hands and feet may move in unison as if they were dancing or following a programmed script. Movement symmetry can be achieved in a beginning fashion by deliberately assuming the posture of the client. This mirroring of nonverbal behavior often brings the therapist to a closer and more complete understanding of the client (see Figure 5.1).

The lack of complementarity and symmetry is also something to observe. The counselor may say something and the client's head may jerk noticeably in the opposite direction. When dissynchronous body movements occur between counselor and client, the interview is often on the wrong track. A solid knowledge and awareness of body language is necessary to consistently observe this type of behavior.

However, once you learn to observe this type of mirroring, it can be a most valuable tool. If you start noting the general pattern of body language of your client and *deliberately assume the same posture, you will find yourself in better synchrony and harmony with that client.* Many scoff at this suggestion, yet, if you try mirroring the body posture of the other, new understandings and communication can develop. Do not use this tool manipulatively, use it to develop increased awareness and new levels of insight.

THE PLACE OF WORDS AND LANGUAGE IN THE INTERVIEW

A person's worldview or map of reality is represented by both nonverbal and verbal sentences. It is important to recognize that *words and sentences form the core of most counseling and psychotherapy approaches.* This section provides an overview of how the language of the interview may be examined to clarify the nature of the counseling process. We will first examine how the grammatical structure of simple sentences tells us much about the counselor and the client. We will then examine how the wording of more complex sentences gives an indication of how the person thinks. Finally, we will examine the concept of surface and deep structure in sentences and consider specific methods through which counselors can bring out the deeper meanings underlying the issues brought by clients.

The Structure of Sentences.   The way people articulate or phrase sentences is an important clue as to how they view the world. Consider the following sentence given by a woman in the early stages of counseling:

HELPEE: My husband tells me what to do and I try to do it. But, I simply can't respond.
HELPER: How would you like to respond to him?
HELPEE: He wants me to please him. I'd like to be able to do that.

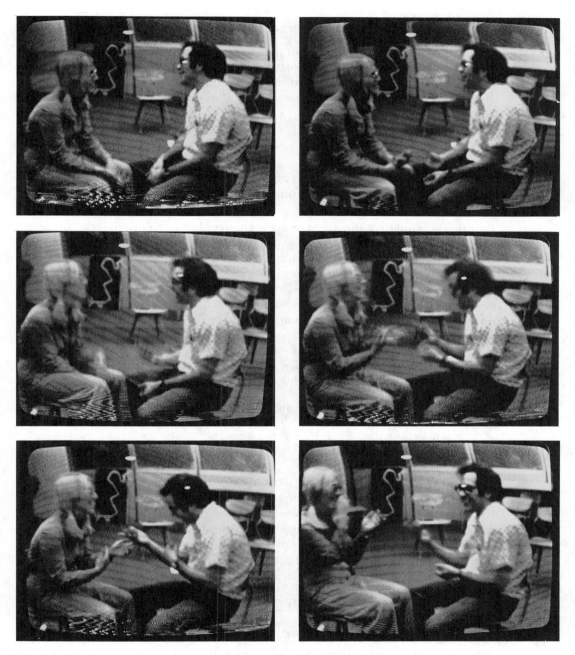

Figure 5.1 Movement symmetry occurs when client and counselor demonstrate body movements that mirror one another. In this series of photos, the client and counselor are discussing an issue of mutual interest. The time for the completion of this series of movements is about one second. Careful examination of videotapes and films of helping interviews will reveal many examples of movement symmetry. Also observe for dissynchronous movement that often indicates failure to communicate effectively.

Photos from Ivey, A. and J. Authier, Microcounseling: Innovations in Interviewing, Counseling, Psychotherapy, and Psychoeducation *(Springfield, IL: Chas. C. Thomas, 1978). Used by permission.*

In the above sentences, the woman puts herself as the object of the sentence in a passive role. The counselor supports this passivity by asking her how she would like to respond to him. A forward-moving, feminist therapist would most likely attempt to put the client in the actor role and in charge of her own life. For example:

HELPER: Anne, what are your personal wishes and desires in this situation? What do you want?

HELPEE: I'm really angry . . . so angry I sometimes just don't want to do anything for him or with him.

Putting the woman as the agent or actor changes her perception of the situation. In the first example, the sentence structure of the counselor put the client in a passive role and reinforced old, ineffective behavior. In the second example, the sentence structure used by the therapist places the client in a stronger, more assertive role and helps remove passive thinking and acting. The woman who has complained about her difficulties with her lover has described her situation via one set of sentences. The same situation could be described via many alternatives. For example:

1. (Original statement) I love him so much. Why won't he respond to me? I've done everything for him: I bring home the money; I clean the apartment. What more can I do?
2. He won't respond to me. He doesn't respond to my attentions. He ignores me no matter what I do. I better try harder.
3. I'm getting ripped off. I do all the work and he just lies around the house. It's time I kicked him out. Yes, I love him, but it isn't worth it.

While more alternative descriptions could be generated, these three are sufficient to illustrate the point. Clients come to counseling sessions with key sentences describing their situations. Often these sentences are routinized into standardized patterns. The task of the therapist is to free the client to generate new sentences. If the young woman went back to the situation using the sentences as described in version 2, it may be predicted that the new sentences would be a result of sexist counseling that moved her from a partially passive, partially assertive role to a completely passive, traditionally feminine character. Phyllis Chesler in *Women and Madness* (1972) speaks passionately and articulately about how a predominantly white male helping profession has served to keep women in subservient roles. The third set of sentences places the young woman in an assertive frame where she is making her own decisions. She is the subject of her sentences and on the basis of these sentences is able to generate new nonverbal behaviors (specifically, throwing him out). The ways in which people view themselves are revealed in their sentences.

Let us imagine that you are driving along the Pennsylvania Turnpike and get off for lunch.* On your return to the Pike, the ticket that comes out of the machine is ripped and you have only half of the ticket. What are you going to tell the collector when you get off the Turnpike at the Ohio border?

1. The ticket ripped.
2. I ripped the ticket.
3. The machine ripped the ticket.
4. Something happened.

The description of even such a small event can be a clue to the way a person views self and the world. Each of the above sentences could be termed a true and accurate description of what happened, but each sentence represents a different worldview. The first represents a descriptive view in that the event is simply described; the second represents a person who takes responsibility for the situation and may be an indication of inner directedness; the third represents outward directedness or an "I didn't do it" view; and the fourth represents a vague, fatalistic, almost mystical view.

From sentence analysis, we may draw some important conclusions for the counseling process: the words used by a client or a therapist to describe an event may say more about the person talking than about the event itself; the grammatical structure of sentences (subjects, verbs, objects) is also an indication of personal worldview. Counseling is a predominantly verbal process, and systematic analysis of the language of counseling is essential to full understanding.

Thought and Language—The Wording of Sentences

> . . . our modes of thinking as well as the artifacts of our culture are at the mercy of the language we speak. (Sapir and Whorf, cited in Deece, 1970)

The world around us and the words we use for description are not one and the same. Our cultural language has given us words that help us to understand ourselves and others. The choice of words we use to describe our situations largely determines how we perceive what is happening. However, language, words, and sentences are not fully adequate to describe our world. The eminent Russian linguist Vygotsky gives us the following example:

> Thought, unlike speech, does not consist of separate units. When I wish to communicate the thought that today I saw a barefoot boy in a blue shirt running down the street, I do not see every item separately: the boy, the shirt, its blue color, the absence of shoes. I conceive of all this in one thought; but I put it into separate words. A speaker often takes several minutes to disclose one thought. (Vygotsky, 1962, p. 150)

---

*We are indebted to Barbara Partee of the University of Massachusetts' Department of Linguistics for this example.

It is important to realize that words and sentence structures can never describe the full range of human experience. The feelings, thoughts, and experiences of the counselor and the client can never be fully shared via words. At best, we make an approximation.

The counselor must realize that when a client describes an event the description is a *representation* of the event and *not* the event itself. As such, therapists receive only a very small portion of their client's life, events, or experiences. There is an infinite number of ways people can describe their world. Some people become blocked and have only one sentence or representation of their world and are unable to generate the many possible ways of describing themselves and their world.

One task for the intentional counselor is to provide the client with an ever increasing array of responses for describing any situation, and this means a broader, more comprehensive worldview. The young woman having difficulties with her lover needs the ability to generate more ways of describing her situation. Particularly, she needs at least one way to describe her world that is more effective for her. The question becomes: Which words are most functional and useful to describe the world? The therapeutic benefit of the counseling process may begin to take effect when useful, satisfying verbal descriptions can be developed.

It is useful for the counselor to start searching the statements of the client for key words and descriptions that provide an indication of how that person views the world. This may be accomplished through the use of empathy, a well-structured interview, and the attending skills of open questions, paraphrasing, reflection of feeling, and summarization. In this manner, the counselor assists the client to describe the world as he or she sees it, with minimal inference on the part of the counselor. A central objective of many theories of counseling is to understand the client's world before taking action to change that world.

Through careful attending to the client, the counselor can begin to see patterns of words and ideas appearing that indicate typical thought processes. For example, the client may always talk in the past tense about negative early experience and find it virtually impossible to talk about present-day concerns with a husband or wife, thus uselessly going over old data. Or a client may always talk in a vague fashion about communication difficulties with a child. Certain words or phrases may appear frequently, such as, "I am responsible; it's my fault," "that's a *little* problem; he's a *small* man; *no big* thing," or, as in the case of the young woman at the beginning of this chapter, "I've *done* for him; I *did* that . . . ," etc. Through examination of these patterns, the underlying thought of the client begins to come through and is more accessible to change. In the case of the woman, we might note her past-tense verb form and the repetitious pattern of her doing things for her male lover. Her underlying thought may be that it is her fault and that she is responsible.

The impact of a therapist or counselor's language system on the client should be stressed. A single client may present a problem concerning impotence. Each therapeutic school will represent that problem in different language systems. A Rogerian client-centered therapist will tend to emphasize feelings about impotence; a behaviorist might stress cause-and-effect "stimulus-response" bonds; while a psychoanalytically oriented counselor will use the language of Freud and perhaps talk about "repressed" anger or an "Oedipal conflict." Through contact in the interview, the client will tend to take on the same language system (and thus the representational system and worldview) of her or his therapist or counselor. The client has indeed been freed to generate new verbal sentences and ways of representing the world, but it is possible that these new ways of responding simply represent the ideas of another person rather than being real and authentic.

Work by Meara, Shannon, and Pepinsky (1979) is particularly interesting here. They examined interviews held by three therapists (Rogers, Perls, and Ellis) with a single client, Gloria. They found that Gloria in each case tended to match the language system of the therapy and therapist. Linguistic matching is not just a hypothetical issue; it occurs regularly. At times, counselors will want to match the language of their clients; at other times, the client may be best served by learning your language and worldview. The power of systematic study of verbal and nonverbal communication cannot be overstated. As you work with these ideas, high ethical standards are vitally important.

Finally, people from varying cultural, racial, ethnic, and socioeconomic backgrounds are likely to develop different representational language systems. Even people of roughly similar backgrounds are likely to use different language in describing the same event. For example, in viewing the sudden religious conversion of several members of former President Nixon's staff, following the problems of Watergate, two white middle-class males might differ in their language systems. A person of a conservative Protestant religious background is likely to welcome and support the new thought patterns and language of the convert. However, a less religious person is likely to view the same event with suspicion and distrust. As another example, an African individual may find the family patterns and relationships in North America, particularly among middle-class whites, diffuse and disorganized, whereas to the middle-class white Americans themselves, they seem normal and appropriate. *Because of personal, historical, and cultural background, representational and language systems will be as diverse as, or perhaps even more varying than, patterns of nonverbal communication.* The counselor must always be aware of the fact that what means one thing to her or him, may mean something totally different to the client.

Since a major task of the counselor is to understand and work with the language of the client, it may be useful at this point to examine some practical implications of language and thought analysis that may occur in the interview.

Moving From Surface Structure to Deep Structure—From the Outside to the Inside. The sentences we use to describe our perceptions and thoughts could be termed *surface structure* sentences. The term *surface structure* is used to describe a situation, person, or event. Surface structure sentence examples in this chapter include: "The ticket ripped," "Sad . . . so sad . . . so sad . . . ," and "I love him so much. Why won't he respond to me?" We have seen that simple rearrangement of the words in a surface structure sentence can change the meaning of an event in the life of a client. A sufficient number of sentence rearrangements by the client can imply that counseling or therapy has been successful and that a life has changed direction.

Counselors and therapists do not generally have their clients change the format of their sentences, although this simple technique proves to be effective if used judiciously. More frequently, therapists are interested in moving clients to the *deep structure*. Deep structure is defined as the set of words, thoughts, and perceptions that underlie surface structure sentences. Through in-depth examinations of key sentences of clients, the counselor can assist in changing perceptions, thoughts, surface structure sentences, and eventually general life functioning, causing an increase in intentionality.

Let us assume that our depressed patient has been in the psychiatric clinic for a period of time. His single partial sentence, "Sad . . . so sad . . . so sad . . . ," has been expanded through skills training, drugs, or an alternative method, and he is able to undergo forms of formalized therapy in a verbalized interview. The task of the therapist is to make the surface structure sentence more complete and to search for the underlying words and ideas represented. The following interchange might occur:

HELPER: Sam, as I was listening to you when you first came to the clinic, you kept saying, "Sad . . . so sad . . . so sad . . . ." First, could you tell me who was or is sad? (From a grammatical point of view, we have no clear subject, verb, or object in the surface sentence.)

HELPEE: I guess I'm sad.

HELPER: What, specifically, do you mean by saying you're sad? (Beginning of search for underlying structure. We now have a complete surface structure sentence. "I am sad.")

HELPEE: I don't seem able to do anything right. I thought I was working hard, but my boss never said I was doing anything right. My wife never seemed interested either.

HELPER: You say you don't seem able to do anything right. Could you tell me about a specific incident where you talked with your boss and you ended up feeling that way? (With this paraphrase and question, the process of finding the deep structure underlying "Sad . . . so sad . . . so sad . . ." has begun. The counselor had an important decision to make in response to the client and could have asked for more elaboration on relations with the boss or with the wife. Staying on both topics at this point offers potential confusion, but the relationship with the wife should be "flagged" and examined at a later point in this interview.)

It may be seen that the process of moving from surface to deep structure is not really that complex. The counselor has asked for specifics or concreteness through the use of open questions. The client is now able to share some of the thoughts and feelings underlying the first surface structure sentence and the process of therapy has begun. A vast array of deep structure sentences underlie the key sentence. Further, as these deep structure sentences are explored, it will be found that still deeper sentences lie below. For example, underlying the relationship with the boss may be a generalized pattern of authority relationship problems that, in turn, stem back to unconscious childhood patterns between son and father. The sentence, "I am scared," may be a representation simultaneously of fear of the boss, strained authority relationships on other jobs, problems in school, and underlying stress and strain between a child and the parents.

The search for deep structure can take years of long-term psychoanalytic therapy. Or the search may be completed within a few short interviews if the therapist amplifies present situations with some supporting materials or imposes her

---

Figure 5.2 *Summary of Key Language Concepts*

1. The grammatical structure of our sentences provides an important indication of how we view the world.

    EXAMPLE: "I can't stop my father from drinking." In this case the client is taking responsibility for the father's drinking problem. A more accurate sentence would be "My father won't stop drinking." The father becomes the subject of the sentence. The client may add the additional sentence, "I feel badly that he doesn't stop."

2. The words we use to describe our world are never a complete description of what is there. At best they are an approximation of what we have experienced. It is important for the counselor to note *which* words the client uses in describing past events. Frequent repetition of words or phrases gives an indication of typical ways a client might think.

    EXAMPLE: "Like the last time he drank, I got scared because I had hidden the bottle and he knew it. I tried to keep it away from him; it's my fault." The event being described is the father's last drinking bout. The words used by the client again indicate that the client is taking responsibility for the father ("I had hidden . . . I tried to keep it away . . . it's my fault."). The word "scared" should also be noted. The words a person uses are their representation of an event and a map of their thinking.

3. Most counseling approaches seek to examine the key surface structure sentences of the client and search for underlying deep structures. In this way, a more complete map of the client's world may be obtained.

    EXAMPLE: The client presents several surface structure sentences in the preceding example. "I got scared," is one potentially important surface sentence for further examination as it is the only sentence that contains an emotionally laden word. The task of the counselor is to search for the underlying associated deeper structures of that sentence. What causes the client fear? Under what conditions does the fear arise? What fantasies does the client have about what might happen in this situation? Exploration of the many sentences underlying this seemingly simple surface sentence will enable the counselor to develop a more complete understanding of the client.

or his theoretical frame and deep structure on the client. Imposition of the counselor's theoretical framework on the client appears in rational-emotive therapy where a new structure for thinking is substituted for diffuse and incoherent patterns. Which method is appropriate? That depends on the theory preferred by the individual counselor. Both methods may change the language representational systems of the client. Research suggests that some theories and methods are better for some people while other systems are better for other people.

The crucial issue for the beginning counselor at this point is to realize that virtually all theories seek to find deep structures of meaning underlying surface structures. The techniques to do this focus on: (1) primarily using attending skills to bring out further specific information; (2) systematically selecting or deciding on one issue at a time for work; and (3) after a surface sentence has been explored, returning to another sentence to search for further data.

INCONGRUITIES AND DISCREPANCIES

Let us return to the young woman who had difficulties with her lover. As she began the interview, her voice became tight and tense; her body became rigid; and she said, "I love him so much . . ." Assume that is all she said. If the verbal message says love, the body and vocal messages are saying something else. We may say that she is presenting discrepancies or incongruities in her behavior. *This discrepancy immediately becomes a central issue for the therapy process. It becomes a surface structure sentence of its own that needs examination. What lies under the double message of differing verbal and nonverbal sentences?*

The young man presents a double message also. His predominant verbal and nonverbal picture is that of a slow-moving depressive. Yet, the constant handscratching at the back of his neck and the occasional rapid-fire, "Sad . . . so sad . . . so sad . . . ," are incongruous with the picture presented. Again, we have an important surface message that needs to be decoded. What lies under the double message?

Double messages, incongruities, and discrepancies appear constantly in counseling interviews. A client may present an open right hand and smile while the left hand is closed in a fist. The counselor may be sitting with an open posture while covering the genital area with both hands. The client may say, "I really like my parents," while sitting in a closed posture with arms crossed over the chest. Double messages appear at the verbal level as well. The "Freudian slip" is a classic example of a mixed verbal message. A Freudian slip occurs when someone says one thing but means another. The client may say, "I liked my parents," when intending to say he or she *likes* them. The past tense *liked* could be interpreted as a "death wish." More directly, some clients will say, "I both love and hate my children and those mixed feelings scare me." Dreams represent a type of mixed and incongruent message as well. The task for the therapist is to identify mixed messages and to search for the underlying meaning or deeper structure.

One of the main tasks of counseling is to assist clients to work through, resolve, or learn to live with incongruities. Incongruities, discrepancies, and mixed or double messages are often at the root of immobility, and the inability to respond creatively. Most counseling theories have as their main focus the resolution of incongruities. Freudians talk about resolving polarities and unconscious conflicts; Gestaltists, about resolving splits; client-centered therapists, about resolving mixed feelings; rational-emotive therapists, about the need to attack incongruent irrational thinking; vocational counselors about the distinction between unreal and real goals . . . the list could continue. The importance of naming and resolving incongruities cannot be overstressed.

The observation of client verbal and nonverbal incongruities is obviously basic to your work as a therapist or counselor and in influencing your clients toward a new and hopefully, more intentional direction. You will tend to work more effectively with your client if you select only one incongruity or discrepancy at a time. Clients can be overwhelmed when you summarize and identify several apparent discrepancies. For example, the young woman who has difficulties with

---

Figure 5.3 *Examples of Verbal Discrepancies Identifiable in Client's Language*

Three types of issues for exploration of deeper structure have been identified by Bandler and Grinder (1975). They suggest that surface structure sentences may suffer from deletions, distortions, and overgeneralizations. Examples follow:

1. *Deletions* may appear in surface structure sentences such as "I'm afraid." The question becomes, "What or whom causes the client fear; Under what conditions; What is an example of a frightening situation or person; Is this fear past or present; Is this fear realistic or unrealistic?" Information to answer these questions isn't presented and the task of the counselor becomes aiding clients to complete their sentences and develop complete representational maps. Out of this process of completion, new surface structure sentences and meanings may evolve.
2. *Distortions* may be described as misconstrued or twisted sentences. These sentences twist the client's perceptions of what actually happened or is currently occurring. A classic distortion sentence at a surface level is, "He makes me mad," when in truth the person who is "made" angry is responsible for her or his own behavior. A more correct form would be, "I become angry when he does that." In this case, the client "owns" the behavior and begins to take control of life direction. Distortions often appear as deletions and are examined in surface sentences. At a deeper level, careful examination of what happened in a person's life history will reveal many present-day distortions of reality. Through the uncovering process of therapy, and the search for deeper structures, distortions may be eliminated.
3. *Generalizations* appear when the client makes conclusions that reach beyond available information. When the depressed patient was asked to specify what makes him sad, he might have said, "People make me sad." Actually, only a few people make him feel sad. Distortions often accompany generalizations. Words associated with generalizations include "all people," "everyone," "always," "never," "same," "continually," "permanent," and "eternal." Generalizations also appear in the deep structure when we discover that clients relate to their spouses and children in much the same fashion as they related to their parents or some other key individual.

her lover may manifest discrepancies in her nonverbals (for example, a clenched fist representing anger in one hand and an inviting pleading gesture with the other), discrepancies in her verbal statements and feeling words (for example, at one time expressing anger at him for impotence, another time expressing love and understanding), verbal discrepancies between her lover and herself (for example, "He feels this . . . , but I feel something else . . ."), and discrepancies between herself as an active feminist and an individual who wants a traditional relationship with a man in the long run. All these discrepancies and more may show in a client in a short time, and bringing them out via confrontation may frighten and drive the client away.

Clients come to counseling for the resolution of their discrepancies and incongruities. While they may not always be consciously aware of the nature of the mixed messages they receive (and they give to others), therapy and counseling are about the resolution of differences. These incongruities may exist within the individual in terms of an unconscious "battle" with one's parents, the inability of a Black person or woman to cope with excessive discrimination, conflict with a spouse, difficulties in vocational choice, or inability to behave in a satisfactory manner in social situations. These incongruities are shown in verbal and nonverbal messages.

Your task as a counselor or therapist is to "read" these nonverbal and verbal messages, get underneath the surface structure, and determine the nature of the conflict. Incongruities and mixed messages are the "stuff" of counseling and psychotherapy, and in their identification and resolution you show your ability and caring as a professional helper.

Now let us turn to possible routes toward resolution of conflict via the ideas of "pacing" and "leading."

PACING AND LEADING: MATCHING AND CHANGING WORLDVIEWS

The client enters counseling or therapy with a distinctive view of his or her situation. You, as counselor, have your own distinctive worldview. You may have intentionally selected a specific theory of therapy to which you are committed, or you may be oriented toward eclecticism or general theory. Regardless, two people with two views of the world are encountering one another. What is to happen? Whose view will prevail? Will both be accommodated and/or enhanced in the process?

Consistently in this book, listening to and understanding the client has been emphasized as critical to the change process. This process of client understanding may also be termed *pacing*, the term used by Lankton (1980) and Richardson and Margulis (1981). These authors also talk about *leading*, which is somewhat parallel to the influencing skills of Chapter 3. However, pacing and leading have special uses that may be of value as you try to understand and help clients develop and grow.

Pacing. The term *pacing* may be defined as a more general concept than attending, rapport development, or empathy—yet it is closely related to all. "Friends pace each other naturally; they have rapport of some sort, they understand each other, . . . they speak the same language" (Lankton, 1980, p. 59). Dancing could also be described as a form of pacing: in dancing two people learn to move together in time; if the lead dancer does not pace the partner well, moving the two together smoothly becomes almost impossible.

Your task as therapist is to learn to pace or match the client as closely as possible. Pacing involves entering the client's worldview and experiencing things as the client does. The literature on pacing, however, provides some very specific things you can do to ensure solid pacing or matching with your client:

1. You may assume the same body posture or use similar gestures, as indicated earlier in the section on movement synchrony.
2. You may match attending behavior patterns of eye contact, body language, vocal tone, and verbal following with those of the client. Some advocate deliberate matching of breathing patterns as well.
3. You may use the *key words* of the client. As noted in paraphrasing and reflection of feeling skills, it is critical that you use the "touchy, main words" that the client uses to describe the situation. Understanding key words of the client will, of course, be facilitated by understanding of the surface and deep-structure language concepts of this chapter.

Central to pacing, of course, is noting the major conflicts, incongruities, and discrepancies of the client. You will find that if you deliberately pace clients, you can more easily enter into and understand how their worldview is constructed.

Useful pacing is deepening the client's experience of the problem or concern. This may be done through the use of perceptual systems.

Perceptual Systems. The term *perceptual systems* refers to how we all take in data through our senses. We gain our worldview through our eyes, ears, and kinesthetic senses. (In addition, taste and odor enrich our perceptions as well.) You will find that you can enhance and deepen your experience of a current or past event by specifically using your main sensory modalities of sight, hearing, and feeling. For just a moment, think back to your experience in high school. Take the time necessary. . . . Remember a specific experience, the first one which comes to your mind. . . . Now *see* yourself in the situation. Note the look of the room or open space. Notice colors, objects, and/or people around you. Gather in as many details as you can. . . . Next, what do you *hear*? Can you hear the voices or sounds around you? If you take a moment you can see and hear much of what transpired in the past. . . . Finally, stay with the scenes and sounds. What do you *feel* in that setting? What is going on in your body? What are your emotions? Take some time to experience what you *see, hear,* and *feel* from the past.

This brief exercise is oriented to helping you *recreate* a situation from the past. If you were successful, you moved your total attention to a past situation and now could describe it in some detail. In counseling and therapy, clients often talk about situations from the past, and you may desire to *recreate* them again in as much detail as you can. Through the use of an exercise such as the one above, you will find your clients can deepen their feelings and become more in touch with what happened specifically in the problem situation, be it 10 years ago or last week. If you watch the work of most experienced therapists and counselors with their clients, you will find them frequently using the words "see," "hear," and "feel," and their variations. Experiencing the *concreteness* of an event seems to be enhanced when the body's senses are involved. In some cases using these sense modalities will bring out a dramatic reliving of prior events and should be used carefully.

You can help your client experience a problem with a spouse, a child, or to relive a past experience through careful use of perceptual systems and pacing. Different people seem to respond differently to parts of the perceptual systems. Most respond best if all systems are used, but some people seem to respond best to the visual portion, others to the auditory or feeling parts. For example, consider the following statement by Jean Piaget, the Swiss developmental theorist, on his own perceptual systems:

> For example, I am absolutely not visual. When I'm out walking, I pull out my watch and sometimes say the time out loud, or I whisper it. If I say what it is and recall the sound of my voice, I can remember the time. If I say nothing, and it's purely visual . . . [I forget]. . . . A minute later I pull out my watch and then I realize it's still the same time. I was conscious the first time, but I completely forgot it. (Bringuier, 1980, p. 5)

Similarly, some of your clients will not be able to "see" events from the past or "hear" the associated voices. The "feelings" may be detached from old experiences. The separation of perceptual systems may be a habitual learning style of your client or may represent emotional trauma from childhood. For example, individuals who have been in an accident or have been raped may often be unable to bring back anything from the trauma except a vague feeling, which itself is not attached to the situation. In such cases, one of the tasks of the therapist may be to work through the issues around the trauma and gradually allow appropriate expression of affect and later reexperiencing of the event. In deep trauma, the event itself may be repressed or forgotten.

At the more basic level, pacing is aimed toward helping you enter the client's frame of reference. If your client has a difficulty with his or her spouse and the surface structure sentences seem vague and inconclusive, you may ask the client to describe a concrete situation using seeing, hearing, and feeling words. With many clients, the experience will be relived and you, as counselor, will have a much *clearer hearing* of how the situation *feels* for the client.

Pacing is obviously closely related to empathy and the attending skills. It is also a useful construct as you seek to enter the worldview of the other person. When combined with the several concepts of the book presented thus far, pacing provides a useful, integrated method of diverse ideas for relating more closely with the client. Pacing provides the basis for understanding that can lead to change.

Leading.   "Once an effective pace has been established, you can gracefully begin to lead the client into a new experience" (Lankton, 1981, p. 61). If you understand and empathize with the client's experience and the client is aware of the relationship, the possibilities for *leading* or influencing change in the client and the client's map of reality (and eventually even the client's worldview) are now more open.

Gracefulness, as Lankton notes, is critical. Understanding and pacing are not enough; the transition to new movements, thoughts, and behaviors must be done judiciously, thoughtfully, and ethically. Techniques for intentionally influencing and directing the client are perhaps what make different theories of helping different from each other; they are virtually infinite and range from sharing your opinion and giving advice to complex theories outlined in beginning form later in this text. The degree of attention that different theories give to pacing (although few would use that word) varies extensively. Rogerian theory gives primary attention to pacing and understanding the client's world. Freudian theory may give some attention to pacing, but the prime effort is influential, to have the client join the therapist in a psychodynamic view of the world. Despite these differences, if you observe the *behavior* of these two often antagonistic theories, you will find them using "see," "hear," and "feel" perceptual systems plus many of the constructs of pacing in their work.

Leading requires you to act on the world of your client through influencing skills and will often require you to use the techniques and theories of counseling and therapy discussed in later chapters. The more polarized or opposite the incongruity, the more likelihood there is of its being an effective source of information. Each theoretical approach deals with incongruities with different counseling techniques. Having identified one polarity or incongruity set, the Gestalt therapist may have the client role-play the situation to an empty chair; the client-centered counselor may simply reflect on the mixed feelings; the Freudian may search for the unconscious childhood determinants of the surface incongruity, etc. The techniques of *therapeutic work* in the counseling interview vary, but all systems are centrally concerned with examining and resolving incongruities. Again, each language or representational system of therapy approaches the same situation differently, often with different results in client representational systems.

Your effectiveness with identifying and working toward resolution will often be immediately apparent. Four possible responses from the client may be noted (Ivey, 1987). The first is *denial*. Here the client may refuse to acknowledge that a contradiction in thought, words, or behavior exists. Your task, most likely, is to recycle the interview to another area where you can work more effectively and return to the denial later. Second, slightly more promising results occur when

Figure 5.4 *Working with Incongruities in the Interview: A Practical Example of Pacing and Leading*

Incongruities have been defined as mixed messages or discrepancies in verbalizations or between nonverbal and verbal behaviors. The identification and working through of incongruities is a central concern of many, perhaps all, counseling theories. A model of coping with incongruities in the interview is presented in this figure. The model will be followed through with a mother who came home and found her 14-year-old son drunk. Assume that the interview is in the midportion and basic descriptions of the situation have been elicited.

1. Identify and Label Incongruities through Pacing

HELPEE: Yes, there he was drunk, falling all over himself. It was sickening.
HELPER: You found the scene really disgusting. Yet as I listen to you, I see a faint smile— almost as if you were proud of him.
HELPEE: No, he's so disgusting. How could he do that to me! He's such a *man,* full of *macho!*
HELPER: I sense you've got real pride in his manliness and strength.
HELPEE: Yeh . . . I really like him. He's way beyond his father.
HELPER: So let me sum up to this point. You seem to be really disgusted and angry over his behavior, but at the same time you have some deep feelings of pride for his manliness and strength. Both the pride and anger seem to come from the same place.

(Comment: The counselor identified the mixed feelings and helped place labels on them for the client. The surface structure sentence, "It was sickening," coupled with the faint smile, has been elaborated and we have a more complete representation or map of how the mother feels and thinks.)

2. Work on a Single Incongruity through Leading
(The counselor in this case is oriented to Gestalt techniques and uses the role-playing format of having the client talk to an empty chair.)

HELPEE: (Sigh) I suppose you're right. The little bugger is really pretty neat. Oh . . . but he gets to me.
HELPER: Imagine he's just sitting there now in that empty chair. What would you tell him? (Client starts to answer) No, don't tell me. Imagine he is sitting there. Talk to him.
HELPEE: Bobbie, you're sitting there so smug. What makes you think you're so hot? You really get to me.
(The first two sentences were said with some heat, the later sentence was spoken in a higher tone and said more rapidly.)
HELPER: Say, "You really get to me," again.
HELPEE: You really get to me. (The voice is even higher in tone.)
HELPER: Again.
HELPEE: You really get to . . . (pause) Yeh, Bobbie gets to me, but he really doesn't get to me. I envy him. He's got it together. So what if he drank a little—I don't want him to do it so much. He's such a neat kid. I need him.

(Comment: Through the techniques of the Gestalt empty chair and psychodynamic repetition, the client has begun to realize her complex feelings toward her son more completely. We are beginning to see the deeper structure of the original surface structure sentence, "It was sickening." The mother has experienced her mixed emotions at a deeper level.)

3. Decide Action for Next Steps—Return to Pacing
(The counselor could develop issues concerning the son in more depth. For example the sentence, "I need him," is a surface structure sentence that might merit further examination. However, in this case, the counselor returns to an earlier statement.)

HELPER: So you have several feelings about your son in this situation. At one level you're angry, but at another level you're proud of his independence. You even envy him a little. Earlier you said he was "way beyond his father." Could you tell me a little more about that?

HELPEE: (Begins an extensive discussion of how the son and father may be compared.)

Comment on Segment: Given a good relationship and a verbal client, the counseling process can move this rapidly. However, one should be fully aware that as often as not the process is slower as clients resist and counselors make errors or miss important points. This brief segment illustrates many points from this chapter. A surface structure sentence, such as "It was sickening," coupled with the faint smile, is labeled immediately by the counselor in the next lead. Through the work in the Gestalt frame, the client experiences the emotion associated with her mixed feelings. Finally, the counselor makes a decision not to pursue that particular incongruity further at that time and introduces a new surface structure sentence for examination: ". . . way beyond his father."

It might be noted that in the first phase of the segment the counselor used pacing attending skills of paraphrasing and reflection of feeling while working with present tense immediacy. The second phase reveals an emphasis on the leading skills of directions with a continued emphasis on the present tense, aimed toward increased concreteness and specificity. As the third phase begins, there is a summary of the material just covered plus an open question relating back to an earlier lead, thus a return to the pacing mode.

the client acknowledges the conflict or discrepancy but only works on a portion of the issue. Pace this partial examination and work later toward a full resolution of the conflict or discrepancy. Third, the client may acknowledge a conflict exists and work on both sides (or more) of the conflict. Here you can use a variety of therapeutic approaches and move toward a successful synthesis. Fourth, the situation occurs in which not all conflict, incongruity, and discrepancy can be resolved. After exploration, your client may decide to live with the situation as it is. This itself represents a higher level of client thinking and should not be regarded as a failure on your part.

This four-point outline of possible client responses has more than theoretical importance. You can monitor the four modes of client response in the interview and change your pacing and leading style accordingly. You may, for example, be working effectively with a client in terms of pacing, listening, and empathy. At that point you may confront the incongruity in the client (leading). If the client denies the confrontation, it is time to return to pacing again and use listening skills to once again join the client's worldview. If the client works on a part of the confrontation, you may continue; but you must notice that your lead has only been partially successful. The other two modes of client responding suggest that the client is accepting your leading and you may be at a new level of communication and possibility.

Figure 5.4 presents an example situation in which client discrepancies are confronted via a variety of techniques. It may be seen that (1) identification of discrepancies represents both problem definition and pacing, and (2) action on discrepancies represents problem resolution and leading. In the figure, the central concepts discussed in this chapter are presented in an action sequence.

The models of language and communication presented here should help basic understanding. Counselors and therapists have problems with their own personal discrepancies and incongruities. Most give mixed messages, at times, to clients. Sometimes this can even be done deliberately for therapeutic benefit. A counselor needs awareness of her or his own limitations. This requires an openness to self-examination, the use of videotape and audiotape recording of interviews, and the sharing of her or his own work with colleagues under appropriate ethical conditions. One must never forget that there are times when the client is more intentional than the counselor. The questions are: How well is the counselor able to handle her or his own deficiencies? Are the incongruities and limitations of the counselor such that it becomes difficult to assist the client? Can the limitations be used as data themselves as the counselor engages in a continuous process of growth, development, and change?

SUMMARY OF THIS CHAPTER

Full mastery of the concepts of this chapter will require considerable clinical practice, work with audiotape and videotape, and further study of verbal and nonverbal dimensions of counseling. By the end of this chapter you should be able to:

1. *Identify key aspects of nonverbal behavior.* Nonverbal dimensions stressed in the chapter are eye contact, body language, vocal tone and speech rate, and the use of physical space and time. Cultural differences in these behaviors have been stressed.

2. *Demonstrate what happens when the structure of a sentence is altered.* If a simple sentence is reordered, the meaning can change. For example, "My wife makes me do it," can be restated as, "I choose to wash the dishes even though my wife is on me all the time and I sometimes feel tempted not to do them." The changing of sentence structure illustrates how easily language changes perceptions of events, the self, and others. Language structure can be used by counselors for identification of incongruities and, as a counseling technique, to resolve polarities.

3. *Manifest a beginning understanding of the relationship between thought and language.* Words and language can never quite describe the perceptual world of any individual. There are so many ways one's perception of the world may be defined with words that the specific words which are selected by the client give a good perspective on that client's way of thinking. Through use of intentional counseling skills, especially in the attending or listening dimensions, the counselor may map client methods of functioning in a wide array of situations. It is also important to keep in mind the fact that different theories of psychotherapy to be described in the following chapters, such as Freudian, behavioral, and rational-emotive, use different language systems and thus produce immensely varying thinking patterns in their clients.

4. *Define the nature of surface structure and deep structure sentences.* One important purpose of therapy is to take key sentences of the client and search for deeper perceptual meanings, experiences, and thoughts. Three types of issues for the exploration of deeper structure of client sentences were defined as deletions, distortions, and generalizations.

5. *Define the concept of incongruity and identify verbal and nonverbal behavior associated with interpersonal discrepancies or incongruity.* An important task of all therapists is to assist clients to identify and work with issues of personal incongruity.

6. *Define and discuss pacing and leading and how they relate to concepts of attending, empathy, and related ideas in this text.* It is suggested the observation of clients' verbal and nonverbal behavior can be integrated with other information in this text to provide a deeper understanding between client and counselor, eventually leading to productive change and growth.

7. *Define and use key terms and concepts in this chapter.* Nonverbal behavior, body language, physical space and time, eye contact, vocal tone and speech rate, movement complementarity, movement symmetry, cultural differences in nonverbal behavior, representational system or map of experience and events, thought and language, surface structure, deep structure, pacing, leading, perceptual systems, deletions, distortions, generalizations, incongruities, discrepancies, and mixed messages.

REFERENCES

BANDLER, J. and R. GRINDER, *The Structure of Magic.* Vol. I. Palo Alto, CA: Behavioral Books, 1975.

BRINGUIER, J., *Conversations with Jean Piaget.* Chicago: University of Chicago Press, 1980.

CHESLER, P., *Women and Madness.* New York: Avon, 1972.

DEECE, J., *Psycholinguistics.* Boston: Allyn & Bacon, 1970.

HALL, E., *The Silent Language.* New York: Fawcett, 1959.

HARPER, R., A. WIENS, and J. MATARAZZO, *Nonverbal Communication: The State of the Art.* New York: Wiley, 1978.

IVEY, A., *Developmental Therapy: Theory Into Practice.* San Francisco: Jossey-Bass, 1986.

LANKTON, S., *Practical Magic.* Cupertino, CA: Meta, 1980.

MEARA, N., J. SHANNON, and H. PEPINSKY, "Comparisons of Stylistic Complexity of Language of Counselor and Client Across Three Theoretical Orientations," *Journal of Counseling Psychology,* 1979, *26,* 181–189.

RICHARDSON, J., and J. MARGULIS, *The Magic of Rapport.* San Francisco: Harbor, 1981.

VYGOTSKY, L., *Thought and Language.* Cambridge, MA: M.I.T. Press, 1962.

SUGGESTED SUPPLEMENTARY READING

The following books provide useful followup to the ideas presented in this chapter:

FARB, P., *Word Play.* New York: Bantam, 1974.

Farb writes exceptionally well and, despite the age of this book, it is still the most interesting, easy to read, and broad-based book available on words and their meanings.

HALL, E., *The Silent Language.* New York: Fawcett, 1959.

One of the most influential books of the past 30 years in bringing us to awareness of cultural differences in communication patterns at both verbal and nonverbal levels.

HALL, E.,   *The Dance of Life*. New York: Anchor/Doubleday, 1983.
A useful updating of Hall's classic work. Interesting summaries of more recent research on nonverbal communication and new ideas on the concept of time as it is played out differently in varying cultures.

LANKTON, S.,   *Practical Magic*. Cupertino, CA: Meta, 1980.
Extensions of pacing and leading with many useful suggested techniques for growth and change in clients.

6
CLIENT ASSESSMENT

GENERAL PREMISE

An integrated knowledge of skills, theory, and practice is essential for culturally intentional counseling and therapy.

Skills form the foundation of effective theory and practice: The culturally intentional therapist knows how to construct a creative decision-making interview and can use microskills to attend to and influence clients in a predicted direction. Important in this process are individual and cultural empathy, client observation skills, *assessment of person and environment*, and the application of positive techniques of growth and change.

Theory provides organizing principles for counseling and therapy: The culturally intentional counselor has knowledge of alternative theoretical approaches and treatment modalities.

Practice is the integration of skills and theory: The culturally intentional counselor or therapist is competent in skills and theory, and is able to apply them to research and practice for client benefit.

Undergirding integrated competence in skills, theory, and practice is an intentional awareness of one's own personal worldview and how that worldview may be similar to and/or different from the worldview and personal constructions of the client and other professionals.

GOALS FOR CLIENT ASSESSMENT

Client assessment is concerned with learning about the individual and his or her background and needs for counseling and therapy. Assessment involves understanding the person and the environmental context within which that individual lives and decides.

This chapter has the following goals:

1. To present Kelly's theories of assessment. Each client has a unique personal history and worldview that has led him or her to interpret his or her life in a relatively consistent fashion. How can Kelly's "psychology of personal constructs" help you understand better how a client constructs his or her worldview?

2. To present an organization of assessment using Kelly's systematic formulation for understanding a client. Specifically, (a) What is the client's problem? (b) How does the client view the world? (c) What is the client's environmental and situational context? (d) How can therapeutic theory be used in assessment? (e) What does assessment tell you about problem solving?

3. To demonstrate how a long-term treatment plan can be organized to help you and the client plan your work together.

The purpose of this chapter is to present a framework for assessing the unique way a client experiences and acts in the world. One useful system for determining the unique perspectives of each client is presented by George Kelly, perhaps the most brilliant personality theorist ever produced in the United States. Kelly's position is that each client is unique in her or his mode of conceptualizing the world; it is the counselor's task to understand the client's perceptions before undertaking action; and each client's perception of life events is heavily determined by her or his cultural background. Therefore, action taken without understanding the *person-environment transaction* may be naive and even dangerous.

THE PSYCHOLOGY OF PERSONAL CONSTRUCTS: HOW THE CLIENT REPRESENTS THE WORLD

"If you don't know what's wrong with a client, ask . . . ; he (or she) may tell you" (Kelly, 1955, p. 201). If you are going to counsel or do therapy with another person, you must have some idea of where he or she is coming from and what is wanted from the contact with you. Kelly's *law of parsimony* in diagnosis and treatment should never be forgotten by any counselor or therapist. It is tempting to use and impose our sophisticated theories and methods on all-too-willing clients without our realizing that sometimes the best way forward is a simple, logical approach.

There is a story, perhaps apocryphal, about Fritz Perls, the founder of Gestalt therapy. A client who suffered terrible headaches during violin concerts came in for therapy. The poor man had been in agony during concerts for years. Physicians had been unable to find anything physically wrong, so he had been referred for long-term treatment through psychoanalysis. That too failed, and thus began many years of treatments by therapists and counselors of many persuasions. None worked, and finally the violinist was referred to Perls. After talking with him for 5 minutes, Perls terminated the session and suggested that the client return for the next interview and bring his violin. The following week, Perls told him to play his violin and keep playing. After about 15 minutes, the headache appeared. The famous therapist observed the violinist carefully and then said, "Move your right foot here and lower this shoulder." As the flow of blood changed with the new body position, the headache disappeared! There was no more need for therapy.

As you delineate the intricate complexities of the interview and become increasingly aware of variations among individuals, you may see or hear things that seem real and important and may be hidden from the client. At the same time, it is also possible, in abstract theorizing, that you will miss the central issue. If one wants to move forward, generally speaking the best route is a straight line ahead.

The purpose of this section is to present a framework for examining the client and the client's world. Out of this assessment/diagnostic process arises a map of the client and the client's interaction with the environment, which makes selection of appropriate therapy methods more than an uninformed guess. The assessment framework presented here is necessarily incomplete, since a full treatment of this issue alone would fill several books. The basic assessment model presented here relies on what we have termed "Kelly's law of parsimony." It starts

George Kelly

with the client's perception of the world, which can be identified and can lead you to make more systematic interventions in your client's life.

People view the world through their own eyes and ears. To the baby, the world must seem a mass of bumbling confusion. Yet, the child gradually learns to *construe*, organize, and understand the world. Through interactions with others, we learn to make sense of what is before us and our own internal experience of what we see, hear, and feel. We learn to distinguish what is our own personhood and what is the external world.

George Kelly argued that humankind are *scientists* constantly testing hypotheses concerning this confusing world we live in. The child tests her or his ideas (hypotheses) through actions (experiments) on the world and the result (finding) leads to conceptualizations and ideas (theory) about the world. Kelly emphasized our

> creative capacity . . . to represent the environment, not merely to respond to it. Because [people] can represent [their] environment, [they] can place alternative constructions upon it and, indeed, do something about it if it doesn't suit [them]. (1955, p. 8)

People look at the world and develop *constructs* that organize and systematize events, people, and the environmental context. Constructs are hypotheses that the person has used to test some idea or behavior on the world and found in some way effective. Constructs, then, are our ideas and representations of the world—in effect, our worldview.

More specifically, constructs and the resulting worldview are groups of *sentences* we generate to describe our experience of being in the world. The spoken sentences (and the nonverbal behavior as well) of the client who comes to you for assistance are immediate and important clues as to how he or she constructs and acts on the world. The critical assessment task of the counselor and therapist is to help that client understand those sentences and their deeper meanings. In most cases of clients who come for interviews, their construct system and worldview have not been fully effective. They may be blocked and unable to intentionally generate new ways of coping effectively.

If you as therapist are to free them for more creative responding, you will want to enter their construct system and examine how they view the world to help them understand their particular system for representing the world. To use Kelly's analogy, you, as therapist, become a scientist consulting or coinvestigating with the client and helping her or him determine where experiments on the world have not worked out as wished.

As an example, some clients construe the world as being full of enemies and obstacles. Somewhere in their past, they have found that the construct "enemy" is a useful way to make the world more safe and organized. That particular construct can permeate a person's whole being so the world is viewed constantly as terrifying and antagonistic. Imagine that you are, for just a few moments, to put on a pair of "enemy glasses." Viewing the world through the lens of the enemy glasses (the construct), you can review the day's events. You will likely find that it is relatively easy to divide your human contacts into enemies and friends. If you keep on the enemy glasses long enough, the construct enemy could eventually permeate and move through your *whole* construct system and worldview until the world becomes enemy. In effect, the constructs you use to view the world determine how the world eventually comes to be in your experience. This simple example is not too distant from what happens with many paranoid schizophrenics. They have a way of viewing the world that worked at one time, but that became so powerful and pervasive that other constructs and alternatives were forced out. They have become fixated *with* and *in* the enemy construct; the construct has become their world.

Consider the following event:

> You are walking down the street and a friend comes up to talk to you. After a brief chat about the weather, she launches into a detailed blow-by-blow description of a fight she had with her husband just that morning. It seems that he was angry at her for not having his shirts laid out neatly and ready for him to go to work. As she was tired and rushing to go to work herself, she became angry and started yelling at him. She arrived late to her own job after she had finished his shirts. Now, she tells you, she thinks perhaps she was "too hard" on her husband. She asks you what she should do.

First, consider the constructs underlying her statements and behavior. What labels or names would you apply to what she is saying. It might be useful to make a list now. These concepts represent your way of seeing her situation or the "glasses" through which you see her.

Some constructs you might use to understand her sentences include "ungrateful," "lazy," "ripped-off," "in need of consciousness-raising," "has a bad family relationship," and "irritable." There are numerous labels, names, and constructs that could be applied to explain the underlying meaning of the interaction with her husband. If you, as helper, construe her behavior as "ungrateful" for all that her husband "has done for her," one set of responses from you is likely to follow. On the other hand, if she seems "ripped-off" by her husband, a different set of responses is likely. In effect, the constructs you have for naming the world represent your worldview and your likely path of action in that world.

Counseling and therapy, however, are different from friendship. Imagine that this is the first interview with the client; she brings up the same information and you want to assess its meaning in her life. A first task of the counselor is to determine/diagnose where the client *is*. One important part of that diagnosis is to understand the client's construct system—through what set of glasses the client views the world. By the skillful use of interviewing techniques and qualities presented in this text, *the counselor can set about understanding how the client organizes and acts on the world. This is the underlying purpose of assessment/diagnosis/interpretation of the client, whether completed by interview, test, or other means.* Effective assessment of another person requires that you become intentional, release your perceptions, and see the world through the client's glasses.

This does not mean, however, that you as therapist negate your own constructs and theories. There will be ample opportunity for you to apply yourself and your ideas to the concerns of the client. Your own constructs and theories about the world will prove useful to the client, especially if you are aware of them and how they color your own perceptions. When we talk with others, we are always using our unique personal constructs and theories. There are dangers in applying your construct system to the client inappropriately. This issue is discussed in detail later in this chapter.

Kelly has suggested that there are several basic issues in effective assessment and diagnosis of clients and their needs. Paraphrased, they are:

1. What is the client's presenting problem? What does the client think is wrong, when does it occur, and what are the results?
2. How does the client view the world? What are the client's constructs and what effect does this representational system have on the problem?
3. What is the client's environmental and situational context? What effect do issues such as socioeconomic class, race, living arrangements, etc. have on the client's personal constructs and life?
4. What are your basic theories and constructs in regard to this unique client? What does this client mean to you? What environmental factors, particularly agency affiliations, impinge on you?
5. What do you and the client do next? How do you handle the immediate problem? If solving the immediate problem is insufficient, then what? What about the development of an overall treatment plan? (Kelly, 1955, pp. 777–779)

The remainder of this chapter will explore these key diagnostic questions in more detail. Yet, as we move toward complexity and increasing awareness of the difficulty of answering the above questions, it seems important to restate Kelly's introductory comment from earlier in this chapter. When one gets confused among the many possibilities for assessing what a client needs or wants, "ask . . . he (or she) may tell you."

What Is the Client's Problem?

Client coming to a welfare window:

CLIENT:	I need food stamps.
COUNSELOR:	You say you need food stamps.
CLIENT:	Yeah, we're completely out of food.
COUNSELOR:	Could you tell me a little bit about your background, your past occupation, for example?
CLIENT:	I don't have a job. Listen, my kids are hungry.
COUNSELOR:	How long have you been out of work?

It would be pleasant if the above were purely mythical and such client-counselor transactions never happened. However, they do, thus dehumanizing the client and wasting valuable time for all concerned. The most logical thing to do for clients who have problems is to help them solve the difficulties as directly and immediately as possible. In this case, the client is clear about an immediate and real problem. Action is needed *now*. Assessment and analysis in more detail can come later. The following is a more positive way of dealing with the issue:

CLIENT: I need food stamps.

COUNSELOR: I sense you want them in a hurry too. Sounds like I may be able to help. It will take a few minutes because I have to ask some questions. Then, I can direct you to the place that will give them to you. Okay if I ask a few questions?

CLIENT: I hate all this detail. I don't have a job. Listen, my kids are hungry.

COUNSELOR: Clearly you want action *now*. Let me see what I can do to speed things up to help. (pause) Well, I can leave out a few items. Okay if I cut the questions as short as possible?

CLIENT: I guess so. Let them fly . . .

Needless to say, the direct and obvious approach doesn't solve all problems. Clients who come for help, whether in a street clinic or a traditional therapist's office, have arrived there because "obvious answers" and usual sources of aid aren't working for them. Assessing the client's status is a complex and involving process requiring skilled use of questioning techniques, broad knowledge of socioeconomic considerations, awareness of alternative life styles, and many other factors.

To obtain a description of the client's problem, Kelly suggests several sources. The first of these is careful analysis of the client's presenting complaint. As the counselor draws out the problem as defined by the client, the presenting problem is often discarded (or saved for later) and other issues are dealt with. For example:

THERAPIST: You say you're not sleeping at night and that your physician referred you to me to find out why. Could you tell me a little bit about what happened last night for example?

CLIENT: Well, my wife just left me and I was trying to sleep when bugs started to crawl out of the wall; they came down and went all over me . . . it was awful.

THERAPIST: Sounds like things are *really* rough right now. What's this about the bugs?

CLIENT: I'm pretty shook up. I've been trying to keep it to myself. Doc Jones has known my family a long time and I can't talk to him. I didn't tell him about the bugs. They just seemed to be coming out all over. I guess it was a dream, but *what* a dream!

THERAPIST: I'm glad you feel free to talk with me. Sometimes people have such dreams after they've been drinking. Did you have anything the night before?

CLIENT: Only a little, but perhaps I had too much that night.

The presenting problem "not sleeping at night" is transformed into likely alcoholism and family concerns. The new problems around which therapy is based do not always come out this quickly. This issue of a presenting problem being transformed into other more "operational" problems is typical of much of counseling and therapy. The importance of careful definition of the problem cannot be overstressed. Beginning counselors and therapists all too often are delighted to "solve" the client's presenting problem and may miss other more important issues.

Extracting and defining the problem may be compared with a newspaper reporter's describing an important event. Considerable care and effort need to be given to:

- *Who* is the individual; what are her or his important characteristics, family background, life style, etc.? What are the important cultural-environmental factors for this individual?
- *What* happened or is happening? The details of the problem are needed. How often does it occur? Under what circumstances? (To understand any individual we need to know as many details as possible.)
- *When* does the problem occur? When did it begin? What are the important time sequences? (Certain problems begin at certain times: Suicide and depression, for instance, are more likely in the spring or just before vacation points in college.) What immediately preceded the problem situation? What were the patterns of this problem over the life cycle of the client?
- *Where* does the problem occur; in what settings; under what conditions; with what people?
- *How* does the client react to the problem? How does the client feel about it?
- *Why* does the problem occur? (Less important in many theories is the search for reasons. However, the careful assessment of the problem often leads to obvious answers.)

To determine the precise nature of the problem, it is also possible to administer psychological tests; search school, employer, and medical records; directly observe the behavior of the client in the interview, on a psychiatric ward, or at home; and interview the family or other associates for information. Through each of these procedures, the same questions of "who," "what," "when," "where," "how," and "why" can be continually asked.

Most counselors and therapists do not use this extensive listing of possibilities for defining the problem and choose to select only those questions and procedures in accord with their theory and what they believe most economical for the client. In admission to some psychiatric hospitals, it may be expected that a fairly complete picture of the problem will be developed with an attempt to provide data from all the possible sources.

Problems can stem from the environment and its pressures. Counselors and therapists typically are satisfied to conduct a thorough review of the individual and often fail to do the same with factors in the environment. A child having nightmares over school may be found to need certain types of psychotherapy to alleviate the problem, when, in fact, an examination of the school classroom may reveal a cruel and sadistic teacher. A woman may be forced to undergo lengthy therapy for depression at the age of 35, when, in actuality, she is facing a life crisis typical of many women in our culture who find themselves bored with a home-maker's role. For her, environmental change in the form of a new job may be more to the point than counseling. A bright Puerto Rican youth may be assessed to be of low intelligence and his inability to speak English may be ignored. These and many other similar cases speak of the danger of failing to consider the total environmental-cultural context.

While there are an infinite number of ways to examine the environment of a client, so are there many ways to consider the client as a person. One of the most important of these for the counselor or therapist is consideration of the life stage of the client. Drawing on the work of many authors, Egan and Cowan (1979) have developed a "developmental map" of the life cycle of the client. This frame-work presented in Figure 6.1 shows many of the considerations a therapist needs to have in mind while working with an individual client.

The first column, "life stage," summarizes an obvious, but telling point: *over the life span, people change.* A child is a different person at ages 2, 4, and 7 and needs different things from the environment. Similarly, adulthood brings its many crises and opportunities. Clients of different ages will have differing needs and expectancies in the interviews.

"Key systems" is closely related to the environmental variables discussed in this chapter. Over the lifespan, the tendency is to move from centering on the family to centering on peers and then to returning to the family. The impact of different environmental factors varies in importance according to a client's life stage.

"Developmental tasks" refers to key learnings for life survival and hap-piness that are typically important to each age grouping. For example, for suc-cessful living in early adulthood, Egan and Cowan point out that the individual must develop the skills of family living, initial parenting, career development, life-style management, and capacity for commitment. Clients who seek counsel-ing at this life stage are likely to have one or more concerns of this type. However, life-stage development will vary from individual to individual and some clients have never learned skills and concepts to cope with these important develop-mental tasks. Thus, the lengthy list of developmental tasks may be important to any individual at any time.

"Developmental resources" refers to what a person needs to accomplish developmental tasks. An infant, for example, cannot develop social attachments unless the resource of security (in terms of support from parents) is available. Similarly, for development of career, the client needs to understand the world of work and her or his own capabilities. A task of the therapist or counselor may be to provide developmental resources for clients or agency referral possibilities.

Each life stage brings with it a special crisis of development. If systems are intact and resources are available, it may be anticipated that the develop-

Figure 6.1   A Developmental Map of the Life Cycle and Its Context*

Life Stage	Key Systems	Developmental Tasks	Developmental Resources	Developmental Crises
Infancy (birth–2)	Family nuclear extended	Social attachment Sense of continued existence of one-self Sensorimotor intelligence & primitive causality Maturation of motor functions	Security Basic need fulfillment Stability	Basic trust or mistrust
Early childhood (2–4)	Family nuclear extended	Self-control Language development Fantasy & play Self-locomotion	Human interaction Sensory stimulation Protected environment Limit setting	Independent sense of self or doubt & shame
Middle childhood (5–7)	Family Neighborhood School	Gender identity Early moral development Concrete mental operations Group play	Appropriate models Explanation of rule setting Consistency in rule enforcement Problem-solving tasks Peer-group interaction	Self as initiator or guilt about self's wishes
Late childhood (8–12)	Family Neighborhood School Peer group	Cooperative social relations Self-evaluation Skill learning Team membership	Cooperative learning environment Cooperative recreational environment Effective skills teaching learning to learn basic interpersonal relationships Feedback on self and performance	Industry or inferiority
Early adolescence (13–17)	Family Peer group School	Physical maturation Formal mental operations Peer group membership Initial sexual intimacy	Physiological information Cognitive problem-solving & decision-making tasks Relationship building skills Knowledge of sex roles & their cultural sources Opportunities for independent moral judgment	Belonging or social isolation
Late adolescence (18–22)	Peer group School or work setting Family Surrounding community	Independent living Initial career decisions Internalized morality Initial sustained intimacy Relativistic thinking	Knowledge and skills for: financial independence, self-exploration, decision making, relationship deepening, dealing with pluralism Responsibility for choices & consequences	Individual identity or identity confusion

Figure 6.1 A Developmental Map of the Life Cycle and Its Context*

Life Stage	Key Systems	Developmental Tasks	Developmental Resources	Developmental Crises
Early adulthood (23–30)	New family Work setting Friendship network Surrounding community	Family living Initial parenting Career development Life-style management Capacity for commitment	Knowledge & skills for: family financial planning & management, interpersonal negotiating & conflict resolution, parenting, role discrimination & integration	Social living competency and intimacy or incompetency & alienation
Pre-middle-age transition (30–35)	Family Work setting Friendship network Surrounding community	Reevaluation & re-dedication re: commitments Parenting of older children Dealing with commitment, reevaluation on part of significant others	Evaluation and renewed decisions re: relationships, career, life style Knowledge & skills to form broadly based interpersonal support	Renewal or resignation
Pre-middle age (36–50)	Friendship network Family Work setting Surrounding community	Midlife evaluation of commitments Children leave home Changes in relationship with spouse Involvement beyond self & nuclear family	Knowledge and skills for higher order role taking Higher order role differentiation & integration	Achievement & meaning in social living or incompetence & meaninglessness
Middle age (51–65)	Family Friendship network Work setting Surrounding community	Involvement beyond family Winding down of career involvement Confrontation with personal mortality	Knowledge and skills for: involvement of self in community systems, teaching & advising Increased reliance on cognitive vs. physical skills	Lasting contribution through involvement with others or self-centered stagnation
Old age (65–death)	Family Friendship network Surrounding community	Increased dependency on others Evaluation of one's life Dealing with deaths of significant others Coping with one's own death	Survival skills given diminished physical resources Capacity to say goodbye and grieve	Sense of meaning & validation of worth or despair

*Developmental map by Gerard Egan and M. Cowan (1979), by permission.

153

mental tasks will be successfully completed, thus minimizing the potential life crisis at any later age. However, if basic difficulties are manifested, sometimes highly disturbing life crises may present themselves. The best known of these is the identity crisis of late adolescence—"Who am I?" and "What does it mean to be me?" If earlier crises are resolved successfully, the individual moves on to further growth and development. If not, the individual still moves on, but may replay old crises again and again in the form of immobility and lack of intentionality. It is difficult, for example, to develop a sense of identity as a late adolescent if one has not developed a sense of industry, competence, and belonging in earlier years. Similarly, failure to obtain a clear identity in the late adolescent stage will result in difficulties in later adulthood.

The value of a developmental map, like that presented by Egan and Cowan, is that it summarizes in graphic form the fact that any individual who comes for a counseling interview has faced and will face a bewildering array of developmental tasks and life crises. Your clients will have met these issues with varying talents and abilities, differing personality factors, and will have worked through these issues in a variety of environmental contexts. The complexity of the human condition cannot be overstressed; nor can the importance of family and culture.

While the client's developmental stage, life facts, and personal definition of the problem are central in basic assessment, an equally important issue is how the client views the problem. For one person, the breaking of a date may be a severe emotional trauma while, for another, no particular thought or feeling may be attached. The way a person represents and thinks about a problem may be as important as, or more important than, the problem itself. It is in this area that Kelly's theory and methods are particularly helpful.

What Are the Client's Constructs for Viewing the World?

Constructs have been defined as sentences and groups of sentences we use to organize and classify our world. They could be described as the "pieces" of a person's worldview. Due to the complexity of life and each person's unique experiences, each client's constructs and worldview will be different and distinct. Before imposing a theory or method to produce change, Kelly emphasized that it was important to understand not only the client and the client's problem, but also the way the client construed or thought about the problem.

The *Repertory Test* (Rep Test) is an instrument developed by Kelly to assist in the determination of the personal constructs of the client. The Rep Test (see Figure 6.2) may be used to determine how the client thinks about important people in her or his life. Much of counseling and psychotherapy revolves around interpersonal issues; the personal constructs clients use to discuss and think about other people are particularly valuable in assessing possible future actions.

The Rep Test asks clients to list significant people in their lives (father, mother, teacher, boss). This is followed by asking for comparisons among these

Figure 6.2   *The Repertory Test (Shortened and Adapted)*

1. *Role Title List*
   List the name of the following individuals:
   1. A teacher you liked (or the teacher of a subject you liked).
   2. A teacher you disliked (or the teacher of a subject you disliked).
   3. Your husband or wife or current man or woman friend.
   4. A person of the opposite sex whom you particularly liked in the past.
   5. A person of the opposite sex whom you particularly disliked in the past (or who disliked and rejected you).
   6. Your mother.
   7. Your father.
   8. Your sister (or a friend who has played a similar role).
   9. Your brother (or a friend who has played a similar role).
   10. A boss or supervisor you particularly liked.
   11. A boss or supervisor you particularly disliked.
   12. A person whom you know well, but with whom you conflict or who may appear to dislike you.
   Be sure that you have 12 different names.
2. *Construct and Contrast*
   Take the people in trios (as indicated below) and for each set ask yourself the following three questions: (a) "From among the three people, which two are the most similar?" (b) "In what way are the two of them alike but different from the third?" (c) "How is the remaining person different?" Record your answers in two columns marked "Construct" and "Contrast."
   Twenty sorts will be used in this brief version, the trios are:

9,12,1	1,2,3
2,10,7	2,3,4
8,10,12	5,6,7
1,2,7	6,7,8
3,4,5	8,9,10
2,11,12	9,10,11
3,7,9	10,11,12
1,2,4	11,12,1
6,7,9	12,1,2
8,9,1	4,5,11

   In making these sorts and defining the constructs and contrasts, it is important that they not be superficial, vague, or a product of the role title. Most effective are qualitative and specific constructs.
3. *Examine the Constructs*
   Both constructs and contrasts are part of one's construct system for viewing the world. There is no specific systematic scoring at this elementary level of the Rep Test. Rather the counselor (sometimes with aid of the client) simply views the constructs developed and classifies them. The words selected often provide a view of important issues to the client. Very often it will be possible to organize constructs in polar opposites: good-bad, tall-short, kind-mean. It has been found that people tend to think about others in characteristic ways. The Rep Test provides a reasonable shortcut for determining how another person thinks, without undue structuring by the counselor or therapist.

people ("How are these people the same and how are they different?"). If a client says, for example, that the boss and a sister are similar in that they are both "kind," *kind* would be noted as a personal construct important to the client. Another client, however, might use "wealthy" or "poor" for the same pairing. Through such a series of comparisons, a relatively stable set of constructs representing the client's view of significant people emerges. This list of personal constructs provides the counselor with a summary of key aspects of the client's worldviews.

The key constructs developed through the administration of one Rep Test were "bright vs. dull," "controlling vs. supporting," and "warm vs. cold and distant." The client in this case was a high-achieving social worker who had difficulty with his supervisor and was seen by colleagues as too deeply involved with clients on a personal level. He was given to frequent arguments with supervisors and appeared arrogant, cold, and distant to other staff members. His work was effective, but his interpersonal relationships were poor. This listing of key constructs provided the therapist with major issues that needed to be considered in the therapeutic process.

Practicing therapists and counselors tend to utilize standardized tests of intelligence, achievement, personality, vocational interests, and others extensively in assessment. Kelly, also, recognizes the potential value of the more commonly used test instruments. He points out, however, that such tests have been developed according to some arbitrary external standard and may miss the way an individual thinks about or construes the world, thus taking the therapist in wrong directions for diagnosis and treatment. On the other hand, tests provide an unbiased source of data about the client. As Kelly observes:

> Testing may broaden the perspective of the therapist. It is easy enough to become preoccupied with certain palpable issues during the course of therapy and forget just what type of client one is dealing with. The therapist's own acceptance of his client tends to bias his judgment. The test is a good way to dispel some of the bias and place the case in a well-balanced frame of reference. (Kelly, 1955, p. 979)

The intentional counselor and therapist should have a thorough knowledge of tests and their potential use in the interviews.

Thus the Rep Test is only one way to assess the personal constructs of the client. Kelly's adage, "ask the client" holds again. If you, as helper, listen carefully, you will find that some key words appear again and again in the client's conversation. These words that appear and reappear are clues to the client's worldview and construct system and should not be ignored. For example, consider the following:

CLIENT 1:   I took the examination and I was flying high. I thought I knew it. I had studied so hard. Then I got the results and I flunked it. That hurt! I guess I really don't have it. I'm a phoney, a fake.

CLIENT 2:   I took the examination and I was flying high. I thought I knew it. I had studied so hard. Then I got the results and I flunked it. I guess I didn't study hard enough. Next time I'll get help. Maybe it's best it happened early in the term. I'll figure it out.

In the above two excerpts, the same situation is construed differently by the two clients. The key constructs of Client 1 include "hurt," "don't have it," and self-images of phoneyness and fakery. The second client, rather than saying he or she "didn't have it," acknowledged the possible need to study harder and seek help. The intention to "figure it out" appears prominently. The two construct systems are vastly different and would suggest different actions on the part of the counselor.

Each client who appears for counseling and therapy is providing ongoing and immediate data about her or his personal construct system. One only has to listen carefully to find key constructs appearing over and over again. It is these repetitious, often blocked or immobilized constructs that may represent loss of intentionality and key issues for intervention in the helping process. If one is able to work in the construct system of the client, language and meaning barriers are removed, and the helping process can proceed more smoothly.

A useful exercise for practice is to tape record a conversation with a friend or client and then to list the key constructs used to describe different situations. Patterns of repetition of key words often emerge relatively early. Perhaps more important, note your own patterning of responses and your own constructs for responding to other people. Through the Rep Test and study of your own and others' construct systems, you will find that much data is available for understanding the client, which you have previously missed.

It is important to examine the nature of *tight* and *loose constructions* the client uses in many different areas of her or his life:

> A client may use loose construction when dealing with people and tight construction when dealing with money. He may show guilt in his relationships to his family, hostility in his relationships to his employer, preemption in his relationship to foreigners. (Kelly, 1955, p. 802)

Tight and loose constructions may be related to the decisional styles described in Chapter 2. The person who manifests unconflicted adherance to a single point of view or theory, with constant repetitions of key words could be defined as a special type of tight-construction thinker. Loose constructions are shown by the client or therapist who constantly changes direction and demonstrates lack of commitment. Kelly points out that different therapeutic modes are required for people whose construct systems are tight or loose. The goal for Kelly is *permeable constructs* that are flexible and able to cope with the changing situations of life. Kelly suggests that any single client may approach an interview with tight constructs in some areas but also manifest loose constructs and some permeable constructs (intentional) in other areas. Therefore, more than one therapeutic mode may be required to reach any single client in all critical areas.

Tight constructions could be represented in the following types of client comments:

1: No, you can't say that. My husband is a good, church-going man. He wouldn't do anything wrong. Our daughter deserved what she got.
2: No, that's not child abuse. That is discipline. It's what I got at home. No way, you social workers ought to stay out of our lives.

Tight constructions of reality are "logic-tight" and often can explain anything at anytime. Your task as therapist is to loosen the constructions of the tight worldview and help the client see alternative ways to frame the situations. A permeable construct in this case might be the following. "I still feel that discipline is important, but I know that we have been too harsh. The assertiveness training and social skills exercises have given me new ways to look at the situation." The stuckness of tight constructions has been replaced with a more vigilant, intentional, decisional style.

By contrast, overly loose constructions would be represented by the following client comments:

1: I don't see the importance of scheduling. I like to be spontaneous. We eat together as a family now and then. I've got so much to do . . . the kids will survive.
2: You wonder why I missed the last appointment. I guess I forgot . . . always doing that, even got fired once for being too late. Our family works best when we do what we feel like. I think the problem with Jane will take care of itself if we just relax and don't worry.

Spontaneity can be fine in some places, but in others it results in a form of immobilization in which the client produces very little except distraction. A permeable set of constructs around the same situation might be: "Now I am getting my act together. We are able to sit down together as a family and do some planning, but I still won't let the schedule dominate me. You were right and it was helpful to learn that a teenager such as Jane does need some rules. After some beginning arguments, she now says she feels I care for her more. . . . Apparently, she used to feel I didn't care." Again, the client has become more vigilant and intentional in decision making.

The goal of a Kelly-type assessment is not to label the client, but to find out how the client thinks and what he or she thinks about. Furthermore, the idea of permeable, changeable constructs is quite different from a fixed concept of what the client *is* or "*should be*." The Diagnostic and Statistical Manual (DSM-III)—see Figure 6.3—is an example of an assessment system oriented toward

---

Figure 6.3 *THE DIAGNOSTIC AND STATISTICAL MANUAL (DSM-III)*

DSM-III: DETERMINATION OF ILLNESS AS A PROBLEM OF ASSESSMENT

If one views the world through the construct system "mental illness," one is likely to construct a world of problems and mental disorders. The most common diagnostic system used today in mental health is that of DSM-III, the *Diagnostic and Statistical Manual* (1980) of the American Psychiatric Association. You will want to familiarize yourself with this framework, which is widely used in the mental health system.

Diagnostic nomenclature of DSM-III is organized into the following major categories (certain subcategories have been added as examples and for clarification):

1. Disorders usually first evident in infancy, childhood, or adolescence: mental retardation; attention deficit disorder; eating disorders (anorexia, bulimia)
2. Organic mental disorders
3. Substance abuse disorders
4. Schizophrenia disorders
5. Paranoid disorders
6. Affective disorders (mania, depression)
7. Anxiety disorders (phobias, anxiety neurosis)
8. Somatoform disorders (conversion, hypochrondriasis)
9. Dissociative disorders (hysterical neuroses, multiple personality)
10. Psychosexual disorders (transvestism, sexual sadism)
11. Factitious disorders (the patient "fakes" or makes up disorder)
12. Adjustment disorder (difficulty in adjusting to life event)
13. Personality disorders (borderline personality, passive-aggressive personality)

The client or patient is evaluated on five "axes," each of which refers to specific diagnostic information. Axis I refers to the presenting problem, and Axis II, to longer-term disorders; together they refer to the "mental disorders" listed above. Axis III refers to physical disorders, Axis IV to severity of psychosocial stressors, and Axis V to "highest level of adaptive functioning" in the past year. Thus a client such as the sad and depressed individual of Chapter 5 might be classified as follows: Axis I: 296.24 major depression, single episode, with psychotic features; Axis II: 300.40 depressive neurosis; Axis III: malnutrition; Axis IV: 6—extreme severity (loss of parents and divorce); Axis 5: 4—fair adaptive functioning (moderate impairment in social and occupational functioning). (In actual practice, the first two axes are primarily used; the remaining three are considered more experimental.)

DSM-III has been criticized severely because it does not suggest what a therapist can do once the diagnosis is established. This may be contrasted with the Kelly approach where assessment is tied close to planned action. DSM-III, however, is a reality of the language of therapy that every helper must acknowledge and know well. It serves as a unifying language among a vast array of therapeutic ideologies and treatments.

---

medical labeling of a client; it neither talks about client history nor suggests what is "to be done" with the client once assessment has been completed. Action to help clients change their modes of thinking and being is part and parcel of the Kelly assessment plan.

DSM–III is presented as it is an important part of the assessment process which is increasingly recognized as basic to the professional practice of therapy and counseling. The approach to assessment suggested by Kelly is not in argument with this system, but rather should be seen as an approach which will help you gain insight into the client for diagnosis, should you work in a setting where DSM–III is utilized.

DSM–III, on the other hand, is not relevant to every counselor and therapist. The specific issue of diagnosis into clear categories of "illness" is not consistent with some orientations to therapy (especially Rogerian and many behavioral therapists). Whether or not you agree with the system and conceptualizations of DSM–III, it is an important part of the field and represents a body of knowledge which you will want to study to develop your own position for your later professional practice.

What Is the Client's Situational and Environmental Context?

> It is a mistake to assume that a psychologically healthy person can immediately adjust himself happily to any kind of situation. Adjustment can only be achieved in relation to something. It makes a difference what one has to adjust to. Diagnosis is not complete until the clinician has some understanding of the milieu in which adjustment is to be sought. This position represents a departure from the common notion that diagnosis involves an analysis of the client only. From our point of view, diagnosis is the planning stage of client management. Therefore, *both* the client and his milieu must be understood. (Kelly, 1955, p. 804)

The classic formula $B = f(P, E)$ or "Behavior is a function of the Person and the Environment" was conceptualized by the psychologist Kurt Lewin (1935). Lewin was concerned with psychology's tendency to consider only individuals and to neglect the fact that people are strongly influenced by their environment. Despite Lewin, counselors and therapists have continued to work primarily with individuals and to ignore potent environmental factors. In recent years, extensive work has been initiated to correct this situation (Bandura, 1978; Kohlberg, 1966; Hunt, 1971; Hunt and Sullivan, 1974; Moos, 1984), but still relatively little consideration is given to these issues in counseling and psychotherapy.

A major question that faces professional and nonprofessional helpers is the degree to which they will emphasize environmental factors and whether they will choose to work with individuals alone or also seek to work on environmental change. There are two major routes towards environmental change. The first is direct action on the part of counselors and therapists on the environment itself (such as working toward family change or assisting in improving community conditions) or to bring clients to a fuller awareness of how the environment impinges on their personal life through direct instruction and consciousness raising (such as informing a welfare client about legal rights or encouraging a client to enter a consciousness-raising group). The following section outlines some critical dimensions of the person-environment transaction that can help counselors conceptualize their choice alternatives to assist clients.

Within the person-environment transaction, it is important to consider the array of environmental factors that may be interacting with any one client. One useful model for conceptualizing this issue is provided by Roberts (1975), who lists seven factors as important in relating to any client: *personal, sexual, familial, ethnic, provincial, social class,* and *cultural.* Counseling and therapy, being predominantly individual-centered, historically gave prime focus to the personal dimension. However, therapists have increasingly learned that differences between men and women, family history, ethnic background, living location, and general sociocultural factors all interact. Further, these seven factors obviously interact with one another. Thus a 40-year-old white homosexual of Lebanese extraction from rural New York, lower-class adoptive parents is a very different person from a 40-year-old white homosexual of Lebanese extraction from *urban* New York, lower-class adoptive parents. The changing of one environmental factor can change the total picture.

The model in Figure 6.4 illustrates briefly the importance of considering interactive environmental factors in any treatment program. Equally important, it is possible to see that a major change in viewpoint within the person can change the meaning of a host of environmental factors. The environment obviously influences the person, but the person and the person's view of the environment influences and shapes that environment. If our 40-year-old homosexual man repeats a behavior several times (for example, saying "I think I'm bad because I'm a homosexual"), the environment tends to accept that definition and will start treating that individual as if he indeed is bad. If that same person defines homosexuality as a valid life alternative and regards himself as "good," then the environment may be expected to react more positively. When he reacts to the environment with anger and hurt, a self-fulfilling cycle of immobility and lack of intentionality is established.

Rosenthal and Jacobson (1968) in a stimulating work on the "self-fulfilling prophecy" have clearly demonstrated that what a person expects will often happen. In a school research study, some classroom teachers were told that their students were above average, whereas in others, teachers were told their students were average. At the end of the year, the "above average" class performed significantly better than the "average" class, although in truth there was no difference between the two groups at the start of the year. What the person expects of an environment is what that environment will produce.

Behavioral psychology's prime spokesperson B. F. Skinner has stated, "In the broadest possible sense, the culture into which an individual is born is com-

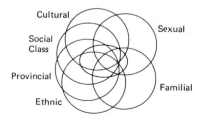

Figure 6.4 Environmental Factors Transacting with the Person

posed of all the variables affecting him which are arranged by other people" (1953, p. 419). While recognizing the importance of physical space, Skinner gives most attention to the *social environment* in which people interacting with one another generate the customs and behavior of a particular culture. The main catalyst in the social environment, of course, is the family who may control the child "through an extension of religious or governmental techniques, by way of psychotherapy, through economic control, or as an educational institution" (p. 419). As the child moves into the broader social environment, peers, schools, and other important people and institutions take over the role of social control. From a Skinnerian view, then, environment and culture can be defined as a massive set of reinforcement and punishment mechanisms designed to shape the behavior of an individual in accord with social tradition. Skinner compares the Russian and U.S. cultures, pointing out that, while there are many similarities, each environment stamps its unique imprint on the child and has its own powerful set of reinforcement, punishment, and control mechanisms.

The aims of a society are transmitted not only by the family but also by its institutions. Educational programs in the schools are believed by many to be particularly important in maintaining societal social-class structures. Bourdieu and Passeron (1977) have stated that education could be considered a "reproductive system" wherein children are socialized to maintain the societal status quo. They demonstrate that the probability of access to higher education in France ranges from approximately 2 percent among farm workers and manual laborers, to 54 percent for industrialists. In an aptly titled article "Once a Blue Collar Worker, Always a Blue Collar Worker?" Dwight (1978) presents data from the United States, reinforcing the statement that parental occupation may be the primary determiner of the occupation of the child.

Symbolic violence is the term Bourdieu and Passeron use to describe the unequal distribution of economic and social power in a society. They argue that the distribution of social power represented in such societies is as violent as if imposed by force or military action. One does not have to accept Bourdieu and Passeron's analysis or terminology to realize the importance of issues like this for the counselor and therapist. At a particularly important choicepoint in his life, Malcolm X described his interaction with a teacher-counselor:

> He told me, "Malcolm, you ought to be thinking about a career. Have you been giving it thought?"
> The truth is, I hadn't. I never have figured out why I told him, "Well, yes, sir, I've been thinking I'd like to be a lawyer." Lansing certainly had no Negro lawyers—or doctors either—in those days, to hold up an image I might have aspired to. All I really knew for certain was that a lawyer didn't wash dishes, as I was doing.
> Mr. Ostrowski looked surprised, I remember, and leaned back in his chair and clasped his hands behind his head. He kind of half-smiled and said, "Malcolm, one of life's first needs is for us to be realistic. Don't misunderstand me, now. We all here like you, you know that. But you've got to be realistic about being a nigger. A lawyer—that's no realistic goal for a nigger. You need to think about something

you *can* be. You're good with your hands—making things. Everybody admires your carpentry shop work. Why don't you plan on carpentry? People like you as a person—you'd get all kinds of work."

The more I thought afterwards about what he said, the more uneasy it made me. It just kept treading around in my mind.

What made it really begin to disturb me was Mr. Ostrowski's advice to others in my class—all of them white. Most of them had told him they were planning to become farmers. But those who wanted to strike out on their own, to try something new, he had encouraged. Some, mostly girls, wanted to be teachers. A few wanted other professions, such as one boy who wanted to become a county agent; another, a veterinarian; and one girl wanted to be a nurse. They all reported that Mr. Ostrowski had encouraged what they had wanted. Yet nearly none of them had earned marks equal to mine.

It was a surprising thing that I had never thought of it that way before, but I realized that whatever I wasn't, I *was* smarter than nearly all of those white kids. But apparently I was still not intelligent enough, in their eyes, to become whatever *I* wanted to be.

It was then that I began to change—inside.

I drew away from white people. I came to class, and I answered when called upon. It became a physical strain simply to sit in Mr. Ostrowski's class.

Where "nigger" had slipped off my back before, wherever I heard it now, I stopped and looked at whoever said it. And they looked surprised that I did.

I quit hearing so much "nigger" and "What's wrong?"—which was the way I wanted it. Nobody, including the teachers, could decide what had come over me. I knew I was being discussed.

In a few more weeks, it was that way, too, at the restaurant where I worked washing dishes, and at the Swerlins'. (Malcolm X, 1964, pp. 36–37)

Given the power of institutions to shape and mold individuals, it is especially important that counselors and therapists be aware of such issues and include them in the therapy process where appropriate. Counselors and therapists can easily fall into symbolic violence through encouraging their clients to adapt to societal demands, thus maintaining social class status quo.

Obviously, the importance of the cultural milieu, particularly as transmitted by the family and institutions, cannot be overstressed. Kelly supports this point, but adds the following caution:

> . . . it is often considered the mark of a sophisticated clinician that he considers all of his clients in terms of the culture groups to which they belong. Yet, in the final analysis, a client who is to be genuinely understood should never be confined to the stereotype of his culture. For the clinician the cultural approach should never be more than a preliminary step in the understanding of his client, the first in a series of approximations which bring the client into sharp focus in a complex matrix of psychological dimensions. (Kelly, 1955, pp. 833–834)

Clients who come for counseling and therapy are individuals first, last, and always. However, each individual must be considered in relationship to her or his unique environment.

When a married woman, age 35 or 40, comes in for counseling, complaining of boredom and vague feelings of anxiety, the modern, feminist therapist is sometimes inclined to classify the woman as needing education in the women's movement, and to consider her problem a normal one of adult adjustment. When a Black person who has just failed to get a job is depressed and suspects racism, the liberal therapist is often likely to discuss the oppression of the economic system. When a teenager complains about parental control, the school guidance counselor may consider this a reaction typical of the student's age. In all three cases, cultural stereotypes may be ruling the actions of the therapist or counselor to the extent that the unique individual before them has not been seen. Each person who comes into counseling and therapy has unique needs, a unique and special way of construing the world, and is different from all other people. While awareness of cultural issues is obviously important, this awareness should never blind the helper to the unique constructs and worldview of the client.

What Are the Counselor's Basic Theories and Constructs?

Just as the client has certain basic ways of construing the world, you, as counselor or therapist, bring your own personal constructions and worldview to the interview. Too often counselors believe that their way of theorizing about the world is *the* correct way and are unable to understand that different clients perceive the world in another potentially valid manner. Such therapists often may seek to impose their point of view on the client. *Too rigid an attachment to your own theories and personal constructs can lead to an inability to hear the client, difficulty in appreciating her or his unique construction of the world, and forcing the client consciously or unconsciously into what you believe the world should be.*

Kelly emphasized constantly that it is necessary to find how each individual represents the world before taking action to produce change. This is different from some other theories to be presented in the following sections of this book. A few therapists and counselors who adhere to a specific theory come to the interview with preconceived ideas about how the world *is* organized, and work with the client within their theoretical framework and personal constructs. Sometimes, the task of the counselor or therapist almost becomes that of "selling" the client on a particular point of view.

From this framework, for one example, it is possible for a therapist of a psychoanalytic orientation to come to an interview with a preconceived set of constructs and representational systems (such as Freudian theory). The process of therapy is to enable the client to see the world through the eyes of Sigmund Freud (at least as interpreted by the Freudian psychotherapist). If the client does not agree with the interpretations of the therapist, he or she is said to be "resisting"; through careful use of counseling skills, the client often comes to accept and embrace the constructs, representational system, and worldview of the analytic tradition. While such therapy may be functional and useful, those interested in the psychology of personal constructs cannot help but be impressed by the relative lack of interest in the person as a unique individual except as she or he fits into the theoretical "glasses" of Freudian psychology. *Fortunately, relatively few therapists are so rigidly fixed to their theories that they impose their points of view on the client.*

Personal construct theory need not be considered in opposition to other theories described in this book, but perhaps as part of a more general theory concerning the counseling and therapeutic process. While Kelly did not expand his theory of personal constructs to the general theory level, it seems but a small extension to suggest that the many competing alternative theories of helping, to be described later in this text, are themselves sets of constructs. For example, in either Rogerian or humanistic theory, you will find helpers consistently using key words and concepts ("stay with the feeling"; "you seem to feel"). In psychodynamic theory, words such as "Oedipal," "projection," and "denial" can be viewed as sets of constructs. Each major theory has a set of constructs tied with it. If the client has personal constructs that relate closely to the constructs of the theory, counseling and psychotherapy may proceed more easily, at least in the early stages. At the same time, diversity of construct systems between counselor and client may be enriching. Thus, it seems logical that the introduction of constructs from the therapist's theory may indeed help free the client for more creative, intentional action in the world. However, it once again seems clear that it would be wise for the therapist to understand the construct system of the client before giving absolute commitment to a single theory.

A counselor's personal and environmental boundaries need constant exploration to avoid rigidity or excessive looseness in personal construct development. Kelly views psychotherapy as a science, and the scientist needs to be objective and systematic in development. "The primary approach should be to help the therapist develop a professional construction system which is printable, psychologically informed, systematically intact, scientifically supported, amenable to searching inquiry, and in process of continuing revision" (Kelly, 1955, p. 1180). Some specific suggestions for examination of yourself as a counselor are given in Figure 6.5. As you move to the second major section of this book and examine psychological theory in more depth, you will likely find some theories more attractive than others. As you make your determinations as to which theories are most compatible for you, keep the psychology of personal constructs in mind. While there may be nothing so useful as a good theory, there likewise may be nothing so harmful as a good theory put to inappropriate use.

A traditional view of the environment was presented in the preceding section. A second consideration of person-environment transaction is now important. *The counselor or therapist is an environment that the client experiences.* In that environment, the counselor influences and is influenced by the client. The counselor through use of different theories and different counseling skills provides the most satisfactory environment possible for the client. (See Figure 6.5.)

Each person you talk to brings to the interview his or her own individual history of environmental transaction. Each has been shaped by unique personal experience, sexual identity, family background, and other environmental factors.

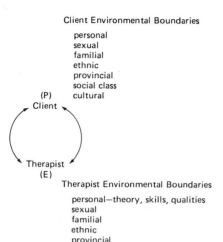

Client Environmental Boundaries

    personal
    sexual
    familial
    ethnic
    provincial
    social class
(P)   cultural
Client

Therapist
(E)

Therapist Environmental Boundaries

    personal—theory, skills, qualities
    sexual
    familial
    ethnic
    provincial
    social class
    cultural

Figure 6.5 Counselor-Client Transaction: Person and Environment

Each, in turn, has influenced, through behavior, some degree of change in her or his own environment. You, as counselor or therapist, bring a similar array of background and experiences. Two people, often from vastly different backgrounds, meet in the interview. You, the counselor, serve as an environment for the client, and the client simultaneously serves as your environment. Whether the result of your transaction will be successful or unsuccessful counseling, both you and the client will change in some way as a result of your interaction.

If the counselor or therapist is to be effective with the client, the maximum "match" between person and environmental factors is to be desired. For example, each kind of client described in Figure 6.1 will likely be more comfortable with a therapist who understands or has experienced her or his background. If the therapist comes from a similar background, a relationship is more easily established. Knowledge of clients who come from different environmental backgrounds can be acquired through study of the many backgrounds of clients and from counseling theory.

There is obviously no end to the possibilities or the need for the counselor and therapist to learn more about different environments of their clients. Furthermore, there is need for counselors to continually learn more both about counseling and therapy theories and about themselves so as to provide the most useful environment for client growth. Figure 6.6 presents an exercise in developmental mapping that has been found to be helpful in enabling counselors and therapists to look at themselves and their environmental history and anticipate the type of environment they provide for their clients. It is an exercise that takes some time and thought, but it also will give you a clearer idea of where you personally stand as a counselor or therapist.

Figure 6.6 *Exercise in Developmental Mapping and Personal Constructs*

Return to the developmental map of the life cycle (Figure 6.1). It provides a useful frame of reference to view the client's development stage. However, it also provides a systematic way for you to examine your own development and to consider how you came to emphasize certain constructs in your own personal worldview. *The developmental map you generate is an important part of the environment that you provide for your client.* This exercise is relatively lengthy, but it can provide useful benefits for understanding some of your strengths and needs as you seek to serve others in the counseling and therapy process.

1. *Life Stage.* Where are you chronologically in terms of your own life stage? What one significant event do you associate with this particular age?

    Next, list one significant event that occurs to you from each earlier stage. Brainstorm brief lists of words for each life event as they occur to you. Significant life events form an important part of your personal construct system.

    Do you note words (constructs) in your brainstorming list that might have impact on your present work with clients, either positively or negatively?
2. *Key Systems.* What are your current key systems (family, work, school, peers, community)? Are your key systems similar to those proposed by Egan and Cowen? What words and constructs do each of these systems use? How do these systems impact on your own personal constructs and behavior?
3. *Developmental Tasks.* What major developmental tasks have you mastered? Which ones were difficult for you? Many clients will come to you as they work through varying developmental tasks. How effectively will you be helping another person with a task you have not yet encountered (for example, an older person winding down career involvement)?
4. *Developmental Resources.* Look through the entire list of developmental resources and rate yourself from one (low) to five (high) on each. How well will you be able to help those individuals whose developmental resources are different from your own?

    You may also wish to add your specific life skills that may be beneficial to your clients (for example, counseling skills, work skills, social skills, knowledge). What areas of client problems will you find easy to understand? Difficult?
5. *Developmental Crises.* How well have you worked through the polarities of the several developmental crises? What is your evaluation of your current developmental crisis? Are you "off" or "on" the chart of Figure 6.1? How might your experiences with these crises relate to your own work in counseling?
6. *Review the above self-examination list.* Look for key words and constructs that repeat themselves and for items that may be of special significance to you as a counselor as you provide an environment for another human being.

    In what areas would you like to develop your potential more fully? Do you plan any action?

Keep this self-study inventory and personal map. It may help you determine how and why you select a particular theory from among the many possibilities. You may find, for example, that key constructs and ideas you have been using are congruent with existing theoretical constructions.

What Is To Be Done?

In emergency cases, such as child-beating, wife abuse, or threats of suicide, it is clear that the therapist's constructions of the client's situation (definition of problem) should take precedence. Referral, hospitalization, supply of overnight housing, and other crisis interventions are the province of the therapist who takes responsibility when the client is unable or unwilling to.

In most cases, however, the design of a treatment plan is conducted jointly between the client and counselor and can allow for a vast array of alternatives:

> . . . treatment can proceed on several fronts. There may . . . be psychotherapy of the individual interview type. There may be orientation sessions for the client's family. There may be groupings of the client with other clients or with other persons in his community. At the same time there may be occupational guidance. There may be recreational supervision . . . we conceive of psychotherapy as involving a great variety of procedures and skills. So widely may these vary from case to case that a procedure which is used predominantly with one client may never be used in precisely the same way with another. . . .
>
> There is a sense in which personal-construct psychology, in accepting a wide variety of psychotherapeutic procedures, is eclectic. The theoretical grounds upon which the varying procedures are accepted do not, however, represent eclecticism. There is no particular objection to eclecticism implied by this. It is interesting to note, in passing, that when eclecticism is itself systematically formulated it loses its eclectic flavor. (Kelly, 1955, pp. 810–811)

Each client will require a uniquely individual treatment plan, and it is unlikely that any one theory will suffice for all clients.

The *treatment plan* is a specific plan of action to use with your client over a series of interviews. It is the result of an effective assessment coupled with an awareness of your own personal constructs and theoretical orientation. One model for outlining your plan for working with your client is summarized in Figure 6.7. Here it may be seen that the information you generate via the interview and assessment may be organized in brief form and used to bring together client data from assessment procedures and testing with additional information generated in the interview. The problems and assets of the client may be summarized along with ideal resolutions of concerns. Critical, of course, is the organization of possibilities for helping clients work through their major issues of incongruity. Here can be listed your own and the client's ideas about resolution and the various available theories and techniques of counseling and therapy. Finally, generalization plans to implement change can be considered. *Assessment and helping interventions that do not include planned change as part of the treatment plan are likely to be ineffective and lost over time.*

Some issues that Kelly has identified as important in determining what is to be done in treatment include the time and emotional investment a client is willing to put into the therapeutic process, the relationship and communication process (and transference) between counselor and client, the emotions of the client

---

Figure 6.7 *Treatment plan (over several interviews)*

1. Rapport/structuring	How does this client develop rapport? What issues are of most comfort/discomfort? How does the client respond to structuring? At what place will structuring be most helpful?
2. Problem definition and summary of assets	List below, in order of importance, the several problem areas of the client. Include a listing of the client's strengths and assets for coping with these issues.
3. Defining outcomes	What are your and the client's ideal outcomes for these issues?
4. Exploring alternatives/ confronting incongruity	What are the main items of client incongruity? How might they best be confronted? What techniques and theories are most appropriate?
5. Generalization	What are your specific plans for generalization of learning from the interview?

From A. Ivey, *Intentional Interviewing and Counseling* (Monterey, CA: Brooks/Cole, 1983), pp. 296–297.

(particularly degree of threat, fear, anxiety, and guilt manifested in the interview), and the precise nature of the presenting complaint.

Kelly, himself, defines psychological disorder as "any personal construction which is used repeatedly in spite of consistent invalidation" (1955, p. 831). It logically follows that the goal of therapy and counseling is to remove blockages and the repeated use of overly loose or overly tight constructs, and to free the person for more creative responding and intentionality. However, Kelly is willing to set a more modest goal. "We may say, simply, that the goal of psychotherapy is to alleviate complaints—complaints of a person about himself and others and complaints of others about him" (Kelly, 1955, p. 831).

Kelly points out that psychodynamic techniques can be useful in loosening clients with overly tight constructs while the more systematic behavioral techniques may be helpful with those with loose construct systems. Given this point of view, the way a person thinks about the world provides the counselor with an important clue as to which treatment may be most appropriate. Fixed-role therapy and Kelly's treatment methods will not be explored in this book. While they are useful, it is believed that Kelly's main contribution concerns his theory about the total nature of psychotherapy processes.

The parallels between Kelly's seminal thinking and the ideas of intentionality should be obvious. Kelly rejects little from the many theories of psychology, while providing helpful integrations of seemingly diverse fields and ideas. Kelly talks about individuals with usable, "permeable" constructs. A permeable construct "works" and has utility for the person using it. Intentionality requires permeable constructs with adequate flexibility, and the ability to commit oneself to action through use of these constructs.

Thus, the question, "What is to be done with the client?," depends on complete and accurate assessment of the client's condition and problem, the con-

Figure 6.8 *Assessment of Clients: A Summary*

In examining clients and their unique needs, the counselor or therapist can consider the five steps of assessment as defined by George Kelly and adapted in this chapter. You will find these dimensions will enrich the five stage model of the interview discussed in Chapter 2.

1. *What Is the Client's Problem? (Relates to Stage 2 of the Five-Stage Model of the Interview)*
   The client's presenting problem may not be the operational problem around which the helping interview should center. The helper needs to balance an awareness of meeting immediate client needs with assisting the client to see the concern in a broader context.
   Developing an understanding of the client's problem involves questioning similar to that of a newspaper reporter. *Who* is the client? *What* happened? *When* does the problem occur? *Where* does it occur? *How* does the client react to the problem? *Why* does the problem occur?
   Particularly important in assessing the client is awareness of the life stage of the client and the particular developmental resources and developmental crises likely to be underlying the client's concern.

2. *What Are the Client's Constructs for Viewing the World? (Stages 1 and 2 and throughout the interview)*
   The way a person thinks about a problem may be as important as, or more important than, the problem itself. The language a client uses to describe her or his world provides a basic clue to the personal construct system. Constructs are sentences or groups of sentences we use to organize and classify our world.
   The Rep Test is a systematic instrument developed by Kelly to examine how clients organize their world of interpersonal relationships. Through comparison of significant figures in one's life, it is possible to develop a list of key personal constructs. It was also suggested that it is feasible to study ordinary day-to-day conversation or the interview itself to define the personal constructs of clients and the counselor or therapist. Psychological tests provide a major alternative for construct assessment.
   Tight constructions are those which force an overly rigid pattern on the world, while loose constructions lack organization and focus. Desired are premeable constructs that allow flexibility *and* direction. Permeable constructs are closely allied to the thinking process one might expect in an individual who demonstrates intentionality.
   The major alternative theories described in this text (Rogerian, behavioral, etc.) are sets of constructs developed by professionals. While these constructs have considerable evidence for their validity, the matching of appropriate theoretical constructs with the personal constructs of the client appears desirable.

3. *What Is the Client's Situational and Environmental Context? (Stages 2, 3, and 5)*
   The person is a product of the environment, and so, too, is the environment a product of the person. It is not possible to consider an individual outside of her or his transaction with the environment. Seven key factors (personal, sexual, familial, ethnic, provincial, social class, and cultural) were identified as critical environmental factors. Family and culture were noted as being key concerns for effective and meaningful individual assessment.
   Special attention needs to be given to the influence of the environment on the individual. It was pointed out that family background rather than individual choice is a major factor in vocational selection. Symbolic violence was identified as being associated with the unbalanced distribution of power and wealth in society.
   As the counselor or therapist assesses the individual and the several alternative treatment possibilities, it is important to study the situational and environmental context, how the individual constructs her or his picture of that context, and to consider whether or not consciousness raising about the nature of the context is to be part of the helping process. Alternatively, the counselor may consider direct intervention with the environment in addition to individual counseling and therapy.

4. *What are the Counselor's Basic Theories and Constructs? (Throughout the interview)*
   The counselor or therapist serves as an environment for the client. The environment may be supportive or destructive of client growth. Therefore, it is critical that the counselor be aware of her or his own personal construct system and environmental history and their potential impact on the client. Too rigid an attachment to one's own theories and personal constructs can lead to an inability to hear the client, difficulty in appreciating her or his unique construction of the world, and forcing the client consciously or unconsciously into what the therapist believes the world should be.

   Thus, as the counselor begins to assess the client, the counselor needs to be able to assess and understand himself or herself and the potential impact of theory and personal constructs on the client.

5. *What is to be Done? (Stages 3,4, and 5)*
   The ultimate assessment issue is a decision for action. Given the assembly of the vast array of data available, the counselor still needs to decide what action is to be taken. Rather than suggesting a single treatment alternative, a multimodal approach to a client's difficulties seems to be called for. This approach may call for individual psychotherapy, family intervention, training in social skills, or even action in the community and environment itself.

   Intentionality and Kelly's concept of permeable constructs (simultaneously tight and loose) are closely related. Thus, the goal of assessment may be said to be finding specific areas where lack of intentionality exists and then developing programs to enable a person to increase her or his response repetoire. Intentionality and permeable constructs offer a general goal of counseling and psychotherapy.

   A major question is, "Which therapy technique should be used for which individual, at what time, under what conditions?" The answer to this complex question is not yet available. However, it is possible to develop a systematic treatment plan based on the five-stage model of the interview (Figure 6.7) and to use the framework to consider the many complexities of assessment and planning that Kelly suggests.

struct system, and awareness of the environmental milieu. There are many alternatives for treatment, including a wide array of theories for individual work, family therapy, groupwork, and interventions in the environment of the client. Underlying the choice of technique is the degree of tightness or looseness in the client construct system; the most effective technique and theory will tend to be that which has the most leverage to promote change. Finding the most likely successful therapy technique or theory for a particular client has haunted the psychotherapy profession for years.

WHICH THERAPY, WHICH INDIVIDUAL, AT WHAT TIME, UNDER WHAT CONDITIONS?

Where once therapists and counselors argued long and loudly about the "most effective" therapy, the trend now is a developing awareness that many different routes toward counseling clients are effective. However, given certain clients, some methods appear to be more effective than others.

A comprehensive understanding of the client and the client's world is required before the counselor is able to initiate successful treatment. In some cases, existing psychological and therapeutic theory will prove invaluable, as many clients find the insights of a certain system growth-producing. But clients do not always easily fit into our preconceived thoughts about them and what we think will be good for them.

Thus, it seems crucial that you, as counselor or therapist, seek to learn as much as possible about *technique* (such as the concepts proposed in this section) and psychological *theory* (such as that described in Part II). Through a solid knowledge of skills and assessment possibilities, coupled with capability in several alternative theoretical persuasions, you will best be able to understand and answer for yourself the question of which method is likely to be most successful. Then, if the method you select isn't working, you will be free to change your theory and techniques to adapt to the special needs of the unique client before you. Too often, counseling and therapy terminate because the client "wasn't ready for help." More likely than not, the counselor failed to demonstrate intentionality and was unable to assess the situation and realize that another approach might have been more suitable.

Throughout the remainder of this book, the question, "Which therapy technique should be used for which individual, at what time, under what conditions?," should be before you. While theory and research are beginning to develop around this important topic, you as an intentional counselor or therapist will have to make some critical decisions and attend carefully to your client's response to your decisions.

Marshall McLuhan, the popular interpreter of modern media, is noted for his phenomenal ability to change thoughts and conversational direction in midstream. Once, when a discussion was not going well on an innovative idea he was developing with some colleagues, he said, "Well, if you don't like that idea, I've got another." Similarly, if your client doesn't like your idea, technique, or theory, you should be able to generate still another which may be better received.

SUMMARY OF THIS CHAPTER

To understand the concepts of this chapter, it is particularly important that you are able to:

1. *Demonstrate an understanding of the person-environment transaction.* People exist in relationship with the environment, which influences them and which they in turn influence. A model for considering this transaction was presented that stressed seven key dimensions. It was pointed out that these variables not only interact with the individual but also with each other, the result of which is that each client who comes for counseling is different from all others.

2. *Recognize that the counselor brings a special environment to the client.* You, as a person who would help others, have your own history of person-environment transac-

tions. When you work in an interview, you become the environment of the client. Too rigid adherence to your own construct system and worldview may result in your imposing it on the client rather than permitting an even, transactional relationship between two individuals who can learn from one another.

3. *Define and discuss Kelly's law of parsimony in diagnosis and treatment.* This chapter presents a wide array of issues underlying the therapeutic process. In the effort to understand an individual completely, it is possible for the counselor to miss the most central issues. Kelly suggests that the most direct way to find out what is troubling a person is to ask, and then perhaps one will be able to act on the person's own direct statement.

4. *Manifest an elementary understanding of the psychology of personal constructs, as presented by George Kelly.* Kelly has stated that different people construe the world differently due to their unique history. Effective assessment and, eventually, effective therapy require understanding the world as the client sees it. Kelly's constructs were related to earlier discussions in this book on intentionality and the generation of new sentences.

5. *Understand and present the five steps of effective assessment of clients in the interview.* These were defined as: (1) defining the client's problem(s); (2) examining the nature of the client's construct system; (3) determining key factors in the client's environmental context; (4) being aware of the basic theories and constructs that you as therapist bring to the interview; and (5) determining the most useful way of acting on the data generated by the client and counselor. Each of these issues was explored in preliminary form in this chapter; it was emphasized that each issue suggests a wide array of possibilities for discussion with the client. It was also suggested that effective selection of treatment procedures depends on a thorough understanding and assessment of the client.

6. *Understand the critical importance of the question, "Which therapy technique should be used for which individual, at what time, under what conditions?"* Clients vary in their problems, their concerns, their particular history of person-environment transaction. The skilled therapist will have more than one approach or theory to meet varied client needs and wishes.

7. *Define and use key terms in this chapter:* person-environment transaction, B = f(P,E), Robert's seven factors, self-fulfilling prophecy, personal construct system, Repertory Test, interaction between family and culture, symbolic violence, assessment in the interview as problem definition in the first stage of the interview process, development of a systematic treatment plan.

REFERENCES

AMERICAN PSYCHIATRIC ASSOCIATION, *Diagnostic and Statistical Manual of Mental Disorders* (3rd ed.). Washington, DC: APA, 1980.

BANDURA, A., "The Self System in Reciprocal Determinism," *American Psychologist,* April 1978, 344–358.

BOURDIEU, P. and J. PASSERON, *Reproduction in Education, Society, and Culture.* Beverly Hills, CA: Sage Publications, Inc., 1977.

DWIGHT, A., "Once a Blue Collar Worker, Always a Blue Collar Worker?" *Vocational Guidance Quarterly,* 1978, *26*, 318–325.

EGAN, G., and M. COWAN, *People in Systems: An Introduction to Human Development.* Monterey, CA: Brooks/Cole, 1979.

FREUD, S., *Civilization and Its Discontents.* London: Hogarth, 1957.

HUNT, D., *Matching Models in Education.* Toronto: Ontario Institute for Studies in Education, 1971.

HUNT, D. and E. SULLIVAN, *Between Psychology and Education.* Hinsdale, IL: Dryden, 1974.

KELLY, G., *The Psychology of Personal Constructs.* Vols. I and II. New York: Norton, 1955.

KOHLBERG, L., "Moral Education in the Schools: A Developmental View," *School Review,* 1966, *74*, 1–30.

LEWIN, K., *A Dynamic Theory of Personality.* New York: McGraw-Hill, 1935.

MALCOLM X, *The Autobiography of Malcolm X.* New York: Grove, 1964.

MOOS, R., "Creating Human Health Contexts: Environmental and Individual Strategies." In J. Rosen and L. Solomon (eds.), *Prevention in Health Psychology.* Hanover, NH: University Press of New England, 1984.

ROBERTS, D., "Treatment of Cultural Scripts," *Transactional Analysis Journal,* 1975, *5*, 29–35.

ROSENTHAL, R., and L. JACOBSON, *Pygmalion in the Classroom: Teacher Expectation and Pupil's Intellectual Development.* New York: Holt, Rinehart & Winston, 1968.

SKINNER, B., *Science and Human Behavior.* New York: Macmillan, 1953.

SUGGESTED SUPPLEMENTARY READING

EGAN, G., and M. COWAN, *Human Development in Human Systems: A Working Model.* Monterey, CA: Brooks/Cole, 1979.
A comprehensive model for the delivery of mental health and other human services in a person-environment transaction.

GOLDSTEIN, G., and M. HERSEN, *Handbook of Psychological Assessment.* New York: Pergamon, 1984.
A comprehensive overview of the assessment process covering topics ranging from interviewing to testing to neuropsychological assessment. This book is perhaps the most broadly based current summary of issues in assessment. No specific chapter on cultural assessment in this particular book, however.

KELLY, G., *The Psychology of Personal Constructs.* Vols. I and II. New York: Norton, 1955.
The work of George Kelly will continue to receive increased recognition as the years pass. This basic series provides a comprehensive overview of his work.

MEEHL, P., *Psychodiagnosis: Selected Papers.* New York: Norton, 1973.
An important figure historically in the diagnostic field, Meehl presents his ideas about diagnosis and assessment in literary and stimulating fashion. His chapter "Why I Do Not Attend Case Conferences" is a must.

SPITZER, R., A. SKODOL, M. GIBBON, and J. WILLIAMS, *DSM-III: Casebook.* Washington, DC: American Psychiatric Association, 1981.
Many case examples of how the diagnostic formulations of DSM-III can be utilized to classify a wide variety of patients.

7

INTEGRATING POSITIVE SKILLS TOWARD PLANNED CHANGE

GENERAL PREMISE

An integrated knowledge of skills, theory, and practice is essential for culturally intentional counseling and therapy.

Skills form the foundation of effective theory and practice: The culturally intentional therapist knows how to construct a creative decision-making interview and can use microskills to attend to and influence clients in a predicted direction. Important in this process are individual and cultural empathy, client observation skills, assessment of person and environment, and *the application of positive techniques of growth and change*.

Theory provides organizing principles for counseling and therapy: The culturally intentional counselor has knowledge of alternative theoretical approaches and treatment modalities.

Practice is the integration of skills and theory: The culturally intentional counselor or therapist is competent in skills and theory, and is able to apply them to research and practice for client benefit.

Undergirding integrated competence in skills, theory, and practice is an intentional awareness of one's own personal worldview and how that worldview may be similar to and/or different from the worldview and personal constructions of the client and other professionals.

GOALS OF INTEGRATING SKILLS AND THE POSITIVE ASSET SEARCH

The skills, qualities, and constructs of the first six chapters of this text may be integrated into a smoothly flowing interview that is greater than the sum of its parts. Once you understand and have mastered skills, you are then prepared to use these abilities in a wide variety of theoretical orientations.

This chapter seeks to:

1. Present an ineffective interview as an example of what not to do. This session will be analyzed using the general theoretical skills model of the first six chapters.
2. Outline and demonstrate the positive asset search. Two additional interviews will be presented to illustrate how skills may be integrated naturally into ongoing interviews. Emphasis will be placed on the positive asset search as a means of reframing client problems from a more optimistic point of view.
3. Point out how the positive asset search is described in several different theoretical orientations. For example, the concept is important in person-centered theory, decisional counseling, and cognitive-behavioral approaches.

As you read the material in the following pages, you will note frequent references to earlier or later chapters. The ideas here form an important bridge between the skills of the first section and the theories of the following chapters. Again, if you master these first chapters, you have basic skills and understandings that can be used with a wide variety of theories. You will find that the content and use of the skill varies, for example, in psychodynamic and behavioral approaches; but the underlying skills and concepts form a foundation for a higher mastery of the new theory.

HOW NOT TO HELP A CLIENT

One of the best ways to clarify the helping process is to look specifically at what helping is *not*. In the following demonstration, prepared for training clarity, the therapist does virtually everything wrong. Let us look at the interview and then analyze the session against the criteria and assumptions of the first chapters of this text.* Later in this chapter, we will present two positive demonstrations of interviewing, one from a transactional analysis perspective (Chapter 12) and one from a general theoretical orientation. ("Mary," the therapist, and "Charles," the client, will be indicated by "M." and "C.")

---

*The interview presented and analyzed in this chapter is taken from a videotape on interpretation and reframing in which Mary Bradford Ivey demonstrates the concepts described in this chapter. An analysis of this interview from a Piagetian cognitive-developmental frame of reference is also available in Ivey (1986). Interview transcript, copyright Microtraining Assoc., 1983, by permission.

Mary Bradford Ivey

1. M:	Would you like to talk a little about the concern that you have to share today, Charles?	1. Open question
2. C:	Well, yes, there's something that even happened this morning, and that is . . . ah . . . the house was a mess. And we had some stuff to do before we went out. So, I knew the kids were busy, so I started to pick up for them. And, as I picked up—I didn't have any feelings, I guess, as I began. But, I began to get more tired and really began to feel angry.	
3. M:	Tired and angry?	3. Encourager
4. C:	Yeah, ah, you see, I've got a lot to do myself. What am I doing picking up this stuff for the kids? . . . So I just went ahead, but, I ended up yelling, and it ended up one of those horrible scenes, Mary.	
5. M:	So you were tired and pushed and you ended up picking up for the kids and doing something you really didn't want to do?	5. Summary

(To this point, Mary has used the basic listening sequence fairly well. She has brought out the main facts of the problem and how the client feels about the facts rather quickly. More concreteness and elaboration on the situation, however, might be helpful. The summary is brief and a little early.)

6. C:	Yeah . . .	
7. M:	You know, it goes back to, it seems to me, you know, we talked about some things like this before. . . . You're very much like your father. . . . You know, he likes to have everything organized and he likes to take charge of things, a little bit compulsive about things.	7. Interpretation

8.	C:	(Somewhat defensively) You feel I'm too compulsive?
9.	M:	Well, I would think so in this situation. You didn't need to do all these things, but you just went ahead and did them anyway.
10.	C:	(More acceptingly) . . . Ah, I hadn't thought of it that way.

9. Feedback/Interpretation

In this brief example, we see clearly the power that the therapist has over the client. Clients lack intentionality when they come to the session: they are often hungry and anxious for a new point of view or perhaps even a new worldview with which to approach their difficulties. Above, we see that Mary, the therapist, listened fairly effectively and readily won the trust of the client. Very shortly, the client was accepting her worldview and using her constructs (for example, "compulsive," "like father").

Viewed from the constructs of the general theory presented in this section, we might note the following problems of the interview:

1. *Intentionality.* The client does have a new frame of reference from which to view the problem, but the view is that of the therapist who has effectively imposed her view on the client. While her view may be correct, it remains "her view."

2. *Creative decision making.* The counselor has supplied the creativity. The goal of the interview has been established by the therapist, not by the client. Given that the therapist has established the goal, chances for implementation of change in behavior or thinking are reduced. In addition, the client's behavior has been viewed negatively and there has been no positive asset search.

3. *Microskill usage.* Given the brevity of the example, the therapist has used the basic listening sequence and managed to bring out the client's main thoughts and feelings about the problem and has summarized them briefly. Her interpretation has been accepted after initial resistance. Clearly, this therapist is influencing her client. Is the impact for good or ill? Persuasive microskill usage is not enough to equal a quality session that facilitates client growth.

4. *Cultural and individual empathy.* The therapist seems to understand the client fairly well, but has not demonstrated this adequately. The client comes from a second-generation Celtic-Anglo background in which emphasis on individual responsibility is sometimes excessive. The behavior of the client, then, is typical of individuals of that particular cultural background. The therapist is of Swedish-Anglo extraction. As such, there is a fair cultural match between the two, but neither are demonstrating awareness of the fact that cultural issues underlie even such a common problem as how one relates to children's "messes." Such lack of awareness of underlying cultural/ethnic differences is relatively common when both therapist and client come from middle-class backgrounds and are white. This would seem to underscore the importance of each individual understanding more about his or her cultural background. What is seen as a "problem" of the father being overly conscientious (compulsive) is a common cultural trait in the Celtic-Anglo tradition. Cultural awareness can help clients understand their "problems" more completely and look at issues in a broader context.

5. *Client observation skills.* The therapist has not given sufficient attention to the client's obvious nonverbal defensiveness and resistance to her interpretation. She has given little attention to his surface structure sentences. She has fairly effectively paced the

client and has used many of his own main words. Her effectiveness here makes it possible for her to lead him to accept her own construction of the world. The confrontation has been implicit rather than explicit and has not allowed the client to generate his own picture of reality.

6. *Person/environment interaction.* In the brief segments presented in this chapter, presentation of any meaningful positive or negative assessment is impossible. However, it may be seen that the therapist has decided her construction of the client is the "correct" one, and we find a general pattern of the client gradually assuming the worldview of the therapist and giving up his own. The client is learning to see the world through the counselor's glasses.

Figure 7.1 (p. 183) presents a summary of issues that may be used to assess your own interviews with clients on the dimensions of the first section of this book. Given these factors, it may be seen that the therapist has done a good number of things in a less than effective manner. This does not mean, however, that the therapist is wrong in her interpretations. Compulsiveness and repeating past patterns of one's parents are common issues, particularly given the cultural background of the client. The question rises, "Would there be a more effective way to facilitate client change and growth in intentionality?"

USING THEORY TO ASSIST CLIENT INTENTIONALITY

It may now be appropriate for a second try at the session. You will find a more positive method of handling the client in the following interviewing segment; as Mary, the therapist, continues her demonstration. The therapist is working from a transactional analysis framework (see Chapter 12), a popular modern theory derived from psychoanalytic and humanistic conceptions of helping. Transactional analysis (TA) is considering especially helpful by many therapists due to its relatively straightforward and clear language system, which explains complex psychoanalytic constructs in understandable form for the client. After you have read this interview, we will again analyze the session using the criteria of the earlier chapters of this text. (The therapist Mary is "M" and the client Charles is "C.")

11. M: OK, I, let's summarize where we were after that awful negative interpretation that I did. Ummm. . . . The house was really a mess . . .   11. Summary

12. C: It sure was.

13. M: And you really were very, very tired and you were angry and you did all the work picking things up. Ummm, have you ever, can you get into that feeling of tired and angry? Have you had that same feeling in other situations? Can you get into that feeling?   13. Summary/Directive

(Here, Mary uses the directive of focused free association, similar to that used by Joann in her interview with Mr. S. This technique can be helpful in understanding repeating patterns of behavior in both current and past situations. You may also note that Mary is using the feeling or kinesthetic perceptual system described in Chapter 5 on client observation skills. She is clearly leading the client.)

14.	C:	Oh yeah, I very much can. Ah . . . in fact, right away it comes to me that my secretary, Georgia . . . and Georgia is a lovely person. And if I detail everything for Georgia to do, she does a marvelous job. But I often find . . .	
15.	M:	You look angry right there.	15. Reflection of feeling

(Using her observation skills of nonverbal communication, Mary notes the incongruity between the positive things Charles is saying and his facial expression. She also used the present-tense concept of immediacy.)

16.	C:	. . . Ah . . . then I end up doing Georgia's work and she sits there reading a magazine. Sometimes it's harder to explain to her what to do, so I just go ahead and do it myself.	
17.	M:	So rather than—	17. Encourager
18.	C:	And, I really don't blow up at her. I think sometimes the poor kids get me blowing up because Georgia isn't doing her job.	

(This could be considered an example of the Freudian defense mechanism of displacement.)

19.	M:	Because she's not doing her job, you're doing Georgia's job, and getting angry at the kids.	19. Interpretation

(Here Mary is supplying the cognitive *linkage* between the two situations. See page 204.)

20.	C:	Yeah, I kinda like Georgia . . . and she comes in and talks about her problems with me and you know, I kinda like to help her when I can . . . and I know she's having some issues right now. So I. . . . Nonetheless, it still leaves it right there on my shoulders. (He touches his shoulders as if to represent the responsibility resting there. This is another example of the individualistic cultural assumptions of many middle-class North Americans.)	
21.	M:	Leaves you tight and angry. Uh-huh . . .	21. Reflection of feeling
22.	C:	Yes . . .	
23.	M:	Remember how we talked about some TA concepts and we talked about the concept of the, ah, critical parent, oh, parenting. And I sometimes wonder in this situation if you're not playing a parent role with her. You know, you . . .	23. Instruction/interpretation

(A common technique among those who employ TA theory is to teach clients important constructs of the theory in a psychoeducational sense and then later use these concepts to interpret the client's behavior.)

24. C: In other words, like the kids, I'm playing the role with Georgia.

(Note that the client is now assuming the language and constructs of the therapist's worldview.)

25. M: Yeah, the same kind of thing. You know, you're doing her work for her and you're letting her get by with not doing it and then you're coming home and, you know, you're taking it out on the kids . . . the same sort of thing with the kids. How does that seem to fit with you?

25. Interpretation/checkout

26. C: (Grabs stomach). . . I feel my body just sort of react to that. Yeah, I hadn't thought about that really. I do tend to be too critical of people. Ah . . . I . . . but, the thing is . . . they just aren't doing the job and . . . the thing is that it makes me feel badly though again. It isn't as bad as compulsive, but, . . . on the other hand . . . being critical all the time . . .

(It is important to note that clients who experience accurate interpretations may initially have extensive verbal and nonverbal incongruences. Charles's nonverbals are mixed and confused. You will also note a number of speech hesitations. This is an indication of his formerly tightly constructed surface structure sentences being loosened. He is taking a new look at his worldview. Critical in this process was the checkout, "How does that seem to fit with you?" This checkout enables Charles to reflect on the interpretation of parallel behavior and feelings in two different situations.)

27. M: Yeah, but there are some positives in that situation, Charles. Can you see some of the positives? I mean, not only are you a critical parent, you're also a nurturing parent, you know.

27. Feedback/Question/open interpretation

(This is a particularly critical lead. Having loosened Charles's construct system or worldview, Mary now seeks to inculcate a more permeable system of thinking. She brings in positive assets and asks Charles to think about what he may be doing right in the situation.)

28. C: Positives? . . . How's that? That doesn't make sense.

29. M: Well, I think that you're really trying to take care of everybody when you're straightening up

29. Interpretation

the house and you know that people are tired.
(C: That's true.) You know your secretary's under a lot of pressure. You know that the kids
have all kinds of work to do, and so in some ways
you can almost reframe what you're doing into
being a positive, ummm . . . , nurturing type
parent. Does that fit?

(This is a classic positive reframing of a negative situation and is discussed in more
detail in the next section, where alternative uses of the positive asset search are
explored. Note that Mary once again wisely used the checkout. She has provided
again important linkage showing to the client the similarity of the situations that,
before her interpretation, were seen as separate. This pointing out of parallels in
situations is characteristic of psychodynamic theory and transactional analysis of
scripts.)

30. C: Yeah, nurturing comes up, it feels right because
           I guess I did say I like the kids . . . you know . . .
           they're busy and I like to help them and I know
           that Georgia is not really in a great spot. . . . But
           it sure ends up with me getting angry. . . . Ah!
           So, in effect, by being nurtur . . . so nurturing,
           I end up being (M: very critical.) . . . very critical
           and very angry . . .

(This might be termed the moment of insight. Charles has now built linkage into
his own construction of the world and has new personal constructs with which to
consider two current troubling situations. Interestingly, the *facts* of the two situations remain the same, but the *emotions* around those same situations are beginning
to change. This is a result that you often aim for in cognitively oriented therapy.)

31. M: Yeah. And my question to you is, where is the   31. Open Question/confron-
           adult? You know how we've talked about the   tation
           parent, adult, and child. Where is the adult in
           the situation that takes change and does some-
           thing?

In the above exchange, we have seen the client move from a negative view
of self and others toward a more positive self-image and, also, a more respectful,
less intrusive relationship with children and his secretary. He has what may be
termed, "a beginning insight." Beginning insights, however, are not actions. Just
because a person understands a situation more fully does not mean that they are
able to act differently. Some sort of generalization plan from the final stage of the
interview (discussed in Chapter 2) is necessary if Charles will change his actions.

It may be useful briefly to review the major general theoretical constructs
of the first six chapters as they relate to this brief segment. First, the client does
demonstrate specific changes in intentionality. Clearly his worldview and construct

Figure 7.1 *Seven Dimensions for Assessing the Effectiveness of an Interview*

The following is a brief summary of the seven major ideas of the first section of this book. Each may be used to assess the completeness and effectiveness of a counselor or therapist's interventions with a client.

1. *Intentionality.* How many ways do you as a counselor have to facilitate client growth and development? Given that your client may be immobilized and stuck at the beginning of counseling and therapy, how many options do they generate by the end of your work?
2. *Creative Decision Making.* Do your clients generate their own goals for therapy or do you provide them with your own goals? Do you include a positive asset search in your problem definition? Do you generate at least three alternatives for action? Is there an action plan for implementation of new alternatives? Is your client vigilant and intentional, or does the decision process appear more limited?
3. *Microskills.* Can you use microskills intentionally to achieve specific impact on your client? Particularly, can you bring out the facts, feelings, and sometimes reasons and meanings underlying your client's problem? Through the use of attending skills and the basic listening sequence, can you describe the world as the client sees, hears, and feels it? Through the use of influencing skills, can your client generate alternative perspectives on his or her situation? Are microskills used in a culturally sensitive manner?
4. *Individual and Cultural Empathy.* Are you able to enter the unique frame of reference of your client through use of individual empathy and related constructs such as immediacy, concreteness, and positive regard? Are you able to modify the empathic constructs to meet the unique cultural background of your client, while simultaneously respecting personal uniqueness? After work with you, is your client more empathic and respectful of *other* individuals and cultures? Your client not only needs to be understood but can also profit from understanding others.
5. *Client Observation Skills.* Are you able to observe and mirror both verbal and nonverbal language of the client? Can you take a surface structure sentence and discover, with the client, the underlying deeper structures and meanings? Are you able to pace the client respectfully and lead them in appropriate new directions? Can you identify discrepancies and resolve them through confrontation? How does your client respond to your confrontations—with denial, a partial examination of the discrepancy, an acknowledgment of the discrepancy, or synthesis with a new construction or new worldview?
6. *Person/Environment Transaction.* Are you able to use Kelly's basic assessment model to maintain the personal uniqueness of your client in a culturally relevant manner? Are you able to provide an appropriate environment for client growth and development?
7. *Integration.* Are you able to integrate the above skills, qualities, and constructs in a smoothly flowing interview that promotes positive change in the client? In particular, are you able to utilize some systematic format from the positive asset search (page 185 and following) to enable your client to construct a worldview that builds at least partially on identified strengths?

system have been enlarged. The general goals for change have again been defined by the therapist. Once you commit yourself to a specific theory, the theory itself sometimes defines the goals of healthy change, although you may modify the goals within this framework. You may also note, however, that the insight-oriented TA segment here provides little in the way of planned behavior change and generalization.

Mary, the therapist, has used microskills rather effectively. She has recovered from the negative demonstration and been able to be an active, influential therapist as she has facilitated change in the client's thoughts and feelings about the situation. Perhaps the most important impact microskills can have on the client is cognitive change in attitudes toward the facts of a situation. In this situation, the facts have not yet changed. However, in the first session, the client feels helpless and guilty. In the second, the client views the same facts with a sense of optimism and a beginning sense of intentionality.

The therapist has demonstrated empathy toward the client. She has been able to view the situation from his perspective, but she has used "additive empathy" to add more to Charles's limited perspective. She is also still working within the self-actualized, individualistic perspective that ultimately lays responsibility on the client. North Americans and Western Europeans tend to be self-actualized and individualistic in their perspectives. This emphasis on the individual seems to be working well with Charles, given his cultural background, but we cannot assume the same would be true if he were Black, Asian-American, Hispanic, or from any of a wide array of cultures that take a more relational orientation. In some cultures, this emphasis on individual self-actualization could be a serious error.

The therapist has done an excellent job of observing her client and noting and using nonverbal and verbal behavior and its incongruities. Her confrontation has been gentle and has included a checkout to allow the client to find "his own space" and construct his own view of the situation. Mary has provided a working environment in which she allows Charles to influence her, which in turn promotes the dialogue of empathy. She takes data from Charles and uses it in an informed and conscious way to produce change. Empathy is not just applying core conditions of helping, it is also being respectful of the individual and using client data and frame of reference (or worldview) to help build new constructions or alternatives for confronting the reality of a complex world.

Finally, it should be noted that the therapist used transactional analysis theory fairly well to help the client broaden his worldview. The client's language system and surface structure (and deep structure) sentences are beginning to change. His nonverbal behavior and speech hesitations indicate the beginning of that change. Given continuation of this effective treatment, it may be anticipated that Charles will become a devotee of TA method and theory. We should note, however, that the language system and worldview of the client has come to resemble that of the therapist.

The word *therapist* is important. Therapy is a remedial process in which the task is to shape the worldview of the client to more effective perspectives. Also, typically important in therapy is the linkage of seemingly different events with one another. In this case, Charles has discovered that the way he behaves with his children is structurally similar to the way he interacts with his secretary. If we were to look further, we would likely find a *pattern* of behavior that Charles often repeats in many different situations. Most of your clients will have patterns of thought and behavior that repeat themselves again and again in different situations. Frozen repetitions such as this represent important examples of the lack of intentionality.

Counseling is also concerned with restructuring repeating patterns of behavior, but psychotherapy is concerned with a total reconstruction of repeating patterns. Repeating patterns of behavior usually come from childhood learning, but they may sometimes come from more recent traumas of living. The task of both counseling and psychotherapy is to change patterns . . . some psychotherapists and clinical psychologists believe that many, many patterns *must* be unearthed and *linked* if long-lasting change is to occur. Most counselors and counseling psychologists would subscribe to the same point, but they, along with many psychotherapists and clinicians, would argue that effective reconstruction of limited areas of patterning may be sufficient to enable long-term positive growth. Once patterns are unearthed and dealt with effectively, the client learns a new, more positive way of coping with situations that are inevitably going to repeat themselves. Some argue that a solid change in one pattern is all that is needed to induce later, larger change in the individual.

One particularly effective way to implement change is for the counselor to give special attention to the positive asset search in its many theoretical variations. Mary's third session with Charles will (later in this chapter) illustrate this point. But, first let us examine the nature of the positive asset search.

THE POSITIVE ASSET SEARCH

Taking a positive approach and noting strengths in the client has been stressed throughout the early portion of this text. You will conduct a more effective decisional interview if you note positive aspects of the client; Joann Griswold demonstrated consistent emphasis on positives with Mr. S. in her interview in Chapter 3. Furthermore, different individuals and different cultural groups will view varying attitudes as positive. For example, in many Asian groups, *dependence* is a positive value, whereas in individualistic North American culture *independence* and *self-actualization* are seen as positives (in much of the rest of the world, this trait is seen as selfish and negative).

If you are empathic toward individuals and their cultural background, you will have taken a major step toward finding positives in their situations. From this observation, you are in a better position to promote growth and development. The environment you provide will more likely be a respectful, culturally appropriate one that promotes varying types of cultural intentionality rather than imposing one single view on the client.

In the interview demonstrating transactional analysis the therapist took client negative thinking and helped the client reinterpret his behavior more positively (M: "Yeah, but there are some positives in that situation, Charles. Can you see some of the positives? I mean, not only are you a critical parent, you're also a nurturing parent, you know"). Theoretically, her actions are based on the "positive asset search" (Ivey, 1983). The positive asset search may be considered a metatheoretical or general concept underlying effective therapy and counseling. However, the idea of being positive with clients is not unique to this text. It is an old and respected tenet of the helping profession. However, what may be considered new about the positive asset search is that it links many different types of therapy in the goal of positively reframing a client's life experience.

Leona Tyler in her classic counseling text of 1953 and 1961 presents some of the underlying thinking which leads to the more general construct of the positive asset search:

> In place of the kind of diagnosis that often preceded therapy, the initial stages of minimum change therapy include a process that might be called *exploration of resources*. The counselor pays little attention to personality weaknesses that are adequately controlled or neutralized. He notes what difficulties are actually blocking the person's forward movement but is on the alert for the possibility that even these may be bypassed rather than attacked. What he is most persistent in trying to locate are ways of coping with anxiety and stress, already existing resources that may be enlarged and strengthened once their existence is recognized. (Tyler, 1953, 1961)

In her discussion, Tyler stresses working with the client's construction of reality rather than imposing an external theoretical model on the client. Tyler also believes that this emphasis on positive assets is typical of counseling as compared to therapy. She presents evidence that this positivistic worldview may provide profound consequences for personal growth and change in the client.

The positive asset search could be said to represent an expansion of the concept of "exploration of resources." The positive asset search seeks to show that much of effective therapeutic work relies on the reframing of life experience, not only from a new point of view, but also from a more positive orientation. This may provide a useful rationale for considering underlying general issues linking alternative therapeutic modalities.

Ivey (1983) has suggested that the positive asset search may be viewed as a special form of the basic listening sequence and thus is not only a theoretical idea, but is also a set of practical skills. To conduct a positive asset search, you need to bring out the positive in a client's situation via the listening skills. What are the facts, feelings, and organization of something positive in the client's life? This identification of positives will often provide clients with the security to look more deeply into negative and troubled areas of their lives. In turn, through the use of a positive interpretation the client may be helped to look at a negative situation more positively.

Figure 7.2 presents in summary form the idea that different modes of helping use different techniques to achieve a somewhat similar goal—the reframing or reconsideration of life from a more positive point of view. At one level, this concept may seem trite; however, the critical force of positive thinking cannot be denied. *The Diary of Anne Frank* is one impressive example of the positive asset search. Anne Frank was forced to grow up as an adolescent in one small room in Holland. As she hid from the Nazi's, she lived and grew through her ability to find good in even the most troubled of situations. The critical force of positive assets cannot be easily denied.

Figure 7.2   *The Positive Asset Search as Found in Varying Theoretical Orientations*

The positive asset search emphasizes the importance of clients' strengths and positives, both in the individual and environmental surround. Characteristic of the positive asset search (PAS) is that it is structured from the worldview of the client and does not impose a theoretically based linguistic system. Each of the following techniques may be considered variations of the PAS and may be employed according to your and your client's needs and interests.

Method and Derivation	Summary of Method; Microskill Sequences
1. Exploration of Resources: Tyler, Counseling Psychology	Locate resources of client that may be enlarged when once recognized—small "minimum changes" may be important in the early stages. Draw out the resource via the basic listening sequence, then clarify it, and finally reinforce client on positives.
2. Positive Regard: Rogers, Humanistic Psychology	Reflect positive meanings and ideas in many client statements that at first glance appear to be negative. In a broader sense, use encourages, paraphrases, and reflections of feelings emphasizing positive dimensions. Offer positive feedback and self-disclosures. Process continues throughout the interview.
3. Finding new meanings: Frankl, Psychodynamic, humanistic	(1) Draw out client's problem using basic listening sequence. Emphasize questions relating to meaning ("What does this mean to you?" "What sense do you make of it?") Reflect meaning. (2) Draw out positive meaning in situation through questions and reflection of meaning. (3) Confront client with, "On one hand, the negatives in your situation are . . . but on the other hand, the positives are . . . ". Clients will tend to synthesize the incongruity into a more positive view of the situation.
4. Focusing: Gendlin, Humanistic	(1) Isolate feeling or emotion of client; (2) ask client to free associate to a specific problem situation; (3) have client feel and experience problem fully through complete attention; (4) find a positive thought or feeling; (5) experience the positive thought or feeling fully; (6) return to the original problem and ask client to experience the same problem using the positive experience. Use auditory, visual, feeling words to magnify the experience.
5. Reframing: Erickson; Bandler and Grinder; Lankton	(1) Establish rapport and match client language and verbal and nonverbal behavior; (2) identify unpleasant experience from past (or present) and use perceptual systems (see, hear, feel) to exaggerate and magnify issue; (3) obtain a positive experience from the past or present and associate it with the past or current problem; (4) ask client to join positive with negative. Alternative: at step 3 ask client what is positive about the old or current experience (similar to Tyler); look to present strengths and assets, and past positives. Make an attempt to have

	the positives overbalance the negatives; at step 4 join the positive with the negative. (If positive does not overcome negative, that is "fine" . . . this is more data and the plan then becomes to use the positive to *lessen* the negative.)
6. Cognitive-behavioral: Beck; Ellis	(1) Recognize maladaptive thinking; (2) note repeating patterns of thinking—automatic thoughts; (3) use distancing or decentering procedures to help clients remove themselves from immediate fears—assess facts and feelings about the situation; (4) change the rules by introducing more positive logic or facts into the situation, thus changing their worldview.
7. Summary	All of the above appear to use the client's main words and constructions of the situation, regardless of their theory. Each tries to first listen to and understand the thoughts and feelings of the client (the basic listening sequence). Then, each tries to find some positive asset in the client and/or situation and suggests that the client use those data to more fully respect themselves and their ability to work through the situation.

In each of the above, the positive asset search may not overcome the negative. In such cases, the client may at times become nervous. This is true in the more dramatic methods—such as reframing and focusing—and less common with the positive asset search, where you have directly asked for positives in the situation, or in Tyler's exploration of resources. If your client appears anxious, reflect and support the feeling as normal and typical of many reactions. The goal then becomes to use the positive asset search techniques to *lessen* the impact of the negative. It is not necessary to resolve the problem all at once. As you use these specific techniques, do not build up unattainable expectations in your client in the early stages.

After you have considered Figure 7.2, you may want to examine other theories of growth and change for their emphasis on positive assets.

THE POSITIVE ASSET SEARCH: ALTERNATIVE THEORETICAL APPROACHES

In this section, several theories of helping that seem to relate clearly to the power of the positive are reviewed with special attention to their methods. These theories will be discussed in more detail later in this book.

Positive Regard

Carl Rogers's positive regard has been reviewed already in Chapter 4. In this construct Rogers gives *selective attention to positive aspects of client verbalization.* Time and time again, you will find Rogers listening to deep client problems and then reflecting the most positive meanings out of complex situations. The following is just one example:

> S: Yes, I realized the position, that I had to get it out, and I did, Tuesday night, and it wasn't that I sat down and I said, "Well, Arnold, let's talk it out, leave us talk it out . . .". I didn't do that. My feeling of hatred towards him was so intense that I was weak already, really I was so weak—I said something and he misunderstood me. And then I misunderstood him and I said, "Arnold, we just don't meet at all, do we Arnold?" Then he said, "Well, let's talk," so we sat down and talked. So he took the initiative, and I started to talk to him for a whole hour and a half. Before it opened up I hated him, I couldn't talk, "Oh, he won't understand," "We don't meet on the same level." To myself, "Let's get away from each other. I can't stand to be with you, you irritate me . . .". Then all of a sudden, I said, "Arnold, do you know that I feel sexually inferior to you," and that did it. The very fact that I could tell him that. Which was, I think that was the very thing, the whole thought to admit, not to admit to myself, because I knew that all the time, but to bring it up so that I could have admitted it to him, which I think was the whole turning point.
>
> R: To be able to admit what you regarded as your deepest weakness.
>
> S: Yes.
>
> R: Just started the ball rolling.
>
> S: This feeling of sexual inadequacy, but now that he knows it—it isn't important any more. It's like I carried a secret with me, and I wanted somebody to share it and Arnold of all people, and finally he knows about it so I feel better. So I don't feel inadequate.
>
> R: The worst is known and accepted. (Rogers, 1951, pp. 86–87)

In the above, it would have been easy to focus on the negative. Rogers, rather, reflects on the more positive dimensions. He is responding to the deep structure of the surface sentences. He uses the skill of reflection of meaning, bringing out the client's main words and ideas for positive reframing. Rogers is "coming from" the worldview of the client.

Frankl's Search for Meaning

Viktor Frankl is considered by many to be the foremost humanistic psychotherapist and philosopher. His positive view of the human condition reflects a lifetime of struggle to find the positives in humankind. Frankl is best-known through his powerful and important book *Man's Search for Meaning* (1959). In this small but highly affecting volume, Frankl describes his experiences in Nazi concentration camps during World War II. While Frankl gives attention to the horrors of the concentration camp, the book is more a testimony to the power of the human spirit and its capability of survival under the most inhuman of conditions.

Following are some quotations from Frankl's book. Just as Rogers found the positive in the seemingly negative client experience, Frankl similarly finds something meaningful in spite of the concentration camp that enables him and others to survive. In the quotes below, the positives in the negative situation are italicized. You will observe that in many cases Frankl moved his attention out of

Viktor Frankl

the immediate situation and focused on the past or the future—the goals that helped him survive.

> We stumbled on in the darkness, over big stones and through large puddles, along the one road leading from the camp. The accompanying guards kept shouting at us and driving us with the butts of their rifles. Anyone with very sore feet supported himself on his neighbor's arm. Hardly a word was spoken; the icy wind did not encourage talk. Hiding his mouth behind his upturned collar, the man marching next to me whispered suddenly: "If our wives could see us now! I do hope they are better off in their camps and don't know what is happening to us."
>
> *That brought thoughts of my own wife to mind. And as we stumbled on for miles,* slipping on icy spots, supporting each other time and again, dragging one another up and onward, nothing was said, but we both knew: *each of us was thinking of his wife.* Occasionally I looked at the sky, where the stars were fading and the pink light of the morning was beginning to spread behind a dark bank of clouds. *But my mind clung to my wife's image, imagining it with an uncanny acuteness. I heard her answering me, saw her smile, her frank and encouraging look. Real or not, her look was then more luminous than the sun which was beginning to rise.*
>
> *A thought transfixed me: for the first time in my life I saw the truth as it is set into song by so many poets, proclaimed as the final wisdom by so many thinkers. The truth—that love is the ultimate and the highest goal to which man can aspire. Then I grasped the meaning of the greatest secret that human poetry and human thought and belief have to impart: The salvation of man is through love and in love. I understood how a man who has nothing left in this world still may know bliss, be it only for a brief moment, in the contemplation of his beloved.* In a position of utter desolation, when man cannot express himself in positive action, when his only achievement may consist in enduring his sufferings in the right way—an honorable way—in such a position man can, through loving contemplation of the image he carries of his beloved, achieve fulfillment. For the first time in my life I was able to understand the meaning of the words, "The angels are lost in perpetual contemplation of an infinite glory."
>
> In front of me a man stumbled and those following him fell on top of him. The guard rushed over and used his whip on them all. Thus my thoughts were inter-

rupted for a few minutes. *But soon my soul found its way back from the prisoner's existence to another world, and I resumed talk with my loved one: I asked her questions, and she answered; she questioned me in return, and I answered.* (Frankl, 1959, pp. 58–60)

The most ghastly moment of the twenty-four hours of camp life was the awakening, when, at a still nocturnal hour, the three shrill blows of a whistle tore us pitilessly from our exhausted sleep and from the longings in our dreams. We then began the tussle with our wet shoes, into which we could scarcely force our feet, which were sore and swollen with edema. And there were the usual moans and groans about petty troubles, such as the snapping of wires which replaced shoelaces. One morning I heard someone, whom I knew to be brave and dignified, cry like a child because he finally had to go to the snowy marching grounds in his bare feet, as his shoes were too shrunken for him to wear. *In those ghastly minutes, I found a little bit of comfort; a small piece of bread which I drew out of my pocket and munched with absorbed delight.* (p. 50)

In the winter and spring of 1945 there was an outbreak of typhus which infected nearly all the prisoners. The mortality was great among the weak, who had to keep on with their hard work as long as they possibly could. The quarters for the sick were most inadequate, there were practically no medicines or attendants. Some of the symptoms of the disease were extremely disagreeable: an irrepressible aversion to even a scrap of food (which was an additional danger to life) and terrible attacks of delirium. The worst case of delirium was suffered by a friend of mine who thought that he was dying and wanted to pray. In his delirium he could not find the words to do so. *To avoid these attacks of delirium, I tried, as did many of the others, to keep awake for most of the night. For hours I composed speeches in my mind. Eventually I began to reconstruct the manuscript which I had lost in the disinfection chamber of Auschwitz, and scribbled the key words in shorthand on tiny scraps of paper.* (p. 55)

In each of the examples above Frankl moved his state of attention from the immediate horror of the here and now and gave it (attending behavior and focusing) to other situations. He paid attention to a crust of bread, he worked on a book secretly, but most of all he thought of his wife. His was the sane response in an insane situation. At a more basic level, Frankl found meaning outside the horror of the immediate situation that gave him strength to cope with life's difficult reality.

In logotherapy, the task of the counselor or therapist is to help the client reflect on the meaning of life in this particular situation rather than *hyperreflect* on negative thoughts. Hyperreflection also includes an overly intensive self-observation and egocentricity. Hyperreflection is a particularly helpful logotherapy construct. Clients often come to us over concentrating (hyperreflecting) on the negatives in their situation. This may be especially typical of successful, middle-class clients who, in effect, have very positive, satisfying lives when compared to the poverty and illness that many people face. The task of logotherapy is to assist clients in finding more satisfying meanings in or beyond their negative situation.

The techniques in Figure 7.2 were developed in Frankl's logotherapy and are summarized in more detail in Chapter 10. A recent description of his techniques may be found in Lukas (1980, 1981).

Gendlin's Focusing

Figure 7.2 presents an interesting therapeutic technique termed "focusing" by Gendlin (1978). Gendlin's focusing has not uniformly won full acceptance by the psychological and psychiatric profession and is considered by some as untested. However, you will note that the structure of his technique in some ways resembles the work of Frankl and the positive regard of Rogers (Gendlin has long been associated with the humanistic thinking of Rogers and is considered his "heir-apparent" by some).

Focusing techniques start with the body and sensory-based perceptual systems. Through this the client learns to magnify and strengthen past and present recall of experience. Finally, the client joins a positive thought or feeling with the problem. The synthesis of positive assets helps alleviate problems. Gendlin gives more attention to body and physical feelings than others; if this approach interests you, you may wish to read more about his methodological and theoretical conceptions in his 1978 book, *Focusing*.

Reframing Life Experience

Another currently popular model of behavior change is that of reframing, which rests originally in the work of Milton Erickson (see Chapter 12). The concept has been made more clear in skills terms by Bandler and Grinder (1975) and Lankton (1980). In reframing, clients "reinterpret" and reconsider past views of problems. Reframing is simply taking an alternative view of an issue.

At this point, you may be aware that many theories and techniques use different terms to describe highly similar phenomena. The terms "positive asset search," "positive regard," "finding positive meanings," and "reframing" are all closely related. They are all concerned with assisting clients to reconstruct ("reconstrue" in George Kelly's terms) their worldview or map of reality. In each system, the facts may remain the same, but the way the client regards those facts may be altered.

As Seneca said in the first century A.D.: "Is it not things, but the way we view things that is important?" Frankl, Rogers, Gendlin, the reframing group, and many other therapists and counselors are concerned with changing the way people view their lives and situations. With a change in view, it then becomes possible to act on that view and change reality if such is necessary. When it is not possible to change reality, one may learn a new way to think about it and live more comfortably with the world as it is.

Cognitive-Behavioral Approaches

The positive asset concepts presented thus far tend to be generated from a psychodynamic or humanistic orientation. Behavioral psychology through the constructions of cognitive-behavioral theory has developed a related system of producing changes in thinking. Beck (1976) has discussed this system of changing a client's thought patterns (also see Chapter 11).

Beck suggests that a major goal of helping is to correct distorted thinking. In Beck's model, the therapist seeks to change the client's thinking patterns and way of constructing his or her worldview. This requires the following steps:

1. Recognizing maladaptive thinking and ideation. This, of course, is similar to noting incongruities in client sentences, thoughts, and behaviors.

2. Noting repeating patterns of ideation that tend to be ineffective. Beck terms such repeating patterns as "automatic thoughts." You may, for example, have been frightened by a dog and now all dogs are scary for you. You "automatically" think all dogs are dangerous. The therapeutic task is to break down the illogical thinking patterns and realize the distinctions between safe and unsafe dogs.

3. Distancing and decentering are techniques that cognitive-behavioral therapists may use to help clients remove themselves from the immediate fear, thought, or problem and help them think about it from a distance (again similar to the reframing or dereflection techniques mentioned earlier). The obsessive thinking becomes less of a "center" for the person's life. As part of this process, the therapist may "authenticate" the conclusions that have been made by the client. In this process, the client often discovers that he or she has been thinking incorrectly. Beck's work may be seen as an extension of that of Albert Ellis, also summarized in Chapter 11.

4. With "changing the rules," the therapist talks with the client about the logic of the situation. For example, the client with the dog phobia may realize that the chances of being bitten by an animal are at best one in 1000, thus learning to rethink the "danger." In this case, the therapist has attacked the logic of the client but has also inserted a positive asset (that is, the true probabilities of the situation) and, as such, is actively altering the worldview of the client.

As this branch of behavioral psychology has developed and matured, a wide array of innovative and powerful techniques for personal growth and change have evolved, many of them using a variety of affective and emotional techniques to supplement the logical example above.

The preceding discussion of positive asset approaches and Figure 7.2 illustrate that much is common even in different theoretical approaches to counseling and therapy. Each approach brings some new positive asset to the situation, although the words and the techniques may vary widely. The positive asset search may be useful to you; it provides a connecting link for you when clients do not seem to change with your usual approach or theory. It is possible that the conceptions and leverage of a quite different approach from your own may be more compatible with the values and worldview of the client. If your first positive idea doesn't work, you've got many others that may.

Now, armed with this introduction to several alternative but seemingly related approaches to human change, let us turn to a specific case example of the positive asset search with our model therapist, Mary.

POSITIVE ASSET SEARCH: AN INTERVIEW EXAMPLE

Let us now turn to an example of the positive asset search used to promote client growth. This is the third demonstration session between therapist Mary and client Charles. In this interview Mary emphasizes a version of Frankl's system of finding positive meanings or "modification of attitudes." Note that the counselor is able to facilitate client development of a new view of the situation primarily using microskills of listening. For the most part, she uses the client's main words as he seeks to reinterpret and look at a past situation more positively.

1. M: I'm going to demonstrate the positive asset search and hunt for more positive meanings in a manner somewhat parallel to those of Frankl. To start this Charles, I'd like to have you move to your shoulders and get with the feeling of the kinds of things we've been talking about.

1. Information/Directive

2. C: Yeah, OK . . . (closes eyes, hands reach to shoulders as if to take on even more responsibility. Mary waits and watches closely).

3. M: Can you feel it even more?

3. Directive

4. C: (Sigh) . . . Yeah

(The client moves into the experience more deeply. He is moving toward deep concentration on the feelings. Mary knows from experience that this client is predominately kinesthetic and thus works directly with the feeling perceptual system. With most clients, you will find a deeper emotional experience with the kinesthetic dimensions than with auditory or visual.)

5. M: Umm-hum . . . umm-hum . . .

5. Encourager

6. C: OK.

(From observation of his nonverbals, Mary knows that the client has entered into emotions fairly fully.)

7. M: Can you go back to a childhood experience or an earlier situation where you felt this heaviness on your shoulders? Can you talk a little bit about it?

7. Directive as closed question

(This is the focused free association technique. See page 220.)

8. C: Oh . . . I was about, about nine, and a friend and I were out—we trespassed on somebody else's property and we were . . . ah . . . pushing logs along a kind of slough or stream. And it was great fun, playing around in the water and just really fun. I didn't quite feel comfortable being there, but . . .

9. M: So it was fun, but not exactly comfortable.

9. Reflection of feeling/confrontation

(This is a confrontation because Mary has selected out the mixed emotions expressed by the client. It is the ambivalent or mixed feelings that are often most important in counseling and therapy.)

10. C:	Well it . . . (pause) . . . you've got it. And then I—we went to cross a cow path and I got stuck and we couldn't move.	
11. M:	Stuck in the path?	11. Encourager
12. C:	And, something like—kind of quicksand because I started to go down deeper. . . . I don't know what really would have happened . . . if it really was quicksand. I was convinced I was going to die. And there we were, where we didn't belong and I couldn't get out. Very, very scary.	
13. M:	So you were feeling very scary and just sinking down?	13. Reflection of feeling and paraphrase
14. C:	Yeah, I just shouldn't have been there. I shouldn't have been there. And I said this is what happens when I don't do the right thing. Ah, I get some of those same feelings of fear in my stomach right now . . . ah . . .	

(At this point, the client is experiencing present-tense immediacy—reliving the past in the present.)

15. M:	So fear and feeling you're going to die, very, very afraid.	15. Reflection of feeling
16. C:	And Jerry tried to dig me out and he couldn't. So then I really got scared. And then Jerry left and I was there all by myself, and nothing I could do. And then, Jerry came back with Mr. Olson, and . . . ah, he yelled at me and he dug me out and everything was OK and I went home. But, I remember I washed my boots off and I wouldn't tell anyone about it and I just felt terribly guilty and it really was something that I shouldn't have done. I just never, we were talking, I just felt—you know—really that I should stay away from other people's space and take care of myself and, you know, in that situation.	

(There are some interesting cultural aspects to this description. Note that the client is still assuming internal responsibility for a childhood event. The word "guilt" is highly characteristic of middle-class youth from his cultural background. You will also note that he takes individual responsibility for his actions and says nothing about the friend who was with him. Other cultural groups might consider playing in this way a "right" and would not have to wash off their boots to "remove" the guilt.)

17. M:	So you had all kinds of feelings associated with this early childhood experience, including, you know, feeling like you shouldn't be doing this . . . feeling guilty, feeling you're in somebody else's	17. Summary

space—you shouldn't be there—lots of negative feelings I hear associated with that.

18. C: Oh God . . . yes . . .

19. M: Is there anything that comes to mind that's positive? I know it sounds like a totally negative experience. Was there anything that you could see that was positive about what happened?

19. Open question

(The positive asset search (modification of attitudes) begins here. Mary has listened to the client carefully and now starts to search out positives in the situation. Verbal clients, experienced in therapy, are likely to respond quickly and easily to this direct approach. Other clients may respond more slowly; or they may prefer one of the several alternative routes toward finding positives in negatives.)

20. C: . . . (pause) . . . Well, it sure felt good when he dug me out. I was scared, but felt guilty, but he at least dug me out.

21. M: So you felt like there was help even though you were afraid and . . .

21. Reflection of feeling

22. C: And you know what? Jerry, you know, really tried to help me and he went and got Mr. Olson. And, ah . . . I was afraid of Mr. Olson after that?

23. M: So, it made you think that you had friends there if you were in trouble.

23. Interpretation

24. C: . . . Well, I didn't really feel that I had friends . . . but, if I start thinking about it, it really does. *I did have friends.* And then actually, Mr. Olson then called next week and asked me to work for him on his farm. . . . I think I've always paid attention to the negative part of that experience. . . . It really was . . . there were people there.

25. M: There were people to help in difficult situations like that.

25. Encourager/Restatement

26. C: Yes, yes . . .

27. M: And Mr. Olson even didn't really blame you for it. In fact, he even . . . ah . . . called and hired you to do other work for him later on.

27. Paraphrase

28. C: I didn't have to take as much on my shoulders as I thought I did.

(This is a particularly important and interesting comment on part of the client. He reinterprets the old situation from a new, more positive frame of reference. He has generated a new perspective on the situation himself with the aid of the therapist. This new view, interestingly, is less self-centered *and more relational* in nature. Note that Mary has been using listening skills almost exclusively.)

29. M: Didn't need as much. Well, how does this relate to all these other things we've been talking about with your secretary and with the kids? If there is any relationship between the two? Do you see any patterns?

29. Encourager/open question/confrontation

(The therapist here searches for repeating patterns and asks the client to examine the old situation from childhood to determine if there are residues in daily life now. The confrontation involves the comparison of the past situation with the present issues.)

30.	C:	Well, the thing that stood out from the first session, Mary, was me being more nurturing than I needed to be. (M: Umm-humm, Umm-humm.) . . . Ahh, and in effect, that's almost like taking more on my shoulders than I need to. And, in one situation back as a kid, I had those feelings of fear. But, now I have these feelings of anger . . . and, you know, somehow I know fear and anger go together.	
31.	M:	How do they go together?	31. Open question
32.	C:	I don't really understand fully, but I know that somehow they are close together, so that's something we need to explore more later . . . more deeply . . .	
33.	M:	Sounds like a pattern, though, of taking on too much responsibility, whether its . . .	33. Interpretation
34.	C:	Whether it's Georgia, the kids . . . or Mr. Olsen . . . sometimes I get angry, other times scared. We've got something for next time.	
35.	M:	So, today, we've looked at a scary situation from way back and we find that even in negative situations there are positives. Perhaps that will give us a clue for the next session.	35. Summary

In this case, the positive asset search has helped the client, Charles, find a new meaning in an old situation. Metaphorically, Charles was trapped in a prison of negative meanings in the situation. With the aid of the therapist, he was able to reconstrue his perceptions of the world and modify his attitudes in a more positive way. Theory holds that this new perception of events will stay with the client and gradually help him to look at new situations, as well, more positively. His worldview has been challenged and a beginning toward change has been made.

Using the seven dimensions for assessing the effectiveness of an interview as presented in Figure 7.1, we would note that the client is now demonstrating more intentionality. Furthermore, the positive asset search with its emphasis on listening skills has enabled the client to generate his own new construction of the situation and perhaps even to make a good start toward a new, more effective worldview. The client does seem to be generating his own goals. However, there has been little to ensure that the insights learned in these three demonstration sessions are actually implemented in practice. Clearly, insight without action is of little help either in the short or long run. Mary will need to give consideration to the generalization of Charles' ideas to daily life.

The therapist's use of microskills in this last session is particularly effective. She brings out the facts, feelings, and underlying meanings that the client has toward the event and enables the client intentionally to generate new meanings. Mary, the therapist, has shown good individual empathy; being sensitive, she is culturally appropriate as well. Nonetheless, the same criticism made earlier holds: the counselor has assumed individualistically oriented therapy is appropriate. The same methods might not be as successful if the client came from a different cultural background.

Obviously, the therapist has demonstrated good client observation skills. She has encouraged the client to find deeper meanings under surface structure sentences. If you were to observe a videotape of the interview, you would discover a great deal of nonverbal mirroring. The therapist encouraged fairly deep experiencing by working through the kinesthetic or feeling system. If she had asked the client to see and hear the past situations as well, the impact of the interview could have been heightened through more concreteness and likely deeper emotional expression. Although no formal assessment is presented, the counselor appears to provide a solid environment within which the client can change, grow, and develop.

CONCLUSION

In this chapter we attempt to summarize the many concepts presented in the first six chapters of the text. In addition we elaborate on the positive asset search, pointing out that many different therapeutic schools use it in some form or another. It may be helpful to you as a therapist or counselor to give attention to several of the alternatives for utilizing the positive asset search. You will find that some clients respond better to one approach and other clients to different ways of thinking. The more options you have available in your repertoire, the more clients you are likely to serve in a helpful, intentional fashion.

The first chapters of this text have focused on the structure and process of therapy and counseling. We can now turn to the second portion of the text where you will consider alternative theoretical methods. Undergirding all these theoretical methods, it is argued, are the microskills and concepts of these early chapters. If you have mastered these concepts, you should be able to study and master quite effectively the distinctive and important alternative theoretical approaches to helping.

A special question you face is which theoretical orientation you will want to take. If you are equipped with a general understanding of counseling and therapy—as provided in this text—you are in a good position to decide whether you wish to adopt a general theoretical approach or orient yourself to one specific theory. Whatever route you take, we would hope that you would be respectful of alternative methods of helping. The field of psychotherapy and counseling has not yet found the method that is the *absolute truth* for all clients.

SUMMARY OF THIS CHAPTER

This chapter summarizes the main ideas of the first seven chapters and demonstrates how they may be integrated into a natural interview. The seven major concepts reviewed in this chapter are summarized in Figure 7.1 so they are only listed here briefly. In addition, there are some new concepts that are important for your mastery of this text:

1. *Seven main concepts of the early chapters.* Intentionality, creative decision making, microskills, cultural and individual empathy, client observation skills, assessment of person/environment interaction, and the several alternatives within the positive asset search.
2. *Alternative routes to the positive asset search.* You will want to master the concepts of Tyler's exploration of resources, Rogers' positive regard, Frankl's finding positive meanings, Gendlin's focusing, reframing, and Beck's cognitive methods. In addition, you may wish to note similarities and differences among the several models and eventually develop competence in several of them, so as to meet the needs and interests of a variety of clients you are likely to face.

REFERENCES

BANDLER, J., and R. GRINDER, *The Structure of Magic.* Vol. I. Palo Alto, CA: Science and Behavior Books, 1975.

BECK, A. *Cognitive Therapy and the Emotional Disorders.* New York: International Universities Press, 1976.

CAMERON-BANDLER, L. *They Lived Happily Ever After.* Cupertino, CA: Meta, 1978.

FRANKL, V., *Man's Search for Meaning: An Introduction to Logotherapy.* New York: Kangaroo, 1959.

GENDLIN, E., *Focusing.* New York: Bantam, 1978.

IVEY, A., *Intentional Interviewing and Counseling.* Monterey, CA: Brooks/Cole, 1983.

IVEY, M., "Interpretation/Reframing." In *Basic Influencing Skills.* Videotape. No. Amherst, MA: Microtraining, 1983.

LANKTON, S., *Practical Magic.* Cupertino, CA: Meta, 1980.

LUKAS, E., "Modification of Attitudes," *The International Forum of Logotherapy,* 1980, *3,* 25–35.

LUKAS, E., "New Ways for Dereflection," *The International Forum of Logotherapy,* 1981, *4,* 13–28.

ROGERS, C., *Client-Centered Therapy.* Boston: Houghton-Mifflin, 1951.

TYLER, L., *The Work of the Counselor.* New York: Appleton-Century-Crofts, 1953, 1961.

SUGGESTED SUPPLEMENTARY READING

BECK, A., *Cognitive Therapy and the Emotional Disorders.* New York: International Universities Press, 1976.
A breakthrough book that clearly brought cognition into the field of behavior therapy. Specific and thoughtful methods for producing behavioral change.

FRANKL, V.,   *Man's Search for Meaning*. New York: Kangaroo, 1959.

A classic counseling and therapy paperback that should be on everyone's shelf. Frankl, well regarded and highly recognized, is one of the few psychotherapists who also ranks highly as a philosopher. This book is easy to read, exciting, and can change lives.

IVEY, A.,   *Developmental Therapy: Theory into Practice*. San Francisco: Jossey-Bass, 1986.

A cognitive-developmental approach to therapy is presented based on an integration of the thinking of Plato and Piaget. In this book specific examples of how to use microskills to move clients to new developmental levels are presented. A dialectical analysis of Mary Bradford Ivey's interview with Charles is presented with illustrations of how therapeutic change may be related to Piagetian developmental concepts.

IVEY, A., and N. GLUCKSTERN,   *Basic Influencing Skills*. Videotapes and book. North Amherst, MA: Microtraining, 1983.

The videotape series contains the actual film of Mary Bradford Ivey conducting the series of interviews mentioned in this chapter.

The International Forum for Logotherapy: Journal of the Search for Meaning. New York: Human Sciences Press.

The official journal of the International Association of Logotherapy. Contains interesting and useful articles on this significant approach to helping. The work of Elisabeth Lukas of the University of Munich is often featured.

8

PSYCHODYNAMIC COUNSELING AND THERAPY

GENERAL PREMISE

An integrated knowledge of skills, theory, and practice is essential for culturally intentional counseling and therapy.

Skills form the foundation of effective theory and practice: The culturally intentional therapist knows how to construct a creative decision-making interview and can use microskills to attend to and influence clients in a predicted direction. Important in this process are individual and cultural empathy, client observation skills, assessment of person and environment, and the application of positive techniques of growth and change.

Theory provides organizing principles for counseling and therapy: *The culturally intentional counselor has knowledge of alternative theoretical approaches and treatment modalities, in this case—psychodynamic methods.*

Practice is the integration of skills and theory: The culturally intentional counselor or therapist is competent in skills and theory, and is able to apply them to research and practice for client benefit.

Undergirding integrated competence in skills, theory, and practice is an intentional awareness of one's own personal worldview and how that worldview may be similar to and/or different from the worldview and personal constructions of the client and other professionals.

GOALS FOR PSYCHODYNAMIC COUNSELING AND THERAPY

The psychodynamic formulations of Sigmund Freud are the original systematic formulations of psychotherapy. More than any other theory, the psychodynamic approach recognizes the power of the past to shape the present. This system of helping may be considered the most theoretically complex of all orientations to helping.

Some specific goals of this chapter are to:

1. Summarize the worldview of psychodynamic theory and illustrate that it is far from a single orthodox framework.
2. Present some central theoretical constructs giving special attention to the unconscious and the object relations developmental framework.
3. Illustrate psychodynamic helping through the presentation of an interview transcript and analysis.
4. Present some central techniques from this theory with practice exercises.
5. Provide you with an opportunity to engage in a beginning psychodynamic interview using the five stages of the interview.

FREUD AS FOUNDATION

Freud brought order out of chaos. Until his brilliant and insightful work was publicized, mental operations and behavior seemed unknowable and almost mystical. His place in history ranks with the major influences of Darwin, Einstein, and Marx. While discussions of the meaning of his legacy sometimes bring more heat than light, there can be no disputing his importance in the development of Western thought.

What does Freud provide for us today? First are his extensive writings which organize human functioning and conceptualize the emotional and irrational feelings underlying behavior. Second, his many disciples provide a constant impetus for change in psychotherapy, through additions to and modifications in his concepts. Those who started from a Freudian perspective include close followers, such as Ernest Jones and revisionists and neo-Freudians such as Alfred Adler, Eric Erikson, Erich Fromm, Karen Horney, Carl Jung, Wilheim Reich, and Harry Stack Sullivan. The currently popular Eric Berne (transactional analysis), Alexander Lowen (bioenergetics), and Fritz Perls (Gestalt therapy) all have their roots in traditional Freudian thought. Psychodynamic theory, as introduced by Freud, may be practiced in a wide array of manners ranging from the orthodox to the wildly innovative.

It must be stressed that the psychodynamic approach being presented here is *not* pure Freudian psychotherapy. Most typically in today's practice, therapists take aspects of Freud's work and shape it toward their own particular ends. Counseling and psychotherapies derived from psychodynamic psychology vary extensively. Specifically, they may range from the orthodox, using only interpretation and adhering strictly to traditional Freudian theory, to the more humanistically oriented transactional analysis, which uses an array of techniques from other schools of counseling in addition to psychoanalysis.

PSYCHODYNAMIC WORLDVIEW

"If Freud's discovery had to be summed up in a single word, that word would without a doubt have to be 'unconscious'," wrote Lapanche and Pontalis (1973, p. 474). The word *unconscious* means lack of awareness of one's own mental functioning. More broadly, it also means all things of which we are not aware at a given moment. Individuals are unaware (unconscious) of what is impelling and motivating them toward action. The concept of unconscious is central to the Freudian worldview.

The Freudian worldview is one that is keenly aware of the difficulties and complexities of life. Freud does not provide easy solutions for the individual. Rather, he suggests that we are ruled by forces of which we are at best only dimly aware. This somewhat harsh view of reality has led the Freudian worldview to be summarized as ". . . essentially pessimistic, deterministic, and reductionistic" (Corey, 1977, p. 12).

However, this negative view of Freud may fail to deal with the true complexity of his theory. Freudian theory is constantly changing and adapting. It is important to remember that much of psychodynamic theory as practiced in North America is based on work of ego psychologists such as Erik Erikson who believe that humans can control their destiny. Transactional analysis (see Chapter 12) is an American derivation of Freudian theory that sees individuals as living life scripts that can be rewritten and relived if they are analyzed and understood fully.

On the other hand, the French psychoanalyst, Jacques Lacan severely criticizes American psychoanalysts for retreating from Freud's basic thinking and argues against ego psychology and individualism in U.S. intepretations of Freud. The practice of psychoanalysis ". . . in the American sphere has been so summarily reduced to a means of obtaining success and a mode of demanding happiness . . . [that it] constitutes a repudiation of psychoanalysis" (Lacan, 1966/1977, pp. 127–128). Lacan calls for a "return to Freud" and that we acknowledge the real power of unconscious mental functioning.

Thus, the psychodynamic establishment clearly has differences of opinion concerning worldview, but all agree on the central importance of the unconscious. The position presented here is basically that of the more optimistic ego psychology, but acknowledges the importance of the Lacanian criticism of this viewpoint.

CENTRAL THEORETICAL CONSTRUCTS

The central goal of psychodynamic therapy is oriented toward uncovering and understanding the unconscious and the forces that guide us. Psychodynamic methods have been described as an "uncovering therapy," in that the goals of therapy are focused on discovering the unconscious processes governing behavior. Once these unconscious processes are discovered in their full complexity, the individual is believed able to reconstruct the personality.

Object Relations Theory and Repeating Patterns of Behavior

Currently important on the psychodynamic scene are the object relations theorists (such as Klein, 1975; Guntrip, 1968; Kernberg, 1980). Object relations is a technical term that may be roughly translated as "past interpersonal relationships." Object relations theory has added to basic Freudian thought through more clearly identifying how past childhood experience is reflected unconsciously in adult patterns of behavior. The object relations model points out that we develop our *patterns* of living or life style from our early relations with significant others, but particularly important is the mother. Stable personality characteristics tend to develop quite early and the goal of therapy is to understand how these childhood patterns are repeated in many variations in adult life.

Object relations theory, thus, clarifies Freudian theory as one's current life style and pattern of living are derived from one's past history. The difficult task of the psychodynamic therapists is to "uncover" the relationship between the past and the present and make the unconscious conscious.

The formulations of object relations theorists may be most valuable to you. Specifically, you will find it helpful to search for consistent patterns of behavior and thinking in your clients that are derived from earlier life events. At the most elementary level, you will find that many of those who have experienced divorce tend to repeat the patterns with their second spouse that defeated them in the first marriage. Or you may find that a person who procrastinates in making a decision about vocational choice also procrastinates in making decisions about buying a car or in deciding to get married. The identification of such repeating patterns is the first step toward later uncovering of unconscious thought processes. These examples of unconscious repetition could be traced back to early childhood experience.

For therapeutic purposes, simply pointing out that a pattern of repetition exists may be helpful. A second level of interpretation occurs when you help the client see how several repetitions are *linked* together and related to childhood experience through affect. A third level of interpretation, less useful to the client generally, is labeling behavior or thought patterns with Freudian or psychodynamic terminology. Mistakenly, some therapists concentrate on labeling and diagnosis, missing the more useful forms of interpretation available through affectively linking present problem behaviors with earlier life experience. This linkage is a specific example of joining conscious and unconscious experience.

Developmental Theory

Freud was perhaps the first developmental psychologist. He not only recognized childhood as the basis of many life problems, he organized development into major stages that each contain certain major developmental tasks for the child. His developmental formulations have deeply influenced our culture and thinking, often without our awareness. For example, in the media and discussion you may find a dependent individual described as having an "oral" character or a person who is controlling or obsessed by detail as "anal." The Oedipal period is less well understood and triggers such sarcastic comments as "Oedipus, smedipus . . . so long as he loves his Mother!"

Some key aspects of Freudian theory, nonetheless, are caught in the above stereotypes. At each stage of child development, the individual has key developmental tasks that must be accomplished or that child may be *stuck* or *immobilized* in that childhood period for life. The therapeutic task of psychodynamic therapy is to work through those developmental tasks so that the adult can be restored to mature intentionality. Object relations theorists have developed useful conceptualizations of the oral period that will be summarized here in brief form.

The central developmental task (or crisis) of the oral period (birth to 2 years) is acquiring the ability to relate to others. This developmental task requires one to be simultaneously *separated* and *attached* (Bowlby, 1969, 1973). To live intentionally, one must learn how to be attached to others in mutually dependent relationships *and* how to be separated from them as a unique individual. Klein (1946/1963) talks about the *holding environment* in which the infant is literally and figuratively "held" by the parents, especially the mother. If the child is held too closely, it may develop excessive feelings of "attachment" or dependence. If the

Melanie Klein

relationship between mother and child is too distant, the child will be "separated" or too independent. Generally speaking, boys are "held" in a more separate fashion than girls, and research evidence even indicates that the first time that boys and girls are picked up after birth, they are held differently. This metaphor of holding expresses itself in thousands of behavioral interactions in which the child eventually experiences itself in relation to others as some balance of separation and attachment. Failure to find a suitable balance at this stage can result in serious and consistent emotional problems in later life.

The anal period (ages 18 months–4 years) may be described as a time in which the child develops a sense of control over destiny. Classic Freudian theory talks about the child's real first chance to control as being in charge of his or her own feces and the act of elimination. The derogatory slang "tight ass" describes an individual who at least partially is still caught in the anal period. If the child learns to control too well, he or she may become stuck in this developmental period resulting in problems of obsessiveness and overattention to detail in later life, perhaps even trying to control the lives of others. Too little control leads to messy rooms and a disorganized life, but may be compensated for by a sense of spontaneity. Again, the task of the child is to find an adequate balance of control versus overcontrol. In most cultures, boys work through this developmental period tending to be encouraged to control. Girls tend to be taught to let others control them. Each person has a unique balance of these dimensions, but each culture has a central tendency of control balance for the sex roles. Again, if the child does not find a culturally suitable balance of control in this period, continuation of emotional difficulties may be expected in adulthood.

The Oedipal period (4–7) is the time at which the child learns to understand the sex role he or she is to undertake. As may be seen from the oral and anal periods, the child has already received considerable training in sex roles through the holding environment and the manner in which the control issues of the anal period have been handled by the culture. What is distinctive about the Oedipal period is that the child develops awareness of the meaning and importance of sex roles themselves and brings together all previous learnings in a total gestalt.

The Oedipal period is also a time of considerable cognitive and physical development. The child starts school, learns to read, acquires friends, becomes truly separate from the parents. Undergirding all these critical developmental tasks is the child's sense of cultural sex role. In "normal development," both boys and girls have through childrearing tended to be closer to the mother than the father. At the Oedipal period, girls learn to become like their mothers, whereas boys model themselves after their fathers. This is a cultural ideal and is not always fulfilled in practice. If the earlier experiences in childhood have oriented the individual differently than the cultural norm, a variety of alternative sex role identifications are possible.

The complexities of the Oedipal period need not be elaborated here. What happens in social learning terms is that each child learns uniquely to model himself or herself as part of both mother and father. The reinforcement over the past history of childhood results in formulations of what the individual is and likely will be.

Erik Erikson (1964) describes some of the same development periods. According to Erikson, the child in the oral period must learn a sense of trust versus mistrust, at the anal stage a sense of autonomy versus shame and doubt, and at the Oepidal period a sense of initation and competence versus guilt. But, unlike Freud whose developmental phases covered only childhood, Erikson's ideas extend the basic developmental constructs throughout the entire lifespan. These developmental tasks or crises that occur throughout life include the teen-age "identity crisis" in which all the aspects of early childhood are replayed once again before the teenager becomes the mature adult. (Figure 6.1 on page 152 outlines a modified version of Erikson's thinking.)

For you as a potential psychodynamic therapist, the Freudian developmental constructs will be invaluable in understanding your clients. Adults who seem either overly independent or separated from others may require interventions in helping them work through aspects of early parent-child relationships. For example, the obsessive personality or phobic may be stuck in the anal period. The confused/distraught Oedipal period brings with it a wide variety of potential opportunities and problems. In each case, you as therapist will seek to help the person *work through* old unresolved developmental crises and tasks. This working through takes considerable time and, obviously, a deep understanding of the theoretical background of how a single individual develops in a culture.

Psychodynamic theory is not a simple theory. It is the most demanding intellectually. The ideas presented here contain many essential elements of the theory, but represent only a beginning. However, you will find that even the very general ideas and conceptualizations presented here can be useful in your understanding of many clients and in using some of the techniques suggested later in this chapter.

Defense Mechanisms

One valuable way to recognize patterns is through emotions and thoughts underlying repeating patterns. These may be disguised, however, through a variety of defense mechanisms. For example, procrastination is a form of defense mechanism in which the individual may be unconsciously hiding true desire. The conscious self may be totally unaware of the pattern and its derivation. Traced back farther, you may find that this individual recalls key life experiences with parents that form the basis for the pattern of procrastination. The parents may have demanded that he or she follow their rigid rules and regulations precisely and that the child never had a chance to make a decision, except perhaps in opposition to the parents. It may be even possible to trace this pattern of opposition and procrastination back to early childhood relationships with the

Sigmund Freud
Courtesy Austrian National Tourist Office

mother. Once the nature and the origin of the pattern is identified, change becomes more possible.

A practical goal for you, then, in psychodynamic therapy is to learn how to search for repeating patterns that may present themselves in a variety of defense mechanisms (see Figure 8.1). Psychodynamic counseling and therapy, however, tend to be awareness centered. Insight about origins of problems is sometimes enough to produce change. But specific plans for generalizing new awareness to daily life often may also be needed.

Id, Ego, Superego

Imperative for uncovering unconscious functioning is understanding of *id, ego,* and *superego* functioning. As Laplanche and Pontalis observe: "The id constitutes the instinctual pole of the personality; its contents, as an expression of the instincts, are unconscious, a portion of them being hereditary and innate, a portion repressed and acquired" (1973, p. 197). It may be noted that the id is almost totally unconscious and may be either playful and creative or destructive. By way of contrast, the superego is totally learned as the child matures in society. Conscience, ideals, and values are within the realm of the superego. Whereas the id is uncontrolled, the superego may seek to control. The superego operates more at the conscious level of experience, although it, too, functions at the unconscious level.

The ego serves as a mediator between the superego (conscious rules from society) and the id (unconscious rebellion or playful storehouse). In traditional Freudian theory, the ego is sometimes seen as being at the mercy of these two

Erik Erikson
Jon Erikson

competing forces. In more modern theory, however, the task of the therapist is seen as helping the ego decide and balance id and superego. Modern theorists, such as Erik Erikson, talk about increasing ego functioning and giving the person more power to control her or his own life. Ego strength may be increased through assisting the client to understand the interplay of ego with id and superego. The ego operates at conscious, preconscious, and unconscious levels of experience, although it is primarily manifested in counseling at the conscious level. Strong ego functioning is imperative to the development of mature intentionality.

Anxiety and tension may result from the conflicts between the id, ego, and superego, from fear caused by conscious or unconscious memories of past experiences from childhood development, from dangerous impulses from the id (such as sexual desires which may be taboo), from superego-derived guilt, or from the inadequacies of the ego to resolve conflict. Anxiety may be attached to a specific object or cause and the reason for anxiety may be clear, or anxiety may be "free-floating," in that the reason for anxiety is lost in the unconscious. A sense of free-floating anxiety without rational explanation is particularly threatening and may be repressed into the ego-defense mechanisms so popular in magazines and newspapers. The complex task of the therapist or counselor is to uncover the structure of anxiety so that personal reconstruction can begin.

The styles or patterns underlying unconscious functioning, of course, originate in the individual's past object relations—of particular importance being the mother, and developmental history.

Let us now turn to an examination of psychodynamic theory in action.

Figure 8.1 *The Ego-Defense Mechanisms*

One central task of the ego is to balance external and internal forces impinging on the individual and to *defend* personal stability. Ego-defense mechanisms are useful in protecting a person from anxiety and threat. The mechanisms operate at an unconscious level and represent varying degrees of psychological "health," depending on the precise nature of the mechanism and the extent of its use. One task of the psychodynamic therapist is to uncover and understand the nature of defense mechanisms used by the client. Ego-defense mechanisms are believed to result from repressed sexuality.

Following are some illustrative defense mechanisms and examples of how these defense mechanisms might be employed by the client (Bob) in the interview typescript presented later in this chapter.

1. *Repression.* Perhaps the most basic defense mechanism, repression, is demonstrated by placing material of life experience in the unconscious. This defense mechanism may manifest itself by forgetting, failure to hear a clear counselor verbalization, a lack of awareness of the meaning of obvious sexual or interpersonal behavior, or simply keeping any item or concept away from consciousness. Repression could be considered the underlying defense mechanism in Bob's behavior in the typescript. As the interview moves through his relationships with first his son and then his father, a considerable amount of unconscious, *repressed* material is brought out. As a generalized defense mechanism, repression has kept unpleasant material out of Bob's awareness.

2. *Denial.* The most difficult and troublesome defense mechanism, denial is shown by the client who refuses to recognize traumatic and troublesome reality. Denial may be shown by a person who refuses to recognize that he or she has actually "flunked out" of college and continues to talk and behave like a regular student or by a person who fails to acknowledge the loss of a limb in an accident or a loved one's death. In short, reality of experience is clear and the client *denies* that it happened or is happening.

   Denial is not demonstrated in the interview typescript. However, if Bob denied obvious anxiety on the fire tower (shown by sweaty palms, rapid breathing, irrational verbalizations) and stated that he was calm and cool, he would be manifesting this defense mechanism. Denial is generally considered one of the most serious defense mechanisms and is a root of psychotic thinking where one "breaks from reality."

3. *Projection.* When a client refuses to recognize behavior in herself or himself and sees or *projects* this behavior in someone else, the defense mechanism of projection is likely to be in operation. One often is troubled most by the behavior of others which is similar to one's own behavior. The individual may deny personal feelings of sexuality but see them in many other people or may point out that many people cheat on examinations while simultaneously and unconsciously denying personal cheating.

   Again, Bob shows no clear examples of projection. However, if he had talked about his son's being afraid of the height while simultaneously denying his own fear, this would be an example of projection. Clients often project their own feelings onto the counselor. For example, when the counselor at 16 reflects Bob's feelings of confusion, Bob could have projected these feelings in the following fashion: "No, I'm not confused, you're the one who's confused. Aren't you listening to me?" It may be seen that projection is a clear movement away from reality.

4. *Reaction-Formation.* When one does precisely the opposite of unconscious wishes, one may be engaging in a *reaction-formation.* If one particularly loves a spouse, a reaction-formation may demonstrate itself in wife-beating. Similarly, extreme anger toward the spouse may be demonstrated in loving behavior. The unconscious roots of reaction-formation may lie at very deep levels.

It is difficult to determine if reaction-formations are present in Bob's interview. However, his statements in the beginning of the interview when he says that things are now going well with his job and wife could be in truth reaction-formations if a deeper analysis of his background reveals deep anger toward his wife and a dislike of his job. The early stages of therapy sometimes are manifested by a "flight into health" in which things get better for the client and defend the ego from uncomfortable, angry, and hostile feelings.

5. *Displacement.* This defense mechanism could be considered a variation of transference, in that the client's feelings or thoughts about a person or object are directed toward another individual or thing. The worker who has a bad day on the job and then treats a waiter badly that evening may be *displacing* his pent-up anger.

   Bob could be said to exemplify displacement in that he has transferred feelings and attitudes toward his father to his own son without conscious awareness. The task of the therapist in such situations, of course, is to make the client aware of displacement and unconscious mental functioning.

6. *Sublimation.* A more positive defense mechanism, sublimation takes repressed sexual energy and utilizes it in constructive work, such as artistic, physical, or intellectual endeavor. A person who is frustrated sexually may turn to movie making, athletics, or creative writing. The person who sublimates unconscious energy is often rewarded by society.

   While we have no direct evidence, it is possible that Bob is subliminating sexual energy into his work as an architect. The symbols of the fire *tower,* the *building* of houses and offices, the *desire* for success can be said to represent repressed sexuality. Psychodynamic theorists often state that much of what is constructive in society comes from sexuality which manifests itself in positive ways through sublimation. Many psychodynamic theorists would argue that most defense mechanisms have an underlying sexual nature.

7. *Other Mechanisms.* The six mechanisms cited here represent only a beginning. Those interested in these concepts should be able to understand and work with the many other defense mechanisms as well. Important among them are *fixation* (being immobilized at an earlier level of development, most likely in childhood), *rationalization* (making up good reasons for irrational or inconsistent behavior), *regression* (returning to early childhood behavior when faced with a new trauma), *conversion* (translating unconscious mental behavior into physical symptoms such as headaches), *identification* (acting and behaving like someone else), and *provocative behavior* (acting in such a way that others are provoked to do to one what one is unable to do to oneself, such as showing anger or love).

THE FIRE TOWER

Bob is in the early stages of psychodynamic counseling and has just come in for his third interview. Bob's presenting problem was his lack of interest in his family, vague feelings of anxiety, and a general lack of involvement in his job. He is 32, a college graduate, and works as an architect. He is married and has one child, age 2. The psychodynamic counselor in this case is nontraditional in that several types of leads beyond pure interpretation are used and that the counselor is oriented to short-term (twenty to thirty sessions) treatment. (It might be pointed out that short-term treatment in other schools of counseling often range from one to five interviews.)

As is typical of many people who enter this approach to therapy, Bob is highly verbal and intellectual and begins to talk just as soon as he sits down.

1. BOB:	Things seem to be going better. I was able to get the blueprints worked out on the apartment complex. Sue hasn't been on me as much lately. Things are pretty good.		COMMENTARY
2. HELPER:	(Silence)		The psychodynamic therapist attempts to remain as neutral as possible, allowing the client's unconscious to direct the interview. An attempt is made to keep nonverbal communications from the therapist to a minimum.
3. BOB:	(Fumbling) . . . I really did a good job on the apartment. Even the boss said so. I really ought to show you what I did . . . (pause) Yeh, things are going pretty well. This weekend I even took Sue and Sonny for a hike.		Bob is searching for an appropriate topic for the interview. Some possible topics for therapist-client discussion include Bob's relationship with his boss, his comment that he "ought to show" the therapist what he did, and the weekend hike.
4. HELPER:	Uh-hummm.		This minimal encourager suggests that Bob continue this line of thinking. It may be anticipated that he will continue talking about the hike. This is an illustration that minimal encouragers have important influence on client talk in the interview. Some believe that the *last* topic presented by a client in a list of problems or issues is the most important.
5. BOB:	Yeh, it was a real change. I haven't done anything like that for ages. We had a real good time, but one funny thing happened when we got to the fire tower near Iron Mountain . . . (pauses, looks to the helper).		It may be noted that Bob is talking about a past event which is highly characteristic of psychodynamic approaches. Some other theories would be more interested in his present feelings and thoughts in *this* interview. Others might be concerned with his behaviors in the specific situation.
6. HELPER:	Uh-hummm.		This second minimal encourager concludes the first decisional phase of this interview. Client and counselor have al-

ready negotiated what they are to talk about for the next several comments. The hike and then the "funny thing" on the fire tower are to be the major topics of this interview. With the next comment, we move to the work phase of the interview.

7. BOB: Well, what happened was really strange. We climbed up the tower after lunch—we had even done some singing—and when we got to the top, I started to enjoy the fantastic view. Then, I noticed I had placed Sonny on the rail and a panic suddenly came over me.

As we move to the work phase, it is time to examine the surface structure sentence. In this case, it is first "One funny thing happened . . ." and then it is made more precise in the sentence "I had placed Sonny on the rail and a panic suddenly came over me." The task of the therapist is to uncover the unconscious deep structure sentences under the elementary surface structure sentence.

It should also be noted that Bob is experiencing the free-floating nonspecific anxiety at a nonverbal level.

8. HELPER: Stay with that feeling of panic and tell me more about it.

The therapist offers a clear directive in the present tense and asks the client to talk about the past in more concrete detail. Directives are not used by all psychodynamic therapists. Most would prefer to wait and let the client take more direction.

9. BOB: Well, I was . . . (suddenly with greater strength) the panic was all over me, I almost shook. I was so afraid that Sonny would fall. I wanted him to hold me . . . I mean I wanted to hold him close. Wow . . . I wonder what that means.

The client responded to the directive with stronger emotion. As emotion gets stronger, unconscious feelings are more likely to appear. In this case we see a "Freudian slip" ("I wanted him to hold me . . .") that is rich in potential meaning. Some psychodynamic helpers might pay close attention to that slip and interpret it immediately, even making a decision to make that slip the new key surface structure sentence for exploration. Others might simply note the slip and move forward.

10. HELPER: Well, let's try. Stay with that feeling of panic and fright and then let your mind run free to your earliest memories possible and tell me the first scene that comes to your mind.

The helper uses another directive and asks the client to *free associate* back to earlier experiences. Free association, the process of letting the mind run free to whatever recollection occurs, is basic to most psychodynamic approaches. Note the strong emphasis on past-tense experience which is reached through observation of the client's present-tense world. The helper is searching for deeper underlying sentences in the client's world.

11. BOB: (Quiet for a moment, his eyes drop to the floor as if in meditation.) I see myself driving up Trail Ridge Road in Rocky Mountain Park. We've come to an overlook and we stop. I was about 5 or 6. Dad was a real "card" at the time. I remember him fooling around on the rail at the dropoff. He got up and started walking on it. I remember Mom and I being in acute panic as we watched him. Then, he lost his balance and almost fell. When he was able to get himself down, he was white as a sheet. I was so scared I almost pee'd in my pants.

It should be noted that Bob is a highly verbal and facile client. This is typical of those who stay with psychodynamic therapy. Those less verbally oriented find free association and the analytical process difficult and often drop out. Bob is able to be very concrete about his past experience and it is fairly easy to see the parallels between his feelings for his father and for his own son. This parallel is particularly important in object relations theory.

12. HELPER: So, when you were up in the fire tower with Sonny you had a real panicked feeling, and when your father almost fell you had similar feelings.

The therapist offers a summary in which father-son feelings in both situations are mentioned. It would be possible for the helper to make the interpretation for the client directly. However, most prefer that the client eventually interpret her or his own personal experience. Psychodynamic theory holds that present reactions to people stem from important past situations. In this example, Bob has feelings toward his son similar to those he felt toward his own father.

13. BOB: Yeh . . . ?

The client is unable to make the connections between the two situations. If a direct interpretation of the parallel had been made, it may be anticipated that he would have rejected it. Interpretations are only effective when the client is ready to hear them.

14. HELPER: Right now, I see your hand shaking.

This feedback is in the present tense and gives special attention to nonverbal communication. Some psychodynamic therapists would never directly refer to nonverbal communication at all while others might use it extensively.

15. BOB: I'm panicked right now. What does it all mean?

Very common to psychodynamic clients and therapists is the search for what an event, behavior, or situation "means." The search for meaning is almost always in the past. It is on this specific issue that humanistically oriented third-force psychology would criticize this interview. They would be more concerned with the client's present experience of the world and give scant attention to its derivation from the past.

16. HELPER: You're confused and puzzled. What do you think it means?

The therapist first reflects here and now immediate feelings and follows this with an open question.

17. BOB: (Relaxing a little) I did seem to have the same feelings with Sonny as I did when I was with my folks (pause) . . . the same feeling of panic . . . both were high places and I never have liked high places.

Building on the prompting from the therapist, Bob begins to put together an explanation for his feelings with Sonny. As he relaxes, his body and thought processes become more genuine or "together." For the first time in this interview, he is beginning to describe parallels in his situation. He is becoming more intentional.

18. HELPER: Right, you do seem to have the same feelings in both settings. Could it be that somehow you are reliving some of your childhood experiences right now?

This is basically an interpretation on the part of the therapist. He does paraphrase Bob's last comment and seems to be asking an open question. However, the open question may be considered a tentative interpretation. Tentativeness in interpretation allows the client room to accept or reject the therapist's ideas and avoids a confrontation between them if the interpretation is too soon or incorrect. This also shows respect for the client.

Important also in this interpretation is the linking of past and present experience. Observation suggests that the most effective psychodynamic counseling interventions are those which help the client see how he or she may be reliving the past in the present. Considerable concreteness is now being developed from the original vague surface structure sentence.

19. BOB: My god! My father never would have anything to do with me. He never showed any interest in me. That trip was one of the few times he stopped working to be with me. He died shortly after that trip, you know . . . (hesitates)

This could be termed the moment of insight. Bob begins to see at a deep emotional level how his father still has a very real grip on his daily life even though his father died years ago. A host of psychodynamic alternative hypotheses could be raised at this point. Among many others are the relationship between resentment toward Bob's absent father and the distance Bob has with Sonny, the feelings of love and anger held toward both, the fear of death being associated with close emotional experience (his father almost fell when things were going well, then he died shortly after a pleasant trip; and the vague anxiety surrounding Sonny on the fire tower), etc. This vast array of possible areas to explore partially explains the long duration of this approach to therapy. It is apparent that for major changes to occur with Bob (at least from this point of view), he must work through many, many experiences and connect them with the past.

20. HELPER: So to sum up to this point, it seems plausible that somehow the experience with Sonny on the tower relates back to your earlier experiences with your own father. A while back you commented that you wanted to hold your son close on the tower. Before that, do you remember what you said—just before that?

The therapist believes that the connections between father and son and father and son are clear to Bob and starts to recycle the interview back for more work. His summary of the interview to this point is accurate, but fails to take into account the present-tense confusion of the client. It would have been preferable to let Bob discuss more feelings about his father. The therapist in this case did not want to move to depth implications of Bob's relationship, so suggested recycling back to the Freudian slip. If the client had been ready, this could have been most effective in uncovering more clearly the parallels between the two relationships.

21. BOB: (A blank look comes over his face) No. Why?

The client was not ready for recycling back to an earlier point. The helper would have been more effective by staying with Bob's discovery at 19. However, errors occur in all interviews and the helper can still salvage the loss.

22. HELPER: Sounds like I'm off track. You were just saying that your father died just after that trip . . .

(The interview continues . . .)

The therapist offers a self-disclosure and then paraphrases one of the client's last important statements. This is a classic illustration of the use of simple attending behavior skills to work with a difficult situation. Generally it is best to admit errors of focus or timing and then to use attending skills to help return to the world of the client.

Microskills of the therapist included minimal encouragers, directives, reflection of feeling/paraphrasing, feedback, self-statement, interpretations, and a summarization. An orthodox psychoanalyst would be expected to use primarily interpretation due to the belief that other verbal statements tend to *direct* the client. The hope of psychodynamic approaches is to free the client to explore the world in her or his own unique fashion through free association. This is in the expectation that basic life patterns will reveal themselves with minimal therapist direction. In truth, most psychodynamic counselors will use skills other than pure interpretation to help move the client ahead faster; yet these other skills are invariably oriented toward interpretation and the generation of new meanings from the psychodynamic framework.

Often the most powerful and meaningful interpretations are based on the nonverbal behaviors of the client. The therapist at 14 did not interpret Bob's behavior, but his observation clearly affected the direction of the session.

Issues of surface and deep structure have been discussed throughout the typescript. Yet, there are several sentences worthy of further exploration and interpretation. One is at Bob: 3: "I really ought to show you what I did." This sentence provides an opportunity to explore authority relationships. "Sue hasn't been on me much lately" provides a chance to examine family situations. Thus, even in one single paragraph from the client, an array of surface structure sentences may appear that are potentially valuable for further exploration. The preceding two examples could lead eventually to those issues being discussed in the work phase of the interview. *While the surface structure sentences may change, the deeper structure remains constant.* The key sentence that was selected related to a major discrepancy at Bob: 5 and 7, in which we hear about a pleasant trip and the sudden feeling of panic. Emphasis in this session was on the deep structure patterns of similarity between fathers and sons. Still deeper levels of structural analysis are likely to occur in later phases of the psychodynamic interviewing process. Given twenty or thirty interviews, it is likely that sexual implications of the tower itself, the fear of falling, feelings of deep love and hate, and so on will become the issues in the counseling process. All these dimensions of psychodynamic theory could be generated from the single surface structure sentence.

While Bob has been able to generate new sentences to describe his situation and is thereby demonstrating more complete intentionality, it must be noted that the treatment has been within a traditional middle-class cultural pattern. Such issues as an achievement-oriented society, the demand for men to perform in certain culturally appropriate patterns, the fact of economic pressures and alienation, and other environmental-situational issues have not been discussed. The therapist and Bob are operating as if the problem is "in" Bob. Psychodynamic counseling and other theories, such as behaviorism and existential/ humanism all tend to focus more or less on individual change. While this may be effective for personal growth, it clearly does not show awareness of the full complexity of person-environment transactions.

In summary, it may be seen that the typescript analysis shows us some central characteristics of psychodynamic counseling. Thus far we have given central attention to the decisional aspects, skills, and qualities of the session. The next section discusses the application of theory to this interview and gives special attention to the practical skills used by the therapist, characteristic of many of those who are committed to psychodynamic uncovering counseling and therapy.

BASIC TECHNIQUES OF PSYCHODYNAMIC INTERVIEWING

Just as the word *unconscious* can be used to summarize Freud's entire theory, so can the technique *free association* be used to summarize psychodynamic methodology. At an elemental level, free association simply encourages the client and the counselor to say anything that comes to mind. A more rigorous definition is:

> Method according to which voice must be given to all thoughts without exception which enter the mind, whether such thoughts are based upon a specific element (word, number, dream-image, or any kind of idea at all) or produced spontaneously. (Laplanche and Pontalis, 1973, p. 169)

Freud developed free association in his early work with hysteria as he encouraged the patients to search for underlying unconscious factors; he refined it in his own self-analysis, particularly in dreams. It was out of dream analysis, in particular, that Freud discovered the "royal road to the unconscious." In allowing oneself to say anything at all that comes to mind (no matter how seemingly irrelevant), he found that a pattern frequently emerges to explain the meaning of a piece of behavior, a dream, or a seemingly random thought.

It is essential to point out that creative decision making, as outlined in Chapter 2, is closely allied with the techniques of free association. The client and counselor start with a definition of a basic issue or problem, the client free associates to whatever comes to mind, and a decision or solution begins to emerge. This process is paralleled in the case of the fire tower. As Bob defines his problem in the first tower, the therapist at 10 suggests that he "Stay with that feeling of panic and fright and then let your mind run free to your earliest memories possible and tell me the first scene that comes to your mind." Out of those free associations a more complete picture of Bob's experience begins to emerge.

More often, the process of free association is seemingly totally random. The following example illustrates how free association can be used in daily life to solve a problem. The same procedures used here are directly parallel to the psychoanalytic hour.

> A radio announcer recently interrupted my reverie to say that a clarinet concerto would next be played—Benny Goodman, soloist. During approximately the next ten seconds there occurred the following: Benny Goodman? That's right, he plays concert music, too. I wonder if I can tell the difference between Goodman and that English fellow, what's his name . . . can't think of it . . . anyhow I wouldn't know the difference . . . and my wife thinks I'm so adept at that type of thing. Look at me, I can't even distinguish Goodman from . . . What *is* his name? . . . I wonder why I cultivate that illusion of hers. I suppose it's because *she* knows so much about painting . . . Still, that is phoney of me. Of course, I *might* have done all right in music. If only that aunt of mine had been less insistent about the violin . . . How did I ever keep from killing that woman? So what if I *had* broken a finger playing baseball? Perhaps now I'd at least be able to distinguish Goodman from . . .

With the elusive name on the tip of my tongue, and with a sense of impending recognition, I was suddenly sitting in the bleachers in Fenway Park in Boston. George Kell, then third baseman for the Red Sox, was at bat and hit a killing line drive, the trajectory of which, from his bat to a point one inch above the wall, formed an absolutely unwavering acute angle. It was the last of the ninth and the Red Sox won by a very well-deserved inch.

George Kell . . . K-E-L-L . . . but, of course: *Reginald Kell* is that English fellow's name. (Jones, 1966, pp. 210–211)

The above example illustrates several key points in the process of free association. First, of course, is the importance of letting the mind wander freely if one wants to find a solution from the preconscious or unconscious. The associations to the disliked aunt at first seem totally irrelevant, but the desire to "kill" the aunt turns very shortly into a baseball scene with George *Kell* (except for one letter the two words are the same). Beyond that we also note other ideas which at the moment seem irrelevant—the competition with the wife, his wondering why he "cultivates that illusion of hers" (cultivation has a sexual connotation), the emphasis on the word Goodman (Good-man), and so forth—all of which are ripe topics for further free association into the unconscious mental functioning of the author. Figure 8.2 presents some additional free-association exercises and offers important practice for any person seriously interested in this approach to counseling.

Free association in the interview typescript was coupled with the technique of *staying with the feeling*. The therapist at 8 and 10 offers directives that the client should stay with the feeling of panic and use that as a base for free association. Through staying with either positive or negative feelings, it is possible to determine underlying messages from the unconscious and thus uncover valuable material for understanding oneself. By staying with the feeling and free associating to an earlier experience, Bob experienced a *focused free association*. This focused free association relates clearly and directly to his feelings toward his son. An even more powerful type of focused free association occurs with *repetition*. The concept of repetition relies heavily on the microskill of directive-giving and could be demonstrated as follows:

HELPER: Stay with that feeling. Make it in the here and now. Say, "I feel panicked."

BOB: I feel panicked.

HELPER: Again.

BOB: I feel panicked!

HELPER: And again.

BOB: (Shaking) I FEEL PANICKED!

HELPER: Now, go back to your past and share what you find.

In this example, Bob would probably go to the same setting as in the typescript, but the emotions associated with the event would be stronger and deeper.

Figure 8.2   *Free Association Exercises and Techniques*

The purpose of these exercises is to illustrate some basic and practical aspects of psychodynamic functioning. The person who moves through each exercise carefully will have a more complete sense of the importance of free association and its potential implementations in the counseling interview. Yet, these exercises are only a minor beginning to an incredibly complex theory.

1. *The symbols of everyday life.* Much of Freudian and psychodynamic thought is based on sexuality and sexual symbolism. A good way to understand symbols and their meanings is to go through a few basic free association/creativity exercises. Take a separate sheet of paper and brainstorm as many words as you can think of when you hear the word "penis." Make this list as long as you can. Now take the word "vagina" and make as extensive a list as you can.

   Now having made the two lists, expand them further. What objects in everyday life remind you of the penis and the vagina? What about types of people; the universe; things in your own living room? Make that list as long and extensive as you can. It can be suggested that brainstorming and creativity are closely allied to the processes of free association.

   Having completed your list, you may find it helpful to turn to the tenth lecture in Freud's *A General Introduction to Psychoanalysis* (1943) widely available in paperback form. You will find that many of the words and symbols you generated are listed in that chapter. It was in a similar, but less structured fashion, that Freud slowly constructed his entire theory of personality.

   As time and interest permits, take the words "intercourse," "death," "love," "hate," "breast," "masturbation," "birth," "body," and other specific words of interest to you. In each case, brainstorming a list of words will reveal a general pattern of the symbols which represent that idea or concept in everyday life.

2. *The "Freudian slip."* Slips of the tongue are often small windows on the unconscious. A student once walked into our office and asked if we gave "objectionable" tests. It takes but a very quick free association to understand this student's unconscious feelings. Not all such slips are as easily understood. But if one allows oneself to free associate, it is often possible to find the meaning of the error in speech. Think back on your own speech errors or those of your friends, then free associate to their meanings.

   The process of examining the psychology of errors may be studied in more detail in Freud's second, third, and fourth lectures (1943). Errors also show in our forgetting appointments, dropping things at crucial times, behavior which seems to repeat itself unnecessarily and in many other ways. Again, free association is a route toward understanding the meaning of these errors.

3. *Dream analysis.* Recall and write down a dream you have had. Then sit back, relax, and *focus* on one aspect of that dream. Letting your free associations lead you, open your mind to whatever comes. Then, see if any patterns or new ideas emerge that help you understand the dream.

   As an alternative, keep the whole dream in mind and relax. This time, free associate back to an early childhood experience. Then, follow that experience and go back to an even earlier childhood experience. In some cases, a third experience association may be helpful. Return to your dream and determine if the dream related to your associations.

   The preceding processes are similar to those employed in analysis of dreams. An examination of Freud's lectures five through fifteen will reveal that you have anticipated some of his constructs and ideas. It is possible, using free association techniques, to realize intuitively many of Freud's concepts before you read them. This direct experiencing of free association should help you to understand the intellective aspects of his theory more fully.

4. *Analysis of resistance.* Resistance is the name given to "everything in the words and actions of the . . . [client] that obstructs his gaining access to his unconscious." (Laplanche and Pontalis, 1973) Most likely, in one of the preceding exercises you "blocked" at some point and couldn't think of a word. Your free associations stopped for a moment. These blockages are mini-examples of resistance and illustrate the operation of the general defense mechanism of repression. To recover the lost association that was blocked, it is important that one first focus on the block itself. The following example may prove helpful. Let us assume you want to understand your feelings toward your parents or some other important person in your life in more depth. One route to this is free associating a list of words that come to your mind in relation to this individual. For example, suppose that one free associates to one's lover the following: "warmth, love, that hike to Lake Supreme, bed, touching, sexuality, (block), tenderness, an argument over my looking at another person, anger, frustration, (block)." First, one can get a general picture of feelings and important thoughts via this free association exercise. It is next appropriate to turn to the block and to use one of the following techniques to understand the block (or resistance): (1) free associate, using the block as a starting point (a clue may come via this route); (2) sing a song, let it come to your mind as you relax, then free associate from that song; (3) draw a picture, and once again free associate; (4) go to the bookshelf and select a book, or go to a dictionary and select a word, and free associate from what you select (sometimes the answer will be there immediately).

   This small set of exercises does not explain resistance in its full complexity. If you have entered into it fully and flexibly, you may have broken through one of your own blocks or resistances and developed a slightly better understanding of yourself. An examination of Freud's nineteenth lecture will amplify these concepts and perhaps suggest additional exercises for you.

5. *Analysis of transference.* We sometimes find people we immediately dislike. Psychodynamic theory suggests that we have transferred past feelings related to someone from our past onto this new individual. Select someone you have problems with and try some of the free associations exercises already suggested. Later, examine Freud's twenty-seventh lecture and compare what you anticipated with what he said.

Dream analysis is another important technique of psychodynamic approaches. Dream analysis can be conducted at a surface level where the *manifest* or *observed content* of the dream is examined again through free association. Underlying the conscious parts of the dream is *latent content* with the deeper structures of meaning. Free association, repetition, and staying with the feeling are used by psychodynamic counselors in the analysis of dreams. The topic of the session with Bob could well have been a dream. The arrangement and framing of the interview would follow the same structure and use the same techniques if the situation at the fire tower had been a dream.

Another important theoretical and methodological issue in psychodynamic approaches is *analysis of resistance*. "Resistance" includes everything in the words and behaviors of the client that prevent access to unconscious material. The temptation in many approaches to helping is to ignore resistance and find another route toward easy client verbalization. The effective psychodynamic counselor or therapist, by contrast, often gives prime attention to resistances. In the process of counseling you will often find a client who fails to hear an important statement from the counselor. The client may say "What?" and a puzzled look appears on her or his face. Alternatively, the client may hear the therapist but forget what was said within a minute or two or between interviews. Other types of resistance appear when the client blocks on something he or she is trying to say, leaves out a key part of a dream, comes late to an interview, or refuses to free associate. Resistances show themselves in many ways as the client unconsciously tries to sabotage the treatment process.

Resistance is best considered an opportunity for a deeper understanding. The task of the psychodynamic counselor is in deciding whether or not to confront a resistance immediately or at a later point. The resistance often represents a major incongruency or discrepancy in the client or in the relationship between the counselor and client. One approach to analysis of resistance is to label or interpret the resistance and then encourage the client to free associate to the facts and feelings associated with the resistance.

The clearest example of resistance in the interview typescript shows at Bob: 21 where Bob has difficulty in hearing the therapist's question. This question, as noted previously, was probably premature. If the counselor wishes to work on this resistance, interpretation or directed free association would be a viable route toward deeper understanding of Bob's unconscious processes at that moment. Further examples of how resistance may be experienced and understood are presented in Figure 8.2.

Analysis of transference and counter-transference are two other important techniques of psychodynamic counselors. Transference refers to feelings and thoughts the client has toward the counselor. Counter-transference refers to feelings and thoughts the counselor has toward the client. In transference analysis, we find the client does not have a clear picture of the nature of the helper due much to the neutrality and objectivity of the counselor. The client is quite likely to *project* an imagined image about the therapist. The client has literally *transferred* feelings and thoughts he or she has toward other people onto the therapist. These data provide the therapist with "here and now" information on the immediate life experience of the client. An example of elementary transference feelings is demonstrated at Bob: 3, where he comments that he ought to show the therapist what he did with the blueprints. The techniques of coping with a transference situation are similar to those of dealing with resistance. The transference is identified and labeled, and free association techniques are used to clarify meaning. Too premature and too direct examination of transference feelings can confuse and trouble the client, so most use of this technique is made in the middle or later stages of therapy (thirty-plus interviews). Virtually all counselors and therapists, regardless of their theoretical orientation, observe transference in their client's comments. However, differing theories vary widely in their use of analysis of transference, and some ignore this concept completely.

Counter-transference often results in counselor "blind spots" and can be destructive and disruptive to the interview process. The feelings that the counselor has toward the client must be identified, isolated, and worked through. A major portion of training in psychoanalytic work is devoted to a form of therapy for the counselor in which the counselor shares feelings, attitudes, and fantasies held toward the client with the psychodynamic training supervisor. The supervisor also analyzes counter-transference feelings through use of free association and the several concepts and methods of psychodynamic counseling. Supervision for the psychodynamic therapist appears very much like typical counselor-client interview. Strong counter-transference feelings and feelings of resistance toward the client may preclude counselors working with some clients until personal counseling or therapy is undertaken. Awareness of feelings toward the client and ability to cope with these feelings are essential to any therapist.

Psychodynamic counseling approaches are interpretive. *Interpretation* is a sophisticated and complex skill in which intellectual knowledge of psychodynamic theory is integrated with clinical data of the client. In Chapter 3, we defined the microskill of interpretation as the renaming of client experience from an alternative frame of reference or worldview. Applied specifically to psychodynamic approaches, the skill of interpretation comes from the worldview of psychoanalysis and seeks to identify wishes, needs, and patterns from the unconscious world of the client. The interpretation at Helper: 18 represents a renaming of Bob's experience with his son. It can be seen at Bob: 19 that the interpretation is accepted and expanded upon. Still deeper interpretations of the same situation are possible ("In some ways, you'd like to kill your son just as you sometimes wanted to kill your father;" "This represents your feelings of sexual inadequacy and ambivalence about the sex act."). Needless to say, such interpretations would be unacceptable and destructive early in therapy, but might be fruitful sources of discussion in the middle portion of therapy (twenty interviews or more). Surface interpretations are generally considered appropriate early in psychotherapy, while depth interpretations wait until a relationship of trust has been developed between counselor and client.

Some specific guidelines for interpretation may be suggested. First, the counselor needs to use attending skills carefully so the data for an interpretation are clear. Next, the interpretation is stated and the client is given time to react. The helper may "check out" the client and ask "How do you react to that?" or "Does that ring a bell?" or "Does that make sense?" The check-out encourages the client to think through, and assimilate or reject the interpretation. This process is demonstrated in Helper: 16 through Helper: 20. However, it is clear at Bob: 21 that insufficient time was given for checking out the client's perceptions.

Intentional psychodynamic therapists produce clients who can make their own interpretations. When a client interprets her or his own story in new words, the client has realized an *insight*. Insight may be described as the ability to look at old information from new perspectives, and thus is directly related to intentionality and creative responding. The person who is able to interpret life experience in new ways through insight is able to generate new sentences to describe the world. However, it is also important to note that these new sentences are almost invariably verbal. A verbal insight or new sentence is useful only if the client is able to take the new information out of the session and use it in daily life. A major criticism of some psychodynamic approaches is the constant emphasis on insight, which produces a client who is searching diligently in the past while continuing to have problems in coping with present-tense everyday living.

To summarize this section on basic techniques of psychodynamic counseling, one central fact should stand out: *Free association is the basis for all the techniques discussed.* We first examined the concept of free association in some detail, and it was pointed out that creativity training, as presented in Chapter 2, is closely allied to this concept. Free association is the most direct route to reach unconscious experience. The techniques discussed (staying with the feeling, focused free association, repetition, dream analysis, analysis of resistance, analysis of transference and counter-transference, and interpretation) all rely on free association in some aspect. To uncover unconscious material, the psychodynamic therapist needs to be skilled in creative free association and in inducing that same verbal skill in clients. However, to this basic skill, psychodynamic counselors add *intellectual discipline.* The next section discusses the immediate practical implications of this approach, so we will first stress the demanding intellectual rigor required of those who would practice this approach to personal development and change.

SOME LIMITATIONS AND PRACTICAL IMPLICATIONS OF PSYCHODYNAMIC APPROACHES

Laplanche and Pontalis have made a careful study of the derivation and meaning of key psychoanalytic concepts, and discuss the concept of *wild analysis:*

> Broadly understood, this expression refers to the procedure of amateur or inexperienced "analysts" who attempt to interpret symptoms, dreams, utterances, actions, etc. on the basis of psychoanalytic notions which they have as often as not misunderstood. In a more technical sense, an interpretation is deemed "wild" if a specific analytic situation is misapprehended in its current dynamics and its particularity, and especially if the repressed content is simply imparted to the client with no heed paid to the resistances and to the transference.
>
> In the article which Freud devoted to "Wild Psycho-Analysis" . . . , he defined it first of all in terms of ignorance. The doctor whose intervention he criticises here has committed errors both *scientific* (regarding the nature of sexuality, repression, anxiety) and *technical:* "Attempts to 'rush' (the patient) at first consultation, by brusquely telling him the secrets which have been discovered by the physician, are technically objectionable . . ." Thus anyone who "knows a few of the findings of psychoanalysis" but has not undergone the required theoretical and technical training . . . can be said to be a practitioner of wild analysis. (Laplanche and Pontalis, 1973, p. 480)

Figure 8.3   *An Exercise in Psychodynamic Interviewing*

The purpose of this exercise is to illustrate how the skills and concepts of the first seven chapters of this text may be used to conduct a basic interview from a psychodynamic perspective. You will find that analysis of a dream or a client's reaction to an authority figure work well in the following framework. Alternatively, you may have identified a repeating life pattern in which the client tends to have a certain style of response, thought, feeling, or behavior in several situations.

If you wish, you could go through the stages by yourself thinking to yourself about one of your own dreams, reactions to authority, or your own repeating patterns.

The framework presented here will provide you with an introduction to *how* psychodynamically oriented counseling and therapy may be conducted.

STAGE 1: RAPPORT/STRUCTURING.

Develop rapport with the client in your own natural way. Inform the client that you will work through some basic psychodynamic understandings about a dream, a relationship with authority, or a life pattern. Decide the issue to be worked on mutually.

STAGE 2: DATA GATHERING.

Use the basic listening sequence (BLS) of questions, encouragers, paraphrasing, and reflection of feeling to bring out the issue in detail. If a dream, be sure that you bring out the facts of the dream, the feelings in the dream, and the client's organization of the dream. If you are working with an authority issue, draw out a concrete situation and obtain the facts, feelings, and organization of the issue. In the case of repeating patterns, draw out several concrete examples of the pattern. Once you have heard the issue presented thoroughly, summarize it using the client's main words and check it out to ensure that have understood the client correctly.

At this point, it is often wise to stop for a moment and use the positive asset search. Specifically, use the BLS to draw out the facts, feelings, and organization of something positive in the client's life. This may or may not be related to the dream or authority figure. Clients tend to move and talk more freely from a base of security.

STAGE 3. DETERMINING OUTCOMES.

Setting up a specific goal of understanding may be useful. A general goal may be to find earlier life experiences that relate to the dream, authority issue, or repeating life pattern. Use the BLS to specify what the client would like to gain from this interview.

STAGE 4. GENERATING ALTERNATIVE SOLUTIONS.

Depending on your purpose and your relationship with this client, there are three major alternatives for analyzing the problem which may be useful.

Alternative 1: Summarize the dream, authority issue, or pattern, and then summarize the desired outcome of the session. Ask your client "What comes to mind as a possible explanation?" If you have communicated the fact that you have been listening, you will often find that clients generate new ideas and interpretations on their own. The structure provided by the interview decisional model and listening is often sufficient to help clients analyze and understand their own problems.

Alternative 2: Summarize the issue and then reflect the central emotion you may have noted in the conflict or ask the client what one single emotion stands out from the first part of the interview. Ask the client to focus on that emotion and *stay with that feeling.* Through the use of the focused free association exercise, direct the client to concentrate on that emotion and then to free associate back to an earlier life experience—the earlier the better. (You will find that free associations are more valuable if made from an emotional state rather than from a state of clear cognitive awareness.) Most clients' first association is with some experience in their teenage years, while others associate to a recent event. In either case, draw out the association using the basic listening sequence.

You now should have the facts, feelings, and organization of the dream, reaction to authority, or pattern and the facts, feelings, and organization of the first association. Based on a clear summary of these two, you and the client should be able to find some *consistent pattern of meaning*. The discovery and notation of these patterns is an example of a basic psychodynamic interpretation.

You will often find repeating *key words* in *both* the association and the original dream or problem. Deeper understandings may come from continuing the exercise as below.

Alternative 3: Continue as in 2 above, but ask your client to free associate to even earlier life experience. Again, use the focused free association technique. Draw out these earlier free associations with the BLS. You may assemble over time a group of recollections and you will find several patterns in the associations that repeat themselves in general daily life.

At this point, the client may make her or his own interpretations of meaning or you may add your own interpretations. Generally speaking, interpretations generated by the client are the more long-lasting.

STAGE 5. GENERALIZATION.

Psychodynamic therapy is not typically oriented to transfer or learnings from the interview to daily life. However, it may be helpful to ask the client to summarize the interview. What did the client summarize as the main facts, feelings, and organization of the interview? As appropriate, you may want to add to the client's perspective and work toward some action.

COMMENT.

It may be observed that the structure of the interview plus microskills of Chapter 3 are most basic to structuring a successful psychodynamically oriented interview. However, cultural and individual empathy, client observation skills (both of verbal and nonverbal behavior, incongruities, pacing, and leading), and the positive asset search are all critical dimensions in a successful session. What psychodynamic theory adds to the process is a *content*, a specific direction and purpose for which to use the skills—*the uncovering of life patterns and relating them back to earlier life experiences with specific theoretical interpretations.*

Thus, the clearest and most immediate practical application of psychodynamic principles is a keen awareness of the practicalities and problems underlying wild analysis. One of the major problems of the psychodynamic approach to counseling has been the amateurs who know a little about the concepts and apply them freely to friends and clients with no real understanding of their meaning and force.

Psychodynamic approaches require not only a general knowledge of the field and a few techniques, they also require and demand extensive study, reading, and supervised practice by carefully trained individuals who have completed years of study. It may be stated that psychodynamic training requires the most rigorous intellectual discipline of all methods. Fullblown psychodynamic practice is not for the beginner.

Nonetheless, there are important learnings from this approach which can be helpful to almost all counselors and therapists. First among these is an *awareness* that what a client presents as a surface problem, concern, or behavior may not be the issue. Underlying a surface structure description of a problem may be a vast array of unconscious or unknown forces, ideas, and thoughts. The technique of assisting clients to free associate through structured directions (*focused free association*), such as those used in the interview typescript, can often bring about a more complete awareness of underlying issues.

Transference. The concept of *transference* occuring in the therapeutic relationship represents one of the central contributions of psychodynamic theory to the entire field of professional helping. It is highly likely your clients will transfer their past history of interpersonal relationships into the interview. Before your eyes, you will find clients repeating with you their past relationships with significant others. If you are working with a client facing a divorce, you may find that client reacting to you personally in the here and now as he or she did with the spouse. You may or may not choose to work on these issues, but awareness of this transferential type of pattern with you is essential regardless of your theoretical orientation.

Countertransference. The repetition of your own life patterns in relationship to the client and/or the client's transference to you is equally possible. This is countertransference. Certain clients "push a button" with us as therapists. These clients may represent through their words and behaviors issues in our own lives which we have not worked through. Dealing with the complex issues of countertransference can be difficult and it is here that supervision and consultation with colleagues and superiors may be most helpful to you and to the client. The best way to deal with your own countertransference toward the client is to openly acknowledge its possible existence.

Yet, once again we would stress the danger of wild analysis—the improper and loose use of elementary understanding of psychodynamic constructs. The greatest danger to any counseling theory is enthusiastic adherents who fail to understand their limitations. Unfortunately, wild analysis is not restricted to beginning therapists and may appear in the work of seasoned professionals who have missed critical issues of resistance, transference, and counter-transference in the interview.

SUMMARY OF THIS CHAPTER

Competence in the ideas presented in this chapter would require that you be able to:

1. *Identify Freud as the first person to explain individual mental functioning in a systematic frame.* Until his arrival, there was no real understanding of mental illness or internal thought process, and no really workable approach to treatment. He leaves

a legacy of thought that has affected Western society and has been amplified by his many important followers, such as Adler, Jung, and Fromm.

2. *Describe some of the important theoretical constructs of psychodynamic therapy.* The Freudian worldview was presented as changing and adapting and its practice varies from the American ego-psychologists to the desire of the followers of Jacques Lacan to "return to Freud." Regardless, all of this general orientation embraces the concept of the unconscious and its power over conscious action. Important theoretical constructs described in this chapter include the patterns of growth stemming from childhood object relations and their linkage to adult behavior and thought. Defense mechanisms were discussed as examples of continuations of childhood experience. The concepts of id, ego, and superego functioning were presented.

3. *Understand basic constructions of developmental theory.* An object relations approach to development was presented with stress on the importance of separation and attachment as basic needs of the developing child and infant. The importance of the holding environment of the mother was discussed and oral, anal, and oedipal developmental issues were considered.

4. *Describe some basic techniques used in psychodynamic interviewing.* Free association was presented as a basic technique which can be implemented by staying with the feeling, focused free association, and repetition. Analysis of resistance and of transference and counter-transference feelings was considered. Interpretation was named as a technique which requires a thorough understanding of psychodynamic theory.

5. *Identify some practical implications of psychodynamic approaches.* Awareness of unconscious behaviors on the part of the client is vital. Direct applications of the techniques above were discussed in practice. One useful modern approach for an understanding of psychodynamic methods is transactional analysis. A practical exercise for this approach was presented in addition to the preceding.

6. *Define and use key terms in this chapter.* Important words and concepts include: unconscious experience, interpretation, free association, staying with the feeling, focused free association, repetition, resistance, transference, countertransference, insight, and wild analysis.

REFERENCES

BOWLBY, J.,   *Attachment.* New York: Basic Books, 1969.

BOWLEY, J.,   *Separation.* New York: Basic Books, 1973.

COREY, G.,   *Theory and Practice of Counseling and Psychotherapy.* Monterey, CA: Brooks/ Cole, 1977.

ERIKSON, E.,   *Childhood and Society* (2nd ed.). New York: Norton, 1964.

FREUD, S.,   *A General Introduction to Psychoanalysis.* Garden City, NY: Doubleday, 1943.

GUNTRIP, H.,   *Schizoid Phenomena, Object Relations, and the Self.* New York: International Universities Press, 1968.

JONES, R.,   *Contemporary Educational Psychology.* New York: Harper and Row, 1966.

KERNBERG, O.,   "Developmental Theory, Structural Organization and Psychoanalytic Technique." In *Rapprochement.* New York: Aronson, 1980.

KLEIN, M.,   *Envy and Gratitude and Other Works, 1946–1963.* London, Hogarth, 1975.

LACAN, J.,   *Écrits: A Selection.* New York: Norton, 1966/1977.

LAPLANCHE, J., and J. PONTALIS,   *The Language of Psychoanalysis.* New York: Norton, 1973.

SUGGESTED SUPPLEMENTARY READING

The format for this reading list will change from preceding chapters. Two introductory books on Freudian constructs will be suggested, followed by a list of important readings from some of those who have adapted and shaped his works but who remain in the psychodynamic tradition.

FREUD, S., *A General Introduction to Psychoanalysis.* Garden City, NY: Doubleday, 1943. (Also available in numerous paperback editions.)

Freud provides the best introduction to his own work and this series of lectures is written in clear prose. Too many read Freud in secondary sources, failing to realize that he is the best presenter of his own ideas.

HALL, C., *A Primer of Freudian Psychology.* New York: NAL (Mentor), 1954.

This popular paperback provides a clear and systematic overview of Freud's work.

Other Suggested Readings

ADLER, A., *The Practice and Theory of Individual Psychology.* New York: Harcourt, Brace, Jovanovich, 1927.

ERIKSON, E., *Childhood and Society* (2nd ed.). New York: Norton, 1964.

FROMM, E., *Escape from Freedom.* New York: Holt, Rinehart & Winston, 1941.

GREENBERG, J., and S. MITCHELL, *Object Relations in Psychoanalytic Theory.* Cambridge, MA.: Harvard, 1983.

HORNEY, K., *Neurosis and Human Growth.* New York: Norton, 1950.

JONES, E., *The Life and Work of Sigmund Freud.* New York: Basic Books, *1,* 1953; *2,* 1955; *3,* 1957.

JUNG, C., *Modern Man in Search of a Soul.* New York: Harcourt, Brace, Jovanovich, 1933.

KLEIN, M., *Envy and Gratitude and Other Works, 1946–1963.* London, Hogarth, 1975.

LACAN, J., *Écrits: A Selection.* New York: Norton, 1966/1977.

LACAN, J., *Feminine Sexuality.* New York: Norton, 1968/1982.

MASTERSON, J., *The Narcissistic and Borderline Disorders: An Integrated Developmental Approach.* New York: Brunner/Mazel, 1981.

RANK, O., *The Trauma of Birth.* New York: Harcourt, Brace, Jovanovich, 1929.

REICH, W., *The Function of the Orgasm.* (Orgone Institute, 1942). New York: Bantam, 1967.

SULLIVAN, H., *The Interpersonal Theory of Psychiatry.* New York: Norton, 1953.

9

BEHAVIORAL THERAPY

GENERAL PREMISE

An integrated knowledge of skills, theory, and practice is essential for culturally intentional counseling and therapy.

Skills form the foundation of effective theory and practice: The culturally intentional therapist knows how to construct a creative decision-making interview and can use microskills to attend to and influence clients in a predicted direction. Important in this process are individual and cultural empathy, client observation skills, assessment of person and environment, and the application of positive techniques of growth and change.

Theory provides organizing principles for counseling and therapy: *The culturally intentional counselor has knowledge of alternative theoretical approaches and treatment modalities, in this case—behavioral therapy.*

Practice is the integration of skills and theory: The culturally intentional counselor or therapist is competent in skills and theory, and is able to apply them to research and practice for client benefit.

Undergirding integrated competence in skills, theory, and practice is an intentional awareness of one's own personal worldview and how that worldview may be similar to and/or different from the worldview and personal constructions of the client and other professionals.

GOALS FOR BEHAVIORAL THERAPY

Insight is not action. Understanding the underlying causes of individual problems does not necessarily change one's everyday life. Behavioral counseling is centrally concerned with concrete change and empowerment of clients—giving them control over their own actions and destiny.

This chapter seeks to:

1. Describe the worldview of behavioral therapy and counseling as one which focuses on what can be seen and the environment's impact on the client.
2. Present applied behavioral analysis, the systematic examination of the client in relation to the environment as a central theoretical and methodological construct of this system.
3. Examine assertiveness training, an especially useful change method, through analysis of an interview transcript.
4. Present some key behavioral techniques which you may find useful, among them relaxation training, systematic desensitization, and relapse prevention.
5. Provide you with an opportunity to assemble these ideas in a model assertiveness training interview that will provide you with a practical introduction to behavioral counseling.

INTRODUCTION

Historically, behavioral counseling is rooted in the work of the behaviorists John Watson and B. F. Skinner. In Skinner's view, our behavior is determined by what happens to us as a result of our behavior. If we are reinforced for what we do, then likely we will continue to engage in that behavior. If we are ignored or punished, the behavior is likely to cease. Behavioral therapy seeks to help control the consequences of our behavior, thus leading us to change our actions.

Humans may be said to be born behaving and the responses (reinforcements) they receive determine the type of person they will become. The task of therapy, then, is to give special attention to the impact of the environment on the client. Skinner made a powerful statement of this point of view in his behavioral novel, *Walden Two* (1968), in which an entire community is trained to work together effectively. Skinner, the prime mover of behaviorism, has taken a radical view about the ability of the individual to control his or her life and destiny. A full Skinnerian view is that we do not control our lives, but are controlled by the reinforcers in our environment. Skinner's radical behavioral philosophy has been criticized, but it also must be recognized as a major force in the growth of the field of psychology, regardless of one's theoretical or philosophical orientation.

B. F. Skinner
Photo by Therese M. Statz

BEHAVIORAL WORLDVIEW

Behavioral psychology is related to the concept of *modernity,* which is a philosophic approach that emphasizes the impact of science. Modernity and behavioral psychology are rooted in the ideal of progress, in the faith of science to solve human problems, and in a devaluation of the past. (Woolfolk and Richardson, 1984) The worldview of behaviorism may be described as antithetical to that of the psychodynamic approaches which emphasize the idea that history drives and directs the present.

Behavioral psychology developed primarily in the United States and is very typically "American": It is scientific, forward-moving, optimistic, and concerned with "what works." This scientific pragmatism, coupled with the headline-making position of Skinner, inevitably raises questions, and behavioral psychology often laments the criticism it receives (Franks, 1982). Much of this criticism stems from the idea of "scientific control of human behavior." While people enjoy the fruits of science and technology, applying similar rational systems to the human species has not been as acceptable to many.

The worldview presented by Skinner suggests that we humans can have the closest approximation to "freedom" through recognizing that we can control and shape behavior in our culture and our families if we choose. We can "choose" what behavior to reinforce. The question, of course, is "who decides?"

In 1974 Albert Bandura, one of the most prominent behavioral psychologists, made a statement that moved the field to an evolving "behavioral humanism" which emphasizes that the client should be deeply involved in the choice and direction of treatment. You will note that behavioral psychology has now become one of the most explicit systems of helping and it emphasizes individual rights in the treatment process. Bandura's current work is on "self-efficacy" (1982), a concept highly similar to intentionality, and stresses that individuals grow best when they feel they are in control of their own destiny.

At this point in time, the worldview of behavioral psychology could be said to be shifting and moving more toward the concepts of Bandura's self-efficacy, although a keen awareness of the power of the environment to shape the individual remains.

SOME CENTRAL THEORETICAL CONSTRUCTS

Behavioral counseling rests on *applied behavioral analysis,* a systematic method of examining the client and the client's environment and, jointly with the client, developing specific interventions to alter life conditions. You will find that applied behavioral analysis is a useful set of constructs that can help you understand your client better, regardless of which orientation to therapy and counseling you select.

Successful applied behavioral analysis rests on four foundations: (1) the *relationship* between the counselor and the client: (2) the definition of the problem through *operationalization of behavior:* (3) the understanding of the full context of the problem through *functional analysis:* and (4) the establishment of *socially important goals* for the client. At the conclusion of this chapter, you will have the opportunity to use some of the concepts of operationalization of behavior as you practice the method in a model assertiveness training exercise. As you read the following you may note that ordering of activities in applied behavioral analysis closely follows the first three stages of the decisional interview presented in Chapter 2. The structure is similar, but the content this time focuses on behavior and not on decisions.

Relationship

At one point in the past, it was thought that those who engaged in behavioral approaches were cold, distant, and mechanical. A research study in 1975 (Sloane, et al.) forever changed this view. Sloane and his colleagues examined expert therapists from a variety of theoretical orientations and found that behavioral therapists exhibited higher level of empathy, self-congruence, and interpersonal contact than other therapists, while levels of warmth and regard were approximately the same. Behavioral therapists may be expected to be as interested in rapport and human growth as any other orientation. If one is to help clients develop, one must be a reinforcing person.

In addition to working toward rapport, behavior therapists engage in careful structuring of the interview. Behavior therapists have very specific methodologies and goals. They are willing and anxious to share their plans with the client in the expectation that the client will share with them in the therapy process.

Operationalization of Behavior

Applied behavioral analysis may perhaps be the most systematic form of gathering information from clients of any form of therapy. Behavioral counseling rests on discovering clear and precise data about client *behavior and action.*

Chapter 2 states that one of your first tasks is to obtain a general summary of the client's problem. Applied behavioral analysis accomplishes this task through focusing on what the client *does* and how he or she *behaves.* There is a constant effort to understand the client's life in terms of concrete behaviors. This may be contrasted with psychodynamic theories and methods which consider overt behavior relatively unimportant and search with the client for explanations underlying the behavior. Behavioral psychology, pragmatic and realistic, works with "what is," what can be seen in the real world and changed through scientific planning.

Let us assume, for example, that you have a client who is depressed and talks about feeling sad. In psychodynamic therapy, you might seek to discover the roots of sadness while in cognitive or humanistic therapies, you might want to change the way the client thinks about the world. However, in behavioral therapy, particularly through applied behavioral analysis, the task is to determine what the patient "does" specifically and concretely when he or she feels depressed:

COUNSELOR: You say you feel depressed. Could you tell me some of the specific things you do when you are depressed?

CLIENT: Well, I cry a lot. Some days I can't get out of bed. I feel sad most of the time.

COUNSELOR: How does your body feel?

CLIENT: It feels tense and drawn all over, almost like little hammers are beating me from inside. It gets so bad sometimes that I can't sleep.

The counselor's two questions have made the behaviors related to the general construct of depression far more obvious. Crying, failure to get out of bed, feelings of bodily tension, and inability to go to sleep are *operational behaviors* which can be seen, measured, and even counted. The feelings of sadness, however, are somewhat more vague and further operationalization of the sentence "I feel sad most of the time," might result in the following, more specific, behaviors:

COUNSELOR: A short time ago you said you feel sad much of the time. Could you elaborate a little more on that?

CLIENT: Well, I cry a lot and I can hardly get moving. My wife says all I do is bitch and complain.

COUNSELOR: So sadness means crying and difficulty in getting moving . . . and you complain a lot . . . You also said you felt tense and drawn inside . . . hammers, I think you said.

In the preceding excerpt, the counselor ties in the vague feelings of sadness with the more concrete operational behaviors mentioned by the client.

The objective of operationalization of behavior, then, is the concretizing of vague words into objective, observable actions. Virtually all behavioral counselors will seek this specificity at some point in the interview, believing it is more possible to work with objective behavior than with vague nonspecific concepts, such as depression and sadness. A simple but basic clue, when engaged in operationalization of behavior, is to ask the question, "Can I see, feel, hear, or touch the words the client is using?" The client may speak of a desire for more warmth from one's spouse; the behavior therapist cannot see, feel, hear, or touch "warmth," and would seek to have this concept operationalized in terms of touching, vocal tone, or certain verbal statements ("I wish my wife would touch me more and say more good things about me").

Functional Analysis

An individual's behavior is directly related to events and stimuli in the environment. A second task of the behavior therapist is to discover how client behaviors occur in the "natural environment." Behavioral counselors and behavior therapists talk about the "A,B,C's" of functional analysis: the study of *antecedent events,* the *resultant behavior,* and the *consequence(s)* of that behavior. For example, the behavioral counselor is interested in knowing what happened just prior to a specific behavior, what the specific behavior or event was, and what the result or consequence of that behavior was on the client and the environment.

COUNSELOR: So far, I've heard that you are generally depressed, that you get these feelings of tiredness and tension. Now could you give me a specific example of a situation where you felt this way? I want to know what happened just before the depression came upon you, what happened as you got those feelings and thoughts, and what resulted after. First, tell me about the last time you had these feelings.

CLIENT: Well, it happened yesterday . . . (sigh) . . . I came home from work and was feeling pretty good. But when I came in the house Bonnie wasn't there, so I sat down and started to read . . .

COUNSELOR: (Interrupting) What was your reaction when your wife wasn't home?

CLIENT: I was a little disappointed, but not much, I just sat down.

COUNSELOR: Go ahead . . .

CLIENT: After about half an hour she came in and just walked by me . . . I said hello, but she was angry at me still from last night when we had that argument. Funny, I always feel relieved and free after we have an argument . . . almost like I get it out of my system.

COUNSELOR: Then what happened?

CLIENT: Well . . . I tried to get her to talk, but she ignored me. After about 10 minutes I got really sad and depressed. I went to my room and lay down until supper. But just before supper, she came in and said she was sorry, but I just felt more depressed.

COUNSELOR: Let's see if I can put that sequence of events together. You were feeling pretty good, but your wife wasn't home and then didn't respond to you because she was angry. You tried to get her to respond and she wouldn't [antecedents]; then you got depressed and felt bad and went to your room and laid down [resultant behavior]; she ignored you for awhile, but finally came to you and you ignored her [consequences]. The pattern seems to be similar to what you've told me about before: (1) you try something; (2) she doesn't respond; (3) you get discouraged, depressed feelings and tensions—sometimes even crying; and (4) she comes back to you and apologizes, but you reject her.

Through this type of examination of functional cause and effect relationships, the counselor comes to understand the sequence of events underlying the overt behavior of a client. Out of such functional patterns, it is possible to design behavioral programs to change the pattern of events.

Important in performing functional analysis is being aware of how behavior develops and maintains itself through a system of rewards or *reinforcers* and punishments. At the simplest level we can state that *whatever follows a particular piece of behavior will influence the probability of its happening again.* In the case of the depressed husband, it may be noted that the husband gained no attention from his wife until he became depressed. At this point, and at this point only, she came to him. It may be seen that his wife's behavior is heavily influencing the probability of his becoming depressed. Skinner has noted:

> Several important generalized reinforcers arise when behavior is reinforced by other people. A simple case is *attention*. The child who misbehaves "just to get

attention" is familiar. The attention of people is reinforcing because it is a necessary condition for other reinforcements from them. In general, only people who are attending to us reinforce our behavior. . . . Attention is often not enough. Another person is likely to reinforce only that part of one's behavior of which he approves, and any sign of his *approval* becomes reinforcing in its own right. (1953, p. 78)

Patterns of attention are particularly important in understanding human relationships. In this case, it may be noted that the husband gets attention only when he becomes depressed, and his wife's attention at that time only reinforces further feelings of depression and hopelessness. If she were to attend to him when he initiated behavior, it is possible—even likely—that certain portions of his pattern of depression would be alleviated. However, it must be noted, as well, that the husband does not attend to (reinforce) his wife's coming to him in the bedroom. He ignores her and helps continue the pattern of mutual lack of reinforcement. Either individual could break the self-defeating pattern of antecedents, behavior, and consequences.

Any meaningful functional analysis must examine the reinforcement patterns maintaining the system of an individual or couple. The social reinforcers of attention and approval are particularly potent and vital in human relationships. However, money, food, grades, and other tangibles are important reinforcers that must be considered in any functional analysis. Other social rewards, such as smiles, affection, and recognition, are often important; and it must be remembered that in many cases negative attention (punishment) is often preferred to being ignored. Ignoring a behaving human being can be the most painful of punishments.

Establishing Behavior Change Goals

If a counselor is to help a client, the behavior change must be relevant to the client. Client involvement is now an axiom in the development of any behavioral change program. It could be argued that, in a sense, modern behavioral counseling involves the client in the change process more as an equal with the counselor than any other theoretical system. Sulzer-Azaroff and Mayer have stated:

Applied behavioral analysis programs assist clients to improve behaviors that will promote their own personal and social development. Consequently, prior to its implementation, a program must clearly communicate and justify how it will assist the client to function more effectively in society, both in the near and distant future. It also must show how any changes that accompany the behavior change of focus will not interfere with the client's or the community's short- and long-range goals. . . . It does not deal with bar pressing. . . . Nor should it serve individuals or agencies whose goals are to the detriment of either clients or their immediate and broader societies. (1977, p. 7)

During the goal-setting phase of the interview, the counselor will work with the client to find highly specific and relevant goals. Rather than, "My goal is not to be depressed anymore," the behavioral counselor will work toward detailed specific plans and goals for the future. One early goal might be as basic as going to a movie or learning to dance. (It is harder to be depressed when one is active and doing something.) Later goals might be to join a community club, start jogging, and find a job. Rather than take "depression" as a broad construct, applied behavioral analysis breaks depression down into manageable behavioral units and teaches clients how to live their lives more happily and effectively.

Throughout applied behavioral analysis, there is an emphasis on concrete doing and action. The individual must "do" something that can be seen, heard, and felt. Thoughts are less important (but become central in behavioral psychology's offspring, cognitive-behavioral psychology discussed in Chapter 11). Interestingly, behavioral psychotherapy often tends to be especially effective with depressives as its emphasis on doing and acting rather than on self-reflection gets the client moving. The emphasis on movement, action, and doing, again, tends to be quite American and pragmatic in orientation.

The matter of relationship and structuring in applied behavioral analysis, of course, relates to the first phase of the five-stages of the interview. Operationalization of behavior is centrally concerned with accurate problem definition (but, of course, from the behavioral point of view). Functional analysis is a deeper, contextual definition of the problem which brings in environmental contingencies and helps the therapist see the context of the total problem. Finally, the setting of joint goals with the client relates specifically to the third phase of the decisional counseling model.

Once having carefully assessed the problem, the therapist is ready for generating answers and solutions with the client. Behavioral therapy has many alternatives for solutions (some of which will be reviewed later in this chapter), but one of the most popular and effective techniques is that of assertiveness training.

ASSERTIVENESS TRAINING

Some individuals passively accept whatever fate hands them. You may think of a friend who serves as a "doormat" and allows friends and family to dominate him or her. This friend may allow others to make decisions, let strangers cut in front while standing in line, or accept being ignored by a waiter for an hour. Individuals who may be overly passive in their behavior can benefit from assertiveness training so that they can learn to stand up for their rights.

You may also think of another friend who is overly aggressive and dominating, who does tell others what to do and what to think. This person may interrupt conversations rudely, cut in front of others in line, and yell at waiters regularly. This aggressive individual can also benefit from assertiveness training.

Assertiveness training involves learning to stand up for your rights—but simultaneously consider the thoughts and feelings of the other person. Assertiveness training does not concern itself with "why" an individual is passive or aggressive, but focuses on observable behavior. An assertiveness trainer may use applied behavioral analysis to identify and understand unassertive behavior. The trainer will then use highly specific techniques to change unassertive behavior into behavior that is assertive and that helps the individual get what he or she wants.

The following case illustrates the process of assertiveness training.

The Case of Joan*

Joan was a 45-year-old woman, separated from her husband and living with her three children and elderly mother. She was returning after twenty-five years of housewifery to the world of full-time work and part-time college. One of her problems was her mother, who was very critical and domineering. Though anxious about her mother's domineering ways, Joan was in conflict because she needed her mother's help with finances, housekeeping, and babysitting. It seemed clear that Joan needed to learn techniques of asserting herself and standing up for her rights against her domineering mother.

First, the counselor, Sharon Bower, had to isolate one or more scenes that were causing Joan's problems. The therapist wanted to know when her mother dominated her, in connection with what subjects, under what circumstances, and where. To illustrate how questions pinpointed the setting of the problem, here is an edited dialogue taped from the second session:

Edited Typescript	*Commentary*
1. COUNSELOR: Joan, last time, you said you needed plans for action, that you wanted to do more than talk. I agree. To know where we should be making plans, I need to ask you what is bothering you most today.	The competent behavioral counselor is interested in the unique person before her or him. Bower starts the session by using the client's name and includes five "you's" in her first statement. The focus of the interview is clearly on the client and the client's needs. At the same time, Bower does not hesitate to share her own opinions. The microskills demonstrated include a summary of the last interview, a brief self-disclosure in the form of an expres-

*This case is abstracted from "Assertiveness Training for Women" by Sharon Anthony Bower and may be found in Krumboltz and Thoresen (1976) *Counseling Methods.* New York: Holt, Rinehart, and Winston. Used by permission.

Sharon Anthony Bower

sion of content ("I agree") and, finally, an open question. One might note the qualitative dimension of respect as being prominent in the counselor's statement. In addition, we note past, present, and future tense immediacy. The question concerning what is "bothering" Joan today is also concrete. In one short statement, Bower demonstrates several important microskills and qualities.

| 2. JOAN: | I'm depressed. I feel like "poor little Joan" all the time. |

The surface structure sentence "I'm depressed" is identified. It may be anticipated that the behavioral counselor will seek to search for the underlying deep structure of this sentence. However, the behavioral counselor is interested in the operationalization of behavior, making the relatively vague term "depression" clear in terms of observable behavioral events and sequences.

| 3. COUNSELOR: | Why do you feel like "poor little Joan"? |

An open question begins the process of uncovering the underlying events surrounding the depression. The following series of questions is oriented toward clarifying the behavioral sequences—antecedents, resultant behavior, and consequences—relating to the depression.

4. JOAN: Oh, my mother—she's always nagging me and the kids.

5. COUNSELOR: What do you mean "nagging"?

An open question focuses on the vague term "nagging," searching for more concreteness.

6. JOAN: She nags. It gets on my nerves.

7. COUNSELOR: What does she say, for instance?

The client has defined nagging as "she nags," and is still vague. The counselor stays on the topic and searches for specifics of what nagging *is*. This is an important point in the interview. A beginning behavioral counselor may have easily gotten off the subject and started asking about "It gets on my nerves." The issue of "nerves" is important, but is ideally saved for later. Asking for specific things said or specific actions is critical in operationalization of behavior.

8. JOAN: That I shouldn't go to a church I like to go to. She says that it's too far away, that it costs too much gasoline, that it takes too much time to get there.

The client is now able to give highly specific instances of what the vague term "nagging" is. Joan's mother's behavior may be considered the *antecedent*.

9. COUNSELOR: What do you say then?

Having determined the antecedent specifics of the term "nagging," the counselor now searches with an open question for Joan's resultant behavior.

10. JOAN: I don't say anything.

11. COUNSELOR: How does that make you feel?

The behavior of doing nothing has been identified and the counselor then searches, via an open question, for the emotions associated with the behavior.

12. JOAN: She just keeps nagging—she tells me what to do—she won't let me live my life.

The client does not answer the question and moves to the vague term "nagging" once again, coupled with the vague and general complaint, "She won't let me live my life."

13. COUNSELOR: I get the picture of a demanding mother, but how do you *feel* when she tells you where to go to church?

The counselor provides a summary interpretation of the mother's behavior, thus acknowledging the client's need to be heard, and then returns

		with increased emphasis to learn about the feelings.
14. JOAN:	I guess I feel like a little girl again, and she's telling me to come along to Sunday school.	
15. COUNSELOR:	How do you feel when she treats you like a little Sunday school girl?	Open question still searching for more specific labeling of emotion.
16. JOAN:	Poor little Joan, that's me.	Note that Joan still does not label the emotion and returns to her first self-definition in her very first interview comment. This type of perseveration is common in many clients and is illustrative of the immobility that brings many people into counseling and therapy.
17. COUNSELOR:	Helpless?	The counselor supplies the missing emotional word for the client. The questioning tone of voice allows the client to accept or reject this label. The feeling or emotional state associated with nagging has been labeled concretely. The label of helplessness and inadequacy is common in clients and may be especially amenable to assertion training.
18. JOAN:	Yes—like I'm not old enough to make my own decisions.	
19. COUNSELOR:	Have you ever told your mother how her behavior makes you feel?	This is a closed question in that it could be answered by the client with a "yes" or "no."
20. JOAN:	Well, she oughta know.	
21. COUNSELOR:	What do you do that should make her know how you feel?	This open question again searches for concreteness. Important in operationalization of behavior is the repetition in some form or another of the key question "what do you do?"
22. JOAN:	Well, when she starts nagging, I throw down my coffee cup, grab my purse, slam the door, and leave as fast as I can get out the driveway.	

With Joan's final statement, the counselor has sufficient data for an "A,B,C" analysis of the general concept of nagging and its effect on Joan:

Antecedent: Joan's mother says don't go to the church that is far away. "It takes too much time and costs too much gas."

Behavior: "I don't do anything." Joan fails to take action. If it continues, Joan throws down the coffee cup and drives away as fast as she can.

Consequence: Joan feels helpless and depressed.

While this one series of events does not provide a full explanation of the depression, the sequence does illustrate highly characteristic behaviors of the depressed individual. The sequence is basically one of: (1) something happens; (2) the depressed individual does nothing; and (3) feelings of helplessness and depression appear.

The task of the behavioral counselor is to break the sequence of events. Sometimes this is done by changing the antecedent conditions (for example, not visiting the mother or moving out of town), but more often it is done by teaching the client to respond differently. In this case, the behavioral counselor is anxious to get Joan to do something, in the belief that almost any action is better than none. When individuals act on their world, feelings of helplessness can disappear. (It should be observed that psychodynamic or humanistic counselors would tend to be more interested in the consequent events in this series; they would focus on feelings and attitudes in the belief that changes in these would ultimately result in changes in behavior as well. The vastly different manner in which different theories would approach this case should be readily apparent.)

Let us now turn to the behavioral interventions common in assertiveness training. The following is greatly abbreviated and represents an edited version of events that would take a counselor an hour or more to complete successfully.

23. COUNSELOR: Let's analyze what happens to make you feel like a child. Let's pretend that I'm you now, drinking coffee in the kitchen, getting ready to go to church. You act out what your mother says and sounds like when she comes into the kitchen. What would you say if you were your mother? You start out as your mother.

This is a counselor *directive* indicating to the client that she is to role-play her mother. Role-plays are common in assertion training and provide clarity as to actual events. Behavioral counselors do not hesitate to offer directives to give the interview precision and direction.

24. JOAN: (as her mother) Joan, don't tell me you're going to that church again? How many times have I told you that church is too far away?

25. COUNSELOR: That's a very strong voice you have when you talk like your mother. Good! Do you feel like a child when you talk like your mother?

The microskill of feedback is used to indicate to Joan how she is speaking more intentionally. The "Good!" is a potentially reinforcing positive comment which indicates to Joan that she can talk louder and still be regarded positively. The counselor then asks a closed question which is probably appropriate late in the interview. At the beginning, such questions can slow interaction. At this point, they can add focus and precision.

26. JOAN: No! I feel really strong—like an adult—but that's not really me!

27. COUNSELOR: Well, let's decide whether you *want* to sound stronger. You need to decide what you want to do, or what you *could* do, about this church-going scene. Let's ask: What do you want to do? For instance, you *could* give in—keep the peace—and not go to the church you have been attending.

The microskills include a mild directive at the beginning ("let's decide"), followed by the open question; finally the counselor asks what goal the client has. This counselor statement is particularly important because it illustrates how behavioral counselors at their most effective are centrally concerned with clients' determining the direction of their own lives. The balancing of the directive, rigorous, and concrete approach with a faith in client self-determination is becoming an axiom of behavioral counseling.

28. JOAN: No! I like this church too much to give it up.

29. COUNSELOR: Well, then, you *could* continue with the same Sunday morning scene.

The counselor is sharing opinion in a mild paradoxical directive.

30. JOAN: That is wearing me out. No, not that anymore.

Note that Joan is making a decision to act. A new and important sentence has been generated.

31. COUNSELOR: You *could* change the scene so it would add more to your life.

Sharing opinion. The counselor has shared two alternatives for action with Joan (giving in and continuing as things are) and now suggests a third alternative—*change!*

The action phase of the interview continues along much the same line. In assertiveness training, the task is to examine the specific behaviors and sequences in more detail, via questioning, role-plays, and deliberate generation of alternatives in a fashion not unlike that described in Chapter 2 on decision making. In this case, Sharon Anthony Bower, the counselor, asked Joan to go through the situation with her mother in "slow motion," eventually dividing the scene into four stages. Bower sought to have Joan describe her mother's behavior to her mother. Next, she wanted Joan to share her feelings with her mother about this behavior. Third, she sought to have Joan specify to her mother desired changes in her behavior and to ask her mother to change to these new behaviors. Finally, the counselor worked with Joan in planning what to do if her mother did not follow the suggestions. This illustrates the importance of helping the client generalize her behavior to daily life.

During the next phase of the interview, further questions, role-plays, and practice with newly learned skills occurred. For example:

32. COUNSELOR: One last step is to stipulate *consequences* for her. Tell her what you'll do if she stops nagging. But to know what are reasonable rewards and punishments, I need to ask you a couple of questions. First, what can you do if your mother does not agree to stop talking—or if she agrees to stop but doesn't live up to the agreement?

Again, the behavioral counselor frequently uses the microskill of directives. These directives, however, are based on client statements of goals. It also may be noted that the planning phase of behavioral approaches and particular assertion training are future oriented (What will you do when such and such happens in the future?). This may be contrasted with the psychodynamic counselor's interest in the past or the humanistic counselor's interest in the present. The emphasis of the behavioral counselor is constantly on enabling change to happen.

33. JOAN: That's the problem. I can't do anything with her.

34. COUNSELOR: You do something now. You throw cups and slam doors.

This paraphrase points out information brought out by the client earlier in the session.

35. JOAN: But it's impossible to get through to her. What can I do?

36. COUNSELOR: Just fantasize for a moment. What would you *like* to do?

This directive/open question is critical in many types of counseling. In the prior lead, the counselor has pointed out what Joan does now in the real situation and, through this lead, is discovering what an ideal solution to the problem might be *in the client's own terms*. When this lead is put together with the preceding counselor lead, we have a classic example of a confrontation in that the present and ideal state and their discrepancies are noted. An underlying trend in many counseling theories is identifying "what is" and "what is desired" and then taking steps to reconcile the two positions.

37. JOAN:	I'd like to walk *calmly* out of the room the first time she mentions church going!	
38. COUNSELOR:	Could you tell her you will walk away calmly if she mentions church going again?	This closed question phrased almost as a directive brings future plans to the present tense by exploring whether or not Joan could do what she would like to do.
39. JOAN:	I should actually tell her what I'll do if she keeps nagging?	
40. COUNSELOR:	Yes, that's part of your new assertive behavior.	This directive continues the line of discussion and indicates faith in the client's ability to take behavior discussed and learned in the counseling hour outside to the "real world."
41. JOAN:	But, if I tell her, I have to be able to see myself really doing that, don't I?	
42. COUNSELOR:	Yes. Is the consequence realistic in this case? Can you see yourself walking calmly out of the room?	
43. JOAN:	Yes.	
44. COUNSELOR:	Fine, then your consequence is realistic and not an empty threat. You could—and would—carry it through. . . .	The client's tentative resolution to the discrepancy of real and ideal self is to attempt to move to the ideal.

As this particular interview continued and moved toward its final stages, the specific behaviors that Joan might employ with her mother were explored in more detail, "scripted" in that ideal words were drafted to be said in accord with new actions, and then practiced or role-played. Behavioral psychologists have learned that discussion of behavior and statements about what one will do can be greatly enhanced with direct and immediate practice in the interview. Practice may be conducted through role-plays with the counselor, working in front of a mirror or a closed circuit video unit, or through audiotape. Bower cites a letter from Joan 4 years after these sessions.

> . . . The role-play *with mirror* stands out in my mind, as well as listening to my own voice. I remember the feeling of complete surprise as I listened to myself trying to be assertive and realizing that I was sounding like a child, being whiney instead of an adult being assertive . . .
>
> Vividly, I recall practicing the "script" we worked out. I had misgivings . . . But when the time came, I remember clearly I used, almost verbatim, the words in the script. I felt a "safety" in using the script. Eventually, I became more sure of myself as I saw the effect of my assertiveness and was able to stop using a script and simply be myself (my *new* self).
>
> . . . I'm working in a very responsible job and enjoying it tremendously. I use my assertiveness on the job frequently and, I feel, very effectively . . . I've learned the importance of using appropriate words and tone of voice . . .

> The situation with mother is well in hand. Stormy at times but I now feel I am in charge of the problems and can handle them as they arise!

As we examine this interview from a microskill viewpoint, we see that the therapist's primary skills were questions and directives. Generally speaking, behavioral counselors are very much "in charge" of their sessions, carefully orchestrating what is happening and what may be expected to happen. Other microskills used by behavioral counselors include advice, opinion, sharing information, and encouragers. The attending skills of paraphrasing, summarization, and reflection of feeling may be used, but not as centrally as in other counseling modes. Self-disclosure in the form of expressions of feeling toward the client may be rare, although skill usage patterns will vary markedly from one behavior therapist to another.

The surface structure sentence, "I'm depressed," has been clarified and expanded throughout this interview. From "poor little Joan," the client has moved to consideration of several alternatives and developed a comprehensive plan of action to change her situation. In this generation of alternatives, she has become more culturally expert and able to generate new verbal and nonverbal behavior and sentences.

In summary, it may be said that this typescript illustrates several key points of behavioral counseling. First, we see the clear and direct effort to understand the antecedents, behaviors, and consequences underlying the client's difficulty through the use of questioning about past life events. This was followed by specific goals for future client life determined by the client, and then implementation plans were developed jointly with the counselor who used questions and directives (particularly role-plays) to understand and script the situation more fully. In the final phase of the interview, more role-plays occurred and more specific plans were made to ensure that behavior learned in the interview could be transferred outside the session. The last point is particularly important because most other types of counseling do not make specific efforts to help clients take interview learnings out of the session. It is necessary to specifically plan any further use of behaviors or ideas the client learned in the session or they will likely disappear over time.

BASIC TECHNIQUES OF BEHAVIORAL COUNSELING AND BEHAVIOR THERAPY

Intentional behavior therapy almost invariably starts with careful applied behavioral analysis. However, in many cases, it is necessary to develop a warm, empathic, and supportive relationship with the client before undertaking the concrete action steps associated with behavior therapy. Thus, in the beginning steps of an interview, behavior therapists may look and sound much the same as psychodynamic, humanistic, or even transpersonal counselors. Thus, the *relationship* between counselor and client is an important prerequisite for applied behavioral analysis or any other interventions. The intentional behavior therapist is increasingly recognized as exhibiting many of the characteristics and skills of intentional counselors and therapists in general.

Applied behavioral analysis was discussed earlier in relationship to underlying theoretical dimensions of behavioral counseling. Behavioral therapy requires ability to operationalize behavior; conduct a functional analysis to determine antecedents, resultant behavior, and consequences; and select socially important behaviors—goals that are codetermined with the client. Unless one can examine behavior and its contexts, behavioral counseling change procedures cannot be instituted wisely.

The fourth dimension of applied behavioral analysis is the judicious use of *behavioral change procedures.* Behavioral change procedures are systematic methods which behavioral counselors use to assist clients in changing their behaviors. Assertion training has been presented in the typescript as one systematic method of behavioral change. A critical task of the behavioral counselor is to select, from among the many possibilities now existing, the most appropriate behavioral change procedure for the individual client. Some of the key behavioral change procedures follow.

Relaxation Training

Physical body tension is characteristic of many clients who enter counseling or therapy. This tension may show itself in a variety of ways, including statements of fear or tension in social situations; direct complaints of sore, constantly tense muscles; impotence and frigidity; difficulties with sleep; and high blood pressure. Surprisingly, simply teaching people the mechanics of systematic relaxation techniques has been sufficient to alleviate many seemingly complex problems. Rather than search for the reasons that a client is unable to sleep, for example, behavioral counselors have found it more effective in many cases to teach the client relaxation techniques. The simple procedure of training clients in relaxation can be an important avenue to bringing totally new views of the world to them. Through finding that they can control their bodies, clients can move on to solve many complex personal difficulties.

It is for this reason that virtually all behavioral counselors are skilled at training clients in relaxation techniques similar to the exercises presented in Figure 9.1. A client may learn the rudiments of relaxation training in a 15-minute session, but many behavioral counselors stress that careful planning and training are needed if relaxation techniques are to become part of a client's life. Wolpe and Lazarus (1966), for example, suggest six interviews, with 20 minutes given to relaxation training, plus having the client spend two 15-minute sessions each day practicing. A variety of systematic relaxation tapes is now available commercially, making it possible for the busy behavioral counselor to pass this training on to the machine and to spend more time training the client in how to use relaxation in specific situations. Relaxation may, for example, be an important part of assertion training. If a client describes physical tension in the stomach when talking with members of

Figure 9.1   *Two Relaxation Exercises*

        Most programs of relaxation rest on a tension-relaxation or direct relaxation procedure. The two systems discussed here usually will be found in some form among the many relaxation exercises, training programs, and audiotapes available in the counseling field. To use the following exercises most effectively, have a friend or family member read them to you slowly while you go through the procedures yourself. Then change roles and help the other person enter the same relaxed state you have just enjoyed. As a final step, adapt the material below into your own relaxation program and place it on audiotape for your own and others' use.

TENSION-RELAXATION CONTRAST

        Many people exist in such a high level of tension that they find it difficult to start relaxing. Tension-relaxation contrast shows the beginner in relaxation what tension is and how it may be controlled systematically. As a first step, the person who is to go through relaxation training should be seated comfortably in a chair or lying on the floor. An easy, casual manner with good rapport is essential.

1. Start the procedure by suggesting that the client close her or his eyes and take a few deep breaths, exhaling slowly each time.
2. Tell the client, "We are going to engage in a systematic relaxation program. You'll find it's something you'll enjoy, but we must go at your pace. If you find I'm moving too fast or too slowly, let me know. In general, I'll know how you are doing as I can watch your response and will time what I'm doing to where you are. First, I'd like you to tighten your right hand— that's right—hold it tight for about 5 seconds. 1, 2, 3, 4, 5. Now let it go, and notice the difference between relaxation and tension. Notice the feeling of ease as you let your hand go. What we'll do is go through your body in much the same fashion, alternatively tightening and letting go of each muscle group. Let's begin . . ."
3. Continue by having the client tighten and loosen the right hand once again. Remember to have the client notice the difference between relaxed and tense body states. Awareness of muscle tensions is one key goal of relaxation training. After you have done the right hand for a second time, continue through the rest of the body in the order suggested in 4, below. Each time, have the client: (1) tighten the muscle group; (2) hold the tension approximately 5 seconds; (3) let the tension go; and (4) notice the difference between tension and relaxation. As the training progresses, it is not necessary to comment on awareness with each muscle group, but mention awareness of the contrasting feelings from time to time. Occasionally, it is helpful to suggest taking a deep breath, holding it, and then exhaling while noting the contrast between tension and relaxation.
4. A suggested order for muscle groups follows:
   right hand
   right arm
   left hand
   left arm
   neck and shoulders together
   neck alone
   face and scalp
   neck and shoulders again
   chest, lungs, back
   abdomen-stomach
   entire upper body—chest, back, lungs, abdomen, face, neck, both arms followed by a deep breath held and then exhaled slowly and gently
   abdomen-stomach again

buttocks
thighs
feet
entire body

5. Complete the exercise by suggesting that the client continue to sit or lie still, enjoying the feelings of relaxation and ease. When he or she wishes, suggest opening the eyes and returning to the world.

DIRECT RELAXATION

Many people prefer this form of relaxation if they find the alternative tensing and loosening tiring and/or uninteresting. However, it has been found that the tension-relaxation procedure is often a good place to start with the beginner in relaxation. Eventually, many people will want to shift to some form of direct relaxation.

One form of direct relaxation is to use the above order of muscle groups and go through them one at a time. However, no tension is used and the client simply lets each muscle group go, one at a time. With practice and experience, the relaxation can be as complete without the practiced tension.

A second form of direct relaxation involves visualization and imagery. Following is one brief example of this approach to relaxation. As in tension-relaxation contrast, the client may sit or lie down. In this form of relaxation, the relationship between the counselor and client is even more important.

1. Start the procedure by suggesting that the client close her or his eyes and notice the feelings inside the body. Take some time and suggest that the client notice the breath going in and out, the feeling of the chair or floor on the buttocks and back, the feeling of the temperature in the room. All this should be done slowly, easily, and comfortably. The effort focuses on bringing the client to here and now awareness of body experience.
2. Then suggest that the client freely think about a scene in the past where he or she felt at ease and comfortable and happy. Suggest that the client go to the scene and enjoy the feelings and thoughts that go with that happy time, noticing as many details and facts as possible. The client may wish to notice the feelings in the body at that time, such as air blowing, temperature, and body movements. Let the client continue with the visualization as long as desired and then become silent, letting him or her determine when to come back.
3. Alternatively, let the client know that he or she will have some time to enjoy the scene and experience, but that you'll come back in awhile. After about 10 minutes, gently say that it is time to return to this room. Suggest that the eyes remain closed and that he or she notes once again the feelings in the body connected with this room, as in the first part of the exercise. Suggest that the eyes may open when the client wishes.

the family or the boss, it is possible to teach him or her to deliberately relax the stomach muscles and remain calm as part of a larger program of assertion training.

Systematic Desensitization

Many people feel anxious in specific situations or in relation to certain objects, animals, or people. Extreme anxieties that are partially or even totally debilitating are termed "phobias." Systematic desensitization is a useful technique to solve more complex personal issues surrounding anxiety and tension. It consists of three primary steps: (1) training in systematic deep muscle relaxation; (2) construction of anxiety hierarchies; and (3) matching specific objects of anxiety from the hierarchies with relaxation training. It is impossible to be simultaneously relaxed and anxious; thus, the purpose of systematic desensitization is to train an automatic relaxation response in conjunction with a previously feared object. Systematic desensitization has proven effective with as varying anxieties as those about snakes, heights, death, sexual difficulties, and examinations.

Examination anxiety is particularly appropriate for desensitization, as the procedure has proven useful with innumerable students in many academic institutions. The first steps in systematic desensitization involve training in relaxation, and applied behavioral analysis of the antecedents, resultant behavior, and consequences relating to the student's examination problems. A typical problem is the student who, upon thinking of a forthcoming examination, experiences mild anxiety, with gradually increasing anxiety and tension until the examination itself appears; at this point the student might block facts important in the examination, feel physically ill, or even leave the examination room.

In the construction of an anxiety hierarchy, it is helpful to develop an anxiety scale. Wolpe and Lazarus suggest: "Think of the worst anxiety you have ever experienced or can imagine experiencing, and assign to this the number 100. Now think of the state of being absolutely calm, and call this 0. Now you have a scale. On this scale how do you rate yourself at this moment?" (1966, p. 73) Two things can be accomplished with this type of scale: (1) the counselor and the client develop a common understanding of how anxious the client is at any time in the past or present; and (2) the beginning and end points of an anxiety hierarchy have been established. Then, through questioning and further applied behavioral analysis, it is possible to fill in experiences associated with examinations and how stress producing they are. An example anxiety hierarchy for a student suffering from examination anxiety is presented below:

0 School is over and I have no more exams for another year.

10 On the first day of class, the professor tells us the course plan and mentions examination plans.

30 About a week before the examination, I realize it is coming.

50 Two days before the examination, I get particularly nervous and begin to find it hard to concentrate.

70 The day before the examination, I get sweaty palms and feel I am forgetting things important to me.

85 The night before the exam, I find I can't sleep and wake up in the middle of the night.

90 As I walk to the exam, I find myself shaking and feeling almost ill.

95 As I enter the room, my hands sweat, I fear I am forgetting everything; I want to leave.

99 When the examination is passed out, I feel almost totally tense, almost unable to move.

100 As I look at the examination I see a question or two which I really don't know and I absolutely panic. I leave the room.

The client is then asked to sit with eyes closed and to visualize a variety of scenes close to the 0 point of anxiety. These scenes may be of school being over, as above, or they may be scenes of comfort and enjoyment for the student, such as a picnic or walking in the woods. The therapist asks the student to note the easy feelings of relaxation and then moves gradually up the hierarchy, visualizing each scene in the hierarchy. If tension is felt, the student may indicate this by a raised finger. For example, if tension were experienced as the student visualized the situation 2 days before the examination, the therapist and student would work to note the tense muscles and relax them while still thinking of the tense scene. Gradually, the client learns to visualize all the scenes in the anxiety hierarchy while relaxed. This type of training may take several interviews, but has been demonstrated to be effective. When students find themselves in similar tension-producing situations, they are able to generate relaxation behaviors to counteract the feelings of tension.

Similar anxiety hierarchies have proven equally effective with many anxiety and phobic situations. Some of the most dramatic demonstrations of desensitization procedures have been with snake phobics who, as a final test, allowed a snake to crawl over them (Bandura, Blanchard, and Ritter, 1969). Frigidity and impotency have been successfully treated in the same fashion. In these cases, couples construct anxiety hierarchies related to sexual experimentation and the sex act. Generally, it is found that the sex act is the most tension producing experience of all. Couples are instructed in systematic relaxation and go through the anxiety hierarchy visualization, much as the student with examination anxiety did. When transferring the newly learned behavior to the bedroom, the couple is often instructed to stop further sexual experimentation until full relaxation is regained.

Modeling

Seeing is believing, it is said, and behavioral psychologists have found that watching films or videotapes of people engaging in successful behavior is sufficient for clients to learn new ways of coping with difficulties. In the snake phobic experiments discussed above, it was found that *live modeling* of snake handling was even more effective than systematic desensitization in teaching snake phobics to cope with their anxieties.

> After observing the therapist interacting closely with the snake, clients were aided through other induction procedures to perform progressively more frightening responses themselves. At each step the therapist himself performed the activities fearlessly and gradually led the clients to touch, stroke, and hold the midsection of the snake's body with gloved and then bare hands for increasing periods. . . . As clients became more courageous, the therapist gradually reduced his level of participation and control over the snake until eventually clients were able to tolerate the squirming snake in their laps without assistance, to let the snake loose in the room and retrieve it, and to let it crawl freely over their bodies. (Bandura, 1976, p. 256)

In a sense, modeling is one of the most simple and obvious ways to teach clients new behaviors. Seeing and hearing directly, either live or via film or tape, brings home a message much more clearly and directly than direct advice and description. Modeling can be combined with relaxation, assertion training, and other behavioral techniques as uniquely individualized programs are developed for clients.

Positive Reinforcement

Perhaps the most direct behavioral technique of all is the provision of rewards for desired behavior. The systematic application of positive reinforcement to human beings began with an important experiment by Greenspoon (1955), who demonstrated that it was possible to condition people to "emit" more plural nouns whenever the "counselor" smiled or nodded the head. In the context of what appeared to be a normal interview, Greenspoon maintained a typical session with the exception that whenever the client uttered a plural noun, the interviewer smiled and nodded. Very soon the clients were providing him with many plural nouns.

Smiles, nods, and the attention of others are particularly reinforcing events. We seek reinforcement and reward. Those who provide us with these rewards tend to be our friends; those who don't we tend to ignore or avoid. Money is another powerful positive reinforcer. It may be said that we work because we are rewarded or reinforced with money. In any applied behavioral analysis that is fully effective, the counselor will be able to note positive reinforcers and rewards maintaining the behavior. The search for the A,B,C's of behavioral sequences will often unravel seemingly complex and mystical behavior.

Although simple and direct, the experimental use of positive reinforcement with human beings has been often used for manipulative rather than constructive purposes. The following experiment is one example:

> The cast: (a) A professor noted for the quality of his knowledge of subject matter. He understands that he will make a presentation and be video-recorded, but is unaware of the purpose of the session. (b) Six students trained in "attending behavior" and who know "how to pay attention" to the professor. Attending behavior is best described as physically and mentally following a professor through eye contact, careful listening, and developed personal involvement.
>
> Outline of plot: The students are told to engage in "typical" classroom behavior for the first portion of the lecture. Then at a signal, they are to "attend" to the professor physically through eye contact and manifestations of physical interest. At another signal, they are to return to typical student nonattending behavior.
>
> The question: What happens to the professor? And the students?
>
> The play in synopsis form: The professor enters the room carrying his notes. He looks up at the T.V. camera peering into the room, then at his notes. He does not look at the assembled students. There is a 30-second pause and he begins. The lecture is heavily laden with references to "exciting" research and clearly shows extensive preparation. Occasionally, the professor looks up from his notes and observes the students engaging in typical classroom behavior of notetaking.

He then returns to his paper and continues on. For ten minutes his hands remain motionless and do not rise above the seminar table.

The signal comes and the students are alerted. They are now focusing all attention on the professor. He, however, is deeply in his notes and does not look up for 30 seconds. When he does, it is only briefly, but he apparently notes a student following him. Shortly he looks up again briefly at the same student and is again reinforced. Again, he looks up for a longer time and sees the student following him closely. He next raises his head and looks around to the rest of the class. They too are attending to him. Immediately, he becomes animated, he gestures for the first time. His verbal rate increases, his physical involvement through gestures and other characteristics is obvious. The students raise a few questions and the professor continues his discussion without notes. The quality of his knowledge of the material is still apparent as the flow of content is constant, but with less reference to specific research. However, a new classroom scene emerges. He is involved and the students are involved.

At another signal, the students stop attending and return to their notepads. The professor continues his talk uninterrupted. He does not stop; but he noticeably slows down. He looks to the students for further support and reinforcement which is not forthcoming. His verbalization slows down further. Resignedly, he returns to his notes and continues through the rest of his lecture once again resting his presentation on others' knowledge instead of his own.

The students comment later that it was difficult to stop attending and return to typical student behavior as they had found the material most stimulating. The students state they had enjoyed his presentation while they had "attended" and felt they had deserted the professor who needed them as they needed and wanted him.

This is nothing but a simple exercise in what psychologists call the "Greenspoon Effect," after Dr. Joel Greenspoon of Temple Buell College. Psychology classes have for years reinforced their professors by alternately smiling and ignoring the professor. Typically, the students have used this as a game to get a professor to stand in a certain place in the classroom or perhaps get him walking back and forth in front of the class much like one of the B. F. Skinner's pigeons. Students have not typically reinforced or rewarded a professor by attending to his presentation. (Ivey and Hinkle, 1968, p. 4)

While this incident is amusing, it is also illustrative of how behavioral techniques can be used to manipulate people and to dehumanize them. Such experimentation with human subjects fortunately is waning. The predominant mode in behavioral counseling now is to share power and expertise with the client. Yet, it can never be forgotten how important and how powerful the shaping techniques of positive reinforcement are. Innumerable concepts and programs for modifying the behavior of children, prisoners, couples, athletes, overeaters, smokers, alcoholics, drug addicts, and many others have been based on the elementary ideas of positive reinforcement and reward. When learning theory concepts, such as extinction, shaping, and intermittent reinforcement, are put together, extremely powerful and effective programs of human change can be developed. At the most sophisticated level, elaborate *token economies* have been developed in prisons, psychiatric hospitals, schools, and other settings, where tangible reinforcers in the form of tokens are given for desired acts *immediately* after they have been performed. At a later point the tokens may be exchanged for candy, cigarettes, or privileges. Important in the success of positive reinforcement and token economies is the clear identification, by the client, of the desired behavior with the reward. Too long a delay in reinforcement dulls its effectiveness in changing behavior.

Charting

One route toward identifying whether or not progress is being made with a behavioral change program is *charting* the changes made by a client. Charting is the specific recording of the number of occurrences of important behaviors before, during, and after treatment. For example, a teacher may be concerned with "out of seat behavior" of a hyperactive child. The behavioral program is to reduce this behavior with a modified token economy in which the child is rewarded for staying at the desk. The chart in Figure 9.2 illustrates the daily frequencies for this behavior before the intervention was instituted, during the treatment, and after treatment was terminated. It is important in such charts to record behavior before the program is instituted so that the effectiveness of the behavioral program can be examined on its inception. "After" charting is important because when the intervention is removed, the behavior sometimes returns to the previous level, indicating that the behavioral program was unsuccessful in maintaining desired outcomes. When charts indicate failure, another type of be-

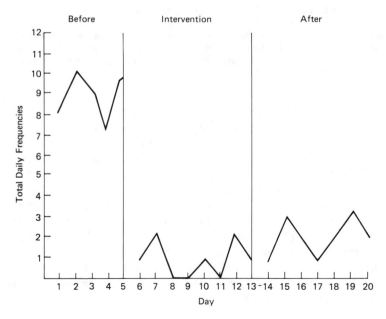

Figure 9.2 Out of Seat Behavior

havioral program (or even another type of counseling intervention, such as psychodynamic or humanistic) needs to be instituted.

Charting is often used in weight control programs, family communication skill training, aiding a child in keeping a room clean, stop-smoking programs, and in a wide variety of interpersonal or classroom situations. The very act of self-recording (charting) sometimes helps an individual to modify her or his behavior without further instruction or counseling.

Relapse Prevention: Systematic Generalization of Behavior

The relapse prevention program (RP) is a set of cognitive/behavioral strategies designed to help clients maintain their behavior and thinking after counseling, therapy, or skills training has ended. It is an axiom of therapy that clients often will lose their insights, their behaviors, and their new skills gained from therapy if the counselor does not take specific action to help maintenance.

The RP model is based on Marlatt's work with alcohol addiction (c.f. Marlatt, 1980, 1982; Marlatt and Gordon, 1985) which was later extended to weight control (Rosenthal and Marx, 1979), and to the maintenance of skills training (Marx, 1982; 1984).

Research in relapse has found that the initial lapse (slip) in treatment is particularly important in the likelihood of future and continued lapses. For example, in weight control, the way the overeater handles the first failure to stay on the diet is highly predictive of what will happen in the future. Because skills developed in therapy have not yet been tested in real life situations, we can expect relapse in nearly 100 percent of our clients in some form. Our task as therapists is to help our clients construct relapse prevention programs (generalization programs in the fifth stage of the interview) to ensure that newly learned behavior and insights are not lost shortly after the session. Research in RP clearly indicates

Alan Marlatt
Courtesy G. Alan Marlatt, University of Washington

Robert Marx

that a systematic program can help clients learn more from their therapy and training programs and maintain the behavioral change for a longer time.

Environmental realities (family, job, the availability of cigarettes, drugs) often conspire to make long-term behavioral maintenance almost impossible. To combat the difficulties of the environment, Marx has a four-point program to help clients become more prepared to manage the post-counseling environment.

Figure 9.3 summarizes the RP program in the form of an exercise which you can use with yourself or with a real or role-play client. Note that RP is skill specific. For example, a client may want to stop overeating. The task of the therapist is to help the client understand the several strategies that are available to help control overeating. Once clients have learned the behavioral techniques to slow down the rate of eating, eat only in specified places and times, monitor calories, understand how emotions affect eating, and eliminate discretionary eating, they are ready to begin preparing for the dangers that exist for dieters once counseling is over and they must manage on their own.

RP provides a set of *self-management* strategies that help the client survive in a world that says, "EAT, EAT, EAT." RP provides control for the individual who faces difficult situations. The strategies can be divided into the following categories:

1. Anticipating difficult situations. Clients can often predict the circumstances that are likely to be threatening to their resolve to maintain their weight or their exercise program. These strategies identify high risk situations that might sabotage new learning and serve as an early warning system so that the client is on guard for a slip or relapse.

2. Regulating thoughts and feelings. Emotions often get out of control and make us feel incompetent, upset, or temporarily irrational. Relapses are less likely to occur if we *expect* these temporary responses and then return to a rational approach to learning from our mistakes.

Figure 9.3 *Relapse Prevention Worksheet*

Self-Management Strategies for Skill Retention
By Robert Marx
(Go through this worksheet by yourself perhaps using one of the microskills of this text or a
behavior you have difficulty in maintaining. Alternatively, use the form to go through the
danger or relapse with a real or role-played client.)

I. CHOOSING AN APPROPRIATE BEHAVIOR TO RETAIN
Describe in detail the behavior you intend to retain:

_____
_____
How often will you use it?_____
How will you know when a slip occurs?_____
_____

II. RELAPSE PREVENTION STRATEGIES
A. *Strategies to help you anticipate and monitor potential difficulties-regulating stimuli.*
             Strategy   *Assessing Your Situation*
1. Do you understand the relapse process?   _____
What is it?   _____
2. What are the differences between learning _____
the behavioral skill or thought and using it in _____
a difficult situation?   _____
3. Support network? Who can help you   _____
maintain the skill?   _____
4. High risk situations? What kind of people, _____
places, or things will make retention   _____
especially difficult?   _____

B. *Strategies to increase rational thinking-regulating thoughts and feelings.*

5. What might be an unreasonable emotional   _____
response to a temporary slip or relapse?   _____
6. What can you do to think more effectively _____
in tempting situations or after a relapse?   _____
                                              _____

C. *Strategies to diagnose and practice related support skills-regulating behaviors.*

7. What additional support skills do you need _____
to retain the skill? Assertiveness?   _____
Relaxation? Microskills?   _____

D. *Strategies to provide appropriate outcomes for behaviors-regulating consequences.*

8. Can you identify some likely outcomes of   _____
your succeeding with your new behavior?   _____
9. How can you reward yourself for a job well- _____
done? Generate specific rewards and   _____
satisfactions.   _____

PREDICTING THE CIRCUMSTANCE OF THE FIRST LAPSE
Describe the details of how the first lapse might occur, including people, places, times,
emotional states.

3. Diagnosing necessary support skills. While we may help clients to become more careful eaters, their eating patterns may suffer when they are in a hurry or when faced with a new tempting variety of ice cream. Additional skills such as assertiveness training, time management, or key cognitive skills may be necessary to avoid eventual relapse. The survival of the skill of not eating, in turn, depends on a variety of behavioral subskills, many of which have been discussed in this chapter.

4. Regulating consequences. A key behavioral concern providing appropriate consequences for behavior. When the client stays away from the refrigerator at midnight, there will be no thunderous applause. That support sometimes must come from the client. The client must learn how to create meaningful rewards for good actions and behavioral maintainance.

Do these techniques really work? A weight-loss treatment program produced a weight loss of 18 pounds per individual. A 1-year follow-up discovered that *only* behavioral weight techniques plus relapse training produced maintenance of weight loss (Perri et al., 1984). A similar study by Rosenthal and Marx (1979) used behavioral techniques to produce an average weight loss of 10 pounds in thirty-six college students. One group received RP, the other was simply encouraged to continue good eating habits. Sixty days after the treatment, the RP group was still losing weight (an additional 3.9 pounds) while the non-RP group had gained 1.4 pounds.

This discussion has focused primarily on relapse in terms of specific eating, drinking, and addictive-type behaviors. However, an individual going through psychotherapy or counseling also relapses. The client may be a spouse or child-abuser, an individual with a compulsion to shoplift, or a person who too easily allows him or herself to become depressed. While depression or child abuse are clearly different problems from overeating, the same general principles of RP may be employed. Specifically, what is the general context in which a depression occurs? What are the antecedents, behaviors, and consequences of a depression? What RP strategies can be used to help understand and cope with depression? A knowledge of RP can be invaluable to you in thinking through alternatives to help your client cope with and deal with difficult and troublesome situations.

RP makes a special and important contribution not only to behavioral counseling, but also to therapy in general. All systems of counseling and therapy have problems with clients who relapse and return to original, sometimes more primitive, ways of behaving. It may well be possible and desirable to study the concepts of RP and its relationship to applied behavioral analysis and to generate with your client new and improved methods for helping your clients maintain new thoughts and feelings (cognitions) and behaviors which come from your work with them.

RP, as applied behavioral analysis, is an extremely valuable tool. But, again, it must be practiced or it will become lost. At this point, it is suggested that you consider working through the processes of the RP model as presented in Figure 9.4 yourself or with a real or role-played client.

Figure 9.4   *An Exercise in Applied Behavioral Analysis and Assertiveness Training*

The purpose of this exercise is to integrate the concepts of this chapter in a practical format that you can use to implement assertiveness training in your own counseling practice. With a role-played client or a classmate who is willing to discuss a specific situation where he or she may have been too passive or too aggressive, work carefully through the following interview:

1. *Rapport/Structuring.* Remember that data indicate that behaviorally oriented counselors and therapists offer as much or more warmth than other orientations to helping. Establish rapport with your client in your own unique way and use attending behavior to "tune in" to the client and client observation skills to note when you have established rapport.

   Give special attention to structuring the interview and telling your client ahead of time what to expect. Behavioral counseling operates on a planned mutuality between counselor and client.

2. *Data Gathering.* Here your goal is to get a clear, behavioral definition of the problem. The basic listening sequence (BLS) will help you draw the specific behavior. You want a clear and specific instance where the individual was not sufficiently assertive. Asking for concrete examples will facilitate operationalizing the present overly passive or overly aggressive behavior.

   Use functional analysis to find out the antecedents of the behavior. What was the context and what happened before the behavior occurred? Define the problem behavior even more precisely. Finally, what were the consequences after the behavior? In each case use questioning skills to describe the behavior.

   A role-play is a particularly useful way to obtain further behavioral specifics. Once you have a clear picture of antecedent-behavior-consequence, have your client role play the situation again with you acting as the other person(s). Make the role-play as real and accurate as you can.

   Finally, draw out positive assets of the client and the situation. What strengths does the client have that will be useful in later problem solution? You may find it necessary to provide your client with positive feedback as nonassertive clients often have trouble identifying any positives in themselves or the situation.

   To repeat, one of the best ways to obtain behavioral data for assertiveness training is to assist your client in conducting a role-play with you in which the situation is recreated in behavioral specificity.

3. *Determining Outcomes.* Develop clear and specific behavioral goals with your client. You will want to use the BLS and operationalization of behavior methods again. Is the goal established by your client clear, specific, and attainable? The goal should be related to the problem of nonassertiveness and be at least some help in being more effective in the difficult situation.

4. *Generating Alternative Solutions.* At this point you have the goals of the client which can be contrasted with the problem as defined. In addition, you have some positive assets and strengths of the client. Note how Sharon Bower helped her client develop new and more assertive behaviors.

   With your client, review the goals and then practice in a role-play with your client the new behaviors represented by those goals. Continue practicing with your client until the client demonstrates the ability to engage in the behavior.

   You may find that relaxation training, charting, modeling, cognitive-behavior therapy, and other behavioral techniques may be useful to supplement and enrich your behavioral program.

5. *Generalization.* It is easy for the successful therapist to stop at the fourth stage. Here it is critical that specific and behavioral plans be made with your client for generalization of the behavior beyond the session. Use the relapse prevention form of Figure 9.3 with your client. Be clear and specific with your behavioral goals and anticipate the likely relapse potential. *Behavior that is not reinforced after training is likely to be lost and lamented two weeks later.*

6. *Followup.* One week after the interview, whether you have another assertiveness training session or not, followup with your client and determine if behavior actually did change. Later followups, of course, can be useful to both you and the client. As necessary, use the relapse form once again to analyze any difficulty with behavioral generalization.

SOME LIMITATIONS AND PRACTICAL IMPLICATIONS OF BEHAVIORAL THERAPY

Ineffective and careless counseling can endanger clients. In the preceding chapter, wild analysis provided an illustration of psychodynamic counseling at its worst. No matter how good the theory or the potential power of a counseling or treatment intervention is, the counselor has the professional and ethical responsibility to be aware of manifestations of false practice. The term *manipulative behavioral counseling* can be used to describe the same phenomenon as the dangers of wild analysis.

Manipulative behavioral counseling occurs when the counselor makes a decision for the client without client awareness or when the counselor has so much power in the client's life that the client has no choice but to agree to the behavioral program whether or not he or she agrees. A focus of behavioral counselors has been to increase "time on task" (amount of time spent working at one's desk) in elementary classrooms. This is obviously a desirable educational goal, but some behavioral interventions have been implemented without child or parent awareness that anything had been changed in the classroom. Manipulative behavior therapy has been used as a means of social control in psychiatric institutions and prisons. Patients and inmates have been placed under behavioral programs and under token economies that have included such "rewards" as tokens thrown on the floor for them to pick up and later exchange for meals. Such horror stories must be contrasted with behavioral humanism where the commitment is to a shared decision-making process between counselor and client. *It is no longer possible to dismiss behavioral counseling as dehumanizing and manipulative.* It is as easy to use psychodynamic or humanistic counseling to the detriment of clients as it is to use behavioral techniques. Counseling theories and techniques are not at fault when abused; rather, the fault lies in the values of the manipulative and careless counselor.

You will find that behavioral techniques "work," that your client often will benefit from and enjoy the specificity of the techniques. At the same time, you may also note that some of your clients change behavior, but still feel "something" is missing. These clients may benefit from the addition of cognitive-behavioral methods (Chapter 11) to your treatment plan or you may find that some want to look back to the reasons their behavior developed as it did. The seemingly antagonistic point of view of psychodynamic therapy can be helpful here. In short, you may find that behavioral counseling benefits from association with other theories in the helping process.

If you practice the exercises of Figures 9.1, 9.3, and 9.4 you have a solid beginning in behavioral counseling and therapy. For the satisfaction of seeing something happen, for the resolution of a specific assertiveness issue and for defining specific goals of therapy, you will find this system of helping most satisfactory. With further study of other techniques not detailed here such as implosive therapy and carefully designed programs of reinforcement, a most impressive array of treatment alternatives may be assembled.

Finally, relapse prevention should be cited as an especially useful set of techniques to add to the final stages of the interview, regardless of what therapeutic technique or theory you are using. The fifth stage of the interview (generalization), Janis' model of transfer of training, followup on clients after the interview, and relapse prevention knowledge are all critical for therapists of all persuasions.

SUMMARY OF THIS CHAPTER

For mastery of the key constructs of this chapter, the following are especially important. You should be able to:

1. *Contrast the action-oriented approach of behavioral counseling with the insight-oriented system of psychodynamic therapy.* In a broad sense, behaviorists are concerned with changing client observable behavior and actions and psychodynamic counselors with changing the way clients think about their actions. Some behaviorists are not concerned with internal dialogue, while most psychodynamic counselors believe that behavior will change once sufficient understanding is developed.

2. *Define and demonstrate the ability to engage in applied behavioral analysis.* Defined are methods which you can use in many settings. Until you have mastered this ability, further action in the behavioral model is likely to be ineffective.

3. *Understand and discuss the structure of assertion training.* Behavioral counseling has many demonstrated effective and useful methods of helping clients take control of their own lives. Assertion training has been selected in this book as one key example of this mode of helping. A five-step model of using assertion training in clinical practice was presented.

4. *Understand and utilize relapse prevention as an effective and systematic method to help clients use learnings from the interview regardless of theoretical orientation.*

5. *Define and discuss the following key terms:* behavioral humanism, applied behavioral analysis, operationalization of behavior, functional analysis, antecedent events, resultant behavior, consequences, assertiveness training, relapse prevention, relaxation, systematic desensitization, modeling, positive reinforcement, charting, token economy.

REFERENCES

ALBERTI, R., and M. EMMONS, *Your Perfect Right.* San Luis Obispo, CA: Impact, 1970.

BANDURA, A., Foreword. In C. Thoresen and M. Mahoney, *Behavioral Self-Control.* New York: Holt, Rinehart & Winston, 1974, pp. v.–vi.

BANDURA, A., "Effecting Change Through Participant Modeling." In J. Krumboltz and C. Thoresen (eds.), *Counseling Methods.* New York: Holt, Rinehart & Winston, 1976, 248–264.

BANDURA, A., "Self-Efficacy: Mechanism in Human Agency." *American Psychologist,* 1982, *37,* 122–147.

BANDURA, A., E. BLANCHARD, and B. RITTER, "The Relative Efficacy of Desensitization and Modeling Approaches," *Journal of Personality and Social Psychology.* 1969, *13,* 173–199.

BOWER, S., Assertiveness Training for Women. In J. Krumboltz and C. Thoresen (eds.), *Counseling Methods.* New York: Holt, Rinehart & Winston, 1976, 467–474.

FRANKS, C., "Behavior Therapy: An Overview." In C. Franks, G. Wilson, P. Kendall, and K. Brownell (eds.) *Annual Review of Behavior Therapy.* New York: Guilford, 1982.

GREENSPOON, J., "The Reinforcing Effect of Two Spoken Sounds on the Frequency of Two Responses," *American Journal of Psychology, 1955, 68,* 409–416.

IVEY, A., and J. HINKLE, "Students, the Major Untapped Resource in Higher Education," *Reach* (A Publication of the Colorado State University *Collegian*), 1968, *6,* 1 and 4.

MARLATT, G., "Relapse Prevention: A Self-Control Program for the Treatment of Addictive Behaviors." Invited Address presented at the International Conference on Behavior Modification, Banff, Alberta, March, 1980.

MARLATT, G., "Relapse Prevention: A Self-Control Program for the Treatment of Addictive Behaviors." In R. Stuart (ed.). *Adherence, Compliance, and Generalization in Behavioral Medicine.* New York: Bruner/Mazel, 1982.

MARLATT, G. and J. GORDON, "Relapse Prevention: Maintenance Strategies in the Treatment of Addictive Behaviors." New York: Guilford, 1985.

MARX, R., "Relapse Prevention for Managerial Training: A Model for Maintenance of Behavior Change," *Academy of Management Review,* 1982, *7,* 433–441.

MARX, R., Self-Control Strategies in Management Training: Skill Maintenance Despite Organizational Realities. Symposium chaired at the American Psychological Association Annual Meeting, Toronto, Canada, August, 1984.

PERRI, M., R. SHAPIRO, W. LUDWIG, C. TWENTYMAN, and W. McADOO, "Maintenance Strategies for the Treatment of Obesity," *Journal of Consulting and Clinical Psychology,* 1984, *52,* 404–413.

ROSENTHAL, B., and R. MARX, A Comparison of Standard Behavior and Relapse Prevention Weight Reduction Programs. Paper presented at the meeting of the Association for the Advancement of Behavior Therapy, San Francisco, December, 1979.

SKINNER, B. F., *Walden Two.* New York: Macmillan, 1948.

SLOANE, R., F. STAPLES, A. CRISTOL, N. YORKSTON, and K. WHIPPLE, *Psychotherapy vs. Behavior Therapy.* Cambridge, MA: Harvard, 1975.

SULZER-AZAROFF, B., *Achieving Educational Success.* New York: Holt, 1985.

SULZER-AZAROFF, B., and G. MAYER, *Applying Behavior-Analysis Procedures with Children and Youth.* New York: Holt, Rinehart & Winston, 1977.

WOLPE, J., and A. LAZARUS, *Behavior Therapy Techniques.* Elmsford, NY: Pergamon Press, 1966.

WOOLFOLK, R., and F. RICHARDSON, "Behavior Therapy and the Ideology of Modernity," *American Psychologist,* 1984, *39,* 777–786.

SUGGESTED SUPPLEMENTARY READING

ALBERTI, R., and M. EMMONS, *Your Perfect Right.* San Luis Obispo, CA: Impact, 1982. The book which popularized assertiveness training. Brief and to the point.

Annual Review of Behavior Therapy: Theory and Practice. New York: Guilford, annual publication.
Behavior therapy has established itself as a major and permanent member of the helping establishment. This annual volume is important not only as a history of theory and practice, but also as a place to learn new techniques and research and their value in daily work.

BOWER, S. A. and G. H. BOWER, *Asserting Yourself: A Practical Guide for Positive Change.* Reading, MA: Addison-Wesley, 1976.

A guide to assertiveness training, written by the author of the case study presented in this chapter. An especially strong feature of this highly regarded book is its emphasis on demonstrated and lasting change.

KRUMBOLTZ, J., and C. THORESEN (eds.), *Counseling Methods.* New York: Holt, Rinehart & Winston, 1976.

A carefully constructed and detailed presentation of a multitude of alternative case approaches to behavioral counseling and behavior therapy. The illustrative material covers issues ranging from sexual dysfunction to overeating, to marital communication difficulties, to snake phobias. Each presentation is clear and methodologically sound.

SKINNER, B. F., *Science and Human Behavior.* New York: Macmillan, 1953.

The prime architect of behavioral psychology presents an overview of his methods and how they might be applied to a wide array of situations ranging from individual change to systematic change in cultures.

10

THE EXISTENTIAL-
HUMANISTIC TRADITION

GENERAL PREMISE

An integrated knowledge of skills, theory, and practice is essential for culturally intentional counseling and therapy.

Skills form the foundation of effective theory and practice: The culturally intentional therapist knows how to construct a creative decision-making interview and can use microskills to attend to and influence clients in a predicted direction. Important in this process are individual and cultural empathy, client observation skills, assessment of person and environment, and the application of positive techniques of growth and change.

Theory provides organizing principles for counseling and therapy: *The culturally intentional counselor has knowledge of alternative theoretical approaches and treatment modalities, in this case three methods of humanistic helping: person-centered, Gestalt, and logotherapy*.

Practice is the integration of skills and theory: The culturally intentional counselor or therapist is competent in skills and theory, and is able to apply them to research and practice for client benefit.

Undergirding integrated competence in skills, theory, and practice is an intentional awareness of one's own personal worldview and how that worldview may be similar to and/or different from the worldview and personal constructions of the client and other professionals.

GOALS FOR EXISTENTIAL-HUMANISTIC THEORY

Existential-humanistic theories have been termed the "third force" in helping. Whereas psychodynamic theory focuses on how history determines the present and behavioral theory on how environmental reinforcement shapes the individual, existential-humanistic theory presents an alternative worldview in which the individual is the locus of control and decision.

The goals of this chapter are to:

1. Describe the general worldview of existential-humanistic theory and how this view may be differentiated and amplified by Carl Rogers, Frederick Perls, and Viktor Frankl.
2. Present central theoretical constructs of the theory, examples of the theory in operation via examination of interview transcripts, and specific techniques associated with each conception.
3. Provide you with an opportunity to practice therapeutic techniques and counseling methods within each framework.

INTRODUCTION

The existential-humanistic view focuses on men and women as people who are empowered to act on the world, and determine their own destiny. The locus of control and decision lies within the individual, rather than in past history or in environmental determinants.

While the roots of the existential-humanistic tradition rest deeply in philosophy, Carl Rogers and his person-centered counseling have been most influential in popularizing the point of view and making it relevant. You will find that his techniques are designed to help you enter the worldview of the client and then to facilitate the client finding his or her own new direction and frame of thinking.

Fritz Perls offers a similar view of the value of individual decision making and control, but his techniques are extremely directive. Whereas Rogers enters in with the client to find and perhaps change a worldview, Perls is active and on the spot directing the change process.

Viktor Frankl provides a balancing force between Rogers and Perls. Rogers might be described as an "attending or listening therapist" and Perls as an "influencing therapist." Frankl appears to use both attending and listening skills, according to the varied needs of the client. All three individuals offer much of practical value to the practice of counseling and therapy.

Let us now turn to the broad worldview and history of the existential-humanistic movement.

THE EXISTENTIAL-HUMANISTIC TRADITION

> [The] world is manifold, and [our] attitudes are manifold. What is manifold is often frightening because it is not neat and simple. [We] prefer to forget how many possibilities are open to [us]. (Kaufmann, 1970, p. 9)

Existentialism is concerned with human *existence* and the infinite possibility of life. However, precise definitions of the key words "existentialism," "existence," and "possibility" are virtually impossible, because existentialism is founded on the belief that each person sees the world uniquely and constructs her or his own reality through transactions with the world. We can know ourselves only through our relationship with others. There is general agreement that existentialism is the study of humankind's *being-in-the-world*. Thus, existentialism is centrally concerned with examining the meaning of life and our place in the world. Existential philosophers constantly seek to find answers to questions of meaning ("What does that mean?" "Why did that happen?" "What really *is?*").

> The mechanism through which persons construct meaning is the decision-making process . . . Indeed existential psychologists view life as a series of decisions continually being made even if the person is unselfconscious of this. Although decisions can obviously vary widely in content, they have an invariant form involving two alternatives: the choice of the future and the choice of the past. (Maddi, 1985, p. 194)

Clients come to you, as noted in Chapter 2, for assistance in making decisions. Those who have decided for the past tend to be reliving old scripts from their history. Those who live for the future are involved in making their own choices and exploring the many possibilities of the future.

A crude, but accurate, analogy may be found in the old joke about the distinction between an optimist and a pessimist:

> Two young people came upon a pile of manure in a barnyard. The first, the pessimist, saw a pile of manure and said "ugh." The optimist started digging in immediately and soon was up to the knees in dung. "Why are you doing that?" asked the first. "Why?" answered the optimist, "Because if there is all this manure piled up, there must be a pony in here somewhere."

One existential position sees difficulties and problems in life's many possibilities. The existential-humanist sees beauty, opportunities, and alternatives. The question of meaning is in the eye of the beholder. A humanistic choice is one which is positive and directed toward a possible future. Humanism is a philosophy that dignifies humankind and conceptualizes people as making their own choices and decisions.

Existentialism's roots may be traced to the Danish philosopher Kierkegaard, but the movement came into full bloom following World War II with the writings of Sartre (1946, 1956) and Camus (1942, 1958). Heidegger (1962), Laing (1967), Husserl (1931), and Tillich (1961) loom large among the many existential philosophers, psychologists, and theologians. May (1958, 1961, 1969) has been particularly important in bringing existential thought to the awareness of counselors and psychologists in the United States.

However, Binswanger (1958, 1963) and Boss (1958, 1963) have been particularly relevant in organizing the many threads of existentialism for the practice of counseling and therapy. Being-in-the-world has been defined as the most fundamental concept of existentialism. We are in the world and acting on that world while it simultaneously acts on us. Any attempt to separate ourselves from the world alienates us and establishes a false and arbitrary distinction. *Alienation* results either from separateness from others and the world or from our inability to choose and act in relationship. The central task of therapy and counseling, then, is to enable the alienated client to see himself or herself in relationship to the world and to choose and act in accordance with what he or she sees.

To facilitate the analysis of the person, existentialists often divide the individual into *eigenwelt* (the person and her or his body), *mitwelt* (other people in the world), and *umwelt* (the biological and physical world). The person may have problems of alienation in one or more areas. Specifically, the person may be alienated from her or his own self and body, from others, or from the world. A general process of existential analysis is to enable the person to study what the world and her or his relationship to that world is like (both *mitwelt* and *umwelt*). Then, having examined the world, the person is assumed free to act, rather than to only be acted upon.

The issue of action, however, brings about another possibility for *existential anxiety*. While existential anxiety may be the result of alienation, it may also be the result of failure to make decisions and the failure to act on the world. Choice and decisions are often difficult, because any time we choose, we must accept the fact that by choosing we deny other alternatives and possibilities. Although choice may be painful, it is likely to be less so than the anxiety of never choosing would be.

Existential *commitment* is deciding to choose and to act; this action can be expected to alleviate anxiety. Yet, the constant nature of choice because of our being-in-the-world constantly reactivates anxiety. It is out of this circle of choice and anxiety that some existentialists (such as Sartre and Kierkegaard) become pessimistic and dubious. Others (such as Buber and Tillich) regard the issue of choice as opportunity rather than as problematic. *Intentionality* is a key existential concept: One that sees choice as opportunity. Intentionality, as used throughout this book, is an existential construct which states that people can be forward moving and act on their world, yet must remain keenly aware that the world acts on them as well. Intentionality provides a bridge to *humanism*, a worldview that finds its full bloom in Carl Rogers and Martin Buber. "Humanism is . . . any philosophy which recognizes the value and dignity of man and makes him the measure of all things . . ." (Abbagnano, 1967, p. 69). The existential-humanistic tradition, then, is one that recognizes the infinite variety of life experience and being-in-the-world as an opportunity rather than as a problem. Basic to this philosophy is assuming the responsibility for choice and acting intentionally on the world.

The person who adopts the existential-humanistic position has made an intentional commitment toward what is positive and possible in human relations. Martin Buber talks of the importance of "I-Thou" relations between people, in which others are seen as people rather than as objects:

> Whoever says *You* (Thou) does not have something for his object. For wherever there is something, there is also another something; every *It* borders on other *Its; It* is only by virtue of bordering on others. But where *You* (Thou) is said, there is no something. *You* has no borders.
>
> Whoever says *You* does not have something; he has nothing. But he stands in relation. (Buber, 1970, p. 55)

The intentional individual will seek "I-Thou" relationships as opposed to "it-it" relationships, in which people are seen as things.

The existential-humanistic tradition ranges from the positivism of Carl Rogers and Viktor Frankl to the valiant negativism of Sartre and Camus. Fritz Perls' Gestalt therapy represents a somewhat more harsh view of reality than that of Rogers and Frankl. Many other theories in helping have been influenced by this "Third Force" of helping ranging from behavioral humanism to rational-emotive therapy and the new consciousness-raising theories of feminist therapy and Black identity development.

The existential-humanistic point of view is an attitude toward the counseling interview and the meaning of life. The main points of this mode of counseling could be summarized as follows:

1. We are in the world; our task is to understand what this means.
2. We know ourselves through our relationship with the world, and in particular through our relationships with other people.
3. Anxiety can result from lack of relationship (with ourselves, with others, or the world at large) *or* from a failure to act and choose.
4. We are responsible for our own construction of the world. Even though we know the world only as it interacts on us, it is we who decide what the world means and who must provide organization for that world.
5. Therefore, the task of the therapist or counselor is to understand the client's world as fully as possible and ultimately to encourage her or him to be responsible for making decisions. However, many existential counselors also share themselves and their worldview immediately and directly with the client.
6. A special problem is that the world is not necessarily meaningful. Existentialists, such as Sartre and Kierkegaard, often find themselves enmeshed in a somewhat dismal and hopeless view as they observe the absurdity and cruelty of life. However, the humanistic existentialists, such as Buber and May, suggest that the very confusion and disorder in the world is an opportunity for growth and beauty. The distinction between the existential position and the existential-humanistic position can be defined as one of philosophy or faith. If a person sees the many

possibilities in the world as a problem, he or she has a problem. A person who sees the same infinite array of possibilities has infinite opportunity, if only he or she will choose to act.

THE ROGERIAN REVOLUTION

Counseling . . . [is] a way of helping the individual help himself. The function of the counselor is to make it possible for the client to gain emotional release in relation to his problems and, as a consequence, to think more clearly and more deeply about himself and his situation. It is the counselor's function to provide an atmosphere in which the client, through his exploration of his situation, comes to see himself and his reactions more clearly and to accept his attitudes more fully. On the basis of this insight he is able to meet his life problems more adequately, more independently, more responsibly than before. (Rogers and Wallen, 1946, pp. 5–6)

This worldview, now commonplace in counseling and therapy and in society's view as well, represented a radical departure, following World War II. Whereas psychodynamic and behavioral counseling and therapy viewed humankind as the often unknowing pawn of unconscious forces and environmental contingencies, existential-humanistic psychology, particularly as represented by Carl

Photo by Nozizwe S.

Carl R. Rogers

Rogers, stressed that the individual could "take charge" of life, make decisions, and act on the world. Undergirding this faith is a worldview that believes that people are positive, forward-moving, basically good, and ultimately self-actualizing. Self-actualization or health may ultimately be defined as experiencing one's fullest humanness. Self-actualizing people enjoy life thoroughly in all its aspects, not only stray moments of triumph. The task of the counselor is to assist the person in attaining the intentionality and the health that is natural to each individual. When a person becomes truly in touch with the inner self, that individual will move to positive action and fulfillment.

It is not hard to see the attraction existing in this positive view of humanity. For people accustomed to thinking of themselves in negative terms, the thought that they can be "good" can be an earthshaking discovery. Whereas Rogers was once laughed at and derided for naiveté and superficiality, he has come to be regarded as a major figure in counseling and therapy, and his ideas are viewed by many as a major social and philosophic force of modern times.

Carl Rogers has never been content with the status quo. He has constantly changed, shaped, and adapted his ideas over the years. This chapter will present three views of Carl Rogers as manifested in his nondirective, client-centered, and modern periods. While his methods change at each stage of his development, the underlying faith in humanity and the individual remains constant. We will first present his major theoretical formulations and then consider sample interviews from each of his major stages of development.

Basic Rogerian Constructs

The central issue in Rogerian and existential-humanistic counseling lies in how the individual perceives the world. "Experience is reality" is a statement that implies both explicitly and implicitly that what one thinks is happening in the world is indeed happening. There are an infinite number of ways in which we might view the world, an infinite number of ways of interpreting that world, and an infinite number of ways of acting on that world. This view is somewhat similar to that of George Kelly and personal construct theory, but emphasizes the individual and tends to give less attention to person-environment transactions. Given the infinite possibilities in life, every person's experience and perceptions will be somewhat different from everyone else's. *A central task of the counselor is to understand and empathize with the unique experiential world of the client.* Basic to existential-humanistic counseling is a consistent effort to understand and experience, as far as possible, the uniqueness that underlies each person.

The importance of this key set of ideas cannot be overstated. If one is to assist another person, one must be able to understand where that other person is "coming from" and the nature of her or his unique perceptions of the world. Perhaps more than anyone else, Carl Rogers was able to listen empathically and carefully to other human beings. And, as he understood them and their perceptions, he consistently found positive, self-actualizing forces in them. Those committed to humanistic counseling theories are almost always able to find positive elements in even the most troubled individual. The following story illustrates this point:

> A small child is attempting to string beads onto a shoelace. The plastic end of the lace has been torn off and the tip is frayed badly. The child sits quietly and determinedly for 15 minutes, attempting an impossible task. Then, with a sudden shout of frustration, the beads and the lace are thrown about the room. At that moment the child's father looks up and strikes the child for "lack of patience."

In this case, the child is obviously forward-moving and purposeful. But the perception of reality is unrealistic, in that the task is impossible, given the frayed string and the age of the child. Viewing the child as we did, it was easy to see that the expression of anger was a normal reaction to growing frustration.

More important to this consideration, however, is the father. His behavior appears immediately despicable and irrational. Where are the forward-moving self-actualized parts in a person who strikes a child? If the father entered counseling and discussed this situation with a Rogerian counselor, he would be encouraged to talk out the situation in considerable detail. There would an be emphasis on the emotional underpinnings of the incident, and, quite likely, the father would share other incidents in which he lost his temper. As this situation is explored in depth, the counselor might uncover the fact that the father had tried very hard that day to find work but was unsuccessful, that the father was a single parent, and that he himself had been abused as a child. Yet, the counselor would tend to focus more on the experience and emotion of the father in his complicated life and give relatively less attention to the facts of the situation. The counselor would reflect the positive elements of the father's behavior (trying to make it, to do the "right thing") and understand and accept the negative behavior. The counselor's strong positive regard would come through, and the father's striking the child could be seen as a natural reaction to frustration quite similar to the child's natural reaction to frustration. This interpretation, however, would not be made explicit. Rather, the counselor would communicate her or his faith that the father could become more intentional and self-actualized if he chose to. This approach may be compared to the psychodynamic therapist, who is interested in *why* the father behaved as he did (usually with an explicit and purposeful examination of childhood patterns), and to the behavioral counselor, who might work with the father to plan systematically for changing the angry behavior itself.

Similarly, husbands who beat their wives, children who fail in school, and individuals who cheat, lie, or steal all have underlying goodness in them. If a therapist can understand their perceptions, the underlying positive traits within them can be exposed. Once this happens, a natural healing process may be expected to occur and individuals will change their behavior and bring perceptions of reality to more positive directions.

A basic dimension of existential-humanistic counseling is to understand where clients are "coming from" and how they organize and experience their world. The attending or listening skills of Chapter 3 are vital in this process, as are the qualitative dimensions of empathy discussed in Chapter 4. A major assumption of this form of counseling is that once people are understood and heard, they will move in positive directions.

A critical issue in Rogerian counseling (presently the most popular existential-humanistic view) is the discrepancy that often occurs between *real self* and *ideal self*. An individual needs to see herself or himself as worthy. Often an individual loses sight of what he or she really is in an effort to attain an idealized image. This discrepancy between thought and reality, between self-perceptions and others' perceptions, or between self and experience leads to incongruities. These incongruities in turn represent places where the person is not truly herself or himself. The father who strikes the child lacks congruence and the objective of therapy is to resolve the discrepancies between ideal and real self, thus eliminating the tension and substituting forward-moving self-actualization.

To be truly empathic and attending with clients, the counselor must also be able to grow personally. The more peaceful and authentic the counselor is, the more able the counselor is to help clients find the same peaceful center in themselves. As a definition of a route toward that center of being, Rogers talks about "The Necessary and Sufficient Conditions of Therapeutic Personality Change" (1957, pp. 95–103) and suggests six basic conditions that, if met adequately, will result in positive forward movement of the client, regardless of theoretical orientation of the therapist or counselor:

1. "Two persons are in psychological contact." A *relationship* must exist between two human beings. Rogers's counseling methods are often called "a relational approach" for the focus of much of the counseling process is on two people who are involved and related with each other.

2. "The first, whom we shall term the client, is in a state of incongruence, being vulnerable and anxious." Incongruence is most easily understood as a discrepancy between the ideal and the real self and leads to anxiety and behavior unsatisfactory to the client and to others. An obvious task of the therapist is helping the client to become increasingly aware of these incongruities and to work toward resolution and synthesis.

3. "The second person, whom we shall term the therapist, is congruent or integrated in the relationship." While counselors may not always be self-actualized persons, it is crucial that they be genuine and authentic in the interview. The concept of genuineness and the absence of mixed messages, emphasized in Chapter 4 on empathy, and the concept of incongruity, as explored in Chapter 5, are particularly important here. Perhaps more than any other theory, Rogers's stresses the importance of authenticity in the interview.

4. "The therapist experiences unconditional positive regard for the client." The counselor is able to view the client with a positive attitude, regardless of her or his overt behavior. This allows the client the freedom to be, to feel accepted and appreciated as a human being without being judged, and to feel safe to share life experiences with the counselor. The communication of warmth, respect, and caring is important in the development of positive regard.

5. "The therapist experiences an empathic understanding of the client's internal frame of reference and endeavors to communicate this experience to the client." The communication of empathy ordinarily occurs through the use of accurate, high quality attending skills of paraphrasing, reflection of feeling, and summarization at a primary level.

6. "The communication to the client of the therapist's empathic understanding and unconditional positive regard is to a minimal degree achieved." All the preceding five dimensions are useless unless the client perceives them. Thus, the six necessary and sufficient conditions become a full circle: the client will perceive the conditions only if a true relationship exists, positive regard and empathy are manifest, and all conditions are met.

These "core conditions" have given rise to extensive research on the counseling process. Their validity has been seriously questioned by the field and this research is presented in more detail in Chapter 13 (pages 393–394). However, given the breadth of Rogers's thinking, it is quite possible that research procedures have not yet been developed that truly measure the broad intent of his approach and the fact that his theories have continued to expand over time. Carl Rogers sees the therapeutic session as a microcosm for human existence, and the issue is the existential question "who am I?" The answer to this question does not come from the therapist, but from the inner being of the client.

Whether one accepts the theory and methods of Rogers, it is clear that his influence has been immense.

A Dynamic Theory of Change and Growth

Rogers believes and acts on his theories. He is a personal demonstration of intentionality and self-actualization, constantly changing and growing. Three main stages* of his process may be identified:

Stage I: 1940–1950—Nondirective. This stage emphasized the acceptance of the client, the establishment of a positive nonjudgmental climate, trust in the client's wisdom, permissiveness, and uses clarification of the client's world as the main technique. His writings give a central emphasis to skills in the counseling process.

Stage II: 1950–1961—Client-centered. This stage centers on reflecting the feelings of the client, incorporates resolving incongruities between the ideal self and real self, avoids personally threatening situations for the client, and uses reflection as the main technique. Skills are not emphasized; rather a major emphasis on the counselor as a person is evolving.

*While three main periods have been identified in Carl Rogers's development, it is also relevant to note his early major work, *Counseling and Psychotherapy* (1942), where he first presented typescripts of his work and commentary on counseling theory. While he talks about nondirective therapy in this book, he gives considerable attention to insight and practical matters of the counseling interview. Further, at that time, Rogers used more questions and interpretations than he did later in his nondirective period. Currently, Rogers is moving more toward work in the world environment, particularly with peace and negotiation.

Stage III: 1961–present—Increased personal involvement. While maintaining consistency with all past work, Rogers has moved increasingly to emphasizing present-tense experience, a more active and self-disclosing role for the counselor, group as well as individual counseling, and consideration of broader issues in society, such as cultural differences and the use of power. The emphasis on skills has remained low as Rogers now emphasizes counselor attitudes rather than interview skills. Coupled with this is an extensive emphasis on experiencing oneself as a person, in relation to others.

In the following pages, brief examples of each of the three major phases of Rogers's growth and development will be explored through the presentation and analysis of brief excerpts from typical sessions of each period.

The Nondirective Period. A special gift of Carl Rogers to the counseling profession was a new openness to what was happening in the interview process. Through detailed notes and discussion and through the new medium of audio-recording, Rogers shared in great detail what he actually did in the counseling interview. Up to that time, the primary mode of training counselors and therapists had been in formal classrooms and one-to-one discussion of what the therapist remembered from an interview. A classic research study by Blocksma and Porter (1947) revealed that what therapists say they do in an interview and what they actually do are two different things. Rogers's ability to share what he was doing, coupled with the work of Blocksma and Porter, has forever changed the nature of counseling and therapy training. There remains strong resistance to this openness, particularly among psychoanalytic therapists, who often prefer more abstract discussions of underlying unconscious conflicts to what actually happens in the session.

The following typescript is taken from Rogers's nondirective phase when he was trying explicitly to draw out the client and impose as little of himself as possible (primary empathy). This was in the belief that interference from the counselor would only slow natural client growth. The microskills in this interview are all attending skills and are extremely clear. Thus, rather than our identifying the skills for you, in the blank space to the left of the typescript, fill in the microskills used. A classification of the microskills will be found on page 279.

Skills		*Interview*
	1. CLIENT:	I wish I knew how to pray.
	2. COUNSELOR:	Do you want to tell me some more about that?*
	3. CLIENT:	I'm all in a mess. I can't sleep. Last night I walked the streets most of the night in a pouring rain. I haven't been able to sleep all the time I've been on leave. I was home for awhile, and I couldn't even talk to my folks there. You see, my buddy was killed, and I just can't get over it.
	4. COUNSELOR:	That's been a pretty upsetting blow to you.*
	5. CLIENT:	Well it has. You see, my buddy was my only real friend—I don't make friends easily, never have had very many—and

he and I always stuck together. [Tells how they met and some of the things they had been through.] We worked on the same gun crew, and we knew each other so well we never had to tell each other what to do. We could just signal by the way we looked. In this particular scrap the enemy planes were coming over plenty. It was pretty hot. The ammunition box was getting empty, and I just glanced at my buddy. He knew what I meant, and he went to get another box. While he was doing that a shell exploded right near him and killed him. (Pause) I just can't get over it. I feel—I feel as though I caused his death.

6. COUNSELOR: You feel that somehow you are to blame for the fact that he was killed.*

7. CLIENT: Yes I do. I don't see why. Well, there's one thing I haven't mentioned. Maybe that has something to do with it. My buddy and I, we got along swell. We hardly ever quarreled, but just the day before this all happened we had quite an argument. [He relates the details of the argument.] We really got sore at each other. I wouldn't even speak to him for several hours afterwards. You know, I think that does have something to do with it. I guess that quarrel makes me feel that I am to blame for what happened.

8. COUNSELOR: You feel that your being angry at him in some way was responsible for killing him.*

9. CLIENT: You know, I think that's it. I haven't thought that through before. Maybe I was scared to think it through. Somehow it helps to talk about things like this. You see, I didn't usually quarrel with my buddy, and I guess it hit me hard to think that we had an argument just the day before he was killed. It doesn't seem so bad when you tell about it. He was really a great guy. [He goes on to tell at some length about his buddy and his buddy's accomplishments and the good relationship they had together. The conversation then turns into other channels, and he talked about his own family and again mentions the fact that he had been very upset while home on leave.] I don't know what you've done sir, but this has sure helped me a lot. I don't see why I felt so much to blame as I did.

10. COUNSELOR: It seems to have helped to get it off your chest. Is that it?*

11. CLIENT: It sure has. I wonder, sir, if it would be too much if I could write to you if I ever feel this way again. I'm probably shipping out pretty quick so I don't think I'll have a chance to see you again, but maybe I could write you a letter.

12. COUNSELOR: I'd be delighted to get a letter from you even if you're not feeling upset. I hope you will write to me.*

13. CLIENT: Well, thanks a lot for talking with me. I've got to go now but you may be hearing from me.

*2. Closed question.
*4. Reflection of feeling.
*6. Paraphrase.

Rogers provides an interesting personal analysis of this interview in which he points out that the counselor does not direct the depth of the interview, but rather attempts to establish conditions so that the client can determine how far or deep to go. Whereas many counselors might have wanted more concreteness and specifics about the situation, the worker in this case accepts the sailor's definition of what happened however he wants to talk about it. A psychodynamic counselor might object to the failure to consider unconscious thought processes underlying the relatively simple surface structure sentences of the sailor; other theorists might have different objections and consider such an interaction superficial. Rogers tends to reply in a particularly disarming fashion to those who criticize his work. He suggests that each therapist must find her or his own way to be authentic with another person, and that those whose views differ from his tend to select counseling theories that work best for them. Thus, we find Rogers exhibiting unusual congruence within himself. Not only does he emphasize and respect the client's ability to determine what is right for herself or himself, but he also respects his critics' ability to determine what is right for themselves.

The Client-Centered Period. The following is illustrative of the work of Rogers's second period. A client, Mrs. Oak, is discussing how hard it is for her to accept any help or positive reactions from others. Note that the complexity of the counselor's sentences have greatly increased since the example from the nondirective period. Yet, the emphasis is still very much on the client and the client's perceptions.

CLIENT: I have a feeling . . . that you have to do it pretty much yourself, but that somehow you ought to be able to do that with other people. [She mentions that there have been "countless" times when she might have accepted personal warmth and kindliness from others.] I get the feeling that I just was afraid I would be devastated. [She returns to talking about the counseling itself and her feeling toward it.] I mean there's been this tearing through the thing myself. Almost to—I mean, I felt it—I mean I tried to verbalize it on occasion—a kind of—at times almost not wanting you to restate, not wanting you to reflect, the thing is *mine*. Course all right, I can say it's resistance. But that doesn't mean a damn thing to me now . . . The—I think in—in relationship to this particular thing, I mean, the—probably at times, the strongest feeling was, it's mine, it's *mine*. I've got to cut it down myself. See?

COUNSELOR: It's an experience that's awfully hard to put down accurately into words, and yet I get a sense of difference here in this relationship, that from the feeling that "this is mine," "I've got to do it," "I am doing it," and so on, to a somewhat different feeling that—"I could let you in."

---

*8. Paraphrase.

*10. Reflection of feeling/paraphrase. Note check-out "Is that it?"

*12. Expression of content and feeling—self-disclosure.

[The counselor's reflection of meaning catches the main points of Mrs. Oak's statement in brief form, thus feeding back to her what her inner world is truly like. In addition, the basic incongruity between real and ideal self is reflected back to the client. Mrs. Oak's statement has a vagueness which would prompt many other counselors to search for more concreteness and to ask for specifics. A psychodynamic therapist might observe the sexual symbolism in the words "I've got to cut it down myself." and the therapist's "I could let you in."]

CLIENT: Yeah. Now, I mean, that's—that it's—well, it's sort of, shall we say, volume two. It's—it's a—well, sort of, well, I'm still in the thing alone, but I'm *not*—see—I'm—

COUNSELOR: M-hm. Yes, that paradox sort of sums it up, doesn't it.

CLIENT: Yeah.

COUNSELOR: In all of this, there is a feeling, it's still—every aspect of my experience is mine and that's kind of inevitable and necessary and so on. And yet that isn't the whole picture either. Somehow it can be shared or another's interest can come in and in some ways it is new.

[There is an interpretive flavor to the last two therapist statements as new meanings are put on old experience. Yet, as they very much come from the client's worldview, this lead is a reflection of meaning, but close to a paraphrase. The increased involvement of the therapist since the first period of Rogers's theory should be apparent. Note also that the therapist goes so far as to use "I" when talking about the client rather than "you;" this could be considered a sign of strong empathy, where the counselor is indeed able to see the world through the client's eyes.]

CLIENT: Yeah. And it's—it's as though, that's how it should be. I mean, that's how it—has to be. There's a—there's a feeling, "and this is good." I mean, it expresses, it clarifies it for me. There's a feeling—in this caring, as though—you were sort of standing back—standing off, and if I want to sort of cut through to the thing, it's a—a slashing of—oh, tall weeds, that I can do it, and you can—I mean you're not going to be disturbed by having to walk through it, too. I don't know. And it doesn't make sense. I mean—

COUNSELOR: Except there's a very real sense of rightness about this feeling that you have, hm?

CLIENT: M-hm. (Rogers, 1961, pp. 84–85)

[It is particularly important to note the emphasis in this paraphrase. The therapist has selectively attended to the positive aspects of the client's message ("this is good") and simultaneously ignored negative aspects ("it doesn't make sense"). Behavioral counselors have often pointed out that Rogerian counseling involves selective attention and that as complete a verbal "shaping" process occurs in this mode of counseling as in more systematic behavioral approaches. Regardless of whether this view is accepted or not, the selective attention to positive, forward-moving aspects of the client is an example of the concepts of the positive regard emphasized strongly in this theory.]

Rogers goes on to comment that this was a turning point for Mrs. Oak, who learned that it was all right to accept others and to discover positive things in herself. This acceptance is, of course, crucial in the development of a positive self-actualizing personality.

The Third Period of Active Counselor Involvement. Stage III of Rogers's development reveals vastly increased involvement and activity on the part of the counselor. To the traditional skills of reflection of feeling and paraphrasing, new skills of self-disclosure, feedback, and questions have been added. The following typescript exemplifies this stage and is taken from an encounter group led by Rogers (the facilitator).

ART: When the shell's on it's, uh . . .

LOIS: It's on!

ART: Yeah, it's on tight.

SUSAN: Are you always so closed in when you're in your shell?

ART: No, I'm so darn used to living with the shell, it doesn't even bother me. I don't even know the real me. I think I've, well, I've pushed the shell away more here. When I'm out of my shell—only twice—once just a few minutes ago—I'm really me, I guess. But then I just sort of pull in a cord after me when I'm in my shell, and that's almost all the time. And I leave the front standing outside when I'm back in the shell.

FACILITATOR: And nobody's back in there with you?

[Art is the focus of group interaction at the moment. He describes his feelings of being shut off from people in a vivid metaphor of life in a shell. Art as a group member is using effective self-disclosure skills. Lois and Susan, through completion of Art's sentence and the focused closed question, show that more people than group leaders and counselors can be helpful. The facilitator's closed question is critical because it brings past and present experience together in one existential moment. Art is experiencing being alone in the shell at this moment as he has in the past in other situations. Yet, paradoxically, he is alone with a supportive facilitator and group. This integration of past and present experience in "moments of truth" appear in most theories of helping and are particularly important.]

ART: (Crying) Nobody else is in there with me, just me. I just pull everything into the shell and roll the shell up and shove it in my pocket. I take the shell, and the real me, and put it in my pocket where it's safe. I guess that's really the way I do it—I go into my shell and turn off the real world. And here—that's what I want to do here in this group, y'know—come out of my shell and actually throw it away.

LOIS: You're making progress already. At least you can talk about it.

FACILITATOR: Yeah. The thing that's going to be the hardest is to stay out of the shell.

ART: (Still crying) Well, yeah, if I can keep talking about it I can come out and stay out, but I'm going to have to, y'know, protect me. It hurts. It's actually hurting to talk about it. (Rogers, 1970, p. 26)

[Lois provides a good example of a feedback statement, and the facilitator expresses his opinion and reaction. Together the two support Art in the immediate moment and help him clarify his own experience.]

In this short example, all leads or statements by the facilitator and the group members would be classified as influencing skills with the exception of the closed questions (and as they were focused so precisely, they tend to resemble influencing skills more than attending skills). The use of group psychotherapy, and in this case, group client-centeredness, provides a great opportunity for clients to share and receive feedback on themselves, in terms of how they are perceived by others in the group. The present-tense immediacy of the group and the relationship between the members provide a point of reflection on the experience of being. The counselor and the group members use much the same skills. However, if one examines the structure of group process, one will often find that the group members gradually learn to utilize the same skills that their facilitator models.

A Person-Centered Theory

Rogers's best known book is entitled *Becoming a Person* (1961) and that title illustrates the theory and the man. In the Rogerian view, there seems to be no definable end to counseling work; this emphasis on process toward possible futures is particularly illustrative of the existential-humanistic orientation that is oriented to a choice for the future.

As noted in the introductory comments of this chapter, Rogerian person-centered theory is one that attempts to enter the worldview of the client and to facilitate understanding and change *only if* the client desires. This may be described as basically a listening approach to therapy, although we note increased use of influencing skills over the years. Figure 10.1 provides you with an opportunity to construct an interview using only listening skills. You may be surprised to find that you can conduct a complete and effective session using only the skills of the basic listening sequence. This exercise does not introduce you to the full range of Rogerian response possibilities, but does illustrate what is possible if one is willing to enter the world of the client and truly attempts to see the world as the other perceives it.

Gendlin summarized in a few brief words the change process that is person-centered therapy throughout its periods and changing styles:

> . . . by saying what the client said, something new will occur, the client will soon say something new, and then we can respond to that. By featuring responsivity at every small, specific momentary step, . . . the therapist carries forward not only what the client verbally stated, but also the client's experiential process . . . *this responsivity to specific felt meaning at each step engenders, carries forward, and changes the individual's ongoing experiential process.* This is the underlying principle that is implicit in client-centered therapy and its early quaint rules for therapist responding. (Gendlin, 1970, pp. 32–33)

In effect, Gendlin is suggesting that when the client shares her or his experience with the counselor, and the counselor responds with accurate listening, the client is moved forward by the interaction. Despite even direct repetition of what the client has said, the client's world has been changed by the very act of being heard. Being heard by another person could be said to be an action on the world. Many, perhaps most, clients do not feel they have power and influence on others or their surroundings. By the giving of himself or herself to the client

Figure 10.1 *An Exercise in Person-Centered Counseling*

A person-centered theorist might argue that our world is too full of advice giving and people telling other people what to do. Your goal in this exercise is to enter the frame of reference of the client and use only listening skills represented by the basic listening sequence and perhaps reflection of meaning. *No advice, suggestions, or interpretation is allowed!* To make the task somewhat easier, you may use questions, but aim each question toward the frame of reference of the client. A good topic for your real or role-played "client" may be the act of procrastination, putting off something until later. However, any of a variety of topics may be used for the practice session.

RAPPORT/STRUCTURING

Begin the interview by establishing rapport until you and the client are comfortable. Remember that rapport is particularly important throughout the session. Structure the interview honestly by saying that you want to understand and listen and not give advice. You might initiate the session by saying, "You wanted to talk about . . ."

DATA GATHERING.

Use primarily the reflective listening skills of encouraging, paraphrasing, and reflection of feeling. Periodically summarize what the "client" says so the session has a continuous structure. After you have heard the problem fairly clearly, you may wish to paraphrase or reflect positive meanings or actions inherent in what the client has been saying. This is a specific way to manifest positive regard and demonstrate the positive asset search.

DETERMINING OUTCOMES.

Your client very likely has implied how he or she would like things to be. As you begin to understand the client's problem, paraphrase or summarize how the client would like things to be. Here, you will likely find it necessary to ask a question related in some form to the following: "How would you like things to be?" You have heard the "real self" and the real problem in Stage 2 and this is the opportunity to draw out the "ideal self" or the ideal solution.

GENERATING ALTERNATIVE SOLUTIONS.

Important in person-centered theory is the distinction between the real and ideal. Summarize this incongruency of real and ideal with the confrontation statement "On one hand, your problem is . . . , but on the other hand your ideal solution is . . . Now what comes to your mind as a possible resolution?" Alternatively, you may wish to talk about how the person views him- or herself and how he or she would like to view him- or herself. Again, the question may not be necessary as the clear summary of the real and ideal often enables clients to start generating their own solutions out of their own personal constructs.

Use the basic listening sequence and reflection of meaning to understand and listen to what the client generates. This may be considered the action phase of the interview in which the client generates a new view on the problem from his or her own internal frame of reference.

GENERALIZATION

Person-centered theory has not traditionally given much attention to generalization and perhaps that is why research as to its effectiveness has not been as promising as once was hoped. You may wish to summarize what the client has generated as alternative solutions and see if the client is interested in actually doing something about her or his situation. As Rogerian theory does not emphasize this phase of helping, you may find it worthwhile to consider generalization techniques from relapse prevention (Chapter 9) or you may simply ask the client "What one thing will you do or think differently this coming day because of our discussion?"

Simply being heard accurately frees many people for creative, intentional responding. This exercise is taken from the nondirective period of Rogerian theory, but may be adapted to include other skills (self-disclosure, feedback) added in later Rogerian periods. You may note that if you have mastered the constructs of the first seven chapters that you can rather rapidly enter into a relatively effective person-centered interview.

through the empathic attending skills, the counselor empowers the client. *The client speaks; the therapist listens carefully and attempts to understand the client's perceptions of the world; the client, having been heard and understood, can move forward.*

GESTALT THERAPY: A SET OF POWERFUL TECHNIQUES

Frederick (Fritz) Perls devised Gestalt theory to fill the theoretical gaps of psychoanalysis. Perls saw human nature as wholistic, consisting of many varied parts, which make a unique individual. We start life more or less "together," but as we grow and develop, we encounter experiences, feelings, and fears in life that cause us to lose parts of ourselves. These "splits" from the whole, or "Gestalt," must be regained if we are to live intentional, self-actualized lives. Thus, Gestalt therapy is centrally concerned with integrating or reintegrating our split-off parts into a whole person.

The Gestalt worldview is that people can be responsible for their actions in the world, and further, that the world is so complex that very little can be understood at any given moment. Thus, Gestalt therapy tends to focus extensively on the present-tense immediate experience of the client. The similarity of these key constructs to the basic existential posture, just discussed, should be obvious. Gestalt could be described as centrally concerned with the totality of one's being-in-the-world. The complexity and possibility of the world can be dealt with, according to existential thought, in a wide variety of ways. Perls chose to emphasize here and now, present-tense experiencing as a way to integrate people in relation to themselves, others, and the world. By doing so, we find a corresponding decrease in emphasis on past or future and on relationships with others and the world. Writes Perls: "Whenever you leave the sure basis of the now and become preoccupied with the future, you experience anxiety" (Perls, 1969 a, p. 30). Perls's suggested mode of being-in-the-world is to center on oneself and get in touch with one's own existential experience, thus making for a very "I-centered," individualistic view of therapy.

It would be possible to discuss Gestalt theory in considerable detail. However, the primary purpose of this section is to examine some powerful techniques for enhancing awareness of interpersonal experiencing developed by Perls and his co-workers. It can be argued that Perls's major contribution is methodological rather than theoretical. Over the years, he developed a wide range of techniques that bring existential experiencing alive. Perls was a charismatic, dynamic therapist, trained in classical psychoanalysis, but profoundly aware of its limitations. He brought his formal knowledge and a formidable clinical talent to the counseling interview. He and his co-workers have been able to document both Gestalt therapy theory and technique in a rather complete form (c.f. Perls, Hefferline, and Goodman, 1951; Fagan and Shepherd, 1970; Perls, 1969 a, 1969 b). However, the most effective way to understand Gestalt therapy is to experience it. The following excerpt is typical of Perls's work. Note particularly the consistent present-tense immediacy in the session.

1. MEG: In my dream, I'm sitting on a platform, and there's somebody else with me, a man, and maybe another person, and—ah—a couple of rattlesnakes. And one's up on the platform, now, all coiled up, and I'm frightened. And his head's up, but he doesn't seem like he's gonna strike me. He's just sitting there and I'm frightened, and this other person says to me—uh—just, just don't disturb the snake and he won't bother you. And the other snake, the other snake's down below, and there's a dog down there.
2. FRITZ: What is there? [Open Question]
3. MEG: A dog, and the other snake.
4. FRITZ: So, up here is one rattlesnake and down below is another rattlesnake and the dog. [Paraphrase]
5. MEG: And the dog is sort of sniffing at the rattlesnake. He's—ah—getting very close to the rattlesnake, sort of playing with it, and I wanna stop—stop him from doing that.
6. FRITZ: Tell him. [Directive]
7. MEG: Dog, stop! /FRITZ: Louder./ *Stop!* /FRITZ: Louder./ (shouts) STOP! /FRITZ: Louder./ (screams) *STOP!*
8. FRITZ: Does the dog stop? [Closed Question]
9. MEG: He's looking at me. Now he's gone back to the snake. Now—now, the snake's sort of coiling up around the dog, and the dog's lying down, and—and the snake's coiling around the dog, and the dog looks very happy.
10. FRITZ: Ah! Now have an encounter between the dog and the rattlesnake. [Directive]
11. MEG: You want me to play them?
12. FRITZ: Both. Sure. This is your dream. Every part is a part of yourself. [Directive, Interpretation]
13. MEG: I'm the dog. (hesitantly) Huh. Hello, rattlesnake. It sort of feels good with you wrapped around me.
14. FRITZ: Look at the audience. Say this to somebody in the audience. [Directive]
15. MEG: (laughs gently) Hello, snake. It feels good to have you wrapped around me.
16. FRITZ: Close your eyes. Enter your body. What do you experience physically? [Directing]
17. MEG: I'm trembling. Tensing.
18. FRITZ: Let this develop. Allow yourself to tremble and get your feelings . . . (her whole body begins to move a little) Yah. Let it happen. Can you dance it? Get up and dance it. Let your eyes open, just so that you stay in touch with your body, with what you want to express physically . . . Yah . . . (she walks, trembling and jerkily, almost staggering) Now dance rattlesnake . . . (she moves slowly and sinuously graceful) . . . How does it feel to be a rattlesnake now? . . . [Directive, Open Question]
19. MEG: It's—sort of—slowly—quite—quite aware, of anything getting too close.
20. FRITZ: Hm? [Encourage]
21. MEG: Quite aware of not letting anything get too close, ready to strike.
22. FRITZ: Say this to us. "If you come too close, I—" [Directive]
23. MEG: If you come too close, I'll strike back!
24. FRITZ: I don't hear you. I don't believe you, yet. [Feedback]
25. MEG: If you come too close, I will *strike back!*
26. FRITZ: Say this to each one, here. [Directive]
27. MEG: If you come too close, I will *strike back!*

28. FRITZ: Say this with your whole body. [Directive]
29. MEG: If you come too close, I will *strike back!*
30. FRITZ: How are your legs? I experience you as being somewhat wobbly. [Open Question, Feedback]
31. MEG: Yeah.
32. FRITZ: That you don't really take a stand. [Interpretation]
33. MEG: Yes, I feel I'm . . . kind of, in between being very strong and—if I let go, they're going to turn to rubber.
34. FRITZ: Okeh, let them turn to rubber. (her knees bend and wobble) Again . . . Now try out how strong they are. Try out—hit the floor. Do anything. (she stamps several times with one foot) Yah, now the other, (stamps other foot) Now let them turn to rubber again. (she lets knees bend again) More difficult now, isn't it? [Directive, Closed Question]
35. MEG: Yeah.
36. FRITZ: Now say again the sentence, "If you come too close—" . . . (she makes an effort) . . . (laughter) . . . [Directive]
37. MEG: If—if you . . .
38. FRITZ: Okeh, change. Say "Come close." (laughter) [Directive]
39. MEG: Come close.
40. FRITZ: How do you feel now? [Open Question]
41. MEG: Warm.
42. FRITZ: You feel somewhat more real? [Interpretation]
43. MEG: Yeah.
44. FRITZ: Okeh . . . So what we did is we took away some of the fear of being in touch. So, from now on, she'll be a bit more in touch. [Interpretation] (Perls, 1969a, 162–164)

A microskill analysis comparing Perls with Rogers is an interesting exercise. The primary area of skill usage within Rogerian counseling is in the attending/listening area, whereas Perls uses predominantly influencing skills of directives, feedback, and interpretation. Where Rogers emphasizes empathy and warmth and positive regard, we find Perls as somewhat personally distant and remote during the session, for his respect for others showed only when they became truly themselves. Although both Rogers and Perls seek genuine encounters with others, Rogers tends to wait patiently for them while Perls may demand that authentic relationships develop.

Both Rogerian and Gestalt therapy are strongly in the tradition of existential-humanism. Both seek authentic relationships where people live in the "now," although Perls gives living in the present tense more prominence than Rogers does. Both theories and therapies are highly focused on the individual, although Rogers emphasizes relationship with others more than Perls does, and Perls emphasizes responsibility of the individual for her or his own fate. One cannot help but be impressed by the consistency of goals between the two and be perplexed by the extreme variation in method. Unfortunately, research studies comparing the two and their differential effectiveness are virtually nonexistent. However, clinical opinion is that Gestalt makes changes occur much faster than Rogerian methods do, but that it also has the potential for more destructive impact on the client if the therapist moves too fast. The Gestalt therapist is often seen by the client as a "guru type," giving the therapist even more power. Lie-berman, Yalom, and Miles (1972) and Strupp and Hadley (1976) have docu-mented well the dangers of the charismatic therapist on fragile clients.

As noted earlier, Fritz Perls has made a major impact on counseling through his exciting and active therapeutic style. Some of the techniques of Ges-talt therapy are outlined below:

1. *Here and now experiencing.* Most techniques of Gestalt therapy are centered on helping the client experience the world *now* rather than in the past or future. What is done is done, and what will be will be. While past experiences, dreams, or future thoughts may be discussed, the constant emphasis is on relating them to immediate present-tense experience.

2. *Directives.* Gestalt therapists are constantly telling their clients what to do. At Meg: 5, for example, we find that Meg is talking in the past tense about her dream. Perls, through the simple directive "Tell him," brings the past to the present. Throughout this session, Perls is constantly directing the movement of the client. Feedback (Fritz: 24), questions relating to feelings (Fritz: 30), and interpretations (Fritz: 32) give additional strength to the directives.

3. *Language changes.* Gestalt clients are encouraged to change questions to state-ments, in the belief that most questions are simply statements about oneself that are hidden ("Do you like me?" may in truth be a statement saying "I am not sure that you like me.") The therapist suggests that the client change questions to "I" statements. Clients are also often asked or told to change vague statements about some subject to "I" statements, thus increasing the personal identification and concreteness in the interview. The client is frequently directed to talk in the pres-ent tense ("Be in the here and now") as this also adds power and focus to the problem. Gestalt therapists point out that the counselor can see and understand only what is before him or her. Talking about problems is considered less effec-tive than experiencing them directly. While questions are generally discouraged, "how" and "what" questions are considered more acceptable than "why" ques-tions, which often lead to intellectualization.

4. *The empty chair technique.* Perhaps the best known and most powerful of the many Gestalt techniques, the empty chair is also one of the easiest to use in counseling practice. When a client expresses a conflict with another person, the client is di-rected to talk to that other person who is imagined to be sitting in an empty chair beside or across from the client. After the client has said a few words, the coun-selor directs the client to change chairs and answer as if he or she were the other person. The counselor directs a dialogue between the client and the imaginary other person by constantly suggesting chair changes at critical points. Through this exercise, the client learns to experience and understand feelings more fully. The client also often learns that he or she was projecting many thoughts onto the other person. (See Figure 10.2.)

5. *Talking to parts of oneself.* A variation of the empty chair technique is to note splits, immobility, or impasses in the client. These two sides of an issue or conflicting parts within the person are drawn out (sometimes details are sought for clarity, other times the counselor moves immediately to the exercise). The two sides of the person then engage in a dialogue, using the empty chair technique. Through the discussion of conflicted issues within the split, the person often spontaneously generates a new solution or answer. A variation on this theme often occurs when the counselor notes incongruities or mixed messages in the body language (or

---

Figure 10.2 *Exercise in Gestalt Counseling: The Empty Chair*

One of the basic exercises in Gestalt training and therapy is the "hot seat." The hot seat is used to work out discrepancies in thoughts and feelings, incongruities, and ambivalent feelings. It is also a method of facing interpersonal and intrapsychic conflicts.

You can do the following exercise by yourself, or you can direct a client. You will need two chairs for the person in the hot seat.

1. Think of a conflict you have with yourself, an ambivalent feeling, or a recent time when you wish you had acted assertively but didn't. Take a moment to review the situation, your feelings, and thoughts.
2. Choose one side—the side that most describes what you represent—and begin to verbally share your thoughts, feelings, and experiences with the other side which is sitting in the empty chair. Show your feelings through your words and descriptions; be angry, be strong, or however you are feeling. When you have run out of things to say, move to the other side, into the empty chair.
3. Now is your chance to provide the counter-argument—your conflicting feelings or thoughts—and challenge the first side of yourself. Share the strength of this side's feelings and thoughts as before, or with whatever amount of emotion is appropriate. When you have shared everything and have nothing else to say, take the seat in the empty chair where you began.
4. Continue being the side represented by this chair, and share your reactions to what side two has just stated. When you are finished here, resume seat two and share those reactions.
5. Continue this process until you feel as though you have established a knowledge of your conflict, ambivalent feeling, or incongruity. Hopefully, but not necessarily, you will find a resolution or solution to your problem.
6. The intentional counselor will be able to assess when a client could benefit from an exercise like the hot seat and how to successfully direct the exercise, and will move the client to a decision for action. The exercise can be applied for relevant problem solving in the client's life, and also as a stimulating source of self-knowledge. It is especially useful in eliciting feelings and emotional incongruities, and thus takes a prominent place in the methodology of Gestalt therapists.

---

between body language and words). In such cases, the Gestalt therapist may have the tense right hand talk to the loose left hand or the jiggling right leg talk to the upset stomach. Through such imaginative games of dialogue, quick and important breakthroughs in understanding often occur.

6. *Top dog and underdog.* Gestalt therapists constantly search for the authoritarian and demanding "top dog," which is full of "should's" and "ought's." By way of contrast, "underdog" is more passive, apologetic, and guilt-ridden. When these two dimensions are observed, the empty chair technique or a dialogue often helps the client to understand and experience them more fully.

7. *Staying with the feeling.* When a key emotion is noted in the interview, particularly through a nonverbal movement, the Gestalt therapist will often move immediately to give attention to the feeling and its meaning. Perls's suggestion in Fritz: 18, that the client let her trembling develop, exemplifies the use of this technique.

8. *Dreamwork.* The typescript presented here is an example of Gestalt dreamwork; it is here that Gestalt most closely resembles its psychoanalytic foundation. Yet,

Gestalt does not use dreams to understand past conflicts, but as metaphors to understand present-day, here and now living. The parts of a dream are considered as aspects of the client. Any piece (person, object, scene, or thing) of a dream somehow is a projection of the client's experiential work, and through acting out the dream it is possible to integrate the split pieces into the whole person.

Through these and other powerful techniques, Perls has made an impressive impact on the practice of counseling and psychotherapy. More than any other therapist, he has been able to show that clients can rapidly be moved to deep understanding of themselves and their condition. While his theoretical foundations have been criticized and there is little empirical evidence validating this approach, there is no question that his work and life are an important expression of the existential-humanistic tradition.

Perls represents therapists who rely on the influencing skills. Although centrally concerned that people develop their own meanings and their own direction in life, Perls never hesitates to share his opinion, interpret, or tell clients what to do (it is important, however, to point out that his use of directives is almost always centered on telling the clients what to do in the interview—outside of the interview he tells them "do your own thing."). This may be contrasted with the predominant use of attending skills by Carl Rogers who brought reflection of feeling and paraphrasing skills to their present prominent place in the helping profession. Rogers may be described as an attending counselor and Perls, as an influencing counselor. Both methods are recognized as intentional and are in wide use.

What Rogers and Perls have in common is the existential-humanistic view that people must select their own direction in life and that each person has unique worth and dignity. Their means to bring out that dignity differ, but the philosophy remains consistent between them. Between the two extreme therapeutic schools of Rogerian and Gestalt theory, we perhaps find the central core of existentialism in the work of Viktor Frankl and his student Elisabeth Lukas. These two represent a balance of listening and effective influencing techniques. Frankl represents a moderate balance between Perls and Rogers and is discussed next.

FRANKL AND LOGOTHERAPY: A FUTURE DIRECTION?

Frankl's positive philosophy and worldview have been summarized in Chapter 7 and form the basis for his logotherapy. Logotherapy holds that the critical issue for humankind is not what happens, but how one views or thinks about what happens. But logotherapy is also concerned with action and change. Frankl's logotherapy is concerned with our search for meaning in life. We have seen that Frankl was able to reframe his life situation in the concentration camp and find positive reasons for living in the midst of negatives. He has faced the existential dilemma of the meaning of life in extremis and won for himself and for others.

The task for the logotherapist is to help the client find meaning and purpose in life. Logotherapy could be described as a therapy balanced between the listening skills of Rogers and the influencing skills of Perls. Logotherapists are interested in carefully learning how the client constructs a worldview, but once they have that understanding of the client, they are willing and ready to move actively to promote client change. One individual can find purpose in serving others, another in a hobby, and still another in quietly observing a sunset. The difficult and important task that logotherapy sets for itself is to engage clients in the search for meaning—to counteract doubt and despair and return the client to intentionality.

The route toward intentionality and meaning is through careful listening to the client's construction or meaning already found in the world. Then, if necessary, the logotherapist will intervene directly and actively to facilitate change in the client's construct or meaning system. This change may be in thought or it may be in action. The listening portion of Frankl's logotherapy seems close to that of Rogers and the influencing portion almost as powerful and direct as that of Perls. The emphasis on both thought and action is also characteristic of the cognitive-behavioral approaches of Chapter 11.

Frankl has framed a theory and a method of helping that seem to be gaining increasing prominence (1946, 1959, 1969). It is especially interesting to note that the three central techniques he developed—dereflection, paradoxical intention, and change of attitudes—are current popular methodological and research areas (Frankl, 1933, 1985a; Lukas, 1984; Fabry, 1984). Frankl's conceptions around change of attitudes and dereflection may be found in varying form in cognitive-behavior modification, rational-emotive therapy, and the structural/systemic family theories. Paradoxical intention is one of the key "new" methods that can be used to produce rapid change, yet it was used by Frankl as early as 1929.

Elisabeth Lukas, Major Theoretician of Logotherapy. (See page 190 for a photo of founder Viktor Frankl.)

Lukas (1984) has outlined four main techniques that therapists can use to facilitate client growth and movement toward meaningful living.

Modification of Attitudes.   A client may have a negative attitude toward the self and experience life in a pessimistic way. A person may be extremely attractive and personable to others, but may see him or herself quite negatively despite what might be an overtly positive life situation. Alternatively, the individual may have really serious problems and be unable to do anything about them. In both cases, the logotherapeutic task is to change the way the person thinks about the situation—a goal quite similar to that of cognitive approaches to change. Modification of attitudes is most often conducted in a rather direct approach through sharing one's opinions, arguing with the client (see Ellis' rational-emotive therapy), or positive suggestions. At issue is assisting the client to take a new view of the situation.

The positive asset search of Chapter 7 is one form of logotherapeutic modulation of attitudes. The following example was demonstrated by therapist Mary Bradford Ivey after she had carefully listened first to the client's construction of the event.

19. M: (referring to the client's fears and guilt over trespassing and thinking himself close to death) Is there anything positive? I know it sounds like a totally negative experience. Was there anything you could see that was positive about what happened?

The past is past, but one can modify and change the way one thinks about it. Thinking of the past negatively is making a "decision for the past." As a result of the questioning of past interpretations, the client makes a decision for the future.

Paradoxical Intention.   This method was developed by Frankl in 1929 and is in increased use in counseling and psychotherapy in recent years. Frankl had a phobic client who was suffering from severe agoraphobia. Analysis and other methods were not working. Improvising, Frankl suggested that the patient—instead of being afraid of fainting on the street—should deliberately *wish* to collapse, have a coronary attack or a stroke. In fact, Frankl unequivocally defines his paradoxical intention technique as "encouraging the patient to do, or wish to happen, the very things he fears—albeit with tongue in cheek" (Frankl, 1985b). The next week the patient was cured. As Frankl did not recall what he had recommended him to do, the patient told him, "I just followed your advice, Doctor. I tried hard to faint but the more I tried the less I could, and consequently—the fear of fainting disappeared!" And the technique was born . . .

Paradoxical intention has become an important therapeutic skill. Ascher and Turner (1979) were the first to come up with a controlled experimental validation of the clinical effectiveness of paradoxical intention in comparison with other behavioral strategies. Even prior to them, Solyom et al. (1972) had proved experimentally that paradoxical intention works.

But Frankl (1985b) warns us of confounding paradoxical intention with so-called symptom prescription. In symptom prescription, the patient is told to exaggerate the symptom, say, a fear. In paradoxical intention, however, the patient is encouraged to wish to happen that of which he is afraid. In other words, not *fear itself* is dealt with, but rather *the object* of fear. At Dr. Frankl's hospital department, for example, a patient suffering from a severe washing compulsion had been washing her hands several hundred times a day. Thereupon one of the doctors suggested that, instead of being afraid of bacteria, the patient should *wish* to contract an infection. "I can't get enough bacteria," she was advised to tell herself, "I want to become as dirty as possible. There is nothing nicer than bacteria." And the patient really followed the advice. She asked the other patients at the hospital department to let her borrow from them as many bacteria as possible and came up with the resolution no longer to wash "the poor creatures" away but, instead, to keep them alive. No one of Frankl's staff would have dreamt of recommending that the patient no longer wash her hands several *hundred* times a day, but—along the lines of "symptom prescription"—that she do so several *thousand* times a day.

As one may see from the above case history, "an integral element in paradoxical intention is the deliberate evocation of humor" (Lazarus 1971). After all, the sense of humor is one of the aspects of what logotherapy regards to be a specifically human capacity, namely that of self-distancing.

Some authorities (for example, Lankton, 1980; Bandler and Grinder, 1982) argue that the client should not know that a paradoxical intervention is being used. However, clinical experience and new research data both suggest that clients can indeed profit from knowing that a paradoxical technique is being used. It may even be helpful to explain to the client your theory as to why the technique works.

Dereflection.   Dereflection as developed by Frankl (1955) "uses our ability to 'forget ourselves' and brings about a therapeutic reordering of attention—turning it from the problem toward other and positive contents of our thinking . . ." (Lukas, 1984). Many of us "hyper-reflect" on our problems and our negative feelings and experiences. The objective of dereflection is systematically to change the focus of our attention. Put in its most simple and directed terms, the task of the therapist is to encourage the client to think about something else other than the problem.

Techniques of dereflection may be as simple as encouraging a person with a loss of limb to start thinking about a new career, helping a cancer patient focus on helping others rather than thinking solely about him- or herself, or helping a retired person find an interesting hobby. In each case, the facts of the situation cannot change and certainly it is difficult to reframe problems of illness, age, and loneliness as having positive components. But what can be done is to find something else on which to focus one's attention. This refocusing of attention changes the "meaning core" of one's life. Instead of being depressed about the loss of a limb, the handicapped person can work toward a new goal, the patient can think about others, and the aging individual may make new friends and enjoy a new hobby. The concept has many important variations that are clearly described in Frankl (1946, 1952) in a chapter on dereflexion. Here you will find special attention given to issues of sexual functioning. Lukas (1984) is another useful source of ideas drawn from this concept.

Dereflection may be especially useful in therapy with sexual dysfunctioning. A case of impotence is often caused by the man giving excessive attention to whether or not he will obtain an erection. He is hyper-reflecting on himself and his problem, which in turn causes more impotence. The route toward therapeutic change via logotherapy in this case would be to dereflect and give attention to the wife, with all their sexual stimuli emanating from her. As one gives attention to another, one cannot think about oneself, and natural autonomic functions start working effectively.

A similar approach may be used with a person having difficulty sleeping at night. Instead of "trying" to fall asleep, the individual decides to use that time to study or some other gainful activity. After a relatively short period of time, you will find that many clients naturally get tired and fall asleep.

In a sense, this is a simple technique, partly born of logic and common sense. But, it takes considerable creativity and expertise to find what each individual client needs to avoid the problem of hyper-reflection. Furthermore, the changing of patterns of attention may require the use of modification of attitudes as discussed in the preceding paragraphs and/or some form of paradoxical intention.

Logotherapy in the application of technique appears to be a very intentional approach to change. There are theoretical and practical reasons for trying to help a client change in a certain direction, but if the first technique doesn't work, logotherapy does not hesitate to "mix and match" and change approach to meet the unique human needs of the client.

The Appealing Technique.   Lukas points out that the three techniques described here require you to work with the client through listening to her or his worldview and then to selectively work to discover the objective meaning of the situation (in the belief that behavior will change once attitudes and beliefs change). The appealing technique, she suggests, may be effective for clients experiencing drug or alcohol detoxification or for those clients you cannot reach via other directions. The appealing technique is reminiscent of the concepts used by Alcoholics Anonymous (AA) and some drug groups. The counselor takes the position that the client's situation is not hopeless and directly attempts to bring the client to a similar awareness. The drug abusing client may be asked to state out loud, for example, "I am not so helpless, I can control and direct my fate."

In some situations with an understanding and supportive counselor or therapist, the appealing technique can work. It is clearly different from the "sophisticated" techniques of psychoanalysis or behavior therapy. Some helpers find themselves embarrassed by this approach—it does not immediately appear deeply laden with theoretical implications. However, if *you* as helper *believe,* you will find that some clients will respond to this exhortative approach. Witness the effectiveness of AA and some drug treatment programs that use similar techniques to logotherapy's appealing process.

Using Positive Therapy Skills.   Frankl was a physician in Vienna before World War II and exchanged letters with Freud. Freud, due to his world wide stature, was able to leave Vienna before the time of the concentration camp. Frankl was just completing his book, *The Doctor and the Soul* (1946) and this was taken from him as he became another number in the death camp.

> This was the lesson I had to learn in three years spent in Auschwitz and Dachau: those most apt to survive the camps were those oriented toward the future, toward a meaning to be fulfilled by them in the future. . . . But meaning and purpose were only a necessary condition of survival, not a sufficient condition. Millions had to die in spite of their vision of meaning and purpose. Their belief could not save their lives, but it did enable them to meet death with heads held high. (Frankl, 1985a, p. 37)

A specific logotherapy interview is not included here because the interview transcript by Mary Bradford Ivey in Chapter 7 demonstrates many of the concepts discussed here. That interview is in the tradition of logotherapy in that it balances listening and influencing skills and does not hesitate to help the client find a positive meaning in his world. Figure 10.3 presents a practice exercise in some dimensions of logotherapy that you may find beneficial for your own work in counseling and psychotherapy.

SOME LIMITATIONS AND PRACTICAL IMPLICATIONS OF THE EXISTENTIAL-HUMANISTIC TRADITION

The beauty and strength of the existential-humanistic tradition lie in a strong faith in humankind, opportunities for personal growth, and the infinite possibility of experience. However, some naive therapists and counselors have taken only the concept of "infinite possibility" and have led clients into destructive, closed circles of existence.

A carefully designed study of seventeen encounter groups with 206 participants was conducted at Stanford University (Lieberman, Yalom, and Miles, 1972). The key finding of the study was that about one-third of the participants benefitted, one-third remained unchanged, and one-third experienced negative experiences as a result of the groups. Most important is the fact that sixteen *severe casualties* and seventeen *negative changers* were found as a result of the brief encounter experience. Among the severe casualties were suicide attempts and psychiatric hospitalization. Encounter group leaders were categorized according to

Figure 10.3   *An Exercise in Logotherapy*

Viktor Frankl and his student, Elisabeth Lukas, give almost as much attention to hearing and understanding the worldview of the client as does Carl Rogers and person-centered therapy. Thus, you can easily adapt Figure 10.1 of this chapter, "An Exercise in Person-Centered Counseling," to logotherapy.

Particularly good topics for this exercise include procrastination, a difficulty with a colleague or housemate, boredom, or concern over illness or the loss of someone important. Indicate to your real or role-played client that you are going to be talking about what the problem means to her or him and that problem solving will be secondary.

STAGES 1, 2, AND 3. RAPPORT/STRUCTURING, DATA GATHERING, DETERMINING OUTCOMES.

It is suggested that you use the same structure of the interview of Figure 10.1 for the first three stages of the interview. Basically, use listening skills and the basic listening sequence to draw out the problem.

However, add one central dimension: Ask yourself and your client, "What does this mean to you?" "What does this say about your deeper values?" "Why is this important?" Ask these meaning-oriented questions after you have heard the problem defined clearly. And, as you reach the third stage of the interview and the goal is established, ask what the goal *means* to the client and why the client *values* that goal. In the process of asking questions about meaning, you will find that a new depth is added to the interview and that clients' frequently start talking about their lives when before they were talking about problems. In this process you will want to add the skill of reflection of meaning. A reflection of meaning is similar to the paraphrase, but focuses more on deeper issues underlying the surface structure sentence.

STAGE 4. GENERATING ALTERNATIVE SOLUTIONS.

Once having heard the client and the client's meaning, you have two central alternatives:

1. You may summarize the problem and its meaning to the client and contrast it with a summary of the ideal goal and its meaning. Through the summary you will have pointed out possible discrepancies and mixed messages in the client's meaning system. Then, through listening skills and reflection of meaning, you can encourage further self-exploration. The goal here is to discover the underlying, more deeply felt meanings guiding the client's action.
2. If the client wishes to act on meaning, select one of the four major techniques of logotherapeutic action (change of attitudes, paradoxical intention, dereflection, or the appealing technique). If the first technique does not work, try another. Logotherapy does not hesitate to try several approaches in an attempt to meet the unique needs of your client.

Out of this portion of the interview, your goal is to facilitate client examination of meaning and through the influencing approach to help your client change and act on her or his meaning system.

STAGE 5. GENERALIZATION.

As with other existential-humanistic orientations, logotherapy does not give extensive attention to generalization and maintenance of behavioral change. It is suggested that you may ask your client to "think about" the interview over the next few days and talk with you personally or by phone. If it seems relevant, ask your client to try one thing differently during the time period before you have a followup talk.

leadership style, and it was found that all but one of the casualities came from five "aggressive stimulator" leaders who were intrusive, challenging, and confrontive to group members. These leaders tended to be authoritarian and sought immediate self-disclosure and expression of deep feelings, giving little concern to the ideas of the individuals in the group. One leader who had three casualties commented, "I saw that most of the group didn't want to do anything, so what I did was to just go ahead and have a good time for myself" (Yalom and Lieberman, 1971, p. 28).

The Lieberman, Yalom, and Miles study, of course, does not define all encounter groups nor does it define even a small portion of existentially-humanistic therapists and counselors. However, the study does illustrate the damage a good theory can do when implemented without consideration of human beings. Individual therapy in the existential-humanistic tradition presents some of the highest hopes of humankind. At the same time, "oddball" and "innovative" therapies may take the existential-humanistic label and develop extreme dependency among clients, even to the point of encouraging sexual relations between therapist and client. Psychodynamic and behavioral counseling, which are sometimes termed "manipulative and dehumanizing," may have a stronger record of ethics and professionalism than the less controlled aspects of existential-humanism.

Another concern that rises with existential-humanistic therapies is the constant emphasis on *individual* growth and possibility. While theory stresses the importance of relationships with others and with the world (*mitwelt* and *umwelt*), the practice of these theories tends to focus on the individual and what he or she wants, with correspondingly little consideration of relationships. The popular Gestalt prayer of Fritz Perls is characteristic of this point of view . . . "You do your thing and I'll do my thing . . . if by chance we meet, it's beautiful." The Gestalt prayer may be criticized for its failure to consider relationship and the need to *work* and be *committed* to someone and something beyond oneself. The infinite possibility of life, stressed within the existential-humanistic tradition, can lead to deep problems of personal alienation from others.

Along with psychodynamic theory, the existential-humanistic approach tends to be highly verbal. Concerned with the meaning of life and individual satisfaction, the therapy tends to be verbose, and therefore appeals mainly to middle-class and upper-class individuals. The positive philosophy of Carl Rogers appears to be particularly applauded by nonwhites and disadvantaged people, but the methods of slow reflection, lack of action, and failure to consider immediate problem solving seem inappropriate for these groups. Again, the tendency for existential-humanistic counseling to ignore person-environment transactions in daily practice is a major limitation among some clients.

Given these problems and concerns, what does the existential-humanistic movement offer the beginning counselor or therapist that is immediately useful? Perhaps the major contribution of Rogers has been his emphasis on empathic and accurate listening and his willingness to open the interview to inspection and research through audiotape and films. The attending skills of Chapter 3 rest heavily on Rogers's classifications and discussion in his early work. The qualitative conditions of Chapter 4 (warmth, respect, concreteness) are derived from his seminal thinking. The methodological message that Rogers has given us is that we, as prospective and active counselors and therapists, must listen to the client and open the interview and ourselves to scrutiny. Only in this way can we grow and learn our own possibilities to enrich the lives of others.

The work of Fritz Perls is significant both for the drama and daring of his life and for a number of highly impactful and powerful therapeutic techniques which may be used not only in Gestalt therapy but also in conjunction with many other theories. Probably more than any other therapist to date, Perls could "make things happen" in the interview.

Current research and theory may lead one to conclude that the balanced listening and influencing approach of Viktor Frankl may gradually come to center stage as the most prominent existential-humanistic theory. Frankl's student, Elisabeth Lukas, offers us helpful discussions of Frankl's work. This approach deals openly and honestly with issues of pain and surmounting these difficulties through personal action and the specific support of the therapist and counselor. A new blend, perhaps including some elements of cognitive-behavioral theory may be on the horizon (Frankl, 1985b). All these theories seem deeply concerned with finding positives in human experience and developing an increasing awareness of person-environment transactions.

SUMMARY OF THIS CHAPTER

In mastering the concepts of this chapter, you should be able to

1. *Define and discuss elementary concepts of existentialism and humanism.* In particular, the terms existence, being-in-the-world, alienation, *eigenwelt, mitwelt, umwelt,* existential anxiety, existential commitment, intentionality, humanism, self-disclosure, and "I-Thou" relationships are important. It is of special importance to understand the relationship of Carl Rogers, Fritz Perls, and Viktor Frankl to the core concepts of the existential-humanistic tradition.

2. *Describe the revolution in counseling and psychotherapy initiated by Carl Rogers.* Until the advent of Rogerian methods, the prime mode of counseling was psychodynamic. The positivistic and clear statement of counseling provided by Rogers has forever changed the face of counseling and psychotherapy.

3. *Define and discuss key aspects of Rogerian theory:* the Rogerian worldview, the importance of understanding the way another person sees the world, the importance of discrepancies between real and ideal self, and the search for self-actualization.

4. *Demonstrate an understanding of the three major phases of Carl Rogers's career:* nondirective, client-centered, and increased personal involvement.

5. *Demonstrate an understanding of the influencing skills and techniques of Fritz Perls as manifested in Gestalt therapy.* Gestalt therapy has been presented as the most pow-

erful and immediate of the many existential-humanistic approaches. As the techniques are powerful, cautions as to their use have been stressed.

6. *Demonstrate an understanding of the logotherapy approach to counseling and psychotherapy.* A philosophy of counseling and life has been developed by Viktor Frankl. Elisabeth Lukas has done much to show how this theory may be implemented in practice. Chapter 7 illustrates aspects of logotherapy modification of attitudes in an interview. Key methodological concepts of this mode of helping are: modification of attitudes, paradoxical intention, dereflection, and the appealing technique.

7. *Discuss some of the problems and limitations of the existential-humanistic tradition and their implications for practice.* At times, some therapists who have labeled themselves of this persuasion have used therapeutic excess to the damage of clients. Further, this system, while philosophically attractive, has a methodology that tends to ignore environmental issues, tends to be highly verbal, and sometimes is inappropriate for nonwhite, nonmiddle-class people.

REFERENCES

ABBAGNANO, N., Humanism. In P. Edwards, ed., *The Encyclopedia of Philosophy.* Vol. III. New York: Macmillan, 1967, 69–72.

ASCHER, L. M., and R. M. TURNER, "Controlled Comparison of Progressive Relaxation, Stimulus Control, and Paradoxical Intention Therapies for Insomnia," *Journal of Consulting and Clinical Psychology,* 1979, 47 (3), 500–508.

BANDLER, R., and J. GRINDER, *Reframing: Neurolinguistic Programming and the Transformation of Meaning.* Moab, UT: Real People Press, 1982.

BECK, J., and S. STRONG, "Stimulating Therapeutic Change with Interpretations: A Comparison of Positive and Negative Connotations," *Journal of Counseling Psychology,* 1982, *29,* 551–559.

BINSWANGER, L., The Existential Analysis School of Thought. In May, R., E. Angel, and H. Ellenberger (eds.) *Existence.* New York: Basic Books, 1958, 191–213.

BINSWANGER, L., *Being-in-the-World; Selected Papers of Ludwig Binswanger.* New York: Basic Books, 1963.

BLOCKSMA, D., and E. PORTER, "A Short-Term Training Program in Client-Centered Counseling," *Journal of Consulting Psychology,* 1947, *11,* 55–60.

BOSS, M., *The Analysis of Dreams.* New York: Philosophical Library, 1958.

BOSS, M., *Psychoanalysis and Daseinanalysis.* New York: Basic Books, 1963.

BUBER, M., *I and Thou.* New York: Scribner's, 1970.

CAMUS, A., *The Stranger.* New York: Random House, 1942.

CAMUS, A., *The Myth of Sisyphus.* New York: Knopf, 1958.

FABRY, J., Personal Communication. International Forum for Logotherapy, 1984.

FAGAN, J., and I. SHEPHERD, *Gestalt Therapy Now.* Palo Alto, CA: *Science and Behavior Books,* 1970.

FELDMAN, D., S. STRONG, and D. DANSER, "A Comparison of Paradoxical and Non-paradoxical interpretations and directives," *Journal of Counseling Psychology,* 1982, *29,* 572–579.

FRANKL, V. E., Wirtschaftskrise und Seelenot. In Socialärztliche Rundschau, Wien, 1933.

FRANKL, V. E., *The Doctor and the Soul.* New York: Bantam, 1946/1952.

FRANKL, V. E., *Man's Search for Meaning.* New York: Pocket, 1959.

FRANKL, V. E., *Psychotherapy and Existentialism*. New York: Simon & Schuster, 1967.

FRANKL, V. E., *The Will to Meaning*. New York: New American Library, 1969.

FRANKL, V. E., *The Unheard Cry for Meaning*. Psychotherapy and Humanism. New York: Simon & Schuster, 1985a.

FRANKL, V. E., Logos, Paradox, and the Search for Meaning. In Mahoney, M. J. and A. Freeman (eds.) *Cognition and Psychotherapy*. Plenum Publishing Corporation, 1985b, 259–275.

GENDLIN, E., A Short Summary and Some Long Predictions. In Hart, J. and T. Tomlinson (eds.) *New Directions in Client-Centered Therapy*. Boston: Houghton-Mifflin, 1970.

HEIDEGGER, M., *Being and Time*. New York: Harper & Row, 1962.

HUSSERL, E., *Ideas: General Introduction to Pure Phenomenology*. London: Allen and Unwin, 1931.

KAUFMANN, W., I and You: A Prologue. In Buber, M., *I and Thou*. New York: Scribner's, 1970, 1–48.

LAING, R., *The Politics of Experience*. New York: Ballantine, 1967.

LANKTON, S., *Practical Magic*. Cupertino, CA: Meta, 1980.

LAZARUS, A. A., *Behavior Therapy and Beyond*. New York: McGraw–Hill, 1971.

LIEBERMAN, M., I. YALOM, and M. MILES, *Encounter Groups: First Facts*. New York, Basic Books, 1972.

LUKAS, E., *Meaningful Living*. Cambridge, MA: Schenkman, 1984.

MADDI, S., "Existential Psychotherapy," In S. Lynn and J. Garske, *Contemporary Psychotherapies*. Columbus, OH: Merrill, 1985, 191–220.

MAY, R., The Origins and Significance of the Existential Movement in Psychology. In May, R., E. Angel, and H. Ellenberger (eds.) *Existence*. New York: Basic Books, 1958, 3–36.

MAY, R., ed., *Existential Psychology*. New York: Random House, 1961.

MAY, R., *Love and Will*. New York: Norton, 1969.

PERLS, F., *Gestalt Therapy Verbatim*. Moab, UT: Real People Press, 1969a.

PERLS, F., *In and Out of the Garbage Pail*. Moab, UT: Real People Press, 1969b.

PERLS, F., R. HEFFERLINE, and P. GOODMAN, *Gestalt Therapy: Excitement and Growth in Human Personality*. New York: Dell, 1951.

ROGERS, C., *Counseling and Psychotherapy*. Cambridge, MA: Houghton-Mifflin, 1942.

ROGERS, C., "The Necessary and Sufficient Conditions of Therapeutic Personality Change," *Journal of Consulting Psychology*, 1957, *21*, 95–103.

ROGERS, C., *On Becoming a Person*. Boston: Houghton-Mifflin, 1961.

ROGERS, C., *On Encounter Groups*. New York: Harper & Row, 1970.

ROGERS, C., and J. WALLEN, *Counseling with Returned Servicemen*. New York: McGraw-Hill, 1946.

SARTRE, J., *No Exit*. New York: Knopf, 1946.

SARTRE, J., *Being and Nothingness*. London: Methuen, 1956.

SOLYOM, L., J. GARZA-PEREZ, B. L. LEDWIDGE, and C. SOLYOM, "Paradoxical Intention in the Treatment of Obsessive Thoughts: A Pilot Study," *Comprehensive Psychiatry*, 1972, 13 (3), 291–297.

STRONG, S., Experimental Studies of Paradoxical Intention. Unpublished Manuscript, Virginia Commonwealth University, 1984.

STRUPP, H., and S. HADLEY, "Contemporary View on Negative Effects in Psychotherapy," *Archives of General Psychiatry*, 1976, *33*, 1291–1302.

TILLICH, P., "Existentialism and Psychotherapy," *Review of Existential Psychology and Psychiatry*, 1961, *1*, 8–16.

YALOM, I., and M. LIEBERMAN, "A Study of Encounter Group Casualities," *Archives of General Psychiatry*, 1971, *25*, 16–30.

SUGGESTED SUPPLEMENTARY READING

BUBER, M., *I and Thou*. New York: Scribner's, 1970.
This book might be described as the "heart" of the existential-humanistic tradition. Buber discusses the nature of the human condition and relationship in poetic terms.

FABRY, J., R. BULKA, and W. SAHAKIAN, eds. *Logotherapy in Action*. New York: Jason Aronson, 1979.
A collection of essays and case studies in logotherapy.

LUKAS, E., *Meaningful Living: A Logotherapy Book*. Berkeley, CA: The Institute of Logotherapy, 1984.
Viktor Frankl's student and colleague presents the *how* of logotherapy with case examples and specific techniques to enable the enactment of Frankl's important philosophy.

MAY, R., E. ANGEL, and H. ELLENBERGER, *Existence*. New York: Simon & Schuster, 1958.
A basic text covering readings by prominent existential authors such as May, Minkowski, and Binswanger.

PERLS, F., *Gestalt Therapy Verbatim*. Moab, UT: Real People Press, 1969.
A series of typescripts by the master therapist with interesting commentary and theoretical insertions.

PERLS, F., *In and Out of the Garbage Pail*. Moab, UT: Real People Press, 1969.
An autobiography of Perls complete with drawings and personal ramblings on a multitude of issues. Delightful to some, appalling to others.

ROGERS, C., *On Becoming a Person*. Boston: Houghton-Mifflin, 1961.
Rogers's best known and classic work. The exposition of method and philosophy is exceptionally clear and well drawn. This book becomes a treasure to many students.

ROGERS, C., *On Encounter Groups*. New York: Harper & Row, 1970.
This book illustrates how much a person can change over a period of ten years. Rogers moved from a prime interest in counseling and psychotherapy to a deep commitment to group work over that time. The descriptions of group process are particularly lucid.

SARTRE, J., *No Exit*. New York: Knopf, 1946.
Existentialism as a philosophy becomes complex with a wide and varied vocabulary. Literature such as *No Exit* is often better at describing existentialism. Sartre has a special gift for presenting the human condition—what exists *exists*. *No Exit* is a play that describes the existential problems of three people committed to hell, which is represented as a single room from which they are unable to leave. The analogies to everyday life experience are implicit but clear.

11

THE COGNITIVE-BEHAVIORAL MOVEMENT

GENERAL PREMISE

An integrated knowledge of skills, theory, and practice is essential for culturally intentional counseling and therapy.

Skills form the foundation of effective theory and practice: The culturally intentional therapist knows how to construct a creative decision-making interview and can use microskills to attend to and influence clients in a predicted direction. Important in this process are individual and cultural empathy, client observation skills, assessment of person and environment, and the application of positive techniques of growth and change.

Theory provides organizing principles for counseling and therapy: *The culturally intentional counselor has knowledge of alternative theoretical approaches and treatment modalities; in this case cognitive-behavioral methods and theory.*

Practice is the integration of skills and theory: The culturally intentional counselor or therapist is competent in skills and theory and is able to apply them to research and practice for client benefit.

Undergirding integrated competence in skills, theory, and practice is an intentional awareness of one's own personal worldview and how that worldview may be similar to and/or different from the worldview and personal constructions of the client and other professionals.

GOALS FOR COGNITIVE-BEHAVIORAL THERAPY

Integration of thought, action, and decision making is the task of cognitive-behavior therapy. Critical in this task is changing the way one thinks about the world, making decisions about the world, *and* then acting/behaving in the world.

This chapter has the following specific goals:

1. To present a currently developing worldview in counseling and psychotherapy that recognizes the importance of *integration* of worldviews into a new synthesis.
2. To describe several important theorists of the cognitive-behavioral orientation (Ellis, Beck, Krumboltz, Meichenbaum, Glasser) and to illustrate their techniques and work.
3. To provide you with some specific constructs and techniques that you can use in your own practice of counseling and therapy.

BACKGROUND LEADING TO THE THEORY

Three major historical forces undergird the helping process—psychodynamic, behavioral, and existential-humanistic. Psychodynamic and existential-humanistic theory primarily work on *cognitions* or thoughts about the world while behavioral psychology emphasizes *behavior* and action in that world.

Cognitive-behavioral theory and methods have arisen to meet the obvious need to *integrate* thought and action, understanding and behavior, and meaning and doing. The cognitive-behaviorist movement seeks to draw from other theories, add some new constructs of its own, and produce a new integration of theory and practice.

Perhaps the first cognitive-behavioral theorist was George Kelly and his psychology of personal constructs (Chapter 6). Kelly saw humans as scientists acting in the world based on their *constructions* or thoughts about that world. Kelly sought to understand the unique client construction of the world through his assessment process and then worked to help clients change their cognitive constructs.

But, Kelly also developed methods so that people would change their behaviors as well. One of these methods he termed "fixed-role" therapy. In fixed-role therapy, the task is to find out the ideal role a client would like to play in real life and then to work out with the client the specific behaviors and actions that the client must take to enact that role. The client then moves from the interview to the real world and engages in the behavior utilizing cognitions or constructs developed in the interview (*role enactment*).

Drawing from Kelly's early work, the task of cognitive-behavioral therapy is dual: (1) to examine how one thinks and if necessary, to change thinking and cognition; and (2) to ensure that clients act on those cognitions through behavior in their daily life. Thus, the term, *cognitive-behavioral.*

There is a third dimension to the cognitive-behavioral trend. Given accuracy of thoughts and behaviors, one must *decide* how one will act. It is this process of decision making that relates the cognitive-behavioral, at least partially, to the existential-humanistic tradition.

Needless to say, much of the material in this book relates to cognitive-behavioral concepts. The decisional model of Chapter 2, for example, talks about listening to the client's problem and clarifying goals in the first part of a counseling interview. In understanding a problem, the therapist or counselor needs to understand both the cognitions and the behaviors of the client. In the fourth phase of the interview, generating alternative solutions, the emphasis again is on finding new thoughts and behaviors for the client and deciding which solution to seek. Finally, generalization of constructs, cognitions, or thoughts requires a decision for action in the world outside. Unless insight is manifested in behavior and thoughts beyond the interview, therapeutic success is most limited. You will also find that psychodynamic, behavioral, and existential-humanistic theory are deeply concerned with issues of cognitive and behavioral change and their meaning—although each handles the balance of thought, action, and decision in very different ways.

Thus, you may find in evolving cognitive-behavioral theory some useful elements to assist you in developing your own conceptualization (*cognitions*) about the therapeutic process and some techniques and actions (*behaviors*) that are useful in helping you *decide* the nature of your own work in the field.

COGNITIVE-BEHAVIORAL WORLDVIEW

Most reviewers of the cognitive-behavioral frame of reference trace the history of the movement to the stoic philosopher, Epictetus, who noted, "Men are disturbed not by events, but by the views they take of them." Changing how one thinks about the world, then, becomes a major goal of cognitive-behavioral points of view.

The idea that one can change the way one thinks about things, of course, is a major dimension of existential-humanistic theory. Viktor Frankl, for example, could not change the concentration camp, but he could change the way he thought about it. In psychodynamic theory, the client often finds new ways to think about the self and the situation. The general construct of the positive asset search as it plays itself out in different theories (Chapter 7, page 187) illustrated how many differing theories facilitate client change in "the views they take of events."

A worldview in which thinking and ideas about the world is central can be traced beyond stoicism to Plato and the philosophies of idealism. The philosophies of idealism emphasize that the *idea* one has about the world is more important than what is "real." In fact, the concept of "reality" may be dismissed by the idealists as a mere "idea about things." More recent adaptations of the idealistic philosophic tradition are manifested in the work of Kant and Hegel. The work of Freud may be described in this tradition; Freud in some ways was a stoic as he felt that little could be done about the human condition except to know it and understand it. Behavioral change may be helpful in this frame of reference, but is still viewed as relatively limited in scope.

But, what is "reality?" How does one act? The British and American logical positivists and pragmatists (Bentham, Mill, William James, Bertrand Russell) have questioned that cognition and idealism are meaningful or sufficient for living in the real world. Out of their philosophic work has arisen the optimistic scientific tradition of hypothesis testing and direct action on the world. Behavioral psychology as represented by Skinner and the cognitive work of George Kelly are obvious extensions of this scientific, realistic orientation.

Existentialist philosophers such as Kierkegaard, Tillich, and Sartre question both idealistic and realistic philosophers and emphasize the act of individual choice and the process of *intentionally* choosing and deciding. Rogers and Perls clearly represent this orientation to helping.

The cognitive-behavioral worldview may be described as a beginning attempt to integrate the three major philosophic traditions of idealism, realism, and existentialism. Albert Ellis, considered the pioneer of cognitive-behavioral theory, first maintained a psychodynamic practice. He then started work on his theory of rational-emotive therapy and was classified in the existential-humanistic tradition for many years. He, however, continued to emphasize the importance of action in his practice, was noticed by behavioral psychology, and now he is considered centrally a cognitive-behaviorist.

Viktor Frankl also began as a psychoanalyst, but moved through life experience to the existential posture. However, in the most recent writings of his student, Elisabeth Lukas, we may note an increased behavioral specificity in the work of and theory in logotherapy.

The worldview of cognitive-behavior therapy, then, may be described as an evolving synthesis of the three major philosophic and psychological traditions of the Western world. *The cognitive-behavioral theorist will ultimately be interested in knowing how the individual developed ideas or cognitions about reality, how the individual chooses and decides from the many possibilities, and how the individual acts and behaves in relationship to reality.* Needless to say, this ambitious goal has yet to be realized, but let us now examine some of the influential work toward this end.

ALBERT ELLIS AND RATIONAL-EMOTIVE THERAPY

Albert Ellis's rational-emotive therapy (RET) originated in the mid-1950s as he became increasingly aware of the ineffectiveness of psychoanalysis to produce change in his patients. He found himself in an extremely successful private practice of psychoanalysis, yet dissatisfied with the results he was obtaining. Gradually, he found himself taking a more active role in therapy, attacking the client's

Albert Ellis

logic, and even prescribing behavioral activities for patients to follow after they left the therapy hour (Ellis, 1983a). The result of this change has come to be known as rational-emotive therapy, the pioneer method of cognitive-behavioral therapy.

Ellis's rational-emotive therapy, however, may be considered as broader and more eclectic than some other cognitive-behavioral approaches. Ellis does not hesitate to use techniques from many differing theoretical orientations, according to the unique needs of the client. With a sexual difficulty, Ellis may use his own cognitive strategies, but he will also use Masters and Johnson's (1970) sensate focusing techniques and the behavioral techniques of progressive relaxation and modeling (Ellis, 1983b). Ellis stresses unconditional acceptance in a manner similar to Carl Rogers. He may use bibliotherapy and have clients read books for deeper understanding. He may use humor or sarcasm as appropriate to the client. He has constantly stressed "homework" as important to the change process, seeking to have clients generalize ideas from the interview to their daily lives. Ellis, however, has not used behavioral techniques and thinking as fully as do Krumboltz and Meichenbaum (to be discussed later in this chapter).

Let us first consider Ellis's approach to therapy in action and then examine the constructs and systems underlying his interviewing style.

An RET Interview Transcript and Analysis

Ellis's early work in sexuality and sexual counseling is particularly noteworthy (Ellis, 1958). He was one of the first to recognize that homosexuality may be an alternative life style rather than a "clinical problem." The following transcript illustrates how Ellis rapidly moves into direct action with the client with the goal of eventually helping the client decide how he wants to live with the idea of homosexuality. Ellis is nonjudgmental about life style issues, he would support either the client's well-thought out desire to accept a homosexual orientation or to change to heterosexuality. But, Ellis would insist that the individual make a logical decision and learn to live with that decision comfortably.

Ellis may or may not spend time developing rapport and will often start the interview effectively and directly. As you will see, he has a unique personal style.

1.	THERAPIST:	What's the main thing that's bothering you? [Open Question]
2.	CLIENT:	I have a fear of turning homosexual—a *real* fear of it!
3.	THERAPIST:	A fear of *becoming* a homosexual? [Encourager]
4.	CLIENT:	Yeah.
5.	THERAPIST:	Because "*if* I became a homosexual—," what? [Open Question]
6.	CLIENT:	I don't know. It really gets me down. It gets me to a point where I'm doubting every day. I do doubt everything, anyway.
7.	THERAPIST:	Yes. But let's get back to—answer the question: "If I were a homosexual, what would that make me?" [Directive, Open Question]
8.	CLIENT:	(Pause) I don't know.
9.	THERAPIST:	Yes, you do! Now, I can give *you* the answer to the question. But let's see if you can get it. [Opinion, Directive]
10.	CLIENT:	(Pause) Less than a person?
11.	THERAPIST:	Yes. Quite obviously, you're saying: "I'm bad *enough*. But if I were homosexual, that would make me a *total* shit!" [Interpretation]
12.	CLIENT:	That's right.
13.	THERAPIST:	Now, why did you just say you don't know? [Open Question]
14.	CLIENT:	Just taking a guess at it, that's all. It's—it's just that the fear really gets me down! I don't know why.
15.	THERAPIST:	(Laughing) Well, you just *gave* the reason why! Suppose you were saying the same thing about—we'll just say—stealing. You hadn't stolen anything, but you *thought* of stealing something. And you said, "If I stole, I would be a thorough shit!" Just suppose that. Then, how much would you then start thinking about stealing? [Expression of Content—Sharing Information-Instruction, Closed Question]
16.	CLIENT:	(Silence)
17.	THERAPIST:	If you believed that: "If I stole it, I would be a thorough shit!"—would you think of it often? occasionally? [Closed Question]
18.	CLIENT:	I'd think of it often.
19.	THERAPIST:	That's right! As soon as you say, "If so-and-so happens, I would be a thorough shit!" you'll get *obsessed* with so-and-so. And the reason you're getting obsessed with homosexuality is this nutty belief, "If I *were* a homosexual, I would be a total shit!" Now, look at that belief for a moment. And let's admit that if you were a homosexual, it would have real disadvantages. Let's assume *that*. But why would you be a thorough shit if you were a homosexual? Let's suppose you gave up girls completely, and you just screwed guys. Now, why would you be a thorough shit? [Encourager, Interpretation, Directive, Open Question]
20.	CLIENT:	(Mumbles incoherently; is obviously having trouble finding an answer)
21.	THERAPIST:	Think about it for a moment. [Directive] (Ellis, 1971, 102–103)

In later stages of the interview, Ellis will seek to have the client decide what he wants to do for logical reasons that are satisfactory emotionally—thus the title "rational-emotive." The individual must *think and feel* a decision is correct. This interviewing style may be most appropriate for Albert Ellis as it is congruent for his personality. It is not wise that you be so forceful and direct if that is not personally authentic for you. Some mistake Ellis's personal style with his theory. It is possible to use the theory of rational-emotive therapy in a fashion that is authentic to you.

The goal of the client and therapist in this session is to change cognitions about homosexuality (cognitive), to make decisions about how one wants to live (cognitive-existential), and to then act/behave according to those decisions (behavioral). In this preceding sentence, you can see the integration of many of the ideas expressed earlier in this text and the expression of the integration of three basic philosophic traditions of idealism, existentialism, and realism.

When encouraging the client to act on his cognitions, Ellis is likely to use role-plays similar to those of social learning theory (modeling) or George Kelly's fixed-role therapy. He almost certainly would assign "homework" in the final stages of the interview to insure that the client does something different as a result of the session. In the followup interview, Ellis could be expected to check carefully on whether or not the client had done anything differently during the time between sessions.

Some Central Theoretical Constructs and Techniques of RET

Ellis and his rational-emotive (RET) approach focuses more on thoughts than on feelings. It is RET's view that people have made themselves victims by their own crooked, incorrect, and mainly *irrational* thinking patterns. While taking an essentially optimistic view toward people, Ellis criticizes humanistic approaches as being too soft at times and failing to cope with the fact that people can virtually "self-destruct" through irrational and muddled thinking. The task of the RET therapist is to correct thought patterns and rid people of irrational ideas.

Perhaps Ellis's most important contribution is his A-B-C theory of personality. The preceding typescript illustrates his theory in action. The A-B-C pattern is illustrated below:

A The objective facts, events, behaviors that an individual encounters.
B The person's belief about A.
C The emotional consequence, or how a person feels about A.

People tend to consider that A causes C or facts cause consequences. Ellis challenges this equation as naïve and failing to consider that it is what people *think* about an event that determines how they feel. Using the A-B-C framework for the typescript, we find:

A The objective fact is the possibility of being a homosexual.
B The client believes being a homosexual is bad, therefore,
C As an emotional consequence, the client experiences guilt, fear, and negative self-thoughts.

In this case the client has short-circuited B and thinks, "If I am a homosexual, I am bad. Thus . . ." Ellis's goal is to attack the belief system. What the client thinks about homosexuality is causing his anxiety and difficulties, *not* by the objective facts of the situation. There are obviously numerous people, both homosexual and heterosexual, who believe that homosexuality is a valid alternative and who do not come to the same conclusion at C that this client does. Ellis's approach in this case, then, becomes one of challenging the client's logic: "If I *were* a homosexual, I would be a total shit." He clarifies the A causes C logic of the statement by challenging the irrationality of the client's logic. It isn't the specific belief that is challenged, but the *unfoundedness* of those beliefs that leads to illogic. The emphasis of the therapy is primarily on changing the way a person thinks about the behavior, rather than mainly on changing the behavior itself.

In a sense, the A-B-C theory is really the nugget of Ellis's theory. It is easy to realize that it is not the event that really troubles us, but it is the way we think about the event. Ellis's theory is closely akin to Frankl's logotherapy (1963) and other humanistic therapies that focus on meaning and the importance of how a person interprets the world. Frankl, for example, survived the horrors of a Nazi concentration camp and discusses how survival depended on his ability to believe certain things about the events around him and find something positive on which to depend. Beliefs were more important to survival than objective facts.

You will find client after client who uses such irrational statements as "If I don't pass this course, it is the end of the world," "Because my parents have been cruel to me as a child, there is nothing I can do now to help myself," "As the economy is lacking jobs, there is no meaning to my life," "If I can't get that scholarship, all is ended," and "The reason I have nothing is that the rich have taken it all." All of these statements at one level are true, but all of them represent "helpless" thinking characteristic of A causes C irrational thinking. Following are five particularly common irrational ideas manifested in our society; the list could be amplified, but more at issue is the therapist's ability to recognize irrational thinking in whatever form it takes.

1. It is a necessity to be loved and approved of by all important people around us. "If he (or she) doesn't love me, it is awful."
2. It is required that one be thoroughly competent, adequate, and achieving if one is to be worthwhile. "If I don't make the goal, it's all my fault."
3. Some people are bad and should be punished for it. "He (or she) did that to me and I'm going to get even."
4. It is better to avoid some difficulties and responsibilities. "It won't make any difference if I don't do that. People won't care."
5. It is awful or catastrophic if things are not the way they are supposed to be. "Isn't it terrible that the house isn't picked up?" (Ellis, 1967, p. 84)

The basic therapeutic maneuver is always to be on the alert for irrational thinking and when it is observed, to work on it directly, concretely, and immediately. RET counselors can vary in their use of microskills, but Ellis uses a large

---

Figure 11.1 *Structured Exercise for Practice in Rational-Emotive Therapy (RET)*

Basic to utilizing this therapeutic method in the counseling process is the ability to identify and understand the irrational ideas of the client. Our society has taught us to ignore the many irrational statements we hear each day, and thus it is desirable that you develop skill in hearing what people are saying and then applying Ellis's *A-B-C* analysis to their ideas. The following progression, if followed carefully over a 1- to 2-week period, will provide a beginning but lasting understanding of the principles of RET.

1. Over a 3-day period, commit yourself to listening for irrational ideas. Once you sense a possible irrational idea in the comment of a friend, acquaintance, store clerk, or family member, simply paraphrase that irrational idea back to them with no comment or evaluation of what you have heard. For example, you may hear "Inflation is so bad that I simply will never be able to make ends meet" or "My kids are so impossible, I must be a bad mother." Make a list of the irrational statements that you paraphrase. You will note that events, facts, or information lead typically to certain statements, behaviors, actions, or thoughts. However, the event, fact, or information need not lead logically to what happens.
2. Having developed the ability to hear irrational ideas, select twenty of the statements that particularly interest you and apply the Ellis *A-B-C* analysis to them, using paper and pencil. For example, "My kids are so impossible, I must be a bad mother," contains the following:
   A *Objective facts.* The children were misbehaving in a store by knocking over a display of canned goods.
   B *The person's belief.* Children who knock over goods in a store are bad. "If I were a 'good' mother, I wouldn't have children who did such things." Therefore,
   C *The emotional consequence.* The mother believes she is "bad" and feels embarrassed or guilty about her children.
   Continue this process until you are able to analyze the *A-B-C* thought patterns easily.
3. Note your own irrational ideas on the spot and apply the *A-B-C* pattern to them. Follow this by asking a friend who gives an irrational statement to sit down with you and explore what he or she has said in more detail. Explain the *A-B-C* pattern to them and together work through the irrational idea, categorizing the person's thought patterns. Try this exercise with several other people who are willing to share their time and thoughts with you.
4. As a final step in practice, test your ability to use the *A-B-C* analysis in a role-played counseling interview. Give your client one of the "problems" expressed via an irrational idea which you identified earlier in your study. Then, using what you have learned plus the microskill of paraphrasing (to make sure that you have heard the irrational idea accurately), attempt an on-the-spot *A-B-C* analysis as part of the counseling role-play. Repeat this exercise, and practice until you become proficient with this basic part of RET counseling.

---

number of open and closed questions, directives, interpretation, and advice and opinion. The listening skills of paraphrasing and reflection of feeling do not play a prominent role in his therapy. At times Ellis moves to what could best be termed an instructional model in which he actively teaches clients how to think. This instructional model is supplemented by homework assignments where clients are told to try out newly learned behaviors and to report back on their success. Ellis often has his clients take audiotape recordings of the interview home with them so that they can review the session during the week.

Basic to RET is confrontation—the direct examination of incongruities and discrepancies in the client's thinking and behavior. The A-B-C pattern is focused on discovering and working on incongruities. The typescript is illustrative, as Ellis often attacks the first incongruent irrational thought that occurs; he need not wait until he has a detailed case analysis. This directness, moreover, is possibly a reason for the success and increasing popularity of this method. Once a client learns the system of examining personal logic, he or she is equipped to examine other issues in life without the aid of the therapist. RET is a therapy that actually can be psychoeducational, for it demystifies the counseling process and shares what is important in the process openly with the client. You will find at many times the RET therapy process much like a teacher-student dialogue (see Therapist: 15, for example).

If the task of the RET counselor is to free the client from irrational thinking, a parallel and more positive goal is to equip the client with beliefs that are satisfactory and functional for everyday life. For example, it is not enough to help free the client presented in the typescript from irrational thoughts about fears of homosexuality. Also needed is an opportunity for this client to explore a new set of beliefs and actions to test their rationality and workability. The RET counselor does not seek to support or challenge any particular belief system; rather, RET counselors tend to be unusually open to alternative life styles and variations among people. But, the RET therapist demands that the client have a rational, workable belief system. In the case of the homosexual anxiety presented in the typescript, once having identified the irrational belief, the RET therapist could support alternative problem resolutions as varying as active adoption of a homosexual life style or an equally active rejection of it. The issue is the logic and rationality of the client's belief system rather than the objective behavior.

One example of a synthesis between behavioral approaches and RET is that of Lange and Jakubowski (1976) who combine the two in an assertiveness training model. In their program they suggest: (1) identifying the situation where assertion is needed clearly and precisely (much as was indicated in Chapter 9); (2) adding the methods of Ellis's RET to bring out the irrational beliefs underlying the lack of assertion; and (3) defining the rights and wishes of the individual in the assertiveness situation. In this way, two major tasks are accomplished simultaneously in assertion training: (1) situation specific behaviors are learned; and (2) the underlying belief system relating to behavior is discovered. The combination of thoughts and actions can lead both to more effective assertion and to a higher probability of the learning generalizing to other situations.

RET could be summarized as an action therapy. The counselor is active, confronting, and involved. The pace of the interview is fast, the number of interviews with each client tends to be fewer, there is heavy emphasis on taking ideas derived in the interview out into daily life. In this sense, RET is a very "American" therapy with its pragmatism and desire to make things "work" as quickly and efficiently as possible. Further, when combined with other approaches, there is some evidence that its power is increased.

AARON BECK AND COGNITIVE THERAPY

Aaron Beck is considered a leading cognitive-behavioral therapist who has been especially effective in working with depression. The strength of Beck is perhaps best illustrated by a case from his well-known book *Cognitive Therapy and the Emotional Disorders* (1976). He describes a depressed patient who had failed to leave his bedside for a considerable period of time. Beck asked him if he could walk to the door of his room. The man said he would collapse. Beck said, "I'll catch you." Through successive steps and longer walks, the man was shortly able to walk all over the hospital and in 1 month was discharged.

How are such "miracles" accomplished? First, Beck is a powerful and caring individual who himself *believes* that change is possible. He is willing to provide himself as a support agent for the client and has specific goals/behaviors in mind for the client. In this case, he sought to change the way the depressed person thought about himself and through slow, successive approximations of shorter walks with Beck's help, the client was able to change his behavior.

Clearly someone who provides this type of change for his clients offers something special, a charisma in its own way as full of impact as that of Ellis. Beck has outlined many important principles for working with many types of patients. Let us first examine his interviewing style in the following transcript and then consider something about his theory and techniques.

An Interview Transcript and Analysis

In the following session, you will see Aaron Beck using a relatively direct interviewing style. When the client says "—now I'm *all alone!*," Beck probes this surface structure sentence for the underlying meaning and logic. In this search for meaning, there are clear parallels to Frankl. In the implicit attack on the logic underlying this overgeneralization or irrational idea, Beck is attempting to pro-

Aaron Beck

duce change in cognitive/thinking processes almost immediately as might be expected in Ellis's work.

Beck, as is typical of the cognitive-behavioral orientation, argues that personal difficulties are very much the result of faulty thinking rather than unconscious motivation. If one thinks more accurately, then useful and healthy behaviors will follow more easily. Thus, Beck asks his clients to look at a situation carefully and think about alternative ways of viewing life.*

> Strain grips the face of the young woman on the television monitor. Hers would be a pretty face were it not for the puffy, reddened eyes, and the glistening tear-tracks splotched on her cheeks.
>
> "My husband wants to leave me," Linda is saying to someone out of camera range. "He wants to go for an unspecified length of time. Then maybe he'll come back. He says it's non-negotiable; he wants no more commitment." She has difficulty controlling her voice; breathy sobs punctuate her recitation.
>
> "I've gotten more and more depressed," Linda continues. "It felt like I had a guillotine over me, or like I had cancer. I told him maybe he'd better leave. And now—" (she begins sobbing in earnest) "—now I'm *all alone!*"
>
> The camera draws back, bringing into view a man seated at the table with Linda. His most striking feature is a thatch of thick white hair smoothed back from his face. Behind his glasses the psychiatrist's eyes are at once gentle and probing. He regards Linda calmly.
>
> "What do you mean, all alone?" asks Dr. Aaron T. Beck '42.
>
> "I don't have Richard!" she gasps, mopping at her eyes with a tissue from the box on the table. "Life wouldn't mean anything without him. I love him so much."
>
> "What do you love about him?" Dr. Beck asks.
>
> "I don't know," Linda says, shaking her head, confused. "I guess I live for him. He's so rotten. But I remember the good stuff."
>
> CLICK. In the darkened viewing room, Dr. Beck pushes a switch and freezes the images of Linda and himself on the monitor. He turns to a visitor and explains his strategy for this emergency therapy session. "First, you always summarize the patient's thoughts to her. This gives clarity and reassures her that you understand. Second, you have to figure out where you're going to move in. It's very difficult in a crisis situation. You have to think on your feet." Dr. Beck explains that according to his theory of depression, the patient will underestimate herself and exaggerate her degree of loss and a negative view of the future. "You have to explore these channels and work it through."
>
> CLICK. The video images move and talk. On the screen, Dr. Beck summarizes for Linda his first therapy session with her six weeks earlier, reminding her that Richard had made certain promises and commitments regarding their marriage. "What happened between then and now?"
>
> "I don't know. I really think he lied to me." She begins to sob again. "This is like a bad dream."
>
> "Richard deceived you?"
>
> "He did. I feel like a fool," Linda cries, "for believing him."

---

*This interview with Aaron Beck and transcript is by Anne Diffily, published in the *Brown Alumni Monthly*, 1984, (pages 39–46) and is used by permission.

CLICK. To his visitor, Dr. Beck says, "This is aggravating the problem; she is feeling deceived, feeling foolish. Which angle am I going to explore—her actual loss, or the hurt to her pride? You have to make a split-second decision."

CLICK. On the screen, Dr. Beck is talking quietly to Linda. "What have you lost?" He is going for the loss angle first.

"I lost my best friend, someone to talk to." She pauses and adds ruefully, "Even though he didn't want to listen to me." What else? "I've lost the father of my children. Financial support, security."

"What hurts you most?" Dr. Beck wonders. "The money?"

"No—losing him. I've lost all my hopes." What hopes? "That things would work out for us." Aren't there other hopes? Dr. Beck asks. Linda looks doubtful. "I guess I'm not letting them come in. But who would want me? He rejected me. I'm not lovable."

"Do you really believe that? Is Richard the supreme arbiter of that?" Dr. Beck says. "Should we trust his judgment?" *Laughter.* Linda, incredibly, is laughing. "Don't make me laugh when I'm crying!" she is saying through a mixture of giggles and sobs.

A brief smile plays across Dr. Beck's face; he continues pressing his point. "Richard broke promises to you on and off for months. And you feel terrible that a guy like that doesn't love you? Why should his problem be reflected in your self-image?"

Dr. Beck asks Linda to list her husband's good and bad qualities. He records them on a long sheet of lined paper divided into two columns. When Linda finishes her list, the "bad" column is twice as long as the "good" column.

"Is this the kind of man you'd want for a mate?" the psychiatrist asks.

"It really sounds dumb when you write it out," she admits.

Eventually Dr. Beck elicits another admission from Linda: Even though she is suffering from dire emotional stress and pain, she can endure it and even adopt a more positive view of her future. "I guess I've been standing it so far," Linda says, "so I can stand it now."

CLICK. Dr. Beck's visitor, moved by the emotions and the glimpse of hope she has viewed on videotape, has a question for him. "Didn't you want to hug Linda, to comfort her, instead of just asking questions?"

"Empathy and understanding," the psychiatrist answers, "are not enough in therapy. As in any branch of medicine, you tend to empathize with the patient. But most reassuring to the patient is your understanding of her problem, and your ability to give her a mastery of the situation." In no way, Dr. Beck emphasizes, was Linda's depression "cured" by this one session; she had to come back for therapy on a regular basis for a while. But using his therapeutic approach—one that has inspired considerable interest and excitement among mental-health professionals world-wide—a therapist can "snap people out of a severe depression very quickly," and allow them to start coping with their problems in a constructive, rewarding way. (Diffily, 1984, pp. 39–46).

Beck's Central Theoretical Constructs and Techniques

Beck gives central attention to the cognitive process. He points out that we have a constant stream of thoughts going through our minds, not all of which we listen to. These thoughts move so rapidly that Beck calls them "automatic thoughts" and points out that it is difficult to stop them. In the case of the woman described in the transcript, she automatically thought her life would be "over" and she would be "alone" without her husband. Beck is concerned with stopping those automatic thoughts and having the person examine his or her mode of thinking and eventually develop new forms of cognition. Beck has a very positive aspect to his therapy. You again may want to review his structure for positive change on page 193 of Chapter 7.

Beck's system has proven particularly effective with depressed clients whose worldview is full of pessimistic automatic thoughts that affect their behavior most forcefully. Beck (1972) has a list of "faulty reasonings" that in many ways is similar to Ellis's conceptualizations of irrational ideas. His list includes such concepts as dichotomous reasoning (assuming things are either all good or all bad—"I'm either perfect or I'm no good"), overgeneralization ("If my husband leaves me, I'm totally alone"), magnification (Ellis terms this "catastrophizing"), and flaws in inference or logic.

Beck suggests a three-step model to produce change in client thinking patterns:

1. Recognize what the client is thinking. Through the use of listening skills, one can identify specifically what the client *is* thinking. It is here that you can search for faulty reasoning or for irrational ideas.
2. Enable the patient to recognize faulty or ineffective thinking patterns. As you perhaps noted in the transcript, Beck uses many listening skills, then challenges the patient's reasoning, and then finally supplies a new frame of reference or worldview. This new frame of reference will be supplied by the therapist using a variety of influencing skills ranging from "Let's walk to the door of your room" to directly challenging faulty logic . . . "Is it really *that* awful?"
3. Obtain feedback to see if the changes developed in reasoning are correct.

Beck's cognitive therapy assumes that clients can examine themselves. Many patients, particularly the depressed, are embedded in their own construction of the world. Beck recognizes that their particularly self-centered worldview may indeed be accurate, but if one thinks about alternatives, these alternatives may be even more useful and, certainly, more growth producing. Important parallels to George Kelly's personal construct theory here should be noted. The depressed individual has a set of ineffective personal constructs, which are hypotheses that the person uses to frame the world. The task of the therapist is to change the constructs in the expectation that if one changes the way one views the world, the way one acts in the world will also change.

Cognitive therapy as practiced by Beck is one of the major alternatives for change in thinking and behavior. You may note that his work is more focused on cognition and thinking than Ellis. Meichenbaum (1985), in fact, has termed Beck's work "cognitive-semantic" through its emphasis on words and ideas. Beck expects cognitive change to lead to behavioral change.

KRUMBOLTZ'S CAREER DECISION MAKING

John Krumboltz (1983) presents a model of cognitively oriented vocational counseling that has broader implications beyond the career area and illustrates how other skills and techniques, particularly those of psychodynamic theory, may be compatible with the cognitive-behavioral orientation. Krumboltz, however, considers himself a behaviorist and evolved his techniques separately.

Krumboltz's Central Theoretical Constructs and Techniques

Krumboltz states that people learn a "set of private rules or beliefs, which they use to make major and minor career decisions" (1983). These private rules are quite similar to Ellis's irrational ideas or to Beck's categories of "faulty reasoning." Some clients have rules or beliefs that are more effective for acting on the world than others. If you are to facilitate client career decision making, the task may be described as understanding these private beliefs and how they interfere (or facilitate) the client. A client may believe that he or she should be completely and totally competent in a career or that the job market is "totally hopeless." Such irrational beliefs or private rules must be clarified if any rational or satisfactory career decision is to be made. No matter what action is taken by the client, the private rules will eventually filter in and interfere with either obtaining, maintaining, and keeping the position.

Given the importance of private rules and their negative consequences, an early task of career counseling is to look for troublesome beliefs that will in-

*Photo by Edward W. Souzan, News and
Publication Service, Stanford University*

John Krumboltz

terfere with career decisions and the work process itself. For example, consider the following classifications of troublesome beliefs suggested by Krumboltz:

1. *Faulty generalizations.*
   "I'm too shy to work as a nurse. I've always been frightened of groups."
   "All people who work in gas stations are dumb."
2. *Self-comparison with a single standard.*
   "I'm not as confident as my Dad. I never could make it in business."
   "This guy I knew in San Francisco. He was a crook. I wouldn't want to go into sales."
3. *Exaggerated estimate of the emotional impact of an outcome.*
   "I wouldn't want to try to get admitted to college. I would be devastated if I didn't get into the one that my friend is going to."
   "It would be terrible if I didn't pass the real estate license test. Such a disgrace."

These statements illustrate only a few of the irrational ideas or thinking underlying vocational decisions. Krumboltz also points out that several other categories of troublesome beliefs exist—for example, *false, causal relationships* ("I didn't get the job because the interviewer didn't like me"); *ignorance of relevant facts* ("I think I can get into a competitive college even though I only have 2 years of math"); and *self-deception* ("The fact that I've lost the last two jobs I had won't hurt me in this application").

Whether you are conducting career assessment or personal counseling and therapy, it can be valuable if you listen carefully for these and other troublesome beliefs. They need not be confronted immediately, but you, as counselor, will want to store these thinking patterns for later examination.

How to Identify Troublesome Beliefs

Krumboltz has several useful techniques that may facilitate uncovering deep-seated patterns of irrational thinking. One route, of course, is direct practice such as that suggested in Figure 11.1 as you seek to identify irrational ideas in your own environment. The following techniques, while developed for vocational counseling, have broader implications and illustrate how other methods can be integrated into the cognitive-behavioral framework.

Reconstruction of Prior Events. The goal is to discuss and describe critical incidents from the past. Each of these past incidents will tell much about how the client constructs the world and how this worldview may have private rules or irrational beliefs that need reconstruction. For example, the client may be seeking a new job and may tell you about a failed interview this past week or even 2 years ago. By carefully questioning, reflecting feelings, paraphrasing, and summarizing, you can obtain a fairly accurate *reconstruction* of the prior event which then can be analyzed for troublesome beliefs. Once this event from the past is recreated, you can change and reinterpret the meaning of the event.

This technique of reconstruction, of course, is highly similar to Figure 8.3, page 226, the exercise in using psychodynamic theory, in which you were encouraged to help a client reconstruct an event from the past or analyze a dream through structured free association. Whereas psychodynamic theory emphasizes the insight generated through this reconstruction, the cognitive-behaviorist would be interested in changing old patterns of faulty reasoning.

Self-Monitoring. Here the client is encouraged to look at the self functioning in the world. Record keeping and self-observation in the tradition of behavioral theory are critical here. The client may be feeling anxious in a classroom and you and the client know that anxiety is "somehow" related to certain types of situations. The client stops the action and takes complete notes on the context of the situation, with whom he or she was talking, and also notes the emotions associated with the situation. Random thoughts (free associations) from this experience may also be listed. The goal of this type of self-monitoring is self-awareness in the belief that behavior change will soon follow. Interestingly, the simple act of awareness often changes irrational thinking on the spot.

Another approach to assessing troublesome beliefs is "thinking aloud" during a variety of tasks. Here you encourage the client to engage in almost any type of task—for example, a problem-solving exercise. As the client works with the task, you ask the client to "think aloud" and report all that crosses the mind during task performance. Of course, this is similar to an exercise in psychodynamic free association, but the intent of the technique and use of the association will be very different.

Psychometric Assessment. Krumboltz lists a variety of brief instruments that are designed to help the counselor assess thinking process. Among those listed are the *Questionnaire to Determine Beliefs about Career Decision Making* (Mitchell and Krumboltz, cited by Mitchell, 1980), *Efficacy Questionnaire* (Mitchell, Krumboltz, and Kinnier, cited in Mitchell, 1980), and *My Vocational Situation* (Holland, Daiger, and Power, 1980). These and other such instruments provide a structured situation in which irrational vocational thinking may be revealed. However, Krumboltz also suggests projective tests such as the Thematic Apperception Test (T.A.T.) as potentially relevant for uncovering troublesome beliefs.

Guidelines for Working with Crucial Cognitions. Once having assessed and determined irrational beliefs, the question "What is to be done?" arises. The first suggestion of Krumboltz is to *examine assumptions and presuppositions of the expressed belief.* Basically, this can be done by talking with the client about a mutually identified troublesome belief. For example, you and the client may have exposed the belief "I can't ever work with a female boss" as troublesome and irrational. The task now is to look at the belief. From where does that belief come? Has it shown in previous situations? The free association exercise may be used to find past situations. You may wish to question the client about his or her intentions behind that statement. You may wish to recreate a situation from the past through role-playing. Through these and a wide variety of techniques suggested here and in other portions of this text, you will find it possible to examine the belief. Through systematic examination, the belief will often change.

You, as counselor, may wish to confront *inconsistencies between words and behavior.* The skill of confrontation has been stressed as critical throughout this text. You may wish to challenge a troublesome belief through variations of the following example:

CLIENT: I simply can't get along with a female boss.

COUNSELOR: As I listen to you, I see you saying firmly that you "can't get along" with your words, but I note your left hand wavering and trembling just a bit as you say that. (Here the counselor has several followup options: (1) it is possible simply to use listening skills and let the client deal with the situation as you provide a supportive relationship; (2) you could move to Gestalt exercises of Chapter 10 and have the client talk to the wavering hand; (3) it would be possible to have the client free associate to an earlier life experience from the emotional contradiction he is expressing; (4) a wide array of other possibilities exist through which the contradiction may be attacked.

Identifying barriers to a goal can be useful in helping the client focus on the real problem. As suggested throughout this text, counseling without specific goals for you and the client often leads to "behavioral circling." Thus, giving special and specific attention to goal setting in the interview is critical. However, Krumboltz wisely suggests that this is not enough. A client may come up with an inappropriate or unrealistic goal. Through careful questioning and listening and, sometimes, interpretation you may be able to help the client find a more suitable workable goal. The client, for example, may say the goal is to be manager of personnel. Through challenge and examination of that goal and barriers to achieving that goal, the intermediate goal of going to college or resolving a problem with a current boss may be discovered to be the real issue in need of counseling.

An Interview Transcript and Analysis

In many ways, the work of Krumboltz will appear similar to that of Ellis and/or Beck. However, he has developed a useful set of three guidelines that summarizes and highlights the cognitive-behavioral mode of interviewing as it relates to attacking faulty reasoning. Once you identify irrational ideas, faulty reasoning, or private rules, he suggests you ask the following three questions to clarify the client's thinking process:

1. How do you know that it is true?
2. What steps could you take to find out if it is true?
3. What evidence would convince you that the opposite is true? (Krumboltz, 1982, p. 29)

You may note that the underlying reasoning behind this system is shown in the following selection from one of Krumboltz's interviews in which he is attempting to facilitate the client becoming more aware of his true values. The client has been denying his materialistic side as related to vocational choice and Krumboltz senses that the issue is more complex. A condensed version of the exchange follows:*

I: You indicated before that you were skeptical of middle-class values.
S: Oh, okay, yeah. That would be a big one. I am skeptical of middle-class values. It scares me to think that everybody, well, a photographer really influenced me, I can't remember his name, but he did. Suburbia was his work. He did it in California, in Santa Barbara, and the important things to those people were, well, "What kind of car am I going to buy next?" for one thing, "Oh, I just got a new gas grill for outdoors."
I: Uh-huh.
S: And "We just got a new pool put in" and "My son Bob rushed for 200 yards last night and he's gonna go to a big school out East and learn how to become an accountant." (laughing) No, no, this can't be. That's like a nightmare. That's like a nightmare.
I: So those kinds of material wealth don't have any appeal to you. . . . Uh-huh. Let me push you a little bit on this.
S: Okay.
I: You said you would like to make a lot of money.
S: But I—
I: But what do you want to do with that money after you make it? Or is just making it and counting it?
S: Oh, I don't think counting it. I think making it is important. Because it's a measure in this society of what one is worth. But what would I do with it after I had it? I have no idea.
I: Uh-huh.
S: I don't even think it would be okay, I'd buy a really nice house and a Lamborghini— you might not know what it is, but it's a very expensive Italian sports car.
                                   . . .
I: Uh-huh.
S: Because, I don't know. That's always been exciting to me.
I: Uh-huh.
S: I might buy a little, oh my god, I don't believe what I'm saying, you know, and then I would be, holy mackerel! (laughing) I don't believe what I'm saying. I was just in another class bracket.
I: You got it.

*Excerpted from Krumboltz, 1983, pp. 12–15. Used by permission.

· · ·

S: I mean, buddy, I tell you, that was a good one. That's the biggest revelation I've had in some time.

I: Uh-huh. (pause)

S: Oh, boy. (pause) So what don't I like, (laughing) that's something. Well, maybe this is it then. Okay, maybe I am a materialist at heart. Maybe I do want that stuff because, yeah, I do want it, all right?

The interchange here forced the client to look at the contradiction in his values. The client expressed a need to avoid materialism, but when pushed admitted his more basic belief and his desire for material things. Now armed with this information, the counselor can move in several alternative directions. At the more superficial level, one could return to vocational counseling and search for a job that allows the opportunity to make "a lot" of money. Alternatively, the client could be encouraged to free associate back to earlier life patterns and examine the desire for materialism and how it developed. When an early pattern is identified, the confrontational style of the counselor might again challenge this pattern of beliefs in the hope of finding a balance between the extremes of anti-materialism and pro-materialism.

As a final portion of vocational counseling (or psychotherapy), the cognitive-behavioral counselor will seek to pinpoint behavior and move the client more directly to action to reach desired goals much as might a behavioral therapist.

MEICHENBAUM'S CONSTRUCTION OF COGNITIVE-BEHAVIOR THERAPY

Donald Meichenbaum has provided an excellent summary of the cognitive-behavioral movement. He notes:

> In summary, the first stage of CBT is concerned with helping the client define his or her problems in terms of making the problem amenable to solution. The second stage is concerned with the actual promotion of cognitive, emotional, and behavioral change. The third stage focuses on the consolidation of changes, the generalization and maintenance of behavior change and the avoidance of relapse. (1985, p. 271)

This view, of course, brings many of the ideas of this book together in one short paragraph. Our task as therapists is to define the problem (and goals) with our clients; we then apply a wide variety of techniques in the fourth stage of the interview to produce cognitive, emotional, and/or behavioral change. Finally, we must act if we are to ensure that behavioral change is to be maintained in the environment of the real world. Whether we commit ourselves to psychodynamic, behavioral, existential/humanistic, or some other orientation, meeting the criteria of the brief outline provided by Meichenbaum should be useful.

Donald Meichenbaum

Meichenbaum's Central Constructs and Techniques

Meichenbaum (1985) summarizes several key components of his conceptions of cognitive-behavioral therapy that include the important work of Beck and Ellis. To the theory presented thus far, the following central constructs should be added.

The Importance of Behavior. Meichenbaum's conceptualizations are important as he emphasizes the tie between behaviorism and cognitive-behavioral theory. In the emphasis on cognition presented by Beck and Krumboltz, and to some extent Ellis, the *behavioral* portion of cognitive-behavioral can sometimes become lost.

Thus, techniques such as assertiveness training, social learning theory's modeling, and relapse prevention are stressed as key aspects of cognitive-behavioral theory. Meichenbaum, in fact, terms Ellis and Beck as "cognitive-semantic" therapists rather than true cognitive-behaviorists.

Pinpointing Behavioral Targets. Applied behavioral analysis, the operationalization of behavior, and functional analysis as discussed in the behavioral chapter are centrally important to Meichenbaum's construction of cognitive-behavioral theory. Whereas some cognitive-behaviorists are satisfied with defining general cognitive and thought difficulties, Meichenbaum stresses *pinpointing* behaviors and thoughts very specifically. Measurable and definable thoughts and behaviors are important in this point of view.

Stress Inoculation. A useful technique is that of teaching clients how to deal effectively with stress (Meichenbaum, 1985; Meichenbaum and Jaremko, 1973).

This training program involves three distinct phases: (1) helping client's develop a cognitive understanding of the role stress plays in one's life; (2) teaching specific coping skills so that one can deal with stress effectively; and (3) working with thoughts and feelings about the stressful situation so that the client may actually be motivated to do something about stress. Meichenbaum makes the important point that cognitive awareness of stress is not enough to produce change nor are skills. One must actually *decide* to do something.

For example, a professional couple may be faced with difficulties in their lives and may very frequently argue with each other. Their problem could be defined as a "marital difficulty" or it could be redefined as a problem in coping with stress. The couple both may work and have two children and be active in the community. There simply isn't time to "do it all" effectively and that becomes a major stressor in itself. The first task in stress inoculation is to help the couple define the problem as one of stress. This itself can be useful as the couple no longer has to "blame" each other for their difficulties and now can see the impact of their environment on the marriage.

Secondly, it would be possible to teach stress reduction procedures such as relaxation training, decision making (so that the couple does fewer things), and social skills so that they might learn alternatives to constant work. These behavioral skills can lead to important change and will likely involve techniques of modeling, role-play, and direct instruction.

Finally, knowing one has a problem with stress and having some skills are not enough. Will the couple decide for action? At the point of generalization, their emotional and cognitive world may again become irrational and faulty thinking will prevent them from a *decision* to act. The techniques of "cognitive-semantic therapy" or relapse prevention (which itself has many cognitive-behavioral components) may be employed to ensure action. The therapist may follow up with this couple to ensure that they actually do implement the systematic plan of behavioral change that has been pinpointed.

The concepts of stress inoculation now have been expanded with specific suggestions as to how to work with victims of trauma (rape, abuse, even victims of terrorist attacks). The framework is increasingly vital as a treatment framework in its own right. Meichenbaum (1985) presents his innovative ideas with many suggested clinical interventions.

Skills Training. An increasingly important part of cognitive-behavioral methods is that of skill training, teaching clients and others specific modes of responding. Skill training is the subject of two important books (Larson, 1984; Marshall and Kurtz, 1983) which present a wide variety of systematic formulations for teaching communication skills, life skills for difficult/delinquent adolescents, marital skills, skills for psychiatric patients, and many others. Skill training, in fact, is beginning to offer itself as a theory of psychotherapy and change in its own right.

Most often skill training involves the following cognitive-behavioral components:

1. *Rapport/Structuring:* Preparing the client/trainee cognitively and emotionally for the instruction.
2. *Cognitive Presentation and Cueing.* Usually, some form of explanation and rationale for the skill is presented. In stress innoculation, Meichenbaum explains the nature of stress and why it is important to learn stress management.
3. *Modeling.* Role-plays, videotapes, audiotapes, and demonstrations are commonly used so that trainees can see and hear the behaviors of the skill in action. Here cognitions from earlier stages are paired with specific observable behaviors.
4. *Practice.* One does not always learn a skill by cognitive understanding and watching. Most skill trainers will require their clients/trainees to engage in the skill through role-played practice possibly supplemented by videotape and audiotape

---

Figure 11.2   *An Exercise in Cognitive-Behavioral Therapy*

The diverse content of cognitive-behavioral theory can be organized into a systematic interview using the following structure. It is suggested that you find a volunteer client who is willing to work through the several stages. A suggested topic for the session is some form of irrational idea, faulty thinking, or private rule. Perhaps the most common and useful topic for this session is the frequent desire many of us have for being "perfect."

1. *Rapport/Structuring.* As before, develop rapport in your own way and inform your client that you would like to work on some aspect of his or her desire for perfection.
2. *Data Gathering.* Using the basic listening sequence, draw out the facts, feelings, and organization of the client's desire for perfection. Try to enter the client's meaning system and reflect the underlying meaning you observe. Point out something positive in the client's meaning system as part of the exploration. Search for irrational ideas or faulty reasoning.
3. *Determining Outcomes.* Pinpoint very specific goals for your client. They should be cognitively and behaviorally specific and measurable. As one rule, can you and the client "see, hear, and feel" concrete change? The concept of concreteness involves specifics, not vague, generalizations: ("Could you give me a specific example of a better resolution of your drive for perfection?") Here you may find your client resisting and retreating once again to faulty, irrational thinking in defining goals.
4. *Generating Alternative Solutions.* Here the world is literally open for you and *you* will have to decide your route toward action. You may wish to attack the faulty, irrational thinking using the Beck or Ellis model, or you may wish to recreate the original situation using some of the free association methods of Krumboltz. Or, you may decide stress innoculation, skills training, or assertiveness training may be called for. Aspects of other theories may occur to you at this point as more appropriate.
5. *Generalization.* Cognitive-behavioral approaches emphasize the importance of taking behavior back home. Several alternatives for ensuring generalization have been made throughout this text. You may wish to have your client fill out a relapse prevention form (Chapter 9) or you may simply assign "homework" and follow up during the week with a phone call to see if cognitive and behavioral change are indeed occurring.

feedback. It is important that the skill be *mastered* to a high level or it is likely to be lost over time.

5. *Generalization.* All skill training emphasizes the decision to take the learning outside and beyond the immediate situation of the training session.

One cognitive-behavioral skill training program is that of the microskills framework of Chapter 3 (Ivey, 1971, 1983) in which counseling and communication skills are taught. It has been found that teaching these skills is not only useful for training in counseling and therapy, but also for a wide variety of patient and client groups. For example, psychiatric patients have benefitted from this form of training as well as management interns, medical personnel, and hospice workers. You will find that skill training itself is a major theoretical and practical form of treatment.

Meichenbaum's work is important as it provides a counterbalance to much of current thinking and work in cognitive-behavioral theory. There has been some tendency to focus too heavily on just the "cognitive" portion of the theory. If behavioral change is to occur, the many useful techniques of behavioral psychology need to be considered. The selection of these techniques will vary from charting through assertiveness training and from relaxation training through free association, but the "bottom line" is always action and change in the client's daily environment.

This chapter will conclude with the presentation of one additional theory, reality therapy, which is sometimes termed an early cognitive-behavior system, although some classify it as a humanistic therapy. However, recent work in reality therapy has moved it ever closer to the tradition of cognitive-behavioral methods discussed here.

REALITY THERAPY

If Albert Ellis's rational-emotive therapy could be summed up as "Be rational and think about things logically," William Glasser's reality therapy could be summarized by saying, "Take responsibility and control of your own life and face the consequences of your actions." Each therapy in this book focuses on a few key words and then elaborates on basic themes as a comprehensive model of change is generated. Although research on reality therapy is limited, it is a frequent treatment of choice if one works with difficult clients, particularly acting-out or delinquent youth or adults.

Central Theoretical Constructs of Reality Therapy

In describing the basic beliefs of reality therapy, Glasser has stated that all clients have been unsuccessful in meeting their needs and that in attempts to

William Glasser

meet their needs they often tend to select ineffective behaviors that virtually assure their failure. Further,

> . . . all patients have a common characteristic: *they all deny the reality of the world around them.* Some break the law, denying the rules of society; some claim their neighbors are plotting against them, denying the improbability of such behavior. Some are afraid of crowded places, close quarters, airplanes, or elevators, yet they freely admit the irrationality of their fears. Millions drink to blot out the inadequacy they feel but that need not exist if they could learn to be different; and far too many people choose suicide rather than face the reality that they could solve their problems by more responsible behavior. Whether it is a partial denial or the total blotting out of all reality of the chronic backward patient in the state hospital, the denial of some or all of reality is common to all patients. Therapy will be successful when they are able to give up denying the world and recognize that reality not only exists but that they must fulfill their needs within its framework.
>
> A therapy that leads all patients toward reality, toward grappling successfully with the tangible and intangible aspects of the real world, might accurately be called a therapy toward reality, or simply *Reality Therapy.* (Glasser, 1965, p. 6)

Reality therapy could best be described as a common-sense approach to counseling. What Glasser advocates is finding out what people want and need, examining their failures and their present assets, and considering factors in the environment that must be met if the needs are to be satisfied. One cannot meet needs except in a *real* world; people must face a world that is imperfect and not built to their specifications and must act positively in this world. The worldview of reality therapy is that people can do something about their fate if they will consider themselves and the environment realistically.

As might be anticipated, reality therapy focuses on conscious, planned behavior, and gives relatively little attention to underlying dimensions of transference, unconscious thought process, and the like. The effort is to consider the past as being past and done with—that the present and the future are what are important. Yet, reality therapy does not emphasize applied behavioral analysis or the detailed plans of assertion training or systematic desensitization. Rather, almost like rational-emotive therapy, reality therapy focuses on responsibility and choice. What is critical is that the client examine her or his life to see how specific behavior is destructive. The more important step, however, is to take responsibility, which Glasser defines as "the ability to fulfill one's needs and to do so *in a way that does not deprive others of the ability to fulfill their needs*" (1965, p. 13). Learning responsibility is a lifelong process.

Given the population that reality therapy often serves (street clinics, prison inmates, school children, and others in institutional settings), it is clear that relationship and trust are particularly important. The institutions with which children and prisoners cope do not easily build the almost automatic trust relationship that seems to come when a person enters the professional office of the highly paid psychoanalyst. The reality therapist as *person* becomes especially important. The qualities of warmth, respect and caring for others, positive regard, and interpersonal openness are crucial. Moreover, the person practicing reality therapy is much more likely to be with her or his clients in settings other than the counseling office. The individual oriented to reality therapy may be expected to be out on the playground with youth in a delinquent detention center, may also serve as a classroom teacher to a child whom he or she is counseling, or perhaps even work as a prison guard. The possible multiplicity of relationships requires a special type of person able to be consistent. This challenge, of course, provides an opportunity for the reality therapist to serve as a continuing model of personal responsibility to the client outside of the counseling session.

An Interview Transcript and Analysis

Similarly, counseling sessions within reality therapy can range from a regularly scheduled 50-minute hour to brief personal encounters in the dining room, classroom, or other setting. For this reason, reality therapy can become a way of life for some people.

A sample interview from the second phase of reality therapy follows. The client is an 18-year-old man on probation for repeated offenses of a minor nature, including selling alcohol to minors, assault, and petty theft. The counselor in this case is a county probation officer and the meeting occurs in the community half-way house. They are just finishing a game of ping-pong.

1. COUNSELOR:	Got ya! 21–18, took me three games, but I finally got one.
2. CLIENT:	Yeah, you pulled it off finally. Man, I'm pooped. (They sit down and have a cup of coffee.)
3. COUNSELOR:	So, how have things been going? [Open question]
4. CLIENT:	Well, I looked for jobs hard last week. But nothing looked any good. The bastards seem to know I'm coming and pull the help wanted sign down just as I come walking in.

5. COUNSELOR: So, you've been looking hard. How many places did you visit? [Paraphrase, closed question, note search for concrete behavior]
6. CLIENT: Oh lots. Nobody will give me a chance.
7. COUNSELOR: Tell me some of the places you've been. [Directive]
8. CLIENT: I tried the gas station down the street. They gave me a bad time. Nobody wants me. It's really tough.
9. COUNSELOR: Where else did you go? [Closed question]
10. CLIENT: I tried a couple other stations too. Nobody wants to look at me. They don't pay too good anyway. Nuts to them!
11. COUNSELOR: So you haven't really done too much looking. Sounds like you want it served on a silver plate, Joe. Do you think looking at a couple of gas stations is really going to get you a job? [Paraphrase, interpretation, closed question]
12. CLIENT: I suppose not. Nobody wants to hire me anyway.
13. COUNSELOR: Let's take another look at that. The economy is pretty rocky right now. Everyone is having trouble getting work. You seem to think "they" are after you. Yet, I've got a friend about your age who had to go to thirty-five places before he got a job. How does that square with you looking at three places and then giving up? Who's responsible—you, the service station owners, or the economy? [Directive, information-giving, open question, note confrontation]
14. CLIENT: Yeh, but, there's not much I can do about it. I tried . . .
15. COUNSELOR: Yeh, at three places. Who's responsible for you not getting a job when you only go to three places when at a time like this you've really got to scramble? Come on, Joe! [Interpretation]

The interview continued to explore Joe's lack of action with an emphasis on responsibility. At points where a Rogerian counselor might have paraphrased or reflected feelings and attitudes (such as Client: 4,8, and 10), the reality therapist honed in for more behavioral specifics through questions and interpretation. The process of examining Joe's behavior is closely akin to that of the behavioral counselor involved in applied behavioral analysis. However, the use of the behavioral data is quite different in reality therapy. Instead of seeking to change behavior, the reality therapist works on changing awareness of responsibility. Once the focus of responsibility has been acknowledged and owned by the client, it is possible to start planning a more effective job search. Later in the interview we begin to see the process of planning:

51. COUNSELOR: So, Joe, sounds like you feel you made a decision this past week not to *really* look for a job . . . almost as if you took responsibility for not getting work. [Reflection of meaning, interpretation]
52. CLIENT: Yeh, I don't like to look at it that way, but I guess I did decide not to do too much.
53. COUNSELOR: And what about next week?
54. CLIENT: I suppose I ought to look again, but I really don't like it.

The reality therapist at this point moved to a realistic analysis of what the client might expect during the coming week on the job market, constantly emphasizing the importance of the client, Joe, taking action and responsibility for

---

Figure 11.3 *Structured Exercise for Practice in Reality Therapy*

More than most other approaches to counseling, reality therapy involves being with clients as more than a counselor or therapist. It also requires being oneself and modeling responsible interpersonal style. For this reason, practice exercises may be more limited in value for learning this particular approach. The following may be helpful, however, in obtaining some sense of the possibilities within reality therapy.

1. Ask yourself the question, "Do I want to be involved with other people?" Authenticity, genuineness, and willingness to be onself truly and be with others is required of the person interested in reality therapy. It is difficult to be a reality therapist who hides in the office, coming out only for coffee and lunch. Are you willing and able to take time to be "out-front" and with people?
   With a friend or with a journal, examine yourself and your commitments.
2. Again, ask yourself, "Am I responsible and do I understand what responsibility means?" Do you believe that you are the director and manager of your own life, that you are "in charge", and that you must face the consequences of your own actions?
   With a friend or with a journal, explore specific instances where you were or were not responsible for your behavior. Apply the Glasser concept of responsibility to yourself, your past and present.
3. Finally, do you believe that it is possible to help others relearn new ways of living through instruction and coping with the realistic, daily problems of life? If you would rather work on past events and the internal psyche, search for the warmth and caring of humanistic self-actualizing therapies, or some other approach; reality therapy may not be for you. Reality therapy requires a rigorous and "hard-nosed" approach to others, coupled with an ability to be equally rigorous and hard-nosed with yourself.
4. If you are personally satisfied with your own reactions to the preceding questions, examine the Structured Exercise for Practice in Rational-Emotive Therapy in Figure 11.1. Use the same exercise for reality therapy, but substitute the word "irresponsibility" for "irrational ideas." Analyze yourself and others for responsibility and coping with reality. Until you are able to identify irresponsibility in others and your own failure to cope with reality at a high level, reality therapy practice will be most difficult.

---

his life. A practice role-play job interview was held, and several alternatives for generating a more effective job search were considered. Joe tried to escape responsibility at several points ("I couldn't do that."), but the counselor confronted him with his excusing style and allowed no excuses or ambivalence.

A reality therapist will use skills and ideas of other theoretical orientations when they serve the purpose of assisting the client to confront reality and move effectively. More likely, the reality therapist will be her or his natural self and use humor, sarcasm, and confrontation in very personal ways to assist the client to understand behavioral patterns and develop new action styles. Role-playing, systematic planning, and actually teaching people how to live more intentionally play a prominent part of reality therapy. Although many people who practice reality therapy approaches may be in power situations (guard, principal, rehabilitation counselor), they still tend to be themselves as they use reality therapy as an extension of themselves, thus adding a tone of genuineness and authenticity to the process at a more significant level than they could with some other approaches. For example, the prison guard trained in reality therapy simply states his position realistically as one of power and control. Then, having clearly established role relationships, the same process of involvement, teaching responsibility, and relearning can take place.

Recent Cognitive Trends in Reality Therapy

A critical part of reality therapy is client awareness of *consequences* of actions. "If you do X, then what is the consequence?" Reality therapy in a highly nonjudgmental fashion attempts to help individuals learn what they can expect when they act in certain ways. In this sense, you may again note a similarity and a difference from rational-emotive therapy. In RET, the consequences are those inside the person (feeling depressed, and so forth) whereas in reality therapy, the consequence may indeed be inside, but the stress is on what happens from the outside world when the client fails to face reality and be responsible.

Glasser has continually expanded his thinking but has remained true to the basic constructs of the method and theory described above. In his 1981 book, *Stations of the Mind,* he builds a comprehensive picture of the workings of the "internal world" of the mind. Glasser notes that the "internal reality" of the mind (cognitions) must be able to understand how the individual relates to external reality. Control is an increasingly important aspect of Glasser's current thinking. "We always have control over what we do" is a chapter head in his most recent book for the popular market, *Take Effective Control of Your Life* (1984). At issue is how one is to exercise that control. You can choose misery as a way of life because it excuses you from trying harder, may get you help from others, may win pity, and so on. A "headaching" person may benefit because this is the only time he or she is able to lay down and rest. Psychosomatic illness is considered a specific type of internal control to help individuals avoid reality. Drugs and alcohol are still other methods whereby an individual can use control to avoid facing reality.

Careful analysis of Glasser's recent work suggests that he is moving closer to the position of Ellis and the cognitive-behavioral position in that he is giving increased attention to the way people think about things. However, he still uses the basic structure of reality therapy to produce change. His theory of control provides an important additional tool to the therapist working with an individual client. This is done through constant attention to the client "owning" thoughts and behavior (including feelings and illness) and being responsible for them. The logic is that if one can control one's mind and body toward seemingly unsatisfactory ends such as drugs, headaches, stealing, and interpersonal conflict, then one could reframe one's mind to take more positive control.

Glasser talks about "positive addictions," which range from friends to jogging to movies to meditation—anything through which an individual can obtain a "high" or more satisfactory way of living. The world offers us the opportunity for negative addiction or for positive addiction. We choose our addiction and our fate. We can have "headaching" or we can have "joying." The choice is ours. We are in control.

Glasser's new emphasis on control, however, indicates that he is moving toward a more immediate, confrontational and cognitive point of view. With certain clients, we may expect direct and forceful confrontations of thought patterns, active teaching of alternative perceptions of reality, and an emphasis that focuses more on internal states and thoughts. Needless to say, the client must be ready for this new challenge. The "how" of control theory has not really been addressed, except by implication. At the moment, traditional reality therapy and the new dimensions of control theory seem somewhat at odds. We may anticipate for the future, however, a more complete integration of Glasser's thinking with illustrations of how a new theory of reality therapy may be used in more practical ways. In the past, Glasser seemed to stress the importance of the client adapting to the world as it is. He now appears to be adding internal cognitive states to his basic view.

SUMMARY OF THIS CHAPTER

To master the central constructs of this chapter, you will want to be able to:

1. *Describe the general orientation of the cognitive-behavioral movement.* At this time, the cognitive-behavioral orientation is growing rapidly and represents a system in which cognitive or thinking therapies may be integrated with behavioral action. George Kelly was described as perhaps the first clear example historically of the cognitive-behavioral movement. The worldview of this orientation is integrationist in nature encompassing both the idea that "It is not things, but our view of things" as well as the need to act and behave in accordance with views of things. The cognitive-behavioral orientation was described as integrating many of the traditional philosophies of idealism, realism, and existentialism.

2. *Describe and utilize constructs of Albert Ellis's rational-emotive therapy.* RET may be considered the modern forerunner of cognitive-behavioral therapy, although Ellis's work tends to be more cognitive than behavioral. Important constructs and methods from this system include irrational ideas, the A-B-C framework of cognitive patterns, and how to integrate methods and ideas from other theoretical orientations in the practice of RET.

3. *Understand the major ideas of Aaron Beck's cognitive therapy.* Important in Beck's system are a positive attitude toward change in thinking, specific patterns of faulty reasoning, a three-step model to produce change in client thinking patterns, and systematic methods to work with automatic thoughts and cognitive patterns.

4. *Discuss and utilize John Krumboltz's career decision making counseling and carry the ideas into personal counseling as well.* Krumboltz presents one of the more broadly based frameworks for cognitive therapy. His concept of private rules and troublesome beliefs in decision making and how they developed are important for extending the cognitive-behavioral model. Useful techniques include reconstruction of prior events, self-monitoring, psychometric assessment, the search for inconsistencies between words and behavior, and identifying barriers to a goal.

5. *Understand Donald Meichenbaum's more behavioral approach to cognitive-behavioral theory.* Meichenbaum integrates much of behavioral technology from Chapter 9 into his work, especially pinpointing behavioral targets. Important methods and ideas stressed in his framework include skills training and social learning and stress innoculation.

6. *Conduct a practice session in cognitive-behavioral therapy.* A structured exercise in the five stages of the interview in this theoretical framework was presented.

7. *Relate cognitive-behavioral approaches to William Glasser's reality therapy.* Reality therapy has not usually been considered a cognitive-behavioral approach, but recent work brings it closer to cognitive-behavioral therapies. Reality therapy attempts to bring the problem behavior in accord with the "reality" of daily living and emphasizes both thinking and doing. Reality therapy is often considered the treatment of choice in cases dealing with delinquency, acting-out youth, or other problems in which individuals may do as they wish without adequately considering the possible problems they may face with reality.

REFERENCES

BECK, A., *Depression: Causes and Treatment.* Philadelphia: University of Pennsylvania Press, 1972.

BECK, A., *Cognitive Therapy and the Emotional Disorders.* New York: International Universities Press, 1976.

DIFFILY, A., *Aaron Beck: A Profile. Brown Alumni Monthly,* Providence, RI: 1984, 39–46.

D'ZURILLA, T. and M. GOLDFRIED, "Problem Solving and Behavior Modification," *Journal of Abnormal Psychology,* 1971, *78,* 107–116.

ELLIS, A., *Sex Without Guilt.* Secaucus, NJ: Lyle Stuart, 1958.

ELLIS, A., Rational-Emotive Psychotherapy. In D. Arbuckle, ed. *Counseling and Psychotherapy.* New York: McGraw-Hill, 1967.

ELLIS, A., *Growth Through Reason.* Palo Alto, CA: Science and Behavior Books, 1971.

ELLIS, A., "The Origins of Rational-Emotive Therapy (RET)," *Voices,* 1983a, *18,* 29–33.

ELLIS, A., "The Use of Rational-Emotive Therapy (RET) in Working for a Sexually Sane Society," In G. Albee, S. Gordon, and H. Leitenberg, eds., *Promoting Sexual Responsibility and Preventing Sexual Problems.* Hanover, VT: University Press of New England, 1983b.

GLASSER, W., *Reality Therapy.* New York: Harper & Row, 1965.

GLASSER, W., *Stations of the Mind.* New York: Harper and Row, 1983.

GLASSER, W., *Take Effective Control of Your Life.* New York: Harper and Row, 1984.

HOLLAND, J., D. DAIGER, and P. POWER, *My Vocational Situation.* Palo Alto, CA: Consulting Psychologists Press, 1980.

IVEY, A., *Microcounseling.* Springfield, IL: Thomas, 1971.

IVEY, A., *Intentional Interviewing and Counseling.* Monterey, CA: Thomas, 1983.

IVEY, A., and N. GLUCKSTERN, *Basic Attending Skills.* North Amherst, MA: Microtraining Associates, 1983.

KRUMBOLTZ, J., *Private Rules in Career Decision Making.* Columbus, OH: The National Center for Research in Vocational Education, 1983.

LANGE, A., and P. JAKUBOWSKI, *Responsible Assertive Behavior: Cognitive/Behavioral Procedures for Trainers.* Champaign, IL: Research Press, 1976.

LARSON, D., ed. *Teaching Psychological Skills.* Belmont, CA: Wadsworth, 1984.

MARSHALL, E., P. KURTZ, and ASSOCIATES. *Interpersonal Helping Skills.* San Francisco: Jossey-Bass, 1982.

MASTERS, W. and V. JOHNSON, *Human Sexual Inadequacy.* Boston: Little-Brown, 1980.

MEICHENBAUM, D., "Cognitive-Behavioral Therapies." In S. Lynn, J. Garske, *Contemporary Psychotherapies*. Columbus, OH, 1985, 261–286.

MEICHENBAUM, D. and M. JAREMKO, *Stress Reduction and Prevention*. New York: Plenum, 1973.

MITCHELL, L., "The Effects of Training in Cognitive Restructuring and Decision Making Skills on Vocational Career Decision Making Behavior, Cognition, and Affect." Ph.D. Dissertation, Stanford University, 1980.

SUGGESTED SUPPLEMENTARY READING

BECK, A., J. RUSH, B. SHAW, and G. EMERY, *Cognitive Therapy of Depression*. New York: Guilford, 1980.

One of the classic works of the cognitive-behavioral movement. A variety of cognitively-oriented techniques to facilitate planning and thinking in dealing with depression.

ELLIS, A., *Growth Through Reason: Verbatim Cases in Rational-Emotive Therapy*. Palo Alto, CA: Science and Behavior Books, 1971.

A particular strength of RET has been a constant emphasis on clarifying what therapists of this persuasion actually do to help people. The typescripts in this book are carefully analyzed and interestingly presented.

GLASSER, W., *Reality Therapy*. New York: Harper & Row, 1965.

The original statement on reality therapy which came to wide national attention. The book is a useful overview of philosophy and method.

GLASSER, W., *Take Effective Control of Your Life*. New York: Harper and Row, 1984.

Glasser's most recent statement of his developing position. Here you will find increasing parallels with the cognitive-behavioral position. Several practical suggestions for daily living are contained in this book written for the popular market.

KRUMBOLTZ, J., *Private Rules in Career Decision Making*. Columbus, OH: National Center for Research in Vocational Education, Ohio State University, 1983.

A cogent and clear summary of the principles of career decision making as proposed by Krumboltz.

MEICHENBAUM, D., *Cognitive-Behavior Modification: An Integrative Approach*. New York: Plenum, 1977.

An overview of the cognitive-behavioral field with special attention to the behavioral side of the equation.

MEICHENBAUM, D., *Stress Innoculation Training*. New York: Pergamon, 1985.

Presents the systematic framework of stress innoculation and shows how this technique may be used in fields as varied as victims of terrorist attacks, rape victims, pain patients, and those who deal with normal stress. Many specific clinical interventions are provided.

12

SYSTEMS THEORIES AND METHODS

GENERAL PREMISE

An integrated knowledge of skills, theory, and practice is essential for culturally intentional counseling and therapy.

Skills form the foundation of effective theory and practice: The culturally intentional therapist knows how to construct a creative decision-making interview and can use microskills to attend to and influence clients in a predicted direction. Important in this process are individual and cultural empathy, client observation skills, assessment of person and environment, and the application of positive techniques of growth and change.

Theory provides organizing principles for counseling and therapy: *The culturally intentional counselor has knowledge of alternative theoretical approaches and treatment modalities, in this case a series of important systems-oriented theories and methods.*

Practice is the integration of skills and theory: The culturally intentional counselor or therapist is competent in skills and theory, and is able to apply them to research and practice for client benefit.

Undergirding integrated competence in skills, theory, and practice is an intentional awareness of one's own personal worldview and how that worldview may be similar to and/or different from the worldview and personal constructions of the client and other professionals.

GOALS FOR SYSTEMS THEORIES

This book thus far has emphasized the individual interview and the wide array of techniques that are available to facilitate individual therapy and development. This chapter seeks to extend that material to current and newly developing concepts that attempt to treat individuals in relationships to others, to families, and to the organizations and communities within which they live and work.

This chapter has the following goals:

1. To present a worldview that is oriented primarily to systems of relationships between and among clients and the environment in which they live.
2. To provide summaries of individual, family, and community/organizational methods that may be used to supplement the individually oriented therapies discussed in this book.
3. To give special attention to the growth of consciousness-raising theories and feminist therapy as special examples of a growing cultural awareness developing in the field.
4. To suggest some practical exercises for you to consider—within this broad frame of change, development, and innovation—so that this material may also be used in your own work.

SYSTEMS AND PERSON/ENVIRONMENT TRANSACTION

In psychiatric hospitals, the staff often talks about the "revolving door." Patients may be well treated, show improvement from individual and group psychotherapy, and then be released to their family and community. Very often in 3 to 6 months, the patients return through the "revolving door" with a repetition of the same illness.

Similarly, an individual goes through extensive and expensive psychodynamic, behavioral, existential-humanistic, or cognitive-behavioral therapy. He or she may make important gains. But often those changes disappear over time as the person returns to the same family and community environment that helped produce the original problem.

Change in psychotherapy is difficult and maintaining that change is sometimes even more difficult. The individual transactions our clients have daily with friends and family subtly and continuously move our "improved client" back to his or her old state of ineffective thinking and behaving. Families and communities are not organized to accept change in their members. And as psychotherapists, we must face the fact that our "cures" are sometimes not welcomed by those who referred their problem members to us.

Psychotherapy and counseling are giving increased attention to prevention of relapse and generalization of behavior from the individual interview. At the same time, however, a group of therapies have developed that seek to examine the "person-in-the-environment" and provide therapy and counseling for both. Although this book has given extensive attention to person and environment interaction (especially through Kelly's model of assessment, an emphasis on cultural differences, and in the chapter on behavioral psychology), the prime thrust of the chapters thus far has been on changing individuals.

The therapies discussed in this chapter also work toward individual change, but also explicitly strive to change the transactions of the individual with the environment and may even attempt environmental change itself.

AN ALTERNATIVE WORLDVIEW OF TRANSACTIONS AND ENVIRONMENT

Each of the major theories of this book talk about the importance of the environment. Freud spoke eloquently of this fact in his classic work *Civilization and Its Discontents*. Skinner's *Walden II* is about environmental change and Frankl's *Man's Search for Meaning* illustrates how one can cope with and manage impossible environments. Cognitive-behavioral theory is an attempt to help the individual *understand and cope* more fully with the environment.

So what is implied in the term "evolving systems theories?" Systems theory, particularly as a developing integrating point of view, is recent as a major theoretical alternative. While new, it clearly builds on the important past work of other theories and through the challenge of this method, we see new developments and changes in older theories as well. Neither psychodynamic, existential-humanistic, or behavioral theory are likely to "lay down and die" due to the competition of new ideas. All in their own way are viable, changing *systems*.

The commonality of the ideas in this chapter is that they build on past theories and methods, but have in common a worldview specifically devoted to *systems*. A systems worldview is one in which the *interaction between and among individuals, families, and environments* is considered the central fact of being in the world. What is new, however, in the systems worldview is that techniques of change try to work directly on the *system* of interaction rather than on one individual "piece" of the system.

Transactional analysis is a humanistic derivative of psychodynamic theory. It is not usually thought of as a "systems" therapy. However, the word "transaction" speaks to systems concepts. In transactional analysis, the goal is to change the *transactions* individuals have with others.

Family therapy and family education seek directly to have impact on a group of individuals. You will find that many principles of individual therapy are useful in understanding this developing mode of helping.

If an individual or a family are to be healthy, they must have a healthy environment in which to live. Thus, recent work in community change and action provide a framework of support for individual and family change and the maintenance of this change from relapse.

Morrill, Oetting, and Hurst (1980) have developed a visual model for systems change efforts that they term the *cube* (see Figure 12.1 for an adapted version of their work). In the cube model, you as a therapist or counselor, in your work, may target individual, family, or organizational change as your goal. Your purpose in this change can be remedial therapy or counseling, or it can be psychoeducational—the teaching of skills to prevent problems from occurring. Skill training, relaxation training, and assertiveness training are all examples of positive preventive/developmental programs, typical of the psychoeducational point of view.

The cube points out that the way you deliver your helping services can vary widely. You can do the work yourself or you may serve as a consultant or trainer and teach groups concepts for more effective living. The skill training programs of relaxation training and assertiveness can be and often are taught to *groups* of individuals and not just single clients. In this way, you can serve the mental health needs of larger populations. Media is a route toward change as well. Those who write books or advice articles in the newspaper, provide mental health pamphlets, and appear on talk shows can facilitate the understanding of large numbers of people. Dr. Ruth Westheimer, currently a popular sex therapist on radio and television, is an example of an individual who is using the media to broaden understanding of mental health issues.

Which method is best? Where should you put your efforts? No one is likely to be able to "do it all!" But a systems worldview in which we recognize that

Figure 12.1
This version is adapted from more detailed formulation, copyrighted by Morrill, Oetting, and Hurst, 1972, 1980

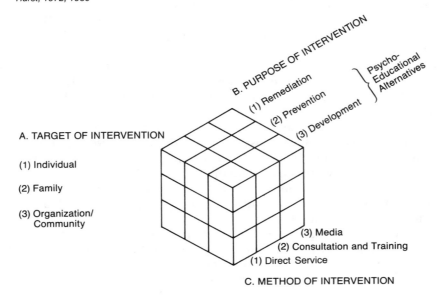

A. TARGET OF INTERVENTION

(1) Individual

(2) Family

(3) Organization/
Community

B. PURPOSE OF INTERVENTION
(1) Remediation
(2) Prevention
(3) Development
Psycho-Educational Alternatives

(3) Media
(2) Consultation and Training
(1) Direct Service

C. METHOD OF INTERVENTION

methods as different as classic psychoanalytic therapy, Gestalt confrontations, family education, and feminist therapy all have a common goal. The cube organizes alternative actions and may be a beginning partial answer as to which treatment alternative is best. Each method and theory contributes in its own way to diversity and intentionality—the generation of new ways of thinking, acting/behaving, and deciding *in relationship to the environment.*

Let us turn first to an example of individual therapy that represents an important beginning step toward extending psychoanalytic concepts to a larger population.

TRANSACTIONAL ANALYSIS

Transactional analysis (TA) first gained national attention in 1964 through the media and the best seller *Games People Play* by Eric Berne. This book was a popularized version of Berne's original work for professionals (c.f. Berne, 1961), but *Games People Play* remains the best known work by the creator of the highly influential TA movement. The titles of some of the early books in the TA movement illustrate the effort to popularize this particular theory: *What Do You Say After You Say Hello?* (Berne, 1972); *I'm OK—You're OK* (Harris, 1967); *Born to Win* (James and Jongeward, 1971); and *What Do You Do With Them Now That You've Got Them? Transactional Analysis for Moms and Dads* (James, 1974).

If TA were simply an advertising phenomenon, it would now be forgotten as a fad. However, TA has matured, developed an increasingly stable body of data, has its own respected professional journal *Transactional Analysis,* and may be considered an important part of the background of a well-trained counselor.

Eric Berne

There are now over 14,000 members of the International Transactional Analysis Association. TA has been especially effective and successful internationally.

Worldview and Central Theoretical Constructs

A special strength of TA has been the development of a language system that communicates with people rather than hides behind vague theoretical constructs. This ability to demystify the process of counseling is a special strength.

> The worldview of TA could perhaps be best summarized by the following: Transactional analysis is a rational approach to understanding behavior and is based on the assumption that all individuals can learn to trust themselves, think for themselves, make their own decisions, and express their feelings. Its principles can be applied on the job, in the home, in the classroom, in the neighborhood—wherever people deal with people. (James and Jongeward, 1971, p. 12)

This lay approach to helping human beings is illustrated by the well known *ego states* of *parent, adult,* and *child.* As we behave, our actions can be construed as existing in one of the main ego states. For example, the parent ego state represents what we have incorporated from our parents and usually appears in the form of "should's" and "ought's." This state roughly corresponds to the superego of psychodynamic psychology and also includes the many cultural prescriptions of what our behavior "ought" to be. TA often talks about two types of parents, the *nurturing parent* who cares for people and the *critical parent* who often tries to get us to "shape up." The child ego state, by way of contrast, is more spontaneous and free and in many ways corresponds to the id. However, TA authorities talk about the child ego state as consisting of the *natural child* (the free, spontaneous expressions), the *little professor* (intuitive, creative thoughts), and the *adapted child* (the natural child modified by demands of the environment). The adult ego state (corresponding roughly to the ego in psychodynamic psychology) processes the data from the world and from the parent and child states and makes decisions. The adult is not emotional and simply "does its best."

However, ego states are learned in *transactions* with the environment. The transactional styles are:

1. I'm O.K.—You're O.K.: The child believes that he or she is validated in the world, can form a self-concept, is acknowledged as an individual, and has a positive self-identity as well as a positive image of those around.
2. I'm O.K.—You're not O.K.: The child believes that he or she is a validated individual and has a positive self-image, but believes that the world and others surrounding the child are enemies and threatening to existence. The child may have been separated from parents, be in a foster home, have experienced the parents once as warm and loving but now as hostile and cruel, or experienced a host of other environmental factors.
3. I'm not O.K.—You're O.K.: The child takes upon himself or herself the blame for things going wrong, is the recipient of negative parental messages, is deluged with guilt, and so on. The child believes himself or herself to be bad and unworthy

of positive feedback from important adults, family members, and others. These types of children often commit crimes, display self-destructive behaviors, and exhibit depression.

4. I'm not O.K.—You're not O.K.: The child has a poor self-image and has hostile and angry feelings about others and the surrounding world. This child has received the messages that he or she is not deserving of positive praise and dislikes those who withhold attention and positive reinforcement. This type of child is often sullen, sarcastic, a problem at home and in school, and unkind to others.

If you refer back to Mary Bradford Ivey's work with the client in the second session of Chapter 7 (page 179), you will see how she used this framework to facilitate understanding. The client, Charles, was deeply into "should's" and "ought's" from the critical parent frame of reference. She reframed his thinking as that of the nurturing parent, thus providing a positive cognition on which later change could follow.

Since ego states are learned in *transactions* with the environment, Charles learned from his environment a basic life position. Looking at the example from Chapter 7, we see Charles at the fourth type of transactional style: "I'm not O.K.—You're not O.K." An individual in this position tends to blame both self and others. The therapist's goal in this case was to move Charles to an "I'm O.K., you're O.K. position," and you will note that she accomplished this through reframing the client's "critical parent" as also containing a "nurturing parent" dimension.

We all develop into one of the basic TA life positions through the lifescripts provided us by our family and our culture. Steiner (1975) talks about the "stroke" economy. Strokes are basically reinforcements provided us by the family and culture that guide and direct our behavior. We are given strokes when we do something well or something others approve. We are so heavily entwined by the environment of the strokes we receive that we sometimes end up living lifescripts over which we have little direction. Lifescripts, of course, go all the way back to infancy ("What a pretty baby!") and move through early childhood ("Don't do that . . . it's dirty!"), to schools ("Pay attention; do your work; you'll get ahead."), to peers ("You're a freak!"), to work ("Be here on time, and be neat!") Due to the many pressures of life, some people end up with stereotyped routinized scripts that they repeat over and over again. Through analysis of lifescripts, it is possible to free the individual for creative intentional responding. The parallels between lifescript analysis and the Freudian analysis of childhood growth patterns should be obvious.

Steiner (1984) talks about "emotional literacy" as one mode of changing past lifescripts. His systematic steps toward emotional understanding include: (1) asking the client for permission to explore feelings; (2) providing strokes (the positive asset search); (3) making a feeling/action statement ("I feel this . . . about that . . .") where emotion and action are closely tied; (4) ensuring that the feeling/action statement is heard by the other. By now, this basic model used in different ways in many theories should by familiar.

There are many, many alternative uses of script analysis. Goulding and Goulding's (1979) *Changing Lives Through Redecision Therapy* is another example. They point out that children make *early decisions* about themselves. The task of therapy (or self-discovery) is to learn about old scripts and then make redecisions. Goulding and Goulding provide a variety of exercises whereby an individual can learn about past scripts and, particularly, how these scripts play themselves out in the present. These methods may include a variety of Gestalt and decisional exercises and direct training and instruction for the individual. At times, the total family system may be involved in rewriting lifescripts.

Transactional analysis is the study of the games people play in the stroke economy as they play out their lifescripts—the examination of transactions between people who may function in the several ego states. A "game" is a routinized set of behaviors and attitudes manifested by an individual in relationship to another individual. The analysis of games, lifescripts, and ego states fills several books on TA, so the following is only a small illustration of one possibility for analysis. Note that we are primarily concerned with identifying the ego state from which each behavior operates in this interaction between a mother and her daughter.

1. DAUGHTER: Let's play dress-up, Mommie.
2. MOTHER: Sounds like such fun, let's do it.

(This is described in TA terms as a *complementary transaction*, as the parties complement each other with their behavior.)

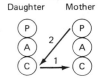

1. DAUGHTER: Let's play dress-up, Mommie.
2. MOTHER: You always make a mess and never pick up.

(This is a *crossed transaction* in which the critical parent in the mother takes over. The nurturing parent might have said: "I love you. OK, let me hold you a minute before we start." As the transaction between mother and child "works," this could be a complementary transaction. Crossed transactions occur where there is conflict or incongruity between the parties, usually at an overt level. For the second response to be fully complementary, the child would have to talk to the parent, rather than to the child in the parent.)

1. DAUGHTER: Let's play dress-up, Mommie.
2. MOTHER: Let's play dress-up, but first I need to hold you . . . and then we can clean up your room before we play.

(This represents what TA calls an *ulterior transaction* in that a double message is apparent. Worse, however, are less explicit ulterior motives ["I *need* to hold you"], which further confuse the child. In this case, the mother is speaking both as a parent and as a child.)

A Sample TA Interview

Each one of us goes through a myriad of interactions with others during a single day, playing the parts of adult, parent, and child in varying combinations. Some people's history in the stroke economy has led them to live as grown-up children, while others have been so socialized that their playful and creative "child" is almost dead. The task of the TA counselor is to help the client understand what is transpiring and to take new action.

The following interview illustrates only a small part of an important theory with a substantial method. The following case is an interview with a 31-year-old woman—referred to in the interview as Clooney—who has been participating in group TA sessions and has had two prior individual meetings about her current social difficulties. The TA counselor in this case is identified as "Dr. Q." Note that education plays an important part in this session and there is an emphasis on how individuals react and live in family environments.

1. CLIENT: I've been thinking about what you told me last week—you said I should grow up. You told me that before, but I wasn't able to listen. My husband has given me permission to grow up, too.
2. DR. Q: I didn't say grow up. I don't think I've ever said that to anybody. I said you had permission to be a woman, which is quite a different thing. Growing up is making progress, but being a woman means that your Adult takes over and you get well. [Information and Instruction]
3. CLIENT: Well, my husband said that when we first got married he needed me to be dependent on him, but now he doesn't need that any more, so I have his permission to become a woman.
4. DR. Q: How did your husband get so smart? [Open Question]
5. CLIENT: He's been here, too, in spirit at least. We talk over what happens here and he's learned a lot about it, so he understands.
6. DR. Q: Your mother was like your husband. She needed you, too. [Interpretation]
7. CLIENT: That's exactly right. She needed me to be dependent on her. (This puzzled Dr. Q, because that was mother's Parent giving directives to Clooney, tell-

ing Clooney to be dependent on her, a directive which Clooney carried into her marriage. But if the script theory was correct, it seemed there should also be an important script control coming from mother's Child. While Dr. Q was pondering this, Clooney changed the subject.)

8. CLIENT: Then you always talk about my bottom, and we know there was something that happened in the bathroom that I've never been able to remember.

9. DR. Q: Well, the scene I'm thinking of is a very common one. The little girl goes into the living room where mother is with her friends, and her diapers fall off and everybody says "Isn't that cute!" [Interpretation]

10. CLIENT: Yes, that happened to me.

11. DR. Q: And then the little kid gets very embarrassed and blushes, and maybe her bottom blushes, too, and that makes it worse because then everybody gets really interested and says: "Now look at that! That really is cute, ho ho ho." [Interpretation]

12. CLIENT: That's really the way I feel.

13. DR. Q: That has something to do with your taking your clothes off at a party. That's one way you know of making contact with people. (At this point Dr. Q drew on the blackboard. . . . It is the custom among transactional analysts to have a blackboard on the wall for the purpose of drawing such diagrams when occasion calls for them.)

14. DR. Q: This diagram shows the relationship between your Child and your husband's Parent. It was the same when you were growing up. Your mother's Parent needed you to depend on her, and your Child went along with that. So you see as far as that part of your marriage goes, your husband really fills in for your mother. [Instruction, also Interpretation]

15. CLIENT: That's right. I married him because he's like my mother.

16. DR. Q: Yes, but somehow your mother's Child must come into it, too. [Interpretation]

17. CLIENT: Oh, yes. She always smiled when something embarrassing happened or when one of us girls did something she thought was naughty. Then she would say: "But isn't it awful?"

18. DR. Q: It's very important to know whether she laughed or smiled first and then said "Isn't it awful?" or said "Isn't it awful?" first and then smiled. [Interpretation]

19. CLIENT: Oh, you mean if she let her Child out first and then apologized to her Parent, or talked with her Parent first and then let her Child out.

20. DR. Q: That's right. [Encourager]

21. CLIENT: I see what you mean. Well, she smiled first.

22. DR. Q: Oh, then she wanted you to do the things she couldn't do, and that really tickled her Child, but then she had to apologize to her Parent. That's exactly what you do: you're always apologizing to your Parent. You go ahead and do your mother's naughties for her, and then you keep saying: "What do I do about guilt feelings?" Like after your mother's Child encourages you to do something, her Parent moves in and clamps down on you. [Interpretation]

23. CLIENT: Yes, I know. But what do I do about the guilt feelings? (Berne, 1972, pp. 380–381)

The TA counselor in this case is quite active and directive. There is almost a complete absence of the attending skills; the predominant skill is interpretation with an extensive amount of instruction in the content of TA theory. Teaching is a common role in the TA approach. While this interview is not representative of all TA counselors, it does illustrate the emphasis on lifescripts, the roots of present experience in childhood, and the examination of important transactions of the client. The immediate situation at a party is related to earlier life events, thus attempting to bring past- and present-tense together. TA counselors tend to be confrontive and work on incongruities and discrepancies constantly.

Figure 12.2   *Structured Exercise for Practice in Transactional Analysis*

Transactional analysis involves a wide array of terms, concepts, and innovative methods. The following will provide one beginning set of activities to serve as a basis for study, which will later result in your being able to use some of the concepts of TA in your own counseling work.

1. *Getting in touch with significant parents, adults, and children.* This exercise is best completed with a friend also interested in learning about TA. However, it can also be helpful to sit down with a journal and write your responses as you look at yourself. Use the following questions for mutual discussion with your friend or for organizing your journal entries.
   a. What were your parents like? Particularly, can you specify incidents of critical parenting? Nurturing, loving parenting? Share the specific incidents that come to mind with your friend or journal.
   b. What adults did you particularly enjoy? Think especially of specific incidents where an adult (your parent or another) made good rational decisions in a mature fashion and solved problems. What did they do that you particularly admired?
   c. Think back on your own childhood. Give an example where you were the playful, creative child, the little professor, and the adapted child. Again, be as specific and concrete as possible.
   d. Look at your present life. What people do you see (children and adults) that play parent, adult, and childlike roles? What do they do in specific situations?
   e. Return to each of the preceding questions. Examine the giving and withdrawal of strokes.
2. *Getting in touch with yourself as parent, adult, and child.* Continue with your friend or your journal, but this time examine yourself in key situations during the past 2 weeks. Where were you behaving as an adult? a parent? a child? Again, be as specific as possible. Do you find any parallels between your behavior and that which you noted from past life? What is the nature of your present stroke economy?
3. *Elementary transactional analysis.* During the past week you undoubtedly had some especially pleasant interactions and, most likely, some that were unpleasant. Apply the parent-adult-child diagrams on page 340 and look at the transactions occurring between you and the other person. Classify your behavior and the behavior of the other as parent, adult, or child and determine whether the transaction was complementary, crossed, or ulterior. Give special attention to the giving or withdrawal of strokes.
4. *Elementary game or script analysis.* Study the important transactions you have identified above. Are any of them repeating patterns which resemble interactions you have had with others (or with the same person over and over again)? What is the sequence of the actions? Do they relate back to the significant adults, parents, and children in your own past history? What is the underlying pattern of the stroke economy?

Transactional analysis (TA) could be summarized as Freudian psycho-dynamic psychology (note the parallels between parent, adult, and child and id, ego, and superego, as well as the emphasis on past life experience relating to present-day functioning), with a more positive humanistic philosophy, and an emphasis on behavior and thought changes (manifested by emphasis on the ability of the person to change scripts and transactions and to make a difference in the world through action), served with Madison Avenue advertising "hype." In short, transactional analysis is viewed as an excellent example of a therapy that is based on solid theory, does not deny the complexities of human life through oversimplification, and shares these insights in an open way with the lay public. Through Eric Berne and his followers, we have learned much about, not only TA, but also about the need to educate our clients to cope with the environment.

Transactional analysis, as with all therapeutic and counseling theory, has limitations. The language of TA at times detracts from the theory and has resulted in TA not being taken as seriously as it might. TA is not known for a strong research tradition, but there are data on its effectiveness. And, just as with all other theories, TA is susceptible to variations of wild analysis and overly controlling and charismatic practitioners.

FAMILY THERAPY AND FAMILY EDUCATION

Just as transactional analysis caught the imagination of the public some 20 years ago, so has family therapy caught the interest and attention of professional counselors and therapists over the past 10 years. Clearly, the family is the place where the individual learns about his or her role in the world. Whereas transactional analysis typically seeks to help the individual cope with the family and the environment, the family therapy movement takes on the more complex task of changing the entire family environment.

Family Therapy Worldview(s)

No single definition of a family therapy worldview is readily available. The field is currently full of a blooming diversity of method, theory, and opinion. However, one dimension that unites the family movement and distinguishes it clearly from individual therapy is the belief that individuals must be considered in relation to the family system; furthermore, that family system is embedded and interrelated with a large array of neighborhood, cultural, and political systems. Each part of the array of systems, whether individual, family, or larger networks has impact on all other systems.

Within this systems framework, family therapists and family educators are quick to point out the importance of the therapist *within* the system. Whereas some individual therapists take a more linear view and consider themselves *outside* of the client system, family-oriented therapists recognize themselves as part of the system that they seek to restructure or change. But the views of how this restructuring or change should occur vary immensely. Let us consider some alternative constructions of the family movement.

Bowen (1978), for example comes from a psychodynamic orientation and gives extensive history to family genealogy and shows how family history determines what happens in the present of both the individual and the family. Patterson and associates (1975) have taken behavioral and cognitive-behavioral methods and applied them to the family. Patterson not only does therapy, but he is also deeply interested in family education as a mode of prevention of problems. Guerney (1977) originates in the person-centered, humanistic tradition and has developed many techniques for both therapy and family education.

However, the strategic/systems-oriented group of individual and family therapists (Erickson, (Haley, 1973); Haley, 1976; Lankton, 1980; Minuchin, 1974; Palazzoli, 1978; Satir, 1967; Weakland, Fisch, Waltzlawick, and Bodin, 1974; Watzlawick, Beavin, and Jackson, 1967; and Whitaker and Keith, 1981) represent a central trend in which the word *system* of relationships becomes central. Needless to say, the strategic/systems-oriented group is not a uniform group and some of the above therapists might object to being placed in the same paragraph with the others.

But, each member of the previously cited group has made unique and important contributions to a developing understanding that individuals grow and develop in a systems relationship to others. Those who adopt the family systems approach believe that change in families is likely to be the most powerful and useful lever for both individuals and their environments. The family itself may be viewed as a small system or network of relationships. What is often sought in the name of "change" is variation in fixed systems of family interaction rather than single change in one individual. Thus, a family with an acting-out delinquent child obtains therapy not only for the child, but also for the total family interactional system that is interrelated with the symptomatic child.

Some Central Theoretical Constructs of Family Therapy

While family therapy represents a very different approach from individual change, you will find that your understanding of individual counseling, skills, and theories helps prepare you for adding the family frame of reference to your thinking and practice. You may, however, find it useful if you modify your theoretical constructs around the concept of "change." Again, individual therapy usually is considered successful if the symptomatic client changes behavior. Family therapy seeks change in *systems of interaction.*

Bowen's Multigenerational Approach. Murray Bowen (1978) identifies two central forces in interpersonal functioning. The first is a movement toward individuality, the second a movement toward togetherness. In the psychody-namic summary on object relations theory, it was pointed out that our view of object relation's theory of infant development talks about two trends in mother-child interaction: (1) the desire for separation; and (2) the desire for attachment. Individuality may be roughly equated with the desire for separation and the to-getherness with the desire for attachment. Bowen adds to this framework the concept of *differentiation*, which he defines as the ability to become involved with others, while simultaneously remaining one's own self. The difficult task is the balancing of individuality and togetherness or separation and attachment.

As might be anticipated, Bowen believes that we develop our unique pat-terns of differentiation through our family relationships. Moving beyond much of object relations theory, he has suggested that even grandparents and great grandparents may be "living in the present" through the model of their lives and stories and cultural messages that have been passed down to family members. An illustration of the way in which we are personally influenced by long-term family messages was presented in Chapter 4 (pages 102–103) where Irish-American and British-American family messages were presented as conflicting patterns that may play themselves out *now* in one person's conflicting internal scripts or mes-sages. Bowen terms this process the *multigenerational transmission process*. As you may sense, one aspect of Bowenian family therapy is to engage the individual and the family in mapping out the intergenerational history of family messages. If you completed the exercise in family messages (Figure 4.4, page 104) you may un-derstand Bowen's concepts at more than a theoretical level. Your personal life style and beliefs are strongly determined by family history.

Once family multigenerational transmission processes are understood, the task is to change the cognitions and behaviors associated with this new aware-ness and to decide what message you as an individual want to pass on to others. With this brief introduction and an understanding of the individual therapy sys-tems of psychodynamic theory and cognitive-behavioral methods, you can im-plicitly generate some of the basics of Bowen's theory and method. The goal in the early stages of the interview and the therapy process is to bring the family to awareness of their history—and how it affects the present—and then to provide techniques to change the way family members think about and act on the past.

A major distinction in family therapy, of course, is that you are working with a *family* and not just an individual. In this case you have the potential to change and differentiate several individuals who can then work together to main-tain the change for the benefit of all.

Communication Approaches.   One route to family understanding is that of facil-itating clear and direct communication among family members. Satir (1967) and Bandler, Grinder, and Satir (1976) are illustrative of this approach. At issue is helping each person understand the worldview or construction of the other in the hope and belief that understanding will lead to change.

A Family Therapy Session*

The following typescript illustrates some possibilities within the family therapy session. For purposes of simplification, only a portion of one session dealing with the husband and wife is presented. At issue is the wife's frigidity and coldness as well as recognizing that two people, not one, have a problem with sexuality.

Typescript	*Commentary*
78. THERAPIST: Dave, you say you went to a movie and you felt close to Betsy for the first time in months.	This paraphrase encourages Dave to elaborate on the surface structure "felt close."
79. DAVE: Yeh, we were sitting on the sofa afterwards and Betsy actually snuggled up. It felt good.	
80. BETSY: Yeh, it was the first time we've touched naturally in ages.	At this point the couple was in relative synchrony or congruence.
81. DAVE: And then, I slowly reached down and touched her breast. She didn't move away. And then, suddenly she did and got angry with me.	The incongruity between Dave and Betsy is identified more concretely.
82. THERAPIST: Betsy, could you elaborate a bit on what was happening with you?	The therapist, through an open question, seeks the meaning of the incongruity to Betsy.
83. BETSY: Yeh, I felt good, then suddenly, for some reason, I tightened up. I really got ticked off at him.	

*While this therapist did not practice transactional analysis counseling, he found it useful to conceptualize the case in TA terms. The pattern of interaction at this point represents the games "frigid woman" and "uproar." (c.f., Berne, 1964, pp. 98–101) In this pattern the husband makes advances on the wife and is rejected. After several rejections a pattern has set in and he "sits back" for awhile. The wife relaxes a bit and feels that the husband is interested in her as a person rather than just for her body. When she has sufficiently relaxed, the husband approaches her naturally; she responds because of his naturalness, but when he stops thinking of her as a person and only thinks of her as a sex object (this being communicated via a variety of verbal and nonverbal means), she again rejects him. At the rejection, the game of "uproar" begins. The game of uproar is clearly demonstrated at Betsy: 86 and Dave: 88. Through careful questioning and examination of both past and present behavior, Dave and Betsy came to understand their patterns of interaction. A high point in the therapeutic process was when Betsy realized her "frigidity" was not frigidity, but was in reality a natural reaction to Dave's using her sexually. Once he sensed his pattern of action, Dave was able to change his approach as he discovered his aggressive actions and lack of sensitivity toward Betsy developed from fear of his own masculinity. Although TA was useful in conceptualizing this case, no TA language or methods were used. Many therapists will think of a case via one theoretical framework, but use the skills and techniques of another.

84. THERAPIST:	Dave, sounds like something happened suddenly, almost for no reason. Tell me a little more about what was happening with you.	The directive following the paraphrase is designed to lead to further concreteness.
85. DAVE:	I remember thinking just after I touched her breast and she didn't move away that "tonight might be the night." But it wasn't!	The deeper structure of Dave's thinking becomes apparent.
86. BETSY:	That's all you ever want is to use me for—sex. Ugh!	
87. THERAPIST:	Right now, Betsy, you seem to feel the same way to Dave that you felt last night. You're really angry.	The interview moves to present-tense interaction from the previous past-tense discussion. Betsy and Dave are reenacting, by analogy at this moment, their conflict of the preceding night.
88. DAVE:	Ah, she's just cold and can't stand sex. To hell with you! (Betsy starts crying)	The problem has moved from a "there and then" discussion to the "here and now." A special advantage of couple or family therapy is that the actual issues between people typically show themselves fairly rapidly. Thus the clinician is able to see before her or him the actual structure of the problem.
89. THERAPIST:	You're both angry and hurt right now. You're at the same place you were last night. What are you aware of in your bodies right now?	The reflection of feeling is followed by an important interpretation ("You're at the same place . . .") that connects the past and the present by pointing out that the problem is being replayed in the present. The present-tense open question concerning body feelings is a useful technique to understand emotional backgrounds of problems, and often builds later to more complete understandings.
90. DAVE:	I'm tight . . . my guts are circling. When Betsy looks at me like that, I feel lost.	
91. THERAPIST:	Say that to Betsy, but also tell her what you mean by "feeling lost."	It is important in family therapy that family members say important things to each other rather than to the therapist. "Feeling lost" is treated by the therapist as a surface structure sentence and the directive

92.	Dave:	Betsy, when you look at me and cry, I feel so guilty for what I've been doing to you. You're so important to me that I am terribly afraid of losing you.	
93.	Betsy:	I'm afraid of losing you too . . . why do we have these silly arguments?	
94.	Therapist:	What are you feeling in your body, Betsy? And what were you feeling when I first asked that question? Tell Dave, not me.	instructs Dave to tell Betsy in more concrete detail what is happening to him.
95.	Betsy:	My thighs were tight, I felt just like shaking. Then when he—I mean—you, Dave, said that, I felt a terrible fear. I really need you so much.	Open question, past and present tense. Note again the directive emphasizing that Betsy share her deeper meanings with Dave.

In the case of Dave and Betsy, we see a family system in which the two individuals interact with one another in a self-defeating circle. The pattern may be considered in the person-environment transaction frame. Dave's relationship with Betsy is produced by Betsy's relationship with him. Dave is Betsy's environment (which she partially produces through her reactions and actions toward him) and Betsy is Dave's environment (which he partially produces through his reactions and actions toward her). Family therapy differs from individual therapy in that the *system* of interaction rather than the individual is the target of change. Through examination of surface structure sentences and deeper meanings, Dave and Betsy studied their incongruities and differences, learned that they were a system interacting one with another, and were able to change their relationship.

What has been accomplished in this brief segment is a redefinition of the problem. Whereas, the problem definition at first was Betsy's so-called "coldness," the couple now realizes that their interaction is very much part of the problem. The focus changes from an "I" or "you" (Betsy) to a "we" (the couple together). The next task of the therapist will be to institute some change procedure. Methods of intervention in family therapy are almost as numerous now as in individual therapy. However, many of the methods of change are closely related to individual methods presented in this text, but always with the sophistication and complexity that a *system of individuals* presents. Whereas individual therapy seeks to act on individual "objects," the family therapist recognizes the flow between "objects within a system."

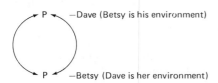

P —Dave (Betsy is his environment)

P —Betsy (Dave is her environment)

This same point is made in different language in Chapters 2 and 6, especially where issues of culture and person/environment transaction are stressed in individual work.

In this example, you may begin to see how one's perception and worldview are affected by the transaction with others, particularly family members. At times, understanding and better communication may be enough to stimulate change spontaneously. At other times, more effective and forceful techniques may be useful.

Strategic Approaches. Surprise and change are manifest in the strategic form of individual and family therapy. Perhaps the drama sometimes associated with this approach is best illustrated by the following individually oriented strategic approach of the distinguished psychiatrist, Milton Erickson. Here you will note the use of paradox and exaggeration, characteristic of Frankl's work.* Erickson was the master of helping individuals cope with their environments and is considered by many to be a pioneer in the family movement, particularly through his development of techniques of change:

> I decided that I could get this young man over his problem of entering this particular restaurant, and in that way I could help him over other fears, particularly his fears of women. I asked him how he felt about going to dinner at the Loud Rooster, and he said he would inevitably faint. Then I described various types of women to him: there is the young naïve woman, the divorcée, the widow, and the old lady. They could be attractive or unattractive. I asked him which was the most undesirable of those four. He said there was no question about it— he was quite afraid of girls, and the idea of association with an attractive divorcée was the most undesirable thing he could think of.
>
> I told him that he was going to take my wife and me out to dinner at the Loud Rooster and there would be someone else going along with us. It might be a young girl, a divorcée, a widow, or an old lady. He should arrive at seven o'clock on Tuesday. I said I would drive because I didn't wish to be in his car when he was likely to faint. He arrived at seven, and I had him wait nervously in the living room until the other person who would accompany us arrived. Of course I had arranged with an extremely attractive divorcée to arrive at seven-twenty. She was one of those charming, easily met people, and when she walked in I asked him to introduce himself. He managed to, and then I told the divorcée our plans. The young man was taking us all out to dinner at the Loud Rooster.
>
> We went to my car, and I drove up to the restaurant and parked the car in the parking lot. As we got out, I said to the young man, "This is a graveled parking lot. That's a nice level spot there where you can fall down and faint. Do you want that place, or is there a better one that you can find?" He said, "I'm afraid it will happen when I get to the door." So we walked over to the door, and I said, "That's a nice-looking sidewalk. You'll probably bang your head hard if you crash. Or how about

---

*If one views the clinical work of Erickson carefully and also examines his philosophy, there are many parallels between him and Frankl. Whereas Frankl experienced the concentration camp and its many confinements, Erickson was bound to a wheelchair for most of his life. Both surmounted their environments through action and helping others.

over here?" *By keeping him busy rejecting my places to faint, I kept him from finding a place of his own choosing.* He didn't faint. He said, "Can we get a table just inside by the door?" I said, "We'll take the table I picked out." We went clear across to an elevated section in the far corner of the restaurant. The divorcée sat beside me, and while we were waiting to give our order, the divorcée and my wife and I talked about matters that were over the young man's head. We told abstruse and private jokes and laughed heartily at them. The divorcée had a master's degree, and we talked about subjects he didn't know anything about and told mythological riddles.

The three of us had a good time and he was out of the swim and feeling increasingly miserable. Then the waitress came to the table. I picked a fight with her. It was a disagreeable, noisy fight, and I demanded to see the manager and then had a fight with him. While the young man sat there intensely embarrassed, the fight culminated with my demand to see the kitchen. When we got there, I told the manager and the waitress that I was ribbing my friend, and they fell in line with it. The waitress began to slam dishes angrily down on the table. As the young man ate his dinner, I kept urging him to clean up his plate. So did the divorcée, adding such helpful comments as "The fat's good for you."

He lived through it and took us home. I had tipped off the divorcée, and she said, "You know, I feel in the mood to go dancing tonight." He could only dance a little bit, having hardly learned it in high school. She took him dancing.

The next night the young man picked up a friend of his and said, "Let's go out to dinner." He took his friend to the Loud Rooster. After what he had been through there, nothing else was to be feared; the worst had happened, and anything else would be a welcome relief. He could also enter other buildings from then on, and this laid the groundwork for getting him over his fear of certain streets. (Haley, 1973, 68–69)

Perhaps the word "change" best summarizes the work of the strategic group. Watzlawick, Weakland, and Fisch (1974) have worked to codify the strategic ideas of Erickson and others and suggest the following four basic steps for producing change in families (which you will find once again closely resemble the five-stage model of Chapter 2). They emphasize that family therapy should: (1) define the family problem (often stressing that the problem is a problem of the family rather than one symptomatic individual); (2) determine what the family has done to resolve the problem (and give emphasis to find out in this process what has *not* worked); (3) establish family goals (here the strategic group points out that the family itself should determine goals, not the therapist—what works for one family may not for another), and (4) construct therapeutic interventions designed to disrupt the typical pattern of interaction sustaining the problem.

The models of strategic therapy typically do not stress rapport and structuring and are very unlikely to tell the client or family what to expect from therapy. Paradoxial instructions or directives may be used to antagonize the family in order to get them to work together "against" the therapist. Generalization techniques are important in this mode of family therapy, but the purpose of the technique may not be shared. This is in the belief that the therapist knows best and that cognitive understanding of "why" may interfere with unconscious assimilation of the change process.

Structural Approaches. Salvatore Minuchin (1974) perhaps has done more than any one other therapist to bring family methods to the popular limelight. He gives special study to the family system and has one technique that most family therapists use in some form or another, but he uses it most explicitly. For example, a family of four may appear with a "problem" of bulemia or anorexia in a female teenager. After a brief introduction, Minuchin often asks each individual to define the "problem." He uses listening skills in a very effective manner as he questions and paraphrases each family member's definition of the problem. One by one, he may draw out each family member's construction of the problem. Typically in this stage of the interview, each person talks about bulemia or anorexia and blames the teenager as *the* problem.

All family therapists seek to avoid the concept of "blame" and emphasize that there is "no fault"; the difficulties are simply a result of a system of relationships that need to be strategically changed or restructured. Minuchin (and most family therapists), moreover, do not accept one person as the problem. Minuchin would very likely say something like the following: "I've heard you say . . ." (and then he would summarize what he has heard), "but it is really not a problem of anorexia and 'Janet,' this is a family problem of interaction and our task is to restructure the family." Here he has changed the *structure* of the problem, hence the term "structural family therapy."

Structural family therapy is interested in changing the way the family is structured. This may mean changes in *power* and the degree of influence each member has in the family. The anorexic or bulemic, it is often found, has developed his or her symptoms as their only way of maintaining power and influence in the family. The teenager in the process of taking power has produced a strong impact on the family and the father and mother, who may, for example, be contemplating a divorce and may stay together for the "good" of their problem daughter.

Minuchin believes that each family is making the best adaptation possible

Salvatore Minuchin, M.D.

to a complex environment of family stress and conflict—the environment of the family may be the cause of difficulties due to a move to a new city or to the environmental context itself (school pressure, economic recession, a grandparent with cancer). Each family problem may result in one or more family members acting out in the form of anorexia, delinquency, failure in school, or sexual delinquency.

Many problem families are likely to be overly *enmeshed* and too involved with each other or overly *disengaged* and separate one from another. These concepts relate closely to object relations' attachment and separation or to Bowen's togetherness and individuality. It may be suggested that the constant repetition of these issues throughout several differing theories, although they use differing language systems, suggests that they are indeed very important ideas that you will want to learn thoroughly.

You will find that many clients or families you face present some variation of the patterns of attachment/togetherness/enmeshment or separation/overindividuation/disengagement. The goal, regardless of the language or theory you prefer is to involve the person(s) in a system of relationships that is adequately differentiated, but still related to others. In other words, your task is to facilitate a cognitive and behavioral balance of the individual or family in relation to the environment.

The therapeutic task with families is to restructure the power and rules of the family with the ultimate goal of balancing enmeshment and detachment through culturally appropriate boundaries between individuals. Important in this process is returning the family "hierarchy" to a situation where parents are in charge, rather than the children. Different cultures, of course, have different patterns of what is "close" and "too close" and may handle the issue of hierarchy very differently. You may recall that the British-American or Yankee family often has greater distance among members than many Jewish, Italian, or Black families. There is no one single "correct" balance.

Some Specific Techniques of Family Therapy

The family movement now has a vast array of techniques and methods to promote change. Many of these are family variations of individual techniques. Some of the important techniques of family therapy include the following.

Joining. Often the family therapist *joins* the family and metaphorically becomes a family member, participating in and naming some of the family rules and family structure. This joining by the therapist immediately changes the structure of the family and produces change on the spot, just as the introduction of a new child changes any family structure. If you use joining as a method of gaining rapport, cultural awareness and respect will be especially essential if you are to maintain an empathic attitude toward this family. In some groups of family therapists, joining means something close to becoming a family member; in other orientations, joining may be discussed as "joining the language system" of the family. Joining for others is a term close to empathic understanding and can be achieved by listening.

Figure 12.3 *A Role-Played Exercise in Family Therapy*

As a first step in this exercise you will need a role-played family with the following characters:

1. An acting out or mildly delinquent teenager.
2. An overly engaged, attached, enmeshed mother who is clearly overprotective.
3. A disengaged father, most concerned with his professional career.
   (Assume the mother and father were having mild marital problems until the teenager acted out.)
4. A younger sibling who wants more attention, but otherwise seems "normal."

Your task with this family is to engage in a rudimentary family therapy session. The structure suggested here is a combination of the several theories above, but will afford you with an opportunity to experience the drama and possibilities of the family therapy session.

STAGE 1. RAPPORT/STRUCTURING.

Because of the dynamics of having four people present, you may find you don't have the time to establish the smooth, easy rapport that you do with one individual. You may find yourself necessarily having to be more active. If so, simply begin by stating, "Glad to be with you; I understand, you've got something you'd like to talk to me about. Who'd like to go first?" Often the first person to talk is the spokesperson for the family and has some special power in the family system.

STAGE 2. DATA GATHERING.

After the first person has spoken, ask each person directly what her or his definition of the problem is. Listen carefully and use the basic listening sequence (BLS) to draw out the problem definition by carefully attending to each person. Once the definition is clear, summarize the family's problem definition . . . (most likely, the acting-out teenager in some way has been identified as "the problem"). But, then reframe or reinterpret this problem as, "This family indeed does have a problem, but it is not an individual problem, it is a problem of the way this family works together." Needless to say, use your own words and constructs for this reframing of the problem and change timing and wording to meet the needs of this unique family. Allow reactions to your reinterpretation, but hold to the problem as that of a total systemic interaction. If you wish, you may mirror verbals and nonverbals of some family members and thus join the structure of the family. In this role, you will gain some personal understanding and empathy for "your" family.

Spend some time searching for family strengths through a positive asset search. What has the family done right? Where does this family work well? You may also examine what has concretely *not* worked for them in their efforts at solution.

At this point, you can spend more time examining the rules and structures of the family and learning specifics of how this family functions. Some family therapists argue that problem definition should take 95 percent of your efforts. If the problem is well-defined, solutions will often present themselves clearly.

STAGE 3. DETERMINING OUTCOMES.

Use the BLS to identify a desired *family outcome*. Do not become trapped into an individually oriented goal for this family. Help the family search for a joint objective that offers something beneficial to each individual and to the total system. You may find your family engaging in irrational and faulty thinking patterns.

STAGE 4. GENERATING ALTERNATIVE SOLUTIONS.

At this point you are facing the challenge of selecting which therapeutic alternative to use with this family and, in the middle of the role play, you are likely beginning to understand that this model of helping, while in some ways similar to other models discussed in this book, is quite demanding in practice. For this exercise, the following alternatives are suggested, although you may wish to consider one of the techniques briefly summarized earlier:

a. Ask the family to sit down and *enact* a typical meal together. During this role-play note the seating arrangement and who speaks after whom. Comment on this and structure a change in seating and speaking order. As part of this process, you may find it helpful to ask the children to play "parent" and the parents to play "children."

b. Note a specific repeating pattern in the family. Comment briefly on that pattern then instruct the family deliberately to repeat that pattern and notice their behavior, thoughts, and feelings. This is a mild paradoxical directive. You may wish to expand this effort into a larger exaggeration.

c. Use circular questioning to uncover family "secrets." Then use positive reframing to encourage a more positive reaction to these secrets.

STAGE 5. GENERALIZATION.

Many family therapy orientations omit this stage. Almost any of the techniques suggested in this book for "homework" and followup can be used in family work. One simple technique that is often helpful is some variation of the mild paradoxical directive. During the coming week, direct the family deliberately to engage in some form of ineffective behavior and to report back to you the following week. If they group together and refuse to engage in your homework, you can be pleased that the group is "working *together* in their own interests" and you may comment on the "failure" of your intervention favorably. If the paradoxical intervention works, you may have new and valuable data for planning. In either case, you have kept the idea of therapy alive after the interview is over.

Enactment. This is another technique, similar to role-playing as it might be used in assertiveness training. But, in this case, you as therapist have the total family before you to role-play the problem situation. In this technique, you simply ask the family to enact (role-play) the problem so you can observe the family interaction. Changes may be produced and suggested by the therapist, but structural therapists do not emphasize specific behavioral change as much as the behavioral or cognitive-behavioral school. Added to enactment may be a paradoxical directive in which the therapist instructs the family to "continue what they are already doing" or to exaggerate the behavior. This may be extended into the following week via a "homework" assignment for the family.

Tracking. This technique involves careful listening to conversational patterns such as who listens to whom and in what order—similar in some ways to the communications example here. This, then, may be followed by pointing out to the family what is going on, suggesting an immediate reenactment of the transaction, and then perhaps joining the family in a way that previous patterns of tracking are impossible for them.

Restructuring Techniques. These techniques focus on relabeling problem behavior (sometimes through the positive asset search), changing who makes the decisions, suggesting different patterns of sitting at the dinner table, or changing the order of speaking. And, the family may be encouraged to discuss how they would like to structure their interactions and practice that role in the interview and then generalize that role during the coming week. This technique, of course, is similar to that of Kelly's fixed-role therapy in which the client plans an ideal role for the future and then acts on it.

Circular Questioning. This is a particularly useful exercise in assessment or intervention. Rather than ask individuals what they think about problems and interactions, you ask one member of a family member what he or she thinks someone else thinks. For example, the therapist might ask a child, "Bill, what does your father think about your mom's starting a new job?" If you had asked the father or mother the same question, the "family secret" might have been kept. Through circular questioning you can bring data into the open that everyone "knows," but doesn't talk about and isn't aware that others also know. Circular questions place behavior in a context and help family members see their part in the symptom of the "identified patient."

Reframing. Reframing is directly parallel to the microskill of interpretation. Here the family problem is reframed or renamed, often from a more positive and useful point of view. The very act of naming a problem as a "family problem" rather than an "individual problem" is itself a very important act of reframing. Family therapy has an array of conceptual methods of reframing, all of which center around helping the family to look at a problem differently. Again, you will see that the goal is *change* in a system that is stuck and immobilized. You might say that the goal of the family therapist is increased flexibility and intentionality for the family as a system. At the same time, a balance of change and stability will be needed in any family. The variety of reframing/reinterpretative and paradoxical techniques are many and the family group has honed them to a fine point. The several theoretical alternatives for the "positive asset search" (Chapter 7, page 187) are themselves a series of reframes that can be adapted to the family therapy approach. Reframing reality is much of what family therapy is about.

Other Techniques. *Accommodation* is parallel to empathy and is another word for acceptance of what is present in the family. *Mimesis* is the direct mirroring of the body language of one or more family members—plus observing which family members mirror each other's body language and in what sequence of unconscious control. This may be particularly helpful in joining the family or in understanding how a particular individual views a problem.

A variety of adaptations may be made in individual techniques discussed throughout this book. Family therapists may use Gestalt techniques, particularly the "hot-seat" exercise to bring out family dynamics more clearly; they may use the dereflection or appealing techniques of Frankl with some families—or, in fact, any individual technique that can produce *change* in the system of interactions.

Strengths and Limitations of Family Therapy

Through a whirlwind tour of the family therapy world, you may see that this group is developing as many alternative constructions of family therapy as individual theorists have for the solo interview. Clearly family therapy is alive and well and will be increasingly important in the years to come. One major difference and contribution of the family movement has been to make us aware of how clients may be viewed from a systems or interactional perspective. The person-environment point of view emphasized in this book is strengthened and clarified by the interactional frame of reference of family therapy.

At the same time, you may observe that if you have solid individual skills and understandings of key theories it is not that hard to at least enter into the family therapy worldview. Many, perhaps most, of the techniques are similar to and may even be derived from individual therapy. Frankl's paradoxical intention was mastered to a fine point by Milton Erickson and now is in frequent use in many family therapy sessions with apparent effectiveness.

A balance of change and stability for the family is sought with a similar blending of separation and attachment, enmeshment and boundaries. Individuals and their family systems are encouraged to differentiate and grow in flexible relationships one with another.

As with all other methods, family therapy has its limitations. Being new on the scene, it has the tendency (common among new therapeutic systems) to claim a special knowledge of *the truth*. This can result in overoptimistic and charismatic therapists whose zeal for the theory sometimes forgets basic ethical issues. For example, family therapists have been known to share videotapes of private sessions with colleagues without client permission. The practice of "wild analysis" is not restricted to those who employ analytic techniques. However, the major limitation of family therapy and its impact may be *individual therapists* who resist change and refuse to learn about family therapy theory and method. Family therapy will become increasingly important and stabilized in the years to come. It seems incumbent on all to learn more about this dynamic development.

Figure 12.3 (pages 354–355) presented a model family therapy exercise which you may want to try in role-played fashion.

An alternative to family therapy is directly working with the family to teach them how to solve their own problems.

Family Education

Recent years have brought forth an array of innovative and promising psychoeducation and developmental approaches to improving family functioning. Gordon's parent effectiveness training (1971) has been taught in widespread fashion through the country and follows a person-centered model. Dinkmeyer and McKay's *Systematic Training for Effective Parenting* (1983) uses an Adlerian model and is also in extensive use in many, many school systems. Patterson (1971)

Louise and Bernard Guerney, Co-Founders of Relationship Enhancement

and Gordon and Davidson (1981) have initiated an important and popular set of training programs for families from a behavioral point of view.

Relationship Enhancement. Relationship Enhancement (Guerney, 1977) is one example of a carefully constructed program for long-term couple and family growth. Relationship enhancement (RE) is based on the ideas of Carl Rogers, B. F. Skinner, and Harry Stack Sullivan and is primarily concerned with teaching skills and principles of living to individuals, couples, and families. Guerney has noted that RE focuses on skills that the individual can transfer to many settings, is a positive approach in that the emphasis is on what's "right" rather than on what's "wrong," and is programmatic in that a planned curriculum of exercises is provided for the participant. Psychoeducation often is provided in systematic, structured formats or curriculum units that are shaped and adapted to the needs and interests of particular individuals and families.

Basic skills taught in relationship enhancement include the "expressive mode," where people learn to state their views clearly and directly; the "empathic responder mode," where listening skills of understanding and acceptance are important; "the facilitator mode," where a third person coaches and guides the work of the expressor and empathic responder; and "mode switching," where individuals learn to work within the several modes of communication. It may be noted that the skills of RE closely relate to the skills of intentional counseling and therapy listed in Chapters 3 and 4 but have been selected and organized to meet family needs for more effective communication.

The relationship enhancement program begins with a carefully constructed intake interview that explains the general program and examines the commitment level of the participants. For those seeking remediation of long-term problems, accepting the idea that one can learn problem resolution through a course of study is sometimes a difficult step. Most people still expect psychotherapy and counseling when they face difficult family concerns.

Following the intake session, actual instruction in RE is undertaken. Guerney provides a series of exercises and structured techniques so that the concepts are fully mastered by the couple or family (or group of families, since RE can also be taught in large group situations). Important instructional procedures include demonstration and modeling of the RE skills by the instructor, moving each family group along according to its own ability to progress, and reinforcing success. Guerney stresses the importance of giving all family group members equal time, and suggests specific responses for the instructor in certain situations. For example, "troubleshooting" (T) responses are suggested when difficulties arise.

The following typescript illustrates the T or troubleshooting response, which may be described as reflections of feeling with a present-tense emphasis. The actions and techniques of the leader in this case are very similar to those identified previously in the discussion of family therapy. The major difference is that the skills of the leader are being made explicit and are shared directly with the family, rather than being held as a special type of expertise that belongs solely to professionals.

LEADER: [to responder, who is crying]: You're terribly hurt by the disappointment Bob [the husband] has expressed in you as a mother.

RESPONDER: [sobbing]: Yes.

LEADER: You want very much to be a good mother, and it's very painful to be told that you're not in some ways.

RESPONDER: [recovering somewhat, but still sobbing occasionally]: It's really not fair of him to think that. He comes home and doesn't know what's been going on. He sees me at a time when I've been putting up with all kinds of pressures all day from the two babies as well as Billy, when I'm exhausted and at my wit's end—when I've lost all the patience I have. Bob has no idea what it's like cooped up there all day with the three of them.

LEADER: You feel hurt; you're hurt not only by what Bob said about you as a mother, but also because it seems so unfair of him to judge you that way, not knowing what your life is like at home all day.

RESPONDER: Yeah! He knows I'm not like that most of the time—if I have some help or get some relief—if he's around to help out. It's an awful thing for him to say.

LEADER: It seems *very* unfair to you. You're very hurt and disappointed in him and angry that he would think that and say that.

RESPONDER: [no longer sobbing]: Yeah!

LEADER: I think it would be good if you would share those feelings with Bob now. Do you think you could clarify the last statement he made now, and take the expressive mode and tell him these feelings directly? (Guerney, 1977, p. 153)

Numerous other crucial trainer responses are taught within the RE program. Several specific formats for workshop instructions are provided, thus providing the therapist with a flexible program suitable for use in many settings.

Family Education vs. Family Therapy

Guerney has made some interesting comments about the parallels and differences between family education and family therapy.

> Now let's look at the distinction between family education and family therapy, starting from the other end—from the perspective of the therapist. The therapist may see the therapeutic task as being one of coming up with the quickest possible solutions to the family's problems. If this is the orientation of a family therapist, he will use whatever techniques—e.g. paradoxical instructions, conditioning, or whatever—that he thinks will do the job. It does not matter to such a therapist whether the family agrees with his diagnosis or not. It does not matter whether the family understands what is going on or not. It does not matter whether the family members learn new ways of thinking about their interpersonal environment and their own behavior. It does not matter whether the participants learn any new skills to carry into the future. . . .
>
> I think family therapists will come to recognize that in general, the most effective and efficient approach to changing the families is one in which the clients understand and can appropriately apply in their own daily lives, new attitudes, new skills, and new behavioral patterns which will allow them to resolve not only the problems which prompted them to come to therapy, but which will allow them to effectively prevent many future conflict problems and better resolve those which do arise. Such an approach is one which I would term skill training family therapy. (Guerney, 1984)

It may be seen that Guerney is suggesting that skill training family therapy from the psychoeducational model provides a more substantial form of treatment than family therapy. Research data on family therapy (c.f. Gurman and Kniskern, 1981) are at best equivocal. Guerney (c.f. Vogelsong, Guerney, and Guerney, 1983; Most and Guerney, 1983) is providing interesting and solid research data backing up his ideas. We should be looking forward to an interesting debate.

PSYCHOEDUCATION AND THE COMMUNITY

In the psychoeducational model, the counselor or therapist becomes a "teacher." Behavioral counseling and therapy, skills training, rational-emotive therapy, reality therapy, and transactional analysis all stress the importance of instructing clients in their theoretical orientation and provide specific guidelines for action. The psychoeducation model was initiated by Guerney and has been summarized as below:

> The practicing psychologist following an educational model is one whose work would derive directly or indirectly from a concern not with "curing" neurosis and not with eliminating symptoms (or complaints) and not with intellectual growth per se but rather with the teaching of interpersonal attitudes and skills which the individual applies to solve present and future psychological problems and to enhance his satisfaction with life. (Guerney, Stollak, and Guerney, 1971, p. 277)

The psychoeducational model, therefore, views the role of the psychological practitioner not in terms of abnormality (or illness) → diagnosis → perscription → therapy → cure; but rather in terms of client-dissatisfaction (or ambition) → goal-setting → skill-teaching → satisfaction (or goal achievement). Likewise, the client is viewed as a pupil rather than a patient. (Authier, 1977, p. 15)

Psychoeducation is possible at the individual level, in families, and in groups. Larson (1984) and Kurtz and Marshall (1983) provide useful overviews of the many alternatives available in psychoeducation or "training as treatment." Psychoeducation at its most sophisticated level, however, may be found at the organizational and community level where large numbers of individuals may be helped at once.

Two specific examples of major community-oriented change efforts will be presented here. The first is the work of Emory Cowen and his associates at the University of Rochester, the second that of Albert Stunkard and his colleagues at the School of Medicine at the University of Pennsylvania. It is important to note that work with a larger community that "makes a difference" is seldom completed by one person. Although Cowen and Stunkard are exceptional examples of leaders in community psychological change, they work closely with many others and offer them recognition for their joint efforts.

The Primary Mental Health Project

The Primary Mental Health Project (PMHP), was initiated 25 years ago in reaction to the fact that schools simply could not meet the increasing mental health needs of the community. The alternatives were either to increase mental health services—almost to an infinite degree—or to work toward prevention of problems. The PMHP has been immensely effective and successful. The project has been adopted by over fifty school districts and is in use in over 300 schools throughout the United States. (Cowen, 1980)

Major projects, however, usually have small beginnings. For example, in response to an identified need by one psychologist in one school in Rochester, New York, a small pilot project was begun. The first task was to identify "problem children" before problems really were resolved. Then, paraprofessionals from the community were trained to work with the children under the supervision of professionals. The project continued for 11 years in just the one school, and data gradually revealed the success and value of the program.

From 1969–1973, the program expanded throughout the Rochester school system. But gathering data about the effectiveness of programs is not enough. Implementation of meaningful programs also means political action and awareness of the complexities of working in a major city. A psychologist might be conducting therapy with a young child in the morning, but might find him- or herself meeting with a school board member in the afternoon, and then presenting a workshop on counseling skills in the evening. The variety of tasks completed by psychologists and counselors on the PMHP team is an outstanding illustration of the role of the psychologist and counselor of the future. *One* aware-ness, *one* expertise, *one* set of theories can never be enough if the profession is to meet the mental health needs of those whom we would serve.

From 1973 to current time, PMHP has evolved toward national dissem-ination of its ideas. Yet, it is not a fixed system, seeking to impose one working program on every school. PMHP intentionally works with each school and pro-gram to help them design unique methods and interventions. PMHP has specific action steps that it uses in each new setting; they are summarized here in brief form:

1. *Data gathering and goal setting.* PMHP staff start with gathering information from mothers of first grade children, group psychological evaluations, classroom ob-servation, and teacher judgment about children. Particularly important at the first stage is the opinion of the teacher who usually refers the child. However, all screening data are brought together at an initial assessment meeting that includes all relevant school personnel and often involves parents as well. At this session, specific action plans are made.
2. *Initial treatment.* Paraprofessional aides are used at the first step of treatment un-der the direction of professionals (see the debate about the use of paraprofes-sionals in helping on pages 395–397). Aides usually work half-time and carry a case load of ten to fourteen children.
3. *Communication* between and among school professionals, mental health staff, and other relevant individuals is stressed. Without continued efforts at communica-tion, even the effective program can become isolated and lose "political clout" and personal effectiveness.
4. *Followup and training/consultation.* PMHP constantly supervises and consults with the aide, the teacher, and others and modifies the treatment plan to meet specific client needs. Data on effectiveness of treatment with one child or an entire school may be collected.

The role of the counselor or psychologist in PMHP does not ordinarily focus on one to one treatment. Rather the staff member acts on the many ther-apeutic, psychoeducational, training, consultation, and research activities out-lined in this book. In effect, PMHP does "everything at once." It is a demanding role for the professional, but it is exciting and constantly satisfying. With the change of program allowed in this type of community intervention, the chances of a professional or aide "burning-out" and giving up are greatly reduced. PMHP includes change and involvement as a natural part of the program.

The program has published over sixty studies on its effectiveness. Among the many interesting findings is the fact that children seen once a week tended to do better than those seen daily. (This led to more emphasis in the pro-gram on spaced versus intensive treatment and also allowed seeing more chil-dren.) The child-aides in the program tended to grow in satisfaction and therapeutic ability. Perhaps the most critical and potentially chilling finding is that children who experience a problematic family background (such as, exces-sive pressure on the child, lack of educational stimulation in the home) *and* the largest number of trauma in the growth process (for example, divorce, abuse, death, major family status change) tend to have the most severe problems and it is difficult to change life patterns. This finding, itself, suggests the need for new and forceful psychoeducational and treatment opportunities that extend beyond the school to the families and to the total community itself. It may be predicted that Cowen's PMHP project is still in the incubation stage. He and his colleagues have a solid beginning, but it appears to be just that . . . a beginning.

The Community and Health

Whereas the PMHP is concerned with emotional conditions, the Stunkard, Felix, and Cohen (1984) Pennsylvania County Health Improvement Program (CHIP) is concerned with general health, of both a psychological and physical nature. Increasingly, you will find psychologists and counselors interested in the contributions that the field can make to physical as well as emotional health.

CHIP has an ambitious goal: "the mobilization of an entire community to improve its health." Lycoming County in Northern Pennsylvania has a population of 118,000. Efforts in CHIP were focused on reducing five risk factors: smoking, hypertension, elevated cholesterol, obesity, and low physical activity. It should be readily apparent that underlying each of these conditions are critical psychological factors.

The method of CHIP obviously is quite different from the PMHP discussed above, yet many of the same principles apply. Important among these are working carefully and effectively with individual clients, bringing in helping professionals and enabling them to work with many others in new ways, and keeping the sociopolitical context constantly in mind.

One of the major efforts of CHIP centered on using mass media such as television, radio, and newspapers to get their health message out to the community. The media campaign introduced the program and was followed by specific action programs focused on treatment of different issues. Within the period 1980–1983, CHIP presented twenty-one exercise and walking classes, eighteen sessions on blood pressure measurement and monitoring, ten weight-loss programs, seven smoking cessation efforts, and two nutrition classes. Contact with industry and schools supplemented the program. The health community, in effect, became allied in a major program of psychological and medical health prevention.

Although the program is still too new for comprehensive evaluation, a number of research studies have been completed. For example, among the many specific results of the weight-loss programs was that participants lost an average of between 7 and 13 pounds. A smoking prevention program reduced the number of high school students smoking from the usual 15 percent to 5.2 percent. A large number of adults have been screened for blood pressure and other risk factors. It will be interesting to see if the community-based program can indeed produce changes in life span.

The two programs generated by Cowen and Stunkard and their colleagues are impressive examples of the mental health professions operating at their highest levels of potential. Here we see all aspects of the cube—individual, group, and family treatment—applied to the community. We see direct and indirect treatment and the effective combination of professionals, paraprofessionals, and lay people in working combinations. Critical to both programs is contact with the media, so important in today's society. The programs focus on remediation of problems, prevention, and development of human potential. Each aspect of the system has been ably covered.

CONSCIOUSNESS-RAISING THERAPIES AND FEMINIST THEORY

It can be argued that the women's movement has done more for the mental health of women than all the therapies in this book. Furthermore, it likewise can be stated that the Black awareness movement has vitally enhanced the mental health of Blacks and also initiated the first awareness among many other underserved groups, leading them also to action.

The raising of personal consciousness requires a change in the way an individual views his or her world. Feminist and Black awareness counselors are concerned with reconstructing the way a Black or a woman views reality. Both are concerned with developing full humanness for individuals *and* groups who have been denied access to a positive worldview. A major goal of the consciousness-raising therapies is to develop awareness of the impact of social and economic forces on the social group (for example, women, Hispanics, Blacks, Asians, handicapped) *and* on the individual. With this awareness, social change becomes important and the client may be enlisted in the process of changing the environment of racism, sexism, ageism, or other forms of oppression.

These consciousness-raising therapies have been included as the closing portion of this chapter as they are the newest and one of the most promising developments in the helping field. Their concepts are gradually becoming more widely accepted as part of effective practice regardless of one's theoretical orientation. These therapies are concerned with extending the direction of the individually oriented methods earlier in this chapter to larger social movements as well. Issues of women, Blacks, and other groups now serve as a standard part of the curriculum in most counseling and therapy training programs. This fact was not so in 1980 when the first edition of this text was completed. A short section on this topic cannot cover all issues and suggested further readings are included at the conclusion of this chapter.

As a beginning step toward understanding of these issues, let us turn to general theories of consciousness-raising as a mental health concern.

Cultural Identity Development

Can a white counsel a Black client? Can a man counsel a woman? The answer to this frequently asked question is not a simple "yes" or "no." The way in which culturally different people identify themselves and their worldview appears to be critical in answering this question. The most highly developed models of cultural identity have been generated by Blacks (Cross, 1971; Jackson, 1975) and Asian-Americans (Sue and Sue, 1971).

A five-stage model of cultural identity has been generated by Atkinson, Morten, and Sue (1979) and is summarized in the following paragraphs. Many believe women and even white ethnic groups follow roughly the same patterns, and examples are included representing women who may be going through similar stages.

Stage 1. *Conformity.* At this level, the group believes in the predominant cultural values to which it is exposed. Thus, women might tend to believe and support the idea that it indeed is a "man's world" and talk about their sons as "all boy." A Black or Asian client may think that "white is right" and feel negatively toward people of his or her own race or background (for example, "My people should work harder").

Stage 2. *Dissonance.* The group or individual finds that things are not necessarily as he or she thought they were. Inconsistencies between what one is capable of doing in society and what one is allowed to do because of racism, sexism, or ageism may become apparent. The individual may start to question previously held values and feel a need to confront these issues of dissonant discrepancies.

Stage 3. *Resistance and Immersion.* The individual or group synthesizes awareness of societal incongruity and reacts with anger and mistrust. Extensive efforts of women and minorities to combat oppression are characteristic of this stage. Hatred of men or whites may be manifested. The group begins to focus on their own cultural interests.

Stage 4. *Introspection.* Individuals again become confronted with discrepancies. Women may find that some men are understanding and supportive. A Native American may find allies for goals among whites. Increased individuality may occur and the person may find herself or himself facing divided loyalties when facing the internal versus the external group.

Stage 5. *Articulation and Awareness.* The individual finds satisfaction in cultural or sexual identity: "I am Black and proud of it"; "I am woman." The individual works from a base of personal and group satisfaction to challenge and to work with the predominant system. Hispanics, proud of themselves, work with the majority, but from a worldview of strength and pride. Women may like and enjoy men, but own their own space and make their own decisions.

If you are working with a client of a different sex or race from you, he or she has some identity (or set of identities) within this framework of identity development. Clearly you cannot work fully effectively as an outsider to the group with clients at Stage 3 (Resistance), and it will be somewhat difficult to work with those at Stages 2 and 4. Some would question whether or not you should counsel any client of a different sex or race if that individual is at Stage 1 (Conforming to "the system")—the issue, they say, is to refer that client to a person of a similar cultural or sexual background to facilitate their development and change. It would seem that all could work with a Stage 5 individual and both help such clients and learn from them. However, Sue emphasizes that the counselor's worldview is critical. It would be very difficult for a Stage 1 counselor to work with a Stage 3 client. You as a prospective therapist with a client different from you must learn about the group—be it women, minorities, or others.

Derald Wing Sue

In short, the client's worldview must be considered. And once you understand that worldview, you may then ask yourself the question "Am I personally, professionally, and culturally prepared to work with this client?" The answer to that question lies in your own cultural and sexual identity and how it is reflected in your worldview.

Sue (1981) gives special attention to internal and external locus of control. Does the client attribute his or her problem to the "individual" or to "society" and the environment? Research clearly indicates that many nonwhite and female clients attribute their difficulties externally—they are keenly aware of problems that society brings to them. The concept of focus (Chapter 3) as a microskill is helpful in understanding and dealing with this issue. For example, Berman (1979) compared Black and white counselor trainees viewing video examples of client problems. The trainees were asked to indicate what they would say next to the client. White males tended to ask questions, white females to reflect feelings and paraphrase, and Blacks tended to give advice and directions. More importantly, Blacks identified the problem as being in society rather than the individual while whites attributed the problem to the individual. Each tended to use the microskill of focusing differently (whites tend to focus on individuals while minority groups on the cultural-environmental context). Atkinson, Marujama, and Matsui (1978) replicated these findings with Asian clients.

Thus, you may expect certain female clients and those of varying racial or ethnic backgrounds to attribute responsibility for their problems differently. Using the microskill of focus, you can identify *how* the client is constructing the problem as internally or externally located. Ballou (1984) believes that feminist therapy deals with the issue of external and internal focus of control in a "both/and position." By this, she states that one needs to be in touch with both positions of control and that separation of the two ultimately may not be wise or possible.

Sue (1977) suggests that microskills need to be used differently with clients of different cultures and those who may have differing levels of consciousness concerning their sexual or ethnic identity. Generally speaking, passive listening approaches (the attending skills) may be viewed with suspicion by those clients who are of differing cultures from your own. Honest self-disclosure, directives, and suggestions may be treatments of choice. Pointing out and helping client's clarify discrepancies in their thinking (confrontation) may be especially helpful, but you must ordinarily have a solid relationship and understand the unique cultural surround of that client.

In the early stages of counseling, it may be helpful to join the client by focusing on the cultural/historical and environmental issues. However, ultimately you are working with an *individual* and you must not fall into cultural or theoretical stereotyping. You will want to focus on how the client before you relates as an individual to the environment. Successful consciousness-raising therapy most often requires that the individual come to terms with both personal and group identity issues.

The theories discussed in the preceding sections provide general guidelines: the theory that follows is specifically oriented to Blacks.

Black Identity Development Theory

Jackson (1975) has proposed a four-stage developmental theory describing how consciousness grows and changes in Blacks. He suggests that diagnosis of consciousness level is essential if a counselor is to work effectively with any client whether they are of similar race or not. What clearly is implied by Jackson's theory is that many nonBlacks will likely be ineffective in working with some Blacks. Furthermore, Black therapists can be expected to have some difficulties themselves with Black clients who have differing worldviews from their own. As such, members of specific groups themselves can profit from understanding these theories.

Stage 1. Acceptance. At this stage, the Black individual thinks of him or herself as "nonwhite." Personal identity is defined by the "other." White may be construed as the correct way of being. This client is likely to be subservient and highly cooperative when working with a white counselor. However, it is at this point that referral to a Black counselor may be most needed and most useful. The stereotype of the "Uncle Tom" who pleases whites is sometimes used to describe this increasingly rare form of Black consciousness.

Stage 2. Resistance. The Black person goes through a critical transformation and recognizes that being Black is an identity in itself. The individual encounters Blackness and its full meaning. At this stage, some individuals experience much anger and may directly refuse to work with a white counselor. The developmental task of this stage is a personal and cultural identity.

Stage 3. Redefinition. The development of awareness of Blackness continues. However, at Stage 2, the Black awareness focused on separation of Black from white, and personal identity is still formed by reaction against whiteness rather than a truly

Bailey Jackson, III

proBlack orientation. At Stage 3, the Black individual may turn more fully away from white culture and become totally immersed in Black history and the Black community. At this point, whites are somewhat irrelevant. The developmental task is the establishment of a firm Black consciousness in its own right.

Stage 4. *Internalization.* The individual becomes a *Black person with pride in self and awareness of others.* This individual makes use of the important dimensions of all stages of development and thus recognizes and accepts the worthwhile dimensions of white culture, fights those aspects that represent racism and oppression, separates self for pride in self and culture, and integrates all the stages in a transcendent consciousness.

Jackson is quick to state that each stage has a special value in personal development. He would argue that all but the first stages are valuable places for a Black person to spend her or his life. While there may be seeming advantages in the fourth level of consciousness, this level involves a division of consciousness that makes action in a racist society sometimes more difficult than if one were at a different level of consciousness. Given the racism and oppression that exists in the United States and throughout the world, we must recognize the validity of more than one relevant state of being.

For counseling, whether one is Black, white, or of another race, it seems critical to maintain awareness of distinctions of cultural identity development. Jackson's concepts have been most useful in understanding personal and group differences.

Feminist Therapy

Shall we attribute the problem to the individual or to the societal/cultural context? Does therapy seek to develop independence or interdependence? Is the therapist an authority figure over the client or an equal in the search? Shall the client adjust to the world as it is or shall the client take personal and group action to work to eliminate oppression? The second alternative in each case, of course, speaks to feminist therapy.

> Feminist therapy holds that traditional systems of psychotherapy are in serious error which stems from traditional sexist assumptions about women. Therefore, research paradigms, personality theory, clinical practices . . . are all suspect. . . . The feminist orientation to therapy is eclectic, endorsing theoretical positions which postulate external factors as causative in the client's problems . . . The client's strengths rather than her weaknesses are emphasized . . . An egalitarian relationship between therapist and client is demanded by feminist therapy. (Ballou and Gabalac, 1984)

It may be readily seen that many of the constructs and theories discussed in this book are open to feminist critique. Furthermore, the structural parallels between feminist therapy and the Black or Asian identity development movements may be clearly seen. All experience the common issue of oppression and the need to find a new group and individual place in society. However, it should be equally clear that the movement toward women's rights is distinct and separate from movements toward more extensive rights and equal treatment for culturally different peoples. Each group has its own struggle and unique set of cultural/historical factors.

Ballou and Gabalac (1984) have summarized the major content areas of feminist therapy. In outline form, they are:

1. *Egalitarian relationship.* The feminist therapist considers herself as a partner with the client and values women and their need for mutual support and exploration. Self-disclosure of one's own personal experiences as a woman is a particularly important part of the therapeutic process.

Mary Ballou

2. *Use of community resources.* Therapy does not end with the completion of an interview. Many clients are referred to women's support groups, community action work, legal aid, and other relevant community services.

3. *An active, participatory counseling style.* Feelings are considered important, but confrontation of discrepancies in the client and between the client and society are important. An example of this might be the client who is full of conflict. The therapist would work with a conflicted client to understand emotions, but also confront the client with the need for growth and resolution. While the therapist may be warm and supportive, a gradual move to independent thought is emphasized. The therapist is likely to use most of the techniques discussed in this book (such as, assertiveness training, Frankl's dereflection, dream analysis, and so forth), but will do so with an awareness of the feminist context of the helping process.

4. *Information giving.* A strong educational component exists in feminist counseling. The client may be instructed in social/historical facts concerning sexism and the impact of cultural conditioning. Sex-role analysis (Carter and Rawlins, 1977) may be used so that women can understand how they have become culturally conditioned to respond in certain ways.

5. *Personal validation.* Many women come from oppressed situations where they have little or no awareness of their own inherent personal worth. Feminist therapy seeks to validate the individual as a unique and valuable person.

A particular value conflict within feminist theory focuses on the issue of when and how women should be confronted with issues of sexism. Clearly, a fragile individual could be overwhelmed and disturbed if suddenly confronted with the social facts of her life. Marriages can be broken through the anger that often comes as a client moves from lower to higher levels of feminist consciousness. One group believes that traditional therapy is more appropriate for the "traditional woman" and that feminist therapy can be used later when the individual has achieved some gains. Alternatively, some see difficulty and personal pain as a necessary part of the route toward a larger, evolving feminist consciousness and would seek to bring all women to a feminist awareness.

Feminist theorists, as the rest of society, may differ on issues of abortion,

Nancy Gabalac

the degree of need for various social/political actions (Equal Rights Amendment, free daycare), the place of lesbians in the larger feminist movement, and the proper relationship of men and women.

This brief summary of feminist therapy illustrates that a clearly articulated alternative approach to counseling and therapy is evolving. The following typescript from an interview conducted by Mary Ballou illustrates some of the issues and the therapeutic approach that one might find in this orientation. You will note that the method here is quite different from other theories to helping. Particularly, consider the mutual exploration of both therapist and client and the manner in which cultural factors undergirding the interview are present.

COUNSELOR: In our first meeting last session you gave me information about your history, current life, focus of concerns and your worldview. We clarified your feminist values orientation and your wish to explore your career/family conflicts as well as the options open to you and your perceptions and feelings about them. I shared with you some information about my orientation to counseling and my feminist worldviews. We also agreed to work together for six sessions and then reevaluate. I am wondering what kind of reactions you have had to our first session and in the intervening time?

CLIENT: Well, there, my reactions are complex and many. I felt easy with you and your explanation of why you needed particular information or why you were suggesting certain things, like the contract, made sense and I relaxed. It was easy to tell you of my history, development, and current confusion. I felt relief that you did not see me as sick or incompetent. It helped when you suggested that many women face similar issues and can resolve them and in different ways. I felt supported, understood, and not trivialized as I often have when I have raised these issues before. Also I felt hopeful that I was not alone but at the same time the options would be mine, not standard sexist or feminist ideology about what women should do.

COUNSELOR: Those reactions are certainly complex and well thought out as well as positive. Were there any other reactions that were less clear or troublesome?

CLIENT: There's one but it is a bit vague. It's, well, I don't know, aha, well, how to think about our interaction. This is not like the counseling I had years ago which was more removed and professionally distant, but it is not like my friends in the feminist support group either.

COUNSELOR: Is there a context or relationship that it is similar to for you.

CLIENT: Perhaps it is like my colleagues with whom I do joint work in the research grant, but in our sessions there seems more room for me and my needs. And it is sort of like the feelings I had with the Licensed Nurse practitioner who worked with me in the home-birth of my last child, but not so focused. But there really is no other model which fits this experience very closely.

COUNSELOR: So our interaction does not fit with your past experiences very well. How is that for you?

CLIENT: Well, I am unsure about how to relate with you. Like do I invite you to lunch, ask personal questions, or treat you like an expert or boss?

COUNSELOR: So the role and boundaries are unclear and, am I right, unsettling?

CLIENT: Yes, yes to both, and I am sort of anxious about it.

COUNSELOR: It is a bit difficult to feel comfortable in an interaction when the roles, boundaries, and expectations are undetermined, unknown, and unexplored. It is similar to being in a new territory. We can talk about our relationship and its boundaries now if that would be useful to you.

CLIENT: Yes. I think it would be.

COUNSELOR: O.K. we will do that—but first I would like to focus on our process for a moment because I think it relates to your general issues in the career/marriage conflicts. I wonder if you would have volunteered this discomfort in our relationship if I had not asked again about your reactions after you told me the positive and clear ones? I also wonder if withholding confusion and/or personal discomfort in relation to others is a pattern for you.

CLIENT: That observation is very accurate, withholding my own discomfort and meeting others' needs in the family and requests on the job are patterns of mine.

COUNSELOR: So our interaction here has just reproduced your general characteristics of giving others' feelings, needs, requests more importance than yourself. What are your thoughts and feelings about that?

CLIENT: It embarrasses me, I don't think I should do that but it is such a habit. Also I guess it angers me its such a self-defeating pattern. I seem to do it naturally.

COUNSELOR: Do you see any connection with this pattern and women's sex role ascribed behavior?

CLIENT: I feel an intuitive rightness but have not made a sex-role linkage. Sexist conditioning would of course affect communication patterns.

COUNSELOR: It is an important point and one we might want to pursue more fully. The novel *A Room of One's Own* illustrates the issues quite well. Perhaps you might read the book and then we can discuss your reactions and any possible relevance to your life. But I interrupted before. Should we now pursue this or return to discussing our relationship, boundaries and expectations? (Mary Ballou, 1984)

ADVANTAGES AND LIMITATIONS OF CONSCIOUSNESS-RAISING THERAPIES

The consciousness-raising therapies have been summarized and illustrated. While each cultural identity group has its distinct needs and style, there do appear to be some overlapping factors in consciousness-development and perhaps even in theories and methods of therapy. While feminist therapy is at present the most clearly identified and articulated change strategy, it is not a large step to suggest that certain aspects of feminist theory are relevant to what may become a large body of literature and theory on specific methods of helping various cultural and ethnic groups.

All therapy is concerned with the uniqueness of the individual. Originally, therapeutic theory and research gave little attention to cultural differences. But, the consistent and insistent emphasis on respect for unique human potential suggests that feminist and racial/ethnic identity theory will become more important over time as the field becomes increasingly aware of cultural, ethnic, and sexual differences relating to the helping process.

The limitations of this newest approach to therapy, which is still in the state of clear definition, cannot be accurately stated at this time. The concepts of Black identity theory, for example, suggest that much of our present systems of therapy are incomplete and perhaps more limited than we would like to admit. The feminist alternative also presents a strong challenge to many of the ideas in this text. The consciousness-raising theories, of course, are subject to the same limitations of overly convinced and charismatic practitioners who may force their ideas on an unready client. Yet, the very nature of these theories suggest that this type of forcefulness is alien to the goals and desires of the theory. The contributions of this group of therapies will become increasingly important over time.

SUMMARY OF THIS CHAPTER

The content of this chapter is diverse and challenging. It represents a summary of one relatively well-established theory (transactional analysis), the burgeoning family therapy field, two examples of dynamic community interventions, and the challenge of the consciousness-raising therapies.

The central objectives in this chapter are to:

1. *Define a systems worldview* in which change efforts are focused on transactions and interactions as compared to individual change. The cube model provides a system to organize the alternative interventions available to you.

2. *Outline the key constructs and techniques of transactional analysis.* Important constructs in this section include: transaction, the four ego states (such as, "I'm O.K., you're O.K."), life scripts, and methods of script analysis.

3. *Summarize the family therapy movement and present some beginning techniques.* Important theories presented were: Bowens' multigenerational approach, communication methods, and strategic/systemic concepts. The key theoretical concept stressed was the parallels between separation and attachment, individuality and togetherness, and disengagement and embeddedness. It was suggested that a balanced, differentiated individual and family is an appropriate goal. Several family therapy techniques were presented.

4. *Discuss family education as an important alternative/supplement to family therapy.* Relationship enhancement was presented as a unique and important route to helping families through teaching them skills.

5. *Discuss community psychology as an integrative model for the practice of counseling and therapy.* Examples of Cowen's work in the schools and Stunkard's in a total community illustrate what can be done when therapeutic, counseling, and psychoeducational interventions are used in concert within the organizations and the community.

6. *Summarize new thinking in the consciousness-raising therapies.* Clients coming to us from different cultures are highly likely to construe the world in a manner far different from that which is often assumed in traditional theories of helping. Identity theories and feminist theory offer new directions for the future that may make it possible for older theories to expand and adapt their thinking as they meet this new intellectual challenge.

REFERENCES

ATKINSON, D., M. MARUJAMA, and S. MATSUI. "The Effects of Counselor Race and Counseling Approach on Asian American's Perception of Counselor Credibility and Utility." *Journal of Counseling Psychology,* 1978, *25,* 76–83.

ATKINSON, D., G. MORTEN, and D. SUE, *Counseling American Minorities: A Cross-Cultural Perspective.* Dubuque, IA: W. C. Brown, 1979.

AUTHIER, J., "The Psychoeducational Model: Definition, Contemporary Roots and Content," *Canadian Counsellor,* 1977, *12,* 15–22.

AUTHIER, J., K. GUSTAFSON, B. GUERNEY, and J. KASDORF, "The Psychological Practitioner as a Teacher: A Theoretical-Historical and Practical Review," *The Counseling Psychologist,* 1975, *5,* 31–50.

BALLOU, M., Interview Transcript (Manuscript). Boston: Northeastern University, 1984.

BALLOU, M. and N. GABALAC, *A Feminist Position on Mental Health.* Springfield, IL: Thomas, 1984.

BANDLER, R., J. GRINDER, and V. SATIR, *Changing With Families.* Palo Alto: Science and Behavior Books, 1976.

BERMAN, J., "Counseling Skills Used by Black and White and Male and Female Counselors," *Journal of Counseling Psychology,* 1979, *26,* 81–84.

BERNE, E., *Transactional Analysis in Psychotherapy.* New York: Grove Press, 1961.

BERNE, E., *Games People Play.* New York: Grove Press, 1964.

BERNE, E., *What Do You Say After You Say Hello?* New York: Grove Press, 1972.

BOWEN, M. *Family Therapy in Clinical Practice.* New York: Aronson, 1978.

CARTER, D., and E. RAWLINS, eds., *Psychotherapy for Women.* Springfield, IL: Thomas, 1977.

COWEN, E., "The Primary Mental Health Project: Yesterday, Today, and Tomorrow," *The Journal of Special Education,* 1980, *14,* 133–154.

CROSS, W. "The Negro to Black Conversion Experience," *Black World,* 1971, *20,* 13–25.

DINKMEYER, D., and G. MCKAY, *Systematic Training for Effective Parenting (STEP).* Circle Pines, MN: American Guidance Service, 1976/1983.

GORDON, S. and N. DAVIDSON, "Behavioral Parent Training." In A. Gurman, and D. Kniskern, eds. *Handbook of Family Therapy.* New York: Brunner/Mazel, 1981, 517–555.

GORDON, T., *Parent Effectiveness Training.* New York: Wyden, 1971.

GOULDING, M. and R. GOULDING, *Changing Lives Through Redecision Therapy.* New York: Brunner/Mazel, 1979.

GUERNEY, B., JR., *Relationship Enhancement: Skill Training Programs for Therapy, Problem Prevention, and Enrichment.* San Francisco: Jossey-Bass, 1977.

GUERNEY, B., JR.,   Personal Communication to Author, 1984.

GUERNEY, B., JR., G. STOLLAK, and L. GUERNEY,   "The Practicing Psychologist as Educator: An Alternative to the Medical Practitioner Model," *Professional Psychology,* 1971, *2,* 276–282.

GUERNEY, B., E. VOGELSONG, and J. COUFAL,   "Relationship Enhancement Versus A Traditional Treatment." In D. Olson and B. Miller, eds. *Family Studies Review Yearbook. Vol. I.* Beverly Hills: Sage, 1983, 738–756.

GURMAN, A. and D. KNISKERN,   "Family Therapy Outcome Research: Knowns and Unknowns." In A. Gurman and D. Kniskern *Handbook of Family Therapy.* New York: Brunner/Mazel, 1981, 742–776.

HALEY, J.,   *Uncommon Therapy: The Psychiatric Techniques of Milton H. Erickson, M.D.* New York: Norton, 1973.

HALEY, J.,   *Problem Solving Therapy.* San Francisco: Jossey-Bass, 1976.

HARRIS, T.,   *I'm OK—You're OK.* New York: Harper & Row, 1967.

JACKSON, B.,   Black Identity Development. *MEFORUM: Journal of Educational Diversity and Innovation,* 1975, *2,* 19–25.

JAMES, M.,   *What Do You Do With Them Now That You've Got Them? Transactional Analysis for Moms and Dads.* Reading, MA: Addison-Wesley, 1974.

JAMES, M., and D. JONGEWARD,   *Born to Win: Transactional Analysis with Gestalt Experiments.* Reading, MA: Addison-Wesley, 1971.

LANGTON, S.,   *Practical Magic.* Cupertino, CA: Meta, 1980.

LARSON, D., ed.,   *Teaching Psychological Skills: Models for Giving Psychology Away.* Monterey, CA: Brooks/Cole, 1984.

MARSHALL, E., D. KURTZ AND ASSOCIATES,   *Interpersonal Helping Skills.* San Francisco: Jossey-Bass, 1983.

MINUCHIN, S.,   *Families and Family Therapy.* Cambridge, MA: Harvard University Press, 1974.

MORRILL, W., E. OETTING, and J. HURST,   "Dimensions of Counselor Functioning." *Personnel and Guidance Journal,* 1974, *52,* 354–359.

MORRILL, W., J. HURST, and E. OETTING,   *Dimensions of Intervention for Student Development.* New York: Wiley 1980.

MOST, R., and B. GUERNEY,   "An Empirical Evaluation of the Training of Lay Volunteers for Premarital Relationship Enhancement," *Family Relations,* 1983, *32,* 239–251.

PALAZZOLI-SELVINI, M.,   *Self-Starvation: From Individual to Family Therapy in the Treatment of Anorexia Nervosa.* New York: Jason Aronson, 1978.

PATTERSON, G.,   *Families.* Champaign, IL: Research Press, 1971.

PATTERSON, G., J. REID, R. JONES, and R. CONGER,   *A Social Learning Approach to Family Intervention, I: Families with Aggressive Children.* Eugene, OR: Castilia, 1975.

SATIR, V.,   *Conjoint Family Therapy.* Palo Alto, CA: Science and Behavior Books, 1967.

STEINER, C., ed.,   *Readings in Radical Psychiatry.* New York: Grove, 1975.

STEINER, C.   "Emotional Literacy." *Transactional Analysis Journal,* 1984, *14,* 162–163.

STUNKARD, A., M. FELIX, and R. COHEN,   "Mobilizing a Community to Promote Health: The Pennsylvania County Health Improvement Project." In J. Rosen and L. Solomon, eds. Hanover, NH: University Press of New England, 1984.

SUE, D.,   *Counseling the Culturally Different.* New York: Wiley, 1981.

SUE, D., and S. SUE,   "Chinese-American Personality and Mental Health" *Amerasia Journal,* 1971, *1,* 36–49.

VOGELSON, E., B. GUERNEY, and L. GUERNEY,   "Relationship Enhancement Therapy with Inpatients and Their Families." In R. Luber and C. Anderson, *Family Intervention with Psychiatric Patients.* New York: Human Sciences, 1983, 48–68.

WATZLAWICK, P., J. BEAVIN, and D. JACKSON,   *Pragmatics of Human Communication.* New York: Norton, 1967.

WEAKLAND, J., R. FISCH, P. WATZLAWICK, and A. BODIN, "Brief Therapy: Focused Problem Resolution," *Family Process,* 1974, *13,* 141–168.

WHITAKER, C., and D. KEITH, "Symbolic-Experiential Family Therapy." In A. Gurman and D. Kniskern, eds. *Handbook of Family Therapy.* New York: Brunner/Mazel, 1981, 187–225.

SUGGESTED SUPPLEMENTARY READING

The Psychoeducational Model

AUTHIER, J., K. GUSTAFSON, B. GUERNEY, JR., and J. KASDORF, "The Psychological Practitioner as Teacher: A Theoretical-Historical and Practical Review," *The Counseling Psychologist,* 1975, *5,* 31–50.
> The roots of the psychoeducational approach, particularly as it relates to psychotherapy, are presented with an extensive review of the literature.

MORRILL, W., J. HURST, and E. OETTING, *Dimensions of Intervention for Student Development.* New York: Wiley, 1980.
> The Colorado State University Counseling Center group of Oetting, Morrill, and Hurst present the cube model that has been influential in this chapter.

Transactional Analysis

BERNE, E., *Games People Play.* New York: Grove Press, 1964.
> The book that launched a movement remains current and vital. This book is particularly useful in understanding basic lifescripts and the parent-adult-child transaction.

JAMES, M., and D. JONGEWARD, *Born to Win: Transactional Analysis with Gestalt Experiments.* Reading, MA: Addison-Wesley, 1971.
> Not only does this book provide a solid overview of transactional analysis, it also contains a wide variety of helpful exercises from Gestalt therapy which can be used for individual analysis and personal growth.

Family Therapy and Family Education

GUERNEY, B., JR., *Relationship Enhancement.* San Francisco: Jossey-Bass, 1977.
> The family education movement and the teaching of family skills are detailed, with a host of practical ideas for family workshops and couples instructions. The author may be considered among the very first to adopt the psychoeducational point of view.

GURMAN, A., and D. RAZIN, *Handbook of Family Therapy.* New York: Brunner/Mazel, 1981.
> One of the definitive summaries of the many alternatives to family therapy offered at a more advanced level. Included is good material on behavioral family therapy and an excellent summary of research.

Community Interventions

DELWORTH, U., E. RUDOW, and J. TAUB, *Crisis Center Hotline: A Guide to Beginning and Operating.* Springfield, IL: Chas. C Thomas, 1972.
> A highly practical guide on how to develop an alternative agency, train staff members, and evaluate effectiveness.

Moos, R., *Human Context: Environmental Determinates of Behavior.* New York: Wiley, 1976.

Moos, R., *Evaluating Educational Environments: Procedures, Methods, Findings, and Policy Implications.* San Francisco: Jossey-Bass, 1979.

Two books by one of the pioneers in social ecology. Again, the emphasis on environmental change as related to individual growth is stressed.

Consciousness-Raising Theory and Feminist Theory

Atkinson, D., D. Morten, and D. Sue, *Counseling American Minorities.* Dubuque, IA: W. C. Brown, 1983.

A useful compendium of counseling and therapy suggestions for counseling and therapy with Native American, Asian American, Black, and Latino clients. Several chapters are written by members of the cultural group themselves.

Ballou, M., and N. Gabalac, *A Feminist Position on Mental Health.* Springfield, IL: Thomas, 1984.

The cutting edge of change and development in therapy in the next decade may well come from the newly developing consciousness-raising theories. From both women and nonwhite individuals, we are seeing the beginning of theory, research, and now practice suggestions for a more comprehensive view of human development. This book is one important contribution to that trend. A transcript by Mary Ballou was featured in this chapter.

13

RESEARCH ON THEORY AND PRACTICE

GENERAL PREMISE

An integrated knowledge of skills, theory, and practice is essential for culturally intentional counseling and therapy.

Skills form the foundation of effective theory and practice: The culturally intentional therapist knows how to construct a creative decision-making interview and can use microskills to attend to and influence clients in a predicted direction. Important in this process are individual and cultural empathy, client observation skills, assessment of person and environment, and the application of positive techniques of growth and change.

Theory provides organizing principles for counseling and therapy: The culturally intentional counselor has knowledge of alternative theoretical approaches and treatment modalities.

Practice is the integration of skills and theory: *The culturally intentional counselor or therapist is competent in skills and theory, and is able to apply them to research* and practice for client benefit.

Undergirding integrated competence in skills, theory, and practice is an intentional awareness of one's own personal worldview and how that worldview may be similar to and/or different from the worldview and personal constructions of the client and other professionals.

GOALS FOR UTILIZATION OF RESEARCH DATA

Counseling and psychotherapy practice are increasingly based on research data. Research empirically tests and demonstrates the impact (or lack of impact) of methods and therapeutic theory and techniques on clients and patients. This chapter serves to summarize some key research findings and to achieve the following goals:

1. Present the central findings on the effectiveness of psychotherapy, with special emphasis on the concept of meta-analysis.
2. Summarize the important work of the Kaiser-Permanente group who are currently demonstrating that short-term planned psychotherapy can make a significant difference in both mental and physical health.
3. Examine some process research dimensions as critical underpinnings of therapeutic outcome.
4. Briefly review examples of community work and a meta-analysis of psychoeducational/community approaches that show equal promise to traditional therapy.

You as a consumer of research—and perhaps a future researcher—will find the material helpful here in examining the central ideas of this book. At the same time, different people develop different constructions and meaning from the same event or data. What is to be your construction and belief system as you examine the data-based world of empirical research?

THE SIGNIFICANCE OF RESEARCH

Research is a means to test the accuracy and meaningfulness of our theories. The world we see is only a view, a description of the world. Counseling and psychotherapy theories represent views of the world that brilliant theoreticians such as Freud, Frankl, and Skinner have *constructed* to describe that world. It seems critical that you constantly recall that theories (including the underlying metatheory of this text) are representations of reality; theories are not real, but are "maps" of the client world. Just as a road map is not the territory through which you are driving, the theories of counseling are not truth; rather they are useful guides.

How accurate and useful are the "maps" provided by our theories? Research has been the major route toward determining the answer to this question. Kurt Lewin stated it succinctly: "No research without action, no action without research" (quoted in Marrow, 1969, p. 193). Counseling and psychotherapy are action fields where the immediate usefulness of our theories is constantly tested by research. Research can help eliminate outmoded and preconceived ideas and enable clinicians to generate new and more useful theories and methods to promote and facilitate client growth.

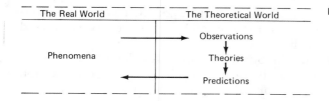

Figure 13.1 A Scheme of the Relationship of Theory to Real Events in the Scentific Model

Research is also an attempt to organize and make sense of the complexity of counselor/client interaction. The problem with research, of course, is that each piece of research takes only a small part of the client/counselor interaction for study. Research follows the scientific model of identifying events in the real world, developing theoretical hypotheses, and testing the hypotheses for their empirical effectiveness. (See Figure 13.1.) As George Kelly (Chapter 6) has noted, the therapist and client both act as scientists testing hypotheses and their effectiveness in the world. Thus you as an interviewer follow similar procedures to those of research. You have an idea (hypothesis) about a client, you test it in the client's world, and revise your idea as you note results.

This chapter has two purposes: (1) to present findings from research on clinical practice and its effectiveness; and (2) to discuss practical implications of research for the counselor or therapist. The first question to be examined is "Does counseling and therapy do any good?" A more detailed analysis of process research examining the interview will follow. Community intervention research will also be considered briefly. *However, having arrived at Chapter 13 in this book, you are likely aware of the true complexity of therapy and counseling. You may want to read the following material using your awareness of the complexity of the "real world" of counseling and therapy. Are the representations of reality by research fully adequate?*

ON THE EFFECTIVENESS OF COUNSELING AND PSYCHOTHERAPY

Studying the extensive data on the effectiveness of psychotherapy, Hans J. Eysenck cast a bombshell on the therapeutic profession in 1952:

> In general, certain conclusions are possible from these data. They fail to prove that psychotherapy, Freudian or otherwise, facilitates the recovery of neurotic patients. They show that roughly two-thirds of a group of neurotic patients will recover or improve to a marked extent within about two years of the onset of their illness, whether they are treated by means of psychotherapy or not. This figure appears to be remarkably stable from one investigation to another, regardless of type of patient treated, standard of recovery employed, or method of therapy used. (Eysenck, 1952, cited in Eysenck, 1966, pp. 29–30)

Eysenck's claim has been ably and sharply rebutted in numerous articles (c.f., Bergin, 1971; Bergin and Suinn, 1975; Luborsky, 1974; Strupp, 1966). Smith and Glass (1978) summarize these arguments and point out that Eysenck was considering approximately only twenty of the over 400 studies then available, and dismiss his work as "tendentious diatribes."

Yet, the fact remains that the burden of proof for the effectiveness of therapy rests with counselors and psychotherapists. The purpose of this section is to explore and summarize key data on the impact of therapy on clients.

Meta-Analysis

In 1977 Smith and Glass assembled 375 studies for a "meta-analysis" of therapy and counseling outcome. Meta-analysis is a complex statistical procedure in which the average impact or *effect size* of counseling and therapy is computed. Effect size is a numerical measure of therapeutic impact. In summarizing this groundbreaking method, the researchers concluded: The average client in these studies was "better off than 75 percent of the untreated controls" (Smith and Glass, 1977, p. 754). This analysis of effectiveness of therapy has been central to discussion among experts ever since.

Glass and Kliegl (1983) updated this work and examined 475 controlled evaluations of psychotherapy. They found the average effect size for psychotherapy was 0.85. This number reveals that the person who receives counseling or therapy is better off than 80 percent of those who don't (that is, the treated group will be 0.85 standard deviation above the untreated). The average duration of psychotherapy was 16 hours and brought together a wide variety of theories for analysis.

Particularly influential on the field has been the data in Figure 13.2, which shows the effect size of psychotherapy for different theoretical orientations. You will note that cognitive approaches to therapy rank first and third in terms of effect size.

> The highest average effect size, 2.38, was produced by cognitive therapies that go by such labels as systematic rational restructuring, rational state-directed therapy, cognitive rehearsal, and fixed-role therapy . . . Cognitive-behavioral therapies such as modeling, self-reinforcement, covert sensitization, self-control desensitization, and behavioral rehearsal were third highest . . . (Glass and Kliegl, 1983, p. 29)

Glass (1984) commented that the high scores earned by the hypnotherapy treatment were due heavily to one single researcher who used several measures in his study. Ivey (1984), however, has shown how hypnosis may be viewed as a special form of cognitive therapy. He points out that most hypnosis involves focused attention and involves similar treatment conditions to those of the other cognitive approaches. It could be argued, then, that the top three techniques in this second meta-analysis all involve some sort of cognitive or cognitive-behavioral approach.

Glass and Kliegl offer some sobering thoughts about their data, however.

Figure 13.2 Average, Standard Deviation, Standard Error, and Number of Effects for Each Therapy Type

TYPE OF THERAPY	AVERAGE EFFECT SIZE, Δ	SD	SE_M	NO. OF EFFECTS (n)*
1. Other cognitive therapies	2.38	2.05	0.27	57
2. Hypnotherapy	1.82	1.15	0.26	19
3. Cognitive-behavioral therapy	1.13	0.83	0.07	127
4. Systematic desensitization	1.05	1.58	0.08	373
5. Dynamic-eclectic therapy	0.89	0.86	0.08	103
6. Eclectic-behavioral therapy	0.89	0.75	0.12	37
7. Behavior modification	0.73	0.67	0.05	201
8. Psychodynamic therapy	0.69	0.50	0.05	108
9. Rational-emotive therapy	0.68	0.54	0.08	50
10. Implosion	0.68	0.70	0.09	60
11. Transactional analysis	0.67	0.91	0.17	28
12. Vocational-personal development	0.65	0.58	0.08	59
13. Gestalt therapy	0.64	0.91	0.11	68
14. Client-centered therapy	0.62	0.87	0.07	150
15. Adlerian therapy	0.62	0.68	0.18	15
16. Placebo treatment	0.56	0.77	0.05	200
17. Undifferentiated counseling	0.28	0.55	0.06	97
18. Reality therapy	0.14	0.38	0.13	9
Total	0.85	1.25	0.03	1761

*The number of effects, not the number of studies; 475 studies produced 1761 effects, or about 3.7 effects per study.

From G. Glass and R. Kliegl, "An Apology for Research Integration in the Study of Psychotherapy." *Journal of Consulting and Clinical Psychology, 31,* 28–41. Copyright 1984 by the American Psychological Association. Reprinted by permission of the author.

For example, 2 years after treatment, the effect size has declined or relapsed to only 0.50. They also found that effect size was larger in therapy which lasted fewer than 10 hours or longer than 20. A marked dip was found in therapies that lasted from 10–20 hours. Therapy of a moderate length did not appear to be as useful as either short time-restricted counseling or long-term therapy. Furthermore, the researchers found that the more unbiased the research instrument, the smaller the effect size of therapy. For example, if therapists rated their own clients, a larger effect size was found than if tests or independent ratings were made.

Given such findings as above, the earlier warning of Smith and Glass should be heeded. The mode of analysis in studies of this type may favor certain types of therapy and the differences that are found may be "somewhat exaggerated in favor of the behavioral . . ." (Smith and Glass, 1977, p. 758).

Although generally applauded by professionals, the Smith and Glass framework of meta-analysis of psychotherapeutic outcome was greeted less than enthusiastically in some quarters. Eysenck, in a letter entitled "An Exercise in Mega-Silliness," points out that Smith and Glass fail to cope with the issue of spontaneous remission (improvement without any therapy) and that their work rests greatly on many poorly designed pieces of research; he also criticizes their computer methodology ("Garbage in, garbage out"). He comments, "If their abandonment of scholarship were to be taken seriously, a daunting but improbable likelihood, it would mark the beginning of a passage into the dark age of scientific psychology" (1978, p. 517). Glass and Smith, then, analyze the Eysenck argument point by point and conclude, "The effects of psychotherapy could hardly have been so treacherous and elusive as to have tricked hundreds of investigators over the past forty years" (1978, p. 518). However, Kurosawa (1984) has recently pointed out that meta-analysis also suffers from "selective publication bias." In other words, journals tend only to publish research that has positive results favoring therapy.

The February 1983 *Journal of Consulting and Clinical Psychology* has a special section on meta-analysis that is perhaps the best description of the issues around the technique. Support for the technique appears in articles by Strube and Hartmann (1983), Shapiro and Shapiro (1983), and Fiske (1983). Wilson and Rachman (1983) repeat the Eysenck critique of the study. The issue of meta-analysis and the effectiveness of therapy is not closed.

Nonetheless, it is tempting to draw comfort from the conclusions of meta-analysis. Psychotherapy does seem to work. Clearly cognitive approaches as well as behavioral do have effect on clients. Even those of a Rogerian or psychodynamic orientation can validly point out that the measures used in meta-analysis do not take into account the broad ambitions for development and client change in these theories. Psychodynamic theoreticians, for example, can turn to the work of Malan (1963; 1976) who studied sixty patients carefully over 20 years and, despite several severe methodological problems, found support for many analytic hypotheses. Thus, it seems unlikely that the data will substantially change the practice of clinicians.

Rachman and Wilson (1980) represent the major alternative critique to the efficacy of psychotherapy. They roundly criticize Smith and Glass, Luborsky et al. (1975), Malan (1963; 1976), and many others. They consider most therapy to be of limited value. They then make several interesting observations about therapy that have implications for research in the future. Among their observations are: (1) research seeks a *cure* and fails to realize that there is no "cure" for *life;* (2) psychotherapy is in truth a learning problem and not a therapy problem (cf. Chapter 12 on psychoeducation); (3) measured personal changes in therapy are narrow and research should reconceptualize outcome measures; and (4) cost-benefit studies of therapy need to be conducted. Some of their objections and problems with research are resolved by the Cummings studies (discussed in the next section), which Rachman and Wilson, interestingly, do not cite in their review of therapy effectiveness. Rachman and Wilson have been associated with the Eysenck point of view and tend to favor behavioral approaches. The work of Cummings and his colleagues tends to be broadly psychodynamic and very much in the clinical action tradition rather than the usual "academic" research.

The Kaiser-Permanente Studies

Cummings (1977), Cummings and Follette (1968; 1976), and Cummings and Vandenbos (1979) have an important—but often ignored—series of studies that examine cost-benefit analysis of psychodynamically oriented eclectic therapy. Working at the Kaiser-Permanente health facility in San Francisco, they found that persons in emotional distress were significantly higher users of inpatient and outpatient medical facilities for physical problems. They found that short-term psychotherapy reduced the use of medical services and "these declines remained constant over five years." Closer analysis of the 16-year study revealed that 85 percent of the patients who were seen an average of 8.6 sessions were found to have a satisfactory adjustment.

Other findings included the fact that long-term patients in therapy lowered their usage of medical services, but had substituted weekly psychotherapy for weekly visits to the physician. The researchers then substituted sessions separated by 30, 60, or 90 days with these patients, and found this form of long-term therapy to yield cost-effective benefits. Cummings found that patients could be maintained through infrequent therapy at a satisfactory level of adjustment. These two findings are particularly interesting as they strongly support meta-analysis in finding that brief, time-limited therapy or counseling may be the treatment of choice and that it offers cost-effectiveness for the client and the helping agency. Short-term counseling (8.3 sessions) or carefully constructed long-term therapy can both be helpful if directed to specific aims.

Cummings (1985, personal communication) has updated the basic findings of the Kaiser group. In essence, the original work continues to maintain itself over time. Psychotherapy is seen as a critical cost-effective benefit by this large medical group. Cummings states that 10 percent of clients need long-term ther-

Nicholas Cummings

apy and these clients can be clearly identified. He now finds that 6.2 sessions are the average length of the therapy/counseling sessions.

Cummings is working on a book in which he plans to detail the specific treatment methods used in this research. Currently, he is engaged in a major research endeavor with 91,000 patients in a large medical practice where the effectiveness of therapy will be measured with the largest number of clients ever studied by any researcher. We can only look forward to the results of this interesting research endeavor.

In light of the issue of cost-benefit analysis, it is interesting to note that neither Rachman and Wilson nor Smith, Glass, and Miller (1980) cite Cummings' pioneering efforts. However, the American Psychiatric Association does mention it in their summary of psychotherapy research (Karasu, 1982). They point out that twenty-eight replications of this research have been completed in widely different settings. Many other key reviews of the psychological literature (c.f. Garfield and Bergin, 1978; Garfield, 1980; Gurman and Razin, 1977; Frances, Clarkin, and Perry 1984; Strupp, 1981; Lambert, Christensen, and DeJulio, 1983) apparently have chosen to ignore the Kaiser-Permanente critical findings.

You as a consumer of research literature and, hopefully, an eventual producer of research may be somewhat puzzled with the summary presented thus far. One conclusion is obviously that conscientious people do differ in their reading of the text of research and what they choose to read and talk about. Furthermore, it is clear that all the answers are not in. Yet, it is also clear that analysis of research will direct the counseling and clinical practice of the future. Two important integrated reviews of research and their potential application to practice follow.

Selecting Specific Treatments for Clients

An interesting and unique approach to the question of appropriate treatment for clients is presented by Goldstein and Stein (1976), who examined psychotherapy research literature to discover what it says about the most appropriate treatment for specific problems or disorders presented by clients. They group psychotherapy research data according to how it relates to specific client issues (phobias, sexual malfunctioning, obsessive-compulsive neuroses) and then summarize the major research findings. For example, they identify seven studies on depression that used a variety of approaches (behavioral, problem-solving, drugs, and supportive psychotherapy), and conclude that for this problem supportive psychotherapy and behavioral approaches may be the treatment of choice. On the other hand, the three identified studies on hysteria were so mixed that they presented no conclusions as to the most appropriate intervention modality. The data and methods illustrate clearly the way that research can inform clinicians as to appropriate clinical practice.

Unfortunately, the promising introduction offered in 1976 has not been followed up (Goldstein, 1985, personal communication). However, Frances, Clarkin, and Perry (1984) have an excellent approach to the differential treatment literature in which they review research and they suggest specific treatment alternatives. (Interestingly, they do not cite the original work by Goldstein and Stein.) These authors review the literature on a specific topic (such as, duration of treatment, which combination of treatments is likely to be effective, etc.) and then make specific suggestions for action. An interesting chapter, "No Treatment as the Recommendation of Choice," for example, points out that no treatment at all can be useful in protecting the patient from harm through incorrect treatment, from wasting time, and by providing the client with an opportunity to find out what he or she can do alone without help. The authors point out that healthy people in crisis often respond quickly with little or no treatment. Furthermore, resistant patients can sometimes develop more interest in therapy if treatment is discontinued for a period of time.

Impact of Counseling on Clients

It is not the intent of this section to review the totality of therapeutic outcome research. The material previously cited and the comprehensive reviews cited provide a good summary of literature regarding whether or not psychotherapists and counselors do make a difference in the lives of their clients. From a review of the data concerning the impact of counseling on clients, the following conclusions are suggested:

1. The evidence about the actual effectiveness of counseling and therapy is mixed, but the bulk of the data suggest that clients do benefit from the individual interviewing process.
2. Available research to date suggests that cognitive-behavioral approaches are more effective than other modes in producing change. However, this effect may be partially due to the research methods of behavioral researchers. Other methods of therapy may profit from examining behavioral research methodology.
3. In all likelihood, it seems that different theories are likely to be differentially effective with different clients who present different problems. A major goal for the future is in matching appropriate treatment with client needs.

The research data, despite many problems, seem to offer some support for the metatheoretical orientation of this text. Specifically, intentionality suggests the importance of the counselor or therapist having many alternatives for helping on which to draw. The microskills approach described in Chapter 3 is based on cognitive understanding, modeling, and rehearsal. The positive asset search shows how several different theories use cognitive reframing techniques to produce positive change in clients. It could be that Glass and Kliegl have identified a trend through their research—the integration of many different theories of helping around a common cause. This common cause appears to be that of cognitively reframing the world and looking at it from a different perspective and then acting on this new knowledge. A special problem of research is that only a *few* of the variables are ever isolated in any one research study. The necessary precision of the scientific method precludes taking all factors into account.

One route toward understanding the complexity of the helping process in more detail is through "process" research discussed in the following section.

RESEARCH ON COUNSELING AND PSYCHOTHERAPY PROCESS

Outcome research is concerned with what happens to clients as a result of counseling and psychotherapy. *Process research* is concerned with examination of the nature of the interview and the determination of the factors that may lead to a successful outcome. Process research is particularly critical for the practitioner, because it specifies variables and behaviors that are useful in deciding which treatments (skills, qualities, theories) are most likely to help a particular client.

This section reviews research literature on counseling skills, qualities, the nature of alternative theoretical orientations to psychotherapy, data on construct development and language, information on the effectiveness of nonprofessionals as compared to more experienced therapists, preliminary data on matching client and therapists, and emerging cultural research.

Attending Behavior, Nonverbal Communication, and Microskills

Attending behavior was identified in Chapter 3 as a basic skill of counseling. Eye contact, nonverbal factors, and verbal following have been given as underlying factors important in all effective communication, whether normal conversation or psychotherapy. The process through which attending was identified as a microskill by a research team (Ivey, Normington, Miller, Morrill, and Haase, 1968) is discussed as follows:

> The basic breakthrough which resulted in the concepts of attending behavior and microcounseling occurred with one of our secretaries. The process consisted of five minutes of videotaping when she was interviewing a student volunteer. This was followed by a replay of the tape, in which her behaviors, which reflected lapses of attending, were pointed out, and direction was given in how to increase identified attending behaviors. She returned to reinterview the student, and, after a moment of artificiality, began to respond in highly impactful ways. In fact, she performed like a highly skilled, highly experienced counselor. The change was not only dramatic, but, when we began to consider the twenty minutes of training, almost shocking! We have had less change of behavior in practicum students in an entire year.
>
> When a hiatus was reached, the lack of training in counseling skills became apparent. The hiatus called for initiation of new areas, and the secretary did not follow one of our counseling traditions. If she had, she would have either waited for the client to respond (nondirective), initiated an expression of her own feeling state (recent client-centered), directed attention to early experience (analytic), presented a discriminative stimulus to elicit verbal responses which could be reinforced (learning theory), induced a trance state (hypnoanalysis), or brought out a Strong Vocational Interest Blank (vocational counseling).

The secretary actually began to talk about an interesting experience in her own immediate past (standard social behavior). However, since she still was attempting to engage in attending behaviors, this led rapidly to a new topic for the student, and she again resembled the highly skilled counselor.

As an indication of the relevance of attending and related constructs to behavior beyond the interview, our secretary entered the office on Monday and could not wait to tell us about attending to people over the weekend. She had developed an entirely new behavioral repertoire which was reinforced by a new kind of excitement and involvement with other people. The impact even on her husband was apparent. (Hackney, Ivey, and Oetting, 1970, p. 344)

This process of identification of researchable dimensions in counseling is cited in detail because it illustrates the sometimes whimsical nature of the research process, in which discoveries are often made by chance rather than by choice. Since the original 1968 study on attending behavior, over 250 studies on the microskill of attending behavior have been completed (cf., Ivey, 1971; Ivey and Authier, 1978; Daniels, 1985). One of the more important findings has been that clients respond better and more positively to counselors who attend to them, are more likely to verbalize at greater length, and indicate a greater willingness to return to attending counselors and therapists. Experienced and sophisticated therapists and counselors seem to have good attending skills, whereas many beginning counselors score poorly on these dimensions. A large number of studies have found eye contact breaks, faulty nonverbal communication, and excessive topic jumping among ineffective or beginning counselors. There is considerable evidence that training in attending behavior improves the skills of both the counselor and clients.

The now extensive literature on nonverbal communication is ably summarized by Harper, Wiens, and Matarazzo (1978) who cite over 200 studies on eye and visual behavior alone. Among the many important findings emphasizing the importance of eye contact is one that Black and white speakers and listeners have differing patterns of eye contact.

> In interaction among whites, a clear indication of attention by the listener is that he looks at the speaker; thus, if the speaker gazes at the listener in order to determine how he is being received, he more often than not finds the listener looking back. Blacks do not look while listening, presumably using other cues to communicate attention. When Blacks and whites interact, therefore, these differences may give rise to communicational breakdowns. The white may feel he is not being listened to, while the Black may feel he is being unduly scrutinized. Further, exchanges of listener-speaker roles become disjunctive, leading to generalized discomfort in the encounter. (Mayo and LaFrance, 1973, p. 7)

While such data are important, it is vital that the counselor and therapist remember that each individual who comes for help may have unique patterns that do not conform to cultural or subcultural expectations (Pederson, 1981). Data on facial expression show both similarities and differences among cultures (cf., Ekman, Friesen, and Ellworth, 1972). The concepts of movement synchrony, discussed in Chapter 5, have been studied extensively by Condon and others.

Examining film and video segments in frame-by-frame analysis, Condon and Ogston (1966, p. 338) comment on "harmonious or synchronous organizations of change between body motion and speech in *both* intra-individual and interactional behavior. Thus, the body of the speaker dances in time with his speech. Further, the body of the listener dances in rhythm with that of the speaker." For the therapist, the identification of incongruence between movements and client speech is of the utmost importance.

The anthropologist Edward Hall (1959) is considered by many to be the originator of systematic study of nonverbal communication. In 1983 he wrote an updated view of this field entitled *The Dance of Life*. He updates the research summary in nonverbal communication and adds *time* to the list of critical nonverbal variables. Hall points out that time is regarded differently in varying cultures and cites research illustrating its key importance in differences among peoples. The Japanese, for example, are very efficient in time usage with careful scheduling. This may be contrasted with some Pacific cultures where time as a construct virtually does not exist.

Vocal tone has been examined by Duncan, et al. (1968) who note that "peak interviews" were characterized by open vocal cord control and soft intonations, whereas poor therapeutic sessions were characterized by a forced, overloud intensity with overhigh pitch, coupled with oversoft patterns at other times. Eldred and Price (1958) have noted that anxiety is marked in the interview by increased breaks and dissonance in speech. Labov and Fanshel (1977) have examined similarities in intonation patterns between therapist and client and consider synchrony as one aspect of good communication. Using an oscilloscope for detailed analysis, they studied rises and falls of intonation and validate many of the more subjective impressions of the importance of vocal tone held by many. Vocal tone synchrony between therapist and client often appears in times of effective communication.

Possibilities for examining various microskills are endless. Particularly interesting work by Strong and his colleagues (c.f. Beck and Strong, 1982; Feldman, Strong, and Danser, 1982) has demonstrated the effectiveness of paradoxical directives. Students were told by their counselors *consciously* to procrastinate one-half hour every day. A comparison group of students was told to plan regular study times. The paradoxical directives were as effective or more effective than straightforward advice and direction. Strong (1983) reports these data as well as the usefulness of positive connotation (positive asset search) on clients.

The importance of identifying patterns of skill usage is suggested by an early study of Blocksma and Porter (1947) who found that students of counseling and therapy reported their behavior in the interview inaccurately when compared to actual study of what transpired. In effect, they found that what a therapist says he or she does may have little relationship to what is actually done. Examining the literature on theoretical orientations of psychotherapists, Sundland (1977, p. 215) concludes: "Extremely important and lacking have been data showing that therapist's beliefs are matched by their behaviors."

Two critical studies on microskills are those of Gill, Berger, and Cogar (1983) and Baker, Scofield, Clayton, and Munson (1984). The first study discovered that *groups of microskills* could be learned rapidly and maintained if cognitive integration was provided for the trainees. The second study provided additional data validating the *cognitive* importance of student trainees thinking about skill usage and planning. These two studies clearly indicate the importance of cognitive/thinking variables in the practice of successful counseling. Ford (1979) found that microskills usage tended to decrease over time. It seems clear that learning skills is not enough. One must conceptualize them cognitively and use them systematically if they are to endure effectively.

Microskills literature may also be criticized (cf. Ivey, 1983) for over emphasis on skill usage and insufficient attention to impact on the client. Ivey makes suggestions for more outcome-oriented skill studies. Future research in this area needs to follow the Meara et al. model discussed below. What is the specific impact of skills on client action?

Data are beginning to emerge to indicate that therapists of differing orientations use different skills. The studies on client-centered and Rogerian therapy, cited earlier, are one example where it has been found that client-centered therapists tend to use the reflective attending skills. Sloane, et al. (1975) discovered that behavior therapists were willing to answer their patient's question by giving information while psychodynamic therapists tended to reflect the question back to the client. Behavior therapists tend to offer more directives telling their clients to do something. Interestingly, "in the psychotherapy group, patients receiving fewer 'clarification and interpretation' statements improved significantly more than those receiving many, but this paradoxical result did not hold true for behavior therapy patients" (p. 222). This tentative finding suggests that the content of interpretation may be important in determining its therapeutic value and that behavioral interpretations may interfere less with the interview than do psychodynamic.

Strupp (1955a; 1955; 1958) asked therapists of different orientations to write responses to written and filmed client statements and found (1) experienced therapists drew from a wider range of responses than inexperienced ones did; (2) experienced psychodynamic therapists used more interpretation and initiation than inexperienced ones did; and (3) experienced client-centered therapists used more exploration and less reflection than inexperienced therapists did. These findings are in accord with the generative theory of intentionality, that, as a therapist matures, he or she develops more options for reaching more clients. Auerbach and Johnson's (1977) review of the literature about levels of therapist experience suggests strongly that more options become available as one learns more about the process.

Examining typescripts of group therapists, Sherrard (1973) found wide difference in skill usage among group leaders devoted to human relations training (Carkhuff), client-centered growth (Lifton), psychodynamic "Bion process group" (Goldberg), and vocational. Fifty percent of Carkhuff's statements were directives, and he also used more expression of content—information leads. Lifton reflected feeling and shared information, while the vocational group leader primarily gave information and paraphrased. Goldberg used interpretation as the primary skill. Interestingly, the patterns of verbal statements among the clients of the more therapeutic groups did not vary extensively.

In a series of classic process studies, researchers (Meara, Shannon, and Pepinsky, 1979; Meara, Pepinsky, Shannon, and Murray, 1981) examined Perls, Ellis, and Rogers interviewing the same client (Shostrum, 1966). Through linguistic analysis, they found that the client, Gloria, tended to assume the language pattern of the therapist. This strongly suggests that the power and social influence of the counselor should be carefully monitored.

Earlier, Bandura notes

> the results of [such] studies show that the therapist not only controls the patient by rewarding him with interest and approval when the patient behaves in a fashion the therapist desires but that he also controls through punishment in the form of mild disapproval and withdrawal of interest when the patient behaves in ways that are threatening to the therapist or run counter to his goals. (1961, p. 154)

Some reassurance on this critical issue, however, is offered by findings that successful white counselors tend to join their Black clients in language patterns rather than trying to impose their own frames either consciously or unconsciously (Fry, Knopf, and Coe, 1980).

Cultural differences in skill usage need consideration. Using a technique close to that of Strupp, cited earlier, Berman (1979) asked Black and white men and women to write therapeutic responses to short client problems presented on videotape. She found that white men tended to ask more questions and give more advice, white women used more reflections of feeling, and Black men and women used more advice and suggestion. Moreover, examination of the focus of response revealed that white counselors tended to focus on the individual ("*You* seem to . . .") whereas the Black counselors tended to focus more often on the cultural and environmental context ("The *system* is getting you because . . ."). These findings are logical and important as they illustrate once again the critical fact that people differ. A reflection of feeling to a person angry about not getting a job may be less useful than advice about how to deal with issues of racial discrimination and job searching. Another illustration of cultural variations in communication patterns is supplied by the anthropologist Briggs (1970), who examined family life and communication in the Central Arctic. Questions are considered rude and intrusive by many Inuit (Eskimo) populations, the direct expression of emotion is discouraged, and one waits patiently for the other person to discuss problems and concerns. Brislin (1983), Hall (1959), Pedersen, Draguns, Lonner, and Trimble (1981), and Harper, Wiens, and Matarazzo (1978), are only four of many references that discuss the impact of cultural differences in communication patterns across different cultural groups. People from Asia, the South Pacific, Europe, South America, and the many subgroups in the United States and Canada have widely varying patterns of communication.

Qualitative Conditions and Empathy

A landmark series of studies by Fiedler (1950a, 1950b, 1951) involved defining the ideal therapeutic relationship and systematic study of therapists of psychoanalytic, Rogerian, and Adlerian persuasion. He found that expert therapists of the several types appeared more similar to each other than they did to inexperienced therapists within their own theoretical orientations. An equally important study was conducted by Barrett-Lennard (1962), who studied level of regard, empathy, congruence, unconditionality of regard, and willingness to be known, as manifested in therapy sessions of inexperienced and experienced counselors. Barrett-Lennard found higher levels of these facilitative conditions among experienced therapists.

These two studies were pivotal in an avalanche of studies of the Rogerian qualitative dimensions during the ensuing years. Useful reviews of this research may be found in Anthony and Carkhuff (1977), Auerbach and Johnson (1977), Carkhuff (1969a and b), and Truax and Mitchell (1971). Studies of the facilitative conditions of empathy, warmth, respect, and so forth have demonstrated these qualities to be closely related to evaluations of effectiveness in counseling and psychotherapy. Further, these dimensions may be more important in some cases than the theoretical orientation of the counselor for it is obvious that a warm and attentive counselor of any orientation would be preferable to most clients than a cold and distant individual who fails to show interpersonal respect.

However, Mitchell, Bozarth, and Krauft read the literature on Rogerian hypotheses and theory quite differently. They concluded, "The recent evidence, although equivocal, does seem to suggest that empathy, warmth, and genuineness are related in some way to client change, but that their potency and generalizability are not as great as was once thought" (1977, p. 483). Rachman and Wilson (1980) state that Rogers and Dymond had insufficient controls in their highly-cited study. Work by Lambert, DeJulio, and Stein (1978) severely criticizes empathy research, suggesting that methods have not always been adequate. Further, they question data on efficacy of skill training approaches. These types of criticisms, coupled with the failure of a major study using person-centered methods with schizophrenics (Rogers, Gendlin, Kiesler, and Truax, 1967) may be leading to a lesser influence of Rogerian theory on the current scene.

Rogers (1975) also points out that many therapists fall short of offering empathic conditions and that therapy and counseling can be for better or worse. Hadley and Strupp (1976) have illustrated this point. Hadley and Strupp reviewed a large number of studies indicating possible deterioration as an effect of the psychotherapeutic process, and point out the importance of a solid relationship appropriate to the need level of the client. Strupp (1977, p. 11) catches the essence of his argument when he says "the art of psychotherapy may largely consist of judicious and sensitive applications of a given technique, delicate decisions of when to press a point or when to be patient, when to be warm and understanding, and when to be remote." Strupp, then, is suggesting that simple application of a few empathic qualities is not enough. These qualities also have to be in synchrony with the client, at the moment, in the interviewing process (cf., Strupp, 1981).

The Sloan et al. study (1975) found that behavior therapists exhibited higher levels of empathy, self-congruence, and interpersonal contact than psychotherapists, while levels of warmth and regard were approximately the same. There was no relationship, however, between these measures and eventual effectiveness of the therapy. It is interesting to note that the behavior therapists, often thought of as cold and distant, proved higher on these dimensions than the psychotherapists. Sloane reviews this landmark study in 1984 and makes this critical summary comment: *Successful patients in both therapies rated their personal interaction with the therapist as the single most important part of treatment.* It is difficult to deny or disregard such a powerful statement by clients.

Chapter 10 on the existential-humanistic therapies gives prominence to the growing interest in Frankl's conceptions. However, to date, specific research verifying his approach is only beginning. Much of it appears in work derivative of his thinking, for example the studies of Strong and his colleagues on paradox cited earlier in this chapter.

Culture as a Process Variable

Empathic qualities manifest themselves differently in different cultures (cf. Brislin, 1983). Touching is appropriate in many South American cultures, but would represent an invasion among many of those from North America. Concreteness is highly desired in this culture, but may be less relevant to certain indirect Asians who use many subtle approaches to communicate important ideas. There is a need for cultural empathy and understanding that the mode of being-in-the-world differs among many peoples. One illustration of basic cultural differences is the Japanese and U.S. conception of the word "love," which in its best sense represents a true empathic feeling toward another human being: There is no direct translation for the word love in Japanese. The closest word is "anan" which describes a fondness, but also includes ideas of dependency; in the United States, love implies an independent, equal relationship. Our understandings from our own culture should not blind us to the fact that other people construct and construe the world differently.

Thus it is critical to remember that what represents empathy in North American culture may be considered rude intrusion in another setting. Whites and Blacks in this culture have differing patterns of being and communicating. Ridley (1984), for example, summarizes theory and research on the clinical treatment of the nondisclosing Black client. He first points out that Blacks vary in their patterns and that stereotyping how a Black client will react is dangerous. He suggests that appropriate counselor self-disclosure may be helpful in enabling the client to feel less vulnerable. Finally, directly facing issues of race is important.

Brodsky (1981) summarizes some of the key research on sex, race, and class. She points out the absence of empathy through stereotyping of all groups, the fact of bias on the part of therapists to favor certain types of clients (usually YAVIS—young, attractive, verbal, intelligent, successful—Schofield, 1964), the need for matching language style, and changing the style and even the place of therapy to fit the unique needs of the client. Finally, she suggests training for counselors on issues of sexism, racism, and classism to enable them to work more effectively. Cultural empathy is no more easily acquired than individual empathy; in fact, the development of cultural empathy may be the most difficult task of all. Without it, no true empathy exists. However, Deaux (1984) in a careful literature review found sex differences to be "surprisingly small."

A careful review of the limited literature on matching therapist and client is provided by Berzins (1977), who reminds us that in some community mental health centers, over 50 percent of Black clients drop out of counseling after the first interview. Most therapists tend to be male (seven out of ten), in their 40s, and from lower middle-class backgrounds. Therapists tend to prefer to work with YAVIS clients. When clients and therapists are matched for socioeconomic class and race, clients tend to self-disclose and talk more easily in the interview. With the advent of the women's movement, gay rights, and other groups, it is increasingly likely that these crucial dimensions will be important. Berzins points out that the data on matching such variables is scanty, but the available data are such that they cannot easily be ignored.

Two useful sources for the development of cultural empathy lie in Sue's *Counseling the Culturally Different* (1981) and McGoldrick, Pearce, and Giordano's *Ethnicity and Family Therapy* (1982). These two books provide rich information about different groups and differential treatment needs. Katz's *White Awareness* (1978) is an especially useful set of exercises for training in racism awareness.

Paraprofessionals

As clarity has developed around issues concerning skills and empathic qualities of effective therapists, a concomitant trend has been the sharing of counseling skills with a growing number of paraprofessionals, mental health volunteers, and lay helpers. This trend has been met with varying reactions:

> Persons without credentials in mental health can have a positive, measurable effect on individuals in need of help . . . whatever enables one person to help another is not the exclusive province of the credentialed mental health professional . . . Few findings in the area of mental health have been replicated as often with such a variety of helpers, helpees, and outcome criteria. (Anthony and Carkhuff, 1977, p. 113)
>
> Unfortunately, the present situation is almost totally out of control. Despite the existence of laws regulating the practice of psychology, social work and psychiatry, essentially nothing prevents a licensed practitioner from originating a new technique, claiming cures, and using it widely on clients. Even more distressing is the fact that thousands of unlicensed persons are now practicing their own versions of psychological therapy under titles and guises that are not legally controlled . . . it is vital that professionals and the public press for uniform state

licensing laws that demand quality therapeutic performance prior to licensure and that restrict unlicensed use of therapy techniques. (Lambert, Bergin, and Collins, 1977, p. 477)

Two statements, both taken from careful reviews of the literature, illustrate the dilemma faced by the helping professions. It is clear that counseling can help *or* harm individuals and the uncontrolled provision of services can actually hurt the public through incompetence and charlatanry. At the same time, the data are clear that unlicensed volunteers, paraprofessionals, and aides can be as effective (and often more effective than certified and licensed counselors, psychologists, social workers, and psychiatrists) (Ivey, 1982, pp. 131–132).

Which of these positions would you take? As you can sense, consensus around the meaning of research is not much easier to find than is consensus about the "most correct" theory.

Given the policy and political implications of paraprofessional versus professional helping and therapy, research on paraprofessional effectiveness becomes especially important. Hattie, Sharpley, and Rogers (1984) discovered 39 studies comparing professional and paraprofessional counselors. Using meta-analysis techniques they concluded that "paraprofessionals are at least as effective, and in many instances more effective, than professional counselors" (p. 540). They did find that paraprofessionals who had experienced longer training were more effective than those who had briefer periods of instruction.

The meta-analysis techniques revealed interesting data on effect size or impact of therapy on client positive growth. Specifically, "the average person who received help from a paraprofessional was better off at the end of therapy than 63 percent of the persons who received help from professionals" (p. 536). This difference may not be large, but it clearly indicates that paraprofessionals can produce as much or more change than professionally trained counselors and therapists.

Hattie, Sharpley, and Rogers (1984) in their meta-analysis provide an important contribution to the field of counseling and therapy. Many of us would like to believe that "professionalization" is the answer to the provision of meaningful services to our clients. The data clearly suggest that the answer is not that simple. Paraprofessionals do seem to work effectively with many clients.

Suh and Strupp (1982) compared a group of psychotherapists with a group of nontrained college professors with a reputation for ability to counsel students and found that both provided a good climate for helping, that neither were especially successful with "difficult, hard to reach clients," and that effectiveness of the two groups did not differ significantly. Strupp, however, does not conclude that nonprofessionals should be studied further or even supported; he actively seeks to maintain strict professionalism in the field, despite his own research which can be interpreted as suggesting the contrary (cf. Williams and Spitzer, 1984).

It is important to note that Suh and Strupp also found that both professors and professionals found it difficult to change their helping style when it was not fully effective, apparently choosing to offer more of the same when their interventions did not work. It appears that intentional change and development is difficult not only for clients, but also for therapists and researchers in the therapeutic process.

The importance of the paraprofessional movement in the delivery of helping services cannot be denied. Rey Carr, for example, has participated in the development of over 500 peer counseling programs in Canada (Carr and Saunders, 1980). A critical future role for this increasingly important group seems secure. It will not be possible to ignore paraprofessional and volunteer helpers. The larger question is the relationship professionals, researchers, and paraprofessionals will share in the future.

Despite interesting evidence that supports the value of paraprofessionals in the helping field, it is equally clear that many professionals do not agree with their use. As you move forward as a professional in therapy and counseling, you will find the issue of paraprofessionals important. Some of your work is likely to center on training these individuals.

Integrating Process and Outcome

The presentation here seems to imply the following central points:

1. Psychotherapy does seem to be effective and produce change (but some would disagree).
2. It appears the cognitive approaches that emphasize the reframing of reality (such as rational-emotive therapy and cognitive-behavioral methods) are the most effective systems. However, if you examine Rogerian, Freudian, or other theories carefully, you will find that they too emphasize the reconstruction of reality that seems to undergird cognitive approaches. Thus, it is possible that research from some theoretical orientations has used limited outcome measures to measure effectiveness of helping. Rachman and Wilson (1980) make an important point when they criticize current research methodology.
3. Short-term therapy and counseling with specific goals appear to be the most effective. Whether one is looking at Cummings' work or those of the cognitive-behavioral group, if one has a specific goal in mind during therapy, the chances are reasonably good that success can be achieved. This would seem to underscore the importance of Stage 3 of the structure of the interview identified in Chapter 2. As Kenneth Blanchard suggests, "If you don't know where you are going (that is, you don't have a goal), you may end up somewhere else." Long-term therapy may turn out to be more effective with clearer subgoals within the treatment process.
4. Microskills, empathic qualities, nonverbal dimensions, cultural dimensions and other identifiable parts of the interview are basic processes necessary for an effective interview. It may be useful to have a goal, do short-term therapy, and emphasize cognitive issues, but unless you have good, solid attending behavior, some level of empathy, and cultural awareness, you are likely to fail.

Given these findings to date, it is reassuring to realize that new models of viewing the reality of research are presently becoming available.

TOWARD A NEW MODEL OF RESEARCH

As Borgen puts it, a key question of research is: "Which approaches work best with which kinds of problems?" (Borgen, 1984). He notes that questions as to the effectiveness of psychotherapy may be insufficiently sophisticated given the complexity of the process. Borgen suggests that new problems should be turned to by researchers: "What are the causes of the problems seen in therapy? What is the nature of therapeutic change? What are the effective ingredients in therapeutic change?" (Borgen, 1984, p. 585). Borgen notes that the profession seems to be moving toward eclecticism and a broader point of view.

As psychotherapy and counseling are so complex, Hill et al. (1983) studied both process *and* outcome in a single case of time-limited counseling intensively. For the most part, therapy research tends to be *either* process or outcome. In this case the client was seen for twelve interviews. The counselor's interviewing style was based on a solid rapport and then emphasized interpretive, confrontive, and experiential work. Process measures revealed the client gradually increased insight and ability to experience in the interview. Most important for this client in change were interpretations or cognitive reframes, feedback, Gestalt exercises, and discussion of the relationship between counselor and client. Outcome measures revealed improvement after the twelve sessions, which were maintained over 2 months, but the client relapsed over a 7-month followup period. The authors state that the client relapsed because "counseling was too brief."

However, the counseling did not include systematic planning for change such as that of relapse prevention (Marlatt and Gordon, 1985; and Marx, 1984). Thus, it might be suggested that counseling was not too brief, but that generalization training was insufficient. The Cummings's Kaiser-Permanente study discussed earlier and recent reviews of research (cf. Frances, Clarkin, and Perry, 1984) all suggest the validity of short-term counseling. Out of this discussion, the differential treatment approach appears to be even more important. Each client is likely to be unique and to require "differential therapeutics." Research literature once talked about the importance of "matching" client and counselor (cf. Berzins, 1977), but it is now appearing that the issue of matching did not recognize the full complexity of the interview. The more comprehensive your therapeutic model, the more likely it is that you can produce change, particularly if you have a solid definition of the problem and a thorough understanding of the client's goals.

New conceptual approaches to research are currently being sought. A special section of the *Journal of Counseling Psychology* outlines the current dilemma in research (Polkinghorne and others, 1984). Suggestions are made that research needs to consider biographical/historical accidents and note how clients often differ from the statistical/research norm (Howard, 1984). Further, there is need for a new phenomenology of research that enables the investigator to view the self of the researcher in the context of research rather than separate from it (Patton,

1984). Ford (1984) applauds these ideas, but notes that they overemphasize single-case-study methodology and fail to consider the emotional aspects of problems. Borgen (1984) questions the scientific model of research and mentions the need for an "eclectic epistemology" and suggests that theory and research may be both considered as metaphor rather than as reality. Ivey (1986) discusses these and other trends and suggests the need for an integration of epistemology and Piagetian developmental theory within the research enterprise.

Research in counseling and psychotherapy is clearly at a crossroads. The directions the research field will take in the next few years will be leading counseling and therapy also in new directions. Concepts from philosophy, logic, and epistemology will likely be entering the field as the search for a restructuring of research methods continues.

Let us conclude this chapter with a brief examination of the importance of research in the family, the community, and the environment.

RESEARCH IN LARGER SYSTEMS

This chapter will conclude with a brief consideration of research on family and community. Counseling and psychotherapy operate within these larger systems and it is often the family and community that will determine the lasting effect of our change efforts on clients.

Family Research

Gurman and Kniskern (1981) have reviewed newly developing research and conclude that controlled studies of the several theories of family therapy together suggest that family therapy is better than no treatment at all. There is some indication that behaviorally oriented family therapy may be particularly effective, if the family problems are moderate, but that an alternative orientation may be preferred when difficulties are more complex.

An analysis of the percentage of family therapy determined as "effective" revealed that 61 percent of marital cases and 73 percent of family therapy cases showed improvement. Needless to say, these figures are not too disparate from the Eysenck critique at the beginning of this chapter. In addition, there does appear to be a 5–10 percent negative impact from therapies of this orientation.

Research on family education shows some promise as an alternative or supplement to family therapy. Guerney, Vogelsong, and Coufal (1983), for example, found that the psychoeducational approach to family adjustment produced more impact of a lasting nature than did traditional family therapy or no treatment at all.

Given these types of findings, it may be anticipated that family therapy research will follow a similar path as that of individual therapy. Furthermore, it may be anticipated that the family therapy and family education movements will be increasingly important areas for research and may provide us with new conceptions of how therapy and counseling can be researched most effectively.

Community Research

The possibilities for community research are, of course, even more extensive than those for examination of individual and group counseling services. Therefore, only four studies will be cited here as representative of the wide array of possibilities. The economy and its effects on jobs and mental health will be considered first, followed by a study on environmental stress and physical health. A long-term evaluation study on the effectiveness of school guidance services will be considered. The first two studies concern the power of the environment over the individual, the third is in regard to professionals' attempts to work on environmental issues. Finally, meta-analysis of community interventions will be summarized.

Brenner (1973) has studied psychiatric hospital admission rates in New York State for the years 1841 to 1967 and has concluded that changes in numbers of patients admitted is greatly determined by changes in the national economy. Specifically, as the economy worsens, psychiatric admissions increase. As the economy improves, admissions decline. The economy, at first glance, would seem to be unimportant in relation to psychiatric distress; but on further thought, the effect of unemployment on personal development, inability to succeed in a culture, financial problems caused by a slow economy, and other factors combine to suggest that economic factors may indeed be critical to the mental health of a society (which in turn reflects on the mental health of individuals).

Observation of Figure 13.3 reveals that admission rates are high during periods of low economic activity (such as 1930s, late 1940s) and lower during times of economic upturn (1940 wartime period, early 1960s boom). It may be noted that the curve for women is different from that for men. Brenner suggests that because of cultural considerations and discrimination, women may be less effected by economic increases and declines. Further, he has discovered that patterns of Black and Puerto Rican admissions also do not follow the chart as closely as those for white men. Again, these findings are the result of probable discrimination (for example, "When things are bad, no one can get a job and it's not my fault," but "When things are good and I still can't get a job, maybe it is my fault." Thus explaining increased hospitalization rates for this group in "good" times).

It follows that the environmental context may need therapy more than the individual does. However, when one thinks of the many people, particularly women and minority populations, who undergo institutionalization, shock and drug therapy, and other forms of psychiatric intervention, one cannot help but wonder if the priorities and skills of the mental health profession are sometimes misplaced. The intensive and extensive attack on the individual in the psychiatric

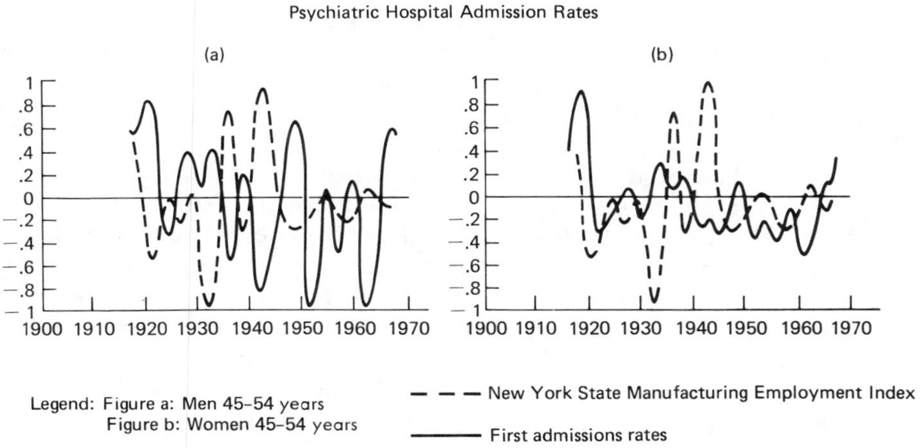

Psychiatric Hospital Admission Rates

Legend: Figure a: Men 45–54 years
Figure b: Women 45–54 years

− − − New York State Manufacturing Employment Index

———— First admissions rates

Figure 13.3 Fluctuations in Employment and Psychiatric Hospital Admission Rates
From H. Brenner, *Mental Illness and the Economy*. Copyright © 1973 Harvard University
Press. Reprinted by permission.

hospital fails to cope with larger systematic, environmental community issues
which cause the distress.

Another example of the importance of environment in determining individual life is provided by Snyder (1978), who examined the lives of women who
were separated from their husbands for long periods of time. The men in this
case were submariners deployed on lengthy missions with little opportunity of
contact with home. An adaptation of Holmes and Rahe's (1967) life stress schedule was used for this study. The schedule is one in which recent problematic
events in the environment are rated. Through the use of this schedule, it has been
found that death, divorce, loss of job, and other stressful events in one's recent
life history are predictive of physical and emotional difficulties. Balancing time
away from and at home, Snyder found that the women visited physicians 368
times while their husbands were gone and only 95 times (62 of which were routine
check-ups) when the husbands were home. In addition, the women noted 329
difficulties that they did not take to a physician when their husbands were gone
and only 34 with their husbands present. Types of illness are also indicative, for
Snyder noted increased problems with blood pressure, emotions, nervousness,
headaches, allergies, and depression with the husband absent.

Once again, one cannot help but visualize the physicians and psychiatrists
treating the specific symptomatic problems brought to them by these women,
when environmental factors are so clearly relevant. The need for preventive psychoeducational developmental services should be readily apparent. Rather than
cope with problems, it would seem appropriate for physicians and mental health
workers to join together in a systematic program to change the environment. Sim-

ilarly, it may be anticipated that unhealthy environments in communities, churches, schools, and business contribute to physical and mental illness.

The work of community psychologists and outreach workers, such as those delineated in Chapter 12, will be increasingly important in attacking the systemic causes of personal distress.

School guidance counselors are concerned with facilitating individuals in their development over many years. The Wisconsin studies (cf., Rothney and Roens, 1950; Rothney, 1958; Merenda and Rothney, 1958) were concerned with the effectiveness of guidance programs, and compared schools that did and did not offer these services. Although differences were not large, it was found that those students who had experienced counseling achieved better academic records, were more realistic about their life choices, were more satisfied with school experience, made more progress in employment, were more likely to be engaged in higher education, participated in more self-improvement activities, and remembered their counseling favorably. One disconcerting finding, however, was that several students in the schools with guidance programs did not recall having been counseled, and some from schools with *no* programs recalled their counseling favorably. Nonetheless, this study, which included a rare 5- and 10-year followup, is indicative that well-planned programs can make a difference in the lives of students. It must be remembered that counseling is only one of the many services provided by school guidance workers, and, with the increasing evidence as to the value of the psychoeducational approach, it may be anticipated that competent counselors, community psychologists, and others are now better prepared to make a larger difference in the lives of those whom they serve.

Meta-analysis of the effectiveness of counseling and therapy has proven an important watershed for the field. By combining research results, meta-analysis has paved the way and clarified the need for new methods and concepts of research. In a similar vein is the work of Baker, Swisher, Nadenichek, and Popowicz (1984) who conducted a meta-analysis of forty primary prevention studies completed in the community. The authors reviewed over 200 prospective studies of community prevention work for effective experimental design and control and finally selected forty studies as meeting requirements for meta-analysis.

Now, critical in Baker and associates' work is the fact that the emphasis is on *prevention* as compared with the focus on *remediation* in the work of Glass and Kleigl reported at the beginning of this chapter. You may recall that Glass and Kliegl found a mean "effect size" of 0.85 as a result of psychotherapy. The corresponding effect size in the primary prevention meta-analysis was 0.55. This specifically means "in terms of percentile ranks, an increase from the 50th to approximately the 73rd percentile" in terms of improvement following participation in a community-based primary prevention program. This figure is impressive when one recalls that the type of measure used for effectiveness of treatment closely resembles the measures used for psychotherapy. As so-called "normals" start at a higher place on evaluation instruments than clients entering psychotherapy, the fact of demonstrated change in this meta-analysis may be considered quite impressive.

Figure 13.4 summarizes the data on the classifications of primary prevention programs. Communication skill programs ranked the highest in the meta-analysis with a remarkable effect size of 3.9. However, one study had an unusual effect size (15.75) and another a very low (0.08). This particular finding illustrates the fact that simply providing a psychoeducational community program is not enough. *Psychoeducation and community change must also be provided effectively.* Just as psychotherapy can be done poorly, so also can psychoeducation be ineffective.

It may be anticipated that research in psychoeducation, community work, and primary prevention will be of increasing importance over the next few years. We have seen that therapy and change efforts often "wash out" and disappear over time. Given this the relapse prevention programs of Marlatt and Marx (see also Chapter 9) and the generalization plans of Janis (see Chapter 2), the consistent stress on the importance of generalization in the fifth stage of the interview

Figure 13.4 Summary of Effects of Primary Prevention Strategies

	N_S	N_{ES}	RANGES ES		%(−)	ES
Combined group of primary prevention studies	42[a]	308	−0.40 to	15.75	9.5	0.91
Combined primary prevention studies without the outlayer (Guzetta '76)	41[a]	302	−0.40 to	1.95	9.8	0.55
Programs designed to enhance career maturity	12	62	−0.08 to	1.40	16.7	1.33
Coping skills training founded on cognitive-behavior modification principles	8	52	−0.40 to	1.02	37.5	0.26
Communication skills training programs	5	87	0.08 to	15.75	0.0	3.90
Communication skills training programs without outlayer (Guzetta '76)	4	81	0.08 to	1.94	0.0	0.93
Deliberate psychological education programs	2	3	0.90 to	1.95	0.0	1.43
Moral education programs	3	21	0.32 to	.56	0.0	0.43
Deliberate psychological education and moral education programs	5	24	0.32 to	1.95	0.0	0.83
Substance abuse prevention programs	7	98	0.08 to	1.13	0.0	0.34
Programs categorized as values clarification in nature	7	44	0.29 to	1.13	0.0	0.69
Programs in which values clarification strategies were blended with other strategies	9	98	−0.08 to	1.41	28.6	0.37
All values clarification programs in combination	16	142	−0.08 to	1.41	14.3	0.51

Note. Key to abbreviations: N_S = number of studies, N_{ES} = number of effect sizes within the total number of studies, Range ES = lowest to highest average effect size across the 40 studies, %(−) = percentage of effect sizes that are negative, ES = estimated effect size.

[a]Two of the forty reports cited report more than a single primary prevention independent variable being investigated.

Baker, S., Swisher, J., Nadenichek, P., and Popowicz, C. "Measured Effects of Primary Prevention Strategies. *Personnel and Guidance Journal*, 1984, *62*, 459–464. Copyright AACD. Reprinted with permission. No further reproduction authorized without further permission of AACD.

seems even more justified. If we do not work toward maintaining the difficult gains made through community work, psychoeducation, and counseling and psychotherapy, there seems insufficient justification for continuing the field. The data base seems clear, despite controversy. The Rothney studies cited earlier provide a particularly clear and cogent statement of the need for generalization training—students often forgot that they had participated in counseling at all or they thought that they had counseling when in fact they did not. Data such as these offer an important challenge to the field.

Research can and must take a wide variety of directions beyond that of traditional individual study of counseling and psychotherapy. The observations from community research inevitably lead to the conclusion that professional counselors and therapists may wish to give more attention to prevention. The early data from Baker and associates' meta-analysis are too strong to be ignored.

For the future, it seems possible that a reasoned and reasonable balance of research and practice will lead to a further integration of process and outcome research—and will lead, perhaps, to the answers to some key questions. Specifically, how does this process variable relate to eventual therapy outcome? And how does outcome itself become a process variable leading to new and later outcomes? How can the data on paraprofessional and lay helper effectiveness be integrated meaningfully in a society in which jobs for professional helpers are becoming ever more competitive? How will the field cope with the promising meta-analysis of psychoeducation and primary prevention? Research to these ends is likely to be nil without careful and systematic planning for generalization and transfer of training.

SUMMARY OF THIS CHAPTER

Discussion in this chapter has been designed to provide a summary of research data from many areas and to illustrate that these data are interpreted very differently according to the reader. For an understanding of the key ideas of this chapter, you should be able to:

1. *Define the relationship of theory and research to the phenomena of the real world.* Theory is an abstraction or description of real events and can confuse or clarify understanding. Research is designed to test these observations and theory for their impact on the real world and to inform the counselor which actions are appropriate. In actual counseling practice, the therapist or counselor operates much like a scientist following basic principles of observation, hypothesis testing, and revising theory according to results with the client.

2. *Discuss the alternative perceptions of the effectiveness of counseling and psychotherapy.* The professional debate around the Eysenck interpretation, concerning possible lack of effectiveness, was compared with that of Glass and his meta-analysis. It was suggested that counseling does make a difference in the life of the client, but that the data are not fully clear. Research suggests that cognitive therapies helping clients find a new worldview may be most effective.

3. *Understand the work of Cummings and the Kaiser-Permanente studies.* Detailed research at Kaiser-Permanente suggests that counseling can be cost-effective and reduce the use of medical services. In addition, short-term psychotherapy (six to eight sessions) around specific problems appears to be the general treatment of choice.

4. *Distinguish between process and outcome research.* Outcome research has been defined as that which studies both the short-term and long-term impact of therapy on clients, whereas process research is concerned with identifying the many variables potentially important in producing positive outcome.

5. *Summarize key findings on attending and nonverbal behavior.* An extensive array of studies was reviewed and appears to attest to the importance of attending behavior and its concomitant nonverbal aspects in the counseling process. Numerous studies have identified the critical importance of eye contact patterns, body language, vocal tone, and verbal following behavior in a variety of contexts.

6. *Discuss central findings of process research.* Data on microskills are extensive and verify that different counselors use different skills, according to personal and theoretical persuasion.

7. *Understand research on qualitative dimensions.* Data suggest that there are certain key qualities (empathy, etc.) that underlie all effective interviews. However, different theoretical orientations may manifest these qualities in various ways.

8. *Be aware of cultural differences in attending and nonverbal behavior, microskill usage, and qualitative dimensions.* In all three areas, data were presented underlining the fact that people listen to one another differently, have different patterns of microskill usage, and express the qualitative dimensions of counseling differently, according to their individual or cultural background.

9. *Summarize the literature on the effectiveness of paraprofessional counselors as compared to professionals.* While the data are mixed, indications are that well-trained paraprofessional counselors can be at least as effective as professionals. This may be due to a greater commonality of background with their clients, since most professional therapists come from more limited family and socioeconomic settings.

10. *Discuss new approaches to counseling and therapy research.* The single case study methods of Hill were highlighted as one specific example of the integration of process and outcome research. In addition, several models that may change the face of research methodology in the future were cited.

11. *Understand the impact of the environment on individual counseling practice.* Family research was briefly examined. A study on the effect of the economy on the mental health of individuals was presented, followed by an example of environmental impact on submariners' wives. The Rothney studies of school guidance effectiveness provide an example of how planned remedial, preventive, and developmental programs can make a difference in the lives of large numbers of clients. Baker's community meta-analysis was reviewed. The treatment of choice may be environmental intervention rather than individual counseling.

REFERENCES

ANTHONY, W., and R. CARKHUFF, "The Functional Professional Therapeutic Agent." In Gurman, A., and A. Razin, eds., *Effective Psychotherapy.* Elmsford, NY: Pergamon Press, 1977, 103–119.

AUERBACH, A., and M. JOHNSON, "Research on the Therapist's Level of Experience." In Gurman, A., and A. Razin, eds., *Effective Psychotherapy.* Elmsford, NY: Pergamon Press, 1977, 84–102.

BAKER, S., M. SCOFIELD, L. CLAYTON, and W. MUNSON, "Microskills Practice Versus

Mental Practice Training for Competence in Decision-Making Counseling," *Journal of Counseling Psychology*, 1984, *31*, 104–107.

BAKER, S., J. SWISHER, P. NADENICHEK, and C. POPOWICZ, "Measured Effects of Primary Prevention Strategies." *Personnel and Guidance Journal*, 1984, *62*, 459–464.

BARRETT-LENNARD, G., "Dimensions of Therapist Response as Causal Factors in Therapeutic Change," *Psychological Monographs*, 1962, *76*, (43, whole No. 562).

BAYES, M., "Behavioral Cues of Interpersonal Warmth," *Journal of Counseling Psychology*, 1972, *39*, 333–339.

BECK, J., and S. STRONG, "Stimulating Therapeutic Change with Interpretations," *Journal of Counseling Psychology*, 1982, *29*, 551–559.

BERENSON, B., and K. MITCHELL, *Confrontation for Better or Worse!* Amherst, MA: Human Resource Development, 1974.

BERGIN, A., "The Evaluation of Therapeutic Outcomes." In Bergin, A., and S. Garfield, eds., *Handbook of Psychotherapy and Behavior Change*. New York: John Wiley, 1971, 217–270.

BERGIN, A., and R. SUINN, "Individual Psychotherapy and Behavior Therapy," *Annual Review of Psychology*, 1975, *26*, 509–556.

BERMAN, J., "Counseling Skills Used by Black and White Male and Female Counselors," *Journal of Counseling Psychology*, 1979, *26*, 81–84.

BERZINS, J., "Therapist-Patient Matching." In Gurman, A., and A. Razin eds., *Effective Psychotherapy*. Elmsford, NY: Pergamon Press, 1977, 222–251.

BLOCKSMA, D., and E. PORTER, "A Short-Term Training Program in Client-Centered Counseling," *Journal of Consulting Psychology*, 1947, *11*, 55–60.

BORGEN, F., "Counseling Psychology." In Rosenzweig, M. and L. Porter, *Annual Review of Psychology*, 1984, *35*, 579–604.

BRENNER, H., *Mental Illness and the Economy*. Cambridge, MA: Harvard University Press, 1973.

BRIGGS, J., *Never in Anger: Portrait of an Eskimo Family*. Cambridge, MA: Harvard University Press, 1970.

BRISLIN, R., "Cross-Cultural Psychology." In Rosenzweig, M. and L. Porter, *Annual Review of Psychology*, 1983, *34*, 363–400.

BRODSKY, A., "Sex, Race, and Class Issues in Psychotherapy Research." In Harvey, J. and M. Parks, *Psychotherapy Research and Behavior Change*. Washington, D.C.: American Psychological Association, 1981, 123–150.

CARKHUFF, R., *Helping and Human Relations*, Vols. I and II. New York: Holt, Rinehart & Winston, 1969a and b.

CARR, R. and G. SAUNDERS, *Peer Counseling Starter Kit*. Victoria, B.C.: Educational Research Institute of British Columbia, 1980.

CONDON, W., and W. OGSTON, "Sound Film Analysis of Normal and Pathological Behavior Patterns," *Journal of Nervous and Mental Disease*, 1966, *143*, 338–346.

CUMMINGS, N., "Prolonged (Ideal) Versus Short-Term (Realistic) Psychotherapy," *Professional Psychology*, 1977, *8*, 491–501.

CUMMINGS, N., Personal Communication, Kaiser-Permanente, San Francisco, February, 1985.

CUMMINGS, N. and W. FOLLETTE, "Psychiatric Services and Medical Utilization in a Prepaid Health Plan Setting," *Medical Care*, 1968, *5*, 31–41.

CUMMINGS, N. and W. FOLLETTE, "Brief Psychotherapy and Medical Utilization: An Eight-Year Follow-Up." In Dorken, H. and associates. *The Professional Psychologist Today*. San Francisco: Jossey-Bass, 1976.

CUMMINGS, N. and G. VANDENBOS, "The General Practice of Psychology," *Professional Psychology*, 1979, *10*, 430–440.

DANIELS, T., Microcounseling: Training in Skills of Therapeutic Communication with R.N. Department Program Nursing Students. Unpublished doctoral dissertation, Dalhousie University, Halifax, Nova Scotia.

DEAUX, K., "From Individual Differences to Social Categories," *American Psychologist,* 1984, *39,* 105–116.

DUNCAN, S., JR., L. RICE, and J. BUTLER, "Therapist's Paralanguage in Peak and Poor Psychotherapy Interviews," *Journal of Abnormal Psychology,* 1968, *73,* 566–570.

EKMAN, P., W. FRIESEN, and P. ELLSWORTH, *Emotion in the Human Face.* Elmsford, NY: Pergamon Press, 1972.

ELDRED, S., and D. PRICE, "A Linguistic Evaluation of Feeling States in Psychotherapy," *Psychiatry,* 1958, *21,* 115–121.

EYSENCK, H., "The Effects of Psychotherapy: An Evaluation," *Journal of Consulting Psychology,* 1952, *16,* 319–324.

EYSENCK, H., *The Effects of Psychotherapy.* New York: International Science, 1966.

EYSENCK, H., "An Exercise in Mega-Silliness," *American Psychologist,* 1978, *33,* 517.

FELDMAN, D., S. STRONG, and D. DANSER, "A Comparison of paradoxical and self-control directives in counseling," *Journal of Counseling Psychology,* 1982, *29,* 572–579.

FIEDLER, F., "A Comparison of Therapeutic Relationships in Psychoanalytic, Nondirective, and Adlerian Therapy," *Journal of Consulting Psychology,* 1950a, *14,* 435–436.

FIEDLER, F., "The Concept of an Ideal Therapeutic Relationship," *Journal of Consulting Psychology,* 1950b, *14,* 239–245.

FIEDLER, F., "Factor Analysis of Psychoanalytic, Nondirective, and Adlerian Therapeutic Relationships," *Journal of Consulting Psychology,* 1951, *15,* 32–38.

FISKE, D., "The Meta-Analytic Revolution in Outcome Research," *Journal of Consulting and Clinical Psychology,* 1983, *51,* 65–70.

FORD, D., "Re-examining Guiding Assumptions," *Journal of Counseling Psychology,* 1984, *31,* 461–466.

FORD, J., "Research on training counselors and clinicians," *Review of Educational Research,* 1979, *49,* 87–130.

FRANCES, A., J. CLARKIN, and S. PERRY, *Differential Therapeutics in Psychiatry: The Art and Science of Treatment Selection.* New York: Brunner/Mazel, 1984.

FRY, P., G. KROPF, and K. COE, "Effects of Counselor and Client Racial Similarity on the Counselor's Response Patterns and Skills," *Journal of Counseling Psychology,* 1980, *27,* 130–137.

GARFIELD, S., *Psychotherapy.* New York: Wiley, 1980.

GARFIELD, S., and A. BERGIN, eds., *Handbook of Psychotherapy and Behavior Change.* New York: Wiley, 1978.

GILL, S., C. BERGER, and G. COGAR, "Evaluating Microcounseling Training," *Evaluation Review,* 1983, *7,* 247–256.

GLASS, G., Personal Communication. University of Colorado, Boulder, CO, November 1984.

GLASS, G., and R. KLIEGL, "An Apology for Research Integration in the Study of Psychotherapy," *Journal of Consulting and Clinical Psychology,* 1984, *51,* 28–41.

GOLDSTEIN, A., Personal Communication. Syracuse University, Syracuse, NY, 1985.

GOLDSTEIN, A., and N. STEIN, *Prescriptive Psychotherapies.* Elmsford, NY: Pergamon Press, 1976.

GUERNEY, B., E. VOGELSONG, and J. COUFAL, "Relationship Enhancement versus a Traditional Treatment." In D. Olson and B. Miller, eds., *Family Studies Review Yearbook.* Beverly Hills: Sage, 1983, 738–756.

GURMAN, A., and D. KNISKERN, eds., *Handbook of Family Therapy.* New York: Brunner/Mazel, 1981, 742–776.

GURMAN, A., and A. RAZIN, eds., *Effective Psychotherapy: A Handbook of Research.* Elmsford, NY: Pergamon Press, 1977.

HACKNEY, R., A. IVEY, and E. OETTING, "Attending, Island, and Hiatus Behavior: A Process Conception of Counselor and Client Interaction," *Journal of Counseling Psychology,* 1970, *17,* 342–346.

HADLEY, S., and H. STRUPP, "Contemporary Views of Negative Effects in Psychotherapy," *Archives of General Psychiatry,* 1976, *33,* 1291–1302.

HALL, E., *The Silent Language.* New York: Doubleday, 1959.

HALL, E., *The Dance of Life.* New York: Anchor/Doubleday, 1983.

HARPER, R., A. WIENS, and J. MATARAZZO, *Nonverbal Communication: The State of the Art.* New York: John Wiley, 1978.

HATTIE, J., C. SHARPLEY, and J. ROGERS, "Comparative Effectiveness of Professional and Paraprofessional Helpers," *Psychological Bulletin,* 1984, *95,* 534–541.

HILL, C., J. CARTER, and M. O'FARRELL, "A Case Study of the Process and Outcome of Time-Limited Counseling," *Journal of Counseling Psychology,* 1983, *28,* 428–436.

HOLMES, T., and R. RAHE, "The Social Readjustment Rating Scale," *Journal of Psychosomatic Research,* 1967, *11,* 213–218.

HOWARD, G., "A Modest Proposal for a Revision of Strategies of Counseling Research," *Journal of Counseling Psychology,* 1984, *31,* 430–441.

IVEY, A., *Microcounseling: Innovations in Interviewing Training.* Springfield, IL: Chas. C. Thomas, 1971.

IVEY, A., "Credentialism: Protection for the Public or the Professional?" In E. Herr and N. Pinson, eds., *Foundations for Policy in Guidance and Counseling.* Washington, D.C.: American Personnel and Guidance Association, 1982, 131–154.

IVEY, A., *Intentional Interviewing and Counseling.* Monterey, CA: Brooks/Cole, 1983.

IVEY, A., *The Current Status of Microtraining.* Keynote address to the Japan Student Counseling Association, November 1984.

IVEY, A., *Developmental Therapy: Theory Into Practice.* San Francisco: Jossey-Bass, 1986.

IVEY, A., and J. AUTHIER, *Microcounseling: Innovations in Interviewing, Counseling, Psychotherapy, and Psychoeducation.* (2nd ed.). Springfield, IL: Chas. C. Thomas, 1978.

IVEY, A., and M. GALVIN, "Microcounseling: A Metamodel for Counseling, Psychotherapy, Business, and Medical Interviews." In Larson, D. *Teaching Psychological Skills: Models for Giving Psychology Away.* Monterey, CA: Brooks/Cole, 1984, 207–228.

IVEY, A., C. NORMINGTON, C. MILLER, W. MORRILL, and R. HAASE, "Microcounseling and Attending Behavior: An Approach to Pre-Practicum Counselor Training," *Journal of Counseling Psychology,* 1968, *15.* (whole Part II, 1–12).

KARASU, K., ed., *Psychotherapy Research,* Washington, D.C.: American Psychiatric Association, 1982.

KATZ, J., *White Awareness: Handbook for Anti-Racism Training.* Norman, OK: University of Oklahoma Press, 1978.

KELLY, G., *The Psychology of Personal Constructs.* New York: Norton, 1955.

KUROSAWA, K., "Meta-Analysis and Selective Publication Bias," *American Psychologist,* 1984, *39,* 73–74.

LABOV, W., and D. FANSHEL, *Therapeutic Discourse.* New York: Academic Press, 1977.

LAMBERT, M., A. BERGIN, and J. COLLINS, "Therapist-induced Deterioration in Psychotherapy." In Gurman, A., and A. Razin, eds., *Effective Psychotherapy.* New York: Pergamon, 1977, 452–481.

LAMBERT, M., E. CHRISTENSON, and S. DEJULIO, eds., *The Assessment of Psychotherapy Outcome.* New York: Wiley, 1983.

LAMBERT, M., S. DEJULIO, and D. STEIN, "Therapist Interpersonal Skills," *Psychological Bulletin,* 1978, *85,* 467–489.

LANDFIELD, A., *Personal Construct Systems in Psychotherapy*. Skokie, IL: Rand McNally, 1971.

LUBORSKY, L., "The Latest Word on Comparative Studies: Is It True That All Have Won So All Shall Have Prizes?" Presidential address at the Fifth Annual Meeting of the Society for Psychotherapy Research. Denver, June 1974.

LUBORSKY, L., B. SINGER, and L. LUBORSKY, "Comparative Studies of Psychotherapy: Is it True that Everyone has Won and All Must have Prizes?" *Archives of General Psychiatry*, 1975, *32*, 995–1008.

MALAN, D., *A Study of Brief Psychotherapy*. New York: Plenum, 1963.

MALAN, D., *The Frontier of Brief Psychotherapy*. New York: Plenum, 1976.

MARLATT, G., and J. GORDON, *Relapse Prevention*. New York: Guilford, 1985.

MARROW, A., *The Practical Theorist*. New York: Basic Books, 1969.

MARX, R., Self-Control Strategies in Management Training: Skill Maintenance Despite Organizational Realities. Symposium chaired at the American Psychological Association Annual Meeting, Toronto, Canada, August, 1984.

MAYO, C., and M. LaFRANCE, Gaze Direction in Interracial Dyadic Communication. Paper presented at the meeting of the Eastern Psychological Association, Washington, D.C., 1973.

McGOLDRICK, M., J. PEARCE, and J. GIORDANO, *Ethnicity and Family Therapy*. New York: Guilford, 1982.

MEARA, N., H. PEPINSKY, J. SHANNON, and W. MURRAY, "Semantic Communication and Expectations for Counseling Across Three Theoretical Orientations," *Journal of Counseling Psychology* 1981, *28*, 110–118.

MEARA, N., J. SHANNON, and H. PEPINSKY, "Comparisons of Stylistic Complexity of the Language of Counselor and Client Across Three Theoretical Orientations," *Journal of Counseling Psychology*, 1979, *26*, 181–189.

MERENDA, P., and J. ROTHNEY, "Evaluating the Effects of Counseling—Eight Years After," *Journal of Counseling Psychology*, 1958, *5*, 163–168.

MITCHELL, K., J. BOZARTH, and C. KRAUFT, "A Reappraisal of the Therapeutic Effectiveness of Accurate Empathy, Nonpossessive Warmth and Genuineness." In Gurman, A., and A. Razin, eds., *Effective Psychotherapy*. New York, Pergamon, 1977, 482–502.

PATTON, M., "Managing Social Interaction in Counseling," *Journal of Counseling Psychology*, 1984, *31*, 442–441.

PEDERSEN, P., "The Cultural Inclusiveness of Counseling." In Pedersen, P., J. Draguns, W. Lonner, and J. Trimble, eds., *Counseling Across Cultures*. Honolulu: University of Hawaii, 1981, 22–60.

PEDERSEN, P., J. DRAGUNS, W. LONNER, and J. TRIMBLE, eds., *Counseling Across Cultures*. Honolulu: University of Hawaii, 1981.

POLKINGHORNE, D., "Further Extensions of Methodological Diversity for Counseling Psychology," *Journal of Counseling Psychology*, 1984, *31*, 416–429.

RACHMAN, S., and G. WILSON, *The Effects of Psychological Therapy*. New York: Wiley, 1980.

RIDLEY, C., "Clinical Treatment of the Nondisclosing Black Client," *American Psychologist*, 1984, *39*, 1234–1244.

ROGERS, C., "Empathic: An Unappreciated Way of Being," *The Counseling Psychologist*, 1975, *5*, 2–9.

ROGERS, C., G. GENDLIN, D. KIESLER, and C. TRUAX, *The Therapeutic Relationship and Its Impact: A Study of Psychotherapy with Schizophrenics*. Madison: University of Wisconsin, 1967.

ROTHNEY, J., *Guidance Practices and Results*. New York: Harper & Row, 1958.

ROTHNEY, J., and B. ROENS, *Guidance of American Youth*. Cambridge, MA: Harvard University Press, 1950.

SCHOFIELD, W., *Psychotherapy, The Purchase of Friendship.* Englewood Cliffs, NJ: Prentice-Hall, 1964.

SHAPIRO, D., and D. SHAPIRO, "Comparative Therapy Outcome Research," *Journal of Consulting and Clinical Psychology,* 1984, *51,* 42–53.

SHERRARD, P., "Predicting Group Leader/Member Interaction: The Efficacy of the Ivey Taxonomy." Unpublished dissertation, Amherst, University of Massachusetts, 1973.

SHOSTRUM, E., producer, *Three Approaches to Psychotherapy.* Santa Ana, CA: Psychological Films, 1966. (Film)

SLOANE, R., and F. STAPLES, "Psychotherapy versus Behavior Therapy: Implications for Future Psychotherapy Research." In Williams, J., and R. Spitzer, eds., *Psychotherapy Research: Where are We and Where Should We Go?* New York: Guilford, 1984, 203–215.

SLOANE, R., F. STAPLES, A. CRISTOL, N. YORKSTON, and K. WHIPPLE, *Psychotherapy Versus Behavior Therapy.* Cambridge, MA: Harvard University Press, 1975.

SMITH, M., and G. GLASS, "Meta-Analysis of Psychotherapy Outcome Studies," *American Psychologist,* 1977, *32,* 752–760.

SMITH, M., and G. GLASS, "Comment." *American Psychologist,* 1978, *33,* 518.

SMITH, M., G. GLASS, and T. MILLER, *The Benefits of Psychotherapy.* Baltimore: Johns Hopkins, 1980.

SNYDER, A., "Periodic Marital Separation and Physical Illness," *American Journal of Orthopsychiatry,* 1978, *48,* 637–643.

STRONG, S., Experimental Studies of Paradoxical Intention. Unpublished paper, Virginia Commonwealth University, 1983.

STRUPP, H., "An Objective Comparison of Rogerian and Psychoanalytic Technique," *Journal of Consulting Psychology,* 1955a, *19,* 1–7.

STRUPP, H., "Psychotherapeutic Technique, Professional Affiliation, and Experience Level," *Journal of Consulting Psychology,* 1955b, *19,* 97–102.

STRUPP, H., "The Performance of Psychiatrists and Psychologists in a Therapeutic Interview," *Journal of Clinical Psychology,* 1958, *14,* 219–226.

STRUPP, H., "Comment." In Eysenck, H., *The Effects of Psychotherapy.* New York: International Science, 1966, 67–71.

STRUPP, H., "A Reformulation of the Dynamics of the Therapist's Contribution." In Gurman, A., and A. Razin, eds., *Effective Psychotherapy.* Elmsford, NY: Pergamon Press, 1977, 1–22.

STRUPP, H., "The Vanderbilt Psychotherapy Research Project." In Williams, J., and R. Spitzer, eds., *Psychotherapy Research: Where are We and Where Should We Go?* New York: Guilford, 1984, 235–246.

STRUBE, M., and D. HARTMANN, "Meta-Analysis: Techniques, Applications, and Functions." *Journal of Consulting and Clinical Psychology,* 1984, *51,* 14–27.

SUE, D., *Counseling the Culturally Different.* New York: Wiley, 1981.

SUH, C., and H. STRUPP, Appropriateness of Residual Gains in Psychotherapy Research. Paper presented at the Conference for the Society for Psychotherapy Research, Burlington, VT, 1982.

SUNDLAND, D., "Theoretical Orientations of Psychotherapists." In Gurman, A., and A. Razin, eds., *Effective Psychotherapy.* Elmsford, NY: Pergamon Press, 1977, 189–221.

TRAUX, C., and K. MITCHELL, "Research on Certain Therapist Skills in Relation to Process and Outcome." In Bergin, A., and S. Garfield, eds., *Handbook of Psychotherapy and Behavior Change.* New York: John Wiley, 1971, 299–344.

WILLIAMS, J., and R. SPITZER, eds., *Psychotherapy Research: Where Are We and Where Should We Go?* New York: Guilford, 1984.

WILSON, G., and S. RACHMAN, "Meta-Analysis and the Evaluation of Psychotherapy," *Journal of Consulting and Clinical Psychology,* 1984, *51,* 54–64.

SUGGESTED SUPPLEMENTARY READING

Annual Review of Psychology.   Palo Alto, CA: Annual Reviews, published yearly.
  Each year under varying editorship and authorship, the *Annual Review* summarizes current research findings in many fields of psychology. The reviews on behavior change, personality, counseling, and psychotherapy are likely to be useful background for any serious student of counseling or psychotherapy.

EYSENCK, H.,   *The Effects of Psychotherapy.* New York: International Science, 1966.
  A stimulating summary of the debate concerning the effectiveness of psychotherapy with interesting commentaries by several authorities.

FRANCES, A., J. CLARKIN, and S. PERRY,   *Differential Therapeutics in Psychiatry: The Art and Science of Treatment Selection.* New York: Brunner/Mazel, 1984.
  A highly readable summary of research on counseling and psychotherapy that specifies to the best of its ability how to use research in clinical practice.

HARPER, R., A. WIENS, and J. MATARAZZO,   *Nonverbal Communication: The State of the Art.* New York: John Wiley, 1978.
  A comprehensive and scholarly consideration of the many issues underlying nonverbal communication.

PEDERSON, P., J. DRAGUNS, W. LONNER, and J. TRIMBLE,   *Counseling Across Cultures.* (2nd ed.). Honolulu: University of Hawaii Press, 1981.
  An examination of intercultural counseling issues, racial and ethnic barriers in counseling, the nature of intercultural psychotherapy, and other questions important to those who wish to incorporate increased cultural sensitivity into their counseling and psychotherapy.

SLOANE, R., F. STAPLES, A. CRISTOL, N. YORKSTON, and K. WHIPPLE,   *Psychotherapy Versus Behavior Therapy.* Cambridge, MA: Harvard University Press, 1975.
  The Sloane et al. study is coming to be recognized as a classic, and is important reading not only for its content and findings but also for its sophisticated methodology.

14

INTEGRATING SKILLS
AND THEORY

GENERAL PREMISE

An integrated knowledge of skills, theory, and practice is essential for culturally intentional counseling and therapy.

Skills form the foundation of effective theory and practice: The culturally intentional therapist knows how to construct a creative decision-making interview and can use microskills to attend to and influence clients in a predicted direction. Important in this process are individual and cultural empathy, client observation skills, assessment of person and environment, and the application of positive techniques of growth and change.

Theory provides organizing principles for counseling and therapy: The culturally intentional counselor has knowledge of alternative theoretical approaches and treatment modalities.

Practice is the integration of skills and theory: The culturally intentional counselor or therapist is competent in skills and theory, and is able to apply them to research and practice for client benefit.

Undergirding integrated competence in skills, theory, and practice is an intentional awareness of one's own personal worldview and how that worldview may be similar to and/or different from the worldview and personal constructions of the client and other professionals.

GOALS FOR INTEGRATING SKILLS, THEORIES, AND PRACTICE

This chapter seeks to demonstrate how skills and theory may be integrated in the practice of counseling and therapy. You may recall that Chapter 7 presents how skills and alternative theories may be integrated into the practice of a single interview. Here the aim is to extend those concepts to a longer-term series of interviews and to consider how skills and theory may be used to plan and to analyze one's therapy and counseling practice.

Specific aims of this chapter are to:

1. Discuss how the five-stage model of the interview may be used to develop a plan for the initial interview. Furthermore, special attention will be given to how the same model may be valuable in generating a systematic long-term treatment plan.
2. Present the several theories of this book in summary chart form. In this way you can compare the worldview, major concepts, and techniques of each theory.
3. Summarize the integration of skills and theory into practice through the presentation of a series of seven interviews with a client.
4. Summarize the idea of an integrated general theory or metatheory and encourage *you* to develop *your* own personal construction of counseling and therapy, be it systematic eclectic or represented by a solid commitment to one single major theoretical orientation.

THE SEARCH FOR THE "BEST" THEORY

"*What* treatment, by *whom,* is most effective for *this* individual with *that* specific problem, and under *which* set of circumstances?" Gordon Paul made this classic statement in 1967 and he catches effectively a growing edge of the profession since that time. Prior to Paul's statement, the basic issue was "Which therapy is *best?*" Even the casual reader would be asked to join a particular bandwagon of "truth." Extensive discussion and argument sometimes filled journals and books attested to some old or new theory as "the best."

The important research by Glass and Kliegl (1983) reviewed in Chapter 13 perhaps provides the "best" answer as to which therapy is "best." The answer there suggests that cognitive-behavioral methods have the most solid research behind them attesting to impact and effectiveness. However, this research review can itself be questioned as resting on a series of studies that do not provide a fully comprehensive and equal examination for varying forms of therapy. Newer therapies such as family and the consciousness-raising theories are not included. Moreover, the current cognitive-behavioral trend may represent a new form of eclecticism in which those oriented to thinking approaches—such as Beck's cognitive psychology, Frankl or Rogers' humanism, and others—may find a common ground with room and respect for differences.

Paul, however, is not asking which therapy is "best." He is acknowledging that different treatments are differentially effective with different people—*dif-*

ferent strokes for different folks. Thus, while one therapy may or may not be generally "best," the growing consensus of the field is heading toward the specific treatment of specific issues such as that exemplified by the cutting edge work of Cummings, also described in Chapter 13 (pages 385 through 386). Cummings is cataloging which treatment diagnostically is likely to result in client improvement. He has found that each client needs and deserves individual treatment, not the strict application of a single theory or method. The careful notation of individual, sexual, age, cultural, and many other differences appears to be critical in working effectively with clients.

Currently, there is no definitive single "best" treatment method that can be defined precisely for the client whom you may face. However, the fields of counseling and psychotherapy are rapidly moving toward prescriptive treatment in which client assessment leads to concrete action that makes a predictable difference in the client's life. The summary work of Glass and Kliegl, the methods of Cummings and his colleagues, and the emerging differential treatment represented by Goldstein and Stein (1976) and Frances, Clarkin, and Perry (1984) all focus on answering the complex and important questions through some form of a general theory or metatheoretical synthesis.

Two important issues are missing from Paul's conception, however. The first of these is the critical issue of *culturally and individually appropriate goals.* The *problem* may be that of mild anxiety as stated by the client in the first session. Toward what *cultural and individually appropriate goal* is the client and his or her therapist oriented? Is the goal self-understanding? Then perhaps a Rogerian or psychodynamic approach may be appropriate. However, if the goal turns out to be feeling less anxious in social situations, the method may be assertiveness training. If the client is a woman, feminist-oriented assertiveness training may be called for. In short, it is not enough to settle for solving the problem, one must also have a clear goal and outcome in mind that is satisfactory to the client, and, ideally, the therapist as well.

Secondly, change in therapy that is not planned will often disappear in the complexities of life after therapy. Specifically, it may be useful to help our client feel less anxious via Rogerian therapy or by implementing assertiveness training. Both techniques may fail if no plan for followup and treatment generalization is made. Thus, to Gordon Paul's classic question may be added "and *how will relapse be prevented?*"

This chapter seeks to summarize the central concepts of this text and thus illustrate the considerable complexity of answering the more broadly-stated question:

> *What* treatment, by *whom,* is most effective for *this* individual with *that* specific problem, with *what* specific culturally and individually appropriate goal, under *which* set of circumstances, and *how* can relapse of treatment be prevented?

To accomplish these multifaceted objectives requires a systematic treatment plan and an integrated methodology for each treatment session.

A GENERAL TREATMENT PLAN FOR THE INTERVIEW

Chapter 2 (page 32) outlined five basic stages of the interview giving special attention to cultural and individual differences. The five-stage structure (rapport/structuring, gathering information/identifying assets, determining outcomes, generating alternative solutions, and generalization/transfer of learning) can serve as a basic model as you plan for your first session with a client. The same model can prove useful in taking interview notes and in planning for longer-term issues.

Specifically, before the first session, you can anticipate client issues only partially, even if you have before you a very comprehensive file. Clients tend to be unpredictable. Thus, it appears to be helpful to have an overview of what is "necessary and sufficient" for a well-structured interview. At the same time, *it is important to recall that different clients with distinct problems and who may come from different cultural backgrounds will require adaptation of the following basic model.*

One Model for the Initial Interview

Baron (1985) specializes in work with young people and families. She has found that many problems are prevented if the treatment outline is carefully structured *before* therapy actually begins. She uses the following set of guidelines as a specific plan for the first interview with a client. A summary of key aspects of her plan for a 90-minute first session follows. See Figure 14.1 (page 419) for a checklist that you may wish to use or adapt for your own initial interview sessions with a client.

The model here presented by Baron is only one of many possibilities. What seems important in her conceptions is the openness of key issues of relationship. In a time of increasingly legal involvement in the helping process, this

Nancy Baron

Baron's Initial Interview Plan

STAGE ONE: RAPPORT AND STRUCTURING

1. *Opening statement.*
   Acknowledge that the initial interview is often a bit scary and uncomfortable for the client and myself. Give some attention to issues of rapport and relationship. 1) Explain my plan for the session: 2) talk about myself and my qualifications; 3) explain the counseling/therapy format; 4) determine why the client has come for treatment; 5) establish initial goals; 6) decision as to whether or not it is best for us to work together.
2. *Background: Both client and me.*
   Explain to the client(s) who I am, my education and training, my prior work experience. Describe the difference in types of therapy available and then describe my personal orientation to counseling and therapy.
   Ask about past experience in therapy. *Have they seen someone else? When? Where? What was their experience? Are they currently in therapy of any type with anyone else?* Ask them for signed release so that I can contact any other therapist if needed.
   Any questions about who I am?
3. *Explanation of therapy format.*
   Usually once a week for 60 minutes, family sessions 90.
   Explain no show policy.
   Describe rules of confidentiality. (All sessions are private unless there is serious danger of suicide or someone being harmed or in the case of a minor if child abuse is involved.)
   Ask the client(s) not to terminate therapy by just not showing up. Discuss the joys and pain of therapy as typical of growth. Point out that continuity and honesty of feelings and thoughts about issues and feelings are critical if therapy is to be fully helpful.
   Formalize and clarify payment.

STAGE 2: PROBLEM DEFINITION AND ASSET SEARCH

4. *Why is the client(s) here?*
   History of problem as client(s) and others see it?
   Why is therapy starting now?
   Referral source?
   Feelings about therapy for themselves and others?
   General goals?
   Cultural issues which may impact treatment?
   Definition of one or more client strengths/assets.
   Much more, depending on the client issue—may be continued in considerable detail in later interviews.

STAGE 3: DETERMINING OUTCOMES

5. *Establish initial goals.*
   Jointly concretize general long-term goals of therapy.
   Establish one or more immediate short-term goals which may be more quickly attainable.
   Discussion of timetable for treatment.

STAGE 4: CONFRONTATION OF INCONGRUITY/GENERATION OF ALTERNATIVES

   (In this example, the basic incongruity or ambiguity is whether or not the client and therapist will engage in treatment. The resolution of this simple, but critical issue is basic to almost any treatment plan.)

6. *Decision as to whether or not we shall work together.*

        Ask client(s) how he/she feels about this session. Does it appear that we have a good working relationship which will allow us to continue?

        Summarize my past experience with cases of this type and indicate to client that I feel I have necessary expertise.

        We then agree to work together or I make a referral.

        "Is there anything I should know about them that would specifically help me how to decide to work with them most effectively?" Another variation of this question is "Is there anything important we missed?"

STAGE 5: GENERALIZATION AND FOLLOWUP

7. *Conclusion of session.*

        Brief review of session and agreed-upon goals.

        Presentation on my part of general treatment plan.

        Confirm time of next appointment.

Nancy Baron, copyright 1985. Used by permission.

step-by-step outline of the procedures can prevent confusion and disharmony in the future.

If you are engaged in short-term counseling, this lengthy first interview may not be feasible, but aspects of it may be useful to clarify your relationship and to maintain maximum communication with your client.

In addition, it is currently becoming increasingly accepted for private practice and public practice to post much of this basic information openly in the waiting room. Washington state, for example, requires the posting of patient rights for all clients to read before entering counseling or therapy.

Baron's framework for the initial interview is only one of many approaches, but is presented as a systematic checklist that you may wish to consider as you look toward your own initial interviews. You will find that many suggested techniques of this text will be useful in your own formulation of initial sessions. For example, the Kelly newspaper diagnostic questions ("who, what, when, where, how, why") can be useful in obtaining a more detailed overview of the client's problem. Alternatively, you may involve yourself deeply in the problem definition stage—even for several interviews—as you administer diagnostic tests, obtain detailed case history, and seek to define the problem in its full complexity. There are those who argue that effective diagnosis can serve as 70 percent or more of effective treatment.

In your first interview, awareness of individual and cultural differences is critical. You may find, for example, that some clients object to starting an interview with problem assessment. Nonverbal clients and those with lower incomes often like to start a session (perhaps even before rapport) with a clear statement of goals. It may be necessary to work on goal clarification (and sometimes even goal attainment) before working back to problem definition and deeper development of rapport. In short, it may be necessary to restructure the interview.

Figure 14.1   *Integrating Ethical Issues into the Initial Interview Format*

This checklist should be completed by the therapist at the end of the initial interview and placed into the client's file. It serves as proof that these ethical issues have been addressed with the client(s) before the onset of treatment.

1. A list of professional ethical standards and client's rights is visibly posted in my office.
2. My professional credentials are visibly posted in my office.
3. I reviewed my professional education and experience and explained how that qualifies me to do therapy.
4. I had the client(s) complete a face sheet with pertinent identifying information.
5. I asked the client about previous therapeutic experiences.
6. I described my theoretical orientation and my style of treatment.
7. I explained my crisis and emergency procedures.
8. I clarified issues around payment.
9. I explained my cancellation and no show policy.
10. I reviewed the professional and state standards on the issue of client/therapist confidentiality.
11. I completed my usual initial interview.
12. The client and I reviewed all the information and determined if we should work together.
13. If we have agreed that I am not the therapist of best choice, I have referred the client(s) to another clinician.
14. If we have agreed to work together, we developed an initial set of goals for treatment.
15. I scheduled the next appointment.

_____   _____
therapist signature   date

Used by permission of Nancy Baron, copyright © 1984

Some counseling and therapy theories, perhaps even most, give little attention to defining outcomes, yet, each therapy has specific general goals for the client. Figure 14.3 (see page 426) outlines and summarizes the goals and methods of several alternative modes of helping. The tendency among some therapists and counselors is to assume that the goal of their therapy is also the client's goal. Thus, we sometimes find client-centered therapists unconsciously imposing a goal of "self-actualization" on a client who comes from a culture (for example, some Asians, Blacks, Native Americans) in which self-actualization is, in truth, considered a selfish and overly individualistic approach to life. Thus, it is suggested that simply asking the client what her or his ideal outcome would be is a critical question in interview planning. It does little good to work on sexual dysfunction when the client's goal is a smooth and easy divorce. Defining goals does not mean that goals always have to be achieved. However, awareness of goals is essential if one is to work in a culturally and individually appropriate treatment plan.

Longer-Term Treatment Plans

The five-stage model of the interview serves as a useful reference point to ensure that you have thought through critical issues in initiating therapy and counseling. The same model, of course, was presented in Chapter 2 as a useful way to conceptualize the interview.

It is in longer term treatment plans that different theories of helping are most radically different. A psychoanalyst may want to work on dreams, the cognitive-behaviorist on thinking patterns, and the Gestalt therapist on body incongruities. Our tendency is to select the treatment we as counselors or therapists think is best. If we do so, we may be unconsciously imposing our goal on the client. For example, the methods of logotherapy may be very effective with certain types of problems, but are likely to miss critical issues of action in the world that are stressed by behavior therapy or serious women's issues faced by feminist therapy. However, behavior therapy and feminist therapy may not adequately deal with the issues of meaning represented by logotherapy.

Obviously, different therapies all seek to resolve contradiction, polarities, incongruencies, and lack of intentionality; but they go about this resolution very differently. Your task as therapist/counselor is to be aware of several alternative routes to personal growth and development and apply these theories in the moment to meet specific client needs and goals.

For the purpose of a treatment plan, you need to be aware of *what you do know* and what your options for treatment are. If your theoretical orientation and goals are not compatible with that of the client, it may be more appropriate to arrange referral. An effective treatment plan, even before seeing a client, includes your awareness of your capabilities and theoretical intentions and goals.

As part of your treatment plan, you will need to plan specific generalization of attitudes or behaviors learned or discussed in the interview. If your theoretical orientation is not focused around generalization (as is much psychodynamic theory, Rogerian, and existential therapy), it is important that you maintain awareness of the fact that you are leaving generalization up to the client.

Thus, at the most basic level, a treatment plan requires you to think through what you plan to do with the client *before* the interview begins. This thinking through or planning, perhaps even with an interview checklist based on the work of Baron will provide you with a map of what is happening and give you a direction for action.

Interestingly, the same five steps of the interview can be used as an organizing principle for your interview notes. You can summarize key issues of rapport that you need to work through in the next session, problem definition information (along with asset summary), and list the goals of the client. The listing of goals may include your own goals for the client that you may or may not have shared with the client. Each state maintains certain legal requirements for note-taking, and you will want to develop your systematic notes in accord with legal and ethical practice. Interview notes in some situations must be open to client inspection and may even be demanded by courts. You no longer can assume that your records are confidential.

Planning and the taking of notes assume ever more critical roles in the helping process due to recent court decisions which challenge long-held beliefs about the nature and process of confidentiality. The client and therapist relationship is changing due to such court decisions as *Tarasoff v. Regents of California* (1974), *Gibson v. Commonwealth* (1975), and changing state regulations regarding the relationship you have with the client or patient. The sum and substance of legal changes means that accountability is entering counseling and therapy practice as never before.

The Tarasoff case illustrates that confidentiality must be viewed more carefully in the future. The patient (Poddar), a student at the University of California, Berkeley, threatened to murder Tania Tarasoff. The therapist notified the police who later released Poddar who then killed Tarasoff. The courts held the defendants negligent in their "duty to warn" (1974, p. 565). Ethically, the therapist was within usual definitions of reasonable treatment, but the courts have changed forever the meaning of confidentiality.

Gibson v. Commonwealth (1975) ruled that a psychiatrist must testify in a criminal case and that physician-patient confidentiality did not hold. Many states now require school or university records to be open to clients and patients and, with children, parents as well. Needless to say, inaccurate, misleading, or incomplete notes and case records may cause serious problems for the therapist or counselor.

One suggested route is to "keep no notes." This, however, may be construed as "inadequate treatment." A second set of notes for your own thinking which is kept from public view may be considered hiding the evidence and evasion of the law. Thus, you as a therapist face critical and changing definitions of proper practice. On one hand, you have the duty to warn in case of danger, but on the other hand you face the danger of a suit if you break confidentiality. In either case, it is clear that solid professional practice and good records are important as protection both for you and for your clientele.

This issue of record keeping and case planning will become increasingly important in the near future as state laws and court decisions join the profession of helping in defining good practice. In the meantime, effective case planning and documentation of reasons for treatment procedures seems essential.

It has been stressed that all therapies tend to focus on and seek to resolve incongruity and mixed messages. Feminist therapy, however, seeks actively to discover and confront contradiction. Once having discovered the contradiction, the feminist therapist seeks to provide individual and cultural resolution to the conflict. Feminist therapy also seems to stress the importance of living with contradiction as a very real part of life. This is a brief, but important, statement that has applications to many other theories of helping as well. If you review any therapy at a deeper level, you will find some attention paid to the fact that we cannot resolve all the problems of life. Effective therapy is about teaching people how to live with and resolve problems. However, "There is no cure for life." We will always encounter contradiction and incongruity.

Gordon Paul's original question in 1967 did not deal clearly with the goals and aims of therapy. Feminist therapy and Black and Asian theorists remind us that cultural and sexual differences result in the need for different orientations to therapy and force us to think more carefully through our goals and what we seek to achieve in the helping process.

Figure 14.2 Expected Amount of Time Spent in Stages of the Interview in Some Example Theories

	DECISIONAL COUNSELING	*PSYCHOANALYTIC PSYCHOTHERAPY*	*ASSERTIVENESS TRAINING*	*PERSON-CENTERED*	*FAMILY THERAPY*
1. Rapport/ Structuring. "Hello!"	Some	Little or none	Some	Little structuring, rapport emphasized throughout	Some
2. Data gathering. "What's the problem?" "What are your strengths?"	Medium	Little or none (However, often begins with careful introductory assessment)	Great	Some	Great
3. Determining Outcomes. "What do you want to have happen?"	Medium	Little or none	Medium	Little or none	Medium
4. Generating Alternative Solutions. Confronting incongruities. "What are we going to do about it?"	Medium	Great	Medium	Great	Medium
5. Generalization and Transfer of Learning. "Will you do it?"	Medium	Little or none	Medium	Little	Varies widely

From *Intentional Interviewing and Counseling* by A. Ivey. Copyright © 1983 by Wadsworth, Inc. Reprinted by permission of Brooks/Cole Publishing Company, Monterey, CA 93940.

Figure 14.2 provides a comparison of how differing theoretical orientations might be viewed from the framework of the five-stage interview structure.

Long-term treatment planning requires you to think through and prioritize the specific issues around which your counseling is oriented. (Also see Chapter 6, page 168 for specifics in long-term treatment planning.) The long-term treatment plan can follow the same five-stage model. For example, if the client comes with a problem of mild anxiety and states the need for a better feeling about self, you may decide in the early stages to use a reflective-listening Rogerian approach and focus your notes and action from that frame of reference. However, by the second interview you may observe issues of sexual dysfunctioning, marital difficulties, and potential child abuse. These new data will enter your treatment plan and may include direct action on your part to inform legal authorities of the abuse, a Masters and Johnson sexual treatment program, and family counseling. You may also note that the client does not have strong parenting skills and you may wish to add instruction in systematic parenting.

The long-term treatment plan, therefore, needs to be updated after each session and the specific client needs for the forthcoming session prioritized. You may, of necessity, find yourself using behavioral methods in one session (for example, to treat sexual dysfunction), family counseling in the next, and many other techniques before you again later return to your own favorite theoretical orientation. Methodologically, you may have departed widely from your original intent in the treatment plan, but philosophically, you will likely be able to maintain a conceptual integrity with your own basic general theoretical approach, be it systematic eclectic or representing a primary allegiance to a single theory.

It may be seen that the five-stage decisional model provides a structured frame of reference from which you can view many alternative constructions of psychotherapy and counseling. The model can be used to plan the first interview, actually be implemented in the interview, and then used as a basis for taking notes and making observations. The model is workable for long-term case planning and treatment. The five-stage model, of course, must be shaped and adapted to fit your own theoretical constructions and the needs and interests of the client. It may be particularly useful in the early stages of your therapeutic career and may be used as a base from which to depart as your experience matures.

The five stages of the interview and the use of skills may be described as a *structure* into which the *content* of theory may be placed. The following section examines this important point in more detail.

AN INTEGRATING FORMAT FOR COMPARING ALTERNATIVE THEORIES

Assuming you have mastered the basic structure of the interview and the skills that are required for working with a client (microskills, empathic skills, observation skills, assessment skills), the major problem remains of how you can formulate the client's concerns and problems. Theory offers us a way to conceptualize the client's worldview. While it is essential that you enter the client's world and walk with her or him in each one's perceptions, it is of great assistance to have a theory of your own to broaden understanding. If you seek to help the client walk or develop in a new direction, you will find a solid theoretical commitment on your part very important.

Theories of therapy, whether psychodynamic, behavioral, or feminist, all provide grounding for our actions. Each theory provides a way of explaining client thinking and behaving. If the client is having difficulty with a loved one, the psychodynamic practitioner may conceptualize the client as having difficulties rooted in childhood difficulties or problems in object relations. This formulation of theory then suggests what type of *practice* may be employed—possibly free association exercises searching for patterns from childhood that repeat themselves in current life.

The behavioral theorist may conceptualize the client as having learned ineffective ways of behavior due to stimulus-response contingencies in the environment. Rather than search for past difficulties, the behaviorist uses theory in a very different way from the psychodynamically oriented practitioner. Instead of searching for "causes," the behaviorist may move directly to combat the relationship problem through thought-stopping, skills training, and assertiveness training. The theoretical formulation in both cases provides a reason and framework for practice and the specific use of skills.

The feminist theorist may view the difficulty with the loved one as a natural result of a culture that forces overly defined sex roles on both men and women. Again, the theoretical formulation is very different in each theory, but each theory does have explanatory power. Drawing on feminist theory, the therapist may explain to the client the roots of cultural oppression and use a variety of egalitarian methods to work with the client toward new views of life and new actions that are possible.

As you can perhaps sense, a humanistically oriented therapist would conceptualize the relationship problem differently from the three theories above. The transactional analyst or family therapist—or cognitive therapist—also would think about the issue in very different ways. Needless to say, each would have different actions that they would take with the same client.

Which is the "correct" theory that you should take into practice? Making that decision is not easy for there are many articulate and persuasive individuals arguing for the value of each theory. The position of this text is that each theory has something to offer and is well worth considering. Clinical experience will reveal that no matter what the research data says about the "best" theory or no matter what your strongest opinion as to the "best" theory, there will be some clients who simply won't agree with either you or research. It is at this time that your own awareness of alternative methods may be most helpful to you.

Intentionality has been suggested as a goal for both therapists and clients—the making of culturally appropriate choices from a set of options. The methods associated with each theory provide you with options for action. While it is essential that you develop a central theoretical commitment (either to one theory or to an integration of several theories), you will find that the ideas of a theory different from your own may be helpful to both you and the client on some occasions.

Figure 14.3 presents thirteen of the major theoretical orientations presented in this book. As has been stated repeatedly, there are many, many other orientations to helping beyond those presented here—well over 200 others! The position of this text is that mastery of skills and decision making ideas, plus the five stages of the interview, will provide you with a format through which you can better consider and utilize the ideas of differing theories. All theories are concerned with *change,* the generation of new ways of thinking, being, deciding, and behaving. Once a stuck or immobilized client experiences a small change, you as therapist have a beginning lever to support further change and personal development. You may find that one theory works best for you in promoting change at one stage in a client's treatment series, and another at a different point. The following section presents a case analysis and shows how theory and skills from differing orientations can be integrated.

The purpose of Figure 14.3 is to show that each theory constructs the world of therapy differently; the figure presents in graph form different worldviews, different major constructs, and even different goals of therapy—some of which are opposed to one another. However, your clients also have multiple goals, some of which are at least partially opposed to one another. The client with a relational problem with a loved one, for example, may seek to be more assertive and will benefit from behavioral methods at one time. Later, it may be useful to examine the roots of childhood experience from a psychodynamic perspective. Issues from feminist counseling or one of the other consciousness-raising therapies may be useful in developing an awareness that cultural racism or sexism may be basic to avoiding the problem in the future. Family therapy may be needed to help change a basic family structure. Psychoeducation or community action may be required to support the family.

The point is that each theory does not have a full grasp of the "truth" of change—each theory can produce change and in many cases will be powerful enough for clients to start their own path toward growth. Yet, you will find many cases where you will want to use more than one theoretical orientation to facilitate your client's development.

At this point, you may want to review Figure 14.3 in detail and to consider its implications for your personal practice of counseling and therapy.

Figure 14.3 provides you with the opportunity to review thirteen approaches to counseling and therapy.

Let us now turn to consideration of how skills and theories manifest themselves in the actual practice of counseling and therapy.

Figure 14.3 Comparison of 13 Psychotherapy/Counseling Approaches

THEORY	WORLDVIEW	MAJOR CONSTRUCTS	MAJOR TECHNIQUES	INCONGRUITY ISSUES	GOALS
Decisional Counseling	Life is a series of decisions. Choosing intentionality from an array of options is desirable. Metatheoretical in worldview in that all other theories may be viewed as cognitive decisions to take a particular worldview. The emphasis on decision and action aligns this method with cognitive-behavioral approaches.	Most counseling and therapy theories follow the five-stage model of the interview in some form. It is particularly important to have clear goals and to followup on goals to ensure that change from the interview survives in the "real" world.	May involve any of a variety of techniques and theories. Particularly important is the creative generation of alternatives for action within the context of client problem(s) (and assets) and client goal. Caution: Client and therapist may become overwhelmed by options. Too early fix on problem definition or goal may stifle creativity.	The distinction between the problem as defined and the ideal goal/outcome of the client. This plays itself out in other theories as real-ideal (Rogers), polarities (psychodynamic), irrational ideas (RET), and others described below.	To free the individual to make more creative and rational decisions within a person-environment context.
Psychodynamic	Deterministic; humankind is impelled by unconscious forces from the past. The biological background of sexual, aggressive, and survival needs is important. In	Development of person rests on early life experience and successful negotiation of critical issues in early life stages. Problems in later life come from early childhood experiences. The	Staying with the emotion, free association, analysis of resistance, analysis of transference, interpretation. Caution: Avoid wild analysis, which is likely to occur with naïve counselors	Uncover polarities and mixed, confused emotions in past life experience and eventually relate these to present issues. Conflicts between id, ego, and superego wishes often serve as the background	To make the unconscious conscious. Personality reconstruction based on working through past issues and developing new syntheses from old conflicts.

426

modern form it tends to be more humanistic and optimistic.	personality is the sum of past experience as manifested in id, ego, and superego. The interaction between person and environment is largely played out in the unconscious.	who fail to understand the complexity of the theory.	for examination of incongruities.	
Behavioral Once defined as mechanistic and deterministic in that people were believed to be totally shaped by their environments and have little choice. Newer frames of reference emphasize increased freedom and choice through understanding of behavioral principles.	Human development stems from the environmental forces shaping the individual, but individual responses in turn shape environment. Behavior is lawful and explainable through systematic study; emphasis is on overt behavior rather than on unconscious forces. Problem behavior comes from faulty learning.	Applied behavioral analysis, relaxation training, assertiveness training, systematic desensitization, modeling, positive reinforcement, behavioral charting, and an expanding array of specific techniques for a wide range of problems. Caution: Manipulative behavior modification places control of the client's future in the hands of the therapist or institution.	Seeks to identify where the client is, behaviorally, and where he or she wants to go. Programs of applied behavioral analysis and alternative treatments will be applied to enable individual to bring actual and desired behavior into congruence.	To eliminate faulty learning and behavior and to substitute more adaptive patterns of behaving. Specific directions for behavior change are decided on by the client.

Figure 14.3 (continued)

THEORY	WORLDVIEW	MAJOR CONSTRUCTS	MAJOR TECHNIQUES	INCONGRUITY ISSUES	GOALS
Existential/Humanistic	A human task is to find meaning and direction in a sometimes seemingly absurd and meaningless world. Some existential approaches can be pessimistic. An emphasis on the infinite possibility that is human life.	Each individual is unique and construes the world differently. Some orientations pay extensive attention to early life development and share many ideas with psychodynamic approaches. A major task of therapy may be coping with basic human issues, such as values, guilt, anxiety. A tendency to emphasize the present with an emphasis on what the person is *becoming*. Most in this orientation consider the person, the person's view of others, and the person's view of being-in-the-world as central.	The existential/ humanistic approach is varied, and no techniques are ordinarily associated with it. The therapist is centrally concerned with meaning and action in the world. Thus the methods of psychodynamic, Rogerian, RET, and even behaviorism may be appropriate. The constant emphasis, however, is on the client's view of the world. Caution: The search for meaning can be full of anxiety and may be especially stressful to fragile individuals. For those whose issues are not existential, the therapy may be considered irrelevant.	The existential paradox in its many manifestations underlies every interview ("to live is to die," "to commit to one action is to miss other possible actions," "the need to make a choice when one can't be sure that choice is possible," etc.).	To find meaning and to take action in the world. To become aware of the very human issues of choice, commitment, and anxiety. Development of mature intentionality.

| Person- Centered, Modern Rogerian | People have potential to move in natural positive directions. Inherent in each client is worth and dignity and the ability to direct one's own life and move toward self-actualization, growth, and health. | Similar to worldview. The view one has of oneself (self-concept) establishes the way one views the world. Real-self/ideal-self congruence is desired because it is viewed as a definition of mental health. Little attention is given to implications of environment on the individual. | Emphasis on present moment, provision of warmth, genuineness, caring in an empathic relationship. In person-centered counseling, almost complete reliance is on primary empathy and attending skills, but little use is made of questioning. In modern Rogerian approaches, therapists may share personal experience and confront the client more directly. Caution: Requires highly verbal client; may be slow; some Rogerians tend to use techniques rigidly and miss the more important philosophic spirit. | Resolution of real-self/ideal-self incongruence. Exploration in depth of mixed and ambivalent emotions. | To release human potential to find its own natural direction and to resolve real-self/ideal-self incongruence, exploration of complex emotions, to facilitate unique human growth. |

Figure 14.3 (continued)

THEORY	WORLDVIEW	MAJOR CONSTRUCTS	MAJOR TECHNIQUES	INCONGRUITY ISSUES	GOALS
Gestalt	Essentially humanistic/ existential. People are wholes; not parts, and are seeking to find completeness in themselves. A person is quite able to take direction of her or his own life.	The natural person may be split or divided into parts. The splitting away from the Gestalt leads to anxiety and pathology. The task of the therapist is to make the person "whole." Gestalt theory emphasizes personal responsibility, completing unfinished business, and actual experiencing of thoughts and feelings from the past in the present.	Extensive emphasis on immediate experiencing. Staying with the feeling, the frequent use of directives, language changes, empty chair technique, talking to parts of oneself, top dog and underdog, and systematic dreamwork are important techniques. Caution: Gestalt techniques are perhaps the most immediately powerful. Extensive emphasis on individual functioning sometimes neglects connections with the rest of the world.	Gestalt has perhaps the most extensive and direct emphasis on incongruities of any theory. Splits, impasses, the emphasis on parts and wholes all illustrate the central importance of incongruity in Gestalt theory.	To become more aware of momentary living and to take responsibility for the direction of one's life.

| Logotherapy | The world exists as you define its meaning. Clients are capable of reframing the meaning of their entire past experience. | Close to existential thinking with a stronger emphasis on personal ability to control meaning and destiny. Meaning can come from action or from thinking. Spiritual aspect of humanity important. Body/mind/spirit are a unity. | Careful listening to the client to understand the unique meanings generated from the past. Use of modification of attitudes, dereflection, and paradoxical intention to assist reframing/behavioral patterns. May use "appealing technique" similar to AA to facilitate individuals seeking "higher" goals. May map out highly specific behavioral action plans. Caution: Paradoxical techniques may be extremely powerful and should be carefully used. | Frank acknowledgement that life itself represents an incongruity—to live is to face death. Given this basic incongruity or paradox in all life, the issue is to live courageously with maximum personal meaning. | To facilitate the development of the "search for meaning" and finding freedom within the "chains" of life. Perhaps best represented by Frankl's ability to find meaning in even the most difficult situation of the concentration camp. |

Figure 14.3 (continued)

THEORY	WORLDVIEW	MAJOR CONSTRUCTS	MAJOR TECHNIQUES	INCONGRUITY ISSUES	GOALS
Cognitive-Behavioral	"It is not things that trouble us, but our view of things." The cognitive-behavioral worldview emphasizes that each individual can construct a unique meaning or thought about an event. The degree to which an individual is in "control" of thinking will vary with the theorist. All will also emphasize *action* and *behaving* in accordance with one's cognitions.	People generate ideas or thoughts about the world to explain themselves and reality. They act on these cognitions. Faulty thinking or irrational ideas may lead to ineffective behaviors. People have the capacity to think more correctly and suffer less pain.	A-B-C analysis of logic of client's thinking patterns, examination of logic, reframing of client's cognitions, teaching client's new ways of thinking and behaving, stress innoculation, recreation of past experience, most of behaviorism's techniques available. Caution: Due to the breadth of the cognitive-behavioral movement, its practitioners may make errors of practice common to all other theories.	Central and consistent focus on incongruities in thinking and logic about oneself and one's world.	Elimination of self-defeating thinking, developing more rational and tolerant view of self and others. Then acting on this knowledge.
Reality Therapy	The belief is that people can develop their own identity and decide for themselves. However, these decisions are made in the context of a *reality* situation in a complex world and the individual must be cognitively able and willing to face	What has happened in the past is not important, the client can act *now* to change her or his situation. Moral judgments and values are important, and one must accept responsibility for actions. A constant emphasis on the person-	Personal involvement of the therapist with the client, teaching and emphasizing responsibility, relearning and planning for new action. A variety of techniques and skills from other theories may be employed in the process. Caution:	Constant emphasis on any deviations from the individual's failure to take responsibility for self. Examination of person and environment incongruities in a reality context.	To fulfill one's own needs in a way that does not interfere with others. To make responsible decisions and to act on them with the full awareness of consequences.

432

Transactional Analysis					
Essentially in the third force existential/humanistic position, TA believes that people can decide for themselves, change, and take charge of their lives. Due to the psychodynamic foundations, TA therapists are often aware of past history and use script analysis for "here and now" understanding.	Psychodynamic constructs have been translated into easily understandable form, such as parent, adult, and child. The emphasis in TA, however, is more often on relationships with others through the stroke economy, script analysis, as part of a system.	the consequences of decisions realistically.	A carefully balanced approach that considers both person and environment is needed; too much emphasis on either may injure the success of therapy.	Teaching people the concepts of TA directly, lifescript analysis, analysis of transactions, examination of the stroke economy, and a variety of games and exercises to highlight and illustrate key points. Influencing skills of interpretation and expression of content sharing information will appear prominently. Caution: Problems such as those associated with RET, psychodynamic, and existential/humanistic are possible.	environment transaction.
					Examination of blocks, conflict, or incongruity within the self in the several ego states or in transaction with others.
					To enable a client to rid self of rigid scripts, patterns, and games, and to enable the development of new and freer decisions based on this awareness.

Figure 14.3 (continued)

THEORY	WORLDVIEW	MAJOR CONSTRUCTS	MAJOR TECHNIQUES	INCONGRUITY ISSUES	GOALS
Family Therapy	Not yet fully articulated. Epistemological in that the roots of knowledge and behavior are examined as a *system*. The family may be described as a system of relationships that influence and prescribe the behaviors of its members. Rather than consider an individual in isolation, the person is always seen in the context of relationships.	The emphasis is on understanding the total system in which the individual or family "symptom" appears. The family is often not to be made aware of the analysis in the belief that change without awareness may be most important.	An increasingly large array of techniques including paradoxical instructions, joining or mirroring family members, enactment, circular questioning, physical rearrangement of family seating arrangements, "no blame," tracking, reframing. Caution: As a relatively new and exciting form of therapy, practitioners may be subject to arrogance in practice as they have "the answer"; thus they may fall prey to the problems of overly charismatic therapists of other theoretical orientations. Desire to keep theory hidden from clients can result in manipulation.	Incongruities are often seen as logical part of family life and the issue is how to live with them effectively. The distinction between what the family "is" and might "want to be" often serves as a basic issue of incongruity. The therapist may point out the difference between the "real family" and the "ideal" that the family holds, often as a secret myth.	To enable individuals and families to change themselves and the systems within which they live. If a critical lever is found for change, many aspects of a person's life will change.

434

| Community/ Psychoeducational | Systemic worldview that believes that education and training may be more effective for prevention and mental health than therapy and remediation. | Individual and family change can only be enacted and *maintained* in healthy communities. Schools are a particularly important organization in the community and represent a "community" in themselves. | The techniques of community psychology and psychoeducation include all the techniques of the therapeutic alternatives plus many, many educational, training, and skills programs. These may range from family education through smoking cessation through the increase of the use of fiber in the diet to prevent cancer. A full community approach would use all facets of the cube model. Caution: The impact and goals of community and psychoeducational programs may become so diffuse as to lose power. Many community and psychoeducational workers suffer from "burnout." | The concept of the ideal community and the goals that represent this ideal may be contrasted with the reality of the present life of the community. | All the positive goals of all therapeutic systems could be said to be the goals of the community/ psychoeducational movement. |

Figure 14.3 (continued)

THEORY	WORLDVIEW	MAJOR CONSTRUCTS	MAJOR TECHNIQUES	INCONGRUITY ISSUES	GOALS
Feminist Therapy*	The world has been predefined by patriarchial male worldviews. A newer, more relational way of thinking and being needs to be defined. This definition is not yet, and perhaps never will be, final.	Development of men and women has been accepted "as is" without examination of basic premises. Much of therapy methods and concepts have been defined by white males. Most worldviews are too male-centered, hierarchial, and individualistic. A real need to construct a new, more egalitarian form of therapy exists.	Will use techniques and methods of all approaches to helping. Special interest in assertiveness training for women, helping women find unique meanings in life as a *woman*, and examining the "cultural unconscious"— how has society and therapy unconsciously defined women. Special attention given to confronting the incongruities abounding in theory and daily life in an atmosphere of equality of client and counselor. Caution: Is the client "ready" for an in-depth cultural or personal analysis that may result in major life change?	Seeks to identify and uncover the multitude of incongruities within the client and the environment/culture and then to actively work on these issues via counseling/therapy, psychoeducational techniques, and community action.	To redefine and make more equal the roles of men and women and to eliminate societal sexism, ageism, and racism.

*Other consciousness-raising theories are not summarized here because currently they have not yet presented fully articulated conceptions. However, review of recommended cultural readings and research should lead in the near future to more clarification on this important issue.

A CASE EXAMPLE OF THERAPEUTIC PLANNING AND TREATMENT

Fukuhara (1984) utilized a variation of the five-stage interviewing model in a successful seven-interview series of therapeutic sessions with a young female university student in Japan who was overly depressed by the loss of her male friend. This case is interesting as it is reported with unusual clarity and is from a Japanese cultural setting. Fukuhara points out that love and relationship are cultural universals that are important to all of us.

The case analysis will be presented in two sections: in the first section, we will see how Fukuhara used microskills and basic structures to produce change and to analyze her own practice. The second section will focus on alternative theoretical constructions of the case.

The Case Presentation

The young woman client in this case was 18 at the time of counseling and was self-referred. She introduced her problem as follows:

> I am in love with a freshman boy who likes me. This spring, I met this boy . . . and thought our love would last a long time. However, when I returned from summer vacation, he did not even seem to want to talk to me. This finally made me so angry that I became aggressive and we had a fight. Surprisingly, my boyfriend seemed to like being told off. Still, he doesn't ask me out and the only time I see him is at the activity club . . . I project into the future and think that if I continue to love him, we would eventually get married. What would my life be then? Would I have to make sacrifices to his will? . . . Would this eventually destroy my love for him? Should I give up on him now?

The early stages of therapy focused on a listening approach so that the client's picture of the world might be understood. In the first interview, the

Machiko Fukuhara

client's perception of the relationship with her boyfriend was "He is mine; I am his" despite the realities of a relationship that had broken down. The client's cognition was "stuck" or immobilized with an unrealistic perception that influenced much of her thinking and behavior and interfered with performance in other areas as well.

Fukuhara charted her use of microskills during each of the seven sessions and her summary may be viewed in Figure 14.4. Briefly, it may be noted that she used primarily person-centered listening skills in the first interviews, confrontational skills (particularly Gestalt-oriented therapy) in the fourth session, and gradually increased her use of influencing skills toward the end of counseling and therapy. This pattern of gradual increase in influencing skills is common among many counselors of many differing orientations. It appears that therapists enter the frame of reference (pacing) through listening skills in the early stages of therapy and then move to influencing skills (leading) in the later sessions.

The use of focus is important in this case. You will find that a person from a relational culture such as Japan often benefits in the early stages of counseling from a "we" orientation in which the therapist joins the clients almost as a family

Figure 14.4   Use of Microskills Compared Over Seven Interviews

Sessions	Basic Attending Skills						Influencing Skills					Focusing			
	Question (open)	Question (closed)	Minimal encouragement	Summarization	Paraphrasing	Reflection of feeling	Feedback	Self-disclosure	Advice, information giving	Interpretation	Confrontation	Client (I)	Main theme	Others (you) he	We
No. 1						x									x
No. 2					x	x									x
No. 3			x		x	x						x			
No. 4				x		x					x	x			
No. 5				x	x	x								x	
No. 6		x		x	x	x				x		x		x	
No. 7						x	x		x	x		x	x	x	

x = Extensive use of microskill in interview

member in the early stages of the sessions. Then, from this "we" orientation, the movement is toward separation and individuation wherein the client separates from the counselor and moves out to the "real world" on her or his own. In much of North American culture, the use of "you" or the client's name in the first session would likely be more preferable. This focus on the individual may be expected to continue throughout much of North American counseling. However, a feminist or family orientation might take an approach more closely approximating the Japanese methods illustrated here.

The first three sessions focused on a basically Rogerian style of listening during which the client moved toward a conceptual frame allowing for more distinctions between herself and her former boyfriend. For example, in interview 3, the client was able to express "He should be different from me, but I cannot admit it." The interview plan at this point called for Fukuhara to enter the client's frame as fully as possible. This close relationship between therapist and client allowed the young woman to start the process of truly separating from her "loved one."

Figure 14.5 presents the client's perception of her relationship with her boyfriend from the beginning of the interview series to the conclusion. You will note that she gradually moves from an overly attached, embedded relational orientation to one in which she is appropriately separated and independent. Three external counselors observed the interview series and rated the client's reality-testing—how realistic was the client's frame of reference toward the world. You will again note that the client became more realistic as therapy progressed.

Interview 4 included more emphasis on confrontation of discrepancies and provided further movement. It was at this point that Gestalt techniques were used to "activate" client thinking and action. The last two interviews used some

Figure 14.5 Client's Descriptions of Relationship and External Evaluations of Reality-Testing Over a Seven-Interview Series

Interview session	Client perception of relationship*	Client reality testing evaluated by three counselors		
		Co. A	Co. B	Co. C**
1	He is mine; I am his.	xx	xx	x
2	His whole existence is for me; my whole existence is for him; I should come up to his expectations.	xx	x	Δ
3	He should be different from me; but I cannot admit it.	x	Δ	Δ
4	I can keep my identity only when I am away from him.***	Δ	Δ	○
5	I have come to understand his own behavior, which is different from mine.	Δ	○	○
6	I am myself; he is himself.	○	○	○
7	I have to do something for my own good.	○	○	○

*As the measure of reality testing, this I-Thou relation was used.
**xx = very poor x = poor Δ = average ○ = good ○ = very good Co. = counselor
***They are separated; he was home for vacation, approx. 100 miles away.

of the concepts of reality therapy and focused on taking newly developed insights into action in daily life. Interview 6 brought a summarization of the past interview together with interpretations on the part of the therapist. The client at this point was able to separate herself fully: "I am myself; he is himself." The final session focused around plans for the future: "I have to do something for my own good." You may note the more extensive use of influencing skills as the therapist plans for transfer of learning and generalization.

Fukuhara's case summary is particularly interesting as it illustrates the cognitive growth and development that can occur in a client in the brief course of counseling and therapy. The client's sentence structure at both a surface and deep structure level has clearly changed. The treatment plan called for listening and entering the client's frame of reference in the early stages. In the mid-part of treatment, confrontation of client discrepancies was emphasized, while the final portion of the treatment moved more toward influencing skills with the closing interview focused on issues of generalization.

It may also be noted that classical issues of separation and attachment (see Chapter 8, pages 204–207) were illustrated in this case. At the beginning of therapy, the client experienced a fusion or overattachment to the male friend. By the end of therapy, the needed separation had been achieved and the client seemed stable on her own terms (a good balance of separation and attachment) and ready to enter the world again.

This case—a college student in Japan—is interesting as it illustrates the crosscultural similarity of a basic male-female issue of love and relationship, separation and attachment. Whereas each culture may play out the script of the interview and the degree of attachment/separation differently, the love and relationship does have crosscultural similarities. Moreover, change in developmental cognition as a result of effective therapy or counseling is clearly a goal of therapy, regardless of one's cultural situation.

The Fukuhara treatment series, in its unusual clarity, provides a model for considering how different theories might have approached the same issues. As we have pointed out, Fukuhara's approach closely resembled the Rogerian listening style in the early stages, but as counseling and therapy continued, a more active style was involved including Gestalt therapy exercises and some dimensions of reality therapy. Fukuhara aptly comments that despite cultural differences, much of "counseling theory is basically applicable to individuals whatever their problems . . . or background."

The description of this case thus far has proceeded from the integrated general theory of Fukuhara. It now may be useful to view the same case as it might be seen from other theoretical orientations.

Alternative Theoretical Views of the Case

Other theoretical orientations might have accomplished much the same results if the client was approached with understanding and cultural empathy. For example, the young woman might have benefitted in the later stages of counseling from assertiveness training so that she might express herself more effectively. Or, psychodynamic free association might have led her to understand the underlying personal and family dynamics that led to the problem in the first place. Furthermore, object relations theory (or family therapy theory) might enable her to understand continuing patterns of separation and attachment that lie in early family relations. The cognitive-behavioral theorist might have focused on the client's illogical thinking processes very directly. The initial statement "He is mine; I am his" is an especially clear example of faulty reasoning patterns.

The clear and cogent results achieved by Fukuhara through a well-constructed treatment plan might also have been achieved with another orientation to therapy—but only if that orientation were comfortable to both the client and the therapist. You will find at times that your own natural orientation to therapy and counseling is not equally comfortable for your client. At that point, you may wish to change your mode of helping and work with a different approach, perhaps even working toward the same basic change goal.

Referring back to Figure 14.3, the final two columns of this figure may be the most important. There you will find summaries of the *goals* of each therapeutic orientation and the major incongruity issues that each orientation attempts to resolve. In the case of this young woman, her original goal seemed to be to resolve what type of relationship she wanted with the young man ("Should I give him up now?"). There, of course, is some lack of realism in this goal as the young man had fairly obviously left the relationship. One of the basic hopes of most orientations to therapy is to increase the accuracy of client reality testing.

A decisional counseling goal would seek to have this client develop "more creative and rational decisions with a person-environment context." The psychodynamic therapist might seek "to make the unconscious conscious," and the behavioral counselor might attempt "to eliminate faulty learning."

The cognitive-behaviorist would aim to bring about the "elimination of self-defeating thinking, developing a more rational and tolerant view of self and others, and *then* acting on this knowledge." The family therapist might seek to "enable individuals and families to change themselves and the systems within which they live" and the family orientation would ideally bring in the young man as well (but this would be possible only if he also were interested in developing better communication with the client). The feminist theorist might see the case as a classic example of the oppressive relationships that exist between men and women and the goal would be "to redefine and make more equal the roles of men and women."

In each example, the desire of the therapist or counselor is to bring thinking and action more in concert with the realities of the present-day environment. Each theoretical system approaches this common goal differently, but if used effectively should provide the young woman with an opportunity for growth that might be as effective as the general theoretical orientation of Fukuhara.

In addition, each of these varying goals leads therapists to search for and find incongruities that match the theory of choice. The feminist theoretician could easily identify the incongruities of cultural sexism, the decisional theorist the marked distinction between the "problem as defined and the ideal goal/outcome of the client," and the psychodynamic theorist would immediately recognize the incongruity of the "mixed, confused emotions in past life and eventually relate these to present issues." The cognitive behaviorist might note the "central and consistent focus on incongruities in thinking and logic," the family therapist between what "is" and what the client "wants to be," while the feminist theorist would identify the "multitude of incongruities in the environment/culture."

Each identification of incongruity in the different theories is, of course, based on a worldview and central set of constructs around the helping process. Finally, the ideas and constructions of each theory lead to the use of specific and widely varying techniques oriented to change.

It is this orientation to change that brings the vastly different views and constructs of each theory back into relative harmony. It was suggested in Chapter 1 of this text that the central goal of counseling and therapy is the reintroduction of intentionality—the ability of the individual to choose and act on thought and behavioral options within the individual's own cultural frame. Change and intentionality appear to be what counseling and therapy are about. The thought patterns and methods of each therapy vary widely, but each offers an opportunity to reach the common goal of positive change and intentionality.

The commonality of these theories does not mean that they are necessarily of equal value. As we have emphasized, at times you will find that different clients will respond differently—very differently—to your theory of choice. At this time, you may find that the issue of which treatment for which individual under what conditions becomes a central issue for your thought and action.

An interesting point to consider is: ". . . *Equal treatment in counseling may be discriminatory treatment!*" (Sue, 1977, p. 423). Given the broad array of client problems that may be presented to a therapist, it seems unrealistic to assume that any one theory or set of techniques will be universally effective. More likely, the more counselors and therapists adapt their interventions and theories to meet the special situations and needs their clients present, the more effective they will be. An aging client lonely for companionship, a teenager concerned over masturbation, a couple contemplating divorce, and a Chicano facing job discrimination all present different problems requiring different solutions. No matter how skillfully the therapist applies a single theory to these different situations, it should be clear that alternative approaches may be more effective than one single favored theory applied in all situations.

As you hear your clients articulate their goals, you may want to compare your clients' statements with the goals and conceptions of the alternative treatment orientation. You will note, for example, that Fukuhara's young client was deeply embedded in issues of complex emotions to the extent that her self was lost (Rogerian person-centered theory), but later she had a wish to fulfill her needs in a way that did not interfere with others (reality therapy), and the techniques of Gestalt therapy were useful in the later stages of therapy (to take responsibility for the direction of her own life). As the client's goals changed, so did the therapeutic and counseling process.

Make use of Figure 14.3! You may find it a useful summary of the major theories of this text and a reference source for determining which theory may be most likely to be useful for your clients. It is suggested that the matching of the language and observational system of the theory to specific client expressed needs may be a beginning wedge to correctly matching theory with client needs. To date, many counselors and therapists simply bring clients to their theoretical frame of reference rather than seeking to join clients in their alternative construction of the world. What do you think—is it more effective to adhere to one theoretical framework—or to adapt as the counseling process continues?

YOU AS GENERAL THEORIST: DECISIONS, DECISIONS, DECISIONS

It is the task of the professional counselor and therapist to know as many theories as possible—their similarities and differences—and to select from each theory that which seems most helpful to a particular client. *Each individual can become her or his own general theorist.* Yet, it must be recognized that skilled therapy and counseling demands that you *master* one orientation particularly well as you learn about others. A "jack of all trades" is not a general theorist.

The theories of behaviorism, psychoanalysis, reality therapy, and others are only "views—descriptions of the world." If the counselor decides that her or his particular theory is *the* correct set of constructs for organizing the world, that decision is a direct rejection of an underlying premise of this book, which is that *theory is simply description, a way to examine reality, a set of constructs.* Those who adapt and accept the idea of "single true answers" have rejected their responsibility as teachers and models for others and have set in motion the imposition of values and ideas.

This awareness of choice can lead to anxiety on the part of the counselor, and you may ask, "Who am I to say which method is right for a particular moment?" And perhaps that is the right question to ask. Indeed, what does give you the right to make decisions for another person? Even if a counselor assumes the person-centered mode, he or she still inevitably influences the style and direction of the interview. When you enter the counseling relationship, you have by definition started influencing another person's life. The awareness that you have made a decision to intervene in another human being's life is critical to self-awareness and your own *and* the client's growth. (And we must remember that the decision not to intervene, not to counsel, is itself a decision that can profoundly affect another person.) *Further, discussion with clients about alternatives may enable them to join with you in deciding the most appropriate treatment.*

The general or metatheoretical position requires that each counselor or therapist develop her or his own conception of the counseling process and should remain constantly open to change and examination. A student working through the draft of this book commented, "I think I've got the point. I find myself rewriting the book in my own way. I use some of it, but ultimately the book I am

Figure 14.6   *Exercise in Generating Your Own General Integrated Theory of Counseling and Therapy*

The purpose of this exercise is to ask you to consider your own construction of counseling and therapy. What is important to you? Where do you stand? Where do you think you are heading?

1. WORLDVIEW

Examine the several worldviews of the theories summarized here. Which appeal to you most? Which might you tend to reject?

In a brief statement, set forth your own worldview and how it relates to the what you think counseling and therapy are about.

2. MAJOR CONSTRUCTS

What major ideas about the helping process help you to organize a theory on which you can later build a practice? Again, turn to the theoretical summaries and search out words and ideas that are important to you.

Write a brief summary of the constructs and ideas of your theory of helping that is most important to you.

3. MAJOR TECHNIQUES

Most of us find that we are comfortable with some techniques and less comfortable with others. We tend to be more successful using techniques and methods we believe in.

List in summary form your favorite techniques for client change. Include both techniques from your own theoretical orientation, but also techniques from other theories that you might consider using at times.

4. INCONGRUITY

The resolution of incongruity, mixed messages, and discrepancies is central to counseling and therapy, regardless of theoretical orientation, but each system considers different issues as central. Again, use Figure 14.3 as a starting point, but then list the important issues of incongruity that you might search for in your clientele.

5. GOALS

Before a review of the goals of different theories, take time to write a brief statement as to what *you* consider the major goals of counseling and therapy.

Then, go back and read the goals of each theoretical orientation. If you wish, change your goal statement. *What do you wish to have happen in your clients as a result of counseling and therapy?*

6. RECONSTRUCTION AND EVALUATION

Using your own goal statement as a primary foundation, go back through the first steps of this exercise and see if you want to add or change any portions. Is your integration of theory and practice consistent? Then write in a summary chart your own revised personal construction of counseling and therapy.

Is this construction one that is primarily oriented to a single theory? Are you eclectic? Systematic eclectic? Do you represent all or part of a general, integrated orientation to helping that systematically utilizes several different orientations to the change process? What does your theoretical summary mean to you? How does your theoretical orientation take issues of cultural understanding and oppression into account? What next steps might you take to implement and act on this orientation to the world?

rewriting in my head is *mine,* my own general theory which is similar in some ways to the book, but in other ways very different."

REFERENCES

BARON, N., *Ethics and the Initial Interview.* Unpublished paper, University of Massachusetts, Amherst, 1985.

CASTANEDA, C., *Tales of Power.* New York: Simon & Schuster, 1974.

FRANCIS, A., J. CLARKIN, and S. PERRY, *Differential Therapeutics in Psychiatry: The Art and Science of Treatment Selection.* New York: Brunner/Mazel, 1984.

FUKUHARA, M., Is Love Universal?—From the Viewpoint of Counseling Adolescents. Paper presented at the 42nd Annual Conference of the International Association of Psychologists, Mexico City, 1984.

GLASS, G., and R. KLIEGL, "An Apology for Research Integration in the Study of Psychotherapy," *Journal of Consulting and Clinical Psychology,* 1984, *51,* 28–41.

GOLDSTEIN, A., and N. STEIN, *Perscriptive Psychotherapies.* Elmsford, NY: Pergamon Press, 1976.

IVEY, A., *Intentional Interviewing and Counseling.* Monterey, CA: Brooks/Cole, 1983.

PAUL, G., "Strategy of Outcome Research in Psychotherapy," *Journal of Consulting Psychology,* 1967, *31,* 109–118.

SUE, D., "Counseling the Culturally Different," *Personnel and Guidance Journal,* 1977, *55,* 422–425.

Legal References

GIBSON V. COMMONWEALTH VA., 219 S.E2d 845 (1975).

TARASOFF V. REGENTS OF THE UNIVERSITY OF CALIFORNIA, 529 P.2d 553 (CA 1974).

ETHICAL PRINCIPLES OF PSYCHOLOGISTS* (1981 REVISION)

This version of the Ethical Principles of Psychologists (formerly entitled: Ethical Standards of Psychologists) was adopted by the American Psychological Association's Council of Representatives on January 24, 1981. The Ethical Principles of Psychologists (1981 Revision) contains both substantive and grammatical changes in each of the nine ethical principles which comprised the Ethical Standards of Psychologists previously adopted by the Council of Representatives in 1979, plus a new tenth principle entitled: Care and Use of Animals. Inquiries concerning the Ethical Principles of Psychologists should be addressed to the Administrative Officer for Ethics; American Psychological Association; 1200 Seventeenth Street, N.W.; Washington, D.C. 20036.

ETHICAL PRINCIPLES OF PSYCHOLOGISTS[1,2]

PREAMBLE

Psychologists respect the dignity and worth of the individual and strive for the preservation and protection of fundamental human rights. They are committed to increasing knowledge of human behavior and of people's understanding of themselves and others and to the utilization of such knowledge for the promotion of human welfare. While pursuing these objectives, they make every effort to protect the welfare of those who seek their services and of the research participants that may be the object of study. They use their skills only for purposes consistent with these values and do not knowingly permit their misuse by others. While demanding for themselves freedom of inquiry and communication, psychologists accept the responsibility this freedom requires: competence, objectivity in the application of skills, and concern for the best interests of clients, colleagues, students, research participants and society. In the pursuit of these ideals, psychologists subscribe to principles in the following areas: 1. Responsibility, 2. Competence, 3. Moral and Legal Standards, 4. Public Statements, 5. Confidentiality, 6. Welfare of the Consumer, 7. Professional Relationships, 8. Assessment Techniques, 9. Research with Human Participants, and 10. Care and Use of Animals.

Acceptance of membership in the American Psychological Association commits the member to adherence to these principles.

Psychologists cooperate with duly constituted committees of the American Psychological Association, in particular, the Committee on Scientific and Professional Ethics and Conduct, by responding to inquiries promptly and completely. Members also respond promptly and completely to inquiries from duly constituted state association ethics committees and professional standards review committees.

PRINCIPLE 1.
RESPONSIBILITY

In providing services, psychologists maintain the highest standards of their profession. They accept responsibility for the consequences of their acts and make every effort to insure that their services are used appropriately.

a. As scientists, psychologists accept responsibility for the selection of their research topics and the methods used in investigation, analysis, and reporting. They plan their research in ways to minimize the possibility that their findings will be misleading. They provide thorough discussion of the limitations of their data, especially where their work touches on social policy or might be construed to the detriment of persons in specific age, sex, ethnic, socioeconomic or other social groups. In publishing reports of their work, they never suppress disconfirming data, and they acknowledge the existence of alternative hypotheses and explanations of their findings. Psychologists take credit only for work they have actually done.

b. Psychologists clarify in advance with all appropriate persons and agencies the expectations for sharing and utilizing research data. They avoid relationships which may limit their objectivity or create a conflict of interest. Interference with the milieu in which the data are collected is kept to a minimum.

c. Psychologists have the responsibility to attempt to prevent distortion misuse, or suppression of psychological findings by the institution or agency of which they are employees.

d. As members of governmental or other organizational bodies, psychologists remain accountable as individuals to the highest standards of their profession.

e. As teachers, psychologists recognize their primary obligation to help others acquire knowledge and skill. They maintain high standards of scholarship by presenting psychological information objectively, fully, and accurately.

f. As practitioners, psychologists know that they bear a heavy social responsibility because their recommendations and professional actions may alter the lives of others. They are alert to personal, social, organizational, financial, or political situations and pressures that might lead to misuse of their influence.

PRINCIPLE 2.
COMPETENCE

The maintenance of high standards of competence is a responsibility shared by all psychologists in the interest of the public and the profession as a whole. Psychologists recognize the boundaries of their competence and the limitations of their techniques. They only provide services and only use techniques for which they are qualified by training and experience. In those areas in which recognized standards do not yet exist, psychologists take whatever precautions are necessary to protect the welfare of their clients. They maintain knowledge of current scientific and professional information related to the services they render.

a. Psychologists accurately represent their competence, education, training, and experience. They claim as evidence of educational qualifications only those degrees obtained from institutions acceptable under the Bylaws and Rules of Council of the American Psychological Association.

b. As teachers, psychologists perform their duties on the basis of careful preparation so that their instruction is accurate, current, and scholarly.

c. Psychologists recognize the need for continuing education and are open to new procedures and changes in expectations and values over time.

d. Psychologists recognize differences among people, such as those that may be associated with age, sex, socioeconomic, and ethnic backgrounds. When necessary, they obtain training, experience, or counsel to assure competent service or research relating to such persons.

e. Psychologists responsible for decisions involving individuals or policies based on test results have an understanding of psychological or educational measurement, validation problems, and test research.

f. Psychologists recognize that personal problems and conflicts may interfere with professional effectiveness. Accordingly, they refrain from undertaking any activity in which their personal problems are likely to lead to inadequate performance or harm to a client, colleague, student, or research participant. If engaged in such activity when they become aware of their personal problems, they seek competent professional assistance to determine whether they should suspend, terminate, or limit the scope of their professional and/or scientific activities.

PRINCIPLE 3.
MORAL AND LEGAL STANDARDS

Psychologists' moral and ethical standards of behavior are a personal matter to the same degree as they are for any other citizen, except as these may compromise the fulfillment of their professional responsibilities, or reduce the public trust in psychology and psychologists. Regarding their own behavior, psychologists are sensitive to prevailing community standards and to the possible impact that conformity to or deviation from these standards may have upon the quality of their performance as psychologists. Psychologists are also aware of the possible impact of their public behavior upon the ability of colleagues to perform their professional duties.

a. As teachers, psychologists are aware of the fact that their personal values may affect the selection and presentation of instructional materials. When dealing with topics that may give offense, they recognize and respect the diverse attitudes that students may have toward such materials.

b. As employees or employers, psychologists do not engage in or condone practices that are inhumane or that result in illegal or unjustifiable actions. Such practices include but are not limited to those based on considerations of race, handicap, age, gender, sexual preference, religion, or national origin in hiring, promotion, or training.

c. In their professional roles, psychologists avoid any action that will violate or diminish the legal and civil rights of clients or of others who may be affected by their actions.

d. As practitioners and researchers, psychologists act in accord with Association standards and guidelines related to the practice and to the conduct of research with human beings and animals. In the ordinary course of events psychologists adhere to relevant governmental laws and institutional regulations. When federal, state, provincial, organizational, or institutional laws, regulations, or practices are in conflict with Association standards and guidelines, psychologists make known their commitment to Association standards and guidelines, and wherever possible work toward a resolution of the conflict. Both practitioners and researchers are concerned with the development of such legal and quasi-legal regulations as best serve the public interest, and they work toward changing existing regulations that are not beneficial to the public interest.

PRINCIPLE 4.
PUBLIC STATEMENTS

Public statements, announcements of services, advertising, and promotional activities of psychologists serve the purpose of helping the public make informed judgments and choices. Psychologists represent accurately and objectively their professional qualifications, affiliations, and functions, as well as those of the institutions or organizations with which they or the statements may be associated. In public statements providing psychological information or professional opinions or providing information about the availability of psychological products, publications, and services, psychologists base their statements on scientifically acceptable psychological findings and techniques with full recognition of the limits and uncertainties of such evidence.

a. When announcing or advertising professional services, psychologists may list the following information to describe the provider and services provided: name, highest relevant academic degree earned from a regionally accredited institution, date, type and level of certification or licensure, diplomate status, APA membership status, address, telephone number, office hours, a brief listing of the type of psychological services offered, an appropriate presentation of fee information, foreign languages spoken, and policy with regard to third-party payments. Additional relevant or important consumer information may be included if not prohibited by other sections of these Ethical Principles.

b. In announcing or advertising the availability of psychological products, publications, or services, psychologists do not present their affiliation with any organization in a manner that falsely implies sponsorship or certification by that organization. In particular and for example, psychologists do not state APA membership or fellow status in a way to suggest that such status implies specialized professional competence or qualifications. Public statements include, but are not limited to, communication by means of periodical, book, list, directory, television, radio, or motion picture. They do not contain: (i) a false, fraudulent, misleading, deceptive, or unfair statement; (ii) a misinterpretation of fact, or a statement likely to mislead or deceive because in context it makes only a partial disclosure of relevant facts; (iii) a testimonial from a patient regarding the quality of a psychologist's services or products; (iv) a statement intended or likely to create false or unjustified expectations of favorable results; (v) a statement implying unusual, unique, or one-of-a-kind abilities; (vi) a statement intended or likely to appeal to a client's fears, anxieties, or emotions concerning the possible results of a failure to obtain the offered services; (vii) a statement concerning the comparative desirability of offered service; (viii) a statement of direct solicitation of individual clients.

c. Psychologists do not compensate or give anything of value to a representative of the press, radio, television, or other communication medium in anticipation of or in return for professional publicity in a news item. A paid advertisement must be identified as such, unless it is apparent from the context that it is a paid advertisement. If communicated to the public by use of radio or television, an advertisement shall be prerecorded and approved for broadcast by the psychologist, and a recording of the actual transmission shall be retained by the psychologist.

d. Announcements or advertisements of "personal growth groups," clinics, and agencies give a clear statement of purpose and a clear description of the experiences to be provided. The education, training, and experience of the staff members are appropriately specified.

e. Psychologists associated with the development or promotion of psychological devices, books, or other products offered for commercial sale make reasonable efforts to insure that announcements and advertisements are presented in a professional, scientifically acceptable, and factually informative manner.

f. Psychologists do not participate for personal gain in commercial announcements or advertisements recommending to the public the purchase or use of proprietary or single-source products or services when that participation is based solely upon their identification as psychologists.

g. Psychologists present the science of psychology and offer their services, products, and publications fairly and accurately, avoiding misrepresentation through sensationalism, exaggeration, or superficiality. Psychologists are guided by the primary obligation to aid the public in developing informed judgments, opinions, and choices.

h. As teachers, psychologists insure that statements in catalogs and course outlines are accurate and not misleading, particularly in terms of subject matter to be covered, bases for evaluating progress, and the nature of course experiences. Announcements, brochures, or advertisements describing workshops, seminars, or other educational programs accurately describe the audience for which the program is intended as well as eligibility requirements, educational objectives, and nature of the materials to be covered. These announcements also accurately represent the education, training, and experience of the psychologists presenting the programs, and any fees involved.

i. Public announcements or advertisements soliciting research participants in which clinical services or other professional services are offered as an inducement, make clear the nature of the services as well as the costs and other obligations to be accepted by the participants of the research.

j. Psychologists accept the obligation to correct others who represent that psychologist's professional qualifications, or associations with products or services, in a manner incompatible with these guidelines.

k. Individual diagnostic and therapeutic services are provided only in the context of a professional psychological relationship. When personal advice is given by means of public lecture or demonstration, newspaper or magazine articles, radio or television programs, mail, or similar media, the psychologist utilizes the most current relevant data and exercises the highest level of professional judgment.

l. Products that are described or presented by means of public lectures or demonstrations, newspaper or magazine articles, radio or television programs, or similar media meet the same recognized standards as exist for use in the context of a professional relationship.

PRINCIPLE 5.
CONFIDENTIALITY

Psychologists have a primary obligation to respect the confidentiality of information obtained from persons in the course of their work as psychologists. They reveal such information to others only with the consent of the person or the person's legal representative, except in those unusual circumstances in which not to do so would result in clear danger to the person or to others. Where appropriate, psychologists inform their clients of the legal limits of confidentiality.

a. Information obtained in clinical or consulting relationships, or evaluative data concerning children, students, employees, and others, are discussed only for professional purposes and only with persons clearly concerned with the case. Written and oral reports present only data germane to the purposes of the evaluation and every effort is made to avoid undue invasion of privacy.

b. Psychologists who present personal information obtained during the course of professional work in writings, lectures, or other public forums either obtain adequate prior consent to do so or adequately disguise all identifying information.

c. Psychologists make provisions for maintaining confidentiality in the storage and disposal of records.

d. When working with minors or other persons who are unable to give voluntary, informed consent, psychologists take special care to protect these persons' best interests.

PRINCIPLE 6.
WELFARE OF THE CONSUMER

Psychologists respect the integrity and protect the welfare of the people and groups with whom they work. When there is a conflict of interest between a client and the psychologist's employing institution, psychologists clarify the nature and direction of their loyalties and responsibilities and keep all parties informed of their commitments. Psychologists fully inform consumers as to the purpose and nature of an evaluative, treatment, educational or training procedure, and they freely acknowledge that clients, students, or participants in research have freedom of choice with regard to participation.

a. Psychologists are continually cognizant of their own needs and of their potentially influential position vis-a-vis persons such as clients, students, and subordinates. They avoid exploiting the trust and dependency of such persons. Psychologists make every effort to avoid dual relationships which could impair their professional judgment or increase the risk of exploitation. Examples of such dual relationships include but are not limited to research with and treatment of employees, students, supervisees, close friends, or relatives. Sexual intimacies with clients are unethical.

b. When a psychologist agrees to provide services to a client at the request of a third party, the psychologist assumes the responsibility of clarifying the nature of the relationships to all parties concerned.

c. Where the demands of an organization require psychologists to violate these Ethical Principles, psychologists clarify the nature of the conflict between the demand and these principles. They inform all parties of psychologists' ethical responsibilities, and take appropriate action.

d. Psychologists make advance financial arrangements that safeguard the best interests of and are clearly understood by their clients. They neither give nor receive any remuneration for referring clients for professional services. They contribute a portion of their services to work for which they receive little or no financial return.

e. Psychologists terminate a clinical or consulting relationship when it is reasonably clear that the consumer is not benefiting from it. They offer to help the consumer locate alternative sources of assistance.

PRINCIPLE 7.
PROFESSIONAL
RELATIONSHIPS

Psychologists act with due regard for the needs, special competencies, and obligations of their colleagues in psychology and other professions. They respect the prerogatives and obligations of the institutions or organizations with which these other colleagues are associated.

a. Psychologists understand the areas of competence of related professions. They make full use of all the professional, technical, and administrative resources that serve the best interests of consumers. The absence of formal relationships with other professional workers does not relieve psychologists of the responsibility of securing for their clients the best possible professional service nor does it relieve them of the obligation to exercise foresight, diligence, and tact in obtaining the complementary or alternative assistance needed by clients.

b. Psychologists know and take into account the traditions and practices of other professional groups with whom they work and cooperate fully with such groups. If a person is receiving similar services from another professional, psychologists do not offer their own services directly to such a person. If a psychologist is contacted by a person who is already receiving similar services from another professional, the psychologist carefully considers that professional relationship and proceeds with caution and sensitivity to the therapeutic issues as well as the client's welfare. The psychologist discusses these issues with the client so as to minimize the risk of confusion and conflict.

c. Psychologists who employ or supervise other professionals or professionals in training accept the obligation to facilitate the further professional development of these individuals. They provide appropriate working conditions, timely evaluations, constructive consultation and experience opportunities.

d. Psychologists do not exploit their professional relationships with clients, supervisees, students, employees, or research participants sexually or otherwise. Psychologists do not condone nor engage in sexual harrassment. Sexual harrassment is defined as deliberate or repeated comments, gestures, or physical contacts of a sexual nature that are unwanted by the recipient.

e. In conducting research in institutions or organizations, psychologists secure appropriate authorization to conduct such research. They are aware of their obligation to future research workers and insure that host institutions receive adequate information about the research and proper acknowledgement of their contributions.

f. Publication credit is assigned to those who have contributed to a publication in proportion to their professional contribution. Major contributions of a professional character made by several persons to a common project are recognized by joint authorship, with the individual who made the principal contribution listed first. Minor contributions of a professional character and extensive clerical or similar nonprofessional assistance may be acknowledged in footnotes or in an introductory statement. Acknowledgement through specific citations is made for unpublished as well as published material that has directly influenced the research or writing. A psychologist who compiles and edits material of others for publication publishes the material in the name of the originating group, if appropriate, with his/her own name appearing as chairperson or editor. All contributors are to be acknowledged and named.

g. When psychologists know of an ethical violation by another psychologist, and it seems appropriate, they informally attempt to resolve the issue by bringing the behavior to the attention of the psychologist. If the misconduct is of a minor nature and/or appears to be due to lack of sensitivity, knowledge, or experience, such an informal solution is usually appropriate. Such informal corrective efforts are sensitive to any rights to confidentiality involved. If the violation does not seem amenable to an informal solution, or is of a more serious nature, psychologists bring it to the attention of the appropriate local, state, and/or national committee on professional ethics and conduct.

PRINCIPLE 8.
ASSESSMENT TECHNIQUES

In the development, publication, and utilization of psychological assessment techniques, psychologists make every effort to promote the welfare and best interests of the client. They guard against the misuse of assessment results. They respect the client's right to know the results, the interpretations made and the bases for their conclusions and recommendations. Psychologists make every effort to maintain the security of tests and other assessment techniques within limits of legal mandates. They strive to assure the appropriate use of assessment techniques by others.

a. In using assessment techniques, psychologists respect the right of clients to have a full explanation of the nature and purpose of the techniques in language that the client can understand, unless an explicit exception to this right has been agreed upon in advance. When the explanations are to be provided by others, the psychologist establishes procedures for insuring the adequacy of these explanations.

b. Psychologists responsible for the development and standardization of psychological tests and other assessment techniques utilize established scientific procedures and observe the relevant APA standards.

c. In reporting assessment results, psychologists indicate any reservations that exist regarding validity or reliability because of the circumstances of the assessment or the inappropriateness of the norms for the person tested. Psychologists strive to insure that the results of assessments and their interpretations are not misused by others.

d. Psychologists recognize that assessment results may become obsolete. They make every effort to avoid and prevent the misuse of obsolete measures.

e. Psychologists offering scoring and interpretation services are able to produce appropriate evidence for the validity of the programs and procedures used in arriving at interpretations. The public offering of an automated interpretation service is considered as a professional-to-professional consultation. The psychologist makes every effort to avoid misuse of assessment reports.

f. Psychologists do not encourage or promote the use of psychological assessment techniques by inappropriately trained or otherwise unqualified persons through teaching, sponsorship, or supervision.

PRINCIPLE 9.
RESEARCH WITH HUMAN PARTICIPANTS

The decision to undertake research rests upon a considered judgment by the individual psychologist about how best to contribute to psychological science and human welfare. Having made the decision to conduct research, the psychologist considers alternative directions in which research energies and resources might be invested. On the basis of this consideration, the psychologist carries out the investigation with respect and concern for the dignity and welfare of the people who participate, and with cognizance of federal and state regulations and professional standards governing the conduct of research with human participants.

a. In planning a study, the investigator has the responsibility to make a careful evaluation of its ethical acceptability. To the extent that the weighing of scientific and human values suggests a compromise of any principle, the investigator incurs a correspondingly serious obligation to seek ethical advice and to observe stringent safeguards to protect the rights of human participants.

b. Considering whether a participant in a planned study will be a "subject at risk" or a "subject at minimal risk," according to recognized standards, is of primary ethical concern to the investigator.

c. The investigator always retains the responsibility for insuring ethical practice in research. The investigator is also responsible for the ethical treatment of research participants by collaborators, assistants, students, and employees, all of whom, however, incur similar obligations.

d. Except for minimal risk research, the investigator establishes a clear and fair agreement with the research participants, prior to their participation, that clarifies the obligations and responsibilities of each. The investigator has the obligation to honor all promises and commitments included in that agreement. The investigator informs the participant of all aspects of the research that might reasonably be expected to influence willingness to participate, and explains all other aspects of the research about which the participant inquires. Failure to make full disclosure prior to obtaining informed consent requires additional safeguards to protect the welfare and dignity of the research participant. Research with children or participants who have impairments which would limit understanding and/or communication, requires special safeguard procedures.

e. Methodological requirements of a study may make the use of concealment or deception necessary. Before conducting such a study, the investigator has a special responsibility to: (i) determine whether the use of such techniques is justified by the study's prospective scientific, educational, or applied value; (ii) determine whether alternative procedures are available that do not utilize concealment or deception; and (iii) insure that the participants are provided with sufficient explanation as soon as possible.

f. The investigator respects the individual's freedom to decline to participate in or to withdraw from the research at any time. The obligation to protect this freedom requires careful thought and consideration when the investigator is in a position of authority or influence over the participant. Such positions of authority include but are not limited to situations when research participation is required as part of employment or when the participant is a student, client, or employee of the investigator.

g. The investigator protects the participants from physical and mental discomfort, harm, and danger that may arise from research procedures. If risks of such consequence exist, the investigator informs the participant of that fact. Research procedures likely to cause serious or lasting harm to a participant are not used unless the failure to use these procedures might expose the participant to risk of greater harm, or unless the research has great potential benefit and fully informed and voluntary consent is obtained from each participant. The participant should be informed of procedures for contacting the investigator within a reasonable time period following participation should stress, potential harm, or related questions or concerns arise.

h. After the data are collected, the investigator provides the participant with information about the nature of the study and attempts to remove any misconceptions that may have arisen. Where scientific or humane values justify delaying or withholding information, the investigator incurs a special responsibility to monitor the research and to assure that there are no damaging consequences for the participant.

i. Where research procedures result in undesirable consequences for the individual participant, the investigator has the responsibility to detect and remove or correct these consequences, including long-term effects.

j. Information obtained about the research participant during the courses of an investigation is confidential unless otherwise agreed upon in advance. When the possibility exists that others may obtain access to such information, this possibility, together with the plans for protecting confidentiality, is explained to the participant as part of the procedure for obtaining informed consent.

PRINCIPLE 10.
CARE AND USE OF ANIMALS

An investigator of animal behavior strives to advance our understanding of basic behavioral principles and/or to contribute to the improvement of human health and welfare. In seeking these ends, the investigator insures the welfare of the animals and treats them humanely. Laws and regulations notwithstanding, the animal's immediate protection depends upon the scientist's own conscience.

a. The acquisition, care, use, and disposal of all animals is in compliance with current federal, state or provincial, and local laws and regulations.

b. A psychologist trained in research methods and experienced in the care of laboratory animals closely supervises all procedures involving animals and is responsible for insuring appropriate consideration of their comfort, health, and humane treatment.

c. Psychologists insure that all individuals using animals under their supervision have received explicit instruction in experimental methods and in the care, maintenance, and handling of the species being used. Responsibilities and activities of individuals participating in a research project are consistent with their respective competencies.

d. Psychologists make every effort to minimize discomfort, illness, and pain to the animals. A procedure subjecting animals to pain, stress, or privation is used only when an alternative procedure is unavailable and the goal is justified by its prospective scientific, educational, or applied value. Surgical procedures are performed under appropriate anesthesia; techniques to avoid infection and minimize pain are followed during and after surgery.

e. When it is appropriate that the animal's life be terminated, it is done rapidly and painlessly.

NOTES

[1] Approved by the Council of Representatives (January 1981).

[2] These Ethical Principles apply to psychologists, to students of psychology and others who do work of a psychological nature under the supervision of a psychologist. They are also intended for the guidance of non-members of the Association who are engaged in psychological research or practice.

ETHICAL STANDARDS OF THE AMERICAN ASSOCIATION FOR COUNSELING AND DEVELOPMENT (3RD REVISION, AACD GOVERNING COUNCIL, MARCH 1988)

PREAMBLE

The Association is an educational, scientific, and professional organization whose members are dedicated to the enhancement of the worth, dignity, potential, and uniqueness of each individual and thus to the service of society.

The Association recognizes that the role definitions and work settings of its members include a wide variety of academic disciplines, levels of academic preparation, and agency services. This diversity reflects the breadth of the Association's interest and influence. It also poses challenging complexities in efforts to set standards for the performance of members, desired requisite preparation or practice, and supporting social, legal, and ethical controls.

The specification of ethical standards enables the Association to clarify to present and future members and to those served by members the nature of ethical responsibilities held in common by its members.

The existence of such standards serves to stimulate greater concern by members for their own professional functioning and for the conduct of fellow professionals such as counselors, guidance and student personnel workers, and others in the helping professions. As the ethical code of the Association, this document establishes principles that define the ethical behavior of Association members. Additional ethical guidelines developed by the Association's Divisions for their speciality areas may further define a member's ethical behavior.

SECTION A: GENERAL

1. The member influences the development of the profession by continuous efforts to improve professional practices, teaching, services, and research. Professional growth is continuous throughout the member's career and is exemplified by the development of a philosophy that explains why and how a member functions in the helping relationship. Members must gather data on their effectiveness and be guided by the findings. Members recognize the need for continuing education to ensure competent service.

2. The member has a responsibility both to the individual who is served and to the institution within which the service is performed to maintain high standards of professional conduct. The member strives to maintain the highest levels of professional services offered to the individuals to be served. The member also strives to assist the agency, organization, or institution in providing the highest caliber of professional services. The acceptance of employment in an institution implies that the member is in agreement with the general policies and principles of the institution. Therefore the professional activities of the member are also in accord with the objectives of the institution. If, despite concerted efforts, the member cannot reach agreement with the

employer as to acceptable standards of conduct that allow for changes in institutional policy conducive to the positive growth and development of clients, then terminating the affiliation should be seriously considered.

3. Ethical behavior among professional associates, both members and nonmembers, must be expected at all times. When information is possessed that raises doubt as to the ethical behavior of professional colleagues, whether Association members or not, the member must take action to attempt to rectify such a condition. Such action shall use the institution's channels first and then use procedures established by the Association.

4. The member neither claims nor implies professional qualifications exceeding those possessed and is responsible for correcting any misrepresentations of these qualifications by others.

5. In establishing fees for professional counseling services, members must consider the financial status of clients and locality. In the event that the established fee structure is inappropriate for a client, assistance must be provided in finding comparable services of acceptable cost.

6. When members provide information to the public or to subordinates, peers, or supervisors, they have a responsibility to ensure that the content is general, unidentified client information that is accurate, unbiased, and consists of objective, factual data.

7. Members recognize their boundaries of competence and provide only those services and use only those techniques for which they are qualified by training or experience. Members should only accept those positions for which they are professionally qualified.

8. In the counseling relationship, the counselor is aware of the intimacy of the relationship and maintains respect for the client and avoids engaging in activities that seek to meet the counselor's personal needs at the expense of that client.

9. Members do not condone or engage in sexual harassment which is defined as deliberate or repeated comments, gestures, or physical contacts of a sexual nature.

10. The member avoids bringing personal issues into the counseling relationship, especially if the potential for harm is present. Through awareness of the negative impact of both racial and sexual stereotyping and discrimination, the counselor guards the individual rights and personal dignity of the client in the counseling relationship.

11. Products or services provided by the member by means of classroom instruction, public lectures, demonstrations, written articles, radio or television programs, or other types of media must meet the criteria cited in these standards.

SECTION B: COUNSELING RELATIONSHIP

This section refers to practices and procedures of individual and/or group counseling relationships.

The member must recognize the need for client freedom of choice. Under those circumstances where this is not possible, the member must apprise clients of restrictions that may limit their freedom of choice.

1. The member's primary obligation is to respect the integrity and promote the welfare of the client(s), whether the client(s) is (are) assisted individually or in a group relationship. In a group setting, the member is also responsible for taking reasonable precautions to protect individuals from physical and/or psychological trauma resulting from interaction within the group.

2. Members make provisions for maintaining confidentiality in the storage and disposal of records and follow an established record retention and disposition policy. The counseling relationship and information resulting therefrom must be kept confidential, consistent with the obligations of the member as a professional person. In a group counseling setting, the counselor must set a norm of confidentiality regarding all group participants' disclosures.

3. If an individual is already in a counseling relationship with another professional person, the member does not enter into a counseling relationship without first contacting and receiving the approval of that other professional. If the member discovers that the client is in another counseling relationship after the counseling relationship begins, the member must gain the consent of the other professional or terminate the relationship, unless the client elects to terminate the other relationship.

4. When the client's condition indicates that there is clear and imminent danger to the client or others, the member must take reasonable personal action or inform responsible authorities. Consultation with other professionals must be used where possible. The assumption of responsibility for the client's(s') behavior must be taken only after careful deliberation. The client must be involved in the resumption of responsibility as quickly as possible.

5. Records of the counseling relationship, including interview notes, test data, correspondence, tape recordings, electronic data storage, and other documents are to be considered professional information for use in counseling, and they should not be considered a part of the records of the institution or agency in which the counselor is employed unless specified by state statute or regulation. Revelation to others of counseling material must occur only upon the expressed consent of the client.

6. In view of the extensive data storage and processing capacities of the computer, the member must ensure that data maintained on a computer is: (a) limited to information that is appropriate and necessary for the services being provided; (b) destroyed after it is determined that the information is no longer of any value in providing services; and (c) restricted in terms of access to appropriate staff members involved in the provision of services by using the best computer security methods available.

7. Use of data derived from a counseling relationship for purposes of counselor training or research shall be confined to content that can be disguised to ensure full protection of the identity of the subject client.

8. The member must inform the client of the purposes, goals, techniques, rules of procedure, and limitations that may affect the relationship at or before the time that the counseling relationship is entered. When working with minors or persons who are unable to give consent, the member protects these clients' best interests.

9. In view of common misconceptions related to the perceived inherent validity of computer generated data and narrative reports, the member must ensure that the client is provided with information as part of the counseling relationship that adequately explains the limitations of computer technology.

10. The member must screen prospective group participants, especially when the emphasis is on self-understanding and growth through self-disclosure. The member must maintain an awareness of the group participants' compatibility

throughout the life of the group.

11. The member may choose to consult with any other professionally competent person about a client. In choosing a consultant, the member must avoid placing the consultant in a conflict of interest situation that would preclude the consultant's being a proper party to the member's efforts to help the client.

12. If the member determines an inability to be of professional assistance to the client, the member must either avoid initiating the counseling relationship or immediately terminate that relationship. In either event, the member must suggest appropriate alternatives. (The member must be knowledgeable about referral resources so that a satisfactory referral can be initiated.) In the event the client declines the suggested referral, the member is not obligated to continue the relationship.

13. When the member has other relationships, particularly of an administrative, supervisory, and/or evaluative nature with an individual seeking counseling services, the member must not serve as the counselor but should refer the individual to another professional. Only in instances where such an alternative is unavailable and where the individual's situation warrants counseling intervention should the member enter into and/or maintain a counseling relationship. Dual relationships with clients that might impair the member's objectivity and professional judgment (e.g., as with close friends or relatives) must be avoided and/or the counseling relationship terminated through referral to another competent professional.

14. The member will avoid any type of sexual intimacies with clients. Sexual relationships with clients are unethical.

15. All experimental methods of treatment must be clearly indicated to prospective recipients, and safety precautions are to be adhered to by the member.

16. When computer applications are used as a component of counseling services, the member must ensure that: (a) the client is intellectually, emotionally, and physically capable of using the computer application; (b) the computer application is appropriate for the needs of the client; (c) the client understands the purpose and operation of the computer application; and (d) follow-up of client use of a computer application is provided to both correct possible problems (misconceptions or inappropriate use) and assess subsequent needs.

17. When the member is engaged in short-term group treatment/training programs (e.g., marathons and other encounter-type or growth groups), the member ensures that there is professional assistance available during and following the group experience.

18. Should the member be engaged in a work setting that calls for any variation from the above statements, the member is obligated to consult with other professionals whenever possible to consider justifiable alternatives.

19. The member must ensure that members of various ethnic, racial, religious, disability, and socioeconomic groups have equal access to computer applications used to support counseling services and that the content of available computer applications does not discriminate against the groups described above.

20. When computer applications are developed by the member for use by the general public as self-help/stand-alone computer software, the member must ensure that: (a) self-help computer applications are designed from the beginning to function in a stand-alone manner, as opposed to modifying software that was originally designed to require support from a counselor; (b) self-help com-

puter applications will include within the program statements regarding intended user outcomes, suggestions for using the software, a description of the conditions under which self-help computer applications might not be appropriate, and a description of when and how counseling services might be beneficial; and (c) the manual for such applications will include the qualifications of the developer, the development process, validation data, and operating procedures.

SECTION C: MEASUREMENT AND EVALUATION

The primary purpose of educational and psychological testing is to provide descriptive measures that are objective and interpretable in either comparative or absolute terms. The member must recognize the need to interpret the statements that follow as applying to the whole range of appraisal techniques including test and nontest data. Test results constitute only one of a variety of pertinent sources of information for personnel, guidance, and counseling decisions.

1. The member must provide specific orientation or information to the examinee(s) prior to and following the test administration so that the results of testing may be placed in proper perspective with other relevant factors. In so doing, the member must recognize the effects of socioeconomic, ethnic, and cultural factors on test scores. It is the member's professional responsibility to use additional unvalidated information carefully in modifying interpretation of the test results.

2. In selecting tests for use in a given situation or with a particular client, the member must consider carefully the specific validity, reliability, and appropriateness of the test(s). General validity, reliability, and related issues may be questioned legally as well as ethically when tests are used for vocational and educational selection, placement, or counseling.

3. When making any statements to the public about tests and testing, the member must give accurate information and avoid false claims or misconceptions. Special efforts are often required to avoid unwarranted connotations of such terms as IQ and grade equivalent scores.

4. Different tests demand different levels of competence for administration, scoring, and interpretation. Members must recognize the limits of their competence and perform only those functions for which they are prepared. In particular, members using computer-based test interpretations must be trained in the construct being measured and the specific instrument being used prior to using this type of computer application.

5. In situations where a computer is used for test administration and scoring, the member is responsible for ensuring that administration and scoring programs function properly to provide clients with accurate test results.

6. Tests must be administered under the same conditions that were established in their standardization. When tests are not administered under standard conditions or when unusual behavior or irregularities occur during the testing session, those conditions must be noted and the results designated as invalid or of questionable validity. Unsupervised or inadequately supervised test-taking, such as the use of tests through the mails, is considered unethical. On the other hand, the use of instruments that are so designed or standardized to be self-administered and self-scored, such as interest inventories, is to be encouraged.

7. The meaningfulness of test results used in personnel, guidance, and counseling functions generally depends

on the examinee's unfamiliarity with the specific items on the test. Any prior coaching or dissemination of the test materials can invalidate test results. Therefore, test security is one of the professional obligations of the member. Conditions that produce most favorable test results must be made known to the examinee.

8. The purpose of testing and the explicit use of the results must be made known to the examinee prior to testing. The counselor must ensure that instrument limitations are not exceeded and that periodic review and/or retesting are made to prevent client stereotyping.

9. The examinee's welfare and explicit prior understanding must be the criteria for determining the recipients of the test results. The member must see that specific interpretation accompanies any release of individual or group test data. The interpretation of test data must be related to the examinee's particular concerns.

10. Members responsible for making decisions based on test results have an understanding of educational and psychological measurement, validation criteria, and test research.

11. The member must be cautious when interpreting the results of research instruments possessing insufficient technical data. The specific purposes for the use of such instruments must be stated explicitly to examinees.

12. The member must proceed with caution when attempting to evaluate and interpret the performance of minority group members or other persons who are not represented in the norm group on which the instrument was standardized.

13. When computer-based test interpretations are developed by the member to support the assessment pro-cess, the member must ensure that the validity of such interpretations is established prior to the commercial distribution of such a computer application.

14. The member recognizes that test results may become obsolete. The member will avoid and prevent the misuse of obsolete test results.

15. The member must guard against the appropriation, reproduction, or modification of published tests or parts thereof without acknowledgement and permission from the previous publisher.

16. Regarding the preparation, publication, and distribution of tests, reference should be made to:

a. "Standards for Educational and Psychological Testing," revised edition, 1985, published by the American Psychological Association on behalf of itself, the American Educational Research Association, and the National Council on Measurement in Education.

b. "The Responsible Use of Tests: A Position Paper of AMEG, APGA, and NCME," *Measurement and Evaluation in Guidance*, 1972, 5, 385–388.

c. "Responsibilities of Users of Standardized Tests," APGA, *Guidepost*, October 5, 1978, pp. 5–8.

SECTION D: RESEARCH AND PUBLICATION

1. Guidelines on research with human subjects shall be adhered to, such as:

a. *Ethical Principles in the Conduct of Research with Human Participants*, Washington, D.C.: American Psychological Association, Inc., 1982.

b. Code of Federal Regulation, Title 45, Subtitle A, Part 46, as currently issued.

c. *Ethical Principles of Psychologists*, American Psyhological Association, Principle #9: Research with Human Participants.

d. Family Educational Rights and Privacy Act (the Buckley Amendment).

e. Current federal regulations and various state rights privacy acts.

2. In planning any research activity dealing with human subjects, the member must be aware of and responsive to all pertinent ethical principles and ensure that the research problem, design, and execution are in full compliance with them.

3. Responsibility for ethical research practice lies with the principal researcher, while others involved in research activities share ethical obligation and full responsibility for their own actions.

4. In research with human subjects, researchers are responsible for the subjects' welfare throughout the experiment, and they must take all reasonable precautions to avoid causing injurious psychological, physical, or social effects on their subjects.

5. All research subjects must be informed of the purpose of the study except when withholding information or providing misinformation to them is essential to the investigation. In such research the member must be responsible for corrective action as soon as possible following completion of the research.

6. Participation in research must be voluntary. Involuntary participation is appropriate only when it can be demonstrated that participation will have no harmful effects on subjects and is essential to the investigation.

7. When reporting research results, explicit mention must be made of all variables and conditions known to the investigator that might affect the outcome of the investigation or the interpretation of the data.

8. The member must be responsible for conducting and reporting investigations in a manner that minimizes the possibility that results will be misleading.

9. The member has an obligation to make available sufficient original research data to qualified others who may wish to replicate the study.

10. When supplying data, aiding in the research of another person, reporting research results, or making original data available, due care must be taken to disguise the identity of the subjects in the absence of specific authorization from such subjects to do otherwise.

11. When conducting and reporting research, the member must be familiar with and give recognition to previous work on the topic, as well as to observe all copyright laws and follow the principles of giving full credit to all to whom credit is due.

12. The member must give due credit through joint authorship, acknowledgement, footnote statements, or other appropriate means to those who have contributed significantly to the research and/or publication, in accordance with such contributions.

13. The member must communicate to other members the results of any research judged to be of professional or scientific value. Results reflecting unfavorably on institutions, programs, services, or vested interests must not be withheld for such reasons.

14. If members agree to cooperate with another individual in research and/or publication, they incur an obligation to cooperate as promised in terms of punctuality of performance and with full regard to the completeness and accuracy of the information required.

15. Ethical practice requires that authors not submit the same manuscript or one essentially similar in content for

simultaneous publication consideration by two or more journals. In addition, manuscripts published in whole or in substantial part in another journal or published work should not be submitted for publication without acknowledgement and permission from the previous publication.

SECTION E: CONSULTING

Consultation refers to a voluntary relationship between a professional helper and help-needing individual, group, or social unit in which the consultant is providing help to the client(s) in defining and solving a work-related problem with a client or client system.

1. The member acting as consultant must have a high degree of self-awareness of his/her own values, knowledge, skills, limitations, and needs in entering a helping relationship that involves human and/or organizational change and that the focus of the relationship be on the issues to be resolved and not on the person(s) presenting the problem.

2. There must be understanding and agreement between member and client for the problem definition, change of goals, and prediction of consequences of interventions selected.

3. The member must be reasonably certain that she/he or the organization represented has the necessary competencies and resources for giving the kind of help that is needed now or may be needed later and that appropriate referral resources are available to the consultant.

4. The consulting relationship must be one in which client adaptability and growth toward self-direction are encouraged and cultivated. The member must maintain this role consistently and

not become a decision maker for the client or create a future dependency on the consultant.

5. When announcing consultant availability for services, the member conscientiously adheres to the Association's Ethical Standards.

6. The member must refuse a private fee or other remuneration for consultation with persons who are entitled to these services through the member's employing institution or agency. The policies of a particular agency may make explicit provisions for private practice with agency clients by members of its staff. In such instances, the clients must be appraised of other options open to them should they seek private counseling services.

SECTION F: PRIVATE PRACTICE

1. The member should assist the profession by facilitating the availability of counseling services in private as well as public settings.

2. In advertising services as a private practitioner, the member must advertise the services in a manner that accurately informs the public of professional services, expertise, and techniques of counseling availabe. A member who assumes an executive leadership role in the organization shall not permit his/her name to be used in professional notices during periods when he/she is not actively engaged in the private practice of counseling.

3. The member may list the following: highest relevant degree, type and level of certification and/or license, address, telephone number, office hours, type and/or desciption of services, and other relevant information. Such information must not contain false, inaccurate,

misleading, partial, out-of-context, or deceptive material or statements.

4. Members do not present their affiliation with any organization in such a way that would imply inaccurate sponsorship or certification by that organization.

5. Members may join in partnership/corporation with other members and/or other professionals provided that each member of the partnership or corporation makes clear the separate specialties by name in compliance with the regulations of the locality.

6. A member has an obligation to withdraw from a counseling relationship if it is believed that employment will result in violation of the Ethical Standards. If the mental or physical condition of the member renders it difficult to carry out an effective professional relationship or if the member is discharged by the client because the counseling relationship is no longer productive for the client, then the member is obligated to terminate the counseling relationship.

7. A member must adhere to the regulations for private practice of the locality where the services are offered.

8. It is unethical to use one's institutional affiliation to recruit clients for one's private practice.

SECTION G: PERSONNEL ADMINISTRATION

It is recognized that most members are employed in public or quasi-public institutions. The funcioning of a member within an institution must contribute to the goals of the institution and vice versa if either is to accomplish their respective goals or objectives. It is therefore essential that the member and the institution function in ways to: (a) make the institutions's goals explicit and public; (b) make

the member's contribution to institutional goals specific; and (c) foster mutual accountability for goal achievement.

To accomplish these objectives, it is recognized that the member and the employer must share responsibilities in the formulation and implementation of personnel policies.

1. Members must define and describe the parameters and levels of their professional competency.

2. Members must establish interpersonal relations and working agreements with supervisors and subordinates regarding counseling or clinical relationships, confidentiality, distinction between public and private material, maintenance and dissemination of recorded information, work load, and accountability. Working agreements in each instance must be specified and made known to those concerned.

3. Members must alert their employers to conditions that may be potentially disruptive or damaging.

4. Members must inform employers of conditions that may limit their effectiveness.

5. Members must submit regularly to professional review and evaluation.

6. Members must be responsible for inservice development of self and/or staff.

7. Members must inform their staff of goals and programs.

8. Members must provide personnel practices that guarantee and enhance the rights and welfare of each recipient of their service.

9. Members must select competent persons and assign responsibilities compatible with their skills and experiences.

10. The member, at the onset of a counseling relationship, will inform the client of the member's intended use of supervisors regarding the disclosure of

information concerning this case. The member will clearly inform the client of the limits of confidentiality in the relationship.

11. Members, as either employers or employees, do not engage in or condone practices that are inhumane, illegal, or unjustifiable (such as considerations based on sex, handicap, age, race) in hiring, promotion, or training.

SECTION H: PREPARATION STANDARDS

Members who are responsible for training others must be guided by the preparation standards of the Association and relevant Division(s). The member who functions in the capacity of trainer assumes unique ethical responsibilities that frequently go beyond that of the member who does not function in a training capacity. These ethical responsibilities are outlined as follows:

1. Members must orient students to program expectations, basic skill development, and employment prospects prior to admission to the program.

2. Members in charge of learning experiences must establish programs that integrate academic study and supervised practice.

3. Members must establish a program directed toward developing students' skills, knowledge, and self-understanding, stated whenever possible in competency or performance terms.

4. Members must identify the levels of competencies of their students in compliance with relevant Division standards. These competencies must accommodate the paraprofessional as well as the professional.

5. Members, through continual student evaluation and appraisal, must be aware of the personal limitations of the learner that might impede future performance. The instructor must not only assist the learner in securing remedial assistance but also screen from the program those individuals who are unable to provide competent services.

6. Members must provide a program that includes training in research commensurate with levels of role functioning. Paraprofessional and technician-level personnel must be trained as consumers of research. In addition, personnel must learn how to evaluate their own and their program's effectiveness. Graduate training, especially at the doctoral level, would include preparation for original research by the member.

7. Members must make students aware of the ethical responsibilities and standards of the profession.

8. Preparatory programs must encourage students to value the ideals of service to individuals and to society. In this regard, direct financial remuneration or lack thereof must not influence the quality of service rendered. Monetary considerations must not be allowed to overshadow professional and humanitarian needs.

9. Members responsible for educational programs must be skilled as teachers and practitioners.

10. Members must present thoroughly varied theoretical positions so that students may make comparisons and have the opportunity to select a position.

11. Members must develop clear policies within their educational institutions regarding field placement and the roles of the student and the instructor in such placement.

12. Members must ensure that forms of learning focusing on self-understanding or growth are voluntary, or if required as part of the educational program, are made known to prospective

students prior to entering the program. When the educational program offers a growth experience with an emphasis on self-disclosure or other relatively intimate or personal involvement, the member must have no administrative, supervisory, or evaluating authority regarding the participant.

13. The member will at all times provide students with clear and equally acceptable alternatives for self-understanding or growth experiences. The member will assure students that they have a right to accept these alternatives without prejudice or penalty.

14. Members must conduct an educational program in keeping with the current relevant guidelines of the Association.

ACKNOWLEDGMENTS

CHAP.	PAGE	
2	26	From Paul Reps, *Zen Flesh, Zen Bones.* Copyright © 1957 by Charles E. Tuttle Co., Inc. Reprinted by permission.
	43	Leon Mann, Flinders University of South Australia, Adelaide, S.A., 1982, by permission.
3	58–68	By permission of Joann Griswold and the client. All key identifying data have been changed in this typescript.
4	92	From E. Gendlin and M. Hendricks, *Rap Manual*, cited in Rogers, *The Counseling Psychologist*, 1975, p. 5. The *Rap Manual* as a whole is now part of *Focusing* by E. T. Gendlin, Everest House, NY, 1978. Reprinted by permission.
6	144ff	Reprinted from George A. Kelly, Ph.D., *The Psychology of Personal Constructs.* Copyright © 1955 by George A. Kelly. Used by permission of W. W. Norton & Co., Inc.
	152–153	From *People in Systems: An Introduction to Human Development* by G. Egan and M. Cowan. Copyright © 1979 by Wadsworth Publishing Co., Inc. Reprinted by permission of the publisher, Brooks/Cole Publishing Co., Monterey, CA.
	163	From *The Autobiography of Malcolm X*, by Malcolm X, with the assistance of Alex Haley. Copyright © 1964 by Alex Haley and Malcolm X. Copyright © 1965 by Alex Haley and Betty Shabazz. Reprinted by permission of Random House, Inc.
7	176ff	From "Basic Influencing Skills Videotapes," Mary Bradford Ivey; Microtraining No. 01059, Amherst, MA, by permission of Microtraining Associates.
	189	From Carl R. Rogers, *Client-Centered Therapy*, pp. 86–87. Copyright © 1951, renewed 1979 by Houghton Mifflin Company. Used by permission.
	190–191	From *Man's Search for Meaning* by Viktor Frankl. Copyright © 1962 by Viktor Frankl. Reprinted by permission of Beacon Press and by permission of Hodder and Stoughton Limited.
9	254–255	From A. Ivey and J. Kinkle, "Students, the Major Untapped Resource in Higher Education," in REACH (a publication of the Colorado State University Collegian), 1968, *6*, 1 and 4. By permission.
10	275–276	From C. Rogers, "The Necessary and Sufficient Conditions of Therapeutic Personality Change," in *Journal of Consulting Psychology, 21*, 1957, 95–103. Copyright © 1957 American Psychological Association. Used by permission.

277–279   From C. Rogers and J. Wallen, *Counseling Returned Servicemen.* Copyright © 1946 by McGraw-Hill, NY. Reprinted by permission.

279–280   From C. Rogers, *On Becoming a Person.* Copyright © 1961 by Houghton Mifflin Company. Used by permission.

281   Specified excerpt from *Carl Rogers on Encounter Groups* by Carl R. Rogers. Copyright © 1970 by Carl R. Rogers. Reprinted by permission of Harper & Row, Publishers, Inc. and by Penguin Books Ltd.

285–286   From Frederick S. Perls, *Gestalt Therapy Verbatim.* Copyright © 1969 by Real People Press. Used by permission.

11   306   From A. Ellis, *Growth through Reason.* North Hollywood, CA: Wilshire Books, 1971. Copyright © by the Institute for Rational-Emotive Therapy, 1971.

319–320   J. Krumboltz, *Private Rules in Decision Making.* Columbus, Ohio: National Center for Research in Vocational Education, Copyright © 1983. Used by permission.

341–342   From *What Do You Say After You Say Hello? The Psychology of Human Destiny* by Eric Berne, M.D. Copyright © 1972 by City National Bank, Beverly Hills, Janice Farbinger. Reprinted by permission of Random House, Inc.

350–351   Selection from Jay Haley, *Uncommon Therapy, The Psychiatric Techniques of Milton H. Erickson, M.D.* Copyright © 1973 by Jay Haley. Reprinted by permission of W. W. Norton & Company, Inc.

359   From B. Guerney, Jr., *Relationship Enhancement.* San Francisco: Jossey-Bass, 1977, pp. 51–53, and p. 153. Used by permission.

Name Index

Subject Index

A

Advice. (*See* Influencing skills, advice)
Age. (*See* Cultural differences)
Appealing technique, 293–294
Assertiveness, 80, 158, 239–245, 336, 441
Assessing the effectiveness of an interview, 147, 197
Assessment, 36, 143–173
Attachment, 205, 440–441
Attending behavior. (*See* Listening skills)
Attending skills, summary chart, 87
Authenticity. (*See* Empathy)

B

Balance Sheet Grid, 43
Basic listening sequence. (*See* Listening skills, basic listening sequence)
Behavioral counseling and therapy, 7–9, 161–162, 231–263, 310, 360, 386, 424, 427
    applied behavioral analysis, 234–236, 249, 260
    basic techniques, 248–262
    behavioral change procedures, 238–239, 249
    behavioral worldview, 233–234
    behaviorism, 232, 302
    operationalization of behavior, 234–236

"Best" theory, 414–415
Black counseling/therapy issues, 12, 22, 162–164, 271, 364–368, 392, 395, 422
Body language, 52–53, 58, 122. (*See also* Nonverbal communication)
Boston Vocational Bureau, 29

C

Case planning, 144ff, 416ff
Charting, 256–257
Check-out, 112–113. (*See also* Empathy, Dialectics)
Client observation skills, 69, 119–141, 178
Client-centered therapy. (*See* Person-centered therapy)
Closed questions. (*See* Listening skills, questions)
Cognitive-behavioral theory, 7, 39, 84, 289, 301–331, 335, 397, 414, 420, 432, 441
    Beck, 311ff
    Ellis, 304–310
    Glasser, 324ff
    Krumboltz, 310–320
    Meichenbaum, 320–323
    worldview, 303–304
Cognitive theory, 311–314
Concreteness. (*See* Empathy)
Confrontation, 86, 106